T0331743

Web Usage Mining Techniques and Applications Across Industries

A.V. Senthil Kumar
Hindusthan College of Arts and Science, India

A volume in the Advances in Data Mining and
Database Management (ADMDM) Book Series

www.igi-global.com

Published in the United States of America by
IGI Global
Information Science Reference (an imprint of IGI Global)
701 E. Chocolate Avenue
Hershey PA, USA 17033
Tel: 717-533-8845
Fax: 717-533-8661
E-mail: cust@igi-global.com
Web site: http://www.igi-global.com

Library of Congress Cataloging-in-Publication Data

Names: Kumar, A.V. Senthil, 1966- editor.
Title: Web usage mining techniques and applications across industries / A.V.
    Senthil Kumar, editor.
Description: Hershey : Information Science Reference, 2016. | Includes
    bibliographical references and index.
Identifiers: LCCN 2016017810| ISBN 9781522506133 (hardcover) | ISBN
    9781522506140 (ebook)
Subjects: LCSH: Information retrieval. | Internet users. | Data mining. | Web
    sites--Design and construction.
Classification: LCC ZA4230 .W437 2016 | DDC 025.5/24--dc23 LC record available at https://lccn.loc.gov/2016017810

This book is published in the IGI Global book series Advances in Data Mining and Database Management (ADMDM)
(ISSN: 2327-1981; eISSN: 2327-199X)

British Cataloguing in Publication Data
A Cataloguing in Publication record for this book is available from the British Library.

All work contributed to this book is new, previously-unpublished material. The views expressed in this book are those of the authors, but not necessarily of the publisher.

For electronic access to this publication, please contact: eresources@igi-global.com.

Advances in Data Mining and Database Management (ADMDM) Book Series

David Taniar
Monash University, Australia

ISSN: 2327-1981
EISSN: 2327-199X

Mission

With the large amounts of information available to organizations in today's digital world, there is a need for continual research surrounding emerging methods and tools for collecting, analyzing, and storing data.

The **Advances in Data Mining & Database Management (ADMDM)** series aims to bring together research in information retrieval, data analysis, data warehousing, and related areas in order to become an ideal resource for those working and studying in these fields. IT professionals, software engineers, academicians and upper-level students will find titles within the ADMDM book series particularly useful for staying up-to-date on emerging research, theories, and applications in the fields of data mining and database management.

Coverage

- Factor Analysis
- Text Mining
- Cluster Analysis
- Data Analysis
- Heterogeneous and Distributed Databases
- Sequence Analysis
- Information Extraction
- Database Testing
- Association Rule Learning
- Data Mining

IGI Global is currently accepting manuscripts for publication within this series. To submit a proposal for a volume in this series, please contact our Acquisition Editors at Acquisitions@igi-global.com or visit: http://www.igi-global.com/publish/.

Titles in this Series

For a list of additional titles in this series, please visit: www.igi-global.com

Collaborative Filtering Using Data Mining and Analysis
Vishal Bhatnagar (Ambedkar Institute of Advanced Communication Technologies and Research, India)
Information Science Reference • copyright 2017 • 309pp • H/C (ISBN: 9781522504894) • US $195.00 (our price)

Effective Big Data Management and Opportunities for Implementation
Manoj Kumar Singh (Adama Science and Technology University, Ethiopia) and Dileep Kumar G. (Adama Science and Technology University, Ethiopia)
Information Science Reference • copyright 2016 • 324pp • H/C (ISBN: 9781522501824) • US $195.00 (our price)

Data Mining Trends and Applications in Criminal Science and Investigations
Omowunmi E. Isafiade (University of Cape Town, South Africa) and Antoine B. Bagula (University of the Western Cape, South Africa)
Information Science Reference • copyright 2016 • 386pp • H/C (ISBN: 9781522504634) • US $210.00 (our price)

Intelligent Techniques for Data Analysis in Diverse Settings
Numan Celebi (Sakarya University, Turkey)
Information Science Reference • copyright 2016 • 353pp • H/C (ISBN: 9781522500759) • US $195.00 (our price)

Managing and Processing Big Data in Cloud Computing
Rajkumar Kannan (King Faisal University, Saudi Arabia) Raihan Ur Rasool (King Faisal University, Saudi Arabia)
Hai Jin (Huazhong University of Science and Technology, China) and S.R. Balasundaram (National Institute of Technology, Tiruchirappalli, India)
Information Science Reference • copyright 2016 • 307pp • H/C (ISBN: 9781466697676) • US $200.00 (our price)

Handbook of Research on Innovative Database Query Processing Techniques
Li Yan (Nanjing University of Aeronautics and Astronautics, China)
Information Science Reference • copyright 2016 • 625pp • H/C (ISBN: 9781466687677) • US $335.00 (our price)

Handbook of Research on Trends and Future Directions in Big Data and Web Intelligence
Noor Zaman (King Faisal University, Saudi Arabia) Mohamed Elhassan Seliaman (King Faisal University, Saudi Arabia) Mohd Fadzil Hassan (Universiti Teknologi PETRONAS, Malaysia) and Fausto Pedro Garcia Marquez (Campus Universitario s/n ETSII of Ciudad Real, Spain)
Information Science Reference • copyright 2015 • 500pp • H/C (ISBN: 9781466685055) • US $285.00 (our price)

www.igi-global.com

701 E. Chocolate Ave., Hershey, PA 17033
Order online at www.igi-global.com or call 717-533-8845 x100
To place a standing order for titles released in this series, contact: cust@igi-global.com
Mon-Fri 8:00 am - 5:00 pm (est) or fax 24 hours a day 717-533-8661

List of Reviewers

Mehul P. Barot, *LDRP College, India*
Himanshu Behera, *Veer Surendra Sai University of Technology, India*
Binod Kumar, *MIT Academy of Engineering, India*
Shailednra Mishra, *Parul Institute of Technology, India*
Saurabh Mittal, *Galaxy Global Group of Institutions, India*
D. S. R. Murthy, *SreeNidhi Institute of Science and Technology, India*
Asoke Nath, *St. Xavier's College, India*
Krishnaiah R. V., *DRK Institute of Science and Technology, India*
Harish Rohil, *Chaudhary Devi Lal University, India*
Jatinderkumar R. Saini, *Narmada College of Computer Application, India*
Suresh Sankaranarayanan, *Institute Teknologi Brunei, Brunei*
Priyanka Sharma, *ISTAR, India*
Ijaz Ali Shoukat, *King Saud University, Saudi Arabia*
Evelyn R. Sowells, *North Carolina A&T State University, USA*
Anusuya Venkatesan, *Saveetha School of Engineering, India*

Table of Contents

Section 2
Applications and Analytics

Section 3
Methodologies and Technologies

Detailed Table of Contents

Section 1
Concepts and Categorization

Chapter 1

Kijpokin Kasemsap, Suan Sunandha Rajabhat University, Thailand

This chapter aims to master web mining and Information Retrieval (IR) in the digital age, thus describing the overviews of web mining and web usage mining; the significance of web mining in the digital age; the overview of IR; the concept of Collaborative Information Retrieval (CIR); the evaluation of IR systems; and the significance of IR in the digital age. Web mining can contribute to the increase in profits by selling more products and by minimizing costs. Web mining is the application of data mining techniques to discover the interesting patterns from web data in order to better serve the needs of web-based multifaceted applications. Mining web data can improve the personalization, create the selling opportunities, and lead to more profitable relationships with customers in global business. Web mining techniques can be applied with the effective analysis of the clearly understood business needs and requirements. Web mining builds the detailed customer profiles based on the transactional data. Web mining is used to create the personalized search engines which can recognize the individuals' search queries by analyzing and profiling the web user's search behavior. IR is the process of obtaining relevant information from a collection of informational resources. IR has considerably changed with the expansion of the Internet and the advent of modern and inexpensive graphical user interfaces and mass storage devices. The effective IR system, including an active indexing system, not only decreases the chances that information will be misfiled but also expedites the retrieval of information. Regarding IR utilization, the resulting time-saving benefit increases office efficiency and productivity while decreasing stress and anxiety. Most IR systems provide the advanced searching capabilities that allow users to create the sophisticated queries. The chapter argues that applying web mining and IR has the potential to enhance organizational performance and reach strategic goals in the digital age.

Web server log file contains information about every access to the web pages hosted on a server like when they were requested, the Internet Protocol (IP) address of the request, the error code, the number of bytes sent to the user, and the type of browser used. Web servers can also capture referrer logs, which show the page from which a visitor makes the next request. As the visit to web site is increasing exponentially the web logs are becoming huge data repository which can be mined to extract useful information for decision making. In this chapter, we proposed a Markov chain based method to categorize the users into faithful, Partially Impatient and Completely Impatient user. And further, their browsing behavior is analyzed. We also derived some theorems to study the browsing behavior of each user type and then some numerical illustrations are added to show how their behavior differs as per categorization. At the end we extended this work by approximating the theorems.

In the current scenario the amount of electronic resources are increasing rapidly. These resources are human readable and understandable. The industries which are managing these resources have various problems for their retrieval. In this chapter, the authors tried to propose folksonomy based information retrieval by generating tag cloud. This model not only helps the industries to manage their electronic resources for retrieval but helps them by providing suggestions for tagging with the usage of similarity metrics. This suggestive mechanism also helps users to understand resources at specific and organizations at general. The authors also have implemented the model to demonstrate the experimental results followed by discussion.

Web Usage Mining (WUM) is the process of discovery and analysis of useful information from the World Wide Web (WWW) by applying data mining techniques. The main research area in Web mining is focused on learning about Web users and their interactions with Web sites by analysing the log entries from the user log file. The motive of mining is to find users' access models automatically and quickly from the vast Web log data, such as similar queries imposed by the various users, frequent queries applied by the user, frequent web sites visited by the users, clustering of users with similar intent etc. This chapter deals with Web mining, Categories of Web mining, Web usage mining and its process, Applications of Web usage mining across the industries and its related works. This Chapter offers a general knowledge about Web usage mining and its applications for the benefits of researchers those performing research activities in WUM.

Chapter 5

An enormous production of databases in almost every area of human endeavor particularly through web has created a great demand for new, powerful tools for turning data into useful, task-oriented knowledge. The aim of this study is to study the predictive ability of Factor Analysis a web mining technique to prevent voting, averaging, stack generalization, meta- learning and thus saving much of our time in choosing the right technique for right kind of underlying dataset. This chapter compares the three factor based techniques viz. principal component regression (PCR), Generalized Least Square (GLS) Regression, and Maximum Likelihood Regression (MLR) method and explores their predictive ability on theoretical as well as on experimental basis. All the three factor based techniques have been compared using the necessary conditions for forecasting like R-Square, Adjusted R-Square, F-Test, JB (Jarque-Bera) test of normality. This study can be further explored and enhanced using sufficient conditions for forecasting like Theil's Inequality coefficient (TIC), and Janur Quotient (JQ).

Section 2
Applications and Analytics

Data mining techniques have potential to unveil the complexity of an event and yields knowledge that can create a difference. They can be employed to investigate natural phenomena; since these events are complex in nature and are difficult to characterize as there are elements of uncertainty involved in their functionality. Therefore, techniques that are compatible with uncertain elements can be employed to study them. This chapter explains the concepts of data mining and discusses at length about the landslide event. Further, the utility of data mining techniques in disaster management using a previous work was explained and provides a brief note on the efficiency of web mining in creating awareness about natural hazard by providing refined information. Finally, a conceptual framework for landslide hazard assessment using data mining techniques such as Artificial Neural Network (ANN), Fuzzy Geometric Mean Model (FGMM), etc. were chosen for description. It was quite clear from the study that data mining techniques are useful in assessing and modelling different aspects of landslide event.

In the present day scenario the World Wide Web (WWW) is an important and popular information search tool. It provides convenient access to almost all kinds of information – from education to entertainment. The main objective of the chapter is to retrieve information from websites and then use the information for website quality analysis. In this chapter information of the website is retrieved through web mining process. Web mining is the process is the integration of three knowledge domains: Web Content Mining, Web Structure Mining and Web Usage Mining. Web content mining is the process of extracting knowledge from the content of web documents. Web structure mining is the process of inferring knowledge from the World Wide Web organization and links between references and referents in the Web. The web content elements are used to derive functionality and usability of the website. The Web Component elements are used to find the performance of the website. The website structural elements are used to find the complexity and usability of the website. The quality assurance techniques for web applications generally focus on the prevention of web failure or the reduction of chances for such failures. The web failures are defined as the inability to obtain or deliver information such as documents or computational results requested by web users. A high quality website is one that provides relevant, useful content and a good user experience. Thus in this chapter, all areas of website are thoroughly studied for analysing the quality of website design.

Chapter 8

R. Umagandhi, Kongunadu Arts and Science College, India
A. V. Senthil Kumar, Hindusthan College of Arts and Science, India

Web is the largest and voluminous data source in the world. The inconceivable boom of information available in the web simultaneously throws the challenge of retrieving the precise and appropriate information at the time of need. The unpredictable amount of web information available becomes a menace of experiencing ambiguity in the web search. In this scenario, Search engine retrieves significant information from the web, based on the query term given by the user. The search queries given by the user are always short and ambiguous and the queries may not produce the appropriate results. The retrieved result may not be relevant all the time. At times irrelevant and redundant results are also retrieved because of the short and ambiguous query keywords. Query Recommendation is a technique to provide the alternate queries as a substitute of the input query to the user to frame the queries in future. A methodology was framed to identify the similar queries and they are clustered; this cluster contains the similar queries which are used to provide the recommendations.

Chapter 9

Rajan Gupta, University of Delhi, India
Sunil K. Muttoo, University of Delhi, India
Saibal K. Pal, DRDO, India

The ever increasing technology usage and the globalization have given rise to the need of quick, accurate and smarter handling of information by organizations, states, nations and the entire globe. For every nation to be under any form of government, it became mandatory to have shorter turnaround time for their interactions with citizens. This pressure gave rise to the concept of e-Governance. It has been implemented by various nations and even UN reported an increase in E-Governance activities around the world. However, the major problems that need to be addressed by developing nations are digital divide and lack of e-Infrastructure. India started its e-Governance plan through a proposal in 2006 with establishment of National e-Governance Plan popularly known as NeGP headed by Ministry of Communications and Information Technology, Government of India. As per the Electronic Transaction and Aggregation Layer, millions of transactions are taking place on regular basis. Within 2015 itself, over 2 billion transactions have been carried out by the Indian citizens in various categories and sectors like agriculture, health, and the likes. For central government projects alone, around 980 million electronic transactions have taken place, while for state government projects, the combined total of all the states is close to 1.2 billion. With the kind of data getting generated through e-Governance initiative in India, it will open up lot of opportunities for data analysts & mining experts to explore this data and generate insights out of them. The aim of this chapter is to introduce various areas and sectors in India where analytics can be applied for e-Governance related entities like citizens, corporate and government departments. It will be useful for researchers, academicians and students to understand various areas in E-Governance where web mining and data analysis can be applied. The theoretical background has been supported by practical case study for better understanding of the concepts of web analysis and mining in the area of E-Governance.

Chapter 10

The explosive growth in the amount of data in the field of biology, education, environmental research, sensor network, stock market, weather forecasting and many more due to vast use of internet in distributed environment has generated an urgent need for new techniques and tools that can intelligently automatically transform the processed data into useful information and knowledge. Hence data mining has become a research are with increasing importance. Since continuation in collection of more data at this scale, formalizing the process of big data analysis will become paramount. Given the vast amount of data are geographically spread across the globe, this means a very large number of models is generated, which raises problems on how to generalize knowledge in order to have a global view of the phenomena across the organization. This is applicable to web-based educational data. In this chapter, the new dynamic and scalable data mining approach has been discussed with educational data.

Section 3
Methodologies and Technologies

Chapter 11

Web usage mining attempts to discover useful knowledge from the secondary data obtained from the interactions of the users with the Web. It is the type of Web mining activity that involves the automatic discovery of out what users are looking for on the Internet. In this chapter methodology of web usage mining explained in detail which are data collection, data preprocessing, knowledge discovery and pattern analysis. The different Web Usage Mining techniques are described, which are used for knowledge and pattern discovery. These are statistical analysis, sequential patterns, classification, association rule mining, clustering, dependency modeling. Pattern analysis is needed to filter out uninterested rules or patterns from the set found in the pattern discovery phase.

Chapter 12

Prashant Srivastava, University of Allahabad, India
Ashish Khare, University of Allahabad, India

The proliferation of huge amount of information has made it essential to develop systems that organize and index them for easy access. The advent of World Wide Web has provided immense opportunity to the people across the world to access and share information for different uses ranging from personal to professional. Today, it is very difficult to keep track of number of research papers based on multiresolution analysis as it is widely used for various image-based applications. Also, there are a number of multiresolution techniques available to achieve this. Multiresolution processing has one big advantage that features that are left undetected at one level get detected at another level which is not the case with single resolution analysis. We demonstrate this fact with the help of an experiment using Discrete Wavelet Transform along with the discussion of various multiresolution techniques for visual information retrieval. The experiment helps in explaining the important properties of multiresolution analysis and also provides future scope of research in this field.

Chapter 13

Ahmed El Azab, Institute of Statistical Studies and Research, Egypt
Mahmood A. Mahmood, Institute of Statistical Studies and Research, Egypt
Abd El-Aziz, Institute of Statistical Studies and Research, Egypt

Web usage mining techniques and applications across industries is still exploratory and, despite an increase in academic research, there are challenge of analyze web which quantitatively capture web users' common interests and characterize their underlying tasks. This chapter addresses the problem of how to support web usage mining techniques and applications across industries by combining language of web pages and algorithms that used in web data mining. Existing research in web usage mining techniques tend to focus on finding out how each techniques can apply in different industries fields. However, there is little evidence that researchers have approached the issue of web usage mining across industries. Consequently, the aim of this chapter is to provide an overview of how the web usage mining techniques and applications across industries can be supported.

Chapter 14

B. Umamageswari, New Prince Shri Bhavani College of Engineering and Technology, India
R. Kalpana, Pondicherry Engineering College, India

Web mining is done on huge amounts of data extracted from WWW. Many researchers have developed several state-of-the-art approaches for web data extraction. So far in the literature, the focus is mainly on the techniques used for data region extraction. Applications which are fed with the extracted data, require fetching data spread across multiple web pages which should be crawled automatically. For this to happen, we need to extract not only data regions, but also the navigation links. Data extraction techniques are designed for specific HTML tags; which questions their universal applicability for carrying out information extraction from differently formatted web pages. This chapter focuses on various web data extraction techniques available for different kinds of data rich pages, classification of web data extraction techniques and comparison of those techniques across many useful dimensions.

Foreword

Today the World Wide Web, which is used to solve and retrieve information, is amazingly swelling in size because of the documents, images, and the multimedia it comprises. Web information is the most sought after powerful platform for working, studying, searching information. The unpredictable amount of web information available becomes a menace of experiencing ambiguity in the web search. The availability of numerous resources in the web as given way for the development of a wide variety of information retrieval techniques with the perspective to cater to the need of the web user. Search engines plays a vital role to explore the web resources through the queries applied by the users. To prevent the web users from getting overwhelmed by the quantity of information available in the web, several strategies are proposed. These strategies attempt to solve the tedious information exploration process of the user, through Information Systems, Information Filtering and Recommendation Systems. Web mining, one of the data mining techniques is used to retrieve the interesting and potentially useful patterns and implicit information from web documents and services. Web mining in turn supports exploring and extracting precisely pragmatic knowledge from web data. Web mining exhibits partitions namely, web content mining, web structure mining and web usage mining based on type of data used for mining process.

Web usage mining, one of the parts of web mining is used to discover the navigation patterns of the surfers from the web data. Web usage mining has seen a rapid increase in interest, from both the research and practice communities. Web usage mining has emerged as the essential tool for realizing more personalized and business optimal web services. Web usage mining proves the support for web site design, personalization server, other business making decision etc. It focuses on techniques that could predict user's behavior while the user interacts with the web. Due to the abnormal growth in web applications and user's interaction with the applications increases, the need for intelligent analysis of the web usage data is given more importance. Usage patterns discovered through web usage mining are effective in capturing item-to-item and user-to-user relationships and similarities at the level of user services.

Web usage mining when applied to e-commerce data enables the discovery of important business intelligence metrics such as customer conversion rations and lifetime values. Web usage mining is an important research area for detecting the web traffic, website reorganization, website personalization, business intelligence, system improvement, usage characterization etc. Web usage mining techniques can be applied in the areas of software engineering, marketing, artificial intelligence and database.

This timely publication shall provide the support for web site design, personalization server, other business making decision etc. It focuses on the systems, techniques and applications that could predict user's behavior while the user interacts with the web. This book shall offer significant contribution towards web information retrieval to the professionals for further research opportunities in this field. This book will provide the application of data mining techniques to the usage logs of large web data repositories in order to produce results that can be applied to many practical subjects, such as improving websites/pages making additional topic or product recommendations, user/customer behavior studies, etc.

This book seeks to address about the various systems, technologies and applications in web data which in turn provides useful information to make easier the web user navigation and to optimize the web server performance. It is hoped that this book will formulate a framework in order to gather useful usage data thoroughly, filter out irrelevant usages data, establish the actual usage data, discover interested navigation patterns, display the navigation patterns clearly, analyze and interpret the navigation patterns correctly, and apply the mining results effectively. This book shall discover interesting user navigation patterns and can be applied to many real-world problems which will be helpful to the professionals for further research opportunities which would be useful for the society.

Amit Dutta
AICTE, India

Amit Dutta *is a faculty in the Department of Computer Science, Barkatullah University, Bhopal. His area of specialization is in the field of Neural Networks. He has published many papers in International Journals. He is a Program Committee Member in various International Conferences and authored a book. Currently he is posted in AICTE as Deputy Director on Deputation.*

Preface

The World Wide Web has variety of information service centers, like news, sites, encyclopedias, education sites, e-commerce etc. Since this massive utility of web resources in recent scenario has turned to be an indispensable commitment for numerous reasons. The inconceivable boom of information available in the websites simultaneously throws the challenge of retrieving the precise and appropriate information at the time of need. Moreover, the web information is the mostly sought after powerful platform for working, studying, searching information, besides, being in touch with our friends. Apparently, the unpredictable amount of web information available becomes a menace of experiencing ambiguity in the web search. In order to successfully retain users in this rapidly developing environments, a website must be built in such a way that supports user personalization. To achieve this, an organization can keep track of user activities while browsing their websites. Besides the challenge to find relevant information, users could also find other difficulties when interacting with the web such as the degree of quality of the information found, the creation of new knowledge out of the information available (Lin & Huang, 2003).

Web Usage Mining is one of the fastest developing areas of web mining (Cooley, Mobeshar & Srivastava, 1997). Web usage mining is the application of data mining technologies to discover interesting usage patterns from web data, in order to understand and better serve the needs of web-based applications. Its attention in analyzing users behavior on the web after exploring access logs made its popularity very rapidly especially in E-services. Its direct application in these areas added its admiration and made it as an inevitable part in computer and information sciences (Lieherman & Letizia, 1995). Web usage mining provides the support for website design, personalization server, other business making decision etc.

Web Usage Mining is an aspect of data mining that has received a lot of attention in recent years. Commercial companies as well as academic researchers have developed an extension array of tools that perform several data mining algorithms on log files coming from web servers in order to identify user behavior on a particular website. Details like user log files, request for resources etc., are maintained in web servers, which is the core mining area of web usage. The analysis of these gives the user browsing patterns and that can be utilized for target advertisement, enhancement of web design, satisfaction of customers and making market analysis. Most of the e-service providers realized the fact that they can apply this tool to retain their customers (Fengrong, 2004).

Web Usage Mining provides better understanding for service the needs of web-based applications (Schafer, Konstan & Reidl, 2001). Site modification, business intelligence, system improvement, personalization and usage characterization are the areas in which the potentials of web usage mining have been recognized and extensively used.

This book, Web Usage Mining Techniques and Applications Across Industries, shall provide the support for web site design, personalization server, other business making decision etc. It focuses on the systems, techniques and applications that could predict user's behavior while the user interacts with the web. This book shall offer significant contribution towards web information retrieval to the professionals for further research opportunities in this field. This book will provide the application of data mining techniques to the usage logs of large web data repositories in order to produce results that can be applied to many practical subjects, such as improving websites/pages making additional topic or product recommendations, user/customer behavior studies, etc.

The audience of this book will widely vary from individuals, researchers, scientists, academics, students, libraries, journalists and development practitioners. This book discovers the navigation patterns of the surfers from the web data and deals with the prediction of the surfer's behavior and interaction with the web which will be useful in furthering their research exposure.

ORGANIZATION OF CHAPTERS

The book has been divided into three sections; Concepts and Categorization, Applications and Analytics, and Methodologies and Technologies. Altogether there are fourteen manuscripts covering wider range of concepts, technologies and applications.

Chapter 1 aims to master web mining and Information Retrieval (IR) in the digital age, thus describing the overviews of web mining and web usage mining; the significance of web mining in the digital age; the overview of IR; the concept of Collaborative Information Retrieval (CIR); the evaluation of IR systems; and the significance of IR in the digital age. The chapter argues that applying web mining and IR has the potential to enhance organizational performance and reach strategic goals in the digital age.

Chapter 2 proposes a Markov chain based method to categorize the users into faithful, partially Impatient and completely Impatient user. And further, their browsing behavior is analyzed. We also derived some theorems to study the browsing behavior of each user type and then some numerical illustrations are added to show how their behavior differs as per categorization. Also the chapter extends the work by approximating the theorems.

Chapter 3 illustrates folksonomy based information retrieval by generating tag cloud. This model not only helps the industries to manage their electronic resources for retrieval but helps them by providing suggestions for tagging with the usage of similarity metrics. This suggestive mechanism also helps users to understand resources at specific and organizations at general. The authors also have implemented the model to demonstrate the experimental results followed by discussion.

Chapter 4 deals Web mining, Categories of Web mining, Web usage mining and its process, Applications of Web usage mining across the industries and its related works. This Chapter offers a general knowledge about Web usage mining and its applications for the benefits of researchers those performing research activities in WUM.

Chapter 5 compares the three factor based techniques viz. principal component regression (PCR), Generalized Least Square (GLS) Regression, and Maximum Likelihood Regression (MLR) method and explores their predictive ability on theoretical as well as on experimental basis. All the three factor based techniques have been compared using the necessary conditions for forecasting like R-Square, Adjusted R-Square, F-Test, JB (Jarque-Bera) test of normality. This study can be further explored and enhanced using sufficient conditions for forecasting like Theil's Inequality Coefficient (TIC), and Janur Quotient (JQ).

Chapter 6 explains the concepts of data mining and discusses at length about the landslide event. Further, the utility of data mining techniques in disaster management using a previous work was explained and provides a brief note on the efficiency of web mining in creating awareness about natural hazard by providing refined information. Finally, a conceptual framework for landslide hazard assessment using data mining techniques such as Artificial Neural Network (ANN), Fuzzy Geometric Mean Model (FGMM), etc. were chosen for description.

Chapter 7 provides the details for a high quality website which is the one that provides relevant, useful content and a good user experience. The chapter also discusses all areas of website are thoroughly studied for analysing the quality of website. design.

Chapter 8 describes Query Recommendation, a technique to provide the alternate queries as a substitute of the input query to the user to frame the queries in future. The chapter also discusses about the methodology framed to identify the similar queries and they are clustered, which contains the similar queries which are used to provide the recommendations.

Chapter 9 presents the details about the kind of data getting generated through E-Governance initiative in India, which will help in opening up lot of opportunities for data analysts and mining experts to explore this data and generate insights out of them. The chapter also introduces areas in India where analytics can be applied for E-Governance related entities - citizens, corporate and government departments.

Chapter 10 discusses about the explosive growth in the amount of data in the field of biology, education, environmental research, sensor network, stock market, weather forecasting and many more due to vast use of internet in distributed environment has generated an urgent need for new techniques and tools that can intelligently automatically transform the processed data into useful information and knowledge. The chapter presents the new dynamic and scalable data mining approach has been discussed with educational data.

Chapter 11 explains in detail about the methodology of web usage mining which are data collection, data preprocessing, knowledge discovery and pattern analysis. The different Web Usage Mining techniques are described, which are used for knowledge and pattern discovery. These are statistical analysis, sequential patterns, classification, association rule mining, clustering, dependency modeling.

Chapter 12 demonstrates visual resolution retrieval with the help of an experiment using Discrete Wavelet Transform along with the discussion of various multiresolution techniques for visual information retrieval. The experiment explained in the chapter helps in explaining the important properties of multiresolution analysis and also provides future scope of research in this field.

Chapter 13 addresses the problem of how to support web usage mining techniques and applications across industries by combining language of web pages and algorithms that used in web data mining. Existing research in web usage mining techniques tend to focus on finding out how each techniques can apply in different industries fields. However, there is little evidence that researchers have approached the issue of web usage mining across industries. Consequently, the aim of this chapter is to provide an overview of how the web usage mining techniques and applications across industries can be supported.

Chapter 14 focuses on various web data extraction techniques available for different kinds of data rich pages, classification of web data extraction techniques and comparison of those techniques across many useful dimensions.

CONCLUSION

Web Usage Mining is becoming an active interesting field of research because of its prospective commercial benefits. Its attention in analyzing users behavior on the web after exploring access logs made its popularity very rapidly. Web usage mining has many benefits which attract business and government agencies towards it. Government agencies utilized the classification and predicting capability of this technology to fight against terrorism and identifying criminal activities. Business sectors are benefited by personalized marketing, customer retention, and customer relationship, and even they got the opportunity to provide promotional offers to specific customers to retain them (Lee, LungLo & Fu, 2011).

A. V. Senthil Kumar
Hindusthan College of Arts and Science, India

REFERENCES

Cooley, R., Mohensher, B., & Srivastava, J. (1997). Web mining information and pattern discovery on the world wide web. In *Proceedings of the 9th IEEE International Conference on Tools and Artificial Intelligence.*IEEE. doi:10.1109/TAI.1997.632303

Fengrong, J. (2004). *Study of web usage mining and discovery of browse interest.* (Thesis). Beijing Science and Technology University, Beijing, China.

Lee, C. H., Lo, Y. L., & Fu, Y. H. (2011). *A novel production model based on hierarchical characteristic of website.* Elsevier.

Lieherman, R., & Letizia. (1995). An agent that assists web browsing. In *Proceedings of the 1995 International Joint Conference on Artificial Intelligence.* Montreal, Canada: IEEE.

Lin, J. G., & Huang, H. H. (2003). Web mining for electronics business application. In *Proceedings of the Fourth International Conference on Parallel and Distribution Computing, Application and Techniques* (pp. 872-876). Academic Press.

Schafer, J. B., Konstan, J. A., & Reidl, R. (2001). E-commerce recommendation applications. *Data Mining and Knowledge Discovery*, 5(5), 115–153. doi:10.1023/A:1009804230409

Acknowledgment

I would like to thank IGI Global for offering me the opportunity to edit this book on Web Usage Mining. I am grateful to Editorial Advisory Board Members and all the valuable contributing authors of this book for the support, assistance, suggestions and contribution. My sincere thanks extends to all reviewers for their extended support during the tiring review process.

I will not have completed this work in time unless continuous support came from my wife, daughter and family members.

Finally, my regards go to the colleagues and friends for their supports and encouragements, without which, I would not have been able to complete this research publication.

A. V. Senthil Kumar
Hindusthan College of Arts and Science, India

Section 1
Concepts and Categorization

Chapter 1
Mastering Web Mining and Information Retrieval in the Digital Age

Kijpokin Kasemsap
Suan Sunandha Rajabhat University, Thailand

ABSTRACT

This chapter aims to master web mining and Information Retrieval (IR) in the digital age, thus describing the overviews of web mining and web usage mining; the significance of web mining in the digital age; the overview of IR; the concept of Collaborative Information Retrieval (CIR); the evaluation of IR systems; and the significance of IR in the digital age. Web mining can contribute to the increase in profits by selling more products and by minimizing costs. Web mining is the application of data mining techniques to discover the interesting patterns from web data in order to better serve the needs of web-based multifaceted applications. Mining web data can improve the personalization, create the selling opportunities, and lead to more profitable relationships with customers in global business. Web mining techniques can be applied with the effective analysis of the clearly understood business needs and requirements. Web mining builds the detailed customer profiles based on the transactional data. Web mining is used to create the personalized search engines which can recognize the individuals' search queries by analyzing and profiling the web user's search behavior. IR is the process of obtaining relevant information from a collection of informational resources. IR has considerably changed with the expansion of the Internet and the advent of modern and inexpensive graphical user interfaces and mass storage devices. The effective IR system, including an active indexing system, not only decreases the chances that information will be misfiled but also expedites the retrieval of information. Regarding IR utilization, the resulting time-saving benefit increases office efficiency and productivity while decreasing stress and anxiety. Most IR systems provide the advanced searching capabilities that allow users to create the sophisticated queries. The chapter argues that applying web mining and IR has the potential to enhance organizational performance and reach strategic goals in the digital age.

DOI: 10.4018/978-1-5225-0613-3.ch001

INTRODUCTION

The development of the World Wide Web has created the successful applications, such as search engines, electronic commerce (e-commerce), weblogs, and social network communications (Yin & Guo, 2013). The analysis of web usage has mostly focused on sites composed of conventional static pages (Berendt & Spiliopoulou, 2000). However, huge amounts of information available in the web derive from databases and are presented to the users in the pattern of the dynamically generated pages (Berendt & Spiliopoulou, 2000). As enterprises expand the increasing information about their business activities on their websites, website data promises as the meaningful source for exploring innovation (Gök, Waterworth, & Shapira, 2015).

With the advent of cost-effective storage systems and high-speed network connectivity, the amount of data gathered by various transactional systems has rapidly increased (Krishna, Jose, & Suri, 2014). Devi et al. (2012) stated that the rising popularity of e-commerce makes data mining a vital technology for several applications, especially online business competitiveness. Web mining is defined as the research focusing on the application of data mining techniques to web data (Borges & Levene, 2007). Markov and Larose (2007) indicated that web mining can be categorized into three domains regarding the nature of data (i.e., web structure mining, web content mining, and web usage mining).

Information retrieval (IR) systems aim to retrieve data that satisfies certain requirements and constitute an important service in many types of networks (Feng & Chin, 2015). IR is a fundamental component of human information behavior (Ruthven, 2008). There is a need for organizing the available information in the meaningful perspective in order to guide and improve the document indexing for the IR applications taking into account more complex data (Codocedo, Lykourentzou, & Napoli, 2014). The key driver of IR system becomes the degree to which a user's search is adapted to the individual user properties and the contexts of use (Steichen, Ashman, & Wade, 2012). The relevant documents from the large data sets are retrieved with the support of ranking function in IR system (Gupta, Saini, & Saxena, 2015).

Increasing amounts of data volume applied on the web and their heterogeneous character make the search for information a challenging task (Besbes & Baazaoui-Zghal, 2015). The design of IR systems must respond to the goals, intentionality, and the domain knowledge of the users (Benoît & Agarwal, 2012). Traditional ranking models for IR lack the ability to make a clear distinction between relevant and non-relevant documents at top ranks if both have similar representations concerning a user's query (Lee, Seo, Jeon, & Rim, 2011). Information requirements recognize the state for individuals seeking information, which includes information search using the IR system (Cole, 2011). Cognitive constructivism takes individual information searchers and their information interaction with IR systems regarding the primary contexts for information behavior in modern organizations (Kasemsap, 2015a).

This chapter aims to bridge the gap in the literature on the thorough literature consolidation of web mining and IR. The extant literatures of web mining and IR provide a contribution to practitioners and researchers by describing the multifaceted applications of web mining and IR to appeal to the different segments of web mining and IR in order to maximize the business impact of web mining and IR in the digital age.

BACKGROUND

The rapid development of the Internet has led to the diverse applications of accessing various web resources, such as web pages, extensible markup language (XML) documents, pictures, and audio files

(Kao & Hsu, 2007). With the rapid increase in web activities, web data mining has become an important research topic and it is receiving a significant amount of interest from both academic and industrial perspectives (Ou, Lee, & Chen, 2008). Data mining is the process of extracting the desirable knowledge and interesting patterns from the existing databases for a certain purpose (Hong, Lin, & Wang, 2002). Data mining can apply the computational methods in showing the unknown data formats in the large data sets (Kasemsap, 2015b). Data mining focuses on the techniques of non-trivial extraction of the implicit and potentially useful information from the large amounts of data (Agrawal & Mehta, 1996). Data mining tools and techniques provide the e-commerce applications with the significant knowledge (Natarajan & Shekar, 2005).

Several techniques exist in data mining, such as association rule (Park, Chen, & Yu, 1997), classification (Yu, 1999), cluster (Perkowitz & Etzioni, 2000), sequential pattern (Agrawal & Srikant, 1995), and time series (Mannila & Ronkainen, 1997). Among web mining categories, web usage mining addresses mining weblog records (Han & Kamber, 2001), which typically include the host name or IP address, remote user name, login name, date stamp, retrieval method, HyperText Transfer Protocol (HTTP) completion code, and number of bytes in the file retrieved. The goal of weblog mining is to discover the user's access behaviors that are embedded in the vast weblogs (Chen, Fu, & Tong, 2003).

The term Information Retrieval was proposed in the late 1940s by an American computer scientist Calvin Mooers, who was a specialist in the area of information theory, for working with information (Mel'nikov, Melikyan, & Maksimov, 2009). Later, Mooers proposed the peculiar computer language TRAC (Text Reckoning And Compiling), which enabled searching in texts in information stores (Mel'nikov et al., 2009). Due to the increasing importance of technology and the World Wide Web, millions of people are engaging in the IR activities when they utilize the search engines. IR engines should be able to cope with the complexity of the new document standards toward providing the new functionalities for information access (Piwowarski & Gallinari, 2005).

Over the past decades, two parallel threads of personalization research have emerged, one originating in the document space in the area of personalized information retrieval (PIR) and the other arising from the hypertext space in the field of adaptive hypermedia (AH) (Steichen et al., 2012). PIR systems take a step further to better satisfy the user's specific information needs by providing search results that are not only of relevance to the query but are also of particular relevance to the user who submitted the query (Ghorab, Zhou, O'Connor, & Wade, 2013). In order to provide the personalized service, PIR system maintains information about the users and the history of their interactions with the system (Ghorab et al., 2013).

Understanding what kinds of web pages are the most useful for the web search engine users is a critical task in web IR systems (Liu, Zhang, Cen, Ru, & Ma, 2007). With the increasing number and diversity of search tools available, interest in the evaluation of search systems, particularly from the user perspective, has grown among practitioners and researchers (Kelly & Sugimoto, 2013). More researchers are designing and evaluating the interactive IR systems and beginning to innovate in the evaluation methods (Kelly & Sugimoto, 2013). IR network is a virtual network involving the World Wide Web server hosts that have search functions (Abe, Taketa, Nunokawa, & Shiratori, 2001).

By using the IR approaches, different types of referential metadata (e.g., data sets, source code, video lectures, presentation slides, online tutorials, and scientific topics) will be automatically retrieved, associated, and ranked (Liu, 2013). Regarding IR systems, typing two or three keywords into a browser has become an easy and efficient way to find information (Hoenkamp & Bruza, 2015). The identification of the behavioral characteristics can help the IR system detect the session of the information search process (Lin & Xie, 2013).

WEB MINING AND INFORMATION RETRIEVAL IN THE DIGITAL AGE

This section emphasizes the overviews of web mining and web usage mining; the significance of web mining in the digital age; the overview of IR; the concept of CIR; the evaluation of IR systems; and the significance of IR in the digital age.

Overview of Web Mining

Web mining refers to the discovery and the analysis of data, documents, and multimedia from the World Wide Web, involving hyperlink structure, statistical usage, and document content mining (Scime, 2004). Web mining can be defined as the application of data mining techniques to web data (Oren, 1996). Etzioni (1996) defined web mining as the adoption of data mining techniques to automatically extract knowledge in the website. Web mining systems exploit the redundancy of data published on the web to automatically extract information from the existing web documents (Shchekotykhin, Jannach, & Friedrich, 2010).

Oyama et al. (2013) stated that the demand for the information technology (IT) services via the World Wide Web has grown as the Internet has evolved. The World Wide Web is the huge network composed of web pages and hyperlinks (Murata, 2007). With the explosive growth of information sources available on the World Wide Web, how to combine the results of multiple search engines has become the valuable problem (Chen, Zou, & Bian, 2009). Wikipedia is characterized by its dense link structure and a large number of articles in different languages, which make it the notable web collection for knowledge extraction and mining, in particular for mining the multilingual associations (Ye, Huang, He, & Lin, 2012).

Web structure mining identifies the authoritative web pages (Cooley, Mobasher, & Srivastava, 1999). Katz and Cothey (2006) investigated the relationships between the Internet and innovation systems by utilizing the website-based indicators from web page counts and links. van de Lei and Cunningham (2006) employed the website data in the future-oriented technology analysis, where it is used to indicate the existing networks that are concerned with technological change. Ladwig et al. (2010) utilized the web structure mining to study the landscape of online resources in the emerging technologies by determining the top search terms and resulting the top-ranked web pages from Google.

Web content mining automatically classifies the web documents and constructs the multilayered web information base (Cooley et al., 1999). Web content mining analyzes various web objects (e.g., text, images, voices, videos, and banners) to extract useful information regarding the websites (Yin & Guo, 2013). Web content mining is broadly applied in website search engine optimization (SEO) (Haveliwala, 2003) and website content redesign (Asllani & Lari, 2007). Arora et al. (2013) developed a similar web content analysis method to examine the activities of small and medium-sized enterprises (SMEs) in the United States, United Kingdom, and China, toward commercializing the emerging graphene technologies.

Webometrics (i.e., the use of metrics based on web presence in measuring scientific performance) has been recognized in science policy literature (Thelwall, 2012). Webometrics approaches utilize both web structure mining and web usage mining (Gök et al., 2015). Webometrics and web mining are two fields where research is focused on the quantitative examination of the web (Lorentzen, 2014). The key difference between the fields is that webometrics has focused on exploratory studies, whereas web mining has been dominated by the research studies focusing on the development of methods and algorithms (Lorentzen, 2014).

Ackland et al. (2010) used the web crawling to capture hyperlinks toward examining the relationships between actors engaged in nanotechnology. Youtie et al. (2012) investigated the current and archived website data of nanotechnology SMEs, with a particular focus on the transition of such technologies from discovery to commercialization. The information leak of web servers can be detected by using web mining techniques on some abnormal weblog and web application log data (Li, Zhang, Gu, & Li, 2003). Chen et al. (2014) indicated that web service tags (i.e., terms annotated by users to describe the functionality or other aspects of web services), are treated as the collective user knowledge for web service mining.

Overview of Web Usage Mining

Web usage mining is a major area of web mining that deals with extracting the useful knowledge from logging the information produced by web servers (Wang & Lee, 2011). Web usage mining discovers the users' access patterns of web pages (Cooley et al., 1999). Carmona et al. (2012) indicated that web usage mining is the process of extracting useful information from the users' history databases associated with an e-commerce website. Web server usually registers the access activities of website users in web server logs (Hung, Chen, Yang, & Deng, 2013).

Many researchers have applied the web usage mining for characterizing usage based on the navigation patterns (Bayir, Toroslu, Demirbas, & Cosar, 2012), for behavior prediction (Dimopoulos, Makris, Panagis, Theodoridis, & Tsakalidis, 2010), and for personalized recommendation (Park, Kim, Choi, & Kim, 2012). In the last decade, the importance of analyzing information management systems logs has grown, because log data constitute a relevant aspect in evaluating the quality of such systems (Agosti, Crivellari, & Di Nunzio, 2012).

The goal of web usage mining is to extract the useful information from web data or weblog files (Devi et al., 2012). Web usage mining aims to discover the browsing patterns based on the click-stream data analysis (Yin & Guo, 2013). Perkowitz and Eizioni (1997) defined adaptive website as sites which automatically improve their organization and presentations by learning from visitor access patterns. Customization-based websites display variable content for each user to satisfy the user's particular requirement, while the transformation-based websites modify the content and reorganize the link structure according to the significant browsing consensus of most users (Perkowitz & Eizioni, 2000). Data mining techniques (e.g., classification, clustering, and association rules) have been used to realize the design of adaptive websites (Mobasher, Cooley, & Srivastava, 1999). Clustering is an unsupervised learning aimed at organizing documents into hierarchical clusters (Chevalier, 2008).

There are various web usage mining techniques, such as the case-based reasoning (Godoy, Schiaffino, & Amandi, 2004), Bayesian networks (Garcia, Amandi, Schiaffino, & Campo, 2007), association rules (Schiaffino & Amandi, 2006), genetic algorithms (Yannibelli, Godoy, & Amandi, 2006), neural networks (Villaverde, Godoy, & Amandi, 2006), and topic modeling (Fujimoto, Etoh, Kinno, & Akinaga, 2011). Web usage mining, used in conjunction with standard approaches to the personalization, can help address the shortcomings of the web usage mining techniques, including the reliance on subjective user ratings, the lack of scalability, and the poor performance in the perspectives of the high-dimensional and sparse data (Mobasher, Dai, Luo, & Nakagawa, 2002).

There is the significant application regarding weblog analyzer in web usage mining that can help users discover the useful knowledge (Dong, Zhuang, & Tai, 2007). Sha et al. (2013) stated that data cleaning is an important step in the preprocessing stage of web usage mining, and it is widely used in many data mining systems. Semantic web usage log preparation model enhances the usage logs with semantic (Zhang, Song, & Xu, 2007). Frequent web navigation patterns generated by using web usage mining techniques provide the valuable information for several applications, such as website restructuring and recommendation (Senkul & Salin, 2012).

Existing web usage mining techniques are based on an arbitrary division of the data (e.g., one log per month) or guided by the presumed results (e.g., what is the customers' behavior for the period of Christmas purchases?) (Masseglia, Poncelet, Teisseire, & Marascu, 2008). The important application of sequential mining techniques is web usage mining, for mining weblog accesses, where the sequences of web page accesses made by the different web users over a period of time, through a server, are recorded (Ezeife & Lu, 2005). Privacy has been widely recognized as one of the major problems of data collections and the web (Berendt, 2012). This perspective concerns data arising from web usage (e.g., querying and transacting) and social networking characterized by the rich self-profiling and relational information (Berendt, 2012).

Significance of Web Mining in the Digital Age

Enterprises utilize their publicly-viewable websites for a wide variety of reasons, including promoting their products and services, directly selling those products and services, presenting information about their development, capabilities and credentials, documenting their achievements, and expanding their customer base, especially in export markets (Fisher, Craig, & Bentley, 2007). Enterprise websites contain valuable information about the company's locations and facilities, specifications of products offered, the orientation of the firm, key personnel, business strategies, and relationships with other companies (Gök et al., 2015). Web mining system creates the hierarchical clustering of web documents retrieved by the commercial web search engines (Schenker, Last, & Kandel, 2005).

Web mining is used in various areas of social sciences (Gök et al., 2015). AleEbrahim and Fathian (2013) developed a method to summarize the customer's online reviews from websites. Al Hassan et al. (2013) investigated whether the North American Industry Classification System code (NAICS) effectively shows the industrial sectors of Fortune 500 firms by analyzing their websites. Battistini et al. (2013) presented the technique for geohazard mapping (e.g., landslides, earthquakes, and floods) by analyzing the online news. Hoekstra et al. (2012) investigated the feasibility and desirability of the automated collection of official statistics (e.g., consumer price index) from websites.

There is a stream of publications concerning the web mining of political opinions from websites, forums, and social media (Sobkowicz, Kaschesky, & Bouchard, 2012). There are attempts to utilize the web mining in the health care industry, such as the mining of social media to discover the drug adverse effects (Yang, Yang, Jiang, & Zhang, 2012). Social media technology can enhance the improved organizational productivity by fostering the communication and collaboration of employees which aids knowledge transfer and makes organizations more profitable (Kasemsap, 2014a). Social media enables the development of knowledge value chain to customize information and delivery for a technological business growth (Kasemsap, 2014b). The capability of social media in building brand in the global marketplace is practically important in modern advertising (Kasemsap, 2015c).

The facility and speed with which business transactions can be executed over the web has been the driving force in the rapid growth of e-commerce (Kohavi, Masand, Spiliopoulou, & Srivastava, 2002). The goal of web portals is to select, organize, and distribute the content in order to satisfy customers (Domingues, Soares, & Jorge, 2013). Web mining refers to the whole of data mining and related techniques that are used to automatically discover and extract information from web documents and services (van Wel & Royakkers, 2004). When used in a business context and applied to some types of personal data, web mining helps companies build the detailed customer profiles toward gaining marketing intelligence (van Wel & Royakkers, 2004). In global business, competitiveness in e commerce requires the successful presence on the web (Spiliopoulou & Pohle, 2001).

Personalization of content returned from the website is an important problem and affects e-commerce (Kamdar & Joshi, 2005). Targeting appropriate information and products to the user can significantly change the user experience on the website (Kamdar & Joshi, 2005). Customer relationship management (CRM) is the major area that can benefit from the advancement of the web mining research (Tuzhilin, 2012). CRM becomes one of the most important business strategies in the digital age, thus involving organizational capability of managing business interactions with customers in an effective manner (Kasemsap, 2015d). Adnan et al. (2011) stated that the amount of data maintained by websites to keep track of the visitors is exponentially growing. Websites are used to establish the company's image, to sell products, and to provide customer support (Spiliopoulou & Pohle, 2001).

For decision management, the result of web usage mining can be used for target advertisement, improving web design, improving satisfaction of customer, guiding the strategy decision of the enterprise and market analysis (Lee & Fu, 2008). Arbelaitz et al. (2013) indicated that web usage mining can be used to extract knowledge from the observed actions. Web practically poses the new challenges to web mining due to its size, the complexity of web pages, its dynamic nature, the broad diversity of user communities, and the low relevance of useful information (Han & Kamber, 2001). The criteria for evaluating the web usage include the download time of the visited web pages (Yen, Hu, & Wang, 2005) and the probability of selling products (Asllani & Lari, 2007) after the reorganization of the website structure.

Regarding web usage mining, website visitor's actions can be logged and this information can be used for the user behavior analysis (Pabarskaite & Raudys, 2007). The behavior of the users of a website quickly changes that it becomes a real challenge to try to make predictions according to the frequent patterns coming from the analysis of an access log file (Masseglia, Teisseire, & Poncelet, 2003). Advances in the data mining technologies have enabled the intelligent web abilities in various applications by utilizing the hidden user behavior patterns discovered from the weblogs (Tseng, Lin, & Chang, 2008). The recent increase in HTTP traffic on the World Wide Web has generated an enormous amount of log records on web server databases (Shyu, Haruechaiyasak, & Chen, 2006). Applying web mining techniques on the server log records can discover the useful patterns and reveal the user access behaviors on the websites (Shyu et al., 2006).

The analysis of customer's behavior in e-commerce websites has attracted much attention in recent years (Liao, Chen, & Lin, 2011). The extraction of predictive knowledge is used to set the personalized recommendations in web use (Zhang & Jiao, 2007). The association rules are used for the descriptive same task (Lazcorreta, Botella, & Fernandez-Caballero, 2008). Predictive and descriptive tasks can hybridize to achieve the same purpose (Kim, Cho, Kim, Kim, & Suh, 2002) and the recommendation of time-varying products (Min & Han, 2005).

Tao et al. (2009) indicated that the intentional browsing data is a new data component for improving web usage mining that uses the weblog files as the primary data source. Intentional browsing data (Tao, Su, & Hong, 2008) is a new data ingredient to be utilized in web usage mining. Intentional browsing data is recognized to improve the estimation of web-related browsing time (Tao, Hong, & Su, 2006) and it is employed in illustrating the web transaction mining algorithms (Yun & Chen, 2000) that explore the role of purchasing behavior in the e-commerce applications.

Overview of Information Retrieval

Due to the contemporary level of development and the widespread adoption of IT, the information resources of a wide variety of volumes and contents become accessible in real time (Vasina, Golitsyna, & Maksimov, 2007). The ability to retrieve information based on a user's need has become increasingly important with the emergence of the World Wide Web and the huge increase in information available online (Cummins & O'Riordan, 2006). IR system has to retrieve the documents that are relevant to a user's query, even if index terms and query terms are not matched (Yun & Seo, 2013). User interactions with IR results have been in the focus of research activities concerning the broad development of web search engines (Keßler, 2012).

IR techniques have been extensively utilized to trace the textual artifacts to each other (Yadla, Hayes, & Dekhtyar, 2005). IR is the major area of natural language processing where statistics have been successfully applied (Fragos & Maistros, 2006). Lillis et al. (2006) stated that IR effectively forms the basis of many information management tasks. Texts in natural languages are the main direct and indirect sources of various knowledge (Kreines, 2009). The needs and expectations regarding multimedia content access have increasingly grown with the rapid development of multimedia technology and the explosion of multimedia content (Hanjalic, 2012). Visual information can be recognized as an enhanced content of the textual document (Jiang, Song, & Huang, 2014).

The application of IT for the scientific activity is related to the problem of the retrieval documentary and factual information necessary for the solution of science-intensive problems (Efremenkova & Krukovskaya, 2009). Adachi et al. (2005) indicated that the needs of efficient and flexible IR on multistructural data stored in database and network are significantly growing. It is important for the IR system to equip with the favorable graphical user interface that organizes the information into the effective visual structure for the searchers to browse during IR process (Cheung & Vogel, 2005). Multilingual IR is understood to organize the retrieval of relevant information in multiple target languages in response to a user's query in a single source language (Si, Callan, Cetintas, & Yuan, 2008). Multilingual IR provides results that are more comprehensive than those of mono- lingual retrieval and cross-lingual retrieval (Rahimi, Shakery, & King, 2015).

IR is the important process concerned with estimating the issues about information need, document, and the likelihood of relevance of the document to the information need (Hsu & Taksa, 2005). Modern IR has come to terms with numerous new media in efforts to help people find information in the diverse settings (Efron, 2011). The quality of IR system's response to an information requirement stated in a query is recognized as effectiveness (El-Khair, 2007). Effectiveness of IR system is calculated in terms of precision, recall, fallout, and miss (Verma, Tiwari, & Mishra, 2011). IR techniques can be utilized to handle a catalogue derived from an existing software package (Pighin & Brajnik, 2000). A patent is a right granted by the government of a country supporting the patent owner with the absolute right to economically utilize an invention within that country. IR tools (e.g., cross-lingual IR, document categorization, and query expansion) are often applied to provide the detailed analysis of patent applications (Rusiñol, de las Heras, & Terrades, 2014).

Personalization of IR tailors search toward individual users to meet their information needs by taking into account information about users and their contexts through the implicit sources of evidence, such as user behaviors (Liu & Belkin, 2015). The Boolean retrieval model is valuable in providing users with the power to make informed searches and have full control over what is found and what is not (Hjørland, 2015). A number of theoretical and practical perspectives on information literacy can be obtained through the examination of tenets of cognitive psychology (Macpherson, 2004). The aspect of cognitive psychology, such as information processing theory, is applied to the development of a two-stage model of the IR process (Macpherson, 2004).

Concept of Collaborative Information Retrieval

Collaborative information retrieval (CIR) is defined as a process involving multiple users which interact with each other in order to solve a specific information need (Hansen & Jarvelin, 2005). The analysis of user intent within an IR task has emphasized the increasing need of collaboration to answer the multifaceted queries (Kashyap, Hristidis, & Petropoulos, 2010) and multitopical queries (Castells, Vargas, & Wang, 2011), where result diversity is expected. Collaboration between searchers favors the synergic effect toward the inclusion of different aspects of the search results (Shah, 2012). CIR involves the retrieval settings in which a group of users collaborates to satisfy the same need (Soulier, Tamine, & Bahsoun, 2014).

CIR models involve either supporting collaboration with adapted tools or developing IR models for a multiple-user context and providing a ranked list of documents adapted for each collaborator (Soulier et al., 2014). Regarding CIR, previous research highlighted the large number of application domains for a collaborative search task, such as medical domain (Morris & Morris, 2011), academic domain (Moraveji, Morris, Morris, Czerwinski, & Riche, 2011), and political domain (Mascaro & Goggins, 2010). The issue of collaboration provides the increase in revisiting search interfaces, IR techniques, and IR models that emphasize the document rankings (Joho, Hannah, & Jose, 2009). The role taxonomy (Golovchinsky, Qvarfordt, & Pickens, 2009) has been proposed assuming that users can be assigned to the different goals in order to solve the shared information requirement.

The CIR setting is characterized by two main dimensions (i.e., the human activity dimension and the spatio-temporal dimension) (Soulier et al., 2014). Shah (2012) indicated that the human activity dimension represents collaboration as a process that exhibits four human behavior activities (i.e., cooperation, coordination, contribution, and communication). On the spatial side of the spatio-temporal dimension, collocated and remote collaboration are distinguished considering the spatial closeness of the users. On the temporal side of the spatio-temporal dimension, the differentiation between synchronous and asynchronous collaboration depends upon whether or not user activities take place at the same time (Shah, 2012).

Foley and Smeaton (2010) stated that CIR involves three principles (i.e., the division of labor, the awareness, and the sharing of knowledge). The division of labor aims at distributing work among users regarding task-based approach and document-based approach. The task-based approach which assigns the distinct search tasks among collaborators, such as looking for diversity and analyzing more in-depth document relevance (Shah, Pickens, & Golovchinsky, 2010). The document-based approach which splits the search results in order to display to the users' distinct document lists (Soulier, Tamine, & Bahsoun, 2013).

The awareness effectively alerts the users of previous submitted queries (Soulier et al., 2014). Collaborative interfaces may support the awareness principle by means of the shared workspaces, enabling users to be informed on the selected documents by the other collaborators (Morris, Paepcke, & Winograd, 2006), enabling to synchronously consider other users' actions. The sharing of knowledge enables the information flow among users by means of the shared workspaces (Gianoutsos & Grundy, 1996).

Evaluation of Information Retrieval Systems

Evaluating the effectiveness of IR systems has been a focus of IR research for decades (Tonon, Demartini, & Cudré-Mauroux, 2015). The performance characteristics of IR system effectively deal with the accuracy of the produced results which are about how effective an IR system is in retrieving the relevant documents (Moghadasi, Ravana, & Raman, 2013). In order to evaluate the effectiveness of IR systems, two different approaches complementing each other can be adopted (i.e., user-based retrieval evaluation and system-based retrieval evaluation) (Moghadasi et al., 2013).

The user-based retrieval evaluation concentrates on observing the user's interactions with the system to quantify their satisfaction levels (Fidel, 1993). The system-based retrieval evaluation focuses on experiments that are aimed to evaluate the performance of the retrieval algorithm (Mandl, 2008). IR evaluators should consider the main factors (e.g., system effectiveness, user effectiveness, user effort, user characteristics, and user expectations) in obtaining user satisfaction (Al-Maskari & Sanderson, 2010).

Bias quantification of retrieval functions with the assistance of document retrievability scores has evolved as an important evaluation measure for the recall-oriented retrieval applications (Bashir & Rauber, 2011). Using a test collection model is a common system-centered approach adopted for IR evaluation (Moghadasi et al., 2013). The system-centered approach is recognized as the Cranfield method based on the Cranfield tests executed between 1957 and 1966 as the origins of the laboratory retrieval evaluation experiments (Cleverdon, 1967). The pooling method has been adopted in the IR evaluation experiments since it produces the sufficient number of judgments for achieving the reliable results (Voorhees, 1998).

Significance of Information Retrieval in the Digital Age

IR is the research area that has generated a great deal of interest over recent years, largely due to the growth in the Internet use and the need to deploy web search engines in order to find information (Fernández-Luna, Huete, & MacFarlane, 2009). IR is related to the situations where a user, having information needs, performs queries on a collection of documents to find a limited subset of the most relevant documents (Farah & Vanderpooten, 2008). IR systems are adopted in various application domains, such as web search, digital library search, blog search, information filtering, recommender system, and social search (Gupta et al., 2015). Users and consumers often browse websites and seek various kinds of information for personal use (Yadav, 2010).

IR is the practice of matching information seekers with the information being sought (Link, Rowe, & Wood, 2011). IR systems on the Internet are developed for searching information and delivering it to users in accordance with specified criteria (Mel'nikov et al., 2009). IR systems have been applied to the distributed computing environment where various hosts store only a part of information partitioned from a very large amount of information (Jung, 2009). The development of IR performance can be increased through the improved search procedures that better match the user's information need (Xu & Benaroch, 2005).

The increasing prominence of information arising from a wide range of sources delivered over electronic media has made traditional IR less effective (Tamine-Lechani, Boughanem, & Daoud, 2010). The volume of information available online become an obstacle to the effective IR (Maleki-Dizaji, Siddiqi, Soltan-Zadeh, & Rahman, 2014). On the heterogeneous web information spaces, users have been suffering from searching for relevant information (Jung, 2007). The major concern of IR is to find the relevant documents related to user's need, modeled through a query from the large data collection in the suitable time interval (Yates & Berthier, 1999). Lang et al. (2008) stated that predicting query performance can provide the valuable feedback for users (e.g., reporting confidence scores for results and asking the users to revise the query).

As the increasing numbers of non-English resources have become available online, the important issue of how web users can retrieve the documents in different languages has arisen (Qin, Zhou, Chau, & Chen, 2006). Cross-language information retrieval (CLIR), the study of retrieving information in one language by the queries expressed in another language, is the promising approach to the problem (Qin et al., 2006). Natural language is vague and uncertain (Subtil, Mouaddib, & Faucout, 1996). Fuzzy logic can organize the uncertainty, vagueness, and impreciseness in the IR system (Zadeh, 1965).

Fuzzy logic transforms the uncertainty of documents, queries, and their characteristics into fuzzy membership functions (Zadeh, 1997). The documents are retrieved by query with the support of the rules framed in the fuzzy inference system (FIS) (Ross, 1997). Gupta et al. (2015) indicated that fuzzy logic utilizes the degrees of memberships to express the relevance unlike the Binary/Boolean model which is based on the binary decision perspectives (i.e., relevant and irrelevant aspects). Rubens (2006) proposed the fuzzy logic-based approach to defining the new ranking function. Three input variables (i.e., term frequency (tf), inverse document frequency (idf), and overlap) and one output variable (i.e., relevance) are used in the IR-related ranking function.

There are different factors which affect the performance of IR system (Lancaster & Warner, 1993). Ranking functions match the documents to a user's query and rank them according to the relevance score in descending order (Gupta et al., 2015). There are different conventional ranking functions in literature, such as Cosine ranking function, Jaccard ranking function (Salton, 1998), and Okapi ranking function (Robertson, Walker, & Hancock-Beaulieu, 2000). Cosine ranking function computes the cosine of the angle between the query and document vector. Jaccard ranking function is defined as the intersection of document and query vectors divided by the union of document and query vectors. Okapi ranking function is developed as the effective ranking function to overcome the shortcomings of Cosine ranking function and Jaccard ranking function (Gupta et al., 2015).

Vector space model (VSM) is applied as an IR model to develop the proposed ranking function due to its IR-related strengths (Gupta et al., 2015). VSM is based on the assumption that the relevance of a document with respect to a query is correlated with the distance between that query and document (Gupta et al., 2015). VSM is considered as one of the most successful IR models (Cordon, Moya, & Zarco, 2004). VSM is the simple model as the documents and queries are represented in the perspectives of vectors in the n-dimensional space, where n is the number of unique terms used to describe the contents of documents and queries (Cordon, Viedma, Pujalte, Luque, & Zarco, 2003).

Regarding IR system, Luk et al. (2002) indicated that XML holds the promise to yield more precise search by providing the additional information in the elements; the better integrated search of documents from the heterogeneous sources; the powerful search paradigm using content specifications; and the data exchange to support the cooperative search. XML arranges the experimental methods by exhibiting the properties of the reasoning assumptions that decide when the document is about a query (Blanke, Lalmas, & Huibers, 2012). Data fusion is broadly used in IR for various tasks (Wu, Li, Zeng, & Bi, 2014). Data fusion has proved to be the useful technology because it is able to improve the IR performance (Larsen, Ingwersen, & Lund, 2009). Ranking IR system is the essential IR-related operation during IR evaluation and data fusion (Efron & Winget, 2010).

Practical information access problems can be solved by analyzing the statistical properties of words in the large volumes of real-world texts (Dumais, 2003). The blogosphere is characterized by the large amounts of noise, including the interrupted content and spam (Ye, He, Wang, & Luo, 2013). The goal in the blog search is to rank the blogs according to their recurrent relevance to the topic of the query (Keikha, Crestani, & Carman, 2012). The content-based classification and the retrieval of real-world audio clips are the challenging tasks in the multimedia IR tasks (Doğan, Sert, & Yazıcı, 2011).

FUTURE RESEARCH DIRECTIONS

The classification of the extant literature in the domains of web mining and IR will provide the potential opportunities for future research. IR products are maturing beyond searching, and now provide the capabilities for knowledge management functions, such as information dissemination. As IR systems mature, they are incorporating the new features that address other areas of knowledge management. Effective knowledge management promotes knowledge creation, productivity, and economic growth. Knowledge management and organizational innovation become a source of competitive advantage in the digital age (Kasemsap, 2016a). Knowledge management is a set of behaviors, processes, and technologies that are designed for managing information more efficiently toward enhancing decision making, learning, and organizational innovation in the learning organizations (Kasemsap, 2016b).

Leaders of virtual support teams may need to assume a coordinating role to ensure effective collaboration and communication among virtual team members (Kasemsap, 2016c). The Semantic Web (also known as Web 3.0) is the technological extension of the current Web 2.0. Data in the Semantic Web is linked in a way that can be utilized for more effective discovery, automation, integration, and reuse across applications. Web mining is the process of discovering and extracting the useful knowledge from the web content mining, web usage mining, and web structure mining of one or more websites. Semantic Web mining is the combination of the Semantic Web and web mining, thus involving the integration of domain knowledge into the web mining process. The relationships among web mining, IR, the Semantic Web, the Semantic Web mining, virtual teams, and knowledge management will be the important topics for future research directions.

CONCLUSION

This chapter highlighted the overviews of web mining and web usage mining; the significance of web mining in the digital age; the overview of IR; the concept of CIR; the evaluation of IR systems; and the significance of IR in the digital age. Web mining can be beneficial to both businesses and individuals. Web mining can contribute to the increase in profits by selling more products and by minimizing costs. In order to do this, marketing intelligence is required. Marketing intelligence can focus on marketing strategy, competitive analyses, and the relationship with the customers. Regarding web mining, the different kinds of web data that are related to customers will be categorized and clustered to build the detailed customer profiles. This perspective helps companies retain the current customers by being able to provide more personalized services toward contributing in the search for potential customers. Web mining is the application of data mining techniques to discover the interesting patterns from web data in order to better serve the needs of web-based multifaceted applications.

Web mining techniques can be applied with the effective analysis of the clearly understood business needs and requirements. Web mining builds the detailed customer profiles based on the transactional data. Web mining is used to create the personalized search engines which can recognize the individuals' search queries by analyzing and profiling the web user's search behavior. Web mining offers more personalized information after filtering out the links that the web users will not be interested in. Mining web data can improve the personalization, create the selling opportunities, and lead to more profitable relationships with customers in global business. Web users can gain the benefit from web mining when the techniques are used to improve the quality of personalized search engines. Web mining assists web users while navigating through the ever-growing web. When companies provide more personalized services on their adaptive websites, the individual web users will obtain the benefit from the services adjusted to the web users' needs and preferences.

Information is a critical business resource. IR is the process of obtaining relevant information from a collection of informational resources. IR is the science of searching for documents and for information within documents, as well as searching relational databases and the World Wide Web. The effective IR system, including an active indexing system, not only decreases the chances that information will be misfiled but also expedites the retrieval of information. Regarding IR utilization, the resulting time-saving benefit increases office efficiency and productivity while decreasing stress and anxiety. IR has considerably changed with the expansion of the Internet and the advent of modern and inexpensive graphical user interfaces and mass storage devices. Beyond the development of search engines and optimization of digital libraries, IR applications encompass automatic classification, discovery, alerting, and routing systems.

IR applications reach out to automatic translation engines, providing companies with business development tools of immediate strategic relevance. Most IR systems provide the advanced searching capabilities that allow users to create the sophisticated queries. IR can help companies generate large amounts of data, ranging from internal memos and e-mail correspondence to customers statistics and market analyses. The fulfillment of web mining and IR is fundamental for modern organizations that seek to serve suppliers and customers, increase business performance, strengthen competitiveness, and achieve continuous success in the digital age. Applying web mining and IR has the potential to enhance organizational performance and gain sustainable competitive advantage in the digital age.

REFERENCES

Abe, K., Taketa, T., Nunokawa, H., & Shiratori, N. (2001). An effective search method for distributed information systems using a self-organizing information retrieval network. *Electronics and Communications in Japan (Part I Communications)*, *84*(3), 29–37.

Ackland, R., Gibson, R., Lusoli, W., & Ward, S. (2010). Engaging with the public? Assessing the online presence and communication practices of the nanotechnology industry. *Social Science Computer Review*, *28*(4), 443–465.

Adachi, F., Washio, T., Fujimoto, A., Motoda, H., & Hanafusa, H. (2005). Multi-structure information retrieval method based on transformation invariance. *New Generation Computing*, *23*(4), 291–313.

Adnan, M., Nagi, M., Kianmehr, K., Tahboub, R., Ridley, M., & Rokne, J. (2011). Promoting where, when and what? An analysis of web logs by integrating data mining and social network techniques to guide ecommerce business promotions. *Social Network Analysis and Mining*, *1*(3), 173–185.

Agosti, M., Crivellari, F., & Di Nunzio, G. M. (2012). Web log analysis: A review of a decade of studies about information acquisition, inspection and interpretation of user interaction. *Data Mining and Knowledge Discovery*, *24*(3), 663–696.

Agrawal, R., & Mehta, M. (1996). *SPRINT: A scalable parallel classifier for data mining*. Paper presented at the 22nd International Conference on Very Large Databases (VLDB 1996), Mumbai, India.

Agrawal, R., & Srikant, R. (1995). *Mining sequential patterns*. Paper presented at the 11th International Conference on Data Engineering (ICDE 1995), Taipei, Taiwan.

Al-Hassan, A. A., Alshameri, F., & Sibley, E. H. (2013). A research case study: Difficulties and recommendations when using a textual data mining tool. *Information & Management*, *50*(7), 540–552.

Al-Maskari, A., & Sanderson, M. (2010). A review of factors influencing user satisfaction in information retrieval. *Journal of the American Society for Information Science and Technology*, *61*(5), 859–868.

AleEbrahim, N., & Fathian, M. (2013). Summarising customer online reviews using a new text mining approach. *International Journal of Business Information Systems*, *13*(3), 343–358.

Arbelaitz, O., Gurrutxaga, I., Lojo, A., Muguerza, J., Perez, J. M., & Perona, I. (2013). Web usage and content mining to extract knowledge for modelling the users of the Bidasoa Turismo website and to adapt it. *Expert Systems with Applications*, *40*(18), 7478–7491.

Arora, S. K., Youtie, J., Shapira, P., Gao, L., & Ma, T. T. (2013). Entry strategies in an emerging technology: A pilot web-based study of graphene firms. *Scientometrics*, *95*(3), 1189–1207.

Asllani, A., & Lari, A. (2007). Using genetic algorithm and multiple criteria web-site optimizations. *European Journal of Operational Research*, *176*(3), 1767–1777.

Bashir, S., & Rauber, A. (2011). On the relationship between query characteristics and IR functions retrieval bias. *Journal of the American Society for Information Science and Technology*, *62*(8), 1515–1532.

Battistini, A., Segoni, S., Manzo, G., Catani, F., & Casagli, N. (2013). Web data mining for automatic inventory of geohazards at national scale. *Applied Geography (Sevenoaks, England)*, *43*, 147–158.

Bayir, M. A., Toroslu, I. H., Demirbas, M., & Cosar, A. (2012). Discovering better navigation sequences for the session construction problem. *Data & Knowledge Engineering*, *73*, 58–72.

Benoît, G., & Agarwal, N. (2012). All-visual retrieval: How people search and respond to an affect-driven visual information retrieval system. *Proceedings of the American Society for Information Science and Technology*, *49*(1), 1–4.

Berendt, B. (2012). More than modelling and hiding: Towards a comprehensive view of web mining and privacy. *Data Mining and Knowledge Discovery*, *24*(3), 697–737.

Berendt, B., & Spiliopoulou, M. (2000). Analysis of navigation behaviour in web sites integrating multiple information systems. *The VLDB Journal*, *9*(1), 56–75.

Besbes, G., & Baazaoui-Zghal, H. (2015). Modular ontologies and CBR-based hybrid system for web information retrieval. *Multimedia Tools and Applications*, *74*(18), 8053–8077.

Blanke, T., Lalmas, M., & Huibers, T. (2012). A framework for the theoretical evaluation of XML retrieval. *Journal of the American Society for Information Science and Technology, 63*(12), 2463–2473.

Borges, J., & Levene, M. (2007). Testing the predictive power of variable history web usage. *Soft Computing, 11*(8), 717–727.

Carmona, C. J., Ramirez-Gallego, S., Torres, F., Bernal, E., del Jesus, M. J., & Garcia, S. (2012). Web usage mining to improve the design of an e-commerce website: OrOliveSur.com. *Expert Systems with Applications, 39*(12), 11243–11249.

Castells, P., Vargas, S., & Wang, J. (2011). *Novelty and diversity metrics for recommender systems: Choice, discovery and relevance.* Paper presented at the 33rd European Conference on IR Research (ECIR 2011), Dublin, Ireland.

Chen, H., Zou, B., & Bian, N. (2009). Optimization of web search engine and its application to web mining. *Wuhan University Journal of Natural Sciences, 14*(2), 115–118.

Chen, L., Wu, J., Zheng, Z., Lyu, M. R., & Wu, Z. (2014). Modeling and exploiting tag relevance for web service mining. *Knowledge and Information Systems, 39*(1), 153–173.

Chen, Z., Fu, A. W. C., & Tong, F. C. H. (2003). Optimal algorithms for finding user access sessions from very large web logs. *World Wide Web (Bussum), 6*(3), 259–279.

Cheung, K. S. K., & Vogel, D. (2005). Complexity reduction in lattice-based information retrieval. *Information Retrieval, 8*(2), 285–299.

Chevalier, M. (2008). Zdravko Markov and Daniel T. Larose, Data mining the web: Uncovering patterns in web content, structure, and usage. *Information Retrieval, 11*(2), 169–174.

Cleverdon, C. (1967). The Cranfield tests on index language devices. *Aslib Proceedings, 19*(6), 173–194.

Codocedo, V., Lykourentzou, I., & Napoli, A. (2014). A semantic approach to concept lattice-based information retrieval. *Annals of Mathematics and Artificial Intelligence, 72*(1), 169–195.

Cole, C. (2011). A theory of information need for information retrieval that connects information to knowledge. *Journal of the American Society for Information Science and Technology, 62*(7), 1216–1231.

Cooley, R., Mobasher, B., & Srivastava, J. (1999). Data preparation for mining World Wide Web browsing patterns. *Journal of Knowledge and Information Systems, 1*(1), 5–32.

Cordon, O., Moya, F., & Zarco, C. (2004). *Fuzzy logic and multi-objective evolutionary algorithms as soft computing tools for persistent query learning in text retrieval environments.* Paper presented at the 14th IEEE International Conference on Fuzzy Systems (FUZZ–IEEE 2004), Budapest, Hungary.

Cordon, O., Viedma, E., Pujalte, C., Luque, M., & Zarco, C. (2003). A review on the application of evolutionary computation of information retrieval. *International Journal of Approximate Reasoning, 34*(3), 241–263.

Cummins, R., & O'Riordan, C. (2006). Evolving local and global weighting schemes in information retrieval. *Information Retrieval, 9*(3), 311–330.

Devi, B. N., Devi, Y. R., Rani, B. P., & Rao, R. R. (2012). Design and implementation of web usage mining intelligent system in the field of e-commerce. *Procedia Engineering, 30*, 20–27.

Dimopoulos, C., Makris, C., Panagis, Y., Theodoridis, E., & Tsakalidis, A. (2010). A web page usage prediction scheme using sequence indexing and clustering techniques. *Data & Knowledge Engineering, 69*(4), 371–382.

Doğan, E., Sert, M., & Yazıcı, A. (2011). A flexible and scalable audio information retrieval system for mixed-type audio signals. *International Journal of Intelligent Systems, 26*(10), 952–970.

Domingues, M. A., Soares, C., & Jorge, A. M. (2013). Using statistics, visualization and data mining for monitoring the quality of meta-data in web portals. *Information Systems and e-Business Management, 11*(4), 569–595.

Dong, Y., Zhuang, Y., & Tai, X. (2007). A novel incremental mining algorithm of frequent patterns for web usage mining. *Wuhan University Journal of Natural Sciences, 12*(5), 777–782.

Dumais, S. (2003). Data-driven approaches to information access. *Cognitive Science, 27*(3), 491–524.

Efremenkova, V. M., & Krukovskaya, N. V. (2009). Information monitoring in the area of science-intensive technologies: Optimisation of information retrieval. *Scientific and Technical Information Processing, 36*(1), 26–38.

Efron, M. (2011). Information search and retrieval in microblogs. *Journal of the American Society for Information Science and Technology, 62*(6), 996–1008.

Efron, M., & Winget, M. (2010). Query polyrepresentation for ranking retrieval systems without relevance judgments. *Journal of the American Society for Information Science and Technology, 61*(6), 1081–1091.

El-Khair, I. A. (2007). Arabic information retrieval. *Annual Review of Information Science & Technology, 41*(1), 505–533.

Etzioni, O. (1996). The World Wide Web: Quagmine or gold mine. *Communications of the ACM, 39*(11), 65–68.

Ezeife, C. I., & Lu, Y. (2005). Mining web log sequential patterns with position coded pre-order linked WAP-Tree. *Data Mining and Knowledge Discovery, 10*(1), 5–38.

Farah, M., & Vanderpooten, D. (2008). An outranking approach for information retrieval. *Information Retrieval, 11*(4), 315–334.

Feng, Z., & Chin, K. W. (2015). A novel data centric information retrieval protocol for queries in delay tolerant networks. *Journal of Network and Systems Management, 23*(4), 870–901.

Fernández-Luna, J. M., Huete, J. F., & MacFarlane, A. (2009). Introduction to the special issue on teaching and learning in information retrieval. *Information Retrieval, 12*(2), 99–101.

Fidel, R. (1993). Qualitative methods in information retrieval research. *Library & Information Science Research, 15*(3), 219–247.

Fisher, J., Craig, A., & Bentley, J. (2007). Moving from a web presence to e-commerce: The importance of a business-web strategy for small-business owners. *Electronic Markets, 17*(4), 253–262.

Foley, C., & Smeaton, A. F. (2010). Division of labour and sharing of knowledge for synchronous collaborative information retrieval. *Information Processing & Management, 46*(6), 762–772.

Fragos, K., & Maistros, Y. (2006). A goodness of fit test approach in information retrieval. *Information Retrieval, 9*(3), 331–342.

Fujimoto, H., Etoh, M., Kinno, A., & Akinaga, Y. (2011). Web user profiling on proxy logs and its evaluation in personalization. In X. Du, W. Fan, J. Wang, Z. Peng, & M. Sharaf (Eds.), *Web technologies and applications.*Lecture notes in computer science (pp. 107–118). Berlin, Germany: Springer–Verlag.

Garcia, P., Amandi, A., Schiaffino, S., & Campo, M. (2007). Evaluating Bayesian networks precision for detecting students learning styles. *Computers & Education, 49*(3), 794–808.

Ghorab, M. R., Zhou, D., O'Connor, A., & Wade, V. (2013). Personalised information retrieval: Survey and classification. *User Modeling and User-Adapted Interaction, 23*(4), 381–443.

Gianoutsos, S., & Grundy, J. (1996). *Collaborative work with the World Wide Web: Adding CSCW support to a web browser.* Paper presented at the 1996 ACM Conference on Computer Supported Cooperative Work (CSCW 1996), Boston, MA.

Godoy, D., Schiaffino, S., & Amandi, A. (2004). Interface agents personalizing web-based tasks. *Cognitive Systems Research Journal, 5*(3), 207–222.

Gök, A., Waterworth, A., & Shapira, P. (2015). Use of web mining in studying innovation. *Scientometrics, 102*(1), 653–671. PMID:26696691

Golovchinsky, G., Qvarfordt, O., & Pickens, J. (2009). Collaborative information seeking. *Computer, 42*(3), 47–51.

Gupta, Y., Saini, A., & Saxena, A. K. (2015). A new fuzzy logic based ranking function for efficient Information Retrieval system. *Expert Systems with Applications, 42*(3), 1223–1234.

Han, J., & Kamber, M. (2001). *Data mining: Concepts and techniques.* San Francisco, CA: Academic Press.

Hanjalic, A. (2012). New grand challenge for multimedia information retrieval: Bridging the utility gap. *International Journal of Multimedia Information Retrieval, 1*(3), 139–152.

Hansen, P., & Jarvelin, K. (2005). Collaborative information retrieval in an information-intensive domain. *Information Processing & Management, 41*(5), 1101–1119.

Haveliwala, T. H. (2003). Topic-sensitive PageRank: A context-sensitive ranking algorithm for web search. *IEEE Transactions on Knowledge and Data Engineering, 15*(4), 784–796.

Hjørland, B. (2015). Classical databases and knowledge organization: A case for Boolean retrieval and human decision-making during searches. *Journal of the Association for Information Science and Technology, 66*(8), 1559–1575.

Hoekstra, R., ten Bosch, O., & Harteveld, F. (2012). Automated data collection from web sources for official statistics: First experiences. *Statistical Journal of the IAOS: Journal of the International Association for Official Statistics*, 28(3/4), 99–111.

Hoenkamp, E., & Bruza, P. (2015). How everyday language can and will boost effective information retrieval. *Journal of the Association for Information Science and Technology*, 66(8), 1546–1558.

Hong, T. P., Lin, K. Y., & Wang, S. L. (2002). Mining linguistic browsing patterns in the World Wide Web. *Soft Computing*, 6(5), 329–336.

Hsu, D. F., & Taksa, I. (2005). Comparing rank and score combination methods for data fusion in information retrieval. *Information Retrieval*, 8(3), 449–480.

Hung, Y. S., Chen, K. L. B., Yang, C. T., & Deng, G. F. (2013). Web usage mining for analysing elder self-care behavior patterns. *Expert Systems with Applications*, 40(2), 775–783.

Jiang, S., Song, X., & Huang, Q. (2014). Relative image similarity learning with contextual information for Internet cross-media retrieval. *Multimedia Systems*, 20(6), 645–657.

Joho, H., Hannah, D., & Jose, J. M. (2009). *Revisiting IR techniques for collaborative search strategies*. Paper presented at the 31st European Conference on IR Research (ECIR 2009), Toulouse, France.

Jung, J. J. (2007). Ontological framework based on contextual mediation for collaborative information retrieval. *Information Retrieval*, 10(1), 85–109.

Jung, J. J. (2009). Consensus-based evaluation framework for distributed information retrieval systems. *Knowledge and Information Systems*, 18(2), 199–211.

Kamdar, T., & Joshi, A. (2005). Using incremental web log mining to create adaptive web servers. *International Journal on Digital Libraries*, 5(2), 133–150.

Kao, S. J., & Hsu, I. C. (2007). Semantic Web approach to smart link generation for web navigations. *Software, Practice & Experience*, 37(8), 857–879.

Kasemsap, K. (2014a). The role of social networking in global business environments. In P. Smith & T. Cockburn (Eds.), *Impact of emerging digital technologies on leadership in global business* (pp. 183–201). Hershey, PA: IGI Global.

Kasemsap, K. (2014b). The role of social media in the knowledge-based organizations. In I. Lee (Ed.), *Integrating social media into business practice, applications, management, and models* (pp. 254–275). Hershey, PA: IGI Global.

Kasemsap, K. (2015a). Theory of cognitive constructivism. In M. Al-Suqri & A. Al-Aufi (Eds.), *Information seeking behavior and technology adoption: Theories and trends* (pp. 1–25). Hershey, PA: IGI Global.

Kasemsap, K. (2015b). The role of data mining for business intelligence in knowledge management. In A. Azevedo & M. Santos (Eds.), *Integration of data mining in business intelligence systems* (pp. 12–33). Hershey, PA: IGI Global.

Kasemsap, K. (2015c). The role of social media in international advertising. In N. Taşkıran & R. Yılmaz (Eds.), *Handbook of research on effective advertising strategies in the social media age* (pp. 171–196). Hershey, PA: IGI Global.

Kasemsap, K. (2015d). The role of customer relationship management in the global business environments. In T. Tsiakis (Ed.), *Trends and innovations in marketing information systems* (pp. 130–156). Hershey, PA: IGI Global.

Kasemsap, K. (2016a). The roles of knowledge management and organizational innovation in global business. In G. Jamil, J. Poças-Rascão, F. Ribeiro, & A. Malheiro da Silva (Eds.), *Handbook of research on information architecture and management in modern organizations* (pp. 130–153). Hershey, PA: IGI Global.

Kasemsap, K. (2016b). The roles of e-learning, organizational learning, and knowledge management in the learning organizations. In E. Railean, G. Walker, A. Elçi, & L. Jackson (Eds.), *Handbook of research on applied learning theory and design in modern education* (pp. 786–816). Hershey, PA: IGI Global.

Kasemsap, K. (2016c). Examining the roles of virtual team and information technology in global business. In C. Graham (Ed.), *Strategic management and leadership for systems development in virtual spaces* (pp. 1–21). Hershey, PA: IGI Global.

Kashyap, A., Hristidis, V., & Petropoulos, M. (2010). *FACeTOR: Cost-driven exploration of faceted query results*. Paper presented at the 19th ACM Conference on Information and Knowledge Management (CIKM 2010), Toronto, Canada.

Katz, J. S., & Cothey, V. (2006). Web indicators for complex innovation systems. *Research Evaluation*, *15*(2), 85–95.

Keikha, M., Crestani, F., & Carman, M. J. (2012). Employing document dependency in blog search. *Journal of the American Society for Information Science and Technology*, *63*(2), 354–365.

Kelly, D., & Sugimoto, C. R. (2013). A systematic review of interactive information retrieval evaluation studies, 1967–2006. *Journal of the American Society for Information Science and Technology*, *64*(4), 745–770.

Keßler, C. (2012). What is the difference? A cognitive dissimilarity measure for information retrieval result sets. *Knowledge and Information Systems*, *30*(2), 319–340.

Kim, J. K., Cho, Y. H., Kim, W. J., Kim, J. R., & Suh, J. H. (2002). A personalized recommendation procedure for Internet shopping support. *Electronic Commerce Research and Applications*, *1*(3/4), 301–313.

Kohavi, R., Masand, B., Spiliopoulou, M., & Srivastava, J. (2002). Web mining. *Data Mining and Knowledge Discovery*, *6*(1), 5–8.

Kreines, M. G. (2009). Models and technologies for the extraction of aggregated knowledge to control processes of the retrieval of non-structured information. *Journal of Computer and Systems Sciences International*, *48*(2), 272–281.

Krishna, V., Jose, J., & Suri, N. N. R. R. (2014). Design and development of a web-enabled data mining system employing JEE technologies. *Sadhana*, *39*(6), 1259–1270.

Ladwig, P., Anderson, A. A., Brossard, D., Scheufele, D. A., & Shaw, B. (2010). Narrowing the nano discourse? *Materials Today*, *13*(5), 52–54.

Lancaster, F. W., & Warner, A. I. (1993). *Information retrieval today*. Arlington, VA: Information Resources Press.

Lang, H., Wang, B., Jones, G., Li, J. T., Ding, F., & Liu, Y. X. (2008). Query performance prediction for information retrieval based on covering topic score. *Journal of Computer Science and Technology*, *23*(4), 590–601.

Larsen, B., Ingwersen, P., & Lund, B. (2009). Data fusion according to the principle of polyrepresentation. *Journal of the American Society for Information Science and Technology*, *60*(4), 646–654.

Lazcorreta, E., Botella, F., & Fernandez-Caballero, A. (2008). Towards personalized recommendation by two-step modified Apriori data mining algorithm. *Expert Systems with Applications*, *35*(3), 1422–1429.

Lee, C. H., & Fu, Y. H. (2008). *Web usage mining based on clustering of browsing features*. Paper presented at the Eighth International Conference on Intelligent Systems Design and Applications (ISDA 2008), Kaohsiung, Taiwan.

Lee, J. T., Seo, J., Jeon, J., & Rim, H. C. (2011). Sentence-based relevance flow analysis for high accuracy retrieval. *Journal of the American Society for Information Science and Technology*, *62*(9), 1666–1675.

Li, J., Zhang, G. Y., Gu, G. C., & Li, J. L. (2003). The design and implementation of web mining in web sites security. *Journal of Marine Science and Application*, *2*(1), 81–86.

Liao, S. H., Chen, Y. J., & Lin, Y. T. (2011). Mining customer knowledge to implement online shopping and home delivery for hypermarkets. *Expert Systems with Applications*, *38*(4), 3982–3991.

Lillis, D., Toolan, F., Mur, A., Peng, L., Collier, R., & Dunnion, J. (2006). Probability-based fusion of information retrieval result sets. *Artificial Intelligence*, *25*(1), 179–191.

Lin, C. W., & Hong, T. P. (2013). A survey of fuzzy web mining. *Wiley Interdisciplinary Reviews: Data Mining and Knowledge Discovery*, *3*(3), 190–199.

Lin, S., & Xie, I. (2013). Behavioral changes in transmuting multisession successive searches over the web. *Journal of the American Society for Information Science and Technology*, *64*(6), 1259–1283.

Link, A. N., Rowe, B. R., & Wood, D. W. (2011). Information about information: Public investments in information retrieval research. *Journal of the Knowledge Economy*, *2*(2), 192–200.

Liu, J., & Belkin, N. J. (2015). Personalizing information retrieval for multi-session tasks: Examining the roles of task stage, task type, and topic knowledge on the interpretation of dwell time as an indicator of document usefulness. *Journal of the Association for Information Science and Technology*, *66*(1), 58–81.

Liu, X. (2013). Generating metadata for cyberlearning resources through information retrieval and meta-search. *Journal of the American Society for Information Science and Technology*, *64*(4), 771–786.

Liu, Y., Zhang, M., Cen, R., Ru, L., & Ma, S. (2007). Data cleansing for web information retrieval using query independent features. *Journal of the American Society for Information Science and Technology*, *58*(12), 1884–1898.

Lorentzen, D. G. (2014). Webometrics benefitting from web mining? An investigation of methods and applications of two research fields. *Scientometrics, 99*(2), 409–445.

Luk, R. W. P., Leong, H. V., Dillon, T. S., Chan, A. T. S., Croft, W. B., & Allan, J. (2002). A survey in indexing and searching XML documents. *Journal of the American Society for Information Science and Technology, 53*(6), 415–437.

Macpherson, K. (2004). An information processing model of undergraduate electronic database information retrieval. *Journal of the American Society for Information Science and Technology, 55*(4), 333–347.

Maleki-Dizaji, S., Siddiqi, J., Soltan-Zadeh, Y., & Rahman, F. (2014). Adaptive information retrieval system via modelling user behaviour. *Journal of Ambient Intelligence and Humanized Computing, 5*(1), 105–110.

Mandl, T. (2008). Recent developments in the evaluation of information retrieval systems: Moving towards diversity and practical relevance. *Informatica, 32*(1), 27–38.

Mannila, H., & Ronkainen, P. (1997). *Similarity of event sequences*. Paper presented at the Fourth International Workshop on Temporal Representation and Reasoning (TIME 1997), Daytona Beach, FL.

Markov, Z., & Larose, D. T. (2007). *Data mining the web: Uncovering patterns in web content, structure, and usage*. Hoboken, NJ: Wiley–Interscience.

Mascaro, C. M., & Goggins, S. (2010). *Collaborative information seeking in an online political group environment*. Paper presented at the Second International Workshop on Collaborative Information Seeking at CSCW 2010, Savannah, GA.

Masseglia, F., Poncelet, P., Teisseire, M., & Marascu, A. (2008). Web usage mining: Extracting unexpected periods from web logs. *Data Mining and Knowledge Discovery, 16*(1), 39–65.

Masseglia, F., Teisseire, M., & Poncelet, P. (2003). HDM: A client/server/engine architecture for real-time web usage mining. *Knowledge and Information Systems, 5*(4), 439–465.

Mel'nikov, V. O., Melikyan, G. S., & Maksimov, O. A. (2009). Characteristics of information retrieval systems on the Internet: Theoretical and practical aspects. *Automatic Documentation and Mathematical Linguistics, 43*(1), 42–50.

Min, D. H., & Han, I. (2005). Detection of the customer time-variant pattern for improving recommender systems. *Expert Systems with Applications, 28*(2), 189–199.

Mobasher, B., Cooley, R., & Srivastava, J. (1999). *Creating adaptive web sites through usage-based clustering of URLs*. Paper presented at the 1999 IEEE Knowledge and Data Engineering Exchange Workshop (KDEX 1999), Chicago, IL.

Mobasher, B., Dai, H., Luo, T., & Nakagawa, M. (2002). Discovery and evaluation of aggregate usage profiles for web personalization. *Data Mining and Knowledge Discovery, 6*(1), 61–82.

Moghadasi, S. I., Ravana, S. D., & Raman, S. N. (2013). Low-cost evaluation techniques for information retrieval systems: A review. *Journal of Informetrics, 7*(2), 301–312.

Moraveji, N., Morris, M., Morris, D., Czerwinski, M., & Riche, N. H. (2011). *ClassSearch: Facilitating the development of web search skills through social learning.* Paper presented at the the 29th Annual ACM Conference on Human Factors in Computing Systems (CHI 2011), Vancouver, Canada.

Morris, M. R., & Morris, D. (2011). *Understanding the potential for collaborative search technologies in clinical settings.* Paper presented at the Third Workshop on Collaborative Information Retrieval (CIR 2011), Glasgow, United Kingdom.

Morris, M. R., Paepcke, A., & Winograd, T. (2006). *TeamSearch: Comparing techniques for co-present collaborative search of digital media.* Paper presented at the First IEEE International Workshop on Horizontal Interactive Human-Computer Systems (TableTop 2006), Adelaide, Australia.

Murata, T. (2007). Discovery of user communities based on terms of web log data. *New Generation Computing, 25*(3), 293–303.

Natarajan, R., & Shekar, B. (2005). Interestingness of association rules in data mining: Issues relevant to e-commerce. *Sadhana, 30*(2/3), 291–309.

Oren, E. (1996). The World Wide Web: Quagmire or gold mine. *Communications of the ACM, 39*(11), 65–68.

Ou, J. C., Lee, C. H., & Chen, M. S. (2008). Efficient algorithms for incremental web log mining with dynamic thresholds. *The VLDB Journal, 7*(4), 827–845.

Oyama, K., Kageura, K., Kando, N., Kimura, M., Maruyama, K., Yoshioka, M., & Takahashi, K. (2003). Development of an information retrieval system suitable for large-scale scholarly databases. *Systems and Computers in Japan, 34*(6), 44–58.

Pabarskaite, Z., & Raudys, A. (2007). A process of knowledge discovery from web log data: Systematization and critical review. *Journal of Intelligent Information Systems, 28*(1), 79–104.

Park, D. H., Kim, H. K., Choi, I. Y., & Kim, J. K. (2012). A literature review and classification of recommender systems research. *Expert Systems with Applications, 39*(11), 10059–10072.

Park, J. S., Chen, M. S., & Yu, P. S. (1997). Using a hash-based method with transaction trimming for mining association rules. *IEEE Transactions on Knowledge and Data Engineering, 9*(5), 813–825.

Perkowitz, M., & Etzioni, O. (1997). *Adaptive web sites: An AI challenge.* Paper presented at the 15th International Joint Conference on Artificial Intelligence (IJCAI 1997), Nagoya, Japan.

Perkowitz, M., & Etzioni, O. (2000). Towards adaptive web sites: Conceptual framework and case study. *Artificial Intelligence, 118*(1/2), 245–275.

Pighin, M., & Brajnik, G. (2000). A formative evaluation of information retrieval techniques applied to software catalogues. *Journal of Systems and Software, 52*(2), 131–138.

Piwowarski, B., & Gallinari, P. (2005). A Bayesian framework for XML information retrieval: Searching and learning with the INEX collection. *Information Retrieval, 8*(4), 655–681.

Qin, J., Zhou, Y., Chau, M., & Chen, H. (2006). Multilingual web retrieval: An experiment in English–Chinese business intelligence. *Journal of the American Society for Information Science and Technology*, *57*(5), 671–683.

Rahimi, R., Shakery, A., & King, I. (2015). Multilingual information retrieval in the language modeling framework. *Information Retrieval Journal*, *18*(3), 246–281.

Robertson, S. E., Walker, S., & Hancock-Beaulieu, M. (2000). Experimentation as a way of life: Okapi at TREC. *Information Processing & Management*, *36*(1), 95–108.

Ross, T. J. (1997). *Fuzzy logic with engineering applications*. Singapore: McGraw–Hill.

Rubens, N. O. (2006). The application of fuzzy logic to the construction of the ranking function of information retrieval system. *Computer Modeling and New Technologies*, *10*(1), 20–27.

Rusiñol, M., de las Heras, L. P., & Terrades, O. R. (2014). Flowchart recognition for non-textual information retrieval in patent search. *Information Retrieval*, *17*(5/6), 545–562.

Ruthven, I. (2008). Interactive information retrieval. *Annual Review of Information Science & Technology*, *42*(1), 43–91.

Schenker, A., Last, M., & Kandel, A. (2005). Design and implementation of a web mining system for organizing search engine results. *International Journal of Intelligent Systems*, *20*(6), 607–625.

Schiaffino, S., & Amandi, A. (2006). Polite personal agent. *IEEE Intelligent Systems*, *21*(1), 12–19.

Scime, A. (2004). Guest editor's introduction: Special issue on web content mining. *Journal of Intelligent Information Systems*, *22*(3), 211–213.

Senkul, P., & Salin, S. (2012). Improving pattern quality in web usage mining by using semantic information. *Knowledge and Information Systems*, *30*(3), 527–541.

Sha, H., Liu, T., Qin, P., Sun, Y., & Liu, Q. (2013). EPLogCleaner: Improving data quality of enterprise proxy logs for efficient web usage mining. *Procedia Computer Science*, *17*, 812–818.

Shah, C. (2012). *Collaborative information seeking: The art and science of making the whole greater than the sum of all*. New York, NY: Springer–Verlag.

Shah, C., Pickens, J., & Golovchinsky, G. (2010). Role-based results redistribution for collaborative information retrieval. *Information Processing & Management*, *46*(6), 773–781.

Shchekotykhin, K., Jannach, D., & Friedrich, G. (2010). xCrawl: A high-recall crawling method for web mining. *Knowledge and Information Systems*, *25*(2), 303–326.

Shyu, M. L., Haruechaiyasak, C., & Chen, S. C. (2006). Mining user access patterns with traversal constraint for predicting web page requests. *Knowledge and Information Systems*, *10*(4), 515–528.

Si, L., Callan, J., Cetintas, S., & Yuan, H. (2008). An effective and efficient results merging strategy for multilingual information retrieval in federated search environments. *Information Retrieval*, *11*(1), 1–24.

Sobkowicz, P., Kaschesky, M., & Bouchard, G. (2012). Opinion mining in social media: Modeling, simulating, and forecasting political opinions in the web. *Government Information Quarterly*, *29*(4), 470–479.

Soulier, L., Tamine, L., & Bahsoun, W. (2013). *A collaborative document ranking model for a multi-faceted search*. Paper presented at the Ninth Asia Information Retrieval Society Conference (AIRS 2013), Singapore.

Soulier, L., Tamine, L., & Bahsoun, W. (2014). On domain expertise-based roles in collaborative information retrieval. *Information Processing & Management, 50*(5), 752–774.

Spiliopoulou, M., & Pohle, C. (2001). Data mining for measuring and improving the success of web sites. *Data Mining and Knowledge Discovery, 5*(1/2), 85–114.

Steichen, B., Ashman, H., & Wade, V. (2012). A comparative survey of personalised information retrieval and adaptive hypermedia techniques. *Information Processing & Management, 48*(4), 698–724.

Subtil, P., Mouaddib, N., & Faucout, O. (1996). *A fuzzy information retrieval and management system and its applications*. Paper presented at the 1996 ACM Symposium on Applied Computing (SAC 1996), Philadelphia, PA.

Tamine-Lechani, L., Boughanem, M., & Daoud, M. (2010). Evaluation of contextual information retrieval effectiveness: Overview of issues and research. *Knowledge and Information Systems, 24*(1), 1–34.

Tao, Y. H., Hong, T. P., Lin, W. Y., & Chiu, W. Y. (2009). A practical extension of web usage mining with intentional browsing data toward usage. *Expert Systems with Applications, 36*(2), 3937–3945.

Tao, Y. H., Hong, T. P., & Su, Y. M. (2006). Improving browsing time estimation with intentional behaviour data. *International Journal of Computer Science and Network Security, 6*(12), 35–39.

Tao, Y. H., Su, Y. M., & Hong, T. P. (2008). Web usage mining algorithm with intentional browsing data. *Expert Systems with Applications, 35*(4), 1893–1904.

Thelwall, M. (2012). A history of webometrics. *Bulletin of the American Society for Information Science and Technology, 38*(6), 18–23.

Tonon, A., Demartini, G., & Cudré-Mauroux, P. (2015). Pooling-based continuous evaluation of information retrieval systems. *Information Retrieval Journal, 18*(5), 445–472.

Tseng, V. S., Lin, K. W., & Chang, J. C. (2008). Prediction of user navigation patterns by mining the temporal web usage evolution. *Soft Computing, 12*(2), 157–163.

Tuzhilin, A. (2012). Customer relationship management and web mining: The next frontier. *Data Mining and Knowledge Discovery, 24*(3), 584–612.

van de Lei, T. E., & Cunningham, S. W. (2006). *Use of the Internet for future-oriented technology analysis*. Paper presented at the Second International Seville Seminar on Future-Oriented Technology Analysis: Impact of FTA Approaches on Policy and Decision-Making, Seville, Spain.

van Wel, L., & Royakkers, L. (2004). Ethical issues in web data mining. *Ethics and Information Technology, 6*(2), 129–140.

Vasina, E. N., Golitsyna, O. L., & Maksimov, N. V. (2007). The architecture of a computerized information retrieval system: Technologies and aids of retrieving in documentary information resources. *Scientific and Technical Information Processing, 34*(3), 117–130.

Verma, A., Tiwari, M. K., & Mishra, N. (2011). Minimizing time risk in on-line bidding: An adaptive information retrieval based approach. *Expert Systems with Applications*, *38*(4), 3679–3689.

Villaverde, J., Godoy, D., & Amandi, A. (2006). Learning styles' recognition in e-learning environments with feed-forward neural networks. *Journal of Computer Assisted Learning*, *22*(3), 197–206.

Voorhees, E. M. (1998). *Variations in relevance judgments and the measurement of retrieval effectiveness*. Paper presented at the 21st Annual International ACM Conference on Research and Development in Information Retrieval (SIGIR 1998), Melbourne, Australia.

Wang, Y. T., & Lee, A. J. T. (2011). Mining web navigation patterns with a path traversal graph. *Expert Systems with Applications*, *38*(6), 7112–7122.

Wu, S., Li, J., Zeng, X., & Bi, Y. (2014). Adaptive data fusion methods in information retrieval. *Journal of the Association for Information Science and Technology*, *65*(10), 2048–2061.

Xu, Y., & Benaroch, M. (2005). Information retrieval with a hybrid automatic query expansion and data fusion procedure. *Information Retrieval*, *8*(1), 41–65.

Yadav, S. B. (2010). A conceptual model for user-centered quality information retrieval on the World Wide Web. *Journal of Intelligent Information Systems*, *35*(1), 91–121.

Yadla, S., Hayes, J. H., & Dekhtyar, A. (2005). Tracing requirements to defect reports: An application of information retrieval techniques. *Innovations in Systems and Software Engineering*, *1*(2), 116–124.

Yang, C. C., Yang, H., Jiang, L., & Zhang, M. (2012). *Social media mining for drug safety signal detection*. Paper presented at the 2012 International Workshop on Smart Health and Wellbeing (SHB 2012). New York, NY.

Yannibelli, V., Godoy, D., & Amandi, A. (2006). A genetic algorithm approach to recognize students learning styles. *Interactive Learning Environments*, *14*(1), 55–78.

Yates, R. B., & Berthier, R. (1999). *Modern information retrieval*. Boston, MA: Addison–Wesley.

Ye, Z., He, B., Wang, L., & Luo, T. (2013). Utilizing term proximity for blog post retrieval. *Journal of the American Society for Information Science and Technology*, *64*(11), 2278–2298.

Ye, Z., Huang, J. X., He, B., & Lin, H. (2012). Mining a multilingual association dictionary from Wikipedia for cross-language information retrieval. *Journal of the American Society for Information Science and Technology*, *63*(12), 2474–2487.

Yen, B., Hu, P., & Wang, M. (2005). *Towards effective web site designs: A framework for modeling, design evaluation and enhancement*. Paper presented at the 2005 IEEE International Conference on e-Technology, e-Commerce and e-Service (EEE 2005), Hong Kong.

Yin, P. Y., & Guo, Y. M. (2013). Optimization of multi-criteria website structure based on enhanced tabu search and web usage mining. *Applied Mathematics and Computation*, *219*(24), 11082–11095.

Youtie, J., Hicks, D., Shapira, P., & Horsley, T. (2012). Pathways from discovery to commercialisation: Using web sources to track small and medium-sized enterprise strategies in emerging nanotechnologies. *Technology Analysis and Strategic Management*, *24*(10), 981–995.

Yu, P. (1999). *Data mining and personalization technologies*. Paper presented at the Sixth IEEE International Conference on Database Systems for Advanced Applications (DASFAA 1999), Hsinchu, Taiwan.

Yun, B. H., & Seo, C. H. (2003). Semantic-based information retrieval for content management and security. *Computational Intelligence, 19*(2), 87–110.

Yun, C. H., & Chen, M. S. (2000). *Using pattern-join and purchase-combination for mining transaction patterns in an electronic commerce environment*. Paper presented at the 24th Annual International Computer Software and Applications Conference (COMP–SAC 2000), Taipei, Taiwan.

Zadeh, L. A. (1965). Fuzzy sets. *Information and Control, 8*(3), 338–353.

Zadeh, L. A. (1997). Toward a theory of fuzzy information granulation and its centrality in human reasoning and fuzzy logic. *Fuzzy Sets and Systems, 90*(2), 111–127.

Zhang, H., Song, H., & Xu, X. (2007). Semantic session analysis for web usage mining. *Wuhan University Journal of Natural Sciences, 12*(5), 773–776.

Zhang, Y., & Jiao, J. (2007). An associative classification-based recommendation system for personalization in B2C e-commerce applications. *Expert Systems with Applications, 33*(2), 357–367.

ADDITIONAL READING

Abbasi, M. K., & Frommholz, I. (2015). Cluster-based polyrepresentation as science modelling approach for information retrieval. *Scientometrics, 102*(3), 2301–2322.

Borg, M., Runeson, P., & Ardö, A. (2014). Recovering from a decade: A systematic mapping of information retrieval approaches to software traceability. *Empirical Software Engineering, 19*(6), 1565–1616.

Chen, J., Knudson, R., & Namgoong, M. (2014). An investigation of effective and efficient multilingual information access to digital collections. *Proceedings of the American Society for Information Science and Technology, 51*(1), 1–3.

Cohen, A., & Nachmias, R. (2011). What can instructors and policy makers learn about web-supported learning through web-usage mining. *The Internet and Higher Education, 14*(2), 67–76.

Dyomin, V. V., & Kamenev, D. V. (2015). Methods of processing and retrieval of information from digital particle holograms and their application. *Radiophysics and Quantum Electronics, 57*(8), 533–542.

Glänzel, W. (2015). Bibliometrics-aided retrieval: Where information retrieval meets scientometrics. *Scientometrics, 102*(3), 2215–2222.

Golitsyna, O. L., & Maksimov, N. V. (2011). Information retrieval models in the context of retrieval tasks. *Automatic Documentation and Mathematical Linguistics, 45*(1), 20–32.

Hagood, J. (2012). A brief introduction to data mining projects in the humanities. *Bulletin of the American Society for Information Science and Technology, 38*(4), 20–23.

Kim, S., Ko, Y., & Oard, D. W. (2015). Combining lexical and statistical translation evidence for cross-language information retrieval. *Journal of the Association for Information Science and Technology*, *66*(1), 23–39.

Koedinger, K. R., D'Mello, S., McLaughlin, E. A., Pardos, Z. A., & Rosé, C. P. (2015). Data mining and education. *Wiley Interdisciplinary Reviews: Cognitive Science*, *6*(4), 333–353. PMID:26263424

Lee, L. H., Juan, Y. C., Tseng, W. L., Chen, H. H., & Tseng, Y. H. (2015). Mining browsing behaviors for objectionable content filtering. *Journal of the Association for Information Science and Technology*, *66*(5), 930–942.

Li, B., & Johan, H. (2013). 3D model retrieval using hybrid features and class information. *Multimedia Tools and Applications*, *62*(3), 821–846.

Liu, C. C., Chang, C. J., & Tseng, J. M. (2013). The effect of recommendation systems on Internet-based learning for different learners: A data mining analysis. *British Journal of Educational Technology*, *44*(5), 758–773.

Lu, K., & Kipp, M. E. I. (2014). Understanding the retrieval effectiveness of collaborative tags and author keywords in different retrieval environments: An experimental study on medical collections. *Journal of the Association for Information Science and Technology*, *65*(3), 483–500.

Moon, S. J., & Yoon, C. P. (2015). Information retrieval system using the keyword concept net of the P2P service-based in the mobile cloud environment. *Peer-to-Peer Networking and Applications*, *8*(4), 596–609.

Niu, X., & Hemminger, B. (2015). Analyzing the interaction patterns in a faceted search interface. *Journal of the Association for Information Science and Technology*, *66*(5), 1030–1047.

Ortiz-Cordova, A., & Jansen, B. J. (2012). Classifying web search queries to identify high revenue generating customers. *Journal of the Association for Information Science and Technology*, *63*(7), 1426–1441.

Priya, R., & Shanmugam, T. N. (2013). A comprehensive review of significant researches on content based indexing and retrieval of visual information. *Frontiers of Computer Science*, *7*(5), 782–799.

Rodriguez, J. M., Crasso, M., Mateos, C., & Zunino, A. (2013). Best practices for describing, consuming, and discovering web services: A comprehensive toolset. *Software: Practice and Experience*, *43*(6), 613–639.

Romero, C., Espejo, P. G., Zafra, A., Romero, J. R., & Ventura, S. (2013). Web usage mining for predicting final marks of students that use Moodle courses. *Computer Applications in Engineering Education*, *21*(1), 135–146.

Santos, O. C., & Boticario, J. G. (2015). User-centred design and educational data mining support during the recommendations elicitation process in social online learning environments. *Expert Systems: International Journal of Knowledge Engineering and Neural Networks*, *32*(2), 293–311.

Sinn, D., & Soares, N. (2014). Historians' use of digital archival collections: The web, historical scholarship, and archival research. *Journal of the Association for Information Science and Technology*, *65*(9), 1794–1809.

Thomas, P. (2012). To what problem is distributed information retrieval the solution? *Journal of the American Society for Information Science and Technology, 63*(7), 1471–1476.

Upadhyaya, B., Tang, R., & Zou, Y. (2013). An approach for mining service composition patterns from execution logs. *Journal of Software: Evolution and Process, 25*(8), 841–870.

van der Meer, J., & Frasincar, F. (2013). Automatic review identification on the web using pattern recognition. *Software: Practice and Experience, 43*(12), 1415–1436.

Xinhua, L., Xutang, Z., & Zhongkai, L. (2012). A domain ontology-based information retrieval approach for technique preparation. *Physics Procedia, 25*, 1582–1588.

KEY TERMS AND DEFINITIONS

Browsing: The exploration of the World Wide Web by following one interesting link to another.

Data Mining: The process of using special software to look at the large amounts of computer data in order to find the useful information.

Information Retrieval: The process of finding stored information on a computer.

Internet: The large system of connected computers around the world that allows people to share information and communicate with each other.

Technology: The purposeful application of information in the design, production, and utilization of products and services.

Web Page: A page of information on the Internet about a certain matter that forms a part of a website.

Website: A set of pages of information on the Internet about a special perspective.

World Wide Web: The system of connected documents on the Internet, usually with pictures, video, and sound, that can be searched for information about a particular subject.

Chapter 2
Analysis of User's Browsing Behavior and Their Categorization Using Markov Chain Model

Ratnesh Kumar Jain
Kendriya Vidyalaya, India

Rahul Singhai
Devi Ahilya University, India

ABSTRACT

Web server log file contains information about every access to the web pages hosted on a server like when they were requested, the Internet Protocol (IP) address of the request, the error code, the number of bytes sent to the user, and the type of browser used. Web servers can also capture referrer logs, which show the page from which a visitor makes the next request. As the visit to web site is increasing exponentially the web logs are becoming huge data repository which can be mined to extract useful information for decision making. In this chapter, we proposed a Markov chain based method to categorize the users into faithful, Partially Impatient and Completely Impatient user. And further, their browsing behavior is analyzed. We also derived some theorems to study the browsing behavior of each user type and then some numerical illustrations are added to show how their behavior differs as per categorization. At the end we extended this work by approximating the theorems.

INTRODUCTION

The discovery and analysis of useful information from the World Wide Web is called *web mining*, or Data Mining efforts associated with web is Web Mining. Web mining term can be used in two different ways, Web Content Mining & web Usage Mining. The first one describes the automatic search of information from the resources that are available on-line i.e. it is the process of information discovery from the sources across World Wide Web, and Web Usage Mining is the process of mining user browsing and access patterns while a web site is visited.

DOI: 10.4018/978-1-5225-0613-3.ch002

DATA PRE-PROCESSING WHILE MINING WEB DATA

One of the important core steps of knowledge discovery is *data pre processing*. The main goal is to create minable objects for knowledge discovery despite the presence of ambiguities and incompleteness in data. Pre-processing consists of converting the usage, content, and structure information contained in the various available data sources into the data abstractions necessary for pattern discovery.

Data Pre-Processing in Content Mining

Web content mining is strongly related to the domain of Text Mining, since in order to process and organize Web pages and their content should be first appropriately processed in order to extract patterns of interest. These selected properties are subsequently used to represent the documents and assist the clustering or classification processes.

Another essential issue during this stage is semantic analysis. Semantic analysis deals mainly with the problems of synonymy (different names for the same concept) and polysemy (different concepts having the same name). Research on the area of "Word Sense Disambiguation" (WSD) has dealt with this problem. Word sense disambiguation is achieved by assigning words to appropriate concepts. The mapping from words to concepts should be done in a reliable way, depending on the relations between words under examination.

Data Pre-Processing in Web Usage Mining

There are some important technical issues that must be taken into consideration during this phase in the context of the Web personalization process. It is necessary for Web log data to be prepared and pre-processed in order to use in the consequent phases of the process. The first issue is data preparation, depending on the application, Web log data may need to be cleaned from entries involving pages that returned an error or graphics file accesses. Furthermore, crawler activity can be filtered out, because such entries do not provide useful information about the site's usability. Another problem is with caching. Accesses to cached pages are not recorded in the Web log, therefore such information is missed. Caching is heavily dependent on the client-side technologies used and therefore cannot be dealt with ease. In such cases, cached pages can usually be inferred using the referring information from the logs. Moreover, a useful aspect is to perform page view identification, determining which page file accesses contribute to a single page view.

Most important of all is the user identification issue. There are several ways to identify individual visitors. The most obvious solution is to assume that each IP address (or each IP address/client agent pair) identifies a single visitor. Nonetheless, this is not very accurate because, for example, a visitor may access the Web from different computers, or many users may use the same IP address. Again, a user that uses more than one browser, even on the same machine, will appear as multiple users. A further assumption can then be made, that consecutive accesses from the same host during a certain time interval come from the same user. So, identification of user's browsing behavior is also one important problem during data pre-processing. More accurate approaches for a priori identification of unique visitors are the use of cookies or similar mechanisms or the requirement for user registration. However, a potential problem in using such methods might be the reluctance of users to share personal information. Assuming a user is identified, the next step is to perform session identification. Before any mining is done on web usage data, sequences of page references must be grouped into logical units representing web transactions or user sessions. A user session is all of the page references made by a user during a single visit to a site. Identifying user session is similar to the problem of identifying individual users as discussed above.

Thus some complex processes are used in order to extract knowledge about users of web site. Pre-processing is therefore is crucial issue for learning.

PROPOSED WORK

In this chapter we have used Markov model to represent the users' past visiting behavior and applied the Markov chain to predict the web page that may be visited next by the user & to categories the users. In this approach web logs are used to represent the previous visiting behavior. Pages that can be accessed by a user in the next click are evaluated based on the current position of user in the web site and his/her visiting history in the Web site stored in the web log. Web site can be represented using a graph called next link graph which is based on user previous access behavior stored in web log. This graph is presented in the form of transition probability matrix called transition matrix in short which contains one-step transition probabilities in the Markov model. The Markov model is then used for next page access prediction by calculating the conditional probabilities of visiting other pages in the future given the user's current position and/or previously visited pages. If we can categorize users of a particular web page into dedicated user or simple user than the prediction of the next page for the user can be more accurate and effective.

In general, reaching on a web page is represented as one state in the Markov chain model but many times we find that after typing the URL the web page is not open. In such case user either switches to other web page or press the refresh button. But web log does not have any entry for refresh button. If we assume that web log has an entry per refresh button click or refresh button click can be detected from the web logs, we can introduce a new state that will represent the refresh button click. Then we can study the impact of the refreshing (using refresh state) on the transition probability which is the theme of this chapter. In this research work based on the refresh button click we divided the user into three categories: faithful user, partially impatient user and completely impatient user and did the simulation study to compare the users' behavior. Thus the main objective of proposed chapter is to categorize the web users based on the number of refreshing attempts and to predict and analyze the user's browsing behavior using Markov chain model.

In Section 2, we firstly defined what the problem is and objective we are focusing in this chapter. In section 3 we explained in detail what is Markov chain model? How can we derive a Markov chain model from the different Web log file? We used an example to explain Markov chain model. We also discuss the applications of Markov chain model. In Section 4 we will propose a new model with a new state i.e. Refresh State. We will discuss the model and the assumptions we will use. We briefly give the Notation and the Transition Probability for each state. Then we will derive the Theorems for calculating the Transition Probability of each category of user of each page at n^{th} attempt. In Section 5 using these theorem we will do simulation study. We will do the study of transition probability of individual user with respect to attempt and with respect to refreshing. In Section 6, we conclude the chapter and discuss future work.

Problems and Objective

Users surf the World Wide Web (WWW) by navigating along the hyperlinks that connect huge amount of content. If we could predict where surfers were going (that is, what they were seeking) we might be able to improve users interactions with the WWW. Indeed, several research and industrial thrusts attempt to predict which type of user is accessing which type of pages, or which user tries to access only a particular web page. This information helps designers to focus on the needs of different type of users and the way they interact.

It is not necessary that when user tries to access the page it will open soon. In such case user may press refresh button. Based on the refresh button click we have categorized the users of a web site into three categories.

- **Faithful Users:** Users that try to open a particular page but press refresh button if page is not open soon and do not switch to other web pages, can be categorized into faithful users.
- **Partially Impatient Users:** A user that try to open a particular page if the page does not open he either press refresh button or he switch to any other page can be categorized as Partially Impatient Users. User has little patient to wait and again try to open that particular page.
- **Completely Impatient Users:** Users that try to open a particular page if it does not open they switch to any other page but do not refresh can be categorized as completely impatient user. User cannot wait or retry he give up the access to the page and go for any other page.

Dividing the users into three categories can help the designer of the web site to improve the contents or services provided on the particular web page according to the category of the users.

First problem in user categorization is that probability function to calculate the probability of the next page access is different for each type of user and require derivation to find the general function. The second problem is that there is no information in the web log for refresh button click. If we assume that web log has an entry per refresh button click or refresh button click can be detected from the web logs, we can introduce a new state that will represent the refresh button click. Then we can study the impact of the refreshing on the transition probability which is the theme of this chapter. Our objective is to develop a Markov chain model with a new state named Refresh state represented by 'R'. And do the simulations study to compare behavior of the different type of users' based on varying probability of refreshing.

Markov Chain Model

Markov chain, named after Andrey Markov, is used to model a stochastic (random) process with the Markov property. Having the Markov property means that, given the present state, future states are independent of the past states. In other words, the description of the present state fully captures all the information that could influence the future evolution of the process. That means future states will be reached through a probabilistic process instead of a deterministic one.

At each instant the system may change its state from the current state to another state, or remain in the same state, according to a certain probability distribution. The changes of state are called transitions, and the probabilities associated with various state-changes are termed transition probabilities.

Definition

A Markov chain is a sequence of random variables $X_1, X_2, X_3, \ldots$ with the Markov property, namely that, given the present state, the future and past states are independent. Formally,

$$P(X_{n+1}= x \mid X_n=x_n,\ldots, X_1= x_1) = P(X_{n+1}= x \mid X_n= x_n)$$

The possible values of X_i form a countable set S called the *state space* of the chain. Markov chains are often described by a directed graph, where each node represents a state, each edge corresponds to a transition from one state to another, and the edges are labeled by the probabilities of going from one state to the other states. This directed graph is used to calculate a transition probability matrix containing one-step transition probabilities in the Markov model.

In general Markov chain model can be defined by a tuple $< X, T, \lambda >$, where

1. X is a set of states called state space
2. Transition Matrix T, and
3. λ is the initial probability distribution on the states in X

Building Markov Models from Web Log Files

Markov models have also been used to analyze web navigation behavior of users. A user's web navigation on a particular website can be modeled using first- or second-order Markov models and can be used to make predictions regarding future navigation and to personalize the web page for an individual user. To understand how is Markov chain model is used to model user access patterns we use the following example. Suppose we have a web site of three pages {I, J, K}. Following are the sequence of user access per session mined from web logs:

1. I, J, K, J
2. I, K, J, K, K
3. J, K, J
4. R, I, J.

Each navigation session suggests the order in which sequence of pages accessed by a user. We can think each page accessed by the user as a state. We introduce two more states say start state S: representing the access to the first page and a final state F: representing the last state. Hence our state space X={S, I, J, K, F}.

The navigation from one page to another can be thought as state transition. In each session, each sequence of two pages say I, J corresponds to a transition from one state (I) to another (J). Figure 1 suggest the transition diagram for first session according to our example. The probability of a transition is estimated by the following formula:

Probability of transition from state U to $V = \dfrac{\text{Number of times page } V \text{ visited after visiting page } U}{\text{Total Number of times page } U \text{ visited}}$

Figure 1. Markov model for first session

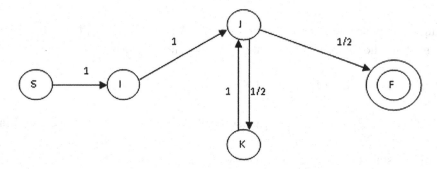

Figure 2 shows the complete model for the set of navigation sessions given in the example.

To record transition probability between states we generally use transition matrix. The initial probability of a state is estimated as the proportion of times the corresponding page was requested as the first page. Since final state is reachable from every other state and there is no out transition from final state, the state F is an absorbing state, hence this model is absorbing Markov chain model.

According to the discussion above we can formally define the Markov chain model for our example as follows:

X={S, I, J, K, F}

λ = <3/15, 6/15, 6/15, 0>

	I	J	K	F
I	0	2/3	1/3	0
T = J	0	0	1/2	1/2
K	1/6	3/6	1/6	1/6
F	0	0	0	1

Figure 2. The complete Markov model for all sessions given in example

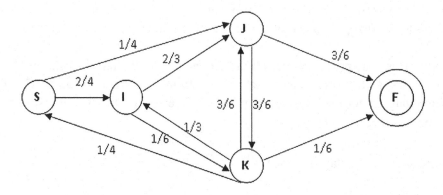

In our model the probability of any access sequence is evaluated using following formula:

Probability of access sequence = Initial probability of the first state in the access sequence × transition probabilities of the enclosed transitions

For example, the estimated probability of I, J, K, J, F is 3/15 x 2/3 x 1/2 x 2/3 x 1/2 = 12/540.

APPLICATIONS OF MARKOV CHAIN MODEL

Markov chain model is best suited for next page access Prediction and Path Analysis. We use Markov Chains to perform *predictive* analysis and modeling of web access sequences. Possible Applications of Markov chain model are:

Searching

The ability to accurately predict user access patterns could lead to a number of improvements in user-WWW interaction. For instance, a search engine assumes that a model of access pattern can lead to improvements in the precision of text-based search engine results. It models user's previous access patterns over the entire WWW link structure. Under this model, user access pattern is viewed as an indicator of user interests, over and above the text keywords entered into a standard search engine.

Recommendation of Related Pages

Recently, tools have become available for suggesting related pages to users. The Netscape browser provides "What's Related" tool button for the recommendations based on content, link structure, and usage patterns. Similar tools for specific repositories of WWW content are also provided by Autonomy. One can think of these tools as making the prediction that "if a user requests page *n*, what will be her most likely next choice". The predictive model of web usage data could be used to enhance the recommendations made by these and other systems.

Web Site Models

Web site designers are often interested in improvements in web site design. Recent research has developed visualizations to show the flow of users through a web site. Businesses have emerged that send simulated users through existing web sites to provide data on web site design. Predictive models of web site users access sequence could help move the state of web site analysis from post-hoc modeling of past user interactions, or a current web site, to predictive models that can accurately simulate users' access sequence through hypothetical web site designs. Web site designers could explore different arrangements of links that promote desired flows of surfers through content.

Latency Reduction

Markov models have significant potential to reduce user-perceived WWW latencies. Year after year, users report WWW delays as their number one problem in using the WWW. One emerging trend of research that aims to improve WWW access times has grown out of research on improving file access time through prefetching and caching methods.

In all these applications Markov chain model can be used in adaptive mode; transition matrix can be updated as new data (example: Web Server Request) arrives. Other application of Markov chain model is Clustering and visualization of web usage data.

MARKOV MODEL WITH REFRESH STATE

Let our web site is consist of three web pages named A, B, C. As in the example in previous section we can introduce two more state namely Start State and Finish State represented by S and F respectively. Since there is no information in the web log for refresh button click. If we assume that web log has an entry per refresh button click or refresh button click can be detected from the web logs, we can introduce a new state that will represent the refresh button click which we named Refresh State and represented by R. The resultant Markov Chain Model with Refresh State is shown in following figure.

As shown in the Figure 3, this Markov chain model consist of six states three for web pages A, B, C and we introduced three additional states named S (Start State), R (Refresh State) and F (Finish State). We have not assigned the constant probability for transition from any state to any other state. Name of the variables indicating the transition probability are shown as the label of the edges. A user can start accessing the Web site by accessing any of the three web pages. Labels on edges from S to other states are indicating the initial probability. As shown in the figure there in no edge from S to R and S to F indicating that without accessing any web page user neither presses the refresh button nor does he close the web site. Hence the tuple $< X, T, \lambda >$ that define Markov chain model is as follows:

$X = \{ S, A, B, C, R, F \}$

$$T = C \begin{array}{c} \\ A \\ B \\ C \\ R \\ F \end{array} \begin{array}{ccccc} A & B & C & R & F \\ \begin{bmatrix} 0 & q_1 & q_2 & q_3 & q_4 \\ q_5 & 0 & q_6 & q_7 & q_8 \\ q_9 & q_{10} & 0 & q_{11} & q_{12} \\ q_{13} & q_{14} & q_{15} & q_{16} & q_{17} \\ 0 & 0 & 0 & 0 & 1 \end{bmatrix} \end{array}$$

$$\lambda = \left\{ p_1, p_2, p_3, 0, 0 \right\}$$

Figure 3. Markov chain model with refresh state

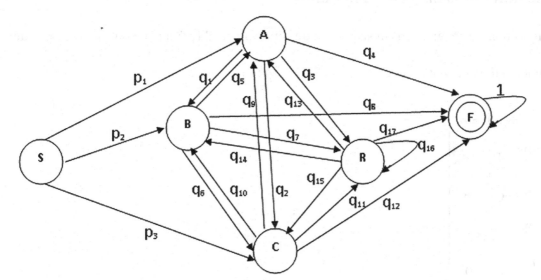

Assumptions

We here summarizing all the assumptions for this model:

1. User can start accessing the web site by directly access any of the web pages the initial probability are:
    a. p_1 for web page A.
    b. p_2 for web page B.
    c. p_3 for web page C.
2. User presses the refresh button if the page is not open or it is taking time. If he uses the URL of the same web page he is in we assume he want to refresh the page. Hence there is no edge from A to A, B to B and C to C. But there is an edge from R to R indicating user can continuously press the refresh button.
3. Without trying to open any web page user neither press the refresh button nor he closes the web site that means initial probability of the Refresh State and Finish State is 0.
4. After going to any of the state user can not return to the Start State. That means there is no transition from any other state to start state.
5. User of the web site can be categorized into three categories:
    a.   **Faithful Users:** Users that try to open a particular page but they press refresh button if page is not open soon and do not switch to other web page can be categorized into faithful users.
    b.   **Partially Impatient Users:** A user that try to open a particular page if the page does not open he either press refresh button and if the page still not open then he switch to any other page can be categorized as Partially Impatient Users.
    c.   **Completely Impatient Users:** Users that try to open a particular page if it does not open they switch to any other page but do not refresh can be categorized as completely impatient user.

Transition Probability between States

In this section we are giving the notation and transition probability from one state to another state:

The initial probability of states are:

$$
\left.
\begin{aligned}
P\left[X^{(0)} = A\right] &= p_1 \\
P\left[X^{(0)} = B\right] &= p_2 \\
P\left[X^{(0)} = C\right] &= p_3 \\
P\left[X^{(0)} = R\right] &= 0 \\
P\left[X^{(0)} = F\right] &= 0
\end{aligned}
\right\}
\tag{1}
$$

If in $(n-1)^{th}$ attempt user is on state A then the probabilities of reaching on state B, C, R and F on n^{th} attempt are represented respectively as given below:

$$
\left.
\begin{aligned}
P\left[X^{(n)} = B \middle/ X^{(n-1)} = A\right] &= q_1 \\
P\left[X^{(n)} = C \middle/ X^{(n-1)} = A\right] &= q_2 \\
P\left[X^{(n)} = R \middle/ X^{(n-1)} = A\right] &= q_3 \\
P\left[X^{(n)} = F \middle/ X^{(n-1)} = A\right] &= q_4
\end{aligned}
\right\}
\tag{2}
$$

If in $(n-1)^{th}$ attempt user is on state B then the probabilities of reaching on state A, C, R and F on n^{th} attempt are represented respectively as given below:

$$
\left.
\begin{aligned}
P\left[X^{(n)} = A \middle/ X^{(n-1)} = B\right] &= q_5 \\
P\left[X^{(n)} = C \middle/ X^{(n-1)} = B\right] &= q_6 \\
P\left[X^{(n)} = R \middle/ X^{(n-1)} = B\right] &= q_7 \\
P\left[X^{(n)} = F \middle/ X^{(n-1)} = B\right] &= q_8
\end{aligned}
\right\}
\tag{3}
$$

If in $(n-1)^{th}$ attempt user is on state C then the probabilities of reaching on state A, B, R and F on n^{th} attempt are represented respectively as given below:

$$\left.\begin{array}{l} P\left[X^{(n)} = A \middle/ X^{(n-1)} = C\right] = q_9 \\[2mm] P\left[X^{(n)} = B \middle/ X^{(n-1)} = C\right] = q_{10} \\[2mm] P\left[X^{(n)} = R \middle/ X^{(n-1)} = C\right] = q_{11} \\[2mm] P\left[X^{(n)} = F \middle/ X^{(n-1)} = C\right] = q_{12} \end{array}\right\} \quad (4)$$

If in $(n-1)^{th}$ attempt user is on state R then the probabilities of reaching on state A, B, C, R and F on n^{th} attempt are represented respectively as given below:

$$\left.\begin{array}{l} P\left[X^{(n)} = A \middle/ X^{(n-1)} = R\right] = q_{13} \\[2mm] P\left[X^{(n)} = B \middle/ X^{(n-1)} = R\right] = q_{14} \\[2mm] P\left[X^{(n)} = C \middle/ X^{(n-1)} = R\right] = q_{15} \\[2mm] P\left[X^{(n)} = R \middle/ X^{(n-1)} = R\right] = q_{16} \\[2mm] P\left[X^{(n)} = F \middle/ X^{(n-1)} = R\right] = q_{17} \end{array}\right\} \quad (5)$$

If in $(n-1)^{th}$ attempt user is on state F then the probabilities of reaching on state F on n^{th} attempt are represented respectively as given below:

$$P\left[X^{(n)} = F \middle/ X^{(n-1)} = F\right] = 1 \quad (6)$$

Where $p_1, p_2, p_3, q_1, q_2, q_3, q_4, q_5, q_6, q_7, q_8, q_9, q_{10}, q_{11}, q_{12}, q_{13}, q_{14}, q_{15}, q_{16}, q_{17}$ are probability between 0 and 1.

Some Results for n^{th} Attempts

As shown above if the starting conditions are:

$$\left.\begin{array}{l} P\left[X^{(0)} = A\right] = p_1 \\[6pt] P\left[X^{(0)} = B\right] = p_2 \\[6pt] P\left[X^{(0)} = C\right] = p_3 \\[6pt] P\left[X^{(0)} = R\right] = 0 \\[6pt] P\left[X^{(0)} = F\right] = 0 \end{array}\right\} \tag{7}$$

As we have discussed, there are three types of users Faithful Users, Partially Impatient Users and Completely Impatient Users. The probability function for n^{th} attempt is different for different type of users. In this section we discuss the nth attempt probability for each type of user in form of theorem.

Nth Attempt Results for Faithful User

A Faithful user at the $(n-1)^{th}$ attempt can be either on a particular web page of which he is a Faithful user (for example he can be at state **A** if he is a Faithful user of page A) or it can be at state R. Then the probability of reaching on states A, B, C on the nth attempt can be calculated using the following theorems:

Theorem 1

The transition probability of reaching on state A at n^{th} attempt when user is faithful:

(i)   When n is even $P\left[X^{(2n)} = A\right] = p_1 q_3^n q_{13}^n$ For n=0,1,2,3...

(ii)   When n is odd $P\left[X^{(2n+1)} = A\right] = 0$ For n= 0,1,2,3...

Proof

For n=0, we have $P[X^{(0)} = A] = p_1$ and $P[X^{(0)} = R] = 0$ then

$$P\left[X^{(1)} = A\right] = P\left[X^{(0)} = R\right] P\left[X^{(1)} = A \Big/ X^{(0)} = R\right] = 0$$

$$P\left[X^{(1)} = R\right] = P\left[X^{(0)} = A\right] P\left[X^{(1)} = R \Big/ X^{(0)} = A\right] = p_1 q_3$$

$$P\left[X^{(2)} = A\right] = P\left[X^{(1)} = R\right] P\left[X^{(2)} = A \Big/ X^{(1)} = R\right] = p_1 q_3 q_{13}$$

$$P\left[X^{(2)} = R\right] = P\left[X^{(1)} = A\right] P\left[X^{(2)} = R \middle/ X^{(1)} = A\right] = 0$$

$$P\left[X^{(3)} = A\right] = P\left[X^{(2)} = R\right] P\left[X^{(3)} = A \middle/ X^{(2)} = R\right] = 0$$

$$P\left[X^{(3)} = R\right] = P\left[X^{(2)} = A\right] P\left[X^{(3)} = R \middle/ X^{(2)} = A\right] = p_1 q_3^2 q_{13}$$

$$P\left[X^{(4)} = A\right] = P\left[X^{(3)} = R\right] P\left[X^{(4)} = A \middle/ X^{(3)} = R\right] = p_1 q_3^2 q_{13}^2$$

$$P\left[X^{(4)} = R\right] = P\left[X^{(3)} = A\right] P\left[X^{(4)} = R \middle/ X^{(3)} = A\right] = 0$$

$$P\left[X^{(5)} = A\right] = P\left[X^{(4)} = R\right] P\left[X^{(5)} = A \middle/ X^{(4)} = R\right] = 0$$

$$P\left[X^{(5)} = R\right] = P\left[X^{(4)} = A\right] P\left[X^{(5)} = R \middle/ X^{(4)} = A\right] = p_1 q_3^3 q_{13}^2$$

$$P\left[X^{(6)} = A\right] = P\left[X^{(5)} = R\right] P\left[X^{(6)} = A \middle/ X^{(5)} = R\right] = p_1 q_3^3 q_{13}^3$$

In the similar way, we can get the proof of the theorem.

Theorem 2

The transition probability of reaching on state B at n^{th} attempt when user is faithful:

(iii) When n is even $P\left[X^{(2n)} = B\right] = p_2 q_7^n q_{14}^n$ For n=0,1,2,3…

(iv) When n is odd $P\left[X^{(2n+1)} = B\right] = 0$ For n= 0,1,2,3…

Proof

For n=0, we have $P[X^{(0)} = B] = p_2$ and $P[X^{(0)} = R] = 0$ then

$$P\left[X^{(1)} = B\right] = P\left[X^{(0)} = R\right] P\left[X^{(1)} = B \middle/ X^{(0)} = R\right] = 0$$

$$P\left[X^{(1)} = R\right] = P\left[X^{(0)} = B\right] P\left[X^{(1)} = R \middle/ X^{(0)} = B\right] = p_2 q_7$$

$$P\left[X^{(2)} = B\right] = P\left[X^{(1)} = R\right] P\left[X^{(2)} = B \middle/ X^{(1)} = R\right] = p_2 q_7 q_{14}$$

$$P\left[X^{(2)} = R\right] = P\left[X^{(1)} = B\right] P\left[X^{(2)} = R \middle/ X^{(1)} = B\right] = 0$$

$$P\left[X^{(3)} = B\right] = P\left[X^{(2)} = R\right] P\left[X^{(3)} = B \middle/ X^{(2)} = R\right] = 0$$

$$P\left[X^{(3)} = R\right] = P\left[X^{(2)} = B\right] P\left[X^{(3)} = R \middle/ X^{(2)} = B\right] = p_2 q_7^2 q_{14}$$

$$P\left[X^{(4)} = B\right] = P\left[X^{(3)} = R\right] P\left[X^{(4)} = B \middle/ X^{(3)} = R\right] = p_2 q_7^2 q_{14}^2$$

$$P\left[X^{(4)} = R\right] = P\left[X^{(3)} = B\right] P\left[X^{(4)} = R \middle/ X^{(3)} = B\right] = 0$$

$$P\left[X^{(5)} = B\right] = P\left[X^{(4)} = R\right] P\left[X^{(5)} = B \middle/ X^{(4)} = R\right] = 0$$

$$P\left[X^{(5)} = R\right] = P\left[X^{(4)} = B\right] P\left[X^{(5)} = R \middle/ X^{(4)} = B\right] = p_2 q_7^3 q_{14}^2$$

$$P\left[X^{(6)} = B\right] = P\left[X^{(5)} = R\right] P\left[X^{(6)} = B \middle/ X^{(5)} = R\right] = p_2 q_7^3 q_{14}^3$$

Continuing in similar way, the proof of the theorem exists.

Theorem 3

The transition probability of reaching on state C at n^{th} attempt when user is faithful:

(v)   When n is even $P\left[X^{(2n)} = C\right] = p_3 q_{11}^n q_{15}^n$ For n = 0,1,2,3...

(vi)   When n is odd $P\left[X^{(2n+1)} = C\right] = 0$ For n = 0,1,2,3...

Proof

For n=0, we have $P[X^{(0)} = C] = p_3$ and $P[X^{(0)} = R] = 0$ then

$$P\left[X^{(1)} = C\right] = P\left[X^{(0)} = R\right] P\left[X^{(1)} = C \middle/ X^{(0)} = R\right] = 0$$

$$P\left[X^{(1)} = R\right] = P\left[X^{(0)} = C\right] P\left[X^{(1)} = R \middle/ X^{(0)} = C\right] = p_3 q_{11}$$

$$P\left[X^{(2)} = C\right] = P\left[X^{(1)} = R\right] P\left[X^{(2)} = C \middle/ X^{(1)} = R\right] = p_3 q_{11} q_{15}$$

$$P\left[X^{(2)} = R\right] = P\left[X^{(1)} = C\right] P\left[X^{(2)} = R \middle/ X^{(1)} = C\right] = 0$$

$$P\left[X^{(3)} = C\right] = P\left[X^{(2)} = R\right] P\left[X^{(3)} = C \middle/ X^{(2)} = R\right] = 0$$

$$P\left[X^{(3)} = R\right] = P\left[X^{(2)} = C\right] P\left[X^{(3)} = R \middle/ X^{(2)} = C\right] = p_3 q_{11}^2 q_{15}$$

$$P\left[X^{(4)} = C\right] = P\left[X^{(3)} = R\right] P\left[X^{(4)} = C \middle/ X^{(3)} = R\right] = p_3 q_{11}^2 q_{15}^2$$

$$P\left[X^{(4)} = R\right] = P\left[X^{(3)} = C\right] P\left[X^{(4)} = R \middle/ X^{(3)} = C\right] = 0$$

$$P\left[X^{(5)} = C\right] = P\left[X^{(4)} = R\right] P\left[X^{(5)} = C \middle/ X^{(4)} = R\right] = 0$$

$$P\left[X^{(5)} = R\right] = P\left[X^{(4)} = C\right] P\left[X^{(5)} = R \middle/ X^{(4)} = C\right] = p_3 q_{11}^3 q_{15}^2$$

$$P\left[X^{(6)} = C\right] = P\left[X^{(5)} = R\right] P\left[X^{(6)} = C \middle/ X^{(5)} = R\right] = p_3 q_{11}^3 q_{15}^3$$

In the similar way, we can get the proof of the theorem.

Nth Attempt Results for Partially Impatient User

If user continuous with attempts to access web pages then at the n-1th attempt he can be at state A, B, C or the user can do refresh which we represent the state R that means user can be at state A or B or C or R then the probability of reaching on states A, B, C on the nth attempt can be calculated using the following theorems.

Theorem 4

The transition probability of reaching on state A at nth attempt when user is partially impatient:

(i)   When n is even

$$P\left[X^{(2n)} = A\right] = p_1 q_1^n q_5^n + p_1 q_2^n q_9^n + 2^n p_1 q_3^n q_{13}^n + p_2 q_6^n q_9 q_{10}^{n-1} + p_3 q_1^{n-1} q_5^n q_{10}$$

For n=1,2,3…

(ii)   When n is odd $P\left[X^{(2n+1)} = A\right] = p_2 q_1^n q_5^{n+1} + p_3 q_2^n q_9^{n+1}$ For n= 0,1,2,…

Proof

For $n = 0$, we have $P[X^{(0)} = A] = p_1$, $P[X^{(0)} = B] = p_2$, $P[X^{(0)} = C] = p_3$, and $P[X^{(0)} = R] = 0$, then

$$P[X^{(1)} = A] = P[X^{(0)} = B] P[X^{(1)} = A/X^{(0)} = B] + P[X^{(0)} = R] P[X^{(1)} = A/X^{(0)} = R]$$
$$+ P[X^{(0)} = C] P[X^{(1)} = A/X^{(0)} = C] + P[X^{(0)} = R] P[X^{(1)} = A/X^{(0)} = R]$$
$$\Rightarrow P[X^{(1)} = A] = p_2 q_5 + p_3 q_9$$

$$P[X^{(1)} = R] = P[X^{(0)} = A] P[X^{(1)} = R/X^{(0)} = A] = p_1 q_3$$

$$P[X^{(2)} = A] = P[X^{(1)} = B] P[X^{(2)} = A/X^{(1)} = B] + P[X^{(1)} = R] P[X^{(2)} = A/X^{(1)} = R]$$
$$+ P[X^{(1)} = C] P[X^{(2)} = A/X^{(1)} = C] + P[X^{(1)} = R] P[X^{(2)} = A/X^{(1)} = R]$$
$$\Rightarrow P[X^{(2)} = A] = p_1 q_1 q_5 + p_1 q_2 q_9 + 2 p_1 q_3 q_{13} + p_2 q_6 q_9 + p_3 q_5 q_{10}$$

$$P[X^{(2)} = R] = P[X^{(1)} = A] P[X^{(2)} = R/X^{(1)} = A] = p_2 q_3 q_5 + p_3 q_3 q_9$$

$$P[X^{(3)} = A] = P[X^{(2)} = B] P[X^{(3)} = A/X^{(2)} = B] + P[X^{(2)} = R] P[X^{(3)} = A/X^{(2)} = R]$$
$$+ P[X^{(2)} = C] P[X^{(3)} = A/X^{(2)} = C] + P[X^{(2)} = R] P[X^{(3)} = A/X^{(2)} = R]$$

$$\Rightarrow P[X^{(3)} = A] = p_1 q_1 q_6 q_9 + p_1 q_2 q_5 q_{10} + p_2 q_1 q_5^2 + p_2 q_2 q_5 q_9 + 2 p_2 q_3 q_5 q_{13} +$$
$$p_2 q_5 q_6 q_{10} + 2 p_2 q_5 q_7 q_{14} + p_3 q_1 q_5 q_9 + p_3 q_2 q_9^2 + 2 p_3 q_3 q_9 q_{13} +$$
$$p_3 q_6 q_9 q_{10} + 2 p_3 q_9 q_{11} q_{15}$$

$$P[X^{(3)} = R] = P[X^{(2)} = A] \, P[X^{(3)} = R / X^{(2)} = A]$$

$$\Rightarrow P[X^{(3)} = R] = p_1 q_1 q_3 q_5 + p_1 q_2 q_3 q_9 + 2 p_1 q_3^2 q_{13} + p_2 q_3 q_6 q_9 + p_3 q_3 q_5 q_{10}$$

$$P[X^{(4)} = A] = P[X^{(3)} = B] \, P[X^{(4)} = A / X^{(3)} = B] + P[X^{(3)} = R] \, P[X^{(4)} = A / X^{(3)} = R]$$
$$+ P[X^{(3)} = C] P[X^{(4)} = A / X^{(3)} = C] + P[X^{(3)} = R] \, P[X^{(4)} = A / X^{(3)} = R]$$

$$P[X^{(4)} = A] = p_1 q_1^2 q_5^2 + 2 p_1 q_1 q_2 q_5 q_9 + 4 p_1 q_1 q_3 q_5 q_{13} + 2 p_1 q_1 q_5 q_7 q_{14} + p_1 q_1 q_5 q_6 q_{10} +$$
$$4 q_1 q_2 q_3 q_9 q_{13} + p_1 q_2 q_6 q_9 q_{10} + 2 p_1 q_2 q_9 q_{11} q_{15} + p_1 q_2^2 q_9^2 + 4 p_1 q_3^2 q_{13}^2 +$$
$$2 p_2 q_1 q_5 q_6 q_9 + p_2 q_2 q_5^2 q_{10} + 2 p_2 q_3 q_6 q_9 q_{13} + p_2 q_2 q_6 q_9^2 + p_2 q_6^2 q_9 q_{10} +$$
$$2 p_2 q_6 q_7 q_9 q_{14} + 2 p_2 q_6 q_9 q_{11} q_{15} + p_3 q_1 q_5^2 q_{10} + p_3 q_1 q_6 q_9^2 + 2 p_3 q_2 q_5 q_9 q_{10} +$$
$$2 p_3 q_5 q_7 q_{10} q_{14} + 2 p_3 q_3 q_5 q_{10} q_{13} + 2 p_3 q_5 q_{10} q_{11} q_{15} + p_3 q_5 q_6 q_{10}^2$$

$$P[X^{(4)} = R] = P[X^{(3)} = A] \, P[X^{(4)} = R / X^{(3)} = A]$$

$$P[X^{(4)} = R] = p_1 q_1 q_3 q_6 q_9 + p_1 q_2 q_3 q_5 q_{10} + p_2 q_1 q_3 q_5^2 + p_2 q_2 q_3 q_5 q_9 +$$
$$2 p_2 q_3^2 q_5 q_{13} + p_2 q_3 q_5 q_6 q_{10} + 2 p_2 q_3 q_5 q_7 q_{14} + p_3 q_1 q_3 q_5 q_9 + p_3 q_2 q_3 q_9^2 +$$
$$2 p_3 q_3^2 q_9 q_{13} + p_3 q_3 q_6 q_9 q_{10} + 2 p_3 q_3 q_9 q_{11} q_{15}$$

$$P[X^{(5)} = A] = P[X^{(4)} = B] \, P[X^{(5)} = A / X^{(4)} = B] + P[X^{(4)} = R] \, P[X^{(5)} = A / X^{(4)} = R]$$
$$+ P[X^{(4)} = C] P[X^{(5)} = A / X^{(4)} = C] + P[X^{(4)} = R] \, P[X^{(5)} = A / X^{(4)} = R]$$

$$P[X^{(5)} = R] = P[X^{(4)} = A] \, P[X^{(5)} = R / X^{(4)} = A]$$

$$P[X^{(5)} = R] = p1q21q3q25 + 2p1q1q2q3q5q9 + 4p1q1q23q5q13 + 2p1q1q3q5q7q14 +$$
$$p1q1q3q5q6q10 + 4p1q2q23q9q13 + p1q2q3q6q9q10 + 2p1q2q3q9q11q15 +$$
$$p1q22q3q29 + 4p1q33q213 + 2p2q1q3q5q6q9 + p2q2q3q25q10 + 2p2q23q6q9q13 +$$
$$p2q2q3q6q29 + p2q3q26q9q10 + 2p2q3q6q7q9q14 + 2p2q3q6q9q11q15 +$$
$$p3q1q3q25q10 + p3q1q3q6q29 + 2p3q2q3q5q9q10 + 2p3q3q5q7q10q14 +$$
$$2p3q23q5q10q13 + 2p3q3q5q10q11q15 + p3q3q5q6q210$$

$$P[X^{(6)} = A] = P[X^{(5)} = B]\,P[X^{(6)} = A/X^{(5)} = B] + P[X^{(5)} = R]\,P[X^{(6)} = A/X^{(5)} = R]$$
$$+ P[X^{(5)} = C]\,P[X^{(6)} = A/X^{(5)} = C] + P[X^{(5)} = R]\,P[X^{(6)} = A/X^{(5)} = R]$$

$$P[X^{(6)} = A] = p_1 q_1^3 q_5^3 + 3p_1 q_1^2 q_2 q_5^2 q_9 + 6p_1 q_1^2 q_3 q_5^2 q_{13} + 2p_1 q_1^2 q_5^2 q_6 q_{10} + 4p_1 q_1^2 q_5^2 q_7 q_{14} +$$
$$p_1 q_1^2 q_6^2 q_9^2 + 3p_1 q_1 q_2^2 q_5 q_9^2 + 12 p_1 q_1 q_2 q_3 q_5 q_9 q_{13} + 4p_1 q_1 q_2 q_3 q_9^2 q_{13} +$$
$$6p_1 q_1 q_2 q_5 q_6 q_9 q_{10} + 3p_1 q_1 q_2 q_5 q_7 q_9 q_{14} + 4p_1 q_1 q_2 q_5 q_9 q_{11} q_{15} + 12 p_1 q_1 q_3^2 q_5 q_{13}^2 +$$
$$4p_1 q_1 q_3 q_5 q_6 q_{10} q_{13} + 6p_1 q_1 q_3 q_5 q_7 q_{13} q_{14} + p_1 q_1 q_5 q_6^2 q_{10}^2 + 4p_1 q_1 q_5 q_6 q_7 q_{10} q_{14} +$$
$$2p_1 q_1 q_5 q_6 q_{10} q_{11} q_{15} + 2p_1 q_1 q_5 q_7^2 q_{14}^2 + 12 p_1 q_2 q_3^2 q_9 q_{13}^2 + 4p_1 q_2 q_3 q_6 q_9 q_{10} q_{13} +$$
$$8p_1 q_2 q_3 q_9 q_{11} q_{13} q_{15} + p_1 q_2^3 q_9^3 + 2p_1 q_2^2 q_3 q_9^2 q_{13} + p_1 q_2^2 q_5^2 q_{10}^2 + 2p_1 q_2^2 q_6 q_9^2 q_{10} +$$
$$4p_1 q_2^2 q_9^2 q_{11} q_{15} + p_1 q_2 q_6^2 q_9 q_{10}^2 + 2p_1 q_2 q_6 q_7 q_9 q_{10} q_{14} + 4p_1 q_2 q_6 q_9 q_{10} q_{11} q_{15} +$$
$$4p_1 q_2 q_9 q_{11}^2 q_{15}^2 + 8p_1 q_3^3 q_{13}^3 + 3p_2 q_1^2 q_5^2 q_6 q_9 + 2p_2 q_1 q_2 q_5^3 q_{10} + 3p_2 q_1 q_2 q_5 q_6 q_9^2 +$$
$$8p_2 q_1 q_3 q_5 q_6 q_9 q_{13} + 2p_2 q_1 q_5 q_6^2 q_9 q_{10} + 2p_2 q_1 q_6^2 q_9 q_{10} + 8p_2 q_1 q_5 q_6 q_7 q_9 q_{14} +$$

$$4p_2 q_1 q_5 q_6 q_9 q_{11} q_{15} + 2p_2 q_2^2 q_5^2 q_9 q_{10} + p_2 q_2^2 q_6 q_9^3 + 4p_2 q_2 q_3 q_5^2 q_{10} q_{13} +$$
$$4p_2 q_2 q_3 q_6 q_9^2 q_{13} + 2p_2 q_2 q_5^2 q_6 q_{10}^2 + 4p_2 q_2 q_5^2 q_7 q_{10} q_{14} + 2p_2 q_2 q_5^2 q_{10} q_{11} q_{15} +$$
$$2p_2 q_2 q_6^2 q_9^2 q_{10} + 2p_2 q_2 q_6 q_7 q_9^2 q_{14} + 4p_2 q_2 q_6 q_9^2 q_{11} q_{15} + 4p_2 q_3^2 q_6 q_9 q_{13}^2 +$$
$$2p_2 q_9 q_6^2 q_9 q_{10} q_{13} + 4p_2 q_9 q_6 q_7 q_9 q_{13} q_{14} + 4p_2 q_9 q_6 q_9 q_{11} q_{13} q_{15} + p_2 q_6^3 q_9 q_{10}^2 +$$
$$4p_2 q_6^2 q_7 q_9 q_{10} q_{14} + 4p_2 q_6^2 q_9 q_{10} q_{11} q_{15} + 4p_2 q_6 q_7^2 q_9 q_{14}^2 + 2p_2 q_6 q_7 q_9 q_{11} q_{14} q_{15} +$$
$$2p_2 q_6 q_9 q_{11}^2 q_{15}^2 + p_3 q_1^2 q_5^3 q_{10} + 2p_3 q_1^2 q_5 q_6 q_9^2 + 4p_3 q_1 q_2 q_5^2 q_9 q_{10} + 2p_3 q_1 q_2 q_6 q_9^3 +$$

$$4p_3 q_1 q_3 q_5^2 q_{10} q_{13} + 4p_3 q_1 q_3 q_6 q_9^2 q_{13} + 2p_3 q_1 q_5^2 q_6 q_{10}^2 + 4p_3 q_1 q_5^2 q_7 q_{10} q_{14} +$$
$$2p_3 q_1 q_5^2 q_{10} q_{11} q_{15} + 2p_3 q_1 q_6^2 q_9^2 q_{10} + 2p_3 q_1 q_6 q_7 q_9^2 q_{14} + 4p_3 q_1 q_6 q_9^2 q_{11} q_{15} +$$
$$4p_3 q_2^2 q_5 q_9^2 q_{10} + 8p_3 q_2 q_3 q_5 q_9 q_{10} q_{13} + 4p_3 q_2 q_5 q_6 q_9 q_{10}^2 + 4p_3 q_2 q_5 q_7 q_9 q_{10} q_{14} +$$
$$8p_3 q_2 q_5 q_9 q_{10} q_{11} q_{15} + 2p_3 q_3 q_5 q_7 q_{10} q_{13} q_{14} + 2p_3 q_3^2 q_5 q_{10} q_{13}^2 +$$
$$2p_3 q_3 q_5 q_{10} q_{11} q_{13} q_{15} + p_3 q_3 q_5 q_6 q_{10}^2 q_{13} + 4p_3 q_5 q_6 q_7 q_{10}^2 q_{14} + p_3 q_5 q_6^2 q_{10}^3 +$$
$$4p_3 q_5 q_6 q_{10}^2 q_{11} q_{15} + 4p_3 q_5 q_7^2 q_{10} q_{14}^2 + 4p_3 q_5 q_7 q_{10} q_{11} q_{14} q_{15} + 4p_3 q_5 q_{10} q_{11}^2 q_{15}^2$$

In the similar way, we can get the proof of the theorem.

Theorem 5

The transition probability of reaching on state B at n^{th} attempt when user is partially impatient:

(iii) When n is even

$$P\left[X^{(2n)} = B\right] = p_2 q_1^n q_5^n + p_2 q_6^n q_{10}^n + 2^n p_2 q_7^n q_{14}^n + p_1 q_2^n q_9^{n-1} q_{10} + p_3 q_1^n q_5^{n-1} q_9$$

For n=1,2,3...

(iv) When n is odd $P\left[X^{(2n+1)} = B\right] = p_1 q_1^{n+1} q_5^n + p_3 q_6^n q_{10}^{n+1}$ For n= 0,1,2,3...

Proof

For $n = 0$, we have $P[X^{(0)} = A] = p_1$, $P[X^{(0)} = B] = p_2$, $P[X^{(0)} = C] = p_3$, and $P[X^{(0)} = R] = 0$, then

$$P[X^{(1)} = B] = P[X^{(0)} = A]\,P[X^{(1)} = B / X^{(0)} = A] + P[X^{(0)} = R]\,P[X^{(1)} = B / X^{(0)} = R]$$
$$+ P[X^{(0)} = C]P[X^{(1)} = B / X^{(0)} = C] + P[X^{(0)} = R]\,P[X^{(1)} = B / X^{(0)} = R]$$

$$\Rightarrow P[X^{(1)} = B] = p_1 q_1 + p_3 q_{10}$$

$$P[X^{(1)} = R] = P[X^{(0)} = B]\,P[X^{(1)} = R / X^{(0)} = B] = p_2 q_7$$

$$P[X^{(2)} = B] = P[X^{(1)} = A]\,P[X^{(2)} = B / X^{(1)} = A] + P[X^{(1)} = R]\,P[X^{(2)} = B / X^{(1)} = R]$$
$$+ P[X^{(1)} = C]P[X^{(2)} = B / X^{(1)} = C] + P[X^{(1)} = R]\,P[X^{(2)} = B / X^{(1)} = R]$$

$$\Rightarrow P[X^{(2)} = B] = p_2 q_1 q_5 + p_3 q_1 q_9 + p_1 q_2 q_{10} + p_2 q_6 q_{10} + 2 p_2 q_7 q_{14}$$

$$P[X^{(2)} = R] = P[X^{(1)} = B]\,P[X^{(2)} = R / X^{(1)} = B] = p_1 q_1 q_7 + p_3 q_7 q_{10}$$

$$P[X^{(3)} = B] = P[X^{(2)} = A]\,P[X^{(3)} = B / X^{(2)} = A] + P[X^{(2)} = R]\,P[X^{(3)} = B / X^{(2)} = R]$$
$$+ P[X^{(2)} = C]P[X^{(3)} = B / X^{(2)} = C] + P[X^{(2)} = R]\,P[X^{(3)} = B / X^{(2)} = R]$$

$$\Rightarrow P[X^{(3)} = B] = p_1 q_1^2 q_5 + p_1 q_1 q_2 q_9 + 2 p_1 q_1 q_3 q_{13} + p_1 q_1 q_6 q_{10} + 2 p_1 q_1 q_7 q_{14} +$$
$$p_2 q_1 q_6 q_9 + p_2 q_2 q_5 q_{10} + p_3 q_1 q_5 q_{10} + p_3 q_2 q_9 q_{10} + p_3 q_6 q_{10}^2 +$$
$$2 p_3 q_7 q_{10} q_{14} + 2 p_3 q_{10} q_{11} q_{15}$$

$$P[X^{(3)} = R] = P[X^{(2)} = B]\,P[X^{(3)} = R / X^{(2)} = B] = p_1 q_2 q_7 q_{10} + p_2 q_1 q_5 q_7 +$$
$$p_2 q_6 q_7 q_{10} + 2 p_2 q_7^2 q_{14} + p_3 q_1 q_7 q_9$$

$$P[X^{(4)} = B] = P[X^{(3)} = A]\,P[X^{(4)} = B / X^{(3)} = A] + P[X^{(3)} = R]\,P[X^{(4)} = B / X^{(3)} = R]$$
$$+ P[X^{(3)} = C]P[X^{(4)} = B / X^{(3)} = C] + P[X^{(3)} = R]\,P[X^{(4)} = B / X^{(3)} = R]$$

$$P[X^{(4)} = B] = p_1 q_1^2 q_6 q_9 + 2p_1 q_1 q_2 q_5 q_{10} + 2p_1 q_2 q_3 q_{10} q_{13} + 2p_1 q_2 q_7 q_{10} q_{14} +$$
$$2p_1 q_2 q_{10} q_{11} q_{15} + p_1 q_2 q_6 q_{10}^2 + p_1 q_2^2 q_9 q_{10} + p_2 q_1^2 q_5^2 + p_2 q_1 q_2 q_5 q_9 +$$
$$2p_2 q_1 q_3 q_5 q_{13} + 2p_2 q_1 q_5 q_6 q_{10} + 4p_2 q_1 q_5 q_7 q_{14} + p_2 q_2 q_6 q_9 q_{10} +$$

$$4p_2 q_6 q_7 q_{10} q_{14} + 2p_2 q_6 q_{10} q_{11} q_{15} + p_2 q_6^2 q_{10}^2 + 4p_2 q_7^2 q_{14}^2 + p_3 q_1^2 q_5 q_9 + p_3 q_1 q_2 q_9^2 +$$
$$2p_3 q_1 q_3 q_9 q_{13} + 2p_3 q_1 q_6 q_9 q_{10} + 2p_3 q_1 q_9 q_{11} q_{15} + 2p_3 q_1 q_7 q_9 q_{14} + p_3 q_2 q_5 q_{10}^2$$

$$P[X^{(4)} = R] = P[X^{(3)} = B] P[X^{(4)} = R \big/ X^{(3)} = B]$$

$$P[X^{(4)} = R] = p_1 q_1^2 q_5 q_7 + p_1 q_1 q_2 q_7 q_9 + 2p_1 q_1 q_3 q_7 q_{13} + p_1 q_1 q_6 q_7 q_{10} + 2p_1 q_1 q_7^2 q_{14} +$$
$$p_2 q_1 q_6 q_7 q_9 + p_2 q_2 q_5 q_7 q_{10} + p_3 q_1 q_5 q_7 q_{10} + p_3 q_2 q_7 q_9 q_{10} + p_3 q_6 q_7 q_{10}^2 +$$
$$2p_3 q_7^2 q_{10} q_{14} + 2p_3 q_7 q_{10} q_{11} q_{15}$$

$$P[X^{(5)} = B] = P[X^{(4)} = A] P[X^{(5)} = B \big/ X^{(4)} = A] + P[X^{(4)} = R] P[X^{(5)} = B \big/ X^{(4)} = R]$$
$$+ P[X^{(4)} = C] P[X^{(5)} = B \big/ X^{(4)} = C] + P[X^{(4)} = R] P[X^{(5)} = B \big/ X^{(4)} = R]$$

$$P[X^{(5)} = B] = p_1 q_1^3 q_5^2 + 2p_1 q_1^2 q_2 q_5 q_9 + 4p_1 q_1^2 q_3 q_5 q_{13} + 2p_1 q_1^2 q_5 q_6 q_{10} + 4p_1 q_1^2 q_5 q_7 q_{14} +$$
$$p_1 q_1 q_2^2 q_9^2 + 4p_1 q_1 q_2 q_3 q_9 q_{13} + 3p_1 q_1 q_2 q_6 q_9 q_{10} + p_1 q_1 q_2 q_7 q_9 q_{14} +$$
$$2p_1 q_1 q_2 q_9 q_{11} q_{15} + 2p_1 q_1 q_3 q_6 q_{10} q_{13} + 4p_1 q_1 q_3^2 q_{13}^2 + 2p_1 q_1 q_3 q_7 q_{13} q_{14} +$$
$$p_2 q_1 q_6^2 q_{10}^2 + 4p_1 q_6 q_7 q_{10} q_{14} + 2p_1 q_1 q_6 q_{10} q_{11} q_{15} + 2p_1 q_1 q_7^2 q_{14}^2 + p_1 q_2^2 q_5 q_{10}^2 +$$
$$2p_2 q_1^2 q_5 q_6 q_9 + 2p_2 q_1 q_2 q_5^2 q_{10} + p_2 q_1 q_2 q_6 q_9^2 + 2p_2 q_1 q_3 q_6 q_9 q_{13} + 2p_2 q_1 q_6^2 q_9 q_{10} +$$

$$4p_2 q_1 q_6 q_7 q_9 q_{14} + 2p_2 q_1 q_6 q_9 q_{11} q_{15} + 2p_2 q_2 q_3 q_5 q_{10} q_{13} + 2p_2 q_2 q_5 q_6 q_{10}^2 +$$
$$p_2 q_2^2 q_5 q_9 q_{10} + 4p_2 q_2 q_5 q_7 q_{10} q_{14} + 2p_2 q_2 q_5 q_6 q_{10}^2 + p_3 q_1^2 q_5^2 q_{10} + p_3 q_1^2 q_6 q_9^2 +$$
$$3p_3 q_1 q_2 q_5 q_9 q_{10} + 2p_3 q_1 q_3 q_5 q_{10} q_{13} + 2p_3 q_1 q_5 q_6 q_{10}^2 + 4p_3 q_1 q_5 q_7 q_{10} q_{14} +$$
$$2p_3 q_1 q_5 q_{10} q_{11} q_{15} + p_3 q_2^2 q_9^2 q_{10} + 2p_3 q_2 q_3 q_9 q_{10} q_{13} + 2p_3 q_2 q_6 q_9 q_{10}^2 +$$
$$4p_3 q_2 q_9 q_{10} q_{11} q_{15} + 2p_3 q_2 q_7 q_9 q_{10} q_{14} + 4p_3 q_6 q_7 q_{10}^2 q_{14} + p_3 q_6^2 q_{10}^3 +$$
$$4p_3 q_6 q_{10}^2 q_{11} q_{15} + 4p_3 q_7^2 q_{10} q_{14}^2 + 4p_3 q_7 q_{10} q_{11} q_{14} q_{15} + 4p_3 q_{10} q_{11}^2 q_{15}^2$$

$$P[X^{(5)} = R] = P[X^{(4)} = B] P[X^{(5)} = R \big/ X^{(4)} = B]$$

$$P[X^{(5)} = R] = p_1 q_1^2 q_6 q_7 q_9 + 2p_1 q_1 q_2 q_5 q_7 q_{10} + 2p_1 q_2 q_3 q_7 q_{10} q_{13} + 2p_1 q_2 q_7^2 q_{10} q_{14} +$$
$$2p_1 q_2 q_7 q_{10} q_{11} q_{15} + p_1 q_2 q_6 q_7 q_{10}^2 + p_1 q_2^2 q_7 q_9 q_{10} + p_2 q_1^2 q_5^2 q_7 + p_2 q_1 q_2 q_5 q_7 q_9 +$$
$$2p_2 q_1 q_3 q_5 q_7 q_{13} + 2p_2 q_1 q_5 q_6 q_7 q_{10} + 4p_2 q_1 q_5 q_7^2 q_{14} + p_2 q_2 q_3 q_6 q_7 q_{10} +$$
$$4p_2 q_6 q_7^2 q_{10} q_{14} + 2p_2 q_6 q_7 q_{10} q_{11} q_{15} + p_2 q_6^2 q_7 q_{10}^2 + 4p_2 q_7^3 q_{14}^2 + p_3 q_1^2 q_5 q_7 q_9 +$$
$$p_3 q_1 q_2 q_7 q_9^2 + 2p_3 q_1 q_3 q_7 q_9 q_{13} + 2p_3 q_1 q_6 q_7 q_9 q_{10} + 2p_3 q_1 q_7 q_9 q_{11} q_{15} +$$
$$2p_3 q_1 q_7^2 q_9 q_{14} + p_3 q_2 q_5 q_7 q_{10}^2$$

$$P[X^{(6)} = B] = P[X^{(5)} = A]\,P[X^{(6)} = B/X^{(5)} = A] + P[X^{(5)} = R]\,P[X^{(6)} = B/X^{(5)} = R]$$
$$+ P[X^{(5)} = C]\,P[X^{(6)} = B/X^{(5)} = C] + P[X^{(5)} = R]\,P[X^{(6)} = B/X^{(5)} = R]$$

$$
\begin{aligned}
P[X^{(6)} = B] =\;& 2p_1 q_1^3 q_5 q_6 q_9 + 3p_1 q_1^2 q_2 q_5^2 q_{10} + 2p_1 q_1^2 q_2 q_6 q_9^2 + 4p_1 q_1^2 q_3 q_6 q_9 q_{13} + \\
& 2p_1 q_1^2 q_6^2 q_9 q_{10} + 4p_1 q_1^2 q_6 q_7 q_9 q_{14} + 2p_1 q_1^2 q_6 q_9 q_{11} q_{15} + 2p_1 q_1 q_2^2 q_5 q_9 q_{10} + \\
& 4p_1 q_1 q_2 q_3 q_5 q_{10} q_{13} + 4p_1 q_1 q_2 q_5 q_6 q_{10}^2 + 8p_1 q_1 q_2 q_5 q_7 q_{10} q_{14} + \\
& 4p_1 q_1 q_2 q_5 q_{10} q_{11} q_{15} + p_1 q_2^3 q_9^2 q_{10} + 2p_1 q_2^2 q_6 q_9 q_{10}^2 + 2p_1 q_2^2 q_7 q_9 q_{10} q_{14} +
\end{aligned}
$$

$$
\begin{aligned}
& 4p_1 q_2^2 q_9 q_{10} q_{11} q_{15} + 4p_1 q_2 q_3^2 q_{10} q_{13}^2 + 2p_1 q_2 q_3 q_6 q_{10}^2 q_{13} + 4p_1 q_2 q_3 q_7 q_{10} q_{13} q_{14} + \\
& 4p_1 q_2 q_3 q_{10} q_{11} q_{13} q_{15} + p_1 q_2 q_6^2 q_{10}^3 + 4p_1 q_2 q_6 q_7 q_{10}^2 q_{14} + 4p_1 q_2 q_6 q_{10}^2 q_{11} q_{15} + \\
& 4p_1 q_2 q_7^2 q_{10} q_{14}^2 + 4p_1 q_2 q_7 q_{10} q_{11} q_{14} q_{15} + 4p_1 q_2 q_{10} q_{11}^2 q_{15}^2
\end{aligned}
$$

$$
\begin{aligned}
& p_2 q_1^3 q_5^3 + 2p_2 q_1^2 q_2 q_5^2 q_9 + 4p_2 q_1^2 q_3 q_5^2 q_{13} + 3p_2 q_1^2 q_5^2 q_6 q_{10} + 6p_2 q_1^2 q_5^2 q_7 q_{14} + p_2 q_1^2 q_6^2 q_9^2 + \\
& 5p_2 q_1 q_2 q_5 q_6 q_9 q_{10} + 4p_2 q_1 q_2 q_3 q_5 q_9 q_{13} + p_2 q_1 q_2^2 q_5 q_9^2 + 4p_2 q_1 q_2 q_5 q_7 q_9 q_{14} + \\
& 2p_2 q_1 q_2 q_5 q_9 q_{11} q_{15} + 4p_2 q_1 q_3^2 q_5 q_{13}^2 + 4p_2 q_1 q_3 q_5 q_6 q_{10} q_{13} + 8p_2 q_1 q_3 q_5 q_7 q_{13} q_{14} + \\
& 12p_2 q_1 q_5 q_6 q_7 q_{10} q_{14} + 4p_2 q_1 q_5 q_6 q_{10} q_{11} q_{15} + p_2 q_1 q_5 q_6^2 q_{10}^2 + 4p_2 q_1 q_5 q_7^2 q_{14} + \\
& 8p_2 q_1 q_5 q_7^2 q_{14}^2 + 4p_2 q_2 q_6 q_7 q_9 q_{10} q_{14} + 12p_2 q_6 q_7^2 q_{10} q_{14}^2 + 6p_2 q_6 q_7 q_{10} q_{11} q_{14} q_{15} + \\
& 6p_2 q_6^2 q_7 q_{10}^2 q_{14} + 8p_2 q_7^3 q_{14}^3 + 2p_2 q_1 q_5 q_6 q_9^2 q_{10} + p_2 q_2^2 q_5^2 q_{10}^2 + p_2 q_2^2 q_6 q_9^2 q_{10} + \\
& 2p_2 q_2 q_3 q_6 q_9 q_{10} q_{13} + 2p_2 q_2 q_6^2 q_9 q_{10}^2 + 4p_2 q_2 q_6 q_9 q_{10} q_{11} q_{15} + p_2 q_6^3 q_{10}^3 + \\
& 4p_2 q_6^2 q_{10}^2 q_{11} q_{15} + 2p_2 q_6 q_7 q_{10} q_{11} q_{14} q_{15} + 2p_2 q_6 q_{10} q_{11}^2 q_{15}^2 +
\end{aligned}
$$

$$
\begin{aligned}
& p_3 q_1^3 q_5^2 q_9 + p_3 q_1^2 q_2 q_5 q_9^2 + 4p_3 q_1^2 q_3 q_5 q_9 q_{13} + 4p_3 q_1^2 q_5 q_6 q_9 q_{10} + 2p_3 q_1^2 q_5 q_9 q_{11} q_{15} + \\
& 4p_3 q_1^2 q_5 q_7 q_9 q_{14} + p_3 q_1 q_2^2 q_9^3 + 4p_3 q_1 q_2 q_3 q_9^2 q_{13} + 4p_3 q_1 q_2 q_6 q_9^2 q_{10} + 4p_3 q_1 q_2 q_9^2 q_{11} q_{15} + \\
& 3p_3 q_1 q_2 q_5^2 q_{10}^2 + 4p_3 q_1 q_3^2 q_9 q_{13}^2 + 4p_3 q_1 q_3 q_6 q_9 q_{10} q_{13} + 2p_3 q_1 q_3 q_9 q_{11} q_{13} q_{15} + 3p_3 q_1 q_6^2 q_9 q_{10}^2 + \\
& 8p_3 q_1 q_6 q_7 q_9 q_{10} q_{14} + 8p_3 q_1 q_6 q_9 q_{10} q_{11} q_{15} + 4p_3 q_1 q_9 q_{11}^2 q_{15}^2 + 2p_3 q_1 q_2 q_7^2 q_9^2 q_{14} + \\
& 4p_3 q_1 q_3 q_7 q_9 q_{13} q_{14} + 4p_3 q_1 q_7 q_9 q_{11} q_{14} q_{15} + 4p_3 q_1 q_7^2 q_9 q_{14}^2 + 4p_3 q_2 q_5 q_7 q_{10}^2 q_{14} + 2p_3 q_2^2 q_5 q_9 q_{10}^2 + \\
& 2p_3 q_2 q_3 q_5 q_{10}^2 q_{13} + 2p_3 q_2 q_5 q_6 q_{10}^3 + 4p_3 q_2 q_5 q_{10}^2 q_{11} q_{15}
\end{aligned}
$$

In the similar way, we can get the proof of the theorem.

Theorem 6

The transition probability of reaching on state C at n^{th} attempt when user is partially impatient:

(v) When n is even

$$P\left[X^{(2n)} = C\right] = p_1 q_1 q_6^n q_{10}^{n-1} + p_2 q_1^{n-1} q_2 q_5^n + p_3 q_2^n q_9^n + p_3 q_6^n q_{10}^n + 2^n p_3 q_{11}^n q_{15}^n$$

For n=1,2,3…

(vi) When n is odd $P\left[X^{(2n+1)} = C\right] = p_1 q_2^{n+1} q_9^n + p_2 q_6^{n+1} q_{10}^n$ For n= 0,1,2,3…

Proof

For $n = 0$, we have $P[X^{(0)} = A] = p_1$, $P[X^{(0)} = B] = p_2$, $P[X^{(0)} = C] = p_3$, and $P[X^{(0)} = R] = 0$, then

$$P[X^{(1)} = C] = P[X^{(0)} = A] P[X^{(1)} = C/X^{(0)} = A] + P[X^{(0)} = R] P[X^{(1)} = C/X^{(0)} = R]$$
$$+ P[X^{(0)} = B] P[X^{(1)} = C/X^{(0)} = B] + P[X^{(0)} = R] P[X^{(1)} = C/X^{(0)} = R]$$

$$\Rightarrow P[X^{(1)} = C] = p_1 q_2 + p_2 q_6$$

$$P[X^{(1)} = R] = P[X^{(0)} = C] P[X^{(1)} = R/X^{(0)} = C] = p_3 q_{11}$$

$$P[X^{(2)} = C] = P[X^{(1)} = A] P[X^{(2)} = C/X^{(1)} = A] + P[X^{(1)} = R] P[X^{(2)} = C/X^{(1)} = R]$$
$$+ P[X^{(1)} = B] P[X^{(2)} = C/X^{(1)} = B] + P[X^{(1)} = R] P[X^{(2)} = C/X^{(1)} = R]$$

$$\Rightarrow P[X^{(2)} = C] = p_1 q_1 q_6 + p_2 q_2 q_5 + p_3 q_2 q_9 + p_3 q_6 q_{10} + 2 p_3 q_{11} q_{15}$$

$$P[X^{(2)} = R] = P[X^{(1)} = C] P[X^{(2)} = R/X^{(1)} = C] = p_1 q_2 q_{11} + p_2 q_6 q_{11}$$

$$P[X^{(3)} = C] = P[X^{(2)} = A] P[X^{(3)} = C/X^{(2)} = A] + P[X^{(2)} = R] P[X^{(3)} = C/X^{(2)} = R]$$
$$+ P[X^{(2)} = B] P[X^{(3)} = C/X^{(2)} = B] + P[X^{(2)} = R] P[X^{(3)} = C/X^{(2)} = R]$$

$$\Rightarrow P[X^{(3)} = C] = p_1 q_1 q_2 q_5 + p_1 q_2^2 q_9 + 2 p_1 q_2 q_3 q_{13} + p_1 q_2 q_6 q_{10} + 2 p_1 q_2 q_{11} q_{15} +$$
$$p_2 q_1 q_5 q_6 + p_2 q_2 q_6 q_9 + p_2 q_6^2 q_{10} + 2 p_2 q_6 q_7 q_{14} + 2 p_2 q_6 q_{11} q_{15} + p_3 q_1 q_6 q_9 +$$
$$p_3 q_2 q_5 q_{10}$$

$$P[X^{(3)} = R] = P[X^{(2)} = C] P[X^{(3)} = R/X^{(2)} = C] = p_1 q_1 q_6 q_{11} + p_2 q_2 q_5 q_{11} +$$
$$p_3 q_2 q_9 q_{11} + p_3 q_6 q_{10} q_{11} + 2 p_3 q_{11}^2 q_{15}$$

$$P[X^{(4)} = C] = P[X^{(3)} = A] P[X^{(4)} = C/X^{(3)} = A] + P[X^{(3)} = R] P[X^{(4)} = C/X^{(3)} = R]$$
$$+ P[X^{(3)} = B] P[X^{(4)} = C/X^{(3)} = B] + P[X^{(3)} = R] P[X^{(4)} = C/X^{(3)} = R]$$

$$P[X^{(4)} = C] = 2p_1q_1q_2q_6q_9 + p_1q_1^2q_5q_6 + p_1q_2^2q_5q_{10} + 2p_1q_1q_6q_7q_{14} + 2p_1q_1q_6q_{11}q_{15} +$$
$$2p_1q_1q_3q_6q_{13} + p_1q_1q_6^2q_{10} + p_2q_1q_2q_5^2 + p_2q_1q_6^2q_9 + p_2q_2^2q_5q_9 + 2p_2q_2q_5q_6q_{10} +$$
$$2p_2q_2q_5q_7q_{14} + 2p_2q_2q_5q_{11}q_{15} + 2p_2q_2q_3q_5q_{13} + p_3q_1q_2q_5q_9 + p_3q_1q_5q_6q_{10} +$$
$$p_3q_2^2q_9^2 + 2p_2q_2q_3q_9q_{13} + 2p_3q_2q_6q_9q_{10} + 4p_3q_2q_9q_{11}q_{15} + p_3q_6^2q_{10}^2 +$$
$$2p_3q_6q_7q_{10}q_{14} + 4p_3q_6q_{10}q_{11}q_{15} + 4p_3q_{11}^2q_{15}^2$$

$$P[X^{(4)} = R] = P[X^{(3)} = C]\, P[X^{(4)} = R \big/ X^{(3)} = C]$$

$$P[X^{(4)} = R] = p_1q_1q_2q_5q_{11} + p_1q_2^2q_9q_{11} + 2p_1q_2q_3q_{11}q_{13} + p_1q_2q_6q_{10}q_{11} + 2p_1q_2q_{11}^2q_{15} +$$
$$p_2q_1q_5q_6q_{11} + p_2q_2q_6q_9q_{11} + p_2q_6^2q_{10}q_{11} + 2p_2q_6q_7q_{11}q_{14} + 2p_3q_6q_{11}^2q_{15} +$$
$$p_3q_1q_6q_9q_{11} + p_3q_2q_5q_{10}q_{11}$$

$$P[X^{(5)} = C] = P[X^{(4)} = A]\, P[X^{(5)} = C\big/X^{(4)} = A] + P[X^{(4)} = R]\, P[X^{(5)} = C\big/X^{(4)} = R]$$
$$+ P[X^{(4)} = B]P[X^{(5)} = C\big/X^{(4)} = B] + P[X^{(4)} = R]\, P[X^{(5)} = C\big/X^{(4)} = R]$$

$$P[X^{(5)} = C] = p_1q_1^2q_2q_5^2 + p_1q_1^2q_6^2q_9 + 2p_1q_1q_2^2q_5q_9 + 4p_1q_1q_2q_3q_5q_{13} + 4p_1q_1q_2q_3q_9q_{13} +$$
$$3p_1q_1q_2q_5q_6q_{10} + 2p_1q_1q_2q_5q_7q_{14} + 2p_1q_1q_2q_5q_{11}q_{15} + p_1q_2^3q_9^2 + 2p_1q_2^2q_6q_9q_{10} +$$
$$4p_1q_2^2q_9q_{11}q_{15} + 4p_1q_2q_3^2q_{13}^2 + 2p_1q_2q_3q_6q_{10}q_{13} + 4p_1q_2q_3q_{11}q_{13}q_{15} + p_1q_2q_6^2q_{10}^2 +$$
$$2p_1q_2q_6q_7q_{10}q_{14} + 4p_1q_2q_6q_{10}q_{11}q_{15} + 4p_1q_2q_{11}^2q_{15}^2 + p_2q_1^2q_5^2q_6 + 2p_2q_1q_2q_5q_6q_9 +$$
$$2p_2q_1q_3q_5q_6q_{13} + 2p_2q_1q_5q_6^2q_{10} + 2p_2q_1q_5q_6q_{11}q_{15} + 4p_2q_1q_5q_6q_7q_{14} + p_2q_2^2q_5^2q_{10} +$$

$$P[X^{(5)} = R] = P[X^{(4)} = C]\, P[X^{(5)} = R\big/X^{(4)} = C]$$

$$P[X^{(5)} = R] = 2p_1q_1q_2q_6q_9q_{11} + p_1q_1^2q5q_6q_{11} + 2p_1q_1q_6q_7q_{11}q_{14} + 2p_1q_1q_6q_{11}^2q_{15} +$$
$$2p_1q_1q_3q_6q_{11}q_{13} + p_1q_1q_6^2q_{10}q_{11} + p_1q_2^2q_5q_{10}q_{11} + p_2q_1q_2q_5^2q_{11} + p_2q_2^2q_5q_9q_{11} +$$
$$2p_2q_2q_5q_6q_{10}q_{11} + 2p_2q_2q_5q_7q_{11}q_{14} + 2p_2q_2q_5q_{11}^2q_{15} + 2p_2q_2q_5q_3q_{11}q_{13} +$$
$$p_2q_1q_6^2q_9q_{11} + p_3q_1q_2q_5q_9q_{11} + p_3q_2^2q_9^2q_{11} + 2p_3q_2q_3q_9q_{11}q_{13} + 2p_3q_2q_6q_9q_{10}q_{11} +$$
$$4p_3q_2q_9q_{11}^2q15 + p_3q_6^2q_{10}^2q_{11} + p_3q_1q_5q_6q_{10}q_{11} + 2p_3q_6q_7q_{10}q_{11}q_{14} + 4p_3q_6q_{10}q_{11}^2q_{15} +$$
$$4p_3q_{11}^3q_{15}^2$$

$$P[X^{(6)} = C] = (4p_1q_1^2q_2q_5q_6q_9 + 2p_1q_1q_2^2q_5^2q_{10} + 8p_1q_1q_2q_3q_6q_9q_{13} + 3p_1q_1q_2^2q_6q_9^2 +$$

$$3p_1q_1q_2q_6q_7q_9q_{14} + 4p_1q_1q_2q_6^2q_9q_{10} + 8p_1q_1q_2q_6q_9q_{11}q_{15} + 4p_1q_2^2q_3q_5q_{10}q_{13} +$$

$$p_1q_2^3q_5q_9q_{10} + 2p_1q_2^2q_5q_6q_{10}^2 + 2p_1q_2^2q_5q_7q_{10}q_{14} + 4p_1q_2^2q_5q_{10}q_{11}q_{15} + 2p_1q_1^2q_5q_6q_{11}q_{15} +$$

$$4p_1q_1q_6q_7q_{11}q_{14}q_{15} + 4p_1q_1q_6q_{11}^2q_{15}^2 + 4p_1q_1q_3q_6q_{11}q_{13}q_{15} + 4p_1q_1q_6^2q_{10}q_{11}q_{15} +$$

$$p_1q_1^3q_5^2q_6 + 4p_1q_1^2q_3q_5q_6q_{13} + 2p_1q_1^2q_5q_6^2q_{10} + 4p_1q_1^2q_5q_6q_7q_{14} + 2p_1q_1q_3q_6^2q_{10}q_{13} +$$

$$4p_1q_1q_3^2q_6q_{13}^2 + 2p_1q_1q_3q_6q_7q_{13}q_{14} + p_1q_1q_6^3q_{10}^2 + 4p_1q_1q_6^2q_7q_{10}q_{14} + 2p_1q_1q_6q_7^2q_{14}^2 +$$

$$p_2q_1^2q_2q_5^3 + 2p_2q_1q_2^2q_5^2q_9 + 4p_2q_1q_2q_3q_5^2q_{13} + 4p_2q_1q_5^2q_6q_{10} + 4p_2q_1q_2q_5^2q_7q_{14} +$$

$$p_2q_1q_2q_6^2q_9^2 + 4p_2q_2^2q_5q_6q_9q_{10} + 4p_2q_2^2q_3q_5q_9q_{13} + p_2q_2^3q_5q_9^2 + 2p_2q_2^2q_5q_7q_9q_{14} +$$

$$4p_2q_2^2q_5q_9q_{11}q_{15} + 4p_2q_2q_3^2q_5q_{13}^2 + 4p_2q_2q_3q_5q_6q_{10}q_{13} + 4p_2q_2q_3q_5q_7q_{13}q_{14} +$$

$$8p_2q_2q_5q_6q_7q_{10}q_{14} + 8p_2q_2q_5q_6q_{10}q_{11}q_{15} + 3p_2q_2q_5q_6^2q_{10}^2 + 4p_2q_2q_5q_7^2q_{14}^2 +$$

$$2p_2q_1q_2q_5^2q_{11}q_{15} + 4p_2q_2q_5q_7q_{11}q_{14}q_{15} + 4p_2q_2q_5q_{11}^2q_{15}^2 + 4p_2q_2q_3q_5q_{11}q_{13}q_{15} +$$

$$2p_2q_1q_6^2q_9q_{11}q_{15} + 2p_2q_1^2q_5q_6^2q_9 + p_2q_1q_2q_6^2q_9^2 + 2p_2q_1q_3q_6^2q_9q_{13} + 2p_2q_2q_6^3q_9q_{10} +$$

$$4p_2q_1q_6^2q_7q_9q_{14} + 2p_2q_1q_6^2q_9q_{11}q_{15} + 2p_2q_2q_5q_6^2q_{10}^2 + p_3q_1^2q_2q_5^2q_9 + p_3q_1q_2^2q_5q_9^2 +$$

$$4p_3q_1q_2q_3q_5q_9q_{13} + 6p_3q_1q_2q_5q_6q_9q_{10} + 4p_3q_1q_2q_5q_9q_{11}q_{15} + 2p_3q_1q_2q_5q_7q_9q_{14} +$$

$$p_3q_2^3q_9^3 + 4p_3q_2^2q_3q_9^2q_{13} + 3p_3q_2^2q_6q_9^2q_{10} + 6p_3q_2^2q_9^2q_{11}q_{15} + 2p_3q_2^2q_5^2q_{10}^2 + 4p_3q_2q_3^2q_9q_{13}^2 +$$

$$4p_3q_2q_3q_6q_9q_{10}q_{13} + +6p_3q_2q_3q_9q_{11}q_{13}q_{15} + 3p_3q_2q_6^2q_9q_{10}^2 + 4p_3q_2q_6q_7q_9q_{10}q_{14} +$$

$$12p_3q_2q_6q_9q_{10}q_{11}q_{15} + 12p_3q_2q_9q_{11}^2q_{15}^2 + 6p_3q_6^2q_{10}q_{11}q_{15} + 4p_3q_1q_5q_6q_{10}q_{11}q_{15} +$$

$$8p_3q_6q_7q_{10}q_{11}q_{14}q_{15} + 12p_3q_6q_{10}q_{11}^2q_{15}^2 + 8p_3q_{11}^3q_{15}^3 + p_3q_1^2q_5^2q_6q_{10} + p_3q_1^2q_6^2q_9^2 +$$

$$2p_3q_1q_3q_5q_6q_{10}q_{13} + p_3q_1q_5q_6^2q_{10}^2 + 4p_3q_1q_5q_6q_7q_{10}q_{14} + 4p_3q_6^2q_7q_{10}^2q_{14} + p_3q_6^3q_{10}^3 +$$

$$4p_3q_6q_7^2q_{10}q_{14}^2$$

In the similar way, we can get the proof of the theorem.

N[th] Attempt Results for Completely Impatient User

A completely impatient user if continuous with attempts to access web pages then at the n-1th attempt he can be at state A, B and C then the probability of reaching on states A, B, C on the nth attempt can be calculated using the following theorems.

Theorem 7

The transition probability of reaching on state A at n[th] attempt when user is completely impatient:

(i) When n is even $P\left[X^{(2n)} = A\right] = p_1 q_1^n q_5^n + p_1 q_2^n q_9^n + p_2 q_2^{n-1} q_6 q_9^n + p_3 q_1^{n-1} q_5^n q_{10}$ For n=1,2,3…

(ii) When n is odd $P\left[X^{(2n+1)} = A\right] = p_2 q_1^n q_5^{n+1} + p_3 q_2^n q_9^{n+1}$ For n= 0,1,2,3…

Proof

For n=0, we have have $P[X^{(0)} = A] = p_1$, $P[X^{(0)} = B] = p_2$ and $P[X^{(0)} = C] = p_3$ then

$$P\left[X^{(1)} = A\right] = P\left[X^{(0)} = B\right] P\left[X^{(1)} = A / X^{(0)} = B\right] + P\left[X^{(0)} = C\right] P\left[X^{(1)} = A / X^{(0)} = C\right]$$

$$\Rightarrow P\left[X^{(1)} = A\right] = p_2 q_5 + p_3 q_9$$

$$P\left[X^{(2)} = A\right] = P\left[X^{(1)} = B\right] P\left[X^{(2)} = A / X^{(1)} = B\right] + P\left[X^{(1)} = C\right] P\left[X^{(2)} = A / X^{(1)} = C\right]$$

$$\Rightarrow P\left[X^{(2)} = A\right] = p_1 q_1 q_5 + p_1 q_2 q_9 + p_2 q_6 q_9 + p_3 q_5 q_{10}$$

$$P\left[X^{(3)} = A\right] = P\left[X^{(2)} = B\right] P\left[X^{(3)} = A / X^{(2)} = B\right] + P\left[X^{(2)} = C\right] P\left[X^{(3)} = A / X^{(2)} = C\right]$$

$$\Rightarrow P\left[X^{(3)} = A\right] = p_1 q_1 q_6 q_9 + p_1 q_2 q_5 q_{10} + p_2 q_1 q_5^2 + p_2 q_2 q_5 q_9 + p_2 q_5 q_6 q_{10} +$$
$$p_3 q_1 q_5 q_9 + p_3 q_2 q_9^2 + p_3 q_6 q_9 q_{10}$$

$$P\left[X^{(4)} = A\right] = P\left[X^{(3)} = B\right] P\left[X^{(4)} = A / X^{(3)} = B\right] + P\left[X^{(3)} = C\right] P\left[X^{(4)} = A / X^{(3)} = C\right]$$

$$\Rightarrow P\left[X^{(4)} = A\right] = \underline{p_1 q_1^2 q_5^2} + 2 p_1 q_1 q_2 q_5 q_9 + p_1 q_1 q_5 q_6 q_{10} + \underline{p_1 q_2^2 q_9^2} + p_1 q_2 q_6 q_9 q_{10} +$$
$$2 p_2 q_1 q_5 q_6 q_9 + p_2 q_2 q_5^2 q_{10} + \underline{p_2 q_2 q_6 q_9^2} + p_2 q_6^2 q_9 q_{10} + \underline{p_3 q_1 q_5^2 q_{10}} +$$
$$p_3 q_1 q_6 q_9^2 + 2 p_3 q_2 q_5 q_9 q_{10} + p_3 q_5 q_6 q_{10}^2$$

$$P\left[X^{(5)} = A\right] = P\left[X^{(4)} = B\right] P\left[X^{(5)} = A\big/X^{(4)} = B\right] + P\left[X^{(4)} = C\right] P\left[X^{(5)} = A\big/X^{(4)} = C\right]$$

$$\Rightarrow P\left[X^{(5)} = A\right] = p_1 q_1^2 q_5^3 + 2p_1 q_1^2 q_5 q_6 q_9 + 2p_1 q_1 q_2 q_5^2 q_{10} + 2p_1 q_1 q_2 q_6 q_9^2 + p_1 q_1 q_6^2 q_9 q_{10} + $$
$$2p_1 q_2^2 q_5 q_9 q_{10} + p_1 q_2 q_5 q_6 q_{10}^2 + 2 p_2 q_1 q_2 q_5^2 q_9 + 2p_2 q_1 q_5^2 q_6 q_{10} + p_2 q_1 q_6^2 q_9^2 + $$
$$p_2 q_2^2 q_5 q_9^2 + 3p_2 q_2 q_5 q_6 q_9 q_{10} + p_2 q_5 q_6^2 q_{10}^2 + p_3 q_1^2 q_5^2 q_9 + 2p_3 q_1 q_2 q_5 q_9^2 + $$
$$3p_3 q_1 q_5 q_6 q_9 q_{10} + p_3 q_2^2 q_9^3 + p_3 q_2 q_5^2 q_{10}^2 + 2p_3 q_2 q_6 q_9^2 q_{10} + p_3 q_6^2 q_9 q_{10}^2$$

$$P\left[X^{(6)} = A\right] = P\left[X^{(5)} = B\right] P\left[X^{(6)} = A\big/X^{(5)} = B\right] + P\left[X^{(5)} = C\right] P\left[X^{(6)} = A\big/X^{(5)} = C\right]$$

$$\Rightarrow P\left[X^{(6)} = A\right] = p_1 q_1^3 q_5^3 + 3p_1 q_1^2 q_2 q_5^2 q_9 + 2p_1 q_1^2 q_5 q_6^2 q_{10} + p_1 q_1^2 q_6^2 q_9^2 + 3p_1 q_1 q_2^2 q_5 q_9^2 + $$
$$6p_1 q_1 q_2 q_5 q_6 q_9 q_{10} + p_1 q_1 q_5 q_6^2 q_{10}^2 + p_1 q_2^3 q_9^3 + p_1 q_2^2 q_5^2 q_{10}^2 + 2p_1 q_2^2 q_6 q_9^2 q_{10} + p_1 q_2 q_6^2 q_9 q_{10}^2 + $$
$$3p_2 q_1^2 q_5^2 q_6 q_9 + 2p_2 q_1 q_2 q_5^3 q_{10} + 4p_2 q_1 q_2 q_5 q_6 q_9^2 + 4p_2 q_1 q_5 q_6^2 q_9 q_{10} + 2p_2 q_2^2 q_5^2 q_9 q_{10} + $$
$$p_2 q_2^2 q_6 q_9^3 + 2p_2 q_2 q_5^2 q_6 q_{10}^2 + 2p_2 q_2 q_6^2 q_9^2 q_{10} + p_2 q_6^3 q_9 q_{10}^2 + p_3 q_1^2 q_5^3 q_{10} + 2p_3 q_1^2 q_5 q_6 q_9^2 + $$
$$4p_3 q_1 q_2 q_5^2 q_9 q_{10} + 2p_3 q_1 q_2 q_6 q_9^3 + 2p_3 q_1 q_5^2 q_6 q_{10}^2 + 3p_3 q_2^2 q_5 q_9^2 q_{10} + 2 p_3 q_1 q_6^2 q_9^2 q_{10} + $$
$$3p_3 q_2 q_5 q_6 q_9 q_{10}^2 + p_3 q_5 q_6^2 q_{10}^3$$

In the similar way, we can get the proof of the theorem.

Theorem 8

The transition probability of reaching on state B at n^{th} attempt when user is completely impatient:

(iii) When n is even $P\left[X^{(2n)} = B\right] = p_1 q_2^n q_9^{n-1} q_{10} + p_2 q_1^n q_5^n + p_2 q_6^n q_{10}^n + p_3 q_1^n q_5^{n-1} q_9$ For

n=1, 2, 3...

(iv) When n is odd $P\left[X^{(2n+1)} = B\right] = p_1 q_1^{n+1} q_5^n + p_3 q_6^n q_{10}^{n+1}$ For n= 0, 1, 2, 3...

Proof

For n=0, we have have $P[X^{(0)} = A] = p_1$, $P[X^{(0)} = B] = p_2$ and $P[X^{(0)} = C] = p_3$ then

$$P\left[X^{(1)} = B\right] = P\left[X^{(0)} = A\right] P\left[X^{(1)} = B\middle/ X^{(0)} = A\right] + P\left[X^{(0)} = C\right] P\left[X^{(1)} = B\middle/ X^{(0)} = C\right]$$

$$\Rightarrow P\left[X^{(1)} = B\right] = p_1 q_1 + p_3 q_{10}$$

$$P\left[X^{(2)} = B\right] = P\left[X^{(1)} = A\right] P\left[X^{(2)} = B\middle/ X^{(1)} = A\right] + P\left[X^{(1)} = C\right] P\left[X^{(2)} = B\middle/ X^{(1)} = C\right]$$

$$\Rightarrow P\left[X^{(2)} = B\right] = p_1 q_2 q_{10} + p_2 q_1 q_5 + p_2 q_6 q_{10} + p_3 q_1 q_9$$

$$P\left[X^{(3)} = B\right] = P\left[X^{(2)} = A\right] P\left[X^{(3)} = B\middle/ X^{(2)} = A\right] + P\left[X^{(2)} = C\right] P\left[X^{(3)} = B\middle/ X^{(2)} = C\right]$$

$$\Rightarrow P\left[X^{(3)} = B\right] = p_1 q_1^2 q_5 + p_1 q_1 q_2 q_9 + p_1 q_1 q_6 q_{10} + p_2 q_1 q_6 q_9 + p_2 q_2 q_5 q_{10} +$$
$$p_3 q_1 q_5 q_{10} + p_3 q_2 q_9 q_{10} + p_3 q_6 q_{10}^2$$

$$P\left[X^{(4)} = B\right] = P\left[X^{(3)} = A\right] P\left[X^{(4)} = B\middle/ X^{(3)} = A\right] + P\left[X^{(3)} = C\right] P\left[X^{(4)} = B\middle/ X^{(3)} = C\right]$$

$$\Rightarrow P\left[X^{(4)} = B\right] = \underline{p_2 q_1^2 q_5^2} + p_1 q_1^2 q_6 q_9 + 2 p_1 q_1 q_2 q_5 q_{10} + p_1 q_2^2 q_9 q_{10} + \underline{p_1 q_2 q_6 q_{10}^2} +$$
$$p_2 q_1 q_2 q_5 q_9 + 2 p_2 q_1 q_5 q_6 q_{10} + p_2 q_2 q_6 q_9 q_{10} + \underline{p_2 q_6^2 q_{10}^2} + \underline{p_3 q_1^2 q_5 q_9} +$$
$$p_3 q_1 q_2 q_9^2 + 2 p_3 q_1 q_6 q_9 q_{10} + p_3 q_2 q_5 q_{10}^2$$

$$P\left[X^{(5)} = B\right] = P\left[X^{(4)} = A\right] P\left[X^{(5)} = B\middle/ X^{(4)} = A\right] + P\left[X^{(4)} = C\right] P\left[X^{(5)} = B\middle/ X^{(4)} = C\right]$$

$$\Rightarrow P\left[X^{(5)} = B\right] = p_1 q_1^3 q_5^2 + 2 p_1 q_1^2 q_2 q_5 q_9 + 2 p_1 q_1^2 q_5 q_6 q_{10} + p_1 q_1 q_2^2 q_9^2 + 3 p_1 q_1 q_2 q_6 q_9 q_{10} +$$
$$p_1 q_1 q_6^2 q_{10}^2 + p_1 q_2^2 q_5 q_{10}^2 + 2 p_2 q_1^2 q_5 q_6 q_9 + 2 p_2 q_1 q_2 q_5^2 q_{10} + p_2 q_1 q_2 q_6 q_9^2 +$$
$$2 p_2 q_1 q_6^2 q_9 q_{10} + p_2 q_2^2 q_5 q_9 q_{10} + 2 p_2 q_2 q_5 q_6 q_{10}^2 + p_3 q_1^2 q_5^2 q_{10} + p_3 q_1^2 q_6 q_9^2 +$$
$$3 p_3 q_1 q_2 q_5 q_9 q_{10} + 2 p_3 q_1 q_5 q_6 q_{10}^2 + p_3 q_2^2 q_9^2 q_{10} + 2 p_3 q_2 q_6 q_9 q_{10}^2 + p_3 q_6^2 q_{10}^3$$

$$P\left[X^{(6)} = B\right] = P\left[X^{(5)} = A\right]P\left[X^{(6)} = B \middle/ X^{(5)} = A\right] + P\left[X^{(5)} = C\right]P\left[X^{(6)} = B \middle/ X^{(5)} = C\right]$$

$$\Rightarrow P\left[X^{(6)} = B\right] = 2p_1q_1^3q_5q_6q_9 + 3p_1q_1^2q_2q_5^2q_{10} + 2p_1q_1^2q_2q_6q_9^2 + 2p_1q_1^2q_6^2q_9q_{10} + 4p_1q_1q_2^2q_5q_9q_{10} +$$
$$4p_1q_1q_2q_5q_6q_{10}^2 + p_1q_2^3q_9^2q_{10} + 2p_1q_2^2q_6q_9q_{10}^2 + p_1q_2q_6^2q_{10}^3 + p_2q_1^3q_5^3 + 2p_2q_1^2q_2q_5^2q_9 +$$
$$2p_2q_1^2q_5^2q_6q_9 + p_2q_1^2q_5^2q_6q_{10} + p_2q_1^2q_6^2q_9^2 + p_2q_1q_2^2q_5q_9^2 + 6p_2q_1q_2q_5q_6q_9q_{10} +$$
$$3p_2q_1q_5q_6^2q_{10}^2 + p_2q_2^2q_5^2q_{10}^2 + p_2q_2^2q_6q_9^2q_{10} + 2p_2q_2q_6^2q_9q_{10}^2 + p_2q_6^3q_{10}^2 + p_3q_1^3q_5^2q_9 +$$
$$2p_3q_1^2q_2q_5q_9^2 + 4p_3q_1^2q_5q_6q_9q_{10} + p_3q_1q_2^2q_9^3 + 2p_3q_1q_2q_5q_6q_{10}^2 + 4p_3q_1q_2q_6q_9^2q_{10} +$$
$$p_3q_1q_6^2q_9q_{10}^2 + 2p_3q_2^2q_5q_9q_{10}^2 + 2p_3q_1q_6^2q_9q_{10}^2 + 2p_3q_2q_5q_6q_{10}^3$$

In the similar way, we can get the proof of the theorem.

Theorem 9

The transition probability of reaching on state C at n^{th} attempt when user is completely impatient:

(v)   When n is even $P\left[X^{(2n)} = C\right] = p_1q_1^nq_5^{n-1}q_6 + p_2q_2^nq_5q_9^{n-1} + p_3q_2^nq_9^n + p_3q_6^nq_{10}^n$ For

   n=1,2,3…

(vi)   When n is odd $P\left[X^{(2n+1)} = C\right] = p_1q_2^{n+1}q_9^n + p_2q_6^{n+1}q_{10}^n$ For n= 0,1,2,3…

Proof

For n=0, we have have $P[X^{(0)} = A] = p_1$, $P[X^{(0)} = B] = p_2$ and $P[X^{(0)} = C] = p_3$ then

$$P\left[X^{(1)} = C\right] = P\left[X^{(0)} = A\right]P\left[X^{(1)} = C \middle/ X^{(0)} = A\right] + P\left[X^{(0)} = B\right]P\left[X^{(1)} = C \middle/ X^{(0)} = B\right]$$

$$\Rightarrow P\left[X^{(1)} = C\right] = p_1q_2 + p_2q_6$$

$$P\left[X^{(2)} = C\right] = P\left[X^{(1)} = A\right]P\left[X^{(2)} = C \middle/ X^{(1)} = A\right] + P\left[X^{(1)} = B\right]P\left[X^{(2)} = C \middle/ X^{(1)} = B\right]$$

$$\Rightarrow P\left[X^{(2)} = C\right] = p_1q_1q_6 + p_2q_2q_5 + p_3q_2q_9 + p_3q_6q_{10}$$

$$P\left[X^{(3)} = C\right] = P\left[X^{(2)} = A\right] P\left[X^{(3)} = C/X^{(2)} = A\right] + P\left[X^{(2)} = B\right] P\left[X^{(3)} = C/X^{(2)} = B\right]$$

$$\Rightarrow P\left[X^{(3)} = C\right] = p_1 q_1 q_2 q_5 + p_1 q_2^2 q_9 + p_1 q_2 q_6 q_{10} + p_2 q_1 q_5 q_6 + p_2 q_2 q_6 q_9 +$$
$$p_2 q_6^2 q_{10} + p_3 q_1 q_6 q_9 + p_3 q_2 q_5 q_{10}$$

$$P\left[X^{(4)} = C\right] = P\left[X^{(3)} = A\right] P\left[X^{(4)} = C/X^{(3)} = A\right] + P\left[X^{(3)} = B\right] P\left[X^{(4)} = C/X^{(3)} = B\right]$$

$$\Rightarrow P\left[X^{(4)} = C\right] = p_1 q_1^2 q_5 q_6 + 2p_1 q_1 q_2 q_6 q_9 + p_1 q_1 q_6^2 q_{10} + p_1 q_2^2 q_5 q_{10} + p_2 q_1 q_2 q_5^2 +$$
$$p_2 q_1 q_6^2 q_9 + p_2 q_2^2 q_5 q_9 + 2p_2 q_2 q_5 q_6 q_{10} + p_3 q_1 q_2 q_5 q_9 + p_3 q_1 q_5 q_6 q_{10} +$$
$$p_3 q_2^2 q_9^2 + 2p_3 q_2 q_6 q_9 q_{10} + p_3 q_6^2 q_{10}^2$$

$$P\left[X^{(5)} = C\right] = P\left[X^{(4)} = A\right] P\left[X^{(5)} = C/X^{(4)} = A\right] + P\left[X^{(4)} = B\right] P\left[X^{(5)} = C/X^{(4)} = B\right]$$

$$\Rightarrow P\left[X^{(5)} = C\right] = p_1 q_1^2 q_2 q_5^2 + p_1 q_1^2 q_6^2 q_9 + 2p_1 q_1 q_2 q_5^2 q_9 + 3p_1 q_1 q_2 q_5 q_6 q_{10} + p_1 q_2^3 q_9^2 + 2p_1 q_2^2 q_6 q_9 q_{10} +$$
$$p_1 q_2 q_6^2 q_{10}^2 + p_2 q_1^2 q_5^2 q_6 + 3p_2 q_1 q_2 q_5 q_6 q_9 + 2p_2 q_1 q_2 q_6^2 q_{10} + p_2 q_2^2 q_5^2 q_{10} + p_2 q_2^2 q_6 q_9^2 +$$
$$2p_2 q_2 q_6^2 q_9 q_{10} + p_2 q_6^3 q_{10}^2 + p_3 q_1^2 q_5 q_6 q_9 + p_3 q_1 q_2 q_5^2 q_{10} + 2p_3 q_1 q_2 q_6 q_9^2 +$$
$$2p_3 q_2^2 q_5 q_9 q_{10} + 2p_3 q_1 q_6^2 q_9 q_{10} + 2p_3 q_2 q_5 q_6 q_{10}^2$$

$$P\left[X^{(6)} = C\right] = P\left[X^{(5)} = A\right] P\left[X^{(6)} = C/X^{(5)} = A\right] + P\left[X^{(5)} = B\right] P\left[X^{(6)} = C/X^{(5)} = B\right]$$

$$\Rightarrow P\left[X^{(6)} = C\right] = p_1 q_1^3 q_5^2 q_6 + 4 p_1 q_1^2 q_2 q_5 q_6 q_9 + 2 p_1 q_1^2 q_5 q_6^2 q_{10} + 2 p_1 q_1 q_2^2 q_5^2 q_{10} + 3 p_1 q_1 q_2^2 q_6 q_9^2 +$$

$$4 p_1 q_1 q_2 q_6^2 q_9 q_{10} + p_1 q_1 q_6^3 q_{10}^2 + 2 p_1 q_2^3 q_5 q_9 q_{10} + 2 p_1 q_2^2 q_5 q_6 q_{10}^2 + p_2 q_1^2 q_2 q_5^3 +$$

$$2 p_2 q_1^2 q_5 q_6^2 q_9 + 2 p_2 q_1 q_2^2 q_5^2 q_9 + 4 p_2 q_1 q_2 q_5^2 q_6 q_{10} + 2 p_2 q_1 q_2 q_6^2 q_9^2 + 2 p_2 q_1 q_6^3 q_9 q_{10} +$$

$$p_2 q_2^3 q_5 q_9^2 + 4 p_2 q_2^2 q_5 q_6 q_9 q_{10} + 3 p_2 q_2 q_5 q_6^2 q_{10}^2 + p_3 q_1^2 q_2 q_5^2 q_9 + 2 p_3 q_1 q_2^2 q_5 q_9^2 +$$

$$p_3 q_1^2 q_5^2 q_6 q_{10} + p_3 q_1^2 q_6^2 q_9^2 + 6 p_3 q_1 q_2 q_5 q_6 q_9 q_{10} + 2 p_3 q_1 q_5 q_6^2 q_{10}^2 + p_3 q_2^3 q_9^3 + p_3 q_2^2 q_5^2 q_{10}^2 +$$

$$2 p_3 q_1 q_5 q_6^2 q_{10}^2 + 3 p_3 q_2^2 q_6 q_9^2 q_{10} + p_3 q_2^2 q_6 q_9^2 q_{10} + 3 p_3 q_2 q_6^2 q_9 q_{10}^2 + p_3 q_6^3 q_{10}^3$$

In the similar way, we can get the proof of the theorem.

SIMULATION STUDY

Initially we observe the behavior of each type of user individually by varying the value of refreshing probability (q_3 and q_{13} for page A, q_7 and q_{14} for page B and q_{11} and q_{15} for page C) of each type of user. We draw the graphs between the number of attempt and Transition probability.

As shown in the Figure 4(a), 4(b), 5(a), 5(b), 6(a) and 6(b), we find that for any value of q_3, q_{13}, q_7, q_{14}, q_{11} and q_{15}, Transition Probability decreases as the number of attempts increases. With higher value of q_3, initially transition probability is high but it decreases rapidly as attempt increases. While for lower value of q_3 initially transition probability is low and it decreases slowly. The same results obtained when we vary the transition probability q_{13} i.e. the transition probability of going from refresh state to state A. The second trend we find is that for faithful user varying the probability of going from page to refresh state and from Refresh state to page does not affect the transition probability. That is transition probability from any page to refresh state and from Refresh state to pages is same. The transition probability for even attempt is decreasing as the attempt is increasing. While the transition probability for odd attempt is zero. That is why we got fluctuating graph. The graphs for web page B and C have same pattern as for page A only difference is their initial probability. This indicates that behavior of the faithful user is same regardless of web pages.

Figure 4. (a) and (b): Faithful user of page A

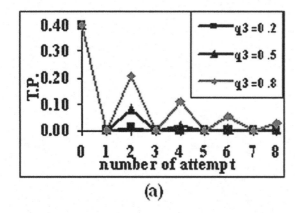
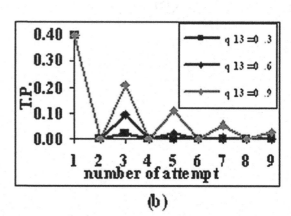

(a)   (b)

Figure 5. (a) and (b): Faithful user of page B

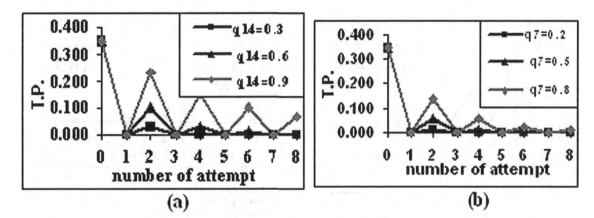

(a)   (b)

Figure 6. (a) and (b): Faithful user of page C

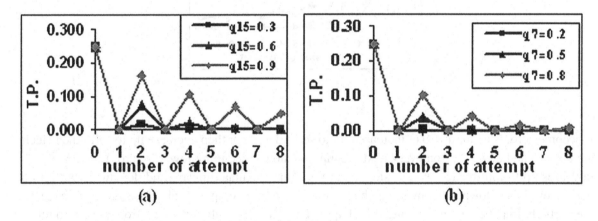

(a)   (b)

The graphs for Partially Impatient Users are different than faithful users and Completely Impatient Users as shown in Figure 7(a), 7(b), 7(c). With the low value (0.2) of q_3 when we vary q_{13} from 0.3 to 0.7, Partially Impatient User's behavior is same. The graph shows that till 5th attempt for even number of attempt, transition probability is high and it drops at odd number of attempt and increases at even number of attempt but for further attempts it becomes zero irrespective of even or odd. For medium value (0.5) of q_3 and different values of q_{13} transition probability with respect to number of attempt is fluctuating but reducing towards zero as the attempt is increasing. Also for higher value of q_{13} graph is fluctuating at the higher side of Transition Probability and for higher valued of q_{13} it fluctuating comparatively lower side of Transition Probability. But after 8th attempt it becomes zero.

Graphs for higher value of q_3 (q_3=0.75) shows very different results. It shows that for higher value of q_{13} (i.e. q_{13}=0.7), possibility of having Partially Impatient user at page A is increasing as the number of attempt increasing, while for moderate value of q_{13} (i.e. q_{13}=0.5) transition probability is decreasing slowly and for lower value of q_{13} (i.e. 0.3) the transition probability is decreasing and it becomes zero from 5th attempt onwards.

In Figure 8 we find same behavior for the lower and medium value of q_7 but for higher value of q_7 (i.e. q_7=0.75) each line shows different behavior. Line for q_{14}=0.3 shows initially fluctuating pattern then

Figure 7. Partially impatient user of page A

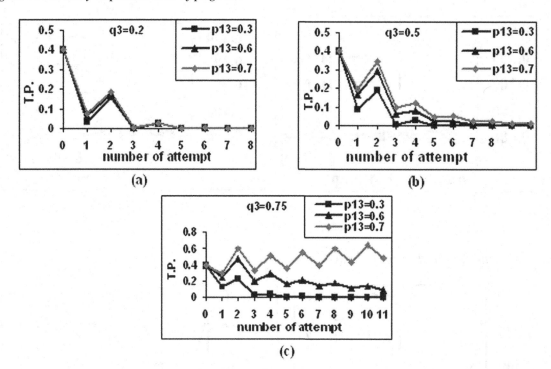

it become zero. Line for q_{14}=0.6, increased up to second attempt then decrease up to forth then fluctuate upward and downward on every next attempt but slowly declining towards zero. Line for q_{14}=0.7, increases up to fourth attempt very slowly but after that fluctuate upward and downward but upward peak goes higher slowly. That means at the higher number of attempt probability of having at page B of the Partially Impatient User is higher if both q_7 and q_{14} (i.e. probability of going from page B to refresh state and from refresh state to page B) are high, zero if any of the q_7 and q_{14} are low and very less (about zero) if both q_7 and q_{14} are medium or if one is medium and one is high.

Figure 9 (b) shows that for q_{11}=0.5 and q_{15}=0.7, transition probability increased on the first attempt, on second attempt it decreases very slowly but on the third attempt transition probability is dropped drastically. And for the further attempt it slowly decline towards zero. For q_{11}=0.5 and q_{15}=0.6, transition probability decreased slowly till second attempt but on the third attempt it decreases drastically and on the further attempt it goes towards zero.

Behavior of the Partially Impatient User when q_{11}=0.7 and q_{15}=0.7 is again fluctuating, for odd terms it is increasing and for even terms it is decreasing. That is, if we draw a line for odd terms only we find an inclined line which means probability of having at page C increase as the attempt increases. But when q_{11}=0.7 and q_{15}=0.6 graph is declined till forth attempt then we get fluctuating graph. For q_{11}=0.7 and q_{15}=0.3 as attempt increases probability of having on page C is decreases rapidly and very soon becomes zero.

One important conclusion we can derive from the graphs from 1 to 7 that to study the users' behavior we should restrict the attempt number till five.

To study the behavior of the Completely Impatient User we again draw the graphs, page wise, between number of attempt and Transition probability as shown in the Figure 10(a), 10(b) and 10(c). With

Figure 8. Partially impatient user of page B

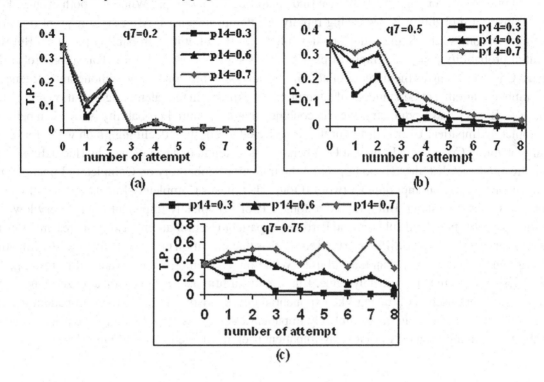

Figure 9. Partially impatient user of page C

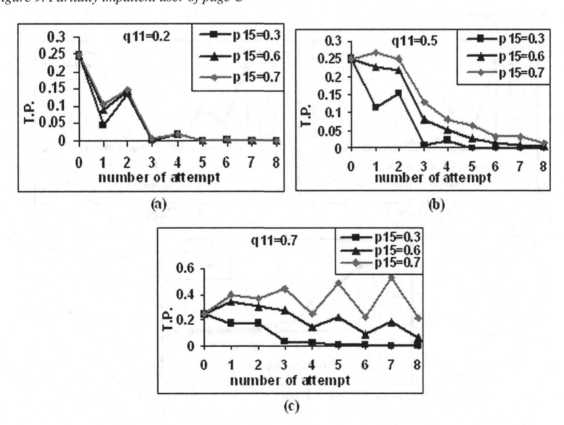

the initial probability for page A p1=0.4 we find again fluctuating graph. Where for both even and odd terms, transition probability is decreasing rapidly as attempt increases. After sixth attempt transition probability becomes zero. Same pattern is shown for page B with initial probability p2=0.35. But with the initial probability p3=0.25, graph for page C shows some different pattern. Transition probability for page C is decreasing as the number of attempt is increasing but constantly without any influence of even number of attempt or odd number of attempt. Since expression for calculating transition probability for page A, B and C have symmetry. We can conclude that if the initial probability is low then behavior of Completely Impatient User is different that is reflected as constant declining graph while for higher initial probability Completely Impatient User behavior is different that is indicated by fluctuating graph.

Figure 11 shows that, there is no impact on the transition probability on Completely Impatient user for any value of q_3 for attempt number two and four. That means Completely Impatient User of page A is not affected by refreshing. But for attempt four, T.P. of Completely Impatient User is very low. The transition probability of Faithful User and Partially Impatient User for attempt two is increasing with the refreshing probability but the difference between both is that transition probability for Partially Impatient Users' growing more rapidly than faithful user. While on 4th attempt, for low value of refreshing, T.P. of all types of user are approximately same. But T.P. of faithful user is approximately zero and T.P of Partially Impatient users' is growing like exponential curve. Also, T.P. of Partially Impatient user for lower refreshing is lower than the Completely Impatient User but as the refreshing rate is increased the probability of having at page A of Partially Impatient user also increased (see Figure 12).

Figure 10. Completely impatient user

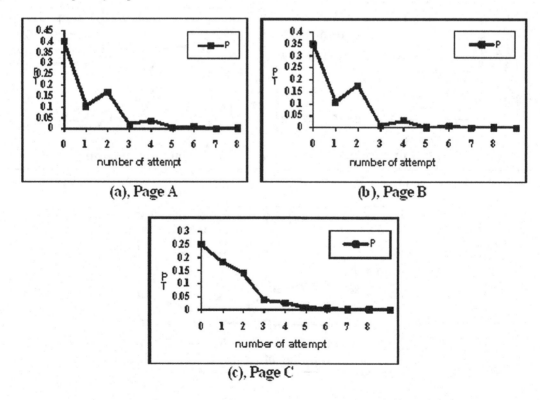

(a), Page A

(b), Page B

(c), Page C

Figure 11. Comparison between different users of page A for even attempt when q_{13} is low

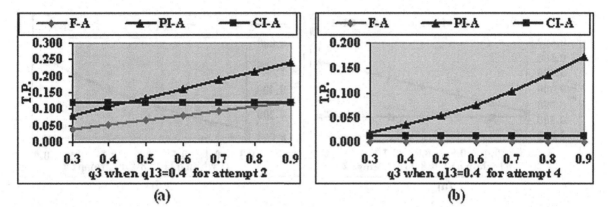

(a)   (b)

Figure 12. Comparison between different users of page A for odd attempt when q_{13} is low

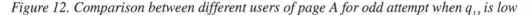
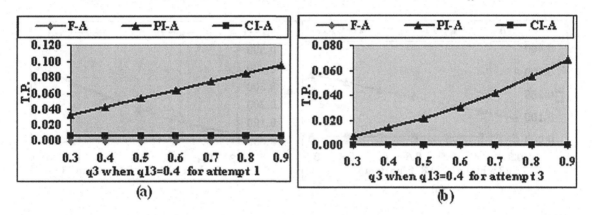

(a)   (b)

For odd number of attempt and lower value of q_{13} T.P. of Partially impatient user is growing with the refreshing probability(q_3) but T.P. of all others are very low approximately zero and not changing.

From Figure 11(a) and 13(a) we can find that transition probability of Completely Impatient user will not be affected by q_{13}. Secondly the T.P. of faithful user is lower than the T.P. of Completely Impatient user for any value of q_3 when q_{13} is low but higher value of q_{13} T.P. of faithful user is initially lower than the Completely Impatient user but as the value of q3 is increased over 0.45 T.P. of faithful user crosses the T.P. of Completely Impatient user (see Figure 13).

As shown in the charts in Figure 11(a), 11(b), 12(a), 12(b), 13(a), 13(b), 14(a) and 14(b) the T.P. is low for lower value of q_{13} and T.P. decreases with the attempt, but T.P. of Partially Impatient user is increased as the Refreshing probability increases.

From Figure 15(a), 15(b), 16(a), 16(b), 17(b), 17(b), 18(b) and 18(b) we can find that, the pattern for page B is similar to pattern for page A the only difference is that since here we taken the lower value of q_{14}=0.5 T.P. is higher. Since there is similarity in the probability calculating function of page A, B and C if we assign the same probability we can not get the difference in the T.P. hence to study the changes in the T.P. we have taken different probabilities. And the resultant changes can be seen from the charts. To study the behavior of different users of page B we used q_6=0.4 and q_{10}=0.6.

Figure 13. Comparison between different users of page A for even attempt when q_{13} is high

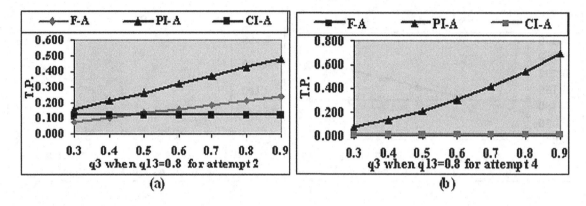

Figure 14. Comparison between different users of page A for odd attempt when q_{13} is high

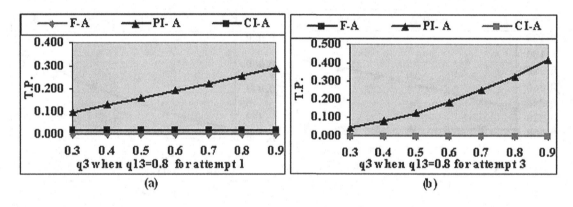

Figure 15. Comparison between different users of page B for even attempt when q_{14} is low

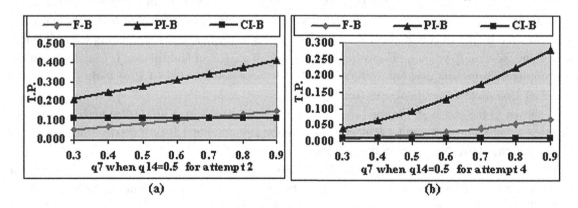

Figure 16. Comparison between different users of page B for odd attempt when q_{14} is low

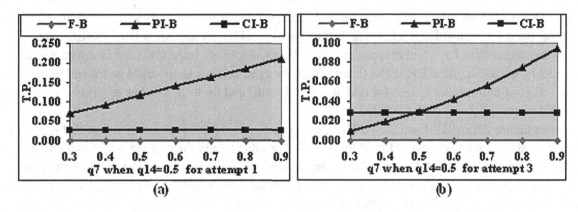

Figure 17. Comparison between different users of page B for odd attempt when q_{14} is high

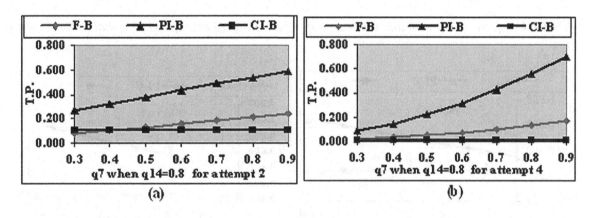

Figure 18. Comparison between different users of page B for odd attempt when q_{14} is high

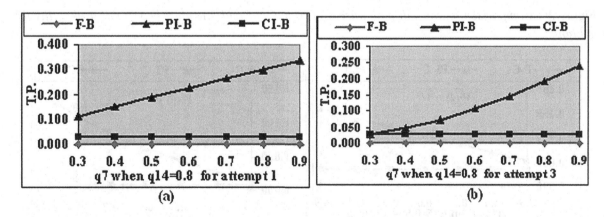

From Figure 19(a), 19(b) and 20(a), 20(b) we can find that, when the initial probability of page C is high that is p_3=0.5 and p_2=p_1=0.25 then for odd attempt T. P. is very low and can not reach to 0.2 while on other hand for even attempt T.P. is reached to approx. 1. For any attempt T.P. of Partially Impatient Users are higher than T.P. of other types of user. T.P. of Completely Impatient User is constant without affected by q_{11} and q_{15}. But T.P. is fluctuating (high for even number terms and low for odd number of terms. T. P. of faithful user is zero for odd number of terms and for even number of terms it is initially low and increased slowly with the value of q_{11}.

From Figure 21(a), 21(b) and 22(a), 22(b), For page C if its initial probability is low that is p_3=0.1, then the pattern found is same as found for p_3=0.5. For odd attempt there is not very much difference in the T.P. for low values of refreshing (q11) but as the refreshing rate increased the difference in the T.P. of different user expand. For odd number of attempt the T.P. of faithful user and T.P. of Completely Impatient User is constant with respect to refreshing. While for even number of attempt the T.P. of Faithful User is increasing with the refreshing but very slowly in comparison to the Partially Impatient user. Also, T.P. of all the users is decreasing with respect to attempt irrespective of even or odd attempt.

Figure 19. Comparison between different users of page C for even attempt when initial probability p3 is high

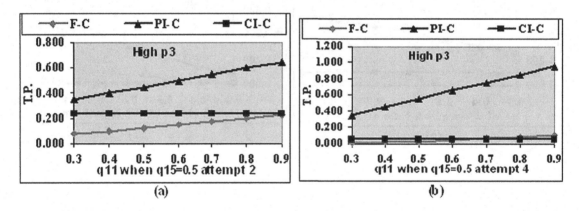

Figure 20. Comparison between different users of page C for odd attempt when initial probability p3 is high

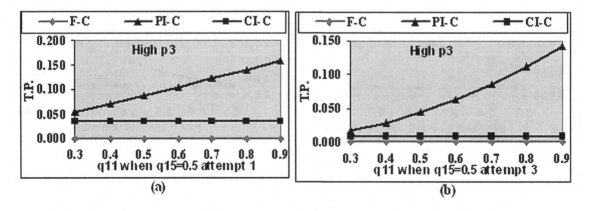

Figure 21. Comparison between different users of page C for even attempt when initial probability p3 is low

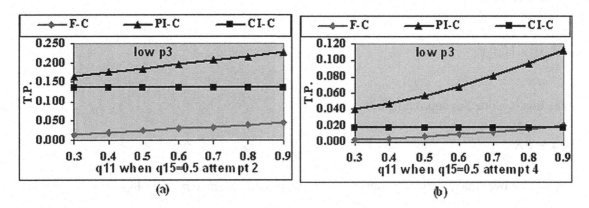

Figure 22. Comparison between different users of page C for odd attempt when initial probability p3 is low

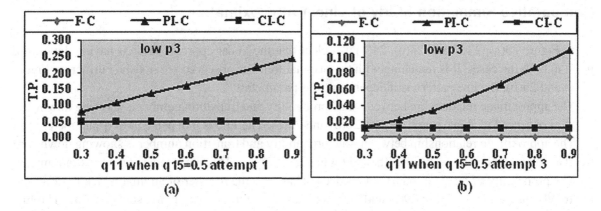

Linear Approximation of Proposed Study

Consider two variables Y and X as

Y = P[X = .] and
X = n

Now we can draw line Y = a + bX using principle of least square.
The two normal equations are

$\Sigma Y = ma + \Sigma X$
$\Sigma XY = a \Sigma X + b \Sigma X2$

Where m is number of pair points available on the graph,

$$\hat{b} = \frac{m\Sigma XY - (\Sigma X)(\Sigma Y)}{m\Sigma X^2 - (\Sigma X)^2}$$

$$\hat{a} = \frac{1}{n}[\Sigma Y - m\Sigma X]$$

The line is plotted as approximation:

$$Y = \hat{a} + \hat{b}X$$

Averaging over many varying parameters p, q etc. provide average relationship-

$$Y = \bar{a} + \bar{b}X$$

Comparative Simulation Study of Linear Approximation

From Figure 23(a), 23(b) and 24(a), 24(b) it is clear that the linear approximation is having downward trend in both the cases. It is matching with the original trend as observed previously. Further, in Figure 25(a) and 25(b), the line pattern is independent of q-parameters.

The approximate relationship between state probability and transition number is showing downward trend as observed in above graph (Figure 26(a) and 26(b). The line is independent of q-parameter.

The approximate relationship between state probability and transition number is showing downward trend as shown in the Figure 27(a),27(b) and Figure 28(a),28(b).. The line is independent of q-parameter.

The probability of reaching on page C is decreasing with the number of attempt which is similar to the trends shown in the Figure 29(a) and 29(b) of previous graph in simulation study section. The line in Figure 30(a) and 30(b) is independent of the q-values.

The graph in Figures 32(a), 32(b) and 32(c) is declining with the number of transaction as in the Figures 31(a), 31(b) and 31(c) which suggest that Figure 32(a), 32(b) and 32(c) is linear approximation of the Figure 31(a), 31(b) and 31(c) and it is independent of the values of p and q.

Figure 23. (a) and (b), previous graphs of faithful user of page A

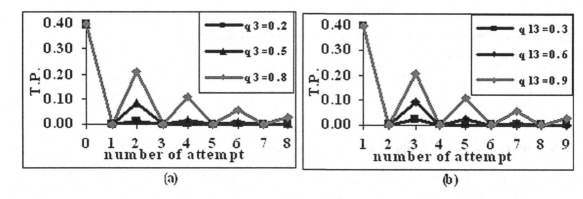

Figure 24. (a) and (b) Faithful user of page A after linear approximation independent of q-values

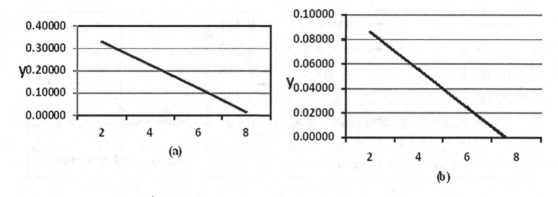

(a)

(b)

Figure 25. (a) and (b), previous graphs of faithful user of page B

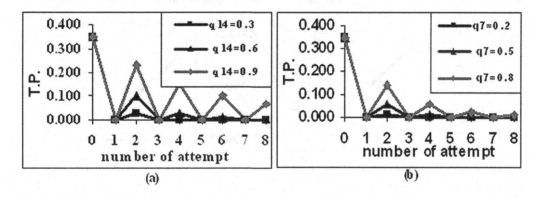

(a)

(b)

Figure 26. (a) and (b), Faithful user of page B after liner approximation independent of q-values

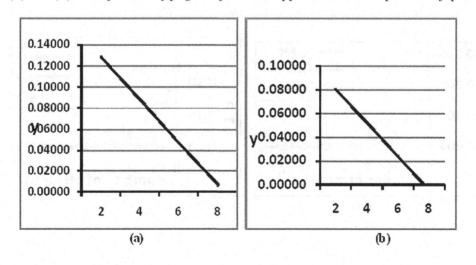

(a)

(b)

Figure 27. (a) and 27(b), previous graphs of faithful user of page

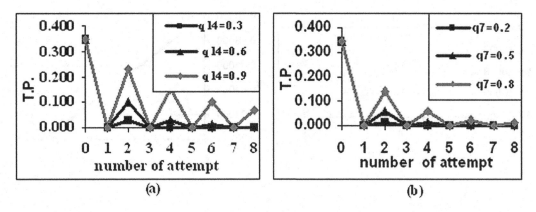

Figure 28. (a) and 28(b), faithful user of page B after liner approximation independent of q-values

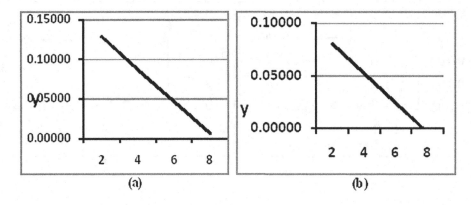

Figure 29. (a) and (b), previous graphs of faithful user of page C

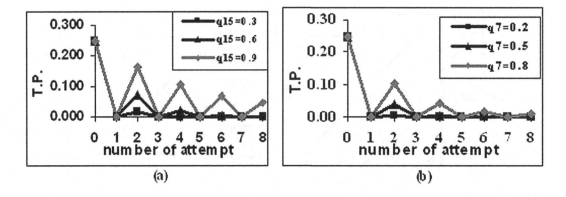

Figure 30. (a) and (b), Faithful user of page C after linear approximation and independent p and q-values

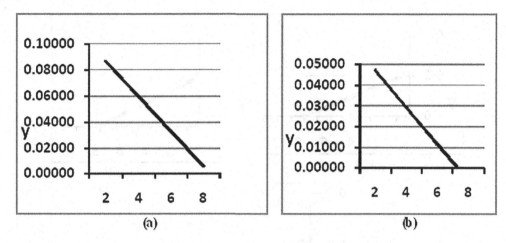

Figure 31. (a), (b) and (c), previous graphs of partially impatient users

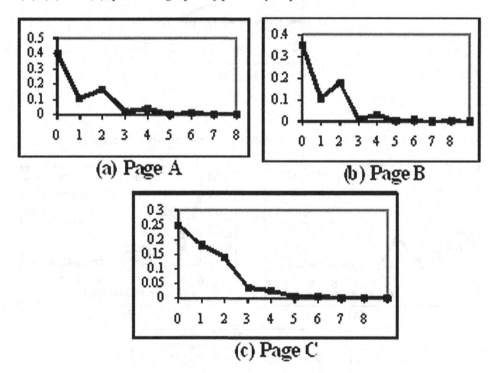

The approximate relationship between state probability and transition number for the completely impatient user of page A is shown in the Figure 34(a), 34(b) and 34(c) which shows similar trends as shown in the Figure 33(a), 33(b) and 33(c).

The approximated behavior of Completely Impatient user of page B is showing (Figure 36(a),36(b),36(c)) downward trend which means the transition probability is decreasing with respect to the number of attempts. This trend is similar to the trend shown in previous graph as drawn in section 5. Which means linear approximation is effective and independent of the p and q-values.

Figure 32. (a), (b) and (c), Approximated partially impatient users independent of values p and q

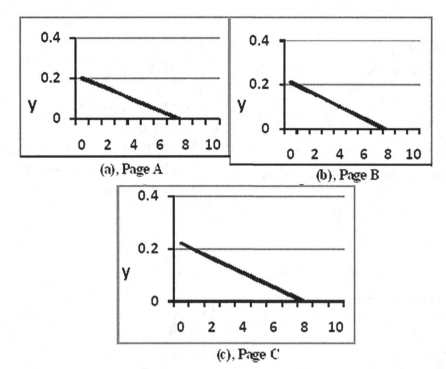

Figure 33. (a), (b) and (c), Previous graph of completely impatient user of page A

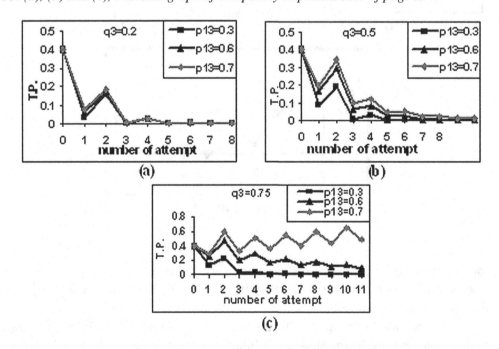

Figure 34. (a), (b) and (c), Approximated behavior of completely impatient user of page A independent of p and q- values

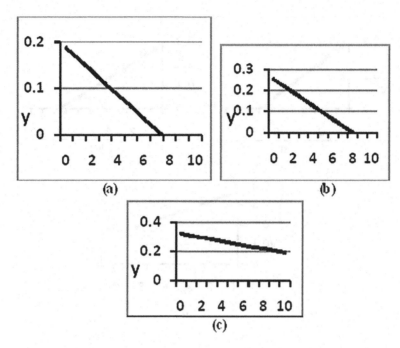

(a)

(b)

(c)

Figure 35. (a), (b) and (c) Previous graph of completely impatient user of page B

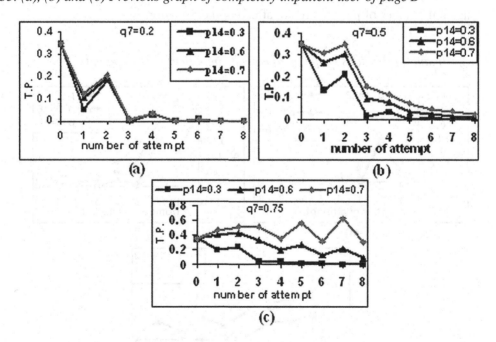

(a)

(b)

(c)

Figure 36. (a), (b) and (c), Approximated behavior of completely impatient user of page B independent of p and q-values

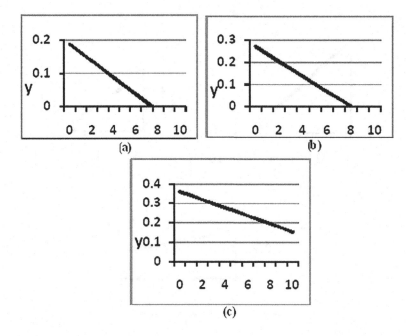

(a)　　　　(b)

(c)

The behavior of completely impatient user of page C in the linear approximation (Figure 37(a),37(b),37(c) and Figure 38(a),38(b),38(c)) is again trending downward which is similar to the previous trend in section 5. Here again the values of p and q are not affecting the behavior.

Figure 37. (a), (b) and (c) Previous graph of completely impatient user of page C

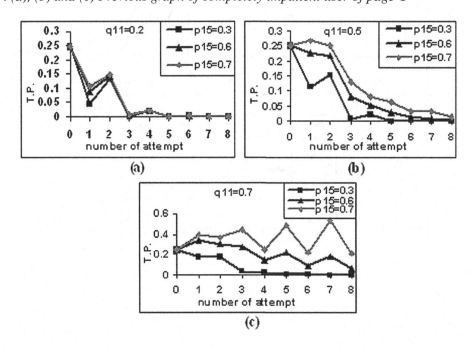

(a)　　　　(b)

(c)

Figure 38. (a), (b) and (c), Approximated behavior of completely impatient user of page C independent of p and q-values

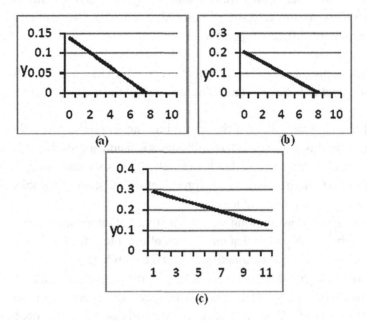

CONCLUSION AND FUTURE DIRECTIONS

In this chapter, The Markov chain model is used to predict the user's browsing behavior. We treated the clicking of Refresh button as another state i.e. Refresh State and on the basis of this assumption we categorized all the users into three category faithful users, partially impatient users and completely impatient users. We proposed some new theorems for calculating the Transition Probability of different category of user (page wise) for odd number of attempt and for even number of attempt. Then using these theorems we did simulation study to prove the categorization. We studied the individual behavior of each categorization with respect to attempt and refreshing. We also did comparative study of behavior of different types of user of each page. The conclusions of this chapter are as follows:

1. Behavior of the faithful user is same regardless of web pages. That is probability of having at a page fluctuate, there is some probability (chances) to be in even number of terms but for odd number of terms probability is zero.
2. If the initial probability is low then behavior of Completely Impatient User is different that is reflected as constant declining graph while for higher initial probability Completely impatient user behavior is different that is indicated by fluctuating graph.
3. The probability of having at a page for Partially Impatient user is fluctuating but in all declines towards zero for lower and medium probability. But for higher refreshing probability being on the page increase with the number of attempt.
4. For odd number of attempt and lower value of q_{13} T.P. of Partially Impatient User is growing with the refreshing probability(q_3) but T.P. of all others are very low approximately zero and not changing.
5. Transition probability of Completely Impatient user of page A is not affected by refreshing. But T.P. of Completely Impatient user decreases with respect to number of attempt.

6.   The Transition probability with respect to refreshing is increased exponentially for Partially Impatient user, constant for Completely Impatient user and slowly increases for faithful user. Hence the T.P. is approximately same for low refreshing but for high refreshing we can see grate difference in the transition probability of different type of user.

The different behavior proves the classification of users. It provides a good method of user classification that can be used for better behavior study. The designer of the web site can focus for any individual category of user.

The drawback of this approach is that if the refreshing rate will be very low then this categorization may be insignificant. Also this approach is basically statistical and approach can be useful only for high visitation sites. One another drawback is that if the web site has so many pages the dimension of the transition matrix will be very high that may cause presentation and memory problems. But this approach is novel and effective for many circumstances.

This approach is based on the assumption that each instance of refreshing can be identified. Thus some good algorithm should be developed so that either each attempt to refreshing a page can be recorded in the web log or by some means it can be identified from the web log.

The linear approximation could be made effectively to the probability values and number of transitions. The basic feature of this approximation is that they are independent of model parameters. One can use the line approximation probabilities directly for computation of state probabilities in the Markov chain model.

REFERENCES

Borges, J., & Levene, M. (2000). Data mining of user navigation patterns. In Proceedings of WEBKDD 99 Workshop on Web Usage Analysis and User Profiling (pp. 31-36). doi:10.1007/3-540-44934-5_6

Borges, J., & Levene, M. (2006). Ranking pages by topology and popularity within web sites. World Wide Web Journal, 9, 301-316.

Chen, M. S., Park, J. S., & Yu, P. S. (1996). Data mining for path traversal patterns in a web environment. In *Proceedings of the 16th International Conference on Distributed Computing Systems* (pp. 385-392). doi:10.1109/ICDCS.1996.507986

Cooley, R., Mobasher, B., & Srivastava, J. (1997). *Grouping web page references into transactions for mining World Wide Web browsing patterns. Technical Report Tr. 97-021*. Minneapolis, MN: University of Minnesota, Dept. of Computer Science.

Cooley, R., Mobasher, B., & Srivastava, J. (1997). Web mining: Information and pattern discovery on the World Wide Web. In *International Conference on Tools with Artificial Intelligence* (pp. 558-567).

Deshpande, M., & Karypis, G. (2004). Selective Markov models for predicting web page accesses. *ACM Transactions on Internet Technology, 4*(4), 163–184. doi:10.1145/990301.990304

Eirinaki, M., & Vazirgiannis, M. (2003). Web mining for web personalization. *ACM Transactions on Internet Technology, 3*(1), 1–27. doi:10.1145/643477.643478

Jain, R. K., Jain, S., Thakur, S. S., & Kasana, R. S. (2009). Web user categorization and behaviour study based on refreshing. *IJANA*, *1*(2), 69–75.

Pei, J., Han, J., Mortazavi-asl, B., & Zhu, H. (2000). Mining access patterns efficiently from web logs. In *Proceedings of the 4th Pacific-Asia Conf. on Knowledge Discovery and Data Mining* (pp. 396-407). doi:10.1007/3-540-45571-X_47

Perkowitz, M., & Etzioni, O. (1998). Adaptive web sites: automatically synthesizing web pages. In *Proceedings of the Fifteenth National Conf. on Artificial Intelligence (AAAI)* (pp. 727-732).

Pirolli, P., Pitkow, J., & Rao, R. (1996). Silk from a sow's ear: extracting usable structures from the web. In *Proceedings of Conference on Human Factors in Computing Systems (SIGCHI)* (pp. 118-125).

Pitkow, J. (1997). In search of reliable usage data on the www. In *Sixth International World Wide Web Conference* (pp. 451-463).

Pitkow, J., & Pirolli, P. (1999). Mining longest repeating subsequences to predict WWW surfing.*Proceedings of 2nd USENIX Symp. Internet Technologies and Systems* (pp. 139-150).

Sarukkai, R. (2000). Link prediction and path analysis using markov chains. In *Proceedings of the 9ᵗʰ International WWW Conference* (pp. 377-386). doi:10.1016/S1389-1286(00)00044-X

Shukla, D., & Singhai, R. (2011). Analysis of user's web browsing behavior using Markov chain model. *International Journal of Advanced Networking & Applications*, *2*(5).

Srikant, R., & Yang, Y. (2001). Mining web logs to improve website organization. In *Proceedings of the 10th International Conference on World Wide Web* (pp. 430 – 437). doi:10.1145/371920.372097

Srivastava, J., Cooley, R., Deshpanda, M., & Tan, P. N. (2000). Web Usage Mining: Discovery and applications of usage patterns from web data. *ACM SIGKDD.*, *1*(2), 12. doi:10.1145/846183.846188

Zhu, J., Hong, J., & Hughes, J. (2002). Using Markov chains for link prediction in adaptive web sites. Proceedings of Software Computing in an Imperfect World (LNCS), (vol. 2311, pp. 60-73). Springer-Verlag. doi:10.1007/3-540-46019-5_5

ADDITIONAL READING

Anderson, C. R., Domingos, P., & Weld, D. S. (2002). Relational markov models and their application to adaptive web navigation. In *Proceedings of the 8th Int. KDD conference*, (pp. 143-152) doi:10.1145/775047.775068

Borges, J., & Levene, M. (2005). Generating Dynamic Higher Order Markov Models in Web Usage Mining. In Proceedings of Ninth European Conf. Principles and Practice of Knowledge Discovery in Databases (PKDD). (pp. 34- 45). doi:10.1007/11564126_9

Chen, X., & Zhang, X. (2007, April). A Popularity-Based Prediction Model for Web Prefetching. *IEEE Transactions on Knowledge and Data Engineering*, *19*, 63–70.

Dongshan, X., & Junyi, S. (2002). A new Markov model for web access prediction. *Computing in Science & Engineering*, 4(6), 34–39. doi:10.1109/MCISE.2002.1046594

Eirinaki, M., Vazirgiannis, M., & Kapogiannis, D. (2005). Web Path Recommendations Based on Page Ranking and Markov Models, Proceedings of Seventh Ann. ACM Workshop on Web Information and Data Management (WIDM í05). (pp. 2-9). doi:10.1145/1097047.1097050

Karlin, S., & Taylor, H. M. (1975). *A First Course in Stochastic Processes* (2nd ed.). New York: Academic Press.

Zhu, J., Hong, J., & Hughes, J. (2001). PageRate: Counting Web Users' Votes. In *Proceedings of ACM Hypertext*.(pp. 131-132).

KEY TERMS AND DEFINITIONS

Data Pre-Processing: Web server log files may contains irrelevant, in consistent and noisy data. If this information is used for analysis purpose then clearly the quality of knowledge extracted will be poor. So log data are processed prior to perform mining tasks.

Markov Chain Model: The stochastic process where both state space and the time are discrete, is called Markov chain. The stochastic process $\left\{ X_n, \ n = 0, 1, 2, \ldots\ldots \right\}$ is called a Markov chain, if, for $j, k, j_1, \ldots\ldots j_{n-1} \in N$ (or any subset of I), $P\left\{ X_n = k / X_{n-1} = j, \ X_{n-2} = j_1, \ X_0 = j_{n-1} \right\} = P\left\{ X_n = k / X_{n-1} = j \right\} = p_{jk}$ Whenever the first member is defined and the set of integer $I = \left\{ \ldots\ldots, -2, -1, 0, 1, 2, \ldots\ldots \right\}$. The outcome values of X_n as $X_n = j_1, \ X_{n-1} = j_2, \ X_{n-2} = j_3, \ldots\ldots$ etc. has an interpretation that j_1, j_2, j_3 are states of Markov chain X_n. While $X_n = j$ we mean at the nth step the random variable X is at the state j. The probability term p_{jk} is the probability of transition from j^{th} state at $(n-1)^{th}$ step to k at the nth step. If the transition probability p_{jk} is independent of n the Markov chain is set to be homogeneous whereas if p_{jk} depends only on n the Markov chain is called non-homogeneous.

Transition Probability: The transition probability pjk satisfies the following(i) $p_{jk} \geq 0$, (ii) $\sum_k p_{jk} = 1$ for all j. These may be written in the form of matrix $P = \begin{matrix} p_{11} & p_{12} & p_{13} & \cdots \\ p_{21} & p_{22} & p_{23} & \cdots \\ \cdots & \cdots & \cdots & \cdots \\ \cdots & \cdots & \cdots & \cdots \end{matrix}$ This matrix p is called the transition probability matrix (t.p.m.) of Markov chains if $\sum_k p_{jk} = 1$ and every $p_{jk} \geq 0$.

The P is a stochastic or Markov chain matrix, i.e. a square with non-negative elements and sums equal to unit value.

User Behavior: User's behavior are determined by the manner they visited websites. This information is recorded in the server log file and is used to personalize the web site.

User Categorization: It is not necessary that when user tries to access the page it will open soon. In such case user may press refresh button. Based on such pressing we have categorized the users of a web site into three categories. 1.Faithful Users; 2. Partially Impatient Users; 3. Completely Impatient Users.

Web Logs (Web Server Log file): A web log file records activity information when a web user submits a request to a web server. Some of the information recorded in log files are: IP address/ domain name of user, user's name and password, entering and exist date and time, Requested URL etc.

Chapter 3

Folksonomy–Based Information Retrieval by Generating Tag Cloud for Electronic Resources Management Industries and Suggestive Mechanism for Tagging Using Data Mining Techniques

Sohil D. Pandya
Sardar Vallabhbhai Patel Institute of Technology (SVIT), India

Paresh V. Virparia
Sardar Patel University, India

ABSTRACT

In the current scenario the amount of electronic resources are increasing rapidly. These resources are human readable and understandable. The industries which are managing these resources have various problems for their retrieval. In this chapter, the authors tried to propose folksonomy based information retrieval by generating tag cloud. This model not only helps the industries to manage their electronic resources for retrieval but helps them by providing suggestions for tagging with the usage of similarity metrics. This suggestive mechanism also helps users to understand resources at specific and organizations at general. The authors also have implemented the model to demonstrate the experimental results followed by discussion.

DOI: 10.4018/978-1-5225-0613-3.ch003

INTRODUCTION

In the current scenario of growth of Information and Communication Technology (ICT), the electronic resources are increasing at dramatic speed. With respect to Electronic Resources Management Industries, they are managing quite sensitive documents of various categories like Finance, Aerospace, Legal, Educational, Administrative, etc. They are providing on-demand services to their clients for Electronic Resources stored in repositories. This industry is required to have setup of sophisticated hardware and software to serve their clients round the clock. They are having certain problems with respect to managing and retrieving electronic resources like – (i) documents may be confidential in nature so the content could not be mined, which leads to difficulty in identification of the resource, (ii) historical documents which needs to be accessed, (iii) the user is not aware of the nomenclature of the documents, etc.

Tags are the strings. Attaching tags to various electronic resources by users or clients themselves will not only help them locate the electronic resources but also help them for quick retrieval. These tags are added by users themselves hence also referred as Folksonmy. As they are added by users, it is easy to recollect them. The system also helps users to get acquainted with the environment and nomenclature.

Authors also generate a tag cloud based representation of the tags, added by users, to search the electronic resources easily. Tag cloud is a well-known representation technique which represents tags in various sizes based on their frequencies. For example, a tag cloud representing population of countries would have a CHINA with the highest font size, followed by INDIA and so on. Authors also incorporated recursive generation tag cloud which is easily accessible to users and let users to search generic to specific electronic resources on the web.

From the previously attached tags and their various properties like frequencies, usage data, relation, etc. a suggestive mechanism for tags is also proposed. This mechanism will merge related tags by usage of Similarity Metrics. The Similarity Metric is a way to identify similarity between two streams. And based on merging and past data users will be having suggestions of tags using data mining techniques. This system helps the users to understand the environment.

All the above will improve the information retrieval in the specific industries and help them to achieve competitive advantage by serving their clients efficiently and timely manner.

Chapter Overview

The chapter starts with the introduction of the topic. After the introduction, back ground information is presented in the next section, which consists of various related information like folksonomy, similarity metrics, social bookmarking and its uses, and related work. In the succeeding section, main focus of chapter is elaborated. It consists of methodology and model, implementation, experimental results and discussion, applications, and limitations of the model. Finally chapter ended with future directions of research, conclusion and references. Required appendices are added at the end of the chapter.

BACKGROUND

Social Bookmarking and its Uses

Social bookmarking is one of the online services which allow users to add, edit and share their bookmarks of web resources. Earlier one has to store one's bookmark of web resources in to one's computer system, which was not accessible to another computer system. But due to social bookmarking services persons can store their bookmark online and have access of them across the world. This service also allow users to share users bookmarks and find from others bookmarks also. Delicious (www.delicious. com), Digg (www.digg.com), BlinkList (www.blinklist.com), Favoor (www.favoor.com), etc. are popular social bookmarking websites. Social bookmarking is also becoming important weapon for Search Engine Optimization (SEO) also. People keep adding their various pages and sites on social bookmarking websites to increase their back links.

Similarity Metric

Similarity metric, also referred as string metric, is used to find out the similarity / distance between two strings or sequences. Basically it is a mathematical way to find out how similar two strings are. Generally it is gives measures between 0 and 1, where 1 is interpreted as identical strings and 0 is interpreted as totally non-identical strings. There various applications of similarity metrics like spell checker, data cleaning, genetics, etc.

There are various similarity metrics are there like Levenshtein Distance, Hamming Distance, Block Distance, Jaccard Similarity, Smith-Watermen, Jaro-Winkler Distance, etc.

In this chapter, we are going to use Jaro-Winkler Distance in our model. The Jaro-Winkler distance d_j between two string s_1 and s_2 can be formulated [18] as in Figure 1.

In Figure 1, m is number of matching characters and t is half the number of transpositions. Table 1 illustrates some examples of results of Jaro-Winkler distance between two strings:

Tag Cloud

Tag cloud is a visual representation of text data. Generally, generally it is based on frequency of text in set. For example, Figure 2 is representing countries of the world. The font size of countries are corresponding to their population. This way of visualization for data is very useful to users, because it gives very good visual effect to users to understand data.

Figure 1. Formula of Jaro-Winkler Distance. Source: http://en.wikipedia.org

$$d_j = \begin{cases} 0 & \text{if } m = 0 \\ \frac{1}{3}\left(\frac{m}{|s_1|} + \frac{m}{|s_2|} + \frac{m-t}{m}\right) & \text{otherwise} \end{cases}$$

Table 1. Illustrations of Jaro-Winkler Distance

String 1	String 2	Jaro-Winkler Distance
Entertainment	Entertanment	0.97863245
Show	Sohw	0.925
University	Unversity	0.91407406
Grass	Grasss	0.9722222
Communication	Comunicaion	0.9641025

Figure 2. Example of tag cloud representing countries as per their population

Related Work

A.W. Rivadeneira (2007) and Kim (2008) studied tag clouds and its evolution. Trant (2009) have proposed a framework for tagging system. Hearst (2008) considered tagging as social signals which needs to be identified and can be used for various situations.

James Sinclair (2007) and Knautz (2008) compared traditional search box and tag cloud approaches to identify users' behavior. They have simulated 10 questions for 89 users and tried to see in which type of questions users were selecting different approaches. And found users' tendency towards tag cloud based approach.

Satoshi Niwa (2006) proposed a web page recommender system using tag generated by users. J Trant (2009) have studied folksonomy and found that this data can be further analyzed using various tools like vocabulary analysis, classification, user interaction theory and social network theory.

Kuo (2007) found that tag cloud offer not only an overview of knowledge but also an interface that enables users to navigate to potentially relevant information hidden.

M A Hearst (2008) found that tag clouds are social signal or mark and are more suggestive device than as a precise depiction of the underlying phenomenon.

Earlier, the access of these tags was limited. But due to availability of open source social bookmarking systems, authors wish to use these meta-data and generate folksonomy based tag cloud for information retrieval.

FOLKSONOMY BASED INFORMATION RETRIEVAL FOR TAG CLOUD AND SUGGESTIVE MECHANISM

Methodology and Model

The proposed model is basically divided in to two major parts: (i) Tag Cloud generation and (ii) Usage of similarity metric for suggestions to tag. Figure 3 represents visual representation of first part.

Part 1

In the first part the user is presented an initial tag generated based on the tags entered by other users on Delicious.

Following is the function to retrieve tags from Delcious:

```
$(function(){
        String word_list[]=getDeliciousTags(String Delicious_Username, Deli-
cious_Password, String t);
});
```

And following is the function to generate tag cloud using JQuery:

```
$(function(){
        $("#div-id").jQCloud(word_list);
});
```

Figure 3. Proposed model of information retrieval and generation of tag cloud

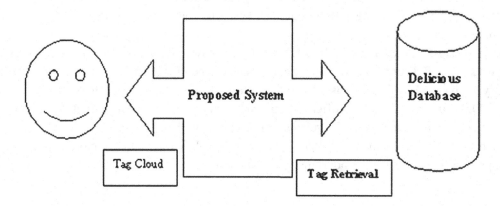

$$S_i = \frac{f_{max} * (t_i - t_{min})}{(t_{max} - t_{min})}$$

Where,

S_i = display font size
f_{max} = max. font size
t_i = count
t_{min} = min. count
t_{max} = max. count

For larger values logarithmic representation may make sense.

The user is able to click on texts of tag cloud to go from generic to specific tags. And at the end of the process users will be narrowing her information requirements.

Part 2

In the second part, the authors propose a suggestive mechanism where users are assisted by suggestive tags by using Clustering technique of Data mining. These suggestions are actually based on matching of entered tags using Similarity Metric, fetched from stored tags in Delicious, and shown in order of frequencies. In this case authors have used Jaro-Winkler Distance to match entered text and stored tags.

Implementation

The implementation of the above model is done using PHP and MySQL. Authors have used Delicious API to fetch data from www.delicious.com. API for Similarity Metrics are also used. Sample code for implementation is given at the end of the chapter.

Experimental Results and Discussion

To experiment the above model authors have selected one of the Universities of India, where all the circulars or notifications of the University are displayed on its website. The authors allow selected users to tag these resources using Delicious. Then after users retrieved these circulars / notifications by proposed model's implementation.

Figure 4 represent an initial tag cloud based on the tags entered by the users. From this tag cloud users are able to see that Diploma Engineering has highest tagging made to circulars and so on.

Figure 5 represents a tag cloud generated after Result is clicked.

Applications

1. Information retrieval
2. Quick visual search
3. Anywhere where generic to specific path approach is followed
4. Studying trends

Figure 4. Initial tag cloud

Figure 5. Tag cloud after 1st selection

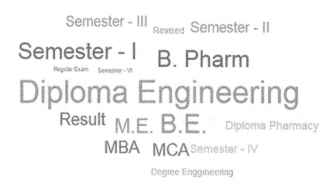

5.   Developing environment to learn local/region/industry specific Folksonomies

Limitation

1.   Resources restricted by people because of private mode may not be accessible to API.
2.   Resources are identified and named by people, hence if people may wrongly / useless /extra / little tagging may lead to wrongly generated tag cloud.
3.   As there are millions of resources available to API, the tag cloud is limited to top 50 tags, which can be further specific in next level (sub) to top 50 tags.

FUTURE RESEARCH DIRECTIONS

In this direction, various commercial research extensions are possible. Following are some of the possible extensions:

1. In this model, one of the similarity metrics is used. One can test and explore other similarity metrics for this and other domains, as we have described in part 2 of the mechanism.
2. Creation of new domain/organization specific taxonomy. The Folksonomy development in the above mentioned model could be base for training and development of new comers in specific industries. For example, the Folksonomy developed in Figure 3 and 4 helps us to determine the words used by people to describe the resources.
3. Combination of taxonomy and folksonomy generated in the above mentioned model for information retrieval.
4. Knowledge Management for learning environment. The Folksonomy developed in the resultant database could be base for the domain for Knowledge Management.

CONCLUSION

The above proposed model will not only improve information retrieval but can be implemented for alternative mechanism over conventional query based search approach. Authors wish to implement the above model and explore experimental results to prove its efficiency. In this paper, we have used Delicious API, but one can explore any other open source social tagging services to generate the tag clouds.

REFERENCES

Ciszak, L. (2008). Application of Clustering and Association Methods in Data Cleaning. In *Proc. of Int. Multiconference on Computer Science and Information Technology.*

Han, J., & Kamber, M. (2006). *Data Mining: Concepts and Techniques.* San Francisco, CA: Morgan Kaufmann Publishers.

Hearst, M. A., & Rosner, D. (2008). Tag clouds: Data analysis tool or social signaller? In *Hawaii International Conference on System Sciences,Proceedings of the 41st Annual.*

Hearst, M. A., & Rosner, D. (2008). Tag clouds: Data analysis tool or social signaller? In *Proceedings of 41st Hawaii International Conference on System Sciences (HICSS 2008), Social Spaces minitrack.*

Kim, Breslin, Yang, & Kim. (2008). Social semantic cloud of tag: Semantic model for social tagging. In *Agent and Multi-Agent Systems: Technologies and Applications.* Springer Berlin Heidelberg.

Knautz, K., Soubusta, S., & Stock, W. G. (2008). Tag clusters as information retrieval interfaces. In *Proceedings of System Sciences (HICSS), 2010 43rd Hawaii International Conference.* doi:10.1109/HICSS.2010.360

Kuo, Hentrich, Good, & Wilkinson. (2007). Tag clouds for summarizing web search results. In *Proceedings of the 16th international conference on World Wide Web.*

Niwa, S., Doi, T., & Honiden, S. (2006). Web Page Recommender System based on Folksonomy Mining. In *Proc. of the Third International Conference on Inforrmation Technology: New Generation (ITNG'06).*

Rivadeneira, A. W., Gruen, D. M., Muller, M. J., & Millen, D. R. (2007). Getting our head in the clouds: Toward evaluation studies of tagclouds. In *Proceedings of the SIGCHI Conference on Human Factors in Computing Systems*. doi:10.1145/1240624.1240775

Russell, T. (2006). Cloudalicious: Folksonomy over time. In *Proceedings of the 6th ACM/IEEEC-CS Joint Conference on Digital Libraries*. doi:10.1145/1141753.1141859

Seifert, C., Kump, B., Kienreich, W., Granitzer, G., & Granitzer, M. (2008). On the beauty and usability of tag clouds. In *Information Visualisation, 2008. IV'08.12th International Conference*. doi:10.1109/IV.2008.89

Sinclair, J., & Cardew-Hall, M. (2007). The folksonomy tag cloud: When is it useful? *Journal of Information Science, 34*(1), 15–29. doi:10.1177/0165551506078083

Trant, J. (2009). Studying social tagging and folksonomy: A review and framework. *Journal of Digital Information, 10*(1).

KEY TERMS AND DEFINITIONS

Application Programming Interface (API): An API is collection of functions and instances for software development.

Folksonomy: A folksonomy is a way to apply public keywords / tags to electronic resources to retrieve them easily.

Similarity Metric: A similarity metric is a function which measures distance between two strings/sequences.

Social Bookmarking: A social bookmarking is an online service which allows users to add/update/share bookmarks of web resources.

Tag Cloud: A tag cloud is a visual representation of data and generally used to represent metadata.

Tagging: A tagging is an act of assigning tag (non-hierarchical term).

APPENDIX 1

The sample code for generating tag cloud:

```
<script type="text/javascript" src="http://ajax.googleapis.com/ajax/libs/jque-
ry/1.4.4/jquery.js"></script>
<script type="text/javascript" src="jqcloud-1.0.4.js"></script>
<script type="text/javascript">

        var products = <?php echo json_encode($associativeArrayBytag) ?>;
        var myStuff= new Array();
        var i=0;
        $.each(products, function(key, value) {
                {
                        myStuff[i] = {text:key, weight:value, handlers:
{click: function() { alert("it worked for " + key); window.location.href =
"tl.php?key="+key; }} };
                        i++;
                }

        });
        $(function() {
                $("#my_favorite_latin_words").jQCloud(myStuff);
        });
</script>
</head>
<body>
    <h1>jQCloud Example</h1>
    <div id="my_favorite_latin_words" style="width: 600px; height: 350px; bor-
der: 1px solid #ccc;" ></div>
        <script type="text/javascript">
                for(i=0;i<myStuff.length;i++)
                {
                        document.write((i+1) + '. ' + myStuff[i]["text"] + ',
');
                }
        </script>
```

APPENDIX 2

The sample code for fetching stored bookmarks from www.delicious.com

```
require_once('delicious.php');

$deli = new delicious('trakesh', 'rt2831986');

$associativeArrayTagCount = array();
$i=1;
foreach ($x->tag as $link) {
        $attrs      = $link->attributes();
        $count      = (string)$attrs->count;
        $tag = (string)$attrs->tag;

        if($i<=20)
                $associativeArrayTagCount[$tag] = $count;
        $i++;
}

if(isset($_GET) && strlen($_GET['key']) > 0)
{
        $newkey = $_GET['key'];
        $_SESSION[$newkey] = $newkey;

        //echo "Request: " . $newkey . "<hr>";
        //echo "After sessio set:  " .$_SESSION[$newkey] ."<br>";
        $newkey = "";
        foreach ($_SESSION as $key=>$val)
        {
                echo $key ." and value  " .$val ."<br/>";
                if(strcmp($key,"start") !=0  and  strcmp($key,"expire") !=0)
                        $newkey .= $val . "+";

        }
        $newkey = rtrim($newkey, "+");

        echo "<br> Your filtering tags are: "  .$newkey ."<br>";

        $tag1 = preg_replace('/\s+/', '%20', $newkey);

        $x = $deli->get_by_tag($tag1);
```

```
        $associativeArrayBytag = array();

        foreach ($x->post as $link) {
                $attrs     = $link->attributes();
                    $tag = (string)$attrs->tag;
                $token = strtok($tag, ",");

                while ($token !== false && strlen($token)>0)
                {
                        $token = (string) strtok(",");
                        if (array_key_exists($token, $associativeArrayTag-
Count)) {
                                if(strlen($_SESSION[$token]) == 0)
                                {

                                        $newcount = $associativeArrayTagCount
[$token];

                                        $associativeArrayBytag[$token] =
$newcount;
                                }
                        }
                }
        }
```

Chapter 4
Applications of Web Usage Mining across Industries

A. V. Senthil Kumar
Hindusthan College of Arts and Science, India

R. Umagandhi
Kongunadu Arts and Science College, India

ABSTRACT

Web Usage Mining (WUM) is the process of discovery and analysis of useful information from the World Wide Web (WWW) by applying data mining techniques. The main research area in Web mining is focused on learning about Web users and their interactions with Web sites by analysing the log entries from the user log file. The motive of mining is to find users' access models automatically and quickly from the vast Web log data, such as similar queries imposed by the various users, frequent queries applied by the user, frequent web sites visited by the users, clustering of users with similar intent etc. This chapter deals with Web mining, Categories of Web mining, Web usage mining and its process, Applications of Web usage mining across the industries and its related works. This Chapter offers a general knowledge about Web usage mining and its applications for the benefits of researchers those performing research activities in WUM.

WEB MINING

Definition of Web Mining

Web mining is a technique used to automatically discover and extract the interesting and potentially useful patterns and implicit information from the web documents and services (Etzioni, O. 1996). Exploring and extracting precisely pragmatic knowledge from web data is also called as web mining. Web mining is indispensable to enhance the utility of web. Application of data mining techniques in the World Wide Web is called as web mining (Srivastava, T. *et al.*, 2005).

Web is the largest and voluminous data source in the world. The plentiful unstructured or semi-structured information on the web leads to a great challenge for the users, who hunt for prompt information.

DOI: 10.4018/978-1-5225-0613-3.ch004

The scenario grows pathetic and distressing to provide personalized service to the individual users from billions of web pages. The unpredictable amount of web information available becomes a menace of experiencing ambiguity in the web search. To prevent the web users from getting overwhelmed by the quantity of information available in the web, search engines are used.

The massive utility of web resources in recent scenario has turned to be an essential commitment for numerous reasons. Clinging on to the web information from a microcosmic level to the macrocosmic level has been growing over the last three decades. At the same time, the inconceivable boom of information available in the websites simultaneously throws the challenge of retrieving the precise and appropriate information at the time of need. To state the precise statistics of active websites, the March 2012 survey of Netcraft (http://news.netcraft.com/archives/2012/01/03/january-2012-web-server-survey.html; March 2012) figures around 644,275,754 websites may be quoted. This survey aids to comprehend how the web appears to be a panacea due to its inevitable applications in several facets of life. Moreover, the web information is the mostly sought after powerful platform for working, studying, searching information, besides, being in touch with our friends. Apparently, the unpredictable amount of web information available becomes a menace of experiencing ambiguity in the web search. To prevent the web users from getting overwhelmed by the quantity of information available in the web, several strategies are proposed. These strategies attempt to solve the tedious information exploration process of the user, through Information System, Information Filtering and Recommendation Systems.

Applications of Web Mining

Web mining is used in four significant fields namely, Resource finding, Information selection and Pre-processing, Generalization and Analysis. Retrieving the anticipated web resource through exploration is called Resource finding. Information selection and Pre-processing is the process of making automatic choices while pre-processing to obtain a definite data from the retrieved web resources. Automatic method to examine general patterns at individual web sites as well as across multiple sites is called Generalization. Analysis is a method of validation and/or interpretation of the mined patterns to reinstate the quality of results observed.

Classification of Web Mining

Web mining is categorized into, web content mining, web structure mining and web usage mining based on type of data used for mining processes. However the prevalent types are web content mining and web usage mining. In one, web structure is considered as part of web content; while in the other, web usage is considered as part of web structure. The main goal of all the three classification types is the method of knowledge discovery of inherent, unidentified and potentially valuable information from the web. Each of them focuses on varied mining objects of the web. Figure 1 describes the web categories and their objects. Subsequently, a brief introduction is given for each of the categories.

Web Content Mining

It is the process of ascertaining information or resource from millions of sources across the WWW. Web content mining will perhaps be distinguished from two perspectives namely, the agent-based technique and the database approach. The first approach aims at enhancing the data finding and filtering. The

Figure 1. Classification of web mining

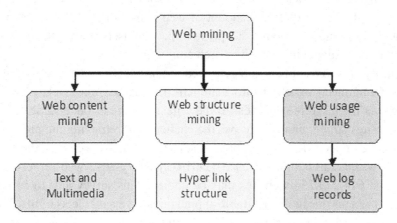

second technique aspires for modelling of the data available on the web into more controlled forms with the intention of applying standard database query mechanism and data mining applications to investigate it. The data on the web deals with unstructured data such as texts, semi-structured data such as Hyper Text Markup Language (HTML) documents, and a more structured data such as data in the tables or database generated in HTML pages, images, audios, videos, metadata and hyperlinks (Kosala, R. *et al.*, 2000). However, much of the web content is unstructured text data. Because of its immense size and data variety, a search query in the web IR results in thousands of web pages and most of them are irrelevant to the user's needs. To prevail over this problem, web content mining provides a path to screen more specific data. The goal of web content mining from the IR view is to improve the information finding or filtering based on user profiles, from the data base view is to model the data on the web and to integrate them so that more sophisticated queries other than the keywords based search could be performed.

Web Structure Mining

It is concerned with discovering the structural summary of the web page and the hyperlinks. Web content mining focuses on intra document structure that is within the document whereas, web structure mining tries to focus on inter-document structure that is within the web (Chakrabarti, S.*et al.*, 1999). In fact, there are several objects related in certain ways in the web. Hence, a peripheral and superficial application of the conventional procedures with an assumption of the existing independence of the web events may lead to disastrous and erroneous conclusions. This model can be used to categorize the web pages and make it possible to compare or integrate different web pages. It is useful to generate information such as the similarity and relationship between different web sites.

Web Usage Mining

It discovers the navigation patterns of the surfers from the web data. It deals with the prediction of the surfer's behaviour and interaction with the web. The web content and structure mining uses the primary data on the web, but web usage mining mines the secondary data, that is, the data from the web server, access logs, proxy server logs, browser logs, user profiles, user queries, registration data, user sessions or transactions etc. (Cooley, R.*et al.*, 1997). The success of usage mining depends on what and how much valid and reliable knowledge one can discover from the huge raw log data (Srivastava, J. *et al.*, 2000). Web usage mining focuses on techniques that could predict user's behaviour while the user interacts with the web.

Web usage mining provides the support for web site design, personalisation server, other business making decision etc. Borges, J.*et al.*, classifies the Web usage mining process into two commonly used approaches (Borges, J. *et al.*, 1999).

- Maps the usage data of the web server into relational tables before an adapted data mining technique is performed.
- Uses the log data directly by utilizing special pre-processing techniques.

The applications of web usage mining could be classified into two main categories: learning a user profile or user modelling in adaptive interfaces and learning user navigation patterns (Kosala, R. *et al.*, 2000). Then the learned knowledge could be used for applications such as personalisation, system improvement, site modification, business intelligence etc. Generally speaking, a web usage mining significantly relies on the essential web applications like through Information System, Information Filtering and Recommendation Systems (Hanani, U.*et al.*, 2001).

Information System (IS) is a process which sustains its support to extract all possible items namely text, video, image, audio etc.

Information Filtering (IF) is an approach which strategically supplies precise and apposite data to those who search for it. The functioning capacity of this process involves a desirable working condition on hefty data with the sustenance of the demographic details obtained through the profiles of the web users besides, their interests. While in the filtering process, main goal is the removal of data from an incoming stream, but the retrieval process focuses on finding relevant data in a stream.

Recommendation Systems (RECSYS) prove itself to have a pivotal function in the recovery of data from the web. This is addressed as web Information Retrieval (IR). The purpose of a recommender system is to observe and fix the user's genuine search intention and to supply the requisite appropriately. A recommender system generally evaluates the user's profile to certain reference features and foresees the rating that a user would give to an item.

Even with a little or hardly any information the user gains the privilege of information retrieval through this system (Resnick, P.*et al.*, 1997). Significantly, this system also advocates alternate suggestions in connection to the genuine intention of the user in a search. This actually helps the users to opt for the quick and best results. RECSYS aspire to procure interesting items besides combining them to the stream of information, whereas IS focuses on elimination of items from the stream. Burke, R. (Burke, R. 2007) defined that the RECSYS are tools that have the effect of guiding the user in a personalised way to interesting or useful objects in a large space of possible options. G. Adomavicius*et al.* (Adomavicius, G.*et al.*, 2005) defined that,

RECSYS is a set of users U, a set of items I, and a utility function $f: U \times I \rightarrow R$, where R is a totally ordered set of recommendations.

With respect to Burke, R.'s works (Burke, R. 2007; Baeza-Yates, R. 2004) the conventional recommendation approaches are classified into five types namely, collaborative, demographic, content-based, case-based and hybrid recommendation.

Collaborative Recommendation

This "people-to-people" (Sarwar, B.*et al.*, 2001) recommendation technique, functions on the preferences deciphered through the similarity of search behaviour of the web users. This may be illustrated with the user U and the query Q. Here, when the user U triggers a query Q, the collaborative filtering system supplies recommendation on the query Q in a couple of steps. Primarily, this system attempts to explore a set of users U with similar interests with respect to Q. Then it musters the queries issued by the users U. Collaborative approaches may also be called as customer-to-customer correlation as they have their firm roots on the perception of other customers. In fact, this similarity may be utilized in recommending the products to their unique customers. Collaborative filtering differentiates the customers' neighbours easily from the history of information.

Demographic Recommendation

The objective of the demographic RECSYS is to categorize people with respect to their personal demographic details (Baeza-Yates, R. 2004), in addition to making suggestions corresponding to the users' demographic profiles. Here, the assumption is that the users within same demographic class would possess similar interests (Ricci, F. *et al.,* 2011). Customizing the suggestions is pursued with the precocious references like the users' age, nativity, linguistic proficiency, and so on.

Content-Based Recommendation

Content-based approach is absolutely dependent on the search histories and navigational behaviour of the user. A content-based approach chooses data items depending on the correlation between the content of the data items and the user's preferences as opposed. The goal of content-based RECSYS is to process the content of the items and to recommend items based on user's profile.

Case-Based Recommendation

Lorenzi, F. *et al.,* defines case-based reasoning (Lorenzi, F. *et al.,* 2005) extremely depends on the computational model that aspires to decipher the search intension with specific reference to the previous problem solving experiences. The solution retrieval of a query is automatically referred at the submission of each new query. Each case experience gets stored in a data-store for futuristic application. A case model is an entry in the data-store with problem and solution descriptions.

Hybrid Recommendation

Hybrid methods combine multiple recommendation techniques to compensate for limitations of single recommendation technique.

The recommendation strategy advises the utility of the previous queries already stored as a web resource and exist in the search histories. A thorough analysis of this previously available search information relevant to one's query, besides, an overt comprehension of the search behavioural pattern of the previous users through the clicks made may be studied from the query log files. The recommendation technique proposed here is actually a hybrid approach, which is a combination of content based and collaborative strategies. A combination of these dual strategies may be suggested for other IR systems also. The consecutive sections brief on process of web usage mining.

PROCESS OF WEB USAGE MINING

Web usage mining refers to the automatic discovery and analysis of patterns in click stream and associated data collected or generated as a result of user interactions with Web resources on one or more Web sites. The goal is to capture, model, and analyze the behavioural patterns and profiles of users interacting with a Web site. The discovered patterns are usually represented as collections of pages, objects, or re-sources that are frequently accessed by groups of users with common needs or interests. Web usage mining process can contain three inter-dependent stages: data collection and pre-processing, pattern discovery and pattern analysis. In the *pre-processing stage*, the click stream data is cleaned and partitioned into a set of user transactions representing the activities of each user during different visits to the site. Other sources of knowledge such as the site content or structure, as well as semantic domain knowledge from site ontologies, may also be used in pre-processing or to enhance user transaction data. In the *pattern discovery stage*, statistical, database, and machine learning operations are performed to obtain hidden patterns reflecting the typical behaviour of users as well as summary statistics on web resources, sessions, and users. In the final stage of the process that is *pattern analysis*, the discovered patterns and statistics are further processed, filtered, possibly resulting in aggregate user models that can be used as input to applications such as recommendation engines, visualization tools, web analytics and report generation tools. The overall process is depicted in Figure 2. The strategically execution of web usage mining is stated subsequently.

Figure 2. Process of web usage mining

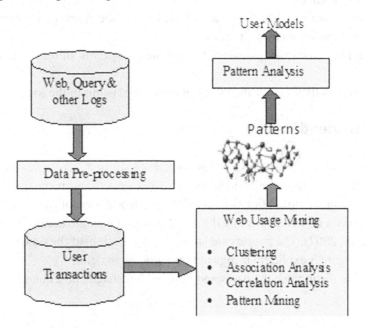

Data Collection

Data collection is the preliminary step of web usage mining. The data authenticity and integrity directly have an effect on the consecutive works smoothly carried on and the final recommendation of characteristic service's quality. Moreover, the web usage mining technology observes the main data origin as the data from the web server, access logs, proxy server logs, browser logs, user profiles, user queries, registration data, user sessions or transactions etc.

Data Pre-Processing

A number of databases are inadequate, inconsistent and incompatible as it exhibits noise. The data pre-treatment is to carry on a unified transformation to those databases. As a result those databases will get integrated and remain consistent. Perhaps, this helps in establishing the database that is potential enough to mine. The data pre-treatment work, mainly include data cleaning, user identification, session identification and path completion.

Data Cleaning

The purpose of data cleaning is to eliminate irrelevant items, and these kinds of techniques are of importance for any type of web log analysis. According to the purposes of different mining applications, irrelevant records in web access log will be eliminated during data cleaning. For instance, the cleaning process in a search engine query log implies the consecutive steps.

- Creation of user profile for each user who set themselves to access textual information. This leads to the automatic removal of requested page comprising the file extension gif, jpeg, bmp (image file extensions) and others.
- The elimination of the corresponding log entries when the requested pages fail to get loaded promptly due to some lapses in the process.
- Removal of the log entries that consists of automated programs similar to that of web robot and so on.
- Exclusion of those methods other than GET and POST existing in the log entries.

User and Session Identification

The task of this section explores and juxtaposes the users and their corresponding sessions from the original access log. User identification is identifying who access the web site and which pages are accessed. The goal of session identification is to divide the page accesses of each user into individual sessions. A session is a series of web pages that the user browse in a single access based on a widely-used rule (White, R.W. *et al.*, 2007). The queries are split into two sessions if the time interval between them exceeds 30 minutes. Figure 3 explicitly brings out this process in detail.

The rules adopted to distinguish the users and sessions are stated subsequently:

Figure 3. Users and session identification

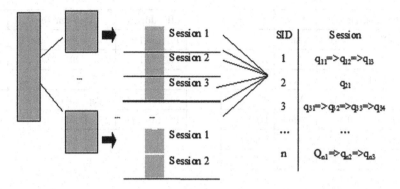

- Distinguishing every single web user through the usage of discrepant Internet Protocol (IP) addresses. A referrer-based method is used for identifying sessions.
- Inferring the differentiation among the users through different browsers and operating systems in case of the utility of the same IP addresses.
- Deciphering the referrer information when the IP address, browsers and operating systems are observed to be the same. Further, the Uniform Resource Locator (URL) field is checked, and a new user session is identified if the URL in the referrer URL field hasn't been accessed previously, or there is a large interval between the accessing time of this record and the previous one if the referrer field is empty.
- The session may contain more than one visit by the same user at different time, the time oriented heuristics is then used to divide the different visits into different user sessions. If all of the IP address, browsers and operating systems are same, the referrer information should be taken into account. The Refer URI is checked, new user's session is identified if the URL in the Refer URI is '-' that is field hasn't been accessed previously, or there is a large interval of more than 30 minutes between the accessing time of this record.

Path Completion

Path Completion should be used acquiring the complete user access path. The incomplete access path of every user session is recognized based on user session identification. If in a start of user session, Referrer as well URI has data value, delete value of Referrer by adding '-'. Web log pre-processing helps in removal of unwanted records from the log file and also reduces the size of original file by 40-50%. Table 1 depicts the log information of a user and the user's session information is displayed in Table 2 and Table 3.

Knowledge Discovery

Statistical method is used to analyse and mine the pre-treated data. Based on the user community's interests an interest model is constructed. The typically used machine learning methods mainly have clustering, association, classifying the relation discovery and the order model discovery.

Table 1. Log information of user 1

IP address	Date and Time	URL	Referrer
192.168.1.41	25/apr/2011:03:04:41	A.html	-
192.168.1.41	25/apr/2011:03:05:34	B.html	A.html
192.168.1.41	25/apr/2011:04:05:39	L.html	-
192.168.1.41	25/apr/2011:03:06:02	F.html	B.html
192.168.1.41	25/apr/2011:04:07:57	R.html	L.html
192.168.1.41	25/apr/2011:03:10:02	O.html	F.html
192.168.1.41	25/apr/2011:03:10:02	G.html	B.html

Table 2. Session 1 of user 1

IP address	Date and time	URL	Referrer
192.168.1.41	25/apr/2011:03:04:41	A.html	-
192.168.1.41	25/apr/2011:03:05:34	B.html	A.html
192.168.1.41	25/apr/2011:03:06:02	F.html	B.html
192.168.1.41	25/apr/2011:03:10:02	O.html	F.html
192.168.1.41	25/apr/2011:03:10:02	G.html	B.html

Table 3. Session 2 of user 1

IP address	Date and time	URL	Referrer
192.168.1.41	25/apr/2011:04:05:39	L.html	-
192.168.1.41	25/apr/2011:04:07:57	R.html	L.html

Pattern Analysis

Challenges of pattern analysis is to filter monotonous information and to visualize and interpret the interesting patterns to the user.

The overall data collection and pre-processing is represented in Figure 4.

An important task in any data mining application is the creation of a suitable target data set to which data mining and statistical algorithms can be applied. This is particularly important in Web usage mining due to the characteristics of click stream data and its relationship to other related data collected from multiple sources and across multiple channels. The process may involve pre-processing the original data, integrating data from multiple sources, and transforming the integrated data into a form suitable for input into specific data mining operations. Collectively, refer this process as data preparation.

SOURCES AND TYPES OF DATA

The information is gathered automatically by web server and stored in web logs and access logs. The web logs is use to track the end user behaviour for WUM. Log files are those files that list the actions that have been occurred. Web server creates and maintains log files for the purpose of getting feedback about activity & performance of the server and the problems occurring in the web server. Log files plays

Figure 4. Process of data collection and pre-processing

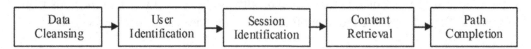

very important role in pattern recognition as analyses of log files helps in identifying relationships and patterns between messages or request from the user. The primary data sources used in Web usage mining are the server log files, which include Web server access logs and application server logs. Log files can be classified into three categories depending on the location of their storage.

- **Web Server Log Files:** These log files resides in web server and notes activity of the user browsing website. There are four types of web server logs i.e., transfer logs, agent logs, error logs and referrer logs.
- **Web Proxy Server Log Files:** These log files contains information about the proxy server from which user request came to the web server.
- **Client Browser Log Files:** These log files resides in client's browser and to store them special software are used.

Log files contain various parameters which are very useful in recognizing user browsing patterns; some of the parameters are, User Name: Identifies the user who has visited the website and this identification normally is IP address, Visiting Path: It is the path taken by the user while visiting the website, Path Traversed: It is the path taken by the user within the website, Time Stamp: It is the time spent by user on each page and is normally known as session, Page Last Visited: It is the page last visited by the user while leaving the website, Success Rate: It is measured by downloads and copying activity carried out on the website, User Agent: It is the browser that user uses to send the request to the server, URL: It is the resource that is accessed by the user and it may be of any format like HTML, Common Gateway Interface (CGI) etc, Request Type: It is the method that is used by the user to send the request to the server and it can be either GET or POST method. Generally three types of log file formats are used by the majority of the servers,

- **Common Log File Format:** It is the standardized text file format that is used by most of the web servers to generate the log files.
- **Combined Log Format:** It is same as the common log file format but with three additional fields referral field, the user agent field, and the cookie field. The following attributes are used in this log format,

```
< host rfc931 username date:time request statuscode bytes referrer user_agent
cookie >
```

The referrer attribute consists the URL which links the user to the web site, user_agent consists of Web browser and platform used by the visitor to the site and cookies are pieces of information that the Hyper Text Transfer Protocol (HTTP) server can send back to client along the with the requested resources. A client's browser may store this information and subsequently send it back to the HTTP server upon making additional resource requests. The HTTP server can establish multiple cookies per HTTP request.

- **Multiple Access Logs:** It is the combination of common log format and combined log file format.

The data obtained through various sources can be categorized into four primary groups.

Usage Data

The log data collected automatically by the Web and application servers represents the fine grained navigational behaviour of visitors. It is the primary source of data in Web usage mining. Each hit against the server, corresponding to an HTTP request, generates a single entry in the server access logs. Each log entry (depending on the log format) may contain fields identifying the time and date of the request, the IP address of the client, the resource requested, possible parameters used in invoking a Web application, status of the request, HTTP method used, the user agent (browser and operating system type and version), the referring Web resource, and, if available, client side cookies which uniquely identify a repeat visitor. Figure 5 depicts the web usage data obtained from the access logs.

Content Data

The content data in a site is the collection of objects and relationships that is conveyed to the user. For the most part, this data is comprised of combinations of textual materials and images. The data sources used to deliver or generate this data include static HTML/XML pages, multimedia files, dynamically generated page segments from scripts, and collections of records from the operational databases. The site content data also includes semantic or structural meta-data embedded within the site or individual pages, such as descriptive keywords, document attributes, semantic tags, or HTTP variables. The under-

Figure 5. Web usage data

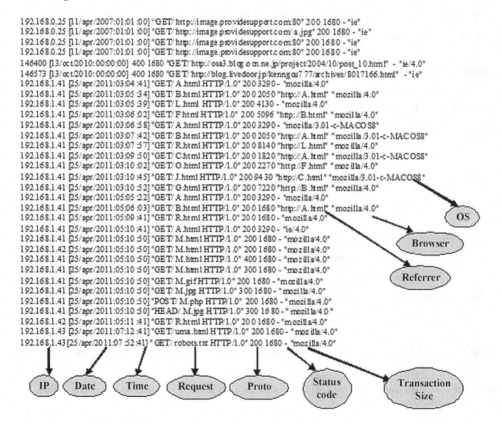

lying domain ontology for the site is also considered part of the content data. Domain ontologies may include conceptual hierarchies over page contents, such as product categories, explicit representations of semantic content and relationships via an ontology language such as RDF, or a database schema over the data contained in the operational databases.

Structure Data

The structure data represents the designer's view of the content organization within the site. This organization is captured via the inter-page linkage structure among pages, as reflected through hyperlinks. The structure data also includes the intra-page structure of the content within a page. For example, both HTML and XML documents can be represented as tree structures over the space of tags in the page. The hyperlink structure for a site is normally captured by an automatically generated "site map." A site mapping tool must have the capability to capture and represent the inter and intra page view relationships. For dynamically generated pages, the site mapping tools must either incorporate intrinsic knowledge of the underlying applications and scripts that generate HTML content, or must have the ability to generate content segments using a sampling of parameters passed to such applications or scripts.

User Data

The operational database(s) for the site may include additional user profile information. Such data may include demographic information about registered users, user ratings on various objects such as products or movies, past purchases or visit histories of users, as well as other explicit or implicit representations of users' interests. Some of this data can be captured anonymously as long as it is possible to distinguish among different users. For example, anonymous information contained in client side cookies can be considered a part of the users' profile information, and used to identify repeat visitors to a site. Many personalization applications require the storage of prior user profile information.

The commonly used technique to augment the users' search experience is the utilization of the knowledge contained within past queries in the query log. A query log, typically, contains information about users, issued queries, clicked results, etc. From this information, knowledge can be extracted to improve the quality in terms of effectiveness and efficiency of their system. For instance, the search histories of American On-Line (AOL) search engine are organized under the following attributes,

```
<AnonID, Query, QueryTime, ItemRank, ClickURL>
```

which are described in Table 4 and Table 5 shows a fragment of the AOL query log.

APPLICATIONS OF WEB USAGE MINING

Web usage mining is the process of discovery and analysis of useful information from the World Wide Web by applying data mining techniques. In the earlier stage, applications of WUM are classified into two main categories: learning a user profile or user modelling in adaptive interfaces (Langley, P. 1999) and learning user navigation patterns (Spiliopoulou, M. 1999).

Table 4. Attributes along with its description

Attribute	Description
AnonID	Anonymous Identifier assigned for every user
Query	Query term supplied by the user
QueryTime	Date and time on which the query is triggered by the user
ItemRank	Rank assigned to each clicked URL
ClickURL	Address of the clicked URL

Table 5. Sample AOL log entries

AnonID	Query	QueryTime	Item Rank	ClickURL
144	www.bostonredsox	2006-03-28 18:12:26	1	http://boston.redsox.mlb.com_
144	www.findmassmoney.com_	2006-04-15 07:34:07	1	http://www.findmassmoney.com_
144	www.herbchambers.com_	2006-04-23 09:23:48	3	http://www.carsearch.com_
144	www.herbchambers.com_	2006-04-23 09:23:48	1	http://www.herbchambers.com_
144	www.eastern bank.com	2006-05-10 10:55:50	1	http://www.easternbank.com_
227	psychiatric disorders	2006-03-02 17:30:36	1	http://allpsych.com_
227	psychiatric disorders	2006-03-02 17:30:36	1	http://allpsych.com_
227	cyclothymia disorders psychiatric	2006-03-02 17:34:08	1	http://www.psycom.net_
227	mental disease	2006-03-02 17:34:08	5	http://www.mental-health-matters.com_
644	Midwestcenter	2006-03-02 17:35:59	1	http://www.carsearch.com_

Web usage mining techniques (Cooley, R. *et al.*, 1997; Srivastava, J. *et al.*, 2000), which capture Web users' navigational patterns, have achieved great success in various application areas such as Web personalization (Mobasher, B, *et al.*, 2000; Mobasher, B. *et al.*, 2002; Pierrakos, D. *et al.*, 2003), Link prediction and analysis (Kushmerick, N. *et al.*, 2000; Sarukkai, R. 2000), Web site evaluation or reorganization (Spiliopoulou, M. *et al.*, 1998; Srikant, R. *et al.*, 2001), Web analytics and ecommerce data analysis (Kohavi, R. *et al.*, 2004), Adaptive Web sites (Perkowitz, M. *et al.*, 1998) and Web pre-fetching (Pitkow, J. 1999).

Most current Web usage mining systems use different data mining techniques, such as clustering, association rule mining, and sequential pattern mining to extract usage patterns from user historical navigational data. Generally these usage patterns are stand alone patterns at the page view level. They, however, do not capture the intrinsic characteristics of Web users' activities, nor can they quantify the underlying and unobservable factors that lead to specific navigational patterns. Web usage mining projects in different areas handled five categories, the data sources used to gather input, the number of users represented in each data set, the number of web sites represented in each data set and the applications area focused by the project. Figure 6 shows some of the applications of WUM.

Figure 6. Applications of WUM

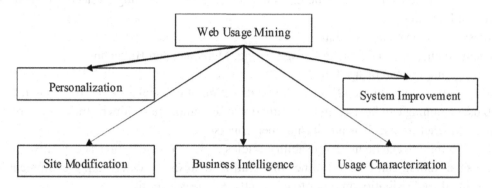

Web usage mining is used in the following areas:

- It offers users the ability to analyze massive volumes of click stream or click flow data, integrate the data seamlessly with transaction and demographic data from offline sources and apply sophisticated analytics for web personalization, e-CRM and other interactive marketing programs.
- Personalization for a user can be achieved by keeping track of previously accessed pages. These pages can be used to identify the typical browsing behavior of a user and subsequently to predict desired pages.
- By determining frequent access behavior for users, needed links can be identified to improve the overall performance of future accesses.
- Information concerning frequently accessed pages can be used for caching.
- In addition to modifications to the linkage structure, identifying common access behaviors can be used to improve the actual design of Web pages and to make other modifications to the site.
- Web usage patterns can be used to gather business intelligence to improve Customer attraction, Customer retention, sales, marketing and advertisement, cross sales.
- Mining of web usage patterns can help in the study of how browsers are used and the user's interaction with a browser interface.
- Usage characterization can also look into navigational strategy when browsing a particular site.
- It focuses on techniques that could predict user behavior while the user interacts with the Web.
- It helps in improving the attractiveness of a Web site, in terms of content and structure.
- Performance and other service quality attributes are crucial to user satisfaction and high quality performance of a web application is expected.
- Web usage mining of patterns provides a key to understanding Web traffic behavior, which can be used to deal with policies on web caching, network transmission, load balancing, or data distribution.
- Web usage and data mining is also useful for detecting intrusion, fraud, and attempted break-ins to the system.
- Web usage mining can be used in
- e-Learning, e-Business, e-Commerce, e-CRM, e-Services, e-Education, e-Newspapers, e-Government, and Digital Libraries.
- Web usage mining can be used in

- Customer Relationship Management, Manufacturing and Planning, Telecommunications and Financial Planning.
- Web usage mining can be used in
- Physical Sciences, Social Sciences, Engineering, Medicine, and Biotechnology.
- Web usage mining can be used in
- Counter Terrorism and Fraud Detection, and detection of unusual accesses to secure data.
- Web usage mining can be used in determination of common behaviors or traits of users who perform certain actions, such as purchasing merchandise.
- Web usage mining can be used in usability studies to determine the interface quality.
- Web usage mining can be used in network traffic Analysis for determining equipment requirements and data distribution in order to efficiently handle site traffic.

The following Section deals with some of the important applications of WUM.

E-Commerce

E-commerce has been growing rapidly keeping the pace with the web. Its rapid growth has made both companies and customers face a new situation. Whereas companies are harder to survive due to more and more competitions, the opportunity for customers to choose among more and more products has increased the burden of information processing before they select which products meet their needs (Kim, E. *et al.*, 2000).With the continued growth and proliferation of e-commerce, Web services, and Web-based information systems, the volumes of click stream and user data collected by Web-based organizations in their daily operations has reached astronomical proportions. Analyzing such data can help these organizations determine the life time value of clients, design cross-marketing strategies across products and services, evaluate the effectiveness of promotional campaigns, optimize the functionality of Web-based applications, provide more personalized content to visitors, and find the most effective logical structure for their Web space.

Yoon Ho Cho et al. (Yoon Ho Cho *et al.*, 2002) proposed a personalized product recommendation system is an enabling mechanism to overcome information overload occurred when shopping in an Internet marketplace. Collaborative filtering has been known to be one of the most successful recommendation methods, but its application toe-commerce has exposed well known limitations such as sparsity and scalability, which would lead to poor recommendations. The suggested methodology is based on a variety of data mining techniques such as web usage mining, decision tree induction, association rule mining and the product taxonomy. Menasce, D. A. *et al.*, (Menasce, D. A. *et al.*, 1999) have presented a state transition graph, called Customer Behaviour Model Graph (CBMG), that is used to describe the behaviour of groups of customers who exhibit similar navigational patterns. VanderMeer, D. *et al.*, (VanderMeer, D. *et al.*, 2000) have developed a user navigation model designed for supporting and tracking dynamic user behaviour in online personalization. The model supports the notion of a product catalogue, user navigation over this catalogue and dynamic content delivery.

E-Learning

Khribi, M. K. *et al.*, (Khribi, M. K.*et al.*, 2009) described an automatic personalization approach to provide online automatic recommendations for active learners without requiring their explicit feedback.

Recommended learning resources are computed based on the current learner's recent navigation history, as well as exploiting similarities and dissimilarities among learners' preferences and educational content. Building automatic recommendations in e-learning platforms is composed of two modules: an off-line module which pre-processes data to build learner and content models, and an online module which uses these models on-the-fly to recognize the students' needs and goals, and predict a recommendation list. Recommended learning objects are obtained by using a range of recommendation strategies based mainly on content based filtering and collaborative filtering approaches, each applied separately or in combination.

Pattern Recognition

Pattern recognition is defined as the act of taking in raw data and making an action based on the 'category' of the pattern. Web usage mining is divided into three parts-Pre-processing, Pattern discovery and Pattern analysis. Pattern recognition is the task of finding useful information from web server logs applying various techniques such as filtering, grouping etc. This extracted knowledge plays a very important role in formulation of important rules and decisions regarding organization website structure, making marketing and advertising more fruitful and effective. Before the process of pattern recognition the log file data has to go through three stages i.e., pre-processing, pattern discovery and pattern analysis. Before the application of pattern recognition, initially log file data is being pre-processed to remove any unwanted entries so that the patterns extracted are useful and relevant.

A significant problem with most of the pattern discovery methods is their difficulty in handling very large scales of data, such as those typically collected on the Web. Despite the fact that most of the Web usage mining process can be done online, the sizes of Web data, particularly access log data, are orders of magnitude larger than those met in common applications of machine learning. In a Web personalization system that is required to operate in real time, the scalability of the pattern discovery method can become critical. Scalability refers to the rate of increase in time and memory requirements with respect to a number of parameters, such as the number of users and pages.

Pattern Discovery

Pattern discovery uses methods and algorithms developed from several fields such as statistics, data mining, machine learning and pattern recognition (Jaideep Srivastava *et al.*, 2000). OLAP and the data cube structure offer a highly interactive and powerful data retrieval and analysis environment. The knowledge that can be discovered is represented in the form of rules, tables, charts, graphs, and other visual presentation forms for characterizing, comparing, predicting, or classifying data from the web access log. Visualization can also be used in web usage mining, and it presents the data in the way that can be understood by users more easily. The pattern discovery methods are Statistical Analysis, Association Rules, Clustering, Classification, Sequential Patterns and Dependency Modelling.

Statistical Analysis: Statistical techniques are the most common method to extract knowledge about visitors to a web site. By analyzing the session file, one can perform different kinds of descriptive statistical analyses (frequency, mean, median, etc) on variables such as page views, viewing time and length of a navigational path.

Association Rules: Association rule generation can be used to relate pages that are most often referenced together in a single server sessions. In the context of web usage mining, association rules refer to sets of pages that are accessed together with a support value exceeding some specified threshold. Association rule mining has been well studied in Data Mining, especially for basket transaction data analysis (Margaret H. Dunham 2003).

Aside from being applicable for e-Commerce, business intelligence and marketing applications, it can help web designers to restructure their web site. The results about the usefulness of such rules in supermarket transaction or in web application have not been reported. People also put some constraints over the mining process, and prune the extracted rules. The association rules may also serve as heuristic for pre fetching documents in order to reduce user-perceived latency when loading a page from a remote site. In electronic CRM, an existing customer can be retained by dynamically creating web offers based on associations with threshold support and/or confidence value (Buchner, A. G. *et al.*, 1998).

Pattern Analysis

The motivation behind pattern analysis is to filter out uninteresting rules or patterns from the set found in the pattern discovery phase. The exact analysis methodology is usually governed by the application for which Web mining is done. End products of such analysis might include the frequency of visits per document, most recent visit per document, who is visiting which documents, frequency of use of each hyperlink and most recent use of each hyperlink. The techniques of Web usage patterns discovery, such as association, path analysis, sequential patterns, etc.The methods like SQL(Structured Query Language) processing and OLAP (Online Analytical Processing) can be used.

Personalization

A Web personalization system can over a variety of functions starting from simple user salutation, to more complicated functionality such as personalized content delivery. Dimitrios*et al.*, distinguish between four basic classes of personalization functions: memorization, guidance, customization and task performance support (Dimitrios *et al.*, 2003).

Memorization

This is the simplest form of personalization function, where the system records and stores in its memory information about the user, such as name and browsing history. When the user returns to the site, this information is used as a reminder of the user's past behaviour, without further processing. Memorization is usually not ordered as a stand-alone function, but as part of a more complete personalization solution.

Guidance

A personalization function refers to the endeavour of the personalization system to assist the user in getting quickly to the information that the user is seeking in a site, as well as to provide the user with alternative browsing options. This personalization function not only increases the users' loyalty but also alleviates in a great extent the information overload problem that the users of a large Web site may face.

Customization

A personalization function refers to the modification of the Web page in terms of content, structure and layout, in order to take into account the user's knowledge, preferences and interests. The main goal is the management of the information load, through the facilitation of the user's interaction with the site.

Task Performance Support

It is a functionality that involves the execution of a particular action on behalf of a user. This is the most advanced personalization function, inherited from a category of Adaptive Systems known as personal assistants (Mitchell, T.*et al.*, 1994), which can be considered as client-side personalization systems. The same functionality can be envisaged for the personalization system employed by a Web server.

RELATED WORKS

Web usage mining tries to make sense of the data generated by the Web surfer's sessions or behaviours. While the Web content and structure mining utilize the real or primary data on the Web, Web usage mining mines the secondary data derived from the interactions of the users while interacting with the Web. The Web usage data includes the data from Web server access logs, proxy server logs, browser logs, user profiles, registration data, user sessions or transactions, cookies, user queries, bookmark data, mouse clicks and scrolls, and any other data as the results of interactions.

Web usage mining focuses on techniques that could predict user behaviour while the user interacts with the Web. The mined data in this category are the secondary data on the Web as the result of interactions. These data could range very widely but generally classify them into the usage data that reside in the Web clients, proxy servers and servers (Srivastava, J. *et al.*, 2000). The Web usage mining process could be classified into two commonly used approaches. The first approach maps the usage data of the Web server into relational tables before an adapted data mining technique is performed. The second approach uses the log data directly by utilizing special pre-processing techniques. As is true for typical data mining applications, the issues of data quality and pre-processing are also very important here. The typical problem is distinguishing among unique users, server sessions, episodes, etc. in the presence of caching and proxy servers (Masand, B. *et al.*, 1999; Srivastava, J. *et al.*, 2000). The Web usage data could also be represented with graphs [17; 98]. Often the Web usage mining uses some background or domain knowledge such as navigation templates, Web content, site topology, concept hierarchies, and syntactic constraints (Spiliopoulou, M. 1999).

Proliferation of information is the order of the day and WWW has become the source for recouping the existing information. Search engines have become the gateway of retrieving the requisite information from the web in terms of web snippets with reference to the query logged in by the user. A query is an array of keywords employed to secure information from the web resources even though desirable results are not retrieved at all times. During certain instances inappropriate and redundant results are retrieved from the web. The incongruous and irrelevant results are procured due to the ambiguous keywords (Wen, J. R.*et al.*, 2001), inadequate knowledge of the user in terms of information need and shorter length queries.

The term "Web Usage Mining" was introduced by Cooley *et al.*, (Cooley *et al.*, 1997) when a first attempt of taxonomy of Web Mining was done; in particular they define Web mining as the discovery and analysis of useful information from the World Wide Web. It is also defined as the application of data mining techniques to large Web data repositories. It is the application of established data mining techniques to analyze Web site usage. . The pattern discovery tasks involve the discovery of association rules, sequential patterns, usage clusters, page clusters, user classifications or any other pattern discovery method (Mobasher *et al.*, 2000a; 2000b). Usage pattern extracted from web data can be applied to a wide range of applications such as web personalization, system improvement, site modification, business intelligence discovery, usage characterization. (Srivastava, J. *et al.*, 2005).

In *Log-based* approach, the query logs are employed to provide the query recommendations. Cao *et al.* (Cao, H. *et al.*, 2008) divided log-based approaches into two categories as *session based* approach and *click-based* approach. For *session-based* approach, Huang *et al.* (Huang, C. K.*et al.*, 2003) recommended mutually similar queries through mining the queries that co-occurred in the same session. For *click-based* approach, similar queries were suggested through bipartite graph model which was built up with the user's click and history information. Wang *et al.* (Wang, J.*et al.* 2004) recommended a method based on the numbers of common URLs clicked between queries. The basic assumption is that two queries are more similar when they share more same clicked URLs. This concept is also exercised in this research to identify the similar queries. Semantic relation between queries is identified at hitting time either using bipartite graph (Mei, Q.*et al.*, 2008) or weighted SimRank (Li, Y. *et al.*, 2010). Jia Li *et al.*,(Jia Li *et al.*,)investigate a novel, which combines usage data, content data, and structure data in a web site to generate user navigational models. These models are then feedback into the system to recommend users shortcuts or page resources. These navigational patterns are then used to generate recommendations based on a user's current status. The items in a recommendation list are ranked according to their importance, which is in turn computed based on web structure information.

In recent years there has been increasing interest in applying *web usage mining* techniques to build web recommender systems. Web usage recommender systems take web server logs as input, and make use of data mining techniques such as association rules and clustering to extract navigational patterns, which are then used to provide recommendations. Web server logs record user browsing history, which contains much hidden information regarding users and their navigation. They could, therefore, be a good alternative to the explicit user rating or feedback in deriving user models. In web usage recommender systems, navigational patterns are generally derived as an off-line process. The most commonly used approach for web usage recommender systems is using association rules to associate page hits (Srivastava, J. *et al.*, 2000; Xiaobin Fu *et al.*, 2000;Lin, C. *et al.*, 2000;Arbee, L.P. *et al.*, 2001).

CONCLUSION AND FUTURE RESEARCH

Rapid growth of the web and its huge size increases the research in the area of web usage mining. This chapter dealt the concept of web mining, types of web mining, content, structure, process and applications of web usage mining. The literature study shows that the proliferation of web usage mining, data pre-processing, pattern discovery and analysis. There are plenty of researches directions are available for the researchers in the field of application of web usage mining like Recommender Systems, Pattern Recognition, Web log analysis, URL recommender systems, Pattern Analysis, Pattern Growth etc.

REFERENCES

Adomavicius, G., & Tuzhilin, A. (2005). Toward the next generation of Recommender systems: A survey of the state-of-the-art & possible extensions. *IEEE Transactions on Knowledge and Data Engineering, 17*(6), 734–749. doi:10.1109/TKDE.2005.99

Arbee, L. P., Wu, & Chen. (2001). Enabling personalized recommendation on the web based on user interests & behaviors. In *11th International Workshop on research Issues Data Engineering.*

Baeza-Yates, R. (2004). Web usage mining search engines. In *Web mining: Applications & techniques* (pp. 307-321). Academic Press.

Borges, J., & Levene, M. (1999). Data Mining of user navigation patterns, In *Proceedings of the WEB-KDD'99 Workshop on Web Usage Analysis & User Profiling* (pp. 31–36). Academic Press.

Buchner, A. G., & Mulvenna, M. D. (1998). Discovering Internet Marketing Intelligence through Online Analytical Web Usage Mining. *ACM SIGMOD, 27*(4), 54–61. doi:10.1145/306101.306124

Burke, R. (2007). Hybrid web recommender systems. In *The adaptive web.* Springer Berlin Heidelberg.

Cao, H., Jiang, D., Pei, J., He, Q., Liao, Z., Chen, E., & Li, H. (2008). Context-aware query suggestion by mining click-through & session data, In *Proceedings of the 14th ACM SIGKDD international conference on Knowledge discovery & data mining* (pp. 875-883). doi:10.1145/1401890.1401995

Chakrabarti, S., Dom, B., Gibson, D., Kleinberg, J., Kumar, S., Raghavan, P., & Tomkins, A. et al. (1999). Mining the link structure of the world wide web. *IEEE Computer, 32*(8), 60–67. doi:10.1109/2.781636

Cooley, R., Mobasher, B., & Srivastava, J. (1997). Web mining: Information & pattern discovery on the world wide web. In *Proceedings of the 9th IEEE International Conference on Tools with Artificial Intelligence.* doi:10.1109/TAI.1997.632303

Pierrakos, Paliouras, Papatheodorou, & Spyropoulos. (2003). Web Usage Mining as a Tool for Personalization: A Survey, User Modeling& User-Adapted Interaction. Kluwer Academic Publishers.

Etzioni, O. (1996). The World Wide Web: Quagmire or gold mine. *Communications of the ACM, 39*(11), 65–68. doi:10.1145/240455.240473

Hanani, U., Shapira, B., & Shoval, P. (2001). Information filtering: Overview of issues, research & systems. *User Modeling and User-Adapted Interaction, 11*(3), 203–259. doi:10.1023/A:1011196000674

Huang, C. K., Chien, L. F., & Oyang, Y. J. (2003, May). Relevant term suggestion interactive web search based on contextual information query session logs. *Journal of the American Society for Information Science and Technology, 54*(7), 638–649. doi:10.1002/asi.10256

Li, J., & Zaïane, O. R. (2004). Combining usage, content, and structure data to improve web site recommendation. In *E-Commerce and Web Technologies* (pp. 305–315). Springer Berlin Heidelberg. doi:10.1007/978-3-540-30077-9_31

Khribi, M. K., Jemni, M., & Nasraoui, O. (2009). Automatic Recommendations for E-Learning Personalization Based on Web Usage Mining Techniques & Information Retrieval. *Journal of Educational Technology & Society, 12*(4), 30–42.

Kim, E., Kim, W., & Lee, Y. (2000). Purchase propensity prediction of EC customer by combining multiple classifiers based on GA. In *International Conference on Electronic Commerce* (pp. 274–280).

Kohavi, R., Mason, L., Parekh, R., & Zheng, Z. (2004). Lessons and challenges from mining retail e-commerce data. *Machine Learning, 57*(1-2), 83–113. doi:10.1023/B:MACH.0000035473.11134.83

Kosala, R., & Blockeel, H. (2000). Web mining research: A survey. *ACM SIGKDD Explorations Newsletter, 2*(1), 1–15. doi:10.1145/360402.360406

Kushmerick, N., McKee, J., & Toolan, F. (2000, January). Towards zero-input personalization: Referrer-based page prediction. In *Adaptive Hypermedia and Adaptive Web-Based Systems* (pp. 133–143). Springer Berlin Heidelberg. doi:10.1007/3-540-44595-1_13

Langley, P. (1999). User modeling adaptive interfaces, In *Proceedings of the Seventh International Conference on User Modeling* (pp. 357–370). Academic Press.

Li, Y., Xu, S., & Wang, B. (2010). Chinese Query Recommendation by Weighted SimRank. *Journal of Chinese Information Processing, 24*(3), 3–10.

Lin, C., Alvarez, S., & Ruiz, C. (2000). *Collaborative recommendation via adaptive association rule mining*. Academic Press.

Lorenzi, F., Ricci, F., Tostes, R. M., & Brasil, R. (2005). Case-based recommender systems: A unifying view. In Intelligent Techniques Web Personalisation. Springer.

Dunham, M. H. (2003). *Data Mining Introductory & Advanced Topics*. Prentice Hall.

Masand, B., & Spiliopoulou, M. (1999). *Workshop on web usage analysis & user profiling*. ACM.

Mei, Q., Zhou, D., & Church, K. (2008). Query suggestion using hitting time. In *Proceedings of the 17th ACM conference on Information & knowledge management* (pp.469-478). ACM.

Menasce, D. A., Almeida, V. A., Fonseca, R., & Mendes, M. A. (1999). A methodology for workload characterization of e-commerce sites. In *Proceedings of ACM E-Commerce* (pp. 119–128). doi:10.1145/336992.337024

Mitchell, T., Caruana, R., Freitag, D., McDermott, J., & Zabowski, D. (1994). Experience with a learning personal assistant. *Communications of the ACM, 37*(7), 81–91. doi:10.1145/176789.176798

Mobasher, B., Cooley, R., & Srivastava, J. (2000a). Automatic personalization based on web usage mining. *Communications of the ACM, 43*(8), 142–151. doi:10.1145/345124.345169

Mobasher, B., Dai, H., Luo, M. N. T., & Nakagawa, M. (2002). Discovery & evaluation of aggregate usage profiles for web personalization. *Data Mining and Knowledge Discovery, 6*(1), 61–82. doi:10.1023/A:1013232803866

Mobasher, B., Dai, H., Luo, T., Sun, Y., & Zhu, J. (2000b). Integrating web usage & content mining for more effective personalization. In *Proceedings of the EC-Web* (pp. 165–176). doi:10.1007/3-540-44463-7_15

Perkowitz, M., & Etzioni, O. (1998). Adaptive web sites: Automatically synthesizing web pages. In *Proceedings of the 15th National Conference on Artificial Intelligence.*

Pierrakos, D., Paliouras, G., Papatheodorou, C., & Spyropoulos, C. (2003). Web usage mining as a tool for personalization: A survey. *User Modeling and User-Adapted Interaction, 13*(4), 311–372. doi:10.1023/A:1026238916441

Pitkow, J., & Pirolli, P. (1999). Mining longest repeating sub sequences to predict www surfing. In *Proceedings of the 2nd USENIX Symposium on Internet Technologies & Systems.*

Resnick, P., & Varian, H. R. (1997). Recommender systems. *Communications of the ACM, 40*(3), 56–58. doi:10.1145/245108.245121

Ricci, F., Rokach, L., Shapira, B., & Kantor, P. B. (2011). Recommender Systems. Springer.

Sarukkai, R. (2000). Link prediction & path analysis using markov chains. In *Proceedings of the 9th International World Wide Web Conference.* doi:10.1016/S1389-1286(00)00044-X

Sarwar, B., Karypis, G., Konstan, J., & Riedl, J. (2001). Item-based collaborative filtering recommendation algorithms. In *ACM Proceedings of the 10th international conference on World Wide Web* (pp. 285-295). doi:10.1145/371920.372071

Spiliopoulou, M. (1999). Data mining for the web. In *Principles of Data Mining & Knowledge Discovery* (pp. 588–589). Academic Press.

Spiliopoulou, M. (2000). Web usage mining for web site evaluation. *Communications of the ACM, 43*(8), 127–134. doi:10.1145/345124.345167

Srikant, R., & Yang, Y. (2001). Mining web logs to improve website organization. In *Proceedings of the 10th International World Wide Web Conference.* doi:10.1145/371920.372097

Srivastava, J., Cooley, R., Deshpande, M., & Tan, P. (2000). Web usage mining: Discovery & applications of usage patterns from web data. *SIGKDD Explorations, 1*(2), 12–23. doi:10.1145/846183.846188

Srivastava, T., Prasanna, D., &Vipin, K. (2005). Web mining–concepts, applications & research directions. In *Foundations & Advances Data Mining.* Springer Berlin Heidelberg.

VanderMeer, D., Dutta, K., & Datta, A. (2000). Enabling scalable online personalization on the web. In *Proceedings of ACM E-Commerce* (pp. 185–196). doi:10.1145/352871.352892

Wang, J., Chen, C., & Peng, B. (2004). *Analysis of the user log for a large-scale Chinese search engine.* South China University of Technology.

Wen, J. R., Jian-Yun, N., & Hong-Jiang, Z. (n.d.). Clustering user queries of a search engine. In *Proceedings of the 10th international conference on World Wide Web* (pp. 162-168).

White, R. W., Bilenko, M., & Cucerzan, S. (2007). Studying the use of popular destinations to enhance web search interaction. In *Proceedings of the 30th Annual International ACM SIGIR Conference on Research & Development Information Retrieval* (pp. 159–166). doi:10.1145/1277741.1277771

Fu, Budzik, & Hammond. (2000). Mining navigation history for Recommendation. *Intelligent User Interfaces*, 106–112.

Cho, Y. H., Kim, J. K., & Kim, S. H. (2002). A personalized recommender system based on web usage mining & decision tree induction. *Expert Systems with Applications*, 23(3), 329–342. doi:10.1016/S0957-4174(02)00052-0

ADDITIONAL READING

Agichtein, E., Brill, E., Dumais, S., & Ragno, R. (2006). Learning user interaction models for predicting web search result preferences. In *Proceedings of the 29th annual international ACM SIGIR conference on Research & development in information retrieval* (pp. 3-10). doi:10.1145/1148170.1148175

Ricardo, B.-Y., Hurtado, C., & Mendoza, M. (2005). Query recommendation using query logs in search engines. Current Trends in Database Technology-EDBT 2004 Workshops (pp. 588-596).

Berendt, B., Mobasher, B., Spilopoulou, M., & Wiltshire, J. (2001). Measuring the accuracy of sessioninzers for web usage analysis. In *Proceedings of the Workshop on Web Mining at the First SIAM International Conference on Data Mining* (pp. 7-14).

Boldi, P., Bonchi, F., Castillo, C., & Vigna, S. (2009). From Dango to Japanese cakes: Query reformulation models and patterns. In *Proceedings of the 2009 IEEE/WIC/ACM International Joint Conference on Web Intelligence and Intelligent Agent Technology. (*Vol. 01 pp. 183-190). doi:10.1109/WI-IAT.2009.34

Chen, J. (2010). UpDown Directed Acyclic Graph Approach for Sequential Pattern Mining. *IEEE Transactions on Knowledge and Data Engineering*, 22(7), 913–928. doi:10.1109/TKDE.2009.135

Chirita Paul-Alexandru., Claudiu, S. F., & Wolfgang N. (2007). Personalized query expansion for the web. In *Proceedings of the 30th annual international ACM SIGIR conference on Research & development in information retrieval.* (pp. 7-14).

Cui, H., Wen, J. R., Nie, J. Y., & Ma, W. Y. (2003). Query expansion by mining user logs. *IEEE Transactions on Knowledge and Data Engineering*, 15(4), 829–839. doi:10.1109/TKDE.2003.1209002

Golfarelli, M., Stefano, R., & Paolo, B. (2011). myOLAP: An approach to express and evaluate OLAP preferences. *IEEE Transactions on Knowledge and Data Engineering*, 23(7), 1050–1064. doi:10.1109/TKDE.2010.196

Mei, Q., Dengyong, Z., & Kenneth, C. (2008). Query suggestion using hitting time. *In Proceedings of the 17th ACM conference on Information & knowledge management*, 469-478.

Neelam, D., & Sharma, A. K. (2011). QUESEM: Towards building a Meta Search Service utilizing Query Semantics. *International Journal of Computer Science*, 8(1).

Neelam, D., & Sharma, A. K. (2010). Rank Optimization & Query Recommendation in Search Engines using Web Log Mining Techniques. *Journal of Computing*, 2(12).

Pei, J., Jiawei, H., Behzad, M., Jianyong, W., Helen, P., Qiming, C., & Mei-Chun, H. et al. (2004). Sequential patterns by pattern-growth: The prefix span approach. *IEEE Transactions on Knowledge and Data Engineering, 16*(11), 1424–1440. doi:10.1109/TKDE.2004.77

Sanderson, M. (2008). Ambiguous queries: test collections need more sense. In *Proceedings of the 31st annual international ACM SIGIR conference on Research & development in information retrieval* (pp. 499-506). doi:10.1145/1390334.1390420

Silverstein, C., Henzinger, M., Marais, H., & Moricz, M. (1998). *Analysis of a very large AltaVista query log. Technical Report.* Systems Research Center, Compaq Computer Corporation.

Speretta, M., & Gauch, S. (2005). Personalized search based on user search histories. In *Proceedings of the IEEE/WIC/ACM International Conference on Web Intelligence* (pp.622-628). doi:10.1109/WI.2005.114

Thada, V., & Sandeep, J. (2011). A Genetic Algorithm Approach for improving the average Relevancy of Retrieved Documents Using Jaccard Similarity Coefficient. *International Journal of Research in IT & Management, 4.*

Umagandhi, R., & Senthilkumar, A. V. (2014). Time Heuristics Ranking Approach for Recommended Queries Using Search Engine Query Logs. *Kuwait Journal of Science, 41*(2), 127–149.

Umagandhi, R., & Senthilkumar, A. V. (2013). Time Dependent Approach for Query and URL Recommendations Using Search Engine Query Logs. *International Journal of Computer Science, 40*(3).

Zahera Hamada, M., & Gamal, F. (2011). Query Recommendation for Improving Search Engine Results. *International Journal of Information Retrieval Research, 1*(1), 45–52. doi:10.4018/ijirr.2011010104

Zhiyong, Z., & Nasraoui, O. (2006). Mining search engine query logs for query recommendation. *Proceedings of the 15th International Conference on World Wide Web,* 1039-1040. doi:10.1145/1135777.1136004

KEY TERMS AND DEFINITIONS

Pattern Analysis: The discovered patterns and statistics are further processed, filtered, possibly resulting in aggregate user models that can be used as input to applications such as recommendation engines, visualization tools, web analytics and report generation tools.

Pattern Discovery: Statistical, database, and machine learning operations are performed to obtain hidden patterns reflecting the typical behaviour of users.

Recommendation Systems: The purpose of a recommender system is to observe and fix the user's genuine search intention and to supply the requisite appropriately.

Web Log: The information is gathered automatically by web server and stored in web logs and access logs. The web logs is use to track the end user behaviour for WUM.

Web Mining: Exploring and extracting precisely pragmatic knowledge from web data is also called as web mining.

Web Usage Mining: It discovers the navigation patterns of the surfers from the web data. It deals with the prediction of the surfer's behaviour and interaction with the web.

Chapter 5
Enhancing Web Data Mining:
The Study of Factor Analysis

Abhishek Taneja
S. A. Jain College, India

ABSTRACT

An enormous production of databases in almost every area of human endeavor particularly through web has created a great demand for new, powerful tools for turning data into useful, task-oriented knowledge. The aim of this study is to study the predictive ability of Factor Analysis a web mining technique to prevent voting, averaging, stack generalization, meta- learning and thus saving much of our time in choosing the right technique for right kind of underlying dataset. This chapter compares the three factor based techniques viz. principal component regression (PCR), Generalized Least Square (GLS) Regression, and Maximum Likelihood Regression (MLR) method and explores their predictive ability on theoretical as well as on experimental basis. All the three factor based techniques have been compared using the necessary conditions for forecasting like R-Square, Adjusted R-Square, F-Test, JB (Jarque-Bera) test of normality. This study can be further explored and enhanced using sufficient conditions for forecasting like Theil's Inequality coefficient (TIC), and Janur Quotient (JQ).

INTRODUCTION

Factor analysis is a collection of techniques employed to explore underlying latent variables/factors which influence the outcomes on a number of measured variables. All of the techniques use common factors in their underlying model which is shown in Figure 1.

This model describes in Figure 1 that in a factor based model every observed measure/prediction from measure 1 to measure 5 is influenced by the underlying latent variables/common factors. These common factors i.e., A1 to A5 are also described latent variables and demonstrates the correlation among the different factors because of the more factors in (Kim, Jae-on., Mueller, Charles W., 1978).

Factor based techniques are actually a one-sample technique (Rencher C. Alvin, 2002). For example, the author thinks a sample X_1, X_2, X_n from an identical population with a mean vector μ and covariance matrix $\sum$. Factor based model represents each variable as a linear collection of essential *common factors*

DOI: 10.4018/978-1-5225-0613-3.ch005

Figure 1. Factor model

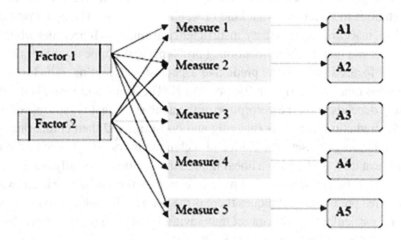

f_1, f_2, f_m, with a linked residual term to account for that part of the variable that is unique. For X_1, X_2, X_p in any observation vector X, the model is as follows:

$$X_1 - \mu_1 = \lambda_1 f_1 + \lambda_{12} f_2 + \cdots + \lambda_{1m} f_m + \varepsilon_1$$

$$X_2 - \mu_2 = \lambda_2 f_1 + \lambda_{22} f_2 + \cdots + \lambda_{2m} f_m + \varepsilon_2$$

...

$$X_p - \mu_p = \lambda_{p1} f_1 + \lambda_{p2} f_2 + \cdots + \lambda_{pm} f_m + \varepsilon_p.$$

If possible, m should be considerably smaller than p; or else the author have not achieved a sensible explanation of the variables as functions of a few underlying factors (Kim, Jae-on & Charles W. Mueller, 1978). In the above equation, f's in random variables that make the X's. The loadings which serve as weights are the coefficients i.e., λ_{ij}. They display how every X_i independently depends on the f's. λ_{ij} *describes* the significance of the jth factor f_j to the ith variable X_i and can also be used in explanation of f_j. The author explains f_2, for example, by examining its coefficients, $\lambda_{12}, \lambda_{22}, \lambda_{p2}$. The larger loadings associate f_2 to its corresponding X's. From these X's, the author deduce a meaning or description of f_2. After estimating the coefficients λ_{ij}'s, it is assumed that they will segregate the variables into parts equivalent to factors. Initially it appears that the MLR and factor analysis are similar techniques but there are fundamentally different because f's in above equations are unobserved and equations above represents one observational vector, whereas MLR represents all n observations.

MAIN FOCUS OF THE CHAPTER

An enormous production of databases in almost every area of human endeavor particularly with the introduction of web has created a great demand for new, powerful tools for turning data into useful, task-oriented knowledge. In this scenario it becomes imperative to explore new algorithms that can determine which technique to select and what kind of web mining to do. The real world data repositories are often incomplete, inaccurate, and/or have insufficient information. It becomes advisable to use those web mining tools that can handle above mentioned problems and can be used in varied environments.

In this chapter is focused only on the predictive aspect of web mining, which is probably its most developed part and has precise description (Berson, A., K. Thearling, and J. Stephen, 1999). The choice of technique largely depends upon the perceptive of the analyst. In that regard lots of time is wasted in trying every singly prediction technique (bagging and boosting) and then comparing which technique best suits for the underlying dataset. The choice of technique plays a large role in the uncertainty of a model. When nonlinear data are fitted to a linear model, the solution is usually biased. When linear data are fitted to a non linear model, the solution usually increases the variance. Hence with the arrival of improved and modified prediction techniques there is the need for the analyst to know which prediction technique suits for a particular type of data set thus saving lot of time by preventing bagging, boosting, and meta-learning (Taneja A., and Chauhan R.K, 2011).

The aim of this study is to compare the predictive ability of factor based linear web mining techniques viz., Principal components analysis (PCA), Generalized Least Square (GLS), and Maximum Likelihood Regression (MLR) to prevent voting, averaging, stack generalization, meta- learning and thus saving much of our time in choosing the right technique for right kind of underlying dataset.

A GENERAL INTRODUCTION TO WEB DATA-MINING

With the substantial increase in the e-commerce, web based information systems, and the introduction of various services now available on the web the data collected through these ventures has reached at astronomical proportions. The swift advancement in digital data possession and storage equipment has led to the fast-growing fabulous and amount of data stored in databases, data warehouses, or other kinds of data repositories such as the *World Wide Web*. Although valuable information may be hiding behind the data, the irresistible data volume makes it difficult, if not impossible, for human beings to extract them without powerful tools. In order to relieve such a data rich but information poor plight, during the late 1980s, a new discipline named web mining emerged, which devotes itself to extracting knowledge from huge volumes of data, with the help of the ubiquitous modern computing device, i.e. computer.

Web usage mining is the automatic discovery and analysis of patterns in clickstream with the interaction of the users with various web resources and web sites. Due to its interdisciplinary nature, web mining has received contributions from a lot of disciplines such as databases, machine learning, statistics, information retrieval, data visualization, parallel and distributed computing, *etc* (Taneja A., 2011), (Pregibon D., 1997). The first three in the list, i.e. database, machine learning, and statistics, are undoubtedly the primary contributors. It is obvious that without the powerful data management techniques donated by the database community and the practical data analysis techniques donated by the machine learning community, web mining would be seeking a needle in the haystack. It is interesting that even recently, a leading statistician raised a cry that the statistics community should embrace web mining (J. H. Friedman, 1997), which exposes that this community had not yet taken web mining seriously at least at that time. However, it is still clear that without the solid theoretical foundation donated by the statistics community, web mining will be building a castle in the air.

Web mining is extraction consistent pattern and/or systematic associations between parameters of interest from huge volume of historical data; it is then used to validate the findings on new subset of data (Giudici, P., 2003), (Berry, M. J. A., 2000).

Web mining tasks are broadly classified as prediction and description. Descriptive web mining includes description of the wide-ranging human interpretable patterns, associations or correlations describing the data in database. The description is focused on the discovery of patterns that represents the data of a complicated database by a comprehensible and exploitable way. A good description could suggest a good description of data behavior. Predictive mining tasks include construction of the data models and performing deduction on the current data in order to make predictions on the new datasets. The major objective of web mining is prediction, which is most common type of web mining and wide applications.

Web mining can be defined as a procedure of discovering new, appealing knowledge, such as patterns, associations, rules, changes, anomalies and significant structures from large amounts of data stored in data repositories and other information repositories. Currently it is regarded as the key ingredient of a much more detailed process called Knowledge Discovery in Databases (KDD). In general, a knowledge discovery process consists of a repetitive sequence of the underlying steps:

1. **Data Selection:** in this step data pertinent to analysis are extracted from the data repository;
2. **Data Cleaning:** it includes smoothing noisy data, removing outliers, and filling missing values.
3. **Data Integration (Enrichment):** where data from various multiple heterogeneous repositories are integrated into one;
4. **Data Transformation (Coding):** here data are transformed or consolidated into forms appropriate for different mining algorithms;
5. **Web Mining:** which is one of the steps in KDD notwithstanding an essential one, where intelligent methods are applied in order to extract hidden and valuable knowledge from data?
6. **Knowledge Representation:** where visualisation and knowledge representation techniques are used to present the mined knowledge in human understandable form to the user.

Web mining is based on the outcome achieved in database systems, statistics, machine learning, statistical learning theory, chaos theory, pattern recognition, neural networks, probabilistic graph theory, fuzzy logic and genetic algorithms. A large set of data analysis methods have been developed in statistics over many years of studies. Machine learning and statistical learning theory have significantly contributed to classification and induction problems. Neural networks have shown their usefulness in classification, prediction, and clustering analysis jobs. One can say that there is no one specific technique that characterizes web mining. Any technique that helps to facilitate extraction of more out of the underlying repositories in an independent and intelligent way may be termed as a web mining technique. Therefore web mining techniques form a quite heterogeneous group.

The procedure of predictive web mining includes of broadly three steps; the primary data examination, model building with validation/verification, and deployment. Exploration at the first step of web mining may require data cleaning to remove noise and to correct inconsistencies in data (Taneja A., 2011), extraction of target dataset or even more target subsets, and data transformations, such as z-score normalization. The second step involves a model building and validation. Depending upon the nature of problem, it may also require a choice of fitting prediction models. A range of models are tested in this phase and the best one, based upon specified criterion function, is chosen. In the last step, the obtained model enables prediction and subsequent interpretation of outcome from new data set.

Predictive models are usually represented in the form of mathematical equations or as a process that input the descriptor variables and calculate and output/estimate for the response or responses. This representation of model in a mathematical form tries to establish the relationship between the input descriptor variables and the output response variables. While establishing these models we should not much focus on whether these models are correct or not, rather we should concentrate on whether these models are useful to our underlying study or not.

There are number of applications of predictive models. Some of them are as under:

- **Setting Priority:** Predictive models can be used in setting priority in a data set that needs to be prioritized. For example, home loan company may build a predictive model to estimate which customers would be the best candidates for some incentives to enhance their financial products. This model could be run over a database of millions of potential customers to identify a subset of the most promising customers.
- **Facilitate Decision Making:** Prediction models can be building upon the historical databases to forecast future events so that knowledgeable action could be taken. For example, prediction models are used to weather forecasting.
- **Identifying and Understanding:** Predictive models facilitate in finding and understanding the relationship between the input descriptor variables and the output response variables. For example, a prediction model can help us out to identify and establish relationship among number of unknown variables under study leading us to understand their relationship.

There are many methods for building prediction models and they are often characterized based on the response variable. When the response is a categorical variable, the model is called a classification model. When the response is a continuous variable, then the model is a regression model (Myatt J. Glenn, 2007).

Broadly there are two different phases for building a predictive model. Each phase requires considering its own set of processes and issues:

- **Building:** At the very outset a mathematical function is established using the existing data called the training dataset. This mathematical function is called the prediction model. This training dataset contains examples with values for the predictor and predicted variables. Initially the training set is used to establish and quantify the associations between the input predictors and the output predicted variables. This training set will be divided into observations. One is used to build the model and other assesses the quality of the model built.
- **Applying:** In this step the predicted model previously built is applied on a new dataset with no output response variables. The model values are fed to this model whose response variable is to be calculated and thus predicting the response variable of the new dataset. Several measures can be used and calculated along-with that reflects the quality of prediction.

PRINCIPAL COMPONENT ANALYSIS

Principal components analysis (PCA) technique describes the correlation structure of a set of predictor variables by reducing the linear combinations of these variables (Al-Kassab M, 2009). This is mainly a dimension reduction technique responsible for producing a reduced set of linear combinations called principal components (PC's). This reduced set of correlation structures of the underlying dataset are formed by using entire set of S variables. The entire variability of the S variables is represented by its corresponding reduced set T, which are the linear combinations of these variables. That specifies to us that the information contained in the set of T variables is equal to the information enclosed in the original S variables (Camdevyren H, Demyr N, Kanik A, Keskyn S, 2005).

This is the reason for using this technique as a dimension reduction leading us to replace the original S variables with the T<S components, resulting in reduced representation of operational data set i.e., ($N \times T$) components rather than ($N \times S$) variables (Amir Reza Razavi, 2005). Where N is the total number of observations.

GENERALIZED LEAST SQUARE

Assume, $y = X\beta + u$, is a linear model, where y is a $n \times 1$ vector of observations on a dependent variable, X is a $n \times k$ matrix of independent variables of full column rank, β is a $k \times 1$ vector of parameters to be estimated, and u is a X 1 vector of residuals (Chipman, J.S., 1979). If A1 $E(u|X) = \mathbf{0}$ (i.e., the residuals have conditional mean zero), and A2 $E(uu'|X) = \sigma^2 \Omega$, where $\Omega = I_n$, is a $n \times n$ identity matrix (i.e., conditional on the X, the residuals are independent and identically distributed or "iid" with conditional variance σ^2), then the ordinary least squares (OLS) estimator $\hat{\beta}_{OLS} = (X'X)^{-1}X'Y$ with variance-covariance matrix $V(\hat{\beta}_{OLS}) = \sigma^2(X'X)^{-1}$ (1) satisfies best linear unbiased estimator (BLUE) properties of β; (2) a consistent estimator of β (i.e., as $n \to \infty$ 1, $\Pr[|\hat{\beta}_{OLS} - \beta| < \varepsilon] = 1$, for any $\varepsilon > 0$, or plim $\hat{\beta}_{OLS} = \beta$) and thus satisfying Gauss-Markov Theorem.

If A2 fails to hold (i.e., $\Omega \neq I_n$, where Ω is a positive definite matrix but not equal to I_n), then $\hat{\beta}_{OLS}$ remains unbiased, but no longer "best", and remains consistent. Relying on $\hat{\beta}_{OLS}$ when A2 doesn't hold risks faulty inferences; without A2, $\hat{\sigma}^2(X'X)^{-1}$ is a biased and inconsistent estimator of $V(\hat{\beta}_{OLS})$, meaning that the estimated standard errors for $\hat{\beta}_{OLS}$ are wrong, invalidating inferences and the results of hypothesis tests. Assumption A2 often fails to hold in practice: e.g., (1) when pooling across disparate units generates disturbances with different conditional variances (*heteroskedasticity*); (2) an analysis of time series data generates disturbances that are not conditionally independent (*serially correlated disturbances*).

When A2 does not hold, it may be possible to implement a *generalized least squares* (GLS) estimator that is BLUE at least asymptotically. For instance, if the researcher knows the exact form of the departure from A2 (i.e., the researcher knows Ω) then the GLS estimator $\hat{\beta}_{GLS} = (X'\Omega^{-1}X)^{-1}X'\Omega^{-1}y$ is BLUE, with variance-covariance matrix $\sigma^2(X'\Omega^{-1}X)^{-1}$. Note that when A2 holds, $\Omega = I_n$ and $\hat{\beta}_{GLS} = \hat{\beta}_{OLS}$ (i.e., OLS is a special case of the more general estimator) (Amemiya, Takeshi., 1985, Cochrane, D. and G.H. Orcutt., 1949).

MAXIMUM LIKELIHOOD REGRESSION

Maximum likelihood regression (MLR) is a method that finds the most likely value for the parameter based on the data set collected (Kleinbaum, David G., Lawrence L. Kupper and Keith E. Muller, 1998).

MLR is by far is the most popular method of parameter estimation and a vital tool for many statistical modeling techniques particularly in non-linear modeling and non-normal data.

According to this technique the preferred probability distribution is the one that makes the observed data most likely and that can be found by finding the value of the parameter vector that maximizes the likelihood function F (w). The resulting parameter which is found by searching the multidimensional parameter space is called as MLR estimate, denoted by $F_{MLR} = (F_{1,MLR}, \ldots \ldots F_{K,MLR})$.

For computational benefit it is suggested that MLR estimate should be attained by maximizing the log likelihood function ln F (w). Assuming the log likelihood function, ln F (w), is differentiable, if W_{MLR} exists, and must satisfy the following likelihood equation (Banbura Marta, Modugno Michele, 2010).

$$\frac{\partial \ln F(w)}{\partial w_i} = 0$$

At $w_i = w_{i,MLR}$ for all i=1,....,k. This equation describes the prerequisite condition for the existence of an MLR estimate. The other condition that need to be satisfied to ensure that $F(W_{MLR})$ is maximum and not a minimum (Dijkstra, T, 1985). Formally the above discussion can be described as:

If $y_1, y_2, \ldots y_n$ is a random sample of size n from a discrete or continuous probability density function, f_Y (yi; θ), where θ is an unknown parameter then the likelihood function is written

$$L(\theta) = \prod_{i=1}^{n} f_Y(y_i; \theta)$$

DATASETS INTRODUCTIONS

The data sets we have selected for this study have an amalgamation of the following unique features: a small number of explanatory attributes, several explanatory attributes, exceedingly collinear attributes, very superfluous attributes, datasets having mixture of categorical & continuous attributes, observations with many missing values and existence of outliers. In this chapter three data sets viz., Marketing, Bank and Parkinson's Telemonitoring data set are taken.

All the data sets before their analysis have been pre-processed and preliminary analysis has been done, just to get superficial knowledge of that data set. This preprocessing step is a vital step in real web mining applications which facilitate in choice of technique to be used for the purpose of mining.

MARKETING DATASET

This dataset has been build by filling 9409 questionnaires containing 502 questions by shopping mall customers in the San Francisco Bay area. This dataset has been extracted from this survey. It consists of 14 demographic attributes. This dataset is the good mixture of continuous and categorical attributes with many attribute values missing. Data set with lot of missing values and mixture of continuous and categorical attributes is a good feature that is required for a web mining purpose.

The target variable in this dataset is *Annual Income* of house hold from rest of other 13 demographics variables. The total number of instances in this dataset are 8993 that has been obtained from the original dataset with 9409 instances. The instances with the target variable missing have been removed. The box plot shown in Figure 3 depicts the dispersion among the variables by comparing the means of various columns. Box plot also helps in identifying outliers if any available in each column/variable. In this regard, it becomes necessary to scale the dataset to reduce the measure of dispersion and bring all the variables of all datasets to the same unit of measure. Linearity among the variables has been conformed by taking double log of all the variables including the target variable. This can be considered an essential step to satisfy the assumptions of linear regression model.

BANK DATASET

This dataset has been synthetically generated by a simulation process that facilitates their customers in choosing their banks. This simulator simulates the queues in series of banks and predicts the part of customers who leave the bank due to full queues. Customers belong to different residential places choose their banks depending upon the distance of the bank from their residence, the complexity of the tasks, and their patience level. Every bank has different queues that open and close depending upon their demand. Customers are allowed to change queues.

In this dataset the target variable is *rej*, which is the rate of rejections. Dataset contains 32 continuous variables and 4500 instances with many variables having missing values. This dataset has also been scaled, preprocessed prior to analysis and to give every variable an equal opportunity to provide all the information contained in the dataset. The box plot of the bank dataset is shown in Figure 4 to show dispersion among the variables and outliers if any.

PARKINSON'S TELE-MONITORING DATASET

This dataset is collected from a range of biomedical voice measurements from 42 people with early stage of Parkinson's disease. They are recruited to a six month trial of a telemonitoring device for remote symptom progression monitoring. All the recordings were automatically done at the patient's homes. There are 22 variables in this dataset with 5875 instances. The target variable in this dataset is "total_UPDRS". The box plot of this data set has been shown in Figure 5, shows the dispersion among the variables. This dataset has been preprocessed before using it for modeling purpose. All the columns have been double logged to make it normal.

From the above discussion it is clear that all the three datasets are unique from the point of view of nature of variables, number of variables, and number of instances, missing values, outliers, and dispersion.

METHODOLOGY

In computational web mining, which do not have an underlying probabilistic model and thus do not allow us to apply the statistical theory of hypothesis testing? For instance, a particular problem of web mining can be modeled using various classes of models. And deployment of wrong web mining model incurs a capital expenditure and investment on the part of company. It the selected model is invalid or does not suit to the underlying problem, it may lead to huge losses to the concerned company (Larose T. Daniel, 2005). In addition to that, the choice of model is also determined by the types of variables. Usually, in exploratory analysis data may be transformed or many of the observations may be removed leading to varied impact on variables. In such scenario various model evaluation criterion are usually used like cross validation-criterion, bootstrap criterion, and bagging and boosting. Cross validation-criterion divides the observations into two samples; a training sample having n-m observations and a validation sample having m number of observations. The first sample is used to build the model and the second is used for validation. This criterion is used to compare models by evaluating the concerned discrepancy function on the m number of observations. Other criteria are based upon the function of internal discrepancy on a single dataset whereas this method compares predicted and observed values directly. This method can be applied to calculate any distance function. For example, in case of neural networks with quantitative output, the Guassian Discrepancy is for each observation *i* in the validation dataset and for each output *j*.

$$\frac{1}{n}\sum_i\sum_j\left(t_{ij}-o_{ij}\right)^2$$

Where

$$t_{ij} \rightarrow fitted\_output$$
$$o_{ij} \rightarrow observed\_output$$

Bootstrap criterion is based on the idea of reproducing the actual distribution of the population with iterative sampling of the observed sample. This method assumes that the observed sample is the population, for which we build the underlying model *f(x)*. To compare different models, we extract a sample from the untrue population and then can use previous results for model comparison. This is an iterative process, and then we calculate the mean discrepancy of the obtained results. In this way we choose that model which minimizes this discrepancy. The biggest drawback of this method is that this method is computationally intensive.

Bagging and boosting methods are based on the principle of combining the results of more than one web mining investigation. They are very similar to Bayesian model averaging methods. In bagging also called bootstrap aggregation, we take up a sample from the available training dataset. This sample has been taken with replacement. For example this procedure may have *m* number of loops; here *m* depends upon the computational resources available. A web mining technique will be applied on each bootstrapped sample, resulting in a set of estimates for each model. These estimates can then be combined to have a final bagged estimate. The final bagged estimate is the mean of all the estimates for each model. For example for a regression tree can be made fit for *M* samples, and thus producing a fitted value $\hat{y}_i$, for each sample as well as for each observation. So, the bagged estimate can be defined as:

$$\frac{1}{M}\sum_{i=1}^{M}\hat{y}_i$$

For complex models like neural networks this procedure will not change the bias but may change the variance.

Boosting which is little variant of bagging, where model is fitted on several weight versions of dataset. The observation with poorest fit will get the largest weight (J. R. Quinlan, 1996). Many criteria can be used to check the predictive ability of web mining technique. This chapter used cross validation method of model evaluation. In this chapter ten model fitness evaluation criteria like MSE, R-square, R-Square adjusted, condition index, RMSE, number of variables included in the prediction model, modified coefficient of efficiency, F-value, and test of normality has been used for assessing and comparing the performance of the web mining techniques.

To compare the said techniques for their predictive performance the author have chosen three unique datasets. The author have used Marketing, Bank, and Parkinson Tele-Monitoring datasets have been acquired from (Traveor Hastie, Robert Tibshirani, Jerome Friedman, 2009), (Carl Rusmussen 1996), and (UCI, 2014) respectively. The datasets selected for the said purpose have been introduced and their preliminary investigation has been done (see Figure 2). The preliminary investigation throws much light on the type of dataset and facilitates us choosing the right technique for the right kind of dataset. At the very first step data has been introduced stating the number of variables it contains, type/s of variables

Figure 2. Methodology for inter evaluation of factor based techniques

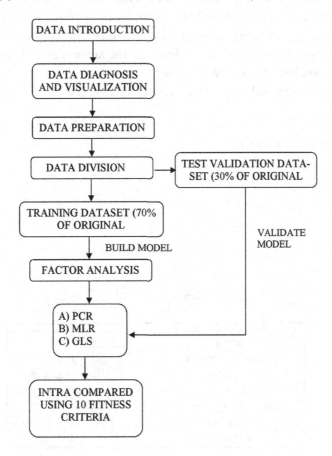

125

it have, missing values it have. This step is followed by data diagnosis and data visualization. In data diagnosis the author take various plots such as partial regression plots, box plots to see how different variables relate with each other and with the dependent variable. Box plots also show the dispersion of the variables (see Figure 3 to 5). Correlation coefficient matrixes have been produced to see the correlation among the input and the output variables. Correlation coefficient matrixes and partial regression plots are not displayed in this chapter due to space limitations.

After preliminary investigation of the individual datasets they have been preprocessed prior to applying three factor based techniques. The preprocessing includes handling missing data, standardizing and scaling the datasets for optimal results. Scaling and standardization is done to fulfill usual assumptions of the linear regression techniques. The author has taken natural log of all the instances of data to make it linear. Otherwise z score normalization has been done for the same purpose (Robert P. Anderson, Daniel Lew, A. Townsend Peterson, 2003). After scaling and standardizing the datasets it is found that all the data sets fulfills usual assumptions of the regression modeling. To ensure linearity of data box plot, histogram, and JB Test (Jarque Bera Test) have been used. This step is considered vital because when non-linear data are fitted to a linear model, solution is usually biased. When linear data are fitted to a non-linear model, solution usually increases the variance. After achieving the data in standard form it is divided into 70:30 ratios as training and test validation set respectively (Myatt J. Glenn, 2007).

For Web mining purpose all regression techniques must satisfy all these usual assumptions and for the reliability of linear regression modeling one can use one more criteria that are the criteria of desirable properties of regression estimator/parameters. These desirable properties are known as BLUE properties i.e., Best, Linear, Unbiased and Efficient. In this study the author has used both stochastic assumptions criteria and BLUE (desirable properties) criteria to check the authenticity of regression modeling. In our study three datasets have been used for web mining to derive inherent characteristics of datasets and four linear regression techniques with their sub modeling have been used.

Figure 3. Box plot of marketing dataset

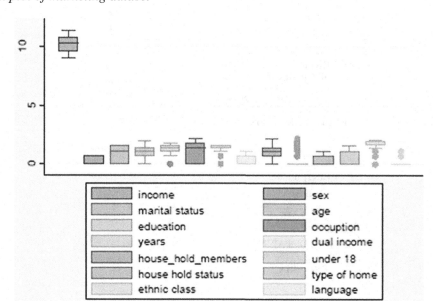

For a more accurate representation of this figure, please see the electronic version of this chapter.

Figure 4. Box plot of bank dataset

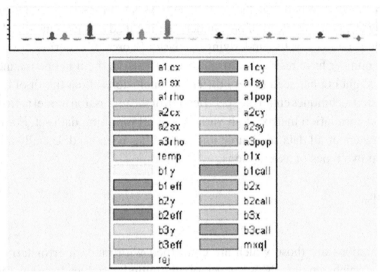

For a more accurate representation of this figure, please see the electronic version of this chapter.

Figure 5. Box plot of Parkinson

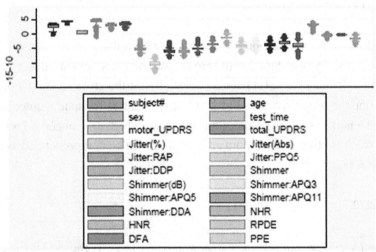

For a more accurate representation of this figure, please see the electronic version of this chapter.

In all linear regression techniques (used in the study) random variable has been found to satisfy all its usual assumptions. For the diagnosis of its normality two criteria have been used one is histogram of μ_i and Jarque-Bera Test. Also is all linear regression a technique of the study linearity has been conformed to the use of natural log of all response and predictor variables of all datasets. There are many different criteria to use to evaluate a statistical data-mining model. So many, in fact it can be a bit mystifying and at times seem like a sporting event where proponents of one criterion are constantly trying to prove it is the best. Every criteria used have different story to tell, so, it is the circumstances that specifies us about the suitability of that criteria. In this study the author has used many model fitness criteria, to evaluate the suitability of the model for the underlying dataset. In a given circumstances one criterion may be better than others but that will change as situations change. Normally it is recommended to use many techniques instead of one, understanding it advantages and disadvantages and then resort to the best one suitable for the underlying scenario. Scores of criterion are trivial deviation of another and a good number have residual sum of squares (RSS) in them in one manner or another. The differences may be slight but can lead to very different conclusions about the fit of a model.

All linear regression techniques entail the specification of the regression model at first. For this purpose the author have used correlation matrix of all variables of all reporting data set. For the linearity of all variables and parameters of all data set double log method has been used. Usually all linear regression models are based on two types of assumptions:

1. Non-Stochastic
2. Stochastic.

Stochastic assumptions are those which are concerned with random error term in the regression model. The variable which captures the influence of all omitted variables from the regression a model.

i. $E(\mu_i) = 0 \rightarrow No\ Biasness$
ii. $\sigma^2_\mu = Constant \rightarrow Homoscedasticity$
iii. $Cov.(\mu_i, \mu_j) = 0 \rightarrow No\ Auto\ Correlation$

Where μ_i is random/stochastic variable? These can be reduced to as $\mu = N(0, \sigma^2_\mu)$. Where random error term should be normally distributed with zero means and constant variance. Changing variance of μ_i in the regression model may cause for heteroscedasticity for the cross-sectional data set of the study. The association among the successive value of μ_i $(1, 2...n)$ causes for spatial autocorrelation for cross-sectional data set. The non-stochastic assumptions are those which are concerned with other part of the regression model, which is other than random error term, It can be comprehended as these assumptions can be comprehended as

$$Y_i = b_0 + b_1x_1 + b_2x_2 + \cdots\cdots + b_nx_n + \mu_i$$

Where Y_i is the total variation, $b_0 + b_1x_1 + b_2x_2 + \cdots\cdots + b_nx_n$ is the explained variation, and μ_i is the non-explained variation. For the purpose of assessment of various statistical web mining techniques the author has used three unique data sets. They should be unique to have a combination of the following characteristics: few predictor variables, many predictor variables, dataset with high multi-collinearity, very redundant variables and presence of outliers. The fundamental condition for general linear regression model is that there is no multi-collinearity among the descriptive variables. This assumption is very important to satisfy otherwise least squares estimators have large variances and become unstable. Therefore, the author chooses biased regression methods for stabilizing the parameter, estimates. Training dataset is used to build the model. The models build are then evaluated on the basis of ten model fitness criteria.

The intra comparison of factor based techniques have been done using parameters like mean square error (MSE), R-square, R-Square adjusted, condition number, root mean square error (RMSE), number of variables included in the prediction model, modified coefficient of efficiency, F-value, and test of normality. For models building and computing the above said ten parameters, the author has used various data mining tools like SPSS 17, XLstat 2009, Stata 10, Unscrambler 10.1, Statgraphics Centurion XVI and MS-Excel 2007.

INTERPRETATION AND RESULTS

Interpretation: On Marketing Dataset

With reference to Figure 6, contains the experimental results of three factor based techniques. With reference to this figure in marketing dataset, the value of R2 and Adj.R2, of maximum likelihood model was found with good explanatory power i.e., 58.9%, which is higher than both PCR and GLS model. Explanatory power value specifies that among all methods of factor analysis, ML model is the one for web mining purpose because almost 59% change in variation in dependent variable was explained by independent variables. So, within factor analysis techniques maximum likelihood model was found best but not up-to the mark. Value of R^2 proposes for using some more regression model. It can also be calculated using the following notations:

$$R^2 = \frac{ESS}{TSS}$$

TSS = Explained Sum Square(ESS)+ Residual Sum Square(RSS)

The Adj. R^2 is maximum again in maximum likelihood. The 58% variation was captured and it explains the overall goodness of fit of the regression model due to use of factor analysis. So, on behalf of first order statistical test (R^2), we can conclude that maximum likelihood model of factor analysis technique is better than multiple regression technique due to explanatory power.

Figure 6. Experiment results

METHOD	R-SQUARE (%AGE)	ADJ. R -SQUARE (% AGE)	MSE	RMSE	MAE	F-VALUE (Df, NO. OF OBSERVTIONS)	CONDITION INDEX	MODIFIED COEFFICIENT OF EFFICIENCY	CRITICAL VALUE OF JB TEST	NUMBER OF VARIABLES
FACTOR ANALYSIS (MARKETING DATASET)										
PCR	58.4	56	0.756	0.869	3.67	323.65 (13, 4819)	12	-6.754	0.665	13
MLR	58.9	57.6	0.775	0.880	3.98	367.45 (13,4819)	18.78	-5.987	0.679	13
GLS	58.7	57.3	0.746	0.860	3.99	386.78 (13,4819)	11	-6.768	0.678	13
FACTOR ANALYSIS (PARKINSON DATASET)										
PCR	63	51	0.456	0.675	0.67	543.5 (19, 4112)	14.87	0.565	0.645	19
MLR	64	54	0.582	0..763	0.66	513.65 (19, 4112)	14.1	0.499	0.598	19
GLS	67	56	0.398	0.63	1.68	665.45 (19, 4112)	12.54	-13.454	0.564	19
FACTOR ANALYSIS (BANK DATASET)										
PCR	74	69	0.643	0.80	0.58	654.45 (34, 3150)	16.86	0.054	0.676	33
MLR	72.8	68.4	0.665	0.815	0.598	675.65 (34, 3150)	16.75	0.055	0.755	33
GLS	71.5	68.2	0.678	0.823	0.612	688.45 (34, 3150)	16.74	0.57	0.544	33

Mean Square Error (MSE) criteria is used for computing un-biasedness and minimum variance property. A minimum MSE estimator will be having smallest MSE, and is defined as: $MSE(\hat{b}) = E(\hat{b}-b)^2$. It can be proved that it is equal to MSE $(\hat{b})$'s $= Var(\hat{b})$'s $+ bias^2 (\hat{b})$

The MSE criteria for un-biasedness and minimum variance were found maximum in case of maximum likelihood model of factor analysis. It signifies that Maximum likelihood MSE is more than all other model's MSE, which further means that under this model of factor analysis of marketing dataset there is more un-biasedness and more variance and is responsible for giving unexpected explanatory power R^2 in marketing dataset.

The comparison all three factor based techniques unexpected MSE for all three which means that under factor analysis all b's are biased but with large variance. Large variance is responsible for high unbiasedness leading to contradictory result under this technique. This forces the author to use alternative measure like RMSE (root mean square error) for this study. RMSE values for these techniques are almost similar. Less variation of RMSE for three factor based models of marketing dataset signifies equal weights for consideration.

The author has used Mean Absolute Error (MAE) to evaluate the predictive performance of different models (Cort J. Willmott, Kenji Matsuura, 2005).

If Y^p be the predicted dependent variable and Y is the actual dependent variable then the MAE can be computed by

$$MAE = \frac{1}{n} \frac{\sum |Y - Y^p|}{Y}$$

In marketing dataset MAE was found less under PCR model, which is less than GLS and maximum likelihood model. MAE value under the PCR model specifies that this model give good prediction results as compared to the other two.

Under factor analysis marketing dataset MAE in all models was found considerably similar but higher than required, therefore we can say factor analysis models for such kind of datasets generate poor prediction performance.

The multi-collinearity index, which is below 100 for factor models in marketing dataset signifies that there is no scope for high multi-collinearity.

In case of maximum likelihood of the same dataset condition number was found lowest than PCR and GLS technique. This means maximum likelihood is better technique to diagnose the effect of multi-collinearity. The high F value in relation to its dF in marketing dataset under GLS model specifies that model is up-to the mark for overall significance.

The prediction power coefficient (modified coefficient of efficiency) has negative values in case of all models of factor analysis on Marketing dataset. The modified coefficient of efficiency reflects that the prediction powers of all the models on Marketing dataset are poor.

Interpretation: On Parkinson's Tele-Monitoring Dataset

For GLS model, the value of R^2 and Adj. R^2 is found to be good and sufficient for explanatory power of the model. No interpolations of observations have been used for computing R^2 and Adj. R^2. The MSE value is low in all the three models of factor analysis but it is the lowest in case of GLS which signifies that GLS technique is better one for the extraction of structural parameters with unbiasness and low variance. RMSE value also shows similar pattern in all the three models as MSE, which signifies the same consideration for unbiasness and variance. The MAE value of GLS model is found higher than the other two models specifying good predictive ability of this model. The modified coefficient of efficiency for getting efficiency in the model was found negative which is not in favour of prediction power of the GLS model.

The multi-collinearity extraction index was found more or less similar in all the three models of factor analysis, which signifies that all are similar as far as diagnosing of multi-collinearity is concerned.

The significance of overall model was found highest in case of GLS, which signifies that overall regression model is better estimated in this model.

Interpretation: On Bank Dataset

Higher value of R^2 and adjusted R^2, in all the three techniques specifies good explanatory power for this dataset. The impact of residual/random error has been minimized which further supports the BLUE properties of regression modeling.

Increasing value of MSE for all models of factor analysis signifies the significance of techniques parameters. The RMSE is also very similar to marketing dataset. It is satisfactory and up-to the mark in all the three techniques.

The similar value of diagnosis index of multi-collinearity in all the techniques specifies their sound capability of identifying multi-collinearity. These methods or techniques yield good and desirable estimates of parameters if and only if when they are fitted to the unique datasets (which are randomly selected). These techniques entail the linearity in parameters and linearity in variables. In our study of three datasets regression models are linear in parameters as well as in variables

With the linear regression model fitted under factor analysis techniques for study, the assumption of least variance of regression model should be satisfied. Out of the three techniques of factor analysis PCR technique is considered as best for least variance and with low effect of multi-collinearity. For large datasets PCR has been found to support results in accordance with theoretical ground in contrast to maximum likelihood which is found to support small datasets like marketing. Theoretically GLS and maximum likelihood techniques of factor analysis are considered to have un-biasedness but with large variances. In our study of three datasets these two also have performed well to satisfy Gauss Markov Theorem (least variance property) than PCR. In all linear techniques factor analysis techniques performed well with least variance of residual and least variance of estimators but this performance differs from one dataset to another dataset.

Intra Comparison of Factor Analysis Models

All the models of factor analysis were found best for Bank dataset. The dataset which consists of more fluctuations in each variable can be estimated for estimators with Factor Analysis models. All the models were found with 70% R^2 and Adjusted R^2, which indicates that these were explaining 70% goodness of fit of regression model for Bank dataset. The biasness parameters and variance parameters are also supporting that PCR, GLS, and Maximum Likelihood were fitted best as the Bank datasets. The overall significance was found high for PCR and Maximum Likelihood methods through F-value, which means the specification error of the regression model for this kind of dataset is low. However all models of

Factor Analysis for all datasets were found to generate normal distribution of residual of all regression model for all datasets, Bank dataset is also one of them.

All the models of Factor Analysis were found with tolerable multi-collinearity with considerable 16 to 17 condition index, which can be removed through the further treatment on the regression model. The modified coefficient of efficiency was also found positive which indicates good prediction power of GLS and PCR model of factor analysis. The ranking of the techniques on the basis of theoretical and studied datasets can be generalized in the Figure 7.

CONCLUSION AND FUTURE WORKS

The techniques under study are supposed to yield good or desirable estimates of parameters if and only if when they are fitted to the unique datasets (which are randomly selected). These techniques necessitate the two conditions need to be satisfied, firstly the linearity in parameters and secondly the linearity in variables. In this study of three datasets the first condition is satisfied for the randomly selected datasets. With first condition being satisfied of regression model fitted under factor analysis techniques for study, the assumption of least variance of regression model should be satisfied. Out of all the factor based techniques, PCR technique is considered as best for least variance and with low effect of multi-collinearity. For large datasets like Bank or Parkinson Tele-monitoring dataset, PCR is also found to support results in accordance to theoretical ground in contrast to maximum likelihood which is suitable for small dataset like marketing. Theoretically GLS and MLR techniques of factor analysis are assumed to have unbiasedness but with large variances. In this study of three datasets, both of them have also performed well to satisfy least variance property than PCR. In all factor based techniques performed well with least variance of residual and least variance of estimators but this performance differs from one dataset to another dataset. This study can be further enhanced by using sufficient condition for forecasting in addition to necessary conditions for forecasting like Theil's inequality coefficient and Janur Quotient.

A systematic measure of the accuracy of the forecasts obtained from an ecoyomepic model has been suggested by (H.Theil, 1966). The Janur Quotient (A. Godd and H.Wold, 1964) has taken into account both the prediction performance of the model in future periods as well as the past periods. The ranking of the techniques on the basis of theoretical and studied datasets can be generalized in the Figure 7.

Figure 7.

ON THE BASIS OF ⟶	THEORITICALLY	STUDIED DATASET
1. *LEAST VARIANCE OF ESTIMATORS*	*PCR and GLS*	*PCR and GLS*
2. *NORMALITY OF DISTRIBUTED VARIANCE OF RESIDUAL*	*PCR and MLR*	*GLS and PCR*
3. *LEAST EFFECT OF MULTICOLLINEARITY*	*PCR and GLS*	*PCR and MLR*
4. *ERROR OF SPECIFICATION*	*GLS and MLR*	*GLS and MLR*
5. *ERROR OF MEASUREMENT*	*GLS and MLR*	*PCR and GLS*

REFERENCES

Abhishek, T., & Chauhan, R.K. (2011). Knowledge Discovery in Databases-An Introduction to Data Mining. New Delhi: Galgotia Publications.

Al-Kassab, M. (2009). A Monte Carlo Comparison between Ridge and Principal Components Regression Methods. *Applied Mathematical Sciences, 3*(42), 2085–2098.

Alvin, R. C. (2002). *Methods of Multivariate Analysis* (2nd ed.). Wiley Interscience.

Amemiya, T. (1985). *Advanced Econometrics*. Cambridge, MA: Harvard University Press.

Anderson, Lew, & Peterson. (2003). Evaluating Predictive Models of Species' Distributions: Criteria for Selecting Optimal Models. *Ecological Modeling, 162,* 211-232.

Belsley, D. A., Kuh, E., & Welsch, R. F. (1980). *Regression Diagnostics: Identifying influential data sources of collinearity*. New York: John Wiley & Sons. doi:10.1002/0471725153

Berry, M. J. A., & Linoff, G. S. (2000). *Mastering Data Mining*. New York: Wiley.

Berson, A., Thearling, K., & Stephen, J. (1999). *Building Data Mining Applications for CRM*. McGraw-Hill.

Camdevyren, H., Demyr, N., Kanik, A., & Keskyn, S. (2005). Use of principal component scores in multiple linear regression models for prediction of Chlorophyll-a in reservoirs. *Ecological Modelling, 181*(4), 581–589. doi:10.1016/j.ecolmodel.2004.06.043

Chipman, J. S. (1979). Efficiency of least squares estimation of linear trend when residuals are autocorrelated. *Econometrica, 47*(1), 115–128. doi:10.2307/1912350

Cochrane, D., & Orcutt, G. H. (1949). Application of Least Squares Relationships Containing Autocorrelated Error Terms. *Journal of the American Statistical Association, 44,* 32–61.

Daniel, L. T. (2005). *Discovering Knowledge in Data*. Wiley Interscience.

Dijkstra, T. (1985). *Latent variables in linear stochastic models: Reflections on maximum likelihood and partial least squares methods* (2nd ed.). Amsterdam, The Netherlands: Sociometric Research Foundation.

Friedman, J. H. (1997). *Data mining and statistics: what is the connection?*. Keynote Speech of the 29th Symposium on the Interface: Computing Science and Statistics, Houston, TX.

Giudici, P. (2003). *Applied Data-Mining: Statistical Methods for Business and Industry*. West Sussex, UK: John Wiley and Sons.

Glenn, M. J. (2007). *Making Sense of Data-A practical guide to exploratory data analysis and data mining. New Jersy*. Wiley-Interscience.

Godd, A., & Wold, H. (1964). *Econometic Model Suideliy*. North Holland.

Hand, D., Mannila, H., & Smyth, P. (2001). *Principles of Data Mining*. Cambridge, MA: MIT Press.

Hastie, T., Tibshirani, R., & Friedman, J. (2009). *The Elements of Statistical Learning-Data Mining, Inference, and Prediction*. Retrieved from http://statweb.stanford.edu/~tibs/ElemStatLearn

Kim, & Mueller. (1978). *Factor analysis: Statistical methods and practical issues*. Beverly Hills, CA: Sage Publications.

Kim, & Mueller. (1978). *Introduction to Factor Analysis-What it is and how to do it*. Sage Publications, Inc.

Kleinbaum, D. G., Kupper, L. L., & Muller, K. E. (1998). *Applied Regression Analysis and Other Multivariate Methods*. Belmont, CA: Duxbury Press.

Little, M. A., McSharry, P. E., Roberts, S. J., Costello, D. A. E., & Moroz, I. M. (2009). Exploiting Nonlinear Recurrence and Fractal Scaling Properties for Voice Disorder Detection. *Biomedical Engineering Online*. PMID:17594480

Marta, B., & Michele, M. (2010). *Maximum Likelihood Estimation of Factor Models on Data Sets With Arbitrary Pattern of Missing Data*. European Central Bank, Working Paper Series, No. 1189.

Pregibon, D. (1997). *Data Mining*. Statistical Computing and Graphics.

Quinlan, J. R. (1996). Bagging, boosting, and C4.5. In *Proc. 13th National Conference on Artificial Intelligence (AAAI'96)*.

Razavi. (2005). *Canonical Correlation Analysis for Data Reduction in Data Mining Applied to Predictive Models for Breast Cancer Recurrence. In Connecting Medical Informatics and Bio-Informatics* (pp. 175–180). ENMI.

Rusmussen, C. (1996). *Website*. Retrieved from http://www.cs.toronto.edu/~delve/data/bank/desc.html

Taneja, A., & Chauhan, R. K. (2011). A Theoretical Framework for Comparison of Data Mining Technique. *International Journal of Advanced Research in Computer Science*, 2(3), 28–33.

Theil, H. (1966). *Applied Economic Forecasting*. North Holland.

UCI-Machine Learning Repository: Center for Machine Learning and Intelligent Systems. (2014). Retrieved from http://archive.ics.uci.edu/ml/datasets.html

Willmott, C. J., & Matsuura, K. (2005). Advantages of the mean absolute error (MAE) over the root mean square (RMSE) in assessing average model performance. *Climate Research*, *30*, 79–82. doi:10.3354/cr030079

ADDITIONAL READING

Daniel, L. T. (2005). *Discovering Knowledge in Data*. Wiley Interscience.

Glenn, M. J. (2007). *"Making Sense of Data-A practical guide to exploratory data analysis and data mining" New Jersy*. Wiley-Interscience.

Goldberg, D. E. (1989). *Genetic Algorithms in Search, Optimization, and Machine Learning*. New York: Addison-Wesley Publishing Company, Inc.

Gujarati, N. Damodar, Sangeetha, (2004) "Basic Econometrics" 4th edition, New York: McGrawHill.

Hand, D., Mannila, H., & Smyth, P. (2001). *Principles of Data Mining*. Cambridge, MA: MIT Press.

Kleinbaum, D. G., Kupper, L. L., & Muller, K. E. (1998). *Applied Regression Analysis and Other Multivariate Methods*. Belmont, California: Duxbury Press.

Lolson, D., and Dursun Delen, (2008) "*Advanced Data Mining Techniques*", Springer, pp. 5-7.

KEY TERMS AND DEFINITIONS

Adjusted R-Square: The improved mathematical measure to penalize those variables which are not useful for prediction purpose. Here the word adjusted means that adjusted for the degree of freedom related with sum of squares entering in the equation of R-Square mentioned above.

Bagging and Boosting: Bagging and boosting methods are based on the principle of combining the results of more than one web mining investigation. They are very similar to Bayesian model averaging methods. In bagging also called bootstrap aggregation, we take up a sample from the available training dataset. Boosting which is little variant of bagging, where model is fitted on several weight versions of dataset. The observation with poorest fit will get the largest weight.

Bias Variance Tradeoff: As the most common method for evaluating the predictive accuracy of the model is MSE. A model with low value of MSE is always preferred. MSE measure combines two other measures i.e., bias and variance: MSE=variance+Bias^2.

Bootstrap Criteria: This method is based on the idea of reproducing the actual distribution of the population with iterative sampling of the observed sample. This method assumes that the observed sample is the population, for which we build the underlying model $f(x)$.

Condition Index: A very important parameter for diagnosis of multicollinearity. Condition index can be computed from the condition number. It is recommended (Belsley, D.A., Kuh, E., and Welsch, R.F., 1980) that a condition number less than 100 specifies no multicollinearity. If the value of condition number is in between 100 and 1000, that means moderate multicollinearity. Condition number more than 1000 signifies serious multicollinearity.

F-Value: Used to check the overall significance of the regression model. It is very similar to T-test. In T-test which is used to find out existence of linear relationship between each predictor variable and the dependent variable. Depending on the number of predictors, separate t-test will be conducted to confirm existence of linear relationship between predictor and the dependent variable.

Mean Adjusted Error (MAE): MAE measure is very similar to RMSE but more natural to RMSE. This measure is the average of errors (difference between predicted and actual value in all the observations; it is the average or prediction error. MAE measure is better than MSE and RMSE measure.

Mean Square Error (MSE): The most common method of evaluating the usefulness of the model for the purpose of prediction. Or in other words MSE of the predictions is the mean of the squares of the difference between the observed values of the predicted variables and the values of the predictor variables that will be predicted by the model.

Modified Coefficient of Efficiency: Used to evaluate the predictive power of the models.

Number of Predictors: How many number of variables included in the regression model determines about the predictive ability of the model.

RMSE: The square root of MSE and is also denoted as standard error. The standard error of estimate (S-value), which is the measure of accuracy of estimates produced by the model, can be computed using MSE.

R-Square: Statistic which is also known as *coefficient of determination*, determines goodness of the regression equation for making predictions. It measures, how well least square regression line fits the observed data.

Test of Normality: For the F-test discussed earlier it is required that the error term should have normal distribution. So, to check normality of the distribution of residual term, some formal test is required.

Section 2
Applications and Analytics

Chapter 6
Application of Conventional Data Mining Techniques and Web Mining to Aid Disaster Management

Akshay Kumar
Birla Institute of Technology, India

Alok Bhushan Mukherjee
Birla Institute of Technology, India

Akhouri Pramod Krishna
Birla Institute of Technology, India

ABSTRACT

Data mining techniques have potential to unveil the complexity of an event and yields knowledge that can create a difference. They can be employed to investigate natural phenomena; since these events are complex in nature and are difficult to characterize as there are elements of uncertainty involved in their functionality. Therefore, techniques that are compatible with uncertain elements can be employed to study them. This chapter explains the concepts of data mining and discusses at length about the landslide event. Further, the utility of data mining techniques in disaster management using a previous work was explained and provides a brief note on the efficiency of web mining in creating awareness about natural hazard by providing refined information. Finally, a conceptual framework for landslide hazard assessment using data mining techniques such as Artificial Neural Network (ANN), Fuzzy Geometric Mean Model (FGMM), etc. were chosen for description. It was quite clear from the study that data mining techniques are useful in assessing and modelling different aspects of landslide event.

DOI: 10.4018/978-1-5225-0613-3.ch006

INTRODUCTION

With advancement in computing technology, there is an exponential rise in the evolution of digital data. From government agencies to private firms, each and every aspect of their working has been shifting to the digital framework. Furthermore, the access of technology has become so easy and user-friendly to different sections of the society that even users from rural areas can easily be seen on various social networking sites. It is not just policies of government agencies that are fueling the growth of digital data, the story of evolution of digital age has its roots in the change of approach in people's way of life; today even a school kid has a social account and an account on social platforms is like an identity for them. Most of the people's significant amount of time passes on computer either working or online shopping etc. It will not be exaggerating if it is said that in coming decades each and every aspect of earth encompassing from human to physical objects will be converted into a data. In fact, with an advent of social networking sites and few government policies, most of the people are already converted into digital identities. Now let the limitation of imagination break, each and every digital identity is further generating a series of data related to them originating from social networking sites, online shopping, health services, travel, or work. That means a trap of million data associated with a digital identity, isn't there is a chance that we can get lost in this data trap! And if that happens, then we can comfortably formulate a hypothesis that we live in a world surrounded by millions of data; however, we are deprived of information, since information requires scientific analysis of data, and if data is not handled with a scientific perspective, then it is just a data which is doomed to die. Therefore, there is an absolute necessity of some technology which can find useful information i.e. knowledge from such a huge data repository and save a user from information loss, so advanced technology like data mining comes into the picture to fill the void created by the fast evolution of data. However, the meaning of knowledge needs to be understood in the right context. The term, 'knowledge' literally represents inference of patterns by processing information that are meaningful and applicable to a decision-making process. At this point, it needs to be outlined that any data sciences ultimately serves the decision-making process. Thus to understand how data sciences work; we need to have a firm understanding of different aspects of the decision-making process. A decision hierarchy is based on alternatives and criteria's, and a closer look at the hierarchy surfaces the fact that criteria's are conditions postulated by the available data. Further, if the data is not processed and refined properly then, the whole process would be dependent on the erroneous information that can lead the results into a wrong direction.

The decision-making process is not just about data cleansing and refinement; it also requires formulation of appropriate conditions that can help to simulate the cognitive aspects of a decision-making process which finally assures precise decision making. Now it needs to be understood that we are not just surrounded by massive digital data, but there is always a need to come across of some decision-making for survival in this world. However it may look superficial theory at one glance, but digging deep will ensure the truth in this hypothesis. That means we just do not need to identify the data that are useful in our decision-making process, but also, there is a requirement of mechanism that can transform the data into a form that can be used for the processing that we call, a transformation of data. Moreover, there are many factors that are responsible and driving factors for origination and evolution of event, and therefore, to extract any meaningful aspect out of an event, we need a firm understanding of that event. If we have an in and out knowledge of an event then only a clear set of steps can be designed to derive information from that event; otherwise, extraction of meaningful information would be imprecise and inaccurate. A complete understanding of an event; be it a social or economic phenomenon or an event occurring in an earth system brings our attention to one absolute fact that there is an enormous amount of complexity involved in their occurrence and sustenance, their evolution is not just a mere of chance. Subsequently, a linear dimension view of the event will not be able to put off the cover from the actual reasons for their birth and growth. There is more to their growth process. It can never be out rightly rejected that there can be many external factors that are not in the widespread realm influence an event in a significant way. Internal factors or we can call it direct causal factors for the occurrence of an event can be identified, and can be used in modelling and simulation very comfortably, but the inclusion of external factors or indirect factors are not so easy for comprehensive studies. They need a proper framework for their integration and processing; otherwise, the interpretation of theirs in a study can go another way around and can give wrong impressions about the event. It should be explicitly mentioned here that internal factors point to the well-perceived directions, and, therefore, their role is significant in those events that work in a one to one mapping that we term as a one-dimensional event. However behavior of external factors are not predictable, their influence on an event can be positive or negative and consequently, they require to be studied in a contextual view rather in an absolute way. We briefed about the nature of events i.e. linear or non-linear and the influence of internal or external factors on the events. However, the need for this discussion was not put forth. There is a need to understand the reasons behind the briefing on nature of events and causal factors. The answer to this question will remove the clutter from the need and significance of data sciences. The questions on the need and scope of data sciences have answers rooted in the complexities of events. We need to understand events to understand precisely the various dimension of data sciences.

Data mining can be defined in various ways, but if put in a straight way, it refers to the process of extraction of output from a set of inputs. However the output must be meaningful in the context of some objective (Weiss & Davison, 2010). It can also be thought of as a process of finding models for data where models can be formed from any of the domains ranging from statistical, machine learning techniques to visualization approaches (Rajaraman & Ullman, 2014). Primarily, it can be represented as a function i.e. a rule that establishes a relationship between raw input and output of the process. There are some steps that need to be followed by the raw data sets to extract meaningful information. Later in the chapter, the steps required to be followed in data mining process will be discussed in detail. Han and Kamber, 2006 argued that the term 'data mining' is not a proper term that fails to reflect the data mining process in its true spirit. Instead of the term data mining, knowledge mining from data should be used as an objective of any data mining process is to discover knowledge from the data. There are also other terms that are used for data mining process, such as knowledge extraction, pattern analysis, etc. Zaki and Meira (2014) highlighted the fact that the technology, i.e. data mining represents a set of algorithms that are employed to understand the intrinsic characteristics of data, and then further establish the relationship among the data to extract knowledge. Further, the fact was insisted that data mining is just a step in the knowledge discovery process. The knowledge discovery process consists of preprocessing and post processing stages. In the preprocessing step, tasks such as data cleaning, extraction, data fusion, and data reduction are involved. While post processing stage focuses on the formation of the hypothesis, and selection of model and its interpretation. The data mining process consists of the steps such as data cleaning, data integration, data selection, data transformation, data mining, pattern evaluation, and knowledge presentation (Han & Kamber, 2006). Data cleaning refers to the process of removing inconsistencies from the raw data. It is entirely possible that raw data contains outliers that are anomalous and does not represent the normal pattern of the data. In that case, it is must to remove all inconsistencies and normalize the data; otherwise, it would affect the accuracy of the results derived from the raw data. Then data integration phase combines data from different sources so that various dimensions of data can be included in the study. Then the relevant data for the analysis are selected in the data selection phase since it is likely that there could be few dimensions of data that are not required in the concerned study and so, needs to be removed. Data transformation stage of the data mining process transforms the data into an appropriate form for application of data mining algorithms. The data need to be compatible with the algorithm, and, therefore, it is required to transform the data into a compatible form. Next step i.e. data mining corresponds to the application of appropriate data mining technique to extract knowledge from the base data. There are different techniques ranging from conventional statistical techniques to soft computing technique employed for data mining tasks. However, the technique for a data mining task needs to be chosen with caution. For a certain task, the compatibility and accuracy of different data mining techniques may differ. For example, if there is an event that consists of an element of uncertainty and has incomplete data set, then conventional statistical techniques should not be applied for mining useful information from the data set. Instead, techniques that can work with an incomplete data set and are effective in an uncertain environment should be employed in data mining tasks. Having applied the data mining techniques, the patterns reflecting the desired pattern needs to identify so that the knowledge can be established in proper form. Furthermore mined knowledge needs to be represented in an effective way to enable the user to access the information easily.

Finally, there is a need to understand as rightly mentioned before; we now are in a digital era where most of the existing entities on the earth, somehow, have a numeric identifier with a strong presence in the cyber space. Subsequently, the need of effective web mining is inevitable. So we need robust data mining methods that can handle extensive data, and its complexity as well, otherwise, the death of the meaning of a digital identity is imminent. But the power of cyberspace cannot be ignored; an enormous amount of information can be uploaded or retrieved from the web. For example, the disaster management authorities can be present on the web with excellent information regarding the real-time data on hazards across the world. Firstly the complexity involved in the understanding of natural hazards is possible with the application of robust data mining methods. Next with the application of content mining, the associative patterns prevailing in the natural hazard data can be provided to the end users which ultimately helps retrieval of more precise information about the natural hazards. Content mining is one of the web mining techniques. For example, other web mining techniques are web structural mining and the web usage mining. In the case of disaster management practices, the content mining will be more useful than the other techniques of web mining.

Landslides are designated as the movement of the rock masses, earth or debris down a mountain slope and contain a broad range of motions whereby flowage, sliding, rock falls and subsidence under the influence of gravitational force. It includes almost all varieties of mass movements on hill slopes topples and debris flows that encompass little or no true sliding (Varnes, 1984). Some landslides are rapid, occurring within seconds, whereas others may take hours, weeks, or even longer to develop. Among the various natural hazards, landslides are the most widespread and destructive hazard. It takes the life of peoples and damage property and natural resources (land, vegetation, soil, etc.) and also hamper developmental projects (bridges, roads, communication lines, etc.) in the area. Landslides frequently occur in areas prone to earthquakes and tectonic activities. The necessary step for assessment and identification of hazard-prone areas based on the degree of real and potential threat. The degree of the landslide problem gets worse with increased urban expansion and change in land use, constituted 4.89% of the natural disasters that occurred worldwide during the years 1990 to 2005 (EM-DAT, 2007). It has been estimated that an average damage caused by landslides in the Himalayan range damage more than US$ 1 billion and also causing more than 200 deaths every year, that considered as 30% of such types of losses occurring all over the world (EMDAT, 2010; Naithani, 1999). According to the database that created by the Centre for Research on Epidemiology of Disasters indicated that Landslides and related processes have killed over 61,000 people the world over in the period between A.D. 1900 and A.D. 2009 (EMDAT, 2010; Pardeshi, Autade, & Pardeshi, 2013).

In the mountainous terrain such as the Himalayas, landslides are the most damaging natural hazards (Figure 1). The Himalayan terrain is highly vulnerable to landslides due to complex geological setting combined with seismic activity, heavy rainfall, varying slopes and relief along with ever increasing hu-

Figure 1. Location map of field photographs shows (a) landslides scars along roadside (b) frontal view of landslide (c) Closer view of landslide in Himalayan terrain

man interference in the ecosystem. The study of landslides has drawn worldwide attention mainly due to increasing awareness of the socio-economic impact of landslides, as well as the increasing pressure of urbanization on the mountain environment (Aleotti & Chowdhury, 1999). Although it is yet difficult to predict a landslide event in space and time, an area may be divided into near-homogeneous domains and ranked (Very high, high, moderate and low) according to degrees of potential hazard due to mass movements (Varnes, 1984).

In recent past there are so many researchers works and adopted different approaches for landslide mapping, hazard zonation and susceptibility mapping (Chung, Fabbri, & Westen, 1995; Gupta & Joshi, 1990; Mehrotra, Sarkar, Kanungo, & Mahadevaiah, 1996; Sarkar, Kanungo, & Mehrotra, 1995). They used different techniques for assignment of numerical weights to the landslide causative factors. Champatiray, Dimri, Lakhera, & Sati, (2007) utilized various geo-environmental parameters such as drainage, lithology, structure, slope, land use, aspect, road excavation, vegetation and vegetation cover can be modeled using information method, weights of evidence modelling and fuzzy logic to prepare landslide hazard zonation maps in the Himalayan region. It indicated that around 60-65% of known landslide was in the high hazardous area. Carrara, Guzzetti, Cardinali, & Reichenbach, (1999) exhibited that the central issue in forecasting landslide or other geological hazards is the identification and collection of the relevant predictors whose nature, character and role will vary depending on the type of disaster and geological, geomorphological and climatic setting of the region affected by the extreme event. Hong, Adler, & Huffman, (2006) revealed that proper assessment of landslide hazard requires an understanding of both where and under what conditions landslides may occur, which requires knowledge of the causative factors for landslides. But decision makers faces a difficulties due to the inconsistency of the data and then they employed a Multi-Criteria Evaluation (MCE) (Saaty, 1994). Yalcin, (2008) performed GIS-based landslide susceptibility mapping using analytical hierarchy process (AHP) and bivariate statistics in Ardesen (Turkey) and carried out a comparison of the results and confirmations. The AHP method gained a wide application in site selection, suitability analysis, regional planning, and landslide susceptibility analysis (Ayalew & Yamagishi, 2005; Barredo, Benavides, Hervas, & Van Westen, 2000; Komac, 2006; Yalcin, 2008). Several authors (Lee & Pradhan, 2006) used frequency ratio model and found reasonably satisfactory results.

MAIN FOCUS OF THE CHAPTER

Functioning of society involves multidimensional and non-linear variables. Therefore, the nature of the interaction between society and environment has complex characteristics. The dynamicity of interaction between societal phenomena and environment can lead to unpredictable consequences. It is a well-accepted fact that the growth of society is dependent upon economic activities. However, variables required to strengthen economic activities can have an adverse effect from the perspective of the environment. For example, an establishment of long-term infrastructure needed to strengthen the economic base of society and consequently play a larger role in the rise of a nation's economy. However unplanned infrastructural establishments as a consequence of anthropogenic activities can be very devastating for environmental sanity. Consequently, disasters' such as urban flood, flash flood, river flood, rainfall induced landslide, earthquake-induced landslide, and earthquakes can cause huge human and monitory losses' across the globe. Furthermore, the aftermath consequences of any disaster are an absolute disaster for any society.

The absence of proper mitigation measures to handle a disaster can leave a long-term negative impact on the sanity of the whole ecosystem.

Any geographical phenomenon or geological phenomenon is a consequence of a combination of geographic or geologic variables respectively. The pattern of the combination of geographic or geologic factors shapes the intensity of the consequence of combination. The proper knowledge of the nature of influencing variables can enable an analyst to understand the significance of the influencing variables in shaping an event. Moreover, the aggregation of the significant variables can output a range of possibilities. Therefore, extraction of the exact required information from a range of possibilities is an absolute necessity. Otherwise, despite having a precise understanding of variables that can trigger a geographic or geologic event, the possible threat of a disaster can be missed. Consequently, mitigation measures to counter a disaster cannot be adequately taken up and therefore, 'huge losses' are inevitable. Therefore, effective disaster management practices need an understanding of influencing variables that can cause a disaster. Then the knowledge of methods to generate the integrated impact of controlling factors and finally, a precise understanding of the science of techniques that can help to extract the useful and valuable information from the final result of the combination of influencing factors.

The present book chapter begins with the elementary description of the need and significance of data mining. Especially it focuses on the utility of data mining techniques in natural sciences and precisely in the realm of disaster management. It explains the data mining process that needs to be employed to infer required information from a set of data. It further goes on explaining different techniques of data mining such as clustering, association, sequential analysis, regression, decision tree, rule induction, neural networks, and nearest neighborhood classification. Further, it adequately provides the description of evolving spatial data mining, which is significant in geospatial analysis. Then it moved on to describe the meaning of disaster management and different stages that need to be followed to perform disaster management such as planning, mitigation, recovery, and response. Prior explanation of disaster management, various types of disaster that can strike and their probable causal factors are explained at length in the proposed chapter. For example, the adequate description of a landslide is provided. Moreover, different types of landslides along with the factors that are responsible for landslide i.e. rainfall, slope, aspect, elevation, geomorphology, and geologic factors are briefed in the proposed chapter. Finally, the landslide was chosen as an event for the demonstration of the significance and utility of data mining techniques in the studies pertaining to natural sciences, and especially, in disaster management.

WEB MINING TECHNIQUES

As discussed earlier in the introduction section, techniques under the realm of data mining are employed to understand, and extract the hidden patterns existing in the dataset. Web mining can be understood as the process of transformation, and application of data mining techniques to retrieve patterns from data in the cyber space which can be termed as web data. The web mining process consists of different phases, such as web content mining, web structure mining, and web usage mining. The need of web mining is a consequence of the huge evolution of digital data due to an exponential growth of e-commerce transactions. Beginning with a brief description of the one of the phases of web mining process i.e. web content mining.

The web content mining refers to the process of deriving productive information from the content of web pages, and the content of web pages may consists of text, images, audio, video etc. The web mining can further be classified into different classes' such as web page content mining and search result mining. There are different techniques available for web content mining, such as unstructured data mining techniques, structured data mining techniques, semi-structured data mining techniques, and multimedia data mining techniques. While web structure mining attempts to explain the structure of the content of the web page, this type of web mining can further be categorized into two broad classes' such as inter page structure and intra page structure. In the inter page structure, there must have some connection between the pages. On the other hand, intra page web mining corresponds to the situation when links are present only within the web page. Finally, the last phase of the web mining process is the web usage mining that explains the process required for discovering the access patterns of the users from the server logs. It is hugely dependent on the application of various data mining techniques for analysis of search patterns.

Primarily, the web usage mining comprised of three different steps. It begins with the preprocessing of the data, derivation of a pattern from the refined data, and finally performing analysis on the derived patterns. The first step which is preprocessing of the data is of utmost significance. The processed and refined data helps in extracting useful patterns from the data. Further, it helps in improving the algorithm used for the web usage mining. It needs to be understood that the data which needs to be preprocessed are of different types, and access of these data are from different websites which further complicates the process.

LANDSLIDES: TRIGGERING FACTORS, EFFICACY AND SIGNIFICANCE OF DATA MINING TECHNIQUES

Causal Factors of Landslides

Landslides are the result of complex interaction among several factors, primarily involving geological, geomorphological and meteorological factors (Sarkar & Kanungo, 2004). In India, almost 0.49 million square meters or 15% of land area is vulnerable to landslide hazard. Out of this, 0.098 million square meters is located in the northeastern region and rest 80% spread over Himalayas, Nilgiris, Ranchi Plateau and Eastern and Western Ghats (GSI, 2006). The Lesser Himalaya Zone is a tectonically active region characterized by a very complex structure of thrust sheets (Kumar & Pande, 1972).

The factors that contribute in landslides are geology of the region, stress in situ, groundwater and precipitation, seismic activity, volcanic eruption and human activity, etc. (Table 1). It can occur as a ground failure of river bluffs, cut-and-fill failures that may accompany highway and building excavations, a collapse of mine-waste piles, and slope failures associated with quarries and opencast mines. Landslides due to groundwater conditions usually involve areas of low relief and small slope gradients in lakes and reservoirs or offshore marine settings. A landslide occurrence in a zone depends on the combination of these factors. The terrain factors such as slope, aspect, relief, lithology, geological structure, land use, lineament and drainage density, geomorphology, etc., are necessary for a landslide to occur in an area (Carrara et al., 1991; Nagarajan, Roy, Vinodkumar, & Khire, 1998; Saha, Gupta, & Arora, 2002). If terrain factors are favorable, e.g., steep slope, unconsolidated rock, high lineament density, etc., then the area is vulnerable to landslide (Jade & Sarkar, 1993; Pachauri & Pant, 1992). Landslides can trigger by rainfall, steep slopes due to flooding or excavation, earthquakes, snowmelt and other natural causes

Table 1. List of caused factors of landslides (USGS, 2004)

1. Geological Causes • Plastic week material • Sensitive material • Collapsible material • Weathered material • Sheared material • Jointed or fissured material • Adversely oriented mass discontinuities (including bedding, schistosity, cleavage) • Adversely oriented structural discontinuities (including faults, unconformities, flexural shears, Sedimentary contacts) • Contrast in permeability and its effects on ground water contrast in stiffness (stiff, dense material over plastic materials)
2. Geomorphological Causes • Tectonic uplift • Volcanic uplift • Glacial rebound • Fluvial erosion of the slope toe • Wave erosion of the slope toe • Glacial erosion of the slope toe • Erosion of the lateral margins • Subterranean erosion (solution, piping) • Deposition loading of the slope or its crest • Vegetation removal (by erosion, forest fire, drought)
3. Physical Processes • Intense, short period rainfall • Rapid melts of deep snow • Prolonged high precipitation • Rapid drawdown following floods, high tides or breaching of natural dams • Earthquake • Volcanic eruption • Breaching of crater lakes • Thawing of permafrost • Freeze and thaw weathering • Shrink and swell weathering of expansive soils
4. Man-Made Processes • Excavation of the slope or its toe • Loading of the slope or its crest • Drawdown (of reservoirs) • Irrigation • Defective maintenance of drainage systems • Water leakage from services (water supplies, sewers, storm water drains) • Mining and quarrying (open pits or underground galleries) • Vegetation removal (deforestation) • Artificial vibration (including traffic, pile driving, heavy machinery) • Creation of dumps of very loose waste

Source: http://pubs.usgs.gov/fs/2004/3072/pdf/fs2004-3072.pdf

as well as human-made causes, such as overgrazing by cattle, terrain cutting and filling and excessive development (Baum, Savage, & Godt, 2002; Dai, Lee, & Nagi, 2002). The impact of these disasters is increasing in less developed regions (Hong et al., 2006).

Types of Investigation Methods

Landslides are considered one of the most horrible natural threats worldwide. The first step to execute quick and safe mitigation strategic planning are the identification of landslides prone and landslide hazard zonation areas. The detailed and consistent knowledge regarding expected frequency, history, character and magnitude of mass movement, triggers in the region is an essential input for mitigation of disasters caused by landslides (Baronˇ & Supper, 2013). Landslide hazard zonation (LHZ) is a process of ranking different parts of an area according to the degrees of actual or potential hazards from landslides (Guzzetti, Carrara, Cardinali, & Reichenbach, 1999; Varnes, 1984). Therefore, the LHZ of an area becomes important, whereby the areas classified as different LHZ ranging from a very low zone, low zone, moderate zone, high and very high hazard zone (Arora, Das Gupta, & Gupta, 2004). Landslides cause enormous loss of life and property every year in mountainous areas. In such regions, landslide hazard zonation is very necessary to delineate the disaster prone areas. So, it is important to be able to delineate landslide hazard areas to develop suitable land-use plans. It is important for future developmental planning and organization of various disaster mitigation programs.

The parameters that contribute directly or indirectly to landslides include lithology and structure, landform, slope, aspect, relief, vegetation cover, climate and human activities. The list of investigation methods shown in Table 2.

The most common investigation methods applied at the monitored sites were the geological mapping, engineering geological and geomorphic techniques. In the recent years, remote sensing technology coupled with global positioning system (GPS) is very much used for identification of landslide hazard zones. Satellite data and aerial photographs have been proved their importance regarding landslide inventory mapping both at the local and regional level. Geospatial technology can also use as an effective aid in any natural hazard investigation, as well as for the purpose of environmental planning.

Table 2. List of investigation method

1. Preliminary Work • Study of archival materials • Terrain reconnaissance • Questionnaire to local people • Conceptual engineering geological model
2. Landslide Investigation • Engineering geological mapping • Longitudinal and cross sections • Boreholes, trial pits, rock and soil sampling, field tests, geophysics • Laboratory tests
3. Depth of Rupture Surface
4. Monitoring • Monitoring of deformation • Monitoring of hydrogeological features, Groundwater level and pore pressure fluctuation, spring yield • Measurement of stress • Indirect methods- geophysics
5. Method of Prediction • Remote sensing and GIS technology • prediction of mechanisms and dimension of failure • Time prediction

Source: http://www.geology.cz/projekt681900/vyukovematerialy/6_Methods_of_landslide_investigation.pdf

Investigation Techniques

The purpose of landslide hazard or susceptibility mapping is to highlight the local distribution of potentially unstable slopes based on a comprehensive study of the factors responsible for a landslide. The generation of landslide hazard zonation maps depends upon the integration of spatial database of various geo-environmental parameters from different sources. The spatial analysis and integration of spatial data are done using landslide hazard zonation models. There are different types of LHZ models developed by various workers out of which the following have been used for the preparation of landslide hazard zonation maps:

1. Analytical Hierarchy Process (AHP)

There are different variables responsible for the occurrence of landslides. Therefore, it is necessary to understand the relative contribution of each variable in triggering landslides (Pardeshi et al., 2013). Consequently, techniques such as Analytic Hierarchy Process (AHP) can be instrumental in the investigations about landslides. Since the AHP method is useful in determining the relative importance of the causal factors for the landslides (Saaty, 1980). The AHP technique is a multi-objective method that effectively scales the importance of each causal factor regarding their significance in triggering the landslide event (Yalcin, 2008). The recent years have witnessed a significant application of the AHP method in landslide susceptibility investigations that was originally developed by Saaty (1980) (Barredo et al., 2000; Komac, 2006). The application of the AHP technique ensures the accuracies in the relative judgments' of the knowledge-based weightings by eliminating the possible inconsistencies in knowledge-based weights (Palcic & Lalic, 2009).

2. Fuzzy Geometric Mean Model

The Analytic Hierarchy Process has been popular in scaling the relative importance of different variables in a study. However it fails to map the inaccuracies associated with the users' perception towards a research problem, and therefore, AHP sometimes may fail miserably in a decision-making problem (Deng, 1999). Furthermore, it needs to be considered that decision-making process confronts uncertainty, and therefore, techniques from fuzzy logic should be considered in the studies (Mikhailov & Tsvetinov, 2004). The limitation as mentioned above of Analytic Hierarchy Process (AHP) in handling the inconsistencies involved in a user's perception can be reduced with the help of a soft computing approach such as fuzzy geometric mean model. In this technique, the first step is to generate a pairwise comparison matrix. The next step is to convert this crisp pair-wise comparison matrix into fuzzy pair-wise comparison matrix. From this fuzzy pair-wise comparison matrix, using the geometric mean method, triangular fuzzy numbers are obtained. Triangular Fuzzy Numbers (TFNs) are commonly used in applications. It is overall accepted that the matrix formulation of a mathematical formula gives additional facility to handle/study the problem. A Triangular Fuzzy Number (TFN) is a fuzzy set that consist of three parameters. Each of the parameters corresponds to a quantified linguistic value with a degree of membership value. A triangular fuzzy number A is defined by three real numbers expressed as A = (aL; aM; aU). The Fuzzy Geometric Mean applies for the triangular fuzzy number through symmetric triangular membership function. By the defuzzification of these triangular fuzzy numbers, the priority vectors for each factor are obtained. These priority vector values are later used for the generation of landslide hazard zonation maps.

3. Frequency Ratio Analysis Model

The frequency ratio model employs probabilistic concepts and is simple to use (Lee & Dan, 2005; Yilmaz, 2009). The Frequency Ratio Model has been used in the past to understand the relationship between landslide occurrence and the causal factors for landslides and has been used in various studies (Lee & Pradhan, 2006). For this method, the primary inputs include the total number of pixels in any class, the percentage of those pixels, the number of landslides in that particular class and the percentage of the landslide in that particular category. The frequency ratio was then computed as the ratio between the rates of the landslide to the percentage of pixels for that particular class. The value of the ratio greater than one corresponds to the significant correlation between landslide occurrence and the causal factors for landslides; otherwise, the relationship is not as significant (Lee & Talib, 2005). So, based on the FR values, the relation of each class of a factor with landslide occurrence can be evaluated. These frequency ratio values are later used for the generation of landslide hazard zonation maps.

4. Artificial Neural Network (ANN)

Artificial Neural Network (ANN) represents an array consisting of elementary processors (Park et al., 1991) It is a non-linear model and proved to be more efficient in landslide hazard assessment (Bui, Pradhan, Lofman & Dick, 2012; Pradhan & Lee 2009). Krishna and Kumar, (2013) performed landslide hazard assessment using ANN. It was outlined in the investigation that landslides occur due to the combination of interrelated factors that are non-linear in characteristics, and therefore, techniques such as ANN can be instrumental in landslide studies (Ercanglu, 2005; Krishna & Kumar, 2013). It further was highlighted that ANN is good in handling uncertainties because of its flexible network architecture. Furthermore, it can solve classification and pattern recognition problem at ease. There are many methods available under the ANN umbrella, such as Multilayer Perceptron Problem (MLP), Support Vector Machines (SVM), etc.

The architecture of the ANN consists of input layers, hidden layers, and output layers. Furthermore, the input layers are associated with the initial weights that may keep on changing in different iterations until the desired output comes. To facilitate the whole process, bias, activation functions, and appropriate learning algorithms are being used to tackle problems about classification and feature extraction problems. Architectures used for the aforementioned problems are feed-forward architectures such as Multilayer Perceptron Problem (MLP); otherwise, recurrent architectures can also be used. The most important thing that needs to be taken care of in the ANN architecture is the decision regarding learning algorithms. There are different learning algorithms are available in the literature, such as supervised learning algorithm, unsupervised learning algorithm, and hybrid learning algorithms. The selection of learning algorithm depends on the context. In one instance, a supervised learning algorithm can be used, while the same supervised learning algorithm cannot be utilized in some other instance. A typical multi-layer feed-forward network has shown in Figure 2 along with input, hidden, and output layers.

5. Logistic Regression (LR) Analysis

The application Logistic Regression (LR) analysis comes handy in assessing the significance of predictor variables on the final outcome the model (Pardeshi et al., 2013; Wang & Sassa, 2005). There are different types of logistic regression analysis. For example, there are binary logistic regression analysis and

Figure 2. Basics elements of an ANN (a) An Artificial Neuron (b) Mathematical representation of an artificial neuron
(Saha 2003)

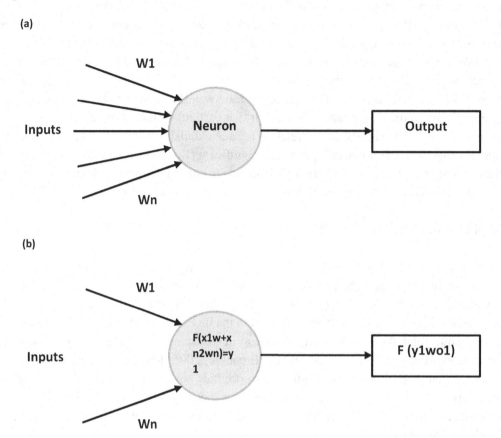

multinomial logistic regression analysis. In binary logistic regression analysis, the dependent variable is dichotomous; while independent variable can be of any type. On the other hand, multinomial logistic regression consists of a dependent variable which has more than two classes. In the studies related to landslide susceptibility mapping, the logistic regression model was found to be instrumental in assessing the relationship between distributions of landslides with the independent variables. The independent variables which are generally used for the relative studies are slope angle, slope aspect, lithology and land use (Ayalew & Yamagishi, 2005). The application of the logistic regression model outputs the model statistics and coefficients. The aforementioned outputs of the model are significant in assessing susceptibility. It was observed that positive coefficients reflect the high possibilities of landslide event. (Guzzetti et al., 1999).

6. Discriminant Analysis Method

In the landslide hazard assessment investigations, the discriminant analysis method is one of the most common methods used in the available literature. The application of discriminant analysis method assures the accurate determination of the impact of independent factors on the occurrence of landslides.

Here the independent factors consist of landslide causal factors (Lee et al., 2008; Pardeshi et al., 2013). For example, the independent factor that is slope is categorized into two classes that landslide-free and landslide affected classes regarding its significance in triggering landslides. Furthermore, the Standardized Discriminant Function Coefficient (SDFC) was computed for each of the independent variables. The SDFC correspond to the relative importance of each causal factors in landslide occurrence event (Pardeshi et al., 2013). It was observed from the investigations that high coefficient variables are strongly associated with the landslide event. In past, there have been many investigations on landslide susceptibility using discriminant analysis across the world (Guzzetti et al., 2005; Calvello, Cascini, & Mastroianni, 2013).

7. Weighted Overlay Method

Weighted overlay method is one of the simplest methods used for combinatorial analysis. It falls under the domain of bivariate statistical analysis. In this method, the weights are associated with the causal factors on the basis of their significance in triggering landslides (Pardeshi et al., 2013). In a recent past, there were many researchers (Panikkar & Subramaniyan, 1997; Sarkar et al., 1995) who employed weighted overlay method for delineation of Landslide Hazard Zonation (LHZ). The method primarily assigns weights to the different significant factors responsible for landslides, and then, the various factors are combined to get the final outcome of the process that corresponds to the possibilities of landslides. Panikkar and Subramaniyan, (1997) performed landslide hazard assessment with the help of GIS and weighted overlay method. The study area where the aforementioned method was demonstrated is Dehradun and Mussoorie, the Uttarakhand State, India. The results of the investigation show rapid deforestation. It further was observed that rapid urbanization has caused landslides in the study area. This primary utility Weighted Overlay Method (WOM) is to assess the relative importance of factors responsible for landslides (Cardinali et al., 2002; Preuth, Glade, & Demoulin, 2010; Pardeshi et al., 2013). In the Weighted Overlay Method (WOM), relative assessment of the significance of the causal factors and their quantification is done using the bi-variate discriminant function (Nagarajan et al., 2000; Pardeshi et al., 2013).

8. Rainfall Threshold Model

Rainfall threshold model is also a widely used model for landslide investigations. Here the rainfall threshold corresponds to the just amount of rainfall necessary to trigger landslides (Varnes, 1984). There are different parameters that required for the design of rainfall threshold model. For example; cumulative rainfall, antecedent rainfall, rainfall intensity, and rainfall duration are such factors that generally considered as input for the Rainfall threshold model. It has been observed that the critical rainfall threshold model is dependent on many factors, such as properties of soil, slope angle, upslope drainage, a bulk density of wet soil, and water density. From past investigations, rainfall thresholds have been determined that can trigger shallow landslides, and this information had been used in the development of early warning systems for landslides. Chelboard et al., (2006) used cumulative rainfall threshold in the landslide investigation. They successfully used the information for prediction of landslides in Seattle, Washington, USA. Further the results of the model validated by historical records of rainfall and landslide events. The results found to be ninety percent accurate. Chang and Chiang (2009) also performed investigation in the line of landslide studies. In their study, an integrated model combining deterministic, statistical and rainfall threshold mode for the landslide susceptibility was proposed, and the model was demonstrated for the typhoon-induced landslides in Taiwan. There were more investigations on the utility of Rainfall Threshold Model for the landslide studies that confirmed the efficacy of the model in assessing and predicting landslides (Gabet et al., 2004).

The models discussed above provide different data incorporation techniques and, therefore, have their own merits and demerits. The AHP and the fuzzy geometric mean method are good in landslide hazard zonation in areas where adequate data on landslide is not available, and the decision maker has a good knowledge of the terrain conditions and parameters. However, the technique such as frequency ratio analysis model should be used to assess the significance of different factors in the eruption of landslides.

Significance of Geospatial Techniques in Disaster Management

The Remote Sensing (RS), Geographic Information System (GIS) and Global Navigation Satellite System (GNSS) techniques are valuable tools for risk and disaster management due to their broad applicability (Thomas et al., 2007). These techniques and data is very important in natural disaster management, and discussions regarding the actual condition of the applications and methodologies permit the identification of gaps in usability and opportunities to facilitate data use (Manfré et al., 2012). The geospatial technology and GNSS tools are often used in applications for disaster management in pre and post-disaster activities. Pre-disaster applications are associated with mitigation and preparedness efforts. Mitigation embraces the activities that reduce the vulnerability of societies to the effect of a disaster and also focused the element exposed to the threat while preparedness refers to activities that facilitate preparation for responding to a disaster when it occurs (Mansourian et al., 2005; Manfré et al., 2012). Post-disaster applications are related to response and recovery efforts. The response is related to the immediate and short-term effects of a disaster while recovery refers to activities that restore communities to pre-disaster conditions, such as reconstruction (Mansourian et al., 2005). The mitigation and preparedness associated with natural hazards (landslide, flood, etc.). It is a part of the planning of land use/land cover (LU/LC) studies and identification of hazard prone areas that is highly vulnerable. The GIS technique is used to analyze, manipulation, visualization, combination and storing the data related to the hazard. It allowed comprehension and the identification of standards and relationships between variables. In GIS environment the topographical, geological and climatological information along with socio-economic data combined for risk assessment to provide planning and preparedness.

Remote Sensing data derived from satellite provides analysis of geospatial products in all types of natural disasters within a relatively short period. There is a diverse and growing constellation of remote-sensing satellites, and studies of natural disasters usually explore different types of images with different characteristics (spatial, spectral, radiometric and temporal resolutions) and different image processing methodologies. Satellite imageries and aerial photographs allow us to map the variability of terrain properties, such as geology, water, vegetation both in space and time. Satellite imageries also provide a synoptic overview and very useful environmental information for a wide range of scales, from continents to details of few meters.

Floods are state of high water flow that submerges the land. Kovar and Natchtnebel (1995) used the combination of morphological data (extracted from DEMs) for mapping flood. They prepare a hydrologic model by using GIS tools. The hydrologic models used for assessing and forecasting flood risk. A simple hydrologic model is represented in Figure 3. A web-based hydrological modelling system also developed by Al-Sabhan, Mulligan, & Blackburn, (2003) that allows the integration of real-time rainfall data from a wireless monitoring network in a spatially distributed GIS-based model. The ETM+ (Enhanced Thematic

Mapper Plus) and UK-DMC (Disaster Monitoring Constellation Satellite) satellite image were used by Yuhaniz and Vladimirova (2009) to map change detection after a flood disaster. They recommended that this mapping could be used in the region affected by any natural disaster that happened due to land cover changes. A methodology suggested by Wikantika, Sinaga, Hadi, & Darmawan, (2007) to recognize damaged buildings and land-use changes in a post-tsunami disaster using IKONOS and Quickbird images immediately after a disaster. To evaluating damage in areas devastated by earthquakes and tsunamis, Yang et al., (2007) used FORMOSAT-2 satellite images because it designed to acquire timely and low-cost daily images. MODIS images were also used for rapid assessments of severe damage to land resources, but due to a moderate resolution, it doesn't provide the land cover type. A methodology also proposed by Butenuth, Frey, Nielsen, & Skriver, (2011) for a near real time analysis immediately after a natural disaster. They used multi-sensor and multi-temporal satellite images and integrated it with GIS data. Di et al., (2010) studied landslide hazards triggered by an earthquake examined with Beijing-1 micro-satellite data in combination with digital elevation and slope gradient maps pre and post disaster event to calculate changes in vegetated areas and to monitor mass movements caused by the earthquake. The AVHRR (Advanced Very High Resolution Radiometer) data is used to detect and monitor the plumes created by large amounts of smoke produced by a fire.

Beyond imagery, out-space technologies are also useful for precise positioning, such as the GNSS, the most popular of which is the Global Positioning System (GPS) (Manfré et al., 2012). It provides information about geographical location i.e. used for mitigation and prevention during and after the disaster. The GPS technology has been frequently applied in natural disasters and the monitoring of geophysical phenomena, mainly landslides, which require the application of a different type of GPS technique (Hastaoglu & Sanli 2011; Manfré et al., 2012).

Figure 3. Remote sensing based hydrodynamic model of flood

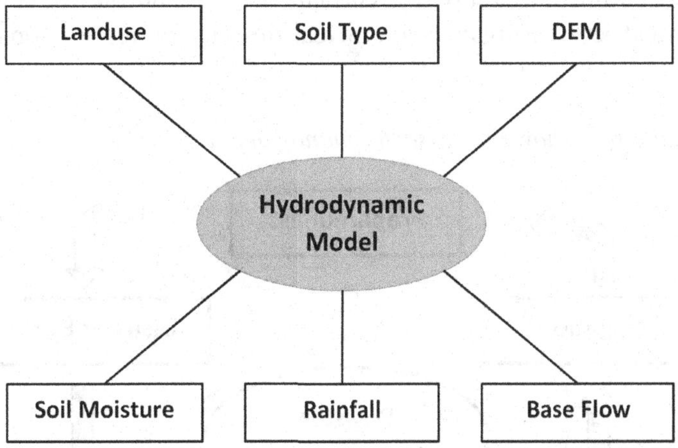

153

DATA MINING TECHNIQUES FOR DISASTER MANAGEMENT: A CONCEPTUAL DEMONSTRATION USING LANDSLIDE AS AN EVENT

Disaster is described as a sudden, unexpected and widespread event that causes great damage, destruction and human suffering, developed from a natural or man-made event that adversely affects human life, social structure, livelihood or industry. It causes a severe disturbance of the functioning of society, widespread human, material, or environmental losses that exceed the capability of the affected society to cope using its resources. In last few decades, the frequency and intensity of natural hazards have increased. According to the World Disaster Report 2011, 4,022 natural disasters occurred between 2001 and 2010 worldwide, reportedly killing a total of 1,221,332 people (IFRC, 2012). The study of Kobiyama et al., (2006) revealed that high population growth along with intense urbanization, industrialization, and unsystematic human activity promote the presence of high-density populations in risk areas that may be responsible for the increase in natural disasters.

Concept and Importance of Disaster Management

A disaster management is a planned approach to the prevention, preparedness, response and recovery from disasters (Figure 4). The actions (efforts to avoid or ameliorate the impact) taken depends in part on the sensitivities of the risk. Disaster management is necessary to minimize deaths and losses. The natural or man-made disasters, such as earthquakes, volcanic eruption, floods, high-rise building collapses, or major nuclear facility malfunctions, pose a constant challenge to public emergency services. To cope with such disasters in a fast and highly synchronized manner, the optimal provision of information or data concerning the situation is an essential pre-requisite. The organizations like the army, police, fire departments, public health and other have to react not only proficiently and individually, but also in a synchronized manner. It provides a coordination between organizations at several hierarchy levels (Auf der Heide, 1989). Since coordination requires current data, and such data must be communicated upstream and downstream within and between organizations in real-time. It requires developing an integrated com-

Figure 4. A schematic diagram shown the disaster management cycle

munication and information system for disaster management that provides efficient, reliable and secure exchange and processing of significant information. This integrated disaster management system must be able to provide relevant data for a post-disaster lessons learned analysis and for training purposes.

Disasters are any tragic events that have an enormous impact on humans and the environment. It is inevitable, we cannot do anything to prevent these, but disaster preparedness is only in our hand. It includes preparation of a disaster plan, anticipating damage evaluation and inspection, repair and recovery, communications and control center, training exercise, monitoring, and forecast or warning of disaster. Government intervention and proper planning, as well as funding, require for disaster management. Disasters are unpredictable although we do not always know when and where they will happen, their worst effects can be partially or wholly prevented by preparation, early warning (hurricane warnings), and instant positive responses. But, it is not necessary that these disasters are always unpredictable. Floods take place in plains and valleys, cyclones in coastal areas, droughts in areas with unstable and low rainfall and oil spills happens in shipping lanes. This predictability provides opportunities to plan for prevent and to lessen the impact of disasters. The main purpose of disaster management to reduce the occurrence of disasters or accidents and to minimize the effects of those cannot prevent. The combined forces of disaster management come into action as soon as possible when it strikes and provide help, relief, rescue and rehabilitation of victims.

Delineation of Landslide Hazard Zonation

The study of physical processes that lead to a landslide is vital for successful landslide hazard zonation of an area. Satellite remote sensing data (ETM+, LISS-III, IV) are now used for mapping of landslides as well as preparation of the thematic layers such as land use/land cover, geology, geomorphology and drainage. High resolution (CARTOSAT-I, II) digital elevation model (DEM) has immense importance in landslide hazard assessment. Various data layer (such as slope, aspect, relief, curvature, drainage, lineaments, watershed and ridges) can be extracted from high-resolution DEM. In recent times, so many researchers used high-resolution DEM to generate spatial information data layer for landslide hazard zonation studies (Ayalew & Yamagishi, 2005; Akbar & Ha, 2011; Balsubramani & Kumaraswamy, 2013; Calvello et al., 2013; Dahl, Mortensen, Veihe, & Jensen, 2010; Ghosh et al., 2009; Jaiswal, van Westen, & Jetten, 2010; Naithani, 2007; Yamagishi, 2005). Moreover, GIS has contributed substantially to the process of making spatial analyses of landslides. Due to geospatial technology, it has become possible to collect efficiently, manipulate, store, integrate and updating a variety of spatial data (such as lithology, geology, geomorphology, land use/land cover, structure and landslide scarp) of an area. These maps can be combined with other terrain maps like slope, aspect, slope morphology, rock weathering and slope-bedding dip relationship in GIS environment to the delineation of landslide hazard zonation (Nagarajan, et al., 1998; Van Westen, 1994).

In recent past, a methodology proposed that involve the use of remote sensing and GIS analyze land cover maps generated through the classification of satellite images with other map information (such as topography, geology, and geomorphology) to delineate the area vulnerable to landslides. The difference between different landslide studies in various geographical areas is the model proposed to integrate data in GIS environment, satellite images types, classification techniques and the methods for assigning weights to each data layer. The weights-of-evidence model (a Bayesian probability model) was used by Lee and Choi (2004) to select variables (maps) and respective weights. Gorsevski and Jankowski (2008) utilized of rough set theory to accommodate the complex terrain characteristics of landslide susceptibility to determine rules relating landslide conditioning factors and landslide events was explored. A multivariate logistic regression model was used by Pradha (2010) to incorporate variables in the GIS and SPOT (Système Pour l'Observation de la Terre) 5 and Landsat TM satellite images to prepared LU/LC map while Chung et al., (1995) used multivariate regression analysis. Finally, the geospatial techniques are very useful for data visualization purposes. Since accurate visualization of factors prevalent and responsible for the earth system phenomenon is required, and therefore, they need to be represented on proper scale and texture. Therefore, the usage of geospatial technologies in the representation of lithology, geological structure, geomorphology, land use/land cover, drainage, landslide scarp, etc. are very common in geospatial investigations. Further, these information's can be used for combinatorial analysis.

Conceptual Methodology for Delineation LHZ

For preparing a landslide hazard zonation map, the data used include high-resolution satellite data (LISS-III, IV) of the study area, Survey of India topographical map on a scale of 1:50,000 and Aster DEM (digital elevation model) are collected. Furthermore, the secondary data used geological map of the study area are procured from Geological Survey of India (GSI). The Survey of India (SOI) topographical map was first georeferenced by using ERDAS Imagine software. The satellite data was then georeferenced by using the image to image registration technique from this topographical map. Once the satellite images were georeferenced, the visual interpretation was performed to delineate landslides in the study area and also to prepare thematic layers on geomorphology and LU/LC. The SOI topographical map was used for the digitization of base map that included roads and drainages. These maps (the road and the drainage map) were updated with the high-resolution satellite data (LISS-IV) so that minor and new roads could be added to the maps. Then, using the Spatial Analyst option in ArcGIS 10.0 software, the road map and drainage map were used to prepare road density map and drainage density map respectively. The lineament map was georeferenced with the help of the topographical map, and the lineaments were delineated. These lineaments were updated with the LISS IV images and finally the lineament density map was generated. Similarly, the geological map was also georeferenced, and the various lithological units were identified and a lithological map was generated. The ASTER DEM was then used for the preparation of thematic layers on a slope, aspect and relief.

All the generated thematic layers (for factors considered responsible for the occurrence of landslides in the region) namely, the geomorphological map, road density map, drainage density map, lineament density map, lithological map, slope map, aspect map and relief map, were used for the development of landslide hazard models which include the analytical hierarchy process, fuzzy AHP, frequency ratio analysis and the fuzzy extent analysis model. The landslide hazard map is also validated by overlaying existing pervious landslides and new landslides (which are not included in modelling) on landslide hazard map. The whole methodological framework are shown in Figure 5 and 6.

In India, landslides are a major problem in mountainous regions such as the Himalayas, Nilgiri Hills, Western Ghats and northeastern part of the country. It takes place most frequently during the monsoon rains, as water is an important catalyst for triggering landslides. In the Himalayas, landslides have been a major and widely spread natural disaster that often strikes life and property and occupy a position of primary concern. The landslides in the Himalayas region are enormous and massive and in most cases the overburden along with the underlying lithology displaced while sliding particularly due to the seismic factor. In the Himalayas, frequent occurrences of landslides and debris flow are very pronounced with high energy environment due to active tectonics, rugged topography with very high relief and highly

Figure 5. Conceptual demonstration of utility of data mining process in landslide hazard prediction investigation

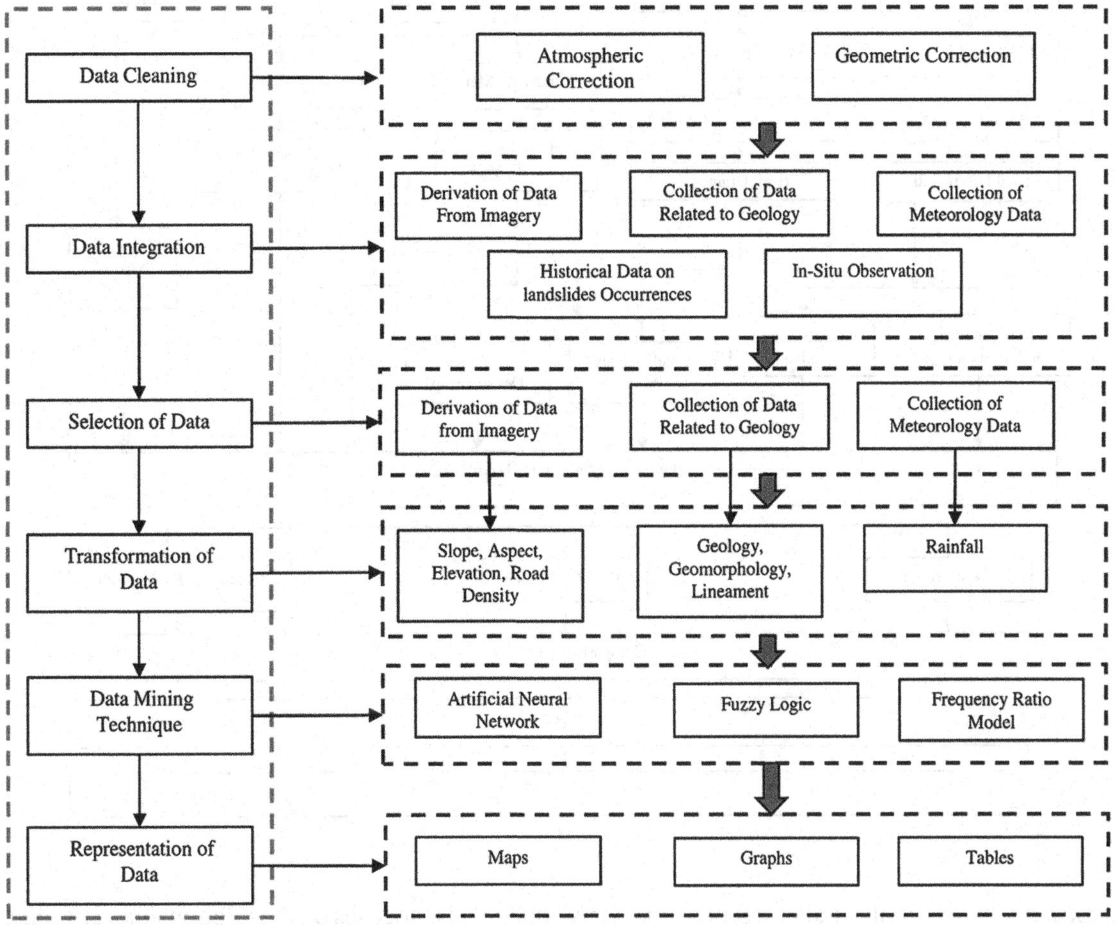

concentrated monsoon precipitation. Moreover, high density of both human and livestock population and consequent change in land use and land cover have caused a further intensification of the processes of landslide and debris flow occurrence.

FUTURE RESEARCH ISSUES

As discussed earlier in the chapter, occurrence of events cannot be understood from a linear view, since their evolution is a consequence of several factors residing in different domains of studies. To understand the basic sciences responsible for their coming into existence, and finally their growth into a full form, data sciences can be helpful by historical data. However, the utility of data sciences lies in understanding the data available on an event which means the process responsible for the evolution of data about an event will be mostly missing in data sciences. Now it has to be understood that extracting pattern from a set of data is not the complete solution to a problem. There must be a sincere effort in back-tracking the process involved in data sciences towards the origin and implications of causal factors in the events, and

Figure 6. Conceptual representation of process for landslides hazard prediction investigation

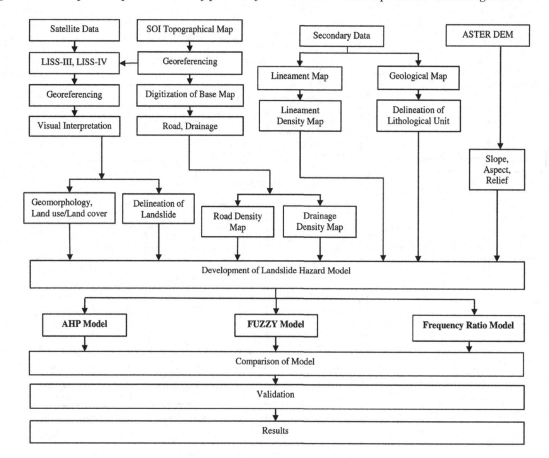

that too beyond sensitivity analysis. Since sensitivity analysis also focuses on the relationship between the different combination of causal factors and the output of a study, it also misses the root of the patterns, and that is we call process. Largely data sciences' sole focus is an extraction of accurate patterns from a set of data, and there is no denial that it is important. However if the process responsible for a pattern is not explained and demonstrated in detail, then events that are equally affected by external factors cannot be understood in entirety. Therefore, a close observation of the natural phenomena will surface an obvious fact that even the most robust sciences and technologies are not able to assess and predict the natural phenomena precisely and accurately in a consistent manner. The reasons are startling; there is an apparent gap between the natural sciences and computational sciences. Natural Sciences' prime focus is on process, whereas a computational science deals with patterns. If data sciences come up with some framework that equally accommodate the variables, or we can say causal factors defining process along with the factors that can unlock hidden patterns of the data, then the problem quoted above can be addressed in an appropriate manner.

Knowing the complexity and unpredictability of natural phenomenon and the issues related to lack of data, it is utmost necessary that intelligent systems should be developed to monitor and predict natural events in real time. That requires robust and intelligent algorithms that can mine patterns from a huge data repository in quick succession of time, so that information about natural hazards can be transmitted to people in time and save lives.

CONCLUSION

This chapter explains in detail regarding the need for an understanding of events and factors be it internal or external for their evolution and growth to understand the requirement and challenges of data sciences. The proposed chapter further briefs the significance of knowledge about the process behind an event to extract the information that can provide a long-term solution to a problem rather have a superficial perspective. It advocates bridging the gap between the process and pattern of the objectives of data sciences to extract meaningful information that can be instrumental in earth system studies. The main differences in the working process of natural sciences and computational sciences has been outlined in the present chapter that creates impedance in the application of computational models in the studies about natural sciences. It further briefs why data sciences fail to assess accurately and precisely natural events, and what measures can be taken sort out the persisting problems in the current data science framework. The fact that linear view of the events and casual factors cannot be effective in unlocking the complexity involved in an event of natural science domain is highlighted in the proposed chapter. Accordingly changes should be made in the data science framework to accommodate the factors that can help to understand the complexity involved in natural science studies.

The proposed chapter intends to highlight the significance of data mining techniques in the investigation of events falling into the realm of natural sciences. Specifically, the utility of data mining techniques in the landslide studies was described based on an earlier work. Since the causal factors of a natural event may be from a different domain and hence, it becomes very complicated to determine the intensity of each factor in triggering any event. Consequently, determination of affected areas due to a natural event is difficult. Further determination of the magnitude of the event is a very complex task. The unavailability of the data related to natural events is a huge impedance to the studies related to disaster management. Therefore, conventional techniques fail to address the issues that fall in the domain of natural phenomena. For example, an occurrence of landslides is affected by different factors and hence, tough to predict its occurrence. Moreover, general data related to landslides are not in complete form and therefore, with incomplete data, any association or classification in the landslide event is not possible. Here advanced data mining techniques can be instrumental in projecting a future scenario using vague data. The chapter discussed landslides in detail to understand the different dimensions of landslides so that the ways of application of data mining techniques can be thought of. In addition to the assessment of the utility of data mining techniques in the investigations of natural events, a short note is also provided on the utility of web mining in providing the more accurate and refined information related to natural hazards.

REFERENCES

Akbar, T., & Ha, S. (2011). Landslide hazard zoning along Himalaya Kaghan Valley of Pakistan-by integration of GPS, GIS, and remote sensing technology. *Landslides*, *8*(4), 527–540. doi:10.1007/s10346-011-0260-1

Al-Sabhan, W., Mulligan, M., & Blackburn, G. A. (2003). A real-time hydrological model for flood prediction using GIS and the WWW. *Computers, Environment and Urban Systems*, *27*(1), 9–32. doi:10.1016/S0198-9715(01)00010-2

Aleotti, P., & Chowdhury, R. (1999). Landslide hazard assessment: Summary review and new perspectives. *Bulletin of Engineering Geology and the Environment, 58*(1), 21–44. doi:10.1007/s100640050066

Arora, M. K., Das Gupta, A. S., & Gupta, R. P. (2004). An artificial neural network approach for landslide hazard zonation in the Bhagirathi (Ganga) Valley, Himalayas. *International Journal of Remote Sensing, 25*(3), 559–572. doi:10.1080/0143116031000156819

Auf der Heide, E. (1989). Disaster Response: Principles of Preparation and Coordination, Mosby. Online Book. Retrieved from http://coe-dmha.org/dr

Ayalew, L., & Yamagishi, H. (2005). The application of GIS-based logistic regression for landslide susceptibility mapping in the Kakuda-Yahiko Mountains, Central Japan. *Geophysical Journal of the Royal Astronomical Society, 65*, 15–31.

Balsubramani, K., & Kumaraswamy, K. (2013). Application of geospatial technology and information value technique in landslide hazard zonation mapping: A case study of Giri Valley, Himachal Pradesh. *Disaster Advances, 6*, 38–47.

Baroň, I., & Supper, R. (2013). Application and reliability of techniques for landslide site investigation, monitoring and early warning—outcomes from a questionnaire study. *Natural Hazards and Earth System Sciences, 13*(12), 3157–3168. doi:10.5194/nhess-13-3157-2013

Barredo, J. I., Benavides, A., Hervas, J., & Van Westen, C. J. (2000). Comparing heuristic landslide hazard assessment techniques using GIS in the Tirajana basin, Gran Canaria Island, Spain. *International Journal of Applied Earth Observation and Geoinformation, 2*(1), 9–23. doi:10.1016/S0303-2434(00)85022-9

Baum, R. L., Savage, W. Z., & Godt, J. W. (2002). U.S. geological survey open-file report:Vol. 02. *TRIGRS—a Fortran program for transient rainfall infiltration and grid-based regional slope stability analysis* (p. 424).

Bui, D., Pradhan, B., Lofman, O., & Dick, O. (2012). Landslide susceptibility assessment in the Hoa Binh Province of Vietnam: A comparison of the Levenberg-Marquardt and Bayesian regularized neural networks. *Geophysical Journal of the Royal Astronomical Society, 172*, 12–29.

Butenuth, M., Frey, D., Nielsen, A. A., & Skriver, H. (2011). Infrastructure assessment for disaster management using multi-sensor and multi-temporal remote sensing imagery. *International Journal of Remote Sensing, 32*(23), 8575–8594. doi:10.1080/01431161.2010.542204

Calvello, M., Cascini, L., & Mastroianni, S. (2013). Landslide zoning over large areas from a sample inventory by means of scale-dependant terrain units. *Geophysical Journal of the Royal Astronomical Society, 182*, 33–48.

Cardinali, M., Reichenbach, P., Guzzetti, F., Ardizzone, F., Antonini, G., Galli, M., & Salvati, P. et al. (2002). A geomorphological approach to estimation of landslide hazards and risks in Umbria, Central Italy. *Natural Hazards and Earth System Sciences, 2*(1/2), 57–72. doi:10.5194/nhess-2-57-2002

Carrara, A., Cardinali, M., Detti, R., Guzzetti, F., Pasqui, V., & Reichenbach, P. (1991). GIS techniques and statistical models in evaluating landslide hazard. *Earth Surface Processes and Landforms, 16*(5), 427–445. doi:10.1002/esp.3290160505

Carrara, A., Guzzetti, F., Cardinali, M., & Reichenbach, P. (1999). Use of GIS technology in the prediction and monitoring of landslide hazard. *Natural Hazards*, *20*(2–3), 117–135. doi:10.1023/A:1008097111310

Champatiray, P., Dimri, S., Lakhera, R., & Sati, S. (2007). Fuzzy based methods for landslide hazard assessment in active seismic zone of Himalaya. *Landslides*, *4*(2), 101–110. doi:10.1007/s10346-006-0068-6

Chang, K., & Chiang, S. (2009). An integrated model for predicting rainfall induced Landslides. *Geophysical Journal of the Royal Astronomical Society*, *105*, 366–373.

Chelboard, F., Baum, R., & Godt, J. (2006). U S Geological Survey Open file report:Vol. 2006-1064. *Rainfall Thresholds for Forecasting Landslides in the Seattle, Washington, Area- Exceedance and Probability* (pp. 1–17). Reston: Verginia.

Chung, C. F., Fabbri, A. G., & van Westen, C. J. (1995). Multivariate Regression Analysis for Landslide Hazard Zonation. In A. Carrara & F. Guzzetti (Eds.), *Geographical Information Systems in Assessing Natural Hazards* (pp. 107–142). Dordrecht, The Netherlands: Kluwer Academic Publishers. doi:10.1007/978-94-015-8404-3_7

Dahl, M., Mortensen, L., Veihe, A., & Jensen, N. (2010). A simple qualitative approach for mapping regional landslide susceptibility in the Faroe Islands. *Natural Hazards and Earth System Sciences*, *10*(2), 159–170. doi:10.5194/nhess-10-159-2010

Dai, E. C., Lee, C. F., & Nagi, Y. Y. (2002). Landslide risk assessment and management: An overview. *Engineering Geology*, *64*(1), 65–87. doi:10.1016/S0013-7952(01)00093-X

Deng, H. (1999). Multicriteria analysis with fuzzy pairwise comparisons. *International Journal of Approximate Reasoning*, *21*(3), 215–231. doi:10.1016/S0888-613X(99)00025-0

Di, B., Zeng, H., Zhang, M., Ustin, S. L., Tang, Y., Wang, Z., & Zhang, B. et al. (2010). Quantifying the spatial distribution of soil mass wasting processes after the 2008 earthquake in Wenchuan, China: A case study of the Longmenshan area. *Remote Sensing of Environment*, *114*(4), 761–771. doi:10.1016/j.rse.2009.11.011

EM-DAT. (2007). Emergency Disasters Data Base, Brussels, Belgium. Centre for Research on the Epidemiology of Disasters. Ecole de Santé, Publique, Université Catholique de Louvain.

EMDAT. (2010). Emergency Disasters Data Base, Brussels, Belgium. Centre for Research on the Epidemiology of Disasters. Ecole de Santé, PubliqueUniversité Catholique de Louvain.

Ercanglu, M. (2005). Landslide susceptibility assessment of SE Bartin (West Black Sea region, Turkey) by artificial neural networks. *Natural Hazards and Earth System Sciences*, *5*(6), 979–992. doi:10.5194/nhess-5-979-2005

Gabet, E., Burbank, D., Putkonen, J., Pratt-Situala, B., & Ojha, T. (2004). Rainfall thresholds for landsliding in the Himalaya of Nepal. *Geophysical Journal of the Royal Astronomical Society*, *63*, 131–143.

Ghosh, S., Van Westen, C., Carranza, E., Ghoshal, T., Sarkar, N., & Surendranath, M. (2009). A quantitative approach for improving BIS (Indian) method of medium-scale landslide susceptibility. *Journal of the Geological Society of India*, *74*(5), 625–638. doi:10.1007/s12594-009-0167-9

Gorsevski, P. V., & Jankowski, P. (2008). Discerning landslide susceptibility using rough sets. *Computers, Environment and Urban Systems*, *32*(1), 53–65. doi:10.1016/j.compenvurbsys.2007.04.001

GSI. (2006). *Geological Survey of India*. Landslide Hazard Studies.

Gupta, R. P., & Joshi, B. C. (1990). Landslide hazard zoning using the GIS approach—a case-study from the Ramganga Catchment, Himalayas. *Engineering Geology, 28*(1–2), 119–131. doi:10.1016/0013-7952(90)90037-2

Guzzetti, F., Carrara, A., Cardinali, M., & Reichenbach, P. (1999). Landslide hazard evaluation: A review of current techniques and their application in a multi study, Central Italy. *Geophysical Journal of the Royal Astronomical Society, 31*, 181–216.

Guzzetti, F., Reichenbach, P., Cardinali, M., Galli, M., & Ardizzone, F. (2005). Probablistic landslide hazard assessment at the basin scale. *Geophysical Journal of the Royal Astronomical Society, 72*, 272–299.

Han, J., & Kamber, M. (2006). *Data Mining: Concepts and Techniques*. New York: Morgan Kaufman Publishers.

Hastaoglu, K. O., & Sanli, D. U. (2011). Monitoring Koyulhisar landslide using rapid static GPS: A strategy to remove biases from vertical velocities. *Natural Hazards, 58*(3), 1275–1294. doi:10.1007/s11069-011-9728-5

Hong, Y., Adler, R., & Huffman, G. (2006). Evaluation of the NASA multi-satellite precipitation analysis potential in global landslide hazard assessment. *Geophysical Research Letters*.

IFRC. (2011). *World Disaster Report*. International Federation of Red Cross and Red Crescent Societies. Available online: http://www.ifrc.org/

Jade, S., & Sarkar, S. (1993). Statistical models for slope stability classification. *Engineering Geology, 36*(1-2), 91–98. doi:10.1016/0013-7952(93)90021-4

Jaiswal, P., van Westen, C., & Jetten, V. (2010). Quantitative assessment of direct and indirect landslide risk along transportation lines in southern India. *Natural Hazards and Earth System Sciences, 10*(6), 1253–1267. doi:10.5194/nhess-10-1253-2010

Kobiyama, M., Mendonça, M., Moreno, D. A., Marcelino, I. P. V. O., Marcelino, E. V., Gonçalves, E. F., & Rudorff, F. M. et al. (2006). *Prevenção de Desastres Naturais* (pp. 20–25). Florianópolis, Brazil: Organic Trading.

Komac, M. (2006). A landslide susceptibility model and multivariate statistics in perialpine Slovenia. *Geomorphology, 74*, 17–28. doi:10.1016/j.geomorph.2005.07.005

Kovar, K., & Natchtnebel, H. P. (1995). *Application of Geographic Information Systems in Hydrology and Water Resources Management. Hydro GIS 93*. Oxford, UK: IAHS Press.

Krishna, A. P., & Kumar, S. (2013). Landslide hazard assessment along a mountain highway in the Indian Himalayan Region (IHR) using remote sensing and computational models. Article In *Proceedings of Spie- The International Society. Optical Engineering (Redondo Beach, Calif.)*. doi:10.1117/12.2029080

Kumar, R., & Pande, I. C. (1972). Deformation of rocks of Simla Hills. *Geologische Rundschau, 61*(2), 430–441. doi:10.1007/BF01896326

Lee, C., Huang, C., Lee, J., Pan, K., Lin, M., & Dong, J. (2008). Statistical approach to storm event-induced landslides susceptibility. *Natural Hazards and Earth System Sciences, 8*(4), 941–960. doi:10.5194/nhess-8-941-2008

Lee, S., & Choi, J. (2004). Landslide susceptibility mapping using GIS and the weight-of-evidence model. *International Journal of Geographical Information Science, 18*(8), 789–814. doi:10.1080/13658810410001702003

Lee, S., & Dan, N. T. (2005). Probabilistic landslide susceptibility mapping in the Lai Chau province of Vietnam: Focus on the relationship between tectonic fractures and landslides. *Environmental Geology, 48*(6), 778–787. doi:10.1007/s00254-005-0019-x

Lee, S., & Pradhan, B. (2006). Probabilistic landslide hazards and risk mapping on Penang Island, Malaysia. *Journal of Earth System Science, 115*(6), 661–672. doi:10.1007/s12040-006-0004-0

Lee, S., & Talib, J. A. (2005). Probabilistic landslide susceptibility and factor effect analysis. *Environmental Geology, 47*(7), 982–990. doi:10.1007/s00254-005-1228-z

Manfre´, L. A., Hirata, E., Silva, J. B., Shinohara, E. J., Giannotti, M. A., Larocca, A. P. C., & Quintanilha, J. A. (2012). An analysis of geospatial technologies for risk and natural disaster management. *ISPRS International Journal of Geo-Information, 1*(2), 166–185. doi:10.3390/ijgi1020166

Mansourian, A., Rajabifard, A., & Valadan Zoej, M. J. (2005). SDI Conceptual Modelling for Disaster Management. In *Proceedings of the ISPRS Workshop on Service and Application of Spatial Data Infrastructure.*

Mehrotra, G. S., Sarkar, S., Kanungo, D. P., & Mahadevaiah, K. (1996). Terrain analysis and spatial assessment of landslide hazards in parts of Sikkim Himalaya. *Geological Society of India, 47*, 491–498.

Mikhailov, L., & Tsvetinov, P. (2004). Evaluation of services using a fuzzy analytic hierarchy process. *Applied Soft Computing, 5*(1), 23–33. doi:10.1016/j.asoc.2004.04.001

Nagarajan, R., Mukherjee, A., Roy, A., & Khire, M. V. (1998). Temporal remote sensing data and GIS application in landslide hazard zonation of part of Western Ghat, India. *International Journal of Remote Sensing, 19*(4), 573–585. doi:10.1080/014311698215865

Nagarajan, R., Roy, A., Vinodkumar, R., & Khire, M. (2000). Landslide hazard susceptibility mapping based on terrain and climatic factors for tropical monsoon region. *Engineering Geology, 58*, 275–287.

Naithani, A. (2007). Macro landslide hazard zonation mapping using uni-variate statistical analysis in parts of Garhwal Himalaya. *Journal of the Geological Society of India, 70*, 353–368.

Naithani, A. K. (1999). The Himalayan Landslides. *Employment News, 23*(47), 20–26.

Pachauri, A. K., & Pant, M. (1992). Landslide hazard mapping based on geological attributes. *Engineering Geology, 32*(1-2), 81–100. doi:10.1016/0013-7952(92)90020-Y

Palcic, I., & Lalic, B. (2009). Analytical Hierarchy Process as a tool for selecting and evaluating projects. *International Journal of Simulation Modelling, 8*(1), 16–26. doi:10.2507/IJSIMM08(1)2.112

Panikkar, S., & Subramaniyan, V. (1997). Landslide hazard analysis of the area around Dehra Dun and Mussoorie, Uttar Pradesh. *Current Science, 73,* 1117–1123.

Pardeshi, S. D., Autade, S. E., & Pardeshi, S. S. (2013). *Landslide hazard assessment: recent trends and techniques.* Springer Plus. doi:.10.1186/2193-1801-2-523

Park, D. C., El-Sharkawi, M. A., Marks, R. J. II, Atlas, L. E., & Damborg, M. J. (1991). Electric load forecasting using an artificial neural network. *IEEE Transactions on Power Engineering, 6*(2), 442–449. doi:10.1109/59.76685

Pradha, B. (2010). Remote sensing and GIS-based landslide hazard analysis and cross-validation using multivariate logistic regression model on three test areas in Malaysia. *Advances in Space Research, 45*(10), 1244–1256. doi:10.1016/j.asr.2010.01.006

Pradhan, B., & Lee, S. (2009). Landslide risk analysis using artificial neural network model focussing on different training sites. *International Journal of Physical Sciences, 4,* 1–15.

Preuth, T., Glade, T., & Demoulin, A. (2010). Stability analysis of a human-influenced landslides in eastern Belgium. *Geophysical Journal of the Royal Astronomical Society, 120,* 4–98.

Rajaraman, A., & Ullman, J. D. (2014). *Mining of Massive Datasets.* New York: Cambridge University Press.

Saaty, T. L. (1980). *The Analytical Hierarchy Process.* New York: McGraw – Hill.

Saaty, T. L. (1994). How to make a decision: The analytic hierarchy process. *Interfaces, 24*(6), 19–43. doi:10.1287/inte.24.6.19

Saha, A. (2003). *Introduction to artificial Neural Network Models.* Retrieved from http://www.geocities.com/adotsaha/-NNinExcel.html

Saha, A. K., Gupta, R. P., & Arora, M. K. (2002). GIS-based landslide hazard zonation in the Bhagirathi (Ganga) Valley, Himalayas. *International Journal of Remote Sensing, 23*(2), 357–369. doi:10.1080/01431160010014260

Sarkar, S., Kanungo, D., & Mehrotra, G. (1995). Landslide hazard zonation: A case study of garhwal Himalaya, India. *Mountain Research and Development, 15*(4), 301–309. doi:10.2307/3673806

Sarkar, S., & Kanungo, D. P. (2004). An integrated approach for landslide susceptibility mapping using remote sensing and GIS. *Photogrammetric Engineering and Remote Sensing, 70*(5), 617–625. doi:10.14358/PERS.70.5.617

Thomas, D. S. K., Eturĝay, K., & Kemeç, S. (2007). The role of Geographic Information System/Remote Sensing in Disaster Management. In H. Rodríguez, E. L. Quarantelli, & R. Dynes (Eds.), *Handbook of Disaster Research* (pp. 83–96). Newark, NJ: Springer. doi:10.1007/978-0-387-32353-4_5

Van Westen, C. J. (1994). GIS in landslide hazard zonation: a review, with examples from the Andes of Colombia. In M. Price & I. Heywood (Eds.), *Mountain environments and geographic information system* (pp. 135–165). London: Taylor and Francis.

Varnes, D. J. (1984). Landslide Hazard Zonation: a review of principles and practice. UNESCO.

Wang, H., & Sassa, K. (2005). Comparative evaluation of landslide susceptibility in Minamata area, Japan. *Environmental Geology*, *47*(7), 956–966. doi:10.1007/s00254-005-1225-2

Weiss, G. M., & Davison, B. D. (2010). *To appear in the Handbook of Technology Management* (H. Bidgoli, Ed.). John Wiley and Sons.

Wikantika, K., Sinaga, A., Hadi, F., & Darmawan, S. (2007). Quick assessment on identification of damaged building and land-use changes in the post-tsunami disaster with a quick-look image of IKONOS and Quickbird (A case study in Meulaboh City, Aceh). *International Journal of Remote Sensing*, *28*(13-14), 3037–3044. doi:10.1080/01431160601091845

Yalcin, A. (2008). GIS – based landslide susceptibility mapping using analytical hierarchy process and bivariate statistics in Ardesen (Turkey): Comparison of results and confirmations. *Catena*, *72*(1), 1–12. doi:10.1016/j.catena.2007.01.003

Yang, M. D., Su, T. C., Hsu, C. H., Chang, K. C., & Wu, A. M. (2007). Mapping of the 26 December 2004 tsunami disaster by using FORMOSAT-2 images. *International Journal of Remote Sensing*, *28*(13-14), 3071–3091. doi:10.1080/01431160601094500

Yilmaz, I. (2009). Landslide susceptibility mapping using frequency ratio, logistic regression, artificial neural networks and their comparison: A case study from Kat landslides (Tokat-Turkey). *Computers & Geosciences*, *35*(6), 1125–1138. doi:10.1016/j.cageo.2008.08.007

Yuhaniz, S. S., & Vladimirova, T. (2009). An onboard automatic change detection system for disaster monitoring. *International Journal of Remote Sensing*, *30*(23), 6121–6139. doi:10.1080/01431160902810638

Zaki, M. J., & Meira, W. Jr. (2014). *Data mining and analysis: fundamental concepts and algorithms*. New York: Cambridge University Press.

ADDITIONAL READING

Belward, A. S., Stibig, H. J., Eva, H., Rembold, F., Bucha, T., Hartley, A., & Mollicone, D. et al. (2007). Mapping severe damage to land cover following the 2004 Indian Ocean tsunami using moderate spatial resolution satellite imagery. *International Journal of Remote Sensing*, *28*(13-14), 2977–2994. doi:10.1080/01431160601091803

Consuegra, D., Joerin, F., & Vitalini, F. (1995). Flood Delineation and Impact Assessment in Agricultural Land Using GIS Technology. In A. Carrara & F. Guzzetti (Eds.), *Geographical Information Systems in Assessing Natural Hazards* (pp. 177–198). Dordrecht, The Netherlands: Kluwer Academic Publishers. doi:10.1007/978-94-015-8404-3_9

Dahl, M., Mortensen, L., Veihe, A., & Jensen, N. (2010). A simple qualitative approach for mapping regional landslide susceptibility in the Faroe Islands. *Natural Hazards and Earth System Sciences*, *10*(2), 159–170. doi:10.5194/nhess-10-159-2010

GSI. (2006). *Geological Survey of India*. Landslide Hazard Studies.

IFRC. (2011). *World Disaster Report.* International Federation of Red Cross and Red Crescent Societies: Geneva, Switzerland. Available online: http://www.ifrc.org/

Saaty, T. L. (1980). *The Analytical Hierarchy Process.* New York: McGraw – Hill.

Varnes, D. J. (1984). Landslide Hazard Zonation: a review of principles and practice. UNESCO, Darantine, Paris, (pp. 1-6).

Wang, H., & Sassa, K. (2005). Comparative evaluation of landslide susceptibility in Minamata area, Japan. *Environmental Geology, 47*(7), 956–966. doi:10.1007/s00254-005-1225-2

Yilmaz, I. (2009). Landslide susceptibility mapping using frequency ratio, logistic regression, artificial neural networks and their comparison: A case study from Kat landslides (Tokat-Turkey). *Computers & Geosciences, 35*(6), 1125–1138. doi:10.1016/j.cageo.2008.08.007

KEY TERMS AND DEFINITIONS

Drainage: Streams and rivers that may induce instability of slope. The effect decreases with increase in the distance on either side from the drainage.

Digital Elevation Model: A quantitative model of a part of the earth's surface in digital form.

Geomorphology: Science of landforms with an emphasis on their origin, evolution, form, and distribution across the physical landscape.

Geographic Information System: It is defined as a powerful set of tools for collecting, storing, retrieving, transforming and displaying spatial data from the real world for a particular set of purposes.

Land Use/Land Cover: Land use refers to man's activities and the various uses which carried on land whereas land covers refers to natural vegetation, water bodies, rock/soil, artificial cover, and others noticed to the land. Land Cover, defined as the assemblage of biotic and a biotic components on the earth's surface is one of the most crucial properties of the earth system.

Lithology: Wide range of rocks in the area.

Lineaments: The structural, topographical, vegetational, soil and lithological alignments identified from remote sensing data. The severity of landslides increases with their decreasing distance from the lineaments.

Lineament Density: Lineament density is derived from lineament.

Relative Relief: The difference between maximum and minimum elevation values within an area or facet.

Slope: The gradient between the center and neighborhood cell with maximum or minimum elevation. The greater the slope, the greater is the probability of landslide occurrence.

APPENDIX: LIST OF ABBREVIATIONS

ASTER DEM: Advanced Space borne Thermal Emission and Reflection Radiometer Digital Elevation Model

AWiFS : Advanced Wide Field Sensor

ANN : Artificial Neural Network

AVHRR: Advanced Very High Resolution Radiometer

DEM : Digital Elevation Model

ETM+ : Enhanced Thematic Mapper Plus

FCC : False Colour Composite

FGMM: Fuzzy Geometric Mean Model

GIS : Geographic Information System

GPS : Global Positioning System

GNSS : Global Navigation Satellite System

GSI : Geological Survey of India

LISS : Linear Imaging Self Scanner Sensor

LULC : Land use/ land cover

LR : Logistic Regression

MLP : Multilayer Perceptron Problem

RS : Remote Sensing

SOI : Survey of India

SPOT : Système Pour l'Observation de la Terre

SDFC : Standardized Discriminant Function Coefficient

SVM : Support Vector Machines

Chapter 7
Analyzing Website Quality Issues through Web Mining:
A Case Study on University Websites in India

G. Sreedhar
Rashtriya Sanskrit Vidyapeetha (Deemed University), India

ABSTRACT

In the present day scenario the World Wide Web (WWW) is an important and popular information search tool. It provides convenient access to almost all kinds of information – from education to entertainment. The main objective of the chapter is to retrieve information from websites and then use the information for website quality analysis. In this chapter information of the website is retrieved through web mining process. Web mining is the process is the integration of three knowledge domains: Web Content Mining, Web Structure Mining and Web Usage Mining. Web content mining is the process of extracting knowledge from the content of web documents. Web structure mining is the process of inferring knowledge from the World Wide Web organization and links between references and referents in the Web. The web content elements are used to derive functionality and usability of the website. The Web Component elements are used to find the performance of the website. The website structural elements are used to find the complexity and usability of the website. The quality assurance techniques for web applications generally focus on the prevention of web failure or the reduction of chances for such failures. The web failures are defined as the inability to obtain or deliver information such as documents or computational results requested by web users. A high quality website is one that provides relevant, useful content and a good user experience. Thus in this chapter, all areas of website are thoroughly studied for analysing the quality of website design.

DOI: 10.4018/978-1-5225-0613-3.ch007

INTRODUCTION

A Website is a collection of Web pages containing text, images, audio and video etc. Thus Web is a vast collection of completely uncontrolled documents. Web pages are of two types, static and dynamic. Static Web pages are static in nature and requires no change in the content. Dynamic Web pages are dynamic in nature and their content is changing frequently. Dynamic Web pages use database for storing end-user information, product information, transaction data and content. Static Web pages are designed using Hypertext Mark up Language (HTML) files. Dynamic Web pages are designed using Dynamic HTML, Scripting Languages and other Web Programming techniques. Today, Web is not only an information resource but also becoming an automated tool in various applications. Over the last few years there has been a remarkable increase in use of the World Wide Web (WWW) for a wide and variety of purposes. There was also a fast growth in its applications. This led the Internet users to realize the importance and the benefits gained from a globally interconnected hypermedia system. The author (Bobby, n.d.) suggested that the sites will be eye-catching, easy to navigate, error free and that they will work in any browser. On the other hand it causes a larger number of useless, meaningless and badly designed websites on the Internet world causing unwanted additional traffic; this is all because of an unorganized non planned websites development processes. This had stake in the challenges in the evaluation task and also in quality assurance task. The management of web sites imposes a constant demand for new information and timely updates due to the increase of services and content that site owners wish to make available to their users, which in turn is motivated by the complexity and diversity of needs and behaviours of the users. Such constant labour intensive effort implies very high financial and personnel costs. Although there exists many design guidelines, and metrics for the evaluation of web sites and applications, most of them lack a well-defined specification framework and even worse a strategy for consultation and reuse. The World Wide Web Consortium (W3C)is an open source organizations and it defines various web standards for designing a website. The W3C is led by web inventor Tim Berners-Lee and CEO. The standards defined by W3C are considered as guidelines and these guidelines help in assessing the quality of website content in presenting the web content. Web mining is the process of investigating various aspects of websites. The growth of internet together with the increasing number of personal computers in the world makes for an increase in accessibility. Thus, a website is indeed a system that utilizes the internet as its underlying infrastructure and the web as its platform.

BACKGROUND

Web Mining: The data on World Wide Web are available in three different formats: web content, web structure and web usage. Web mining is usually defined as the use of data mining techniques to automatically discover and extract information from web documents and services. The authors of O. Etzioni (1996) and R. Cooley (1997) discuss in their research that web data mining can be defined in two distinct forms: first, it is defined as chain of order tasks and second, it is defined considering type of web data used in web data mining process. Web mining is the application of data mining techniques to extract knowledge from web data, i.e. web content, web structure, and web usage data. Web Data Mining extracts and analyses useful information from huge amounts of data stored in different data sources to provide additional information and knowledge that are crucial of decision making process. A decision support system is a computer-based information system that supports business and organizational decision-making activities. According to J. Srivastava et al. (2002) also web data mining is commonly categorized into three areas:

1. **Web Content Mining:** Web content data is web pages content availed to users to satisfy their needs of information. This can be in the form of text, HTML pages, images, audio, video etc. In this category, the HTML pages are common and more familiar form of web content data. Because of variety of internal formats and browsers way of interpretation, theHTML document may appear differently in different browsers while viewing. Still thebasic document structure is similar. The author S. Nestorov et al. (1998) discuss in their research that HTML documents are often considered as semi structured as different elements of documents are not designed according to specific schema. In HTML, elements are tagged in a way to enable designing layout of document. Generally, HTML elements are of two types: first concerns with way of displaying documents in browser and second concerns with information about document itself like title and other document relationship. XML document is another known form of web content data which enables storing and transporting information. It is having structured information and includes contents and information about contents. Each XML document has specific structure and XML is a mark-up language which allows identifying document structure and adding the information. In XML, there are no predefined tags and it is language to describe and add mark-up to documents using XML specification. The applications processing XML document or the style sheets decide the semantics of XML document. Another type of web content data is dynamic server pages which are processed by the web server and generated result is sent to web browser. In contrast, without any change, the static contents are sent to browser. Some of familiar dynamic server page contents are like JSP (Java Server Page), ASP (Active Server Page) and PHP (Pre-Hypertext Processor). The author Manoj Pandia et al. (2011) said that Web Content Mining is the task of extracting knowledge from the content of documents on World Wide Web. The web documents may consists of text, images, audio, video or structured records like tables and lists. According to (Sarwar Hadi, n.d.) Web Content Mining is a form of text data mining applied to the web domain, and has to do with finding the content of documents, classifying documents, and clustering documents. HTML documents are semi structured data. Others like data in tables and databases, generated HTML pages are the more structured data and most of the data is unstructured text data. Due to this unstructured nature, web content mining becomes more complex. Web content mining focuses on automatic search of information resources online. Mining can be applied on the web documents as well the results pages produced from a search engine. There are two types of approach in content mining called agent based approach and database based approach. The agent based approach concentrate on searching relevant information using the characteristics of a particular domain to interpret and organize the collected information. The database approach is used for retrieving the semi-structure data from the web.

2. **Web Structure Mining:** Web structure data represents linkage and relationship of web contents to others. Two types of structure namely intra-page and inter-page structure can be considered. In specific web page, information about arrangement of different HTML tags is intrapage structure information. The pages are connected with other pages using hyperlinks. This is inter-page structure information. Hyperlinks of web pages collectively form a graph called web graph and it

describes the whole structure of the web site. Web graph is a common way of showing the links from one web page to another in whole site and depicts overall structure. The author M. Gandhi et al. (2004) said that that it is a representation of WWW for specific site describing structure of links and relationship to the HTML documents. Web document is depicted as a node in graph and edge is HTML link connecting one page with another. In two different ways, the edges of the graph are presented. A hyperlink stopping at related page is presented as outgoing arcs and hyperlinks using which related page can be found is presented as incoming arcs. Web graph can be used in some applications like web searching, indexing and web communities detection (Murat Ali Bayir, n.d.). Web Structure Mining focuses on discovering structure information from the Web to identify relevant documents. It describes the connectivity in the Web subset based on the given collection of interconnected Web documents. The goal of the Web Structure Mining is to generate the structural summary about the Web site and Web page. It tries to discover the link structure of the hyperlinks at the inter-document level. The structure of a typical Web graph consists of Web pages as nodes, and hyperlinks as edges connecting related pages. Based on the topology of the hyperlinks, Web Structure mining will categorize the Web pages and generate the information like similarity and relationship between different Web sites. This type of mining can be performed at the document level (intra-page) or at the hyperlink level (inter-page). It is important to understand the Web data structure for Information Retrieval. Mining the site structure and Web page structure can help to guide the classification and clustering of pages to find authoritative pages to improve retrieval performance. Web structure mining is the process of discovering structure information from the web. Another task of web structure mining is to discover the nature of the hierarchy or network of hyperlink in the web sites of a particular domain. This may help to generalize the flow of information in Web sites that may represent some particular domain; therefore the query processing can be performed easier and more efficient. Web structure mining has a strong relation with the web content mining.

3. **Web Usage Mining:** Web usage data involves log data collected by web server and application server which is the main source of data. When user interacts with web site, web log data is generated on web server in form of web server log files. Application Server Data is common in commercial application servers. The importance of these data types comes from their feature to track various types of business events and log them in application server logs. Application Level Data is another source for web usage data. With this type of data it is possible to record various kinds of events in an application. These data are used for generating histories about selected special events. The data in this category can be divided into three categories based on the source of its collection: on the server side, the client side, and the proxy side. Other additional data sources are demographic data, site files, cookies etc. Generally, web server is assigned a domain name and has IP address. When user sends request for page to web server through browser, request is processed by server and page is sent to user. As a result of user interaction with web site and server, data are generated on server and resource request, success, error etc. information are recorded into server log files. Different types of usage log files are created on server such as access log, error log, referrer log, agent log. Information stored in web access log includes IP Address, username, date and time, request. Error information like file not found, no data, aborted transmission etc. are recorded into Error logs. The information about browser, its version and operating system of user making request is stored into Agent logs. Different server log file formats are available such as Common Log file Format and Extended Log file Format. The Common Log file Format includes IP Address, date, time, login

name of a user, bytes transferred, status code, URL requested. Extended Log file Format includes IP Address, bytes sent and received, request query, server name, port, requested service name, time elapsed for transaction to complete, version of transfer protocol used, user agent showing browser used for request, cookie ID, and referrer. Using web traffic analyser software, log files of web server can be analysed and a useful information can be derived which helps to improve structure of web site. Web Usage Mining which is also known as web log mining aims to find out interesting and frequent user access patterns from web browsing data that are stored in web server log. Such discovered knowledge is useful in analysing how the web pages are accessed or what are seeking for by the users. According to Srivastava. J (2000) for the task of applying data mining techniques, information from web data is extracted in order to understand and better serve the needs of users navigating on the web. Web usage mining focuses on techniques that could predict user behavior while the user interacts with the web. Usage analysis includes straightforward statistics, such as page access frequency, as well as more sophisticated form of analysis such as finding the common traversal paths through a Website. Web Usage Mining is the process of applying data mining techniques to discover interesting patterns from Web usage data. Web usage mining provides better understanding for serving the needs of Web-based applications. Web Usage data keeps information about the identity or origin of Web users with their browsing behaviour in a web domain. Web Usage Mining is the process of extracting useful information from the secondary data derived from the interactions of the user while surfing on the Web. It extracts data stored in server access logs, referrer logs, agent logs, client-side cookies, user profile and Meta data. The authors G. Chang et al. (2001) discuss in their research that web usage mining is the application of data mining techniques to discover interesting usage patterns from web usage data, in order to understand and better serve the needs of web-based applications. The web log files on the web server are major source of data for Web Usage Mining. When user requests resources of web server, each request is recorded in the web log file on web server. As a consequence, users browsing behaviour is recorded into the web log file. In Web Usage Mining, data can be collected from server log files that include web server access logs and application server logs. The data collected in web log file is incomplete and not suitable for mining directly. Pre-processing is necessary to convert the data into suitable form for pattern discovery. Pre-processing can provide accurate, concise data for data mining. Data pre-processing, includes data cleaning, user identification, user sessions identification, path completion and data integration.

METHODOLOGY

The methodology consists of two phases. In phase I, the complete information of the website is retrieved using web mining process and in phase II, using the information of phase I quality of website is analysed.

Phase I

The information retrieved from web mining process is used for analysing quality of website. In order to retrieve information from web a prototype is developed which consists various modules. These are Web Content Module, Web Structure Module and Web Components Module. To strengthen the functionality of web mining process, different standard web tools are adapted in each module.

Web Content Module

The contents of website are retrieved in web content module. A standard web tool Website Extractor is used to extract complete content of the website. Website Extractor is a great tool for researchers, journalists, students, equity analysts, business and marketing executives. Website Extractor automatically lets you download any files that were not copied due to transfer errors or bad connections. The program is equipped to run through a proxy server and download only revised or new files, bypassing documents that have already been copied. Website Extractor is essentially an intelligent search robot that navigates the hyperlinks of cyberspace and downloads the websites and pages you want to store on user hard drive. With Website Extractor, on can *Limit search* by domain types (.com, .net, .uk, .in, .org, .ac, etc.) by using the sophisticated filtering options based on a list of key words and other options, *Scan websites* both online and offline (on your own hard drive) using the built-in browser, *change html-links* to relative names, allowing you to easily move information to CD-ROM, floppy disk, or to another hard drive, *select the documents* and one can download by type and name using the superb filtering features and *set download depth* for websites. Website Extractor is easy to use and can be configured to your individual needs. The tool accepts home page address of the website and produces list of web pages with detailed web content. The snapshot of the website extractor is shown in Figure 1.

Web Components Module

In this module complete list of components are analysed during web mining process. They are as follows:

- **Links:** Links are the main feature on web sites. They constitute the mean of transport between pages and guide the user to certain addresses without the user knowing the actual address itself.

Figure 1. Website extractor to retrieve web content

- **Forms:** Forms are used to submit information from the user to the host, which in turn gets processed and acted upon in some way. Forms can used both on client side and server side and they can be designed using scripting languages such as JavaScript, VBScript, Perl, etc.
- **Cookies:** Cookies are used often used to store information about the user and his actions on particular site. When a user accesses a site that uses cookies, the web server sends information about the user and stores it on the client computer in form of a cookie. These can be used to create more dynamic and custom made pages.
- **Web Indexing:** There are number of different techniques and algorithms used by different search engines to search the internet. Depending on how the site is designed using Meta tags, frames, HTML syntax, dynamically created pages, passwords or different languages, the site will be searchable in different ways.
- **Dynamic Interface Components:** Web pages are not just presented in static HTML any more. Demands for more dynamic features, custom made sites and high interactivity have made the internet a more vivid place than before. Dynamic interface components reside and operate both on server and client side of the web, depending on the application. The most important include java applets, java servlets, Active X Controls, JavaScript, VBScript, CGI, ASP, CSS and third party plug-ins.
- **Programming Language:** Differences in web programming language versions or specifications can cause serious problems on both client and server side. For example, when HTML is generated dynamically it is important to know how it is generated. When development is done in a distributed environment where developers, for instance, are geographically separated, this area becomes increasingly important. Make sure that specifications are well spread throughout the development organization to avoid future problems.
- **Databases:** Databases play an important role in web application technology, housing the content that the web application manages, running queries and fulfilling user requests for data storage. The most commonly used type of databases in web applications is the relational database and its managed by SQL to write, retrieve and editing of information.
- **Navigation:** Navigation describes the way users navigate within a page, between different user interface controls (buttons, boxes, lists, windows, etc.,) or between pages via links.
- **Graphics:** The graphics of web site include images, animations, borders, colors, movie clips, fonts, backgrounds, buttons etc.
- **Content:** Content should be correct, accurate and relevant to the information presented in the website.
- **Platform (OS):** There are several different operating systems that are being used on the market today, and depending on the configuration of the user system, compatibility issues may occur. Different applications may work fine under certain operating systems.
- **Web Browsers:** The web browser is the most central component on the client side of the web. Browsers come in different brands and versions and have different support for Java, JavaScript, ActiveX, plug-ins or different HTML specifications.
- **Settings and Preferences:** Depending on settings and preferences of the client machine, web applications may behave differently. These settings include screen resolution, color depth, etc,
- **Connection Speed:** Users may differ greatly in connection speed. Users expect minimum download time of the website.

All these components of website are retrieved using web components module. Website analysing and optimizing has became one of the key task that a webmaster has to perform in order to make the website run efficiently. By analysing a website one can identify the problems related to loading time, size, keyword effectiveness etc. A lot of online website analysing tools are available that can be used freely to analyse the website and which gives an insight view of the problems and area of improvement. Web page optimization streamlines web content to maximize display speed. Fast display speed is the key to success with website. It increases profits, decreases costs, and improves customer satisfaction. To maximize display speed the developer can employ the following nine techniques:

1. Minimize HTTP requests.
2. Resize and optimize images.
3. Optimize multimedia.
4. Convert JavaScript behaviour to CSS.
5. Use server-side sniffing.
6. Optimize JavaScript for execution speed and file size.
7. Convert table layout to CSS layout.
8. Replace inline style with CSS rules.
9. Minimize initial display time.

A standard web tool Web Page Analyser is used to retrieve all components of website. The tool accepts of URL address of each page which is retrieved in web content module and generates a report containing details like number of image files, number of HTML files, number of script files, and download time of each component of the web page. The screen shot of web page analyser is shown in Figure 2.

Figure 2. Web page analyser to retrieve website components

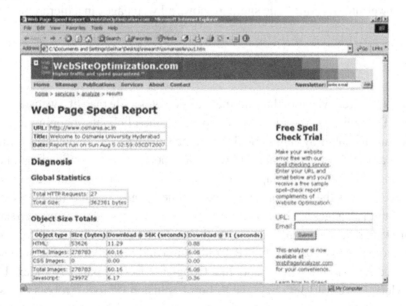

Web Structure Module

Website navigability is termed as the easiness that the users find the required piece of information by moving through a website. Website Navigability is one of attribute of usability and navigability is depending on structure of the website. Website structure is depending on the number of hyperlinks in the website. With the advent of the web new sources of information became available, one of them being the *hyperlinks* between documents and records of the user behaviour. Structural complexity emerges from the relationships among the pages of the website. The most basic and important relationship is that a page is linked to another through hyperlinks. The hyperlinks between web pages of a website form the navigational paths through which users browse the website to find the information that they want. The more complex that the web pages are inter-linked, the more likely that a user becomes lost in the information ocean, and hence, the more difficult to navigate. Thus structural complexity metrics are based on the study of website links. The structurally simplest system consists of a single page with no links. For more complex systems, structural complexity depends on the structure of the graph model of the website. To be precise, *hypertexts* (that is collections of documents connected by hyperlinks) have existed and have been studied for a long time. What was new was the large number of hyperlinks created by independent individuals. Hyperlinks provide a valuable source of information for web information retrieval as we will show in this article. This area of information retrieval is commonly called *link analysis*. A hyperlink is a reference of a web page, which is contained in a web page. When the hyperlink is clicked on in a web browser, the browser displays page. This functionality alone is not helpful for web information retrieval. However, the way hyperlinks are typically used by authors of web pages can give them valuable information content. Typically, authors create links because they think they will be useful for the readers of the pages. Thus, links are usually either navigational aid that, for example, brings the reader back to the homepage of the site, or links that point to pages whose content augments the content of the current page. The second kinds of links tend to point to high-quality pages that might be on the same topic as the page containing the link. Every website must have sitemap to know the organization of web pages in the website structure. The sitemap shows all web pages in a hierarchical tree with home page as root of the tree.

PowerMapper

The PowerMapper is a web crawler tool that automatically creates a site map of a website using thumbnails of each web page. The online web tool PowerMapper is a one-click site mapping tool that eliminates weeks of intensive manual labor by automatically creating site maps and content inventories. It produces visual site maps in a variety of styles, and allows data export to other applications and databases for additional processing. The tool PowerMapper scans each page of a site, capturing page thumbnails and metadata, and then examines the page for links to un-scanned pages. It scans the newly found pages and repeats this process until all pages have been scanned. Pages are requested from the web server in the same way that a web browser requests them. This means the product works with password protected pages as well as server technologies like ASP.NET, JSP, ColdFusion and SharePoint. This process is called web crawling, and is used by search engine agents like Googlebot to find pages to index. Like other well-behaved web crawlers, PowerMapper obeys the Robots Exclusion Protocol (robots.txt) which describes areas of sites that are off limits to web crawlers. A web tool PowerMapper is used in the methodology to construct a sitemap for the website. It selects URL address of website and generates the tree structure for all web pages of website. In this process only markup files (html, asp, php, xml, etc.,) are considered and remaining components like graphic files, script files, etc., are not included because these files do not have any significance in website structure. The sitemap of a website may be organized into various levels depending on its design. Some websites have one or two levels and some may have three or more levels. PowerMapper is a one-click site mapping tool that eliminates weeks of intensive manual labor by automatically creating site maps and content inventories. It produces visual site maps in a variety of styles, and allows data export to other applications and databases for additional processing. PowerMapper stores site structure in a binary .site file, with rendered maps and page thumbnails stored in an associated folder. The web tool PowerMapper produces two types of sitemaps. They are visual sitemaps and XML sitemaps. Visual sitemaps are graphical or textual representations of a website's structure and sitemap works very similar to an organization chart. The XML sitemaps are lists of the pages on the website and are designed to let search engines like Google know which pages website has. There are several special purpose extensions available for XML site maps. They are image sitemaps, mobile sitemaps and video sitemaps. The image sitemaps describe images and are used by Google Image Search. The mobile sitemaps are used for listing mobile web pages and Video sitemaps are used for describing video sites like YouTube etc., the snapshot of sitemap is shown in Figure 3.

Figure 3. Website structure using PowerMapper

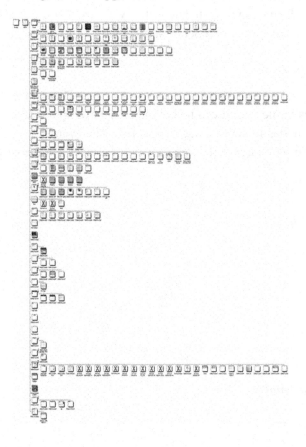

Phase II

The quality of website is analyzed in three modules. These are Website Structure Analysis module, Website Quality Analysis Module and Website Download time Performance module.

Website Structure Analysis Module

analyzes the quality of website structure. The procedure of the quality assessment of website structure involves four modules: creating a sitemap, computing path length metric, evaluating structural complexity of website, and finding broken link error index.

Creating a Sitemap

Every website must have sitemap to know the organization of web pages in the website structure. The sitemap shows all web pages in a hierarchical tree with home page as root of the tree. A web tool *Power-Mapper* is used to construct a sitemap for the website. It selects URL address of website and generates the tree structure for all web pages of website. In this process only markup files (html, asp, php, xml, etc.,) are considered and remaining components like graphic files script files, etc., are not included because these files do not have any significance in website structure. The sitemap of a website may be organized into various levels depending on its design. Some websites have one or two levels and some may have more levels. This idea was further investigated in by T.J. Mc Cabe (1976). A metric for website structure complexity was defined as the sum of number of simple paths from the home page to each page.

Evaluating Path Length Metric

A path length is used to find average number of clicks per page. The path length of the tree is the sum of the depths of all nodes in the tree. It can be computed as a weighted sum, where weightage at each level with its number of nodes its level using Equation 1. The average number of clicks is computed using Equation 2. The width of a tree is the size of its largest level and the height of a tree is the length of its longest root path.

$$path\ length = \sum_{i=1}^{n} l_i m_i \qquad (1)$$

where

l_i: Level number i
m_i: Number of nodes at level i

$$Avg\ no.\ of\ clicks = path\ length / n \qquad (2)$$

where

n: number of nodes in the tree

To illustrate the above for a design with three levels path length is computed as detailed below in Figure 4.

Path length = 0*1 + 1*3 + 2*3 + 3*6 = 27

AvgClicks = 27/13 = 2.07

Structural Complexity

Structural Complexity emerges from the relationships among the web pages of the website. The most basic and important relationship is that a web page is linked to another through hyperlinks. The hyperlinks between web pages of a website form the navigational paths through which users browse the website to find the required information. The more complex that the web pages are inter-linked, the more likely that a user becomes lost in the information ocean and hence, the more difficult to navigate. The structural complexity metrics are therefore based on the study of website links. The structurally simplest website consists of a single web page with no links. For more complex systems, structural complexity depends on the structure of the graph model of the website. It was decided to keep the navigation of the sites fairly simple. The home page of web site would link to all the main topics on the web site. The details of content and its relevant shall be accommodated in the pages at sub levels. Jin, Zhu and Hall (1993) proposed an abstract model of hypertext application systems as a directed graph, which one in general applicable to websites. In this model, a website can be modeled as a pair <G, S>, where G=(V,E) is a directed graph representing the website, V is the set of nodes representing web pages, E is the set of edges representing links between web pages and S is the start node of the graph, i.e. the home page of the website. The directed graph must also satisfy the condition that all nodes v in V are reachable, i.e., there is at least one path from the home page to node v. They suggested the use of the Number of Independent Paths (NOIP) as a measure of hypertext navigation complexity. The larger the NOIP, the more complex the website structure is, the easier for a user to get lost in the network and the poor navi-

Figure 4. Tree structure of a website

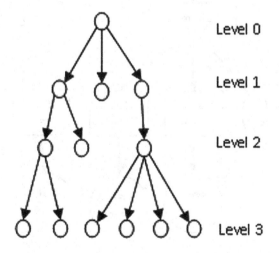

gability. The structural complexity of website is determined with Mc. Cab's Cyclomatic Complexity Metric, which identifies NOIP in the website. This metric is used to know navigation path for a desired web page. The Cyclomatic Complexity metric is derived in graph theory as follows. A tree graph is constructed with home page as root. The tree consists of various sub trees and leaf nodes. An example tree is shown in Figure 5.

A tree graph is constructed for a website by considering various hyperlinks in the website. Each sub tree of the graph represents a web page which has further hyperlinks to the next web pages and leaf node represent a web page which do not have any further links to the web pages. In tree graph, at each level all web pages that do not have further links are represented with one leaf node at that level and a sub tree at each level consists of links to the web pages to the next level. The structural complexity is computed using *Cyclomatic Complexity* and it can be calculated as defined in Equation 3. According McCabe value of *Cyclomatic Complexity Metric (CC$_{Metric}$)* should be less than or equal to 10.

$$Cyclomatic\ Complexity\ Metric\,(CCMetric) = \frac{(e - n + d + 1)}{n} \qquad (3)$$

Where

e: number of web page links
n: number of nodes in the graph
d: number of leaf nodes in the graph

Figure 5. Tree graph for a website

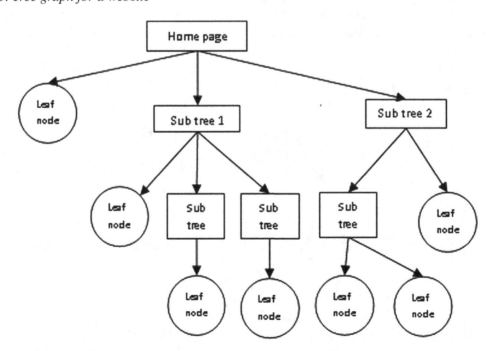

Broken Link Calculation

In a website structure, navigation problem raised due to broken links. The broken link may involve at various levels of web site structure. Broken links are identified by broken link checker module. In a sitemap of website, broken links are counted at various levels and broken error index is calculated based on percentage of broken links involved in sitemap. The percentage of broken links is calculated using Equation 4.

$$PBL = \left(NBL / n \right) * 100 \tag{4}$$

where

PBL: Percentage of broken links
NBL: Total number of broken links in the Web site
n: number of Web pages

10-Point Scale Metric for Evaluating Quality of Website Structure

The quality of website structure for each University is evaluated in 10-point scale. The 10-point scale value for a website is based on organization of web pages in sitemap structure, cyclomatic complexity of website, average number of clicks and broken link error index. The 10-point scale value for sitemap structure (SMP) is evaluated using SMP_{Metric} defined in Equation (5).

$$SMP_{Metric} = \begin{cases} 10 & if \ \ webpage \ is \ \ home \ page \ \& \ wps = n \ \& \ wps \leq 20 \\ 10 & if \ \ wps \geq 10 \ \& \ wps \leq 20 \\ 9 & if \ \ wps = 9 \ or \ 21 \\ 8 & if \ \ wps = 8 \ or \ 22 \\ 7 & if \ \ wps = 7 or \ 23 \\ 6 & if \ \ wps = 6 \ or \ 24 \\ 4 & if \ \ wps = 4 \ or \ 26 \\ 3 & if \ \ wps = 3 \ or \ 27 \\ 2 & if \ \ wps = 2 \ or \ 28 \\ 1 & if \ \ wps = 1 \ or \ 29 \\ 0 & otherwise \\ 10 & if \ \ webpage \ is \ home \ page \ \& \ wps = n \ \& \ wps \leq 20 \end{cases} \tag{5}$$

where

SMP_{Metric}: Site Map Structure Metric
wps: number of web page links in a subtree of sitemap

$$CC_{Metric} = \begin{cases} 10 & if \;\; CC \leq 1 \\ 9 & if \;\; CC \leq 2 \\ 8 & if \;\; CC \leq 3 \\ 7 & if \;\; CC \leq 4 \\ 6 & if \;\; CC \leq 5 \\ 5 & if \;\; CC \leq 6 \\ 4 & if \;\; CC \leq 7 \\ 3 & if \;\; CC \leq 8 \\ 2 & if \;\; CC \leq 9 \\ 1 & if \;\; CC \leq 10 \\ 0 & otherwise \end{cases} \qquad (6)$$

where

CC: Cyclomatic Complexity
CC_{Metric}: Cyclomatic Complexity Metric

10-Point Scale value for website structure is derived using Equations 5 and 6.

$$10_{WS} = (SMP_{Metric} + CC_{Metric}) / 2 \qquad (7)$$

where

10_{WS}: 10 Point Scale Value for Web site structure

The Web Page Click (WP_{Click}) value is determined using Equation 8 and 10-point scale value is refined using the additional information of number of clicks as defined in Equation 9.

$$WP_{Click} = \begin{cases} 0.75 & if \;\; AvgClicks \leq 3 \\ 0.5 & if \;\; AvgClicks \leq 4 \\ 0.25 & if \;\; AvgClicks \leq 5 \end{cases} \qquad (8)$$

where

WP_{Click}: Web page click

The refined 10_{WS} value can be defined as

$$10_{WS} = 10_{WS} + WP_{click} \qquad (9)$$

Also the 10_{WS} can be improved using BLE and in turn BLE can be defined using PBL defined in Equation 10 as follows

$$BLE = \begin{array}{ll} 1 & if\ PBL \geq 10 \\ 0.75 & if\ PBL \geq 5 \\ 0.5 & if\ PBL \geq 2 \\ 0.25 & if\ PBL > 0 \end{array} \tag{10}$$

where

BLE: Broken Link Error Index
PBL: Percentage of Broken Links

Thus the improved 10_{WS} metric is ultimately defined as

$$10_{WS} = 10_{WS} - BLE \tag{11}$$

Website Quality Analysis

Web design encompasses many different skills and disciplines in the production and maintenance of websites. The different areas of web design include web graphic design, interface design, authoring, including standardized code and proprietary software, user experience design and search engine optimization. Web design is the planning and creation of websites. This includes the information architecture, user interface, site structure, navigation, layout, colors, fonts, and imagery. A high quality website is one that provides relevant, useful content and a good user experience. However, there are many individual factors that need to be considered. Website Standards Association (WSA) proposed following collection of some of the components that will confirm a quality website.

1. General website characteristics
   a. Website Structure
   b. Page Depth
   c. Popup use
   d. Clear Entrance and Exit pages
2. Visual layout
   a. Decorative or functional
   b. Text Size
   c. Layout
   d. Page printing
   e. Image use

3. General content
    a. Is it detailed
    b. Grammatical and spelling
    c. Content tone
    d. Regularly updated
    e. Browser support
    f. Navigation
    g. Navigation positioning
    h. Has primary, secondary and tertiary navigation
    i. Consistency
    j. Navigation Hierarchy
    k. Back to top button
    l. Navigation clarity
    m. Tool tips
    n. Order of navigation items
    o. Navigation feedback
    p. Colour combinations
    q. Current location indication
    r. Can pages be book marked
4. Search
    a. Accessible
    b. Useful
5. Navigation aids
    a. Website sitemap
    b. Sitemap Scope
    c. Sitemap up-to-date
6. Site optimisation
    a. Linking
    b. Back links
    c. Google sitemap
    d. Keywords usage and proximity
    e. Meta tags used correctly
7. Form usage

This module mainly focuses on the quality of website content. The Website Quality analysis module evaluates various quality assurance parameters of the website. The quality assurance parameters include errors, accessibility, compatibility, privacy, search, standards according W3C guidelines and usability aspects of website. The website quality analysis module accepts URL address of a Website and processes the first 100 web pages in the website. The output report of the website quality analysis module demonstrates the number of pages that suffer with quality issues due to lack of accessibility, lack of compatibility, lack of privacy, lack of search facilities, lack of standards and lack of usability factors. The screen shot of Website Quality Analysis is shown in Figure 6.

Figure 6. Website quality analysis

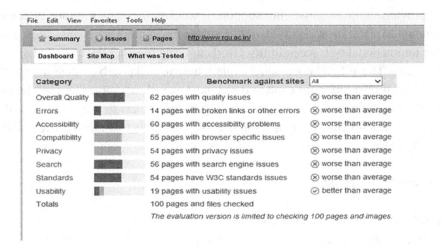

10-Point Scale Metrics for Analyzing Website Quality

Having defined various quality assurance aspects, at this part of the chapter, it is tried to evolve 10-point scale. Thus 10-point scale is a metric towards defining quality of web content. In this connection it is interpreted the 10-point scale indicates such that '0' always represent poorer side and '10' always represent the best side of quality aspect. The 10-point scale metrics for various qualitative measures are formulated using empirical evaluation. Here 10-point scale of web content depends on the value computed using measures and its level competence based on performance. Thus the 10-point scale measurements of various quality assurance aspects are defined below.

Website Accessibility

Use of the Web is spreading rapidly into most areas of society and daily life. In many countries, the Web is increasingly used for government information and services, education and training, commerce, news, workplace interaction, civic participation, health care, recreation, entertainment, and more. In some cases, the Web is replacing traditional resources. Therefore, it is essential that the Web be accessible in order to provide equal access and equal opportunity to people with disabilities. Web accessibility refers to the inclusive practice of removing barriers that prevent interaction with, or access to websites, by people with disabilities. When sites are correctly designed, developed and edited, all users have equal access to information and functionality. Making a Web site accessible can be simple or complex, depending on many factors such as the type of content, the size and complexity of the site, and the development tools and environment. When developing or redesigning a site, evaluating accessibility early and throughout the development process can identify accessibility problems early when it is easier to address them. Simple techniques such as changing settings in a browser can determine if a Web page meets some accessibility guidelines. A comprehensive evaluation to determine if a site meets all accessibility guidelines is much more complex. Much of the focus of web accessibility has been on the responsibilities of web content developers. This view misses the crucial interdependence of other components of web development and interaction, including browsers, assistive technologies, and authoring tools. Improvements in browsers, authoring tools, and other components could significantly reduce the amount of effort spent on accessibility overall and substantially improve web accessibility. For example, if the few hundred authoring tools provided ample accessibility support, it would save many millions of content developers an untold amount of effort on accessibility and result in much more accessible sites. The W3C WAI helps coordinate international web accessibility efforts to bring together the technical and human component considerations. The WCAG documents explain how to make web content accessible to people with disabilities. WCAG is written for content developers as well as, authoring tool developers to use to create tools that generate accessible content; User agent developers to use to create tools that render accessible content; Evaluation tool developers to use to create tools that identify accessibility issues in content. The checklist for accessibility of website is as follows.

Website Accessibility Checklist

- Whether website load-time is reasonable?
- Whether there is adequate text-to-background contrast?
- Whether font size/spacing is easy to read?
- Whether Flash and add-ons are used sparingly?
- Whether Images have appropriate ALT tags?
- Whether website has custom not found/404 page?

The accessibility parameter of website is calculated using the Equation (12).

$$Accessibility = \left(10 - \left(\frac{No.\ of\ Accessibility\ issues}{10}\right)\right) \tag{12}$$

Website Usability

Website Usability testing is the best way to get detailed insights into the usability problems of a web site or app, and how to fix them. Usability testing can be conducted at all stages in a website development. The main reason that usability is so important is because there are so many similar websites that people will go to the next site if the first one they visit is not usable. You can have the most beautiful website in the world, but people will leave immediately if they are unable to figure out how to navigate your site quickly. Web usability is the ease of use of a website. Some broad goals of usability are the presentation of information and choices in a clear and concise way, a lack of ambiguity and the placement of important items in appropriate areas. One important element of web usability is ensuring that the content works on various devices and browsers. Another concern for usability is ensuring that the website is appropriate for all ages and genders. Usability is comprised of Learnability, memorability, efficiency, satisfaction and errors. Learnability is how easy it is for a new user to accomplish tasks the first time they visit your website. Memorability is how easy it is for someone to come back to using your website after they haven't used it for a period of time. Efficiency is how quickly users can complete tasks on your site after they are familiar with its use. Satisfaction is whether users enjoy the design of your site and errors refers to the number of errors users make when they use your site, the severity of the errors and how easy they are to recover from. The usability checklist is as follows.

Website Usability Checklist

- Whether Company logo is prominently placed
- Whether Tag line makes company's purpose clear
- Whether Home page is digestible in 5 seconds
- Whether clear path to company information
- Whether clear path to contact information
- Whether Main navigation is easy identifiable
- Whether Navigation labels are clear and concise
- Whether Number of buttons/links is reasonable
- Whether Company logo is linked to home page
- Whether Links are consistent and easy to identify
- Whether website search is easy to access
- Whether Major headings are clear and descriptive
- Whether Critical content is above the 'fold'
- Whether Styles and colors are consistent
- Whether Emphasis (bold, etc) is used sparingly
- Whether Ads and pop-ups are unobtrusive
- Whether Main copy is concise and explanatory
- Whether URLs are meaningful and user friendly
- Whether HTML page titles are explanatory

The 'usability' parameter of website is calculated using the Equation (13).

$$Usability = \left(10 - \left(\frac{No. \ of \ Usability \ issues}{10}\right)\right) \qquad (13)$$

Website Privacy

The Internet privacy involves the right or mandate of personal privacy concerning the storing, repurposing, provision to third parties, and displaying of information pertaining to oneself via the Internet. Internet privacy is a subset of data privacy. Privacy concerns have been articulated from the beginnings of large scale computer sharing Privacy can entail either *Personally Identifying Information* (PII) or non-PII information such as a site visitor's behavior on a website. PII refers to any information that can be used to identify an individualInternet users may protect their privacy through controlled disclosure of personal information. The revelation of IP addresses, non-personally-identifiable profiling, and similar information might become acceptable trade-offs for the convenience that users could otherwise lose using the workarounds needed to suppress such details rigorously. The 'privacy' parameter of website is calculated using the Equation (14).

$$Privacy = \left(10 - \left(\frac{No.\ of\ \text{Privacy issues}}{10}\right)\right) \qquad (14)$$

Website Compatibility

Internet users have wider choice of browsers when it comes to surfing the net. It is the responsibility of designers and developers to ensure that websites are compatible for most of the commonly used browsers. Cross Browser Testing is a process to test web applications across multiple browsers. Cross browser testing involves checking compatibility of web application across multiple web browsers and ensures that web application works correctly across different web browsers. The following checklist is used to identify compatibility issues of web application.

- CSS validation
- HTML or XHTML validation
- Page validations with and without JavaScript enabled
- Ajax and JQeury functionality
- Font size validation
- Page layout in different resolutions
- All images and alignment
- Header and footer sections
- Page content alignment to center, LHS or RHS
- Page styles
- Date formats
- Special characters with HTML character encoding
- Page zoom-in and zoom-out functionality

These checks give early warning of browser compatibility problems without the associated cost of manual testing on different platform and browser combinations. The 'compatibility' of website is calculated using the Equation (15).

$$Compatibility = \left(10 - \left(\frac{No.\ of\ Compatibility\ \text{issues}}{10}\right)\right) \qquad (15)$$

Website Search

Search engine optimization (SEO) is the process of affecting the visibility of a website or a web page in a search engine's unpaid results, often referred to as natural, organic, or earned results. In general, the earlier (or higher ranked on the search results page), and more frequently a site appears in the search results list, the more visitors it will receive from the search engine's users. SEO may target different kinds of search, including image search, local search, video search, academic search, news search and industry-specific vertical search engines. The quality parameter 'website search' is calculated using the Equation (16).

$$Search = \left(10 - \left(\frac{No.\ of\ search\ \text{issues}}{10}\right)\right) \qquad (16)$$

Website Correctness

Website correctness is depending on the website errors. Following areas of errors are verified in website correctness.

- Broken links and anchors in HTML, CSS, Flash, PDF and Office documents
- Missing or corrupt images
- Server configuration issues like inconsistent MIME types and character set encodings
- Script errors
- Domains about to expire
- SSL certificate problems
- Placeholder text like "Lorem Ipsum" and "TODO"
- Empty pages
- Page code and content larger than a specified size (page weight)
- Pages containing specified text (e.g. inappropriate language, competitor brand names)
- Pages missing required text (e.g. disclaimers or analytics tags)
- server configuration errors, expired domains and faulty SSL certificates
- spelling errors in multiple languages
- Custom dictionary for unusual words like product names Uses page LANG attributes to choose spelling dictionary
- Choice of default spelling language for pages without LANG attributes

The quality parameter 'correctness' of the website is calculated using the Equation (17).

$$Correctness = \left(10 - \left(\frac{No.\ of\ errors}{10}\right)\right) \qquad (17)$$

Website Standards

Web standards are rules and guidelines established by the World Wide Web Consortium (W3C) developed to promote consistency in the design code which makes up a web page. Without getting technical, simply it's the guideline for the mark-up language which determines how a web page. Website Standards Association Inc. has been set up to identify the minimum website standards that websites should meet and educate internet users about how to get the most out of their websites. Web standards are the formal, non-proprietary standards and other technical specifications that define and describe aspects of the World Wide Web. The advantages in adhering to these standards are many:

- Web pages will display in a wide variety of browsers and computers, including new technology like iPhones, Droids, iPads, PDA devices, mobile phones, which greatly increases the viewing audience.
- W3C Standards promote the use of "Cascading Style Sheets" (CSS) or design code which is attached to the web page rather than embedded in the page. The use of style sheets significantly reduces the page file size which means not only a faster page loading time but lower hosting costsfor frequently visited sites due to using less bandwidth.
- Design features such as colours and fonts can be easily changed by just modifying one style sheet instead of editing every individual page in a web site, reducing the costs to modify your site.
- Search Engines are able to access and index pages designed to web standards with greater efficiency.

The quality parameter 'web standards' is calculated using the Equation (18).

$$Standards = \left(10 - \left(\frac{No. \; of \; standards \; issues}{10} \right) \right) \tag{18}$$

Website Download Time Performance

The World Wide Web (WWW) has become an important channel for information retrieval, electronic commerce and entertainment. However, long Web page download times have remained a major cause of frustration among Web. Although various technologies and techniques have been implemented to alleviate the situation and to comfort the impatient users, little research has been done to assess what constitutes an acceptable and tolerable waiting time for Web users. The long waiting time for downloading Web pages is often not tolerable even in the wired environment. Due to the increasing and excessive use of multimedia data (i.e. audio and video clips) on Web pages, this concern is continuously growing. Web page download time is affected by the performance of the browser, the speed of the Internet connection, the local network traffic, the load on the remote host, and the structure and format of the Web page requested. The acceptable or tolerable waiting time for Web page download can be defined from various perspectives. The tolerable waiting time (TWT for short) is defined as *the amount of time users are willing to wait before giving up on the download of a Web page*. The TWT for downloading a Web page may depend on various factors such as level of experience and age of users, individual user's characteristics (i.e. propensity to wait), task type, expected content of the Web page, expected download time, and information available about the wait. Such variability and its associated research challenge should not deter us from studying the 'waiting time' phenomenon and Web users' waiting behaviour. According to Nielsen (1996, 2000), Web users may be willing to tolerate up to 15 seconds for a Web page download. The size of a website is measured considering all its images, sounds, videos and textual components. For each page, the size in bytes can be obtained. The size of pages is an important issue in order to appreciate the site efficiency. The download time (T) is related with the size of a page (τ) and the speed in the established connection line (c) and this relation is shown in Equation 19.

$$T_{Download} = f(\tau, c) \tag{19}$$

This download time is directly proportional to the page size and inversely proportional to the speed of a given connection line. A function may be created in order to classify pages as quick or slow access pages, according to a minimum threshold of time (e.g. 10 seconds) for a given speed of a connection line.

$$g(T_{Download}) = \frac{Quick\ Access \quad T_{Download} < T_{max}}{Slow\ Access \quad T_{Download} \geq T_{max}} \tag{20}$$

The website size is dependent on various components of the website. These components include Images Size, Documents size, Media Size, Programs or Scripts Size, CSS Size and other objects. As the components sizes increase then automatically the size of website is also increases. The relation between website size and web components is shown in Equation 21.

$$WEBSIZE = f(IMAGESIZE, DOCSIZE, MEDIASIZE, \\ SCRIPTSIZE, OTHEROBJSIZE) \tag{21}$$

where

WEBSIZE: Web site size
IMAGESIZE: Image size
DOCSIZE: Document size
MEDIASIZE: Multimedia size
SCRIPTSIZE: Scripts or Programs Size
OTHEROBJSIZE: Other objects size (e.g. ActiveX control objects, Applets, etc.)

A regression analysis is carried out to analyse the relationships among these variables. The analysis is carried out through the estimation of a relationship using equation. The results serve the following two purposes.

- Answer the question of how much web size changes with changes in each of the web component's size and
- Forecast or predict the value of web size based on the values of the web component's size

The download time performance of the website is measured based on home page time. A standard web tool GTmetrix is used to know the download time performance of the website. GTmetrix has a suite of features and options to make optimizing your website clear and easy. GTmetrix's Report Page neatly summarizes web page performance based off key indicators of page load speed. GTmetrix uses Google PageSpeed and Yahoo YSlow, two of the major speed analysis tools, to grade web site's performance and provide actionable recommendations to fix these issues. The speed of a page is made up of both Front-end and Server-side components. GTmetrix assesses the front-end structure of web page to ensure that it is delivered as optimally as possible to visitors, but an optimized server-side is also an important part of the equation in offering a fast and seamless site experience. With PageSpeed and YSlow, it's easy to put too much emphasis on the front-end and forget about the server-side. It's important to remember that even though you may have high PageSpeed and YSlow scores, the developer can make web page faster by optimizing web server-side. GTmetrix finds each web page's Page Load Time, Total Page Size and Total number of Requests. Using the GTmetrix API, user can integrate performance testing into development environment. The download time performance is measured in A, B, C, D, E and F grades as described in Table 1. A screen shot of download time performance module is shown in Figure 7.

Table 1. Description of download time performance grades

Download Time Performance Grade	Description
A	Very Good
B	Good
C	Better than Average
D	Average
E	Poor
F	Very Poor

Figure 7. Website download time performance

Evaluation

As part of quality analysis, in this chapter quality assurance aspects of various University websites are evaluated using the methodology specified above and some of the universities are shown in Table 2. During the quality evaluation process, the quality issues such as errors, accessibility issues, compatibility issues, privacy issues, search issues, standards issues and usability issues along with the download time performance grades of University websites are shown in Table 3. The 10-point metric quality assurance values related to website design viz., correctness, accessibility, compatibility, privacy, search, standards, usability, website structural complexity, website download time performance, overall quality and performance of various University websites are summarized in Table 4.

The quality status of University websites in India is shown in Table 4 after thoroughly evaluating quality assurance aspects of the various University websites. Also the status of the University websites in India in terms of quality of web design is depicted in Figure 8.

Table 2. Central universities with codes

Central University Name	Code
1. English and Foreign Language University, Hyderabad	EFLUH
2. Moulana Azad National Urdu University, Hyderabad	MANUUH
3. University of Hyderabad, Hyderabad	UOH
4. Rajiv Gandhi University, Itanagar	RGUI
5. Assam University	AUS
6. Tezpur University	TU
7. Central University of Bihar	CUB
8. Nalanda University	NU
9. Central University of Haryana	CUH
10. Central University of Himachal Pradesh	CUHD
11. Central University of Jammu	CUJ
12. Central University of Kashmir	CUK
13. Central University of Jharkhand	CUJR
14. Central University of Karnataka	CUKAR
15. Central University of Kerala	CUKER
16. Guru Ghasidas Visvavidyalaya, Bilaspur	GGVB
17. Dr. Harisingh Gour Viswavidyalaya, Sagar	HGVS
18. Indira Gandhi National Tribal University	IGNTU
19. Mahatma Gandhi Antharashtriya Visvavidyalaya	MGAV
20. Central Agricultural University, Manipur	CAUM

Table 3. Number of quality assurance issues related to university websites (per 100 pages)

University	Errors	Accessibility issues	Compatibility issues	Privacy issues	Search issues	Standards issues	Usability issues	Download time performance
1. EFLUH	29	88	13	88	23	88	62	F
2. MANUUH	93	95	19	0	95	95	95	A
3. UOH	96	96	0	96	96	96	96	E
4. RGUI	14	60	55	54	56	54	19	E
5. AUS	38	66	43	18	46	47	48	F
6. TU	45	62	27	47	48	48	49	F
7. CUB	87	88	8	88	90	88	90	F
8. NU	13	35	17	30	31	33	31	F
9. CUH	45	74	10	47	47	47	47	B
10. CUHD	8	15	11	8	8	8	8	B
11. CUJ	12	56	6	43	45	11	44	F
12. CUK	7	33	11	7	7	7	7	D
13. CUJR	13	51	20	33	34	36	36	B
14. CUKAR	19	50	37	35	36	37	37	D
15. CUKER	87	89	20	0	87	87	87	E
16. GGVB	17	68	52	59	59	59	59	B
17. HGVS	54	58	6	5	50	58	58	D
18. IGNTU	36	46	18	36	36	36	36	B
19. MGAV	18	53	39	38	38	39	38	C
20. CAUM	22	65	11	65	66	50	65	B

Figure 8. Quality status of university websites

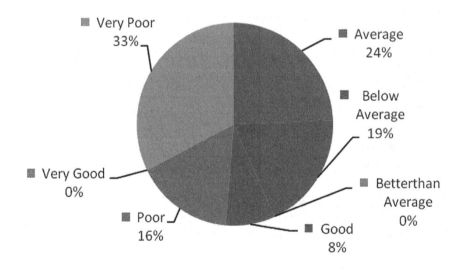

Table 4. 10-Point Metric values of various quality assurance aspects

University	Correctness	Accessibility	Compatibility	Privacy	Search	Standards	Usability	10-WS	10-PDT	Overall Quality	Overall Performance
1. EFLUH	7.1	1.2	8.7	1.2	7.7	1.2	3.8	4.1	0	3.9	Very Poor
2. MANUUH	0.7	0.5	8.1	10	0.5	0.5	0.5	3.2	10	3.8	Very Poor
3. UOH	0.4	0.4	10	0.4	0.4	0.4	0.4	3.6	2	2	Very Poor
4. RGUI	8.6	4	4.5	4.6	4.4	4.6	8.1	4.6	2	5	Below Average
5. AUS	6.2	3.4	5.7	8.2	5.4	5.3	5.2	5.1	0	4.9	Poor
6. TU	5.5	3.8	7.3	5.3	5.2	5.2	5.1	5.2	0	4.7	Poor
7. CUB	1.3	1.2	9.2	1.2	1	1.2	1	2.3	0	2	Very Poor
8. NU	8.7	6.5	8.3	7	6.9	6.7	6.9	5.7	0	6.3	Average
9. CUH	5.5	2.6	9	5.3	5.3	5.3	5.3	4.3	8	5.6	Below Average
10. CUHD	9.2	8.5	8.9	9.2	9.2	9.2	9.2	8.2	8	8.8	Good
11. CUJ	8.8	4.4	9.4	5.7	5.5	8.9	5.6	6.1	0	6	Average
12. CUK	9.3	6.7	8.9	9.3	9.3	9.3	9.3	7.2	4	8.1	Good
13. CUJR	8.7	4.9	8	6.7	6.6	6.4	6.4	5.6	8	6.8	Average
14. CUKAR	8.1	5	6.3	6.5	6.4	6.3	6.3	5.2	4	6	Average
15. CUKER	1.3	1.1	8	10	1.3	1.3	1.3	2.4	2	3.2	Very Poor
16. GGVB	8.3	3.2	4.8	4.1	4.1	4.1	4.1	3.7	8	4.9	Poor
17. HGVS	4.6	4.2	9.4	9.5	5	4.2	4.2	4.1	4	5.5	Below Average
18. IGNTU	6.4	5.4	8.2	6.4	6.4	6.4	6.4	5.4	8	6.6	Average
19. MGAV	8.2	4.7	6.1	6.2	6.2	6.1	6.2	6.5	6	6.2	Average
20. CAUM	7.8	3.5	8.9	3.5	3.4	5	3.5	3.5	8	5.2	Below Average

CONCLUSION AND FUTURE RESEARCH DIRECTION

The chapter identifies the various factors that influence the quality of website design. The methodology is very much comprehensive and will applicable to web application product because web application is the integration of number of different components. In this chapter, a significant effort is made to evaluate the quality assurance aspects related to website design. The chapter has shown the path and cautiousness to be adopted in web design process for the web designers not only on design but also quality of design. The importance of the quality assurance of Web Design is essential in the light of enormous growth of web applications. In this connection the theme of the chapter shows a direction to improve the web applications more viable to the need of common man and to achieve user friendly websites. Thus the presented methodology is quite helpful to address this and to achieve the end user accessibility of website which is imperative in today's context. Also, the quality web design process removes the unnecessary contents of the website and provides information that was quite useful for the user. The chapter is well illustrated with a case study on university websites in India which clearly explains the quality analysis of process of websites in more interesting to the users, web developers or researchers. The researchers further extends the work in terms of website security, authentication and other areas of website quality analysis process.

REFERENCES

Bayir. (n.d.). *A New Reactive Method for Processing Web Usage Data.* Retrieved from http://etd.lib. metu.edu.tr/upload/12607323/index.pdf

Chang, G., Healy, M. J., McHugh, J. A. M., &Wang, J. T. L. (2001). *Mining the World Wide Web: An Information Search Approach.* Kluwer Academic Publishers.

Cooley, R., Mobasher, B., & Srivastava, J. (1997). Web Mining: Information and Pattern Discovery on the Word Wide Web. *Proceedings ICTAI.* doi:10.1109/TAI.1997.632303

Etnoteam S. P. A. Marzo . (2000). Retrieved from http://ww.etnoteam.it/webquality

Etzioni, O. (1996). The World Wide Web: Quagmire or Gold Mine. Communications of the ACM, 39(11), 65-68.

Gandhi, M., Jeyebalan, K., Kallukalam, J., Rapkin, A., Reilly, P., & Widodo, N. (2004). *Web Research Infrastructure Project Final Report.* Cornell University.

Ivory, M. Y. (2001). *An Empirical foundation for Automated Web Interface Evaluation, Doctoral dissertations, University of California.* Berkeley, CA: Computer Science Department.

McCabe, T. J. (1976). A Complexity Measure. *IEEE Transactions on Software Engineering, SE-2*(4), 308–320. doi:10.1109/TSE.1976.233837

Nestorov, S., Abiteboul, S., & Motwani, R. (1998). Extracting schema from semistructured data. In ACM SIGMOD. doi:10.1145/276305.276331

Nielsen, J. (1996). *Top ten mistakes in Web design.* Jakob Nielsen's Alertbox. Retrieved from www. useit.com/alertbox/9605.html

Nielsen, J. (2000). *Designing Web Usability: the practice for simplicity.* Indianapolis, IN: New Riders.

Pandia, , Pani, , & Padhi, , Panigrahy, & Ramakrishna. (2011). A Review of Trends in Research on Web Mining.International Journal of Instrumentation. *Control and Automation, 1*(1), 37–41.

Srivastava, J., Cooley, R., Deshpande, M., & Tan, P. N. (2000). Web usage mining: Discovery and applications of usage patterns from web data. *ACM SIGKDD Explorations Newsletter, 1*(2), 12–23. doi:10.1145/846183.846188

Srivastava.Desikan, J. P., & Kumar, V. (2002). Web Mining:*Accomplishments and Future Directions. National Science Foundation Workshop on Next Generation Data Mining.*

Valet. (n.d.). Retrieved from http://valet.webthing.com/access/url.html

Zhu, H., & Hall, P. (1993). Test data adequacy measurement. *Journal of Software Engineering, 8*(1), 21–30. doi:10.1049/sej.1993.0004

ADDITIONAL READING

Bobby. Retrieved fromhttp://webxact.watchfire.com/

EvalIris. Retrieved fromhttp://www.sc.ehu.es/acwbbpke/evaliris.html

Extractor, W. Retrieved from www.internet-soft.com/extractor.htm

GTMetrix Web Speed & Performance Optimization. Retrieved from www.gtmetrix.com

Rose, G. M., Evaristo, R., & Straub, D. (2003). Culture and consumer responses to web download time: A four-continent study of mono and polychronism. *IEEE Transactions on Engineering Management*, *50*(1), 31–44. doi:10.1109/TEM.2002.808262

Selvidge, P. (1999).How long is too long for a website to load? Usability New, 1(2).Retrieved from http://psychology.wichita.edu/surl/usabilitynews/1s/time_delay.htm

Sitemap for website. Retrieved from www.powermapper.com

University websites in India. Retrieved from www.ugc.ac.in

User effect.Retrieved from www.usereffect.com

W3C guidelines. Retrieved from www.w3c.org

KEY TERMS AND DEFINITIONS

Accessibility: Web accessibility refers to the inclusive practice of removing barriers that prevent interaction with, or access to websites, by people with disabilities. When sites are correctly designed, developed and edited, all users have equal access to information and functionality.

Correctness: Website correctness is depending on the website errors. These errors include broken links, image load errors, script errors etc.

Privacy: The Internet privacy involves the right or mandate of personal privacy concerning the storing, repurposing, provision to third parties, and displaying of information pertaining to oneself via the Internet. Internet privacy is a subset of data privacy.

Usability: Website Usability testing is the best way to get detailed insights into the usability problems of a web site or app, and how to fix them. Usability testing can be conducted at all stages in a website development.

Web Content Mining: Web Content Mining is a form of text data mining applied to the web domain, and has to do with finding the content of documents, classifying documents, and clustering documents.

Web Mining: Web mining is the application of data mining techniques to extract knowledge from web data, i.e. web content, web structure, and web usage data.

Web Standards: Web standards are rules and guidelines established by the World Wide Web Consortium (W3C) developed to promote consistency in the design code which makes up a web page. Web standards are the formal, non-proprietary standards and other technical specifications that define and describe aspects of the World Wide Web.

Web Structure Mining: The goal of the Web Structure Mining is to generate the structural summary about the Web site and Web page. It tries to discover the link structure of the hyperlinks at the inter-document level. The structure of a typical Web graph consists of Web pages as nodes, and hyperlinks as edges connecting related pages. Based on the topology of the hyperlinks, Web Structure mining will categorize the Web pages and generate the information like similarity and relationship between different Web sites.

Web Usage Mining: Web Usage Mining which is also known as web log mining aims to find out interesting and frequent user access patterns from web browsing data that are stored in web server log. Such discovered knowledge is useful in analysing how the web pages are accessed or what are seeking for by the users.

Website Compatibility: Website Compatibility also known as Cross Browser Testing is a process to test web applications across multiple browsers. Cross browser testing involves checking compatibility of web application across multiple web browsers and ensures that web application works correctly across different web browsers.

Website Download Time Performance: The download time performance of the website is measured based on home page time. A standard web tool GTmetrix is used to know the download time performance of the website. The download time performance is measured in A, B, C, D, E and F grades.

Website Quality Analysis: The Website Quality analysis module evaluates various quality assurance parameters of the website. The quality assurance parameters include errors, accessibility, compatibility, privacy, search, standards according W3C guidelines and usability aspects of website.

Website Search: Website Search is the process of affecting the visibility of a website or a web page in a search engine's unpaid results, often referred to as natural, organic, or earned results. SEO may target different kinds of search, including image search, local search, video search, academic search, news search and industry-specific vertical search engines.

Website Structure Analysis: Website Structure analysis module analyzes the quality of website structure. The procedure of the quality assessment of website structure involves four modules: creating a sitemap, computing path length metric, evaluating structural complexity of website, and finding broken link error index.

Chapter 8
Search Query Recommendations in Web Information Retrieval Using Query Logs

R. Umagandhi
Kongunadu Arts and Science College, India

A. V. Senthil Kumar
Hindusthan College of Arts and Science, India

ABSTRACT

Web is the largest and voluminous data source in the world. The inconceivable boom of information available in the web simultaneously throws the challenge of retrieving the precise and appropriate information at the time of need. The unpredictable amount of web information available becomes a menace of experiencing ambiguity in the web search. In this scenario, Search engine retrieves significant information from the web, based on the query term given by the user. The search queries given by the user are always short and ambiguous and the queries may not produce the appropriate results. The retrieved result may not be relevant all the time. At times irrelevant and redundant results are also retrieved because of the short and ambiguous query keywords. Query Recommendation is a technique to provide the alternate queries as a substitute of the input query to the user to frame the queries in future. A methodology was framed to identify the similar queries and they are clustered; this cluster contains the similar queries which are used to provide the recommendations.

INTRODUCTION

The exhaustive information available in the World Wide Web indeed, unfolds the challenge of exploring the apposite, precise and relevant data in every search result. The plentiful unstructured or semi-structured information on the web leads to a great challenge for the users, who hunt for prompt information. The scenario grows pathetic and distressing to provide a personalised service to the individual users from billions of web pages. At the end of the nineties the size of the web to be around 200 million static pages (Bharat, K. *et al.*, 1998). The number of indexable documents in the web exceeds 11.5 billion (Antonio, G. *et al.*, 2005). According to the survey done by Netcraft, Internet Services Company, England there

DOI: 10.4018/978-1-5225-0613-3.ch008

is 739,032,236 sites in September 2013 and 22.2M more than the month August 2013. Every year, millions of web sites are newly added in the information world. Hence a proper tool is needed to search the information on the web.

Search Engine retrieves significant and essential information from the web, based on the query term given by the user. The retrieved result may not be relevant all the time. At times irrelevant and redundant results are also retrieved by the search engine because of the query keywords which are short and ambiguous (Mark, S. 2008). The unpredictable amount of web information available becomes a menace of experiencing ambiguity in the web search. To prevent the web users from getting overwhelmed by the quantity of information available in the web, several strategies are proposed with the advent of data mining techniques.

Search engines are used to retrieve the information from web based on the query term given by the user in terms of web snippets. A web snippet denotes the title, abstract, and URL of a web page returned by the search engines. Apparently, in such instances of web-searching, Query Recommendations is the ultimate application in information retrieval. The Query Recommendation technique provides alternative queries to the user to frame a meaningful and relevant query in the future and rapidly satisfies their information needs. Search engine leaves the search information to the user for further references in the form of query logs. Query log is an important repository, which records the user's search activities. The mining of these logs can improve the performance of search engines. Query log file is a repository contains every query request and its navigation in the search engine and maintained either in the system desktop or in the proxy server. This Chapter deals the new approach for queries recommendations based on:

- The analysis on query log to observe the web users and their sessions, frequent access patterns.
- The proposed query recommendation technique is based on the combined similarity measure on various attributes. Both the positive and negative concepts preference help to explore the string of similarity between the concepts generated which in turn leads to cluster the users with similar intentions.
- The hybrid approach generates the time variant and invariant query clusters; this cluster contains the similar queries based on the attribute time which is used to provide the recommendations.
- The recommendation is based on the user's real search intention which is identified from the hybrid user profile and the recommended queries are prioritized and evaluated using the proposed technique.

The rest of the chapter is organized under background which deals with the review of literature, Basic terms which describes the terms and their definitions used in this chapter and Architecture which describes the methodology used in the proposed work. Next, Identification of similar users and queries identifies the similarity between the users' interms of their queries and Experimental results shows the evidence and the results for the proposed technique. Finally the chapter is concluded.

BACKGROUND

Dupret*et al.* (Dupret, G.,& Mendoza, M. 2006) addresses the non-trivial patterns prevalent in query log data as *Query Log Mining*. After the processing of log files, the data mined explicitly assumes three applications namely, *Query Recommendation*, *Document Recommendation* and *Query Classification*.

- **Query Recommendation:** As the initial input query leads to inappropriate results, query recommendation technique is trusted to provide the appropriate alternative queries to the user where actually the initial input query is applied. Query recommendation application helps in a precise way to explore and formulate the original query.

- **Document Recommendation:** The identification of appropriate documents related to the original query shall be easily achieved with these kinds of applications. The aim of this application is fetching appropriate documents relevant to the users based on their similarity of queries posed by them.

- **Query Classification:** This technique is a methodical identification of appropriate queries and documents and assigns it to one or more predefined categories, based on its topics.

Interpret the human queries into search keyword is never simpletask (BaragliaRanieri*et al.*, 2009). Especially search engine users are inexperienced and they are usually casual. They have very limited background knowledge about the domain they are searching for. Most of the time the queries are coined on the spot in front of the search engine. A study done by C. Silverstein (Silverstein, C., *et al.*, 1998) on Alta Vista Query Log has shown that more than 85% of the queries contain less than three terms and the average length of the query is 2.35 terms. So the shorter length query does not provide any meaningful, relevant and needed information to the users. Table 1 shows some of the examples for ambiguous query keywords. Sanderson M. (Sanderson, M. 2008) reported that up to 23.6% of web search queries are ambiguous, this causes poor retrieval results.

Actually, the query recommendations of a search engine depend on the authentic and the genuine intention of the user, significantly investigated from the search histories. For instance, a search pursued by feeding the query term 'apple' obtains the exclusive recommendations for 'apple iPod' and not for 'apple fruit'. This recommendation is carried out with an assumption of the user's interest fixed to 'apple iPod'. At this juncture, with reference to the previous probe of the same user on 'apple iPod', query recommendation system attempts to supply the results if the query term 'apple' is tried by the same user next time.Consider another example, user U_1 wants to get the information on 'Android applications'. Not keeping in mind of its keyword he enters the query keyword as 'mobile applications'. The top documents do not have the information on 'Android applications'. After a long searching process U_1 gets the result and clicks the correct *URL*. But another user U_2 enters the correct query on Android applications by using the correct keywords and clicks the same *URL*which is clicked by U_1. Our algorithm generates the cluster which contains the users who have the similar intents (that is U_1 and U_2), the query keywords and the URLs are clicked for the queries. The cluster is used to provide the query recommendations to the first user U_1 by using the keywords of U_2. Here the query recommendation is a collaborative technique, which is based on the intent of more than one user.

Search engines provide the assistance to frame the queries in the form of automatic query completion (Chirita Paul-Alexandru*et al.*, 2007; Mei Qiaozhu*et al.*, 2008) at hitting time and query recommendation

Table 1. Ambiguous query keywords

Query	Search Topics
Java	Programming Language, Bike, Country
Apple	Company, Fruit, System

(Ma Hao*et al.*, 2010; Li Ruirui*et al.*, 2012; Baeza-Yates *et al.*, 2005) as a future reference. Automatic query completion technique helps the user to frame the query at hitting time. Query recommendation as shown in Figure 1 is used to provide the set of recommendations to the user to frame the queries in future. Human mentality is to get a choice for everything and select an option from the given choice. Here the user's real intent is analysed based on the given query and historical click-through features. The recommendation is based on the input query, user's real intent and similarity with other users.

CNNIC 2009 search behaviour survey report says that 78.2% of the users change their query by using the recommended queries. Users may select the recommended queries instead of framing the new queries. The recommendation methods are typically trivariatedas stated subsequently (Stefanidis, K.,*et al.*, 2009; Khemiri, R. *et al.*, 2013):

Content-based approach (Khemiri, R. *et al.*, 2013) gives the recommendation based on the past queries and navigational behavior of individual user.

Collaborative approach (Golfarelli, M. *et al.,* 2011) is based on the preferences of other similar users and the queries from similar users are recommended.

Hybrid approach (Stefanidis, K. *et al.*, 2009) combines both content-based and collaborative approach.

The recommendation process shall be fed with the input in the form of a user profile, query log or an external source like ontology, web pages, etc. The recommendation may be provided in three ways namely, in advance to querying, during querying or after querying. The juxtaposition of the previously existing techniques along with the innovative strategy of query recommendation proposed in this study is overtly presented in Table 2.

Umagandhi et al. (Umagandhi, R.*et al.*, 2014) follows hybrid approach which provides the recommendation after querying and it uses the query log file as the input. The queries are recommended from the access log of the similar users.

Figure 1. Query recommendation

Table 2. Query recommendation approaches – a comparison

Research Works		Stefanidis*et al.*, 2009	Chatzopoulou*et al.*, 2009	Khoussainova*et al.*, 2010	Golfarelli*et al.*, 2011	Khemiri*et al.*, 2012	Umagandhi et al., 2014
Recommendation Type	Content Based	X				X	X
	Collaborative	X	X	X	X		X
Recommendation Time	While			X		X	
	After	X	X		X		X
Recommendation Input Data	Log file	X	X	X		X	X
	User Profile				X		

Search activities of the users is analysed by using the query log and semantic meaning of the query have been described (Baeza-Yates *et al.*, 2005). Neelam, D. *et al.* (Neelam, D. *et al.* 2011) Recommendation of the query is by using the semantic meaning of the input query and the semantics have been identified from yourdictionary.com. CucerzanSilviu*et al.* (CucerzanSilviu*et al.* 2007) find the query keywords similarity and click URL similarity. Many researchers have used this similarity measure to cluster the similar queries. Liu, Y. *et al.* (Liu Yiqun*et al.* 2001) have recommended the query in which keywords are recommended because of their appearance in clicked snippets instead of similarity with previous one. The recommendation process is analysed based on the user's perspective. The recommendation is based on the snippet click model and there is a possibility for redundant recommendations. Much research has been done in query expansion, Query suggestions and Query recommendations (Limam, L.*et al.*, 2010; Zahera Hamada, M.*et al.*, 2011). The similar queries in the log entries are clustered based on similarity measure. (Fu, L.*et al.*,2004; Neelam, D.*et al.*, 2010) Recommend the query using similarity based query cluster.

Query recommendations are often based on clustering methods with the inconvenience that queries falling in the same cluster are sometime more ambiguous and less helpful than the original query (Bodon, F. *et al.*, 2005). The frequently used queries and URLs in the log file are identified using Prefix Span (Pei, J. *et* al., 2005) or Up down Directed Acyclic Graph (Chen, J. *et* al., 2006). The similar queries and URLs are clustered; the cluster recommends the queries. Hub and authority weight is calculated for each unique URL (Kleinberg, J. M. 1999). The total weight value is considered for generating the query cluster.

A good query recommendation system should observe the following properties (Li, R. *et al.*, 2012).

- **Relevance:** Recommended queries should be semantically relevant to the user search query.
- **Redundancy Free:** The recommendation should not contain redundant queries that repeat similar search intents.
- **Diversity:** The recommendation should cover search intents of the different interpretations of the keywords given in the input query.
- **Ranking:** Highly relevant queries should be ranked first ahead of the less relevant ones in the recommendation list.
- **Efficiency:** Query recommendation provides online help. Therefore, the recommendation algorithms should achieve fast response times.

ARCHITECTURE

Figure 2 describes the architecture for the proposed query recommendations. Information about the user is gathered by means of registration and stored in the user log. The registered users, by means of this interface, either apply the search query to the search engine or keep them posted with the general status. With the aid of the keywords, the proposed technique pre-processes the query keywords and acquires the search results from Google. The query recommendations can be made by integrating this technique directly into any search engine. It also facilitates the renewal of the user's status against the query and a separate profile is created for each query of the user. Only a single profile of the user is generated by most existing recommenders (Speretta, M. *et al.*, 2005;Agichtein, E. *et al.*, 2006) which is applied to every query posted by the user. Nevertheless, the user's preference is not stable and it differs across queries. In conjunction with the resultant web snippets, ultimately the set of queries is recommended to the user.

The user submits the query through search engine interface. The users request and their navigational behaviours are recorded in the query log file. The user scans the search result from the top to the bottom and decides that the retrieved results are either relevant or irrelevant for their request. Sometimes the user scans the search result andwill be satisfied with the information available in the abstract of the web snippets. For these cases the user does not click any URL, so the message "NoClick" is assigned to the attribute ClickURL. From the pre-processed log entries in the query log file, the users with similar intent and the similar queries are identified. The similarity between the users is identified by using the day wise query access. The concepts stored in the clicked snippets are retrieved and the relationship between the concepts is stacked in the concept log.

The user preferences explicitly given in the login process, the query taken from similar users and the similar queries based on keywords, URLs and concepts, concepts retrieved from the concept log are clustered. This cluster provides the similar queries for the input query as recommendations and it is ranked.

The four different cases of search user U and query Q are identified, such as;

Figure 2. Architecture for query recommendation process

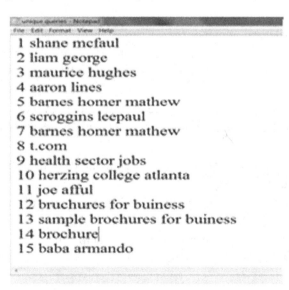

- The query log may comprise U and Q that is absolutely new to the search process.
- U is new and the query keyword Q may exist already.
- U exists previously in the query log and Q is new.
- The U and Q already exist in the query log.

IDENTIFICATION OF SIMILAR USERS AND QUERIES

Similarity between Queries

The similarity between the users and queries are generated. The similarity between the queries in terms of keywords andURLs are calculated using the Equations (1) and (2). This is similar to Jaccard Coefficient (Thada, V. *et al.*, 2011)

$$\text{Keyword Similarity}\left(Qi, Qj\right) = \frac{\text{Number of Common Keywords in the queries } Qi \text{ and } Qj}{\text{Total number of keywords in } Qi \text{ and } Qj} \tag{1}$$

$$\text{Keyword Similarity}\left(Qi, Qj\right) = \frac{\text{keywords}\left(Qi \cap Qj\right)}{\text{keywords}\left(Qi\right) + \text{keywords}\left(Qj\right)}$$

If the queries Qiand Qj share some common terms in their keywords then the queries are similar.

$$\text{URL Similarity}\left(Qi, Qj\right) = \frac{\text{Number of Common URLs clicked for } Qi \text{ and } Qj}{\text{Total number of URLs clicked for } Qi \text{ and } Qj} \tag{2}$$

$$\text{URL Similarity}\left(Qi, Qj\right) = \frac{\text{count}\left(\text{URL}\left(Qi\right) \cap \text{URL}\left(Qj\right)\right)}{\text{count}(\text{URL}\left(Qi\right) + \text{count URL}\left(Qj\right))}$$

The function count is used to find the number of URLs clicked for the given query. The URL count is calculated by using the algorithm HASHURLCOUNT (Umagandhi, R. *et al.*, 2009). The combined similarity measure is calculated by using the Equation (3).

$$\text{Combined Similarity } (Qi, Qj) = \alpha * \text{Keyword Similarity}\left(Qi, Qj\right) + \beta * \text{URL Similarity } (Qi, Qj) \tag{3}$$

For instance, a discussion on the query, $Q1$ = "*grooming in harrisburg pa*" triggered by the user 227 on 2006-03-22 16:39:29 in addition to the submission of another query $Q2$ = "*parking garage in harrisburg pa*" by the same user on 2006-05-07 00:37:17 paves an obvious route to the subsequent observations. At this juncture, it is noteworthy that the proposed research focuses on time as the major constituent of the search process to make every search an effective one. The substantiation of this time factor may be observed successfully through the queries triggered at discrepant time periods. As the proposed work is time independent, the time occurrence of the queries is not considered. With respect to the observation, totally 9 terms are available in *Q1* and *Q2*, out of this three terms are common.

Keyword Similarity (*Q1, Q2*)= 3/9 = 0.3333

When the query *"grooming in harrisburg pa"* is supplied, the user, 227, clicks 3 URLs namely, http:// www.switchboard.com, http://www.magicyellow.com *and* http://harrisburg.citysearch.com. Whereas, for the submission of the consecutive query, *"parking garage in harrisburg pa"*, only a single URL, http:// harrisburg.citysearch.com is clicked. Studying the results of both the above stated queries make evident that the commonly chosen URL is http:// *harrisburg.citysearch.com.*

URL Similarity (*Q1,Q2*) = ¼ = 0.25 Combined Similarity = 0.3333 + 0.25 = 0.5833

If the similarity threshold is 0.5 then the combined similarity measure satisfies the threshold value and the queries *"grooming in harrisburg pa"* and *"parking garage in harrisburg pa"* are considered as similar and they are clustered. Figure 3 shows the bipartite representation of the queries *"grooming in harrisburg pa"* and *"parking garage in harrisburg pa"*.

Clustering of Queries

The clustering of the queries is carried out with the help of combined similarity measure as substantiated in Equation 7. The algorithm *FavouriteQueryIdentifier* illustrated by Umagandhi, R. *et al.*, strengthens the means of finding the favourite query of every query cluster. As soon as the input query is encountered in the searching process, the cluster gets fixed to where the query actually belongs to. Simultaneously, the favorite query of that cluster is recommended. Further, the frequently occurred queries are explored.

For instance exploring the user and their activities around 5 days is elucidated below. The queries Qi, $1 \leq i \leq 6$ are triggered by the user on Day$j$, $1 \leq j \leq 5$.

Figure 3. Query and clicked URL - bipartite representation

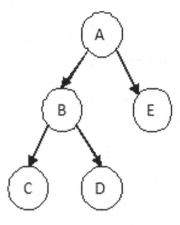

Day 1 – *Q1, Q3, Q4* Day 2 – *Q1, Q4, Q5* Day 3 – *Q1, Q2, Q3, Q6*
Day 4 – *Q3, Q4, Q5* Day 5 – *Q1, Q2, Q6*

The queries *Q1, Q3* and *Q4* are comprehended to have been supplied on Day 1. Consider the minimum support threshold is 2. The queries which satisfy the minimum support threshold are considered to be frequently occurred queries: {*Q1, Q2, Q3, Q4, Q5,* and *Q6*}. To find the combination of frequently occurred queries, the queries issued are to be comprehended by the user in any order. For example, the Queries *Q1* and *Q3* are triggered sequentially on day1. But on day 3, *Q4* is triggered in between *Q1* and *Q3*. However, the support count for *Q1* and *Q3* is 2. While, the frequently occurred queries with the combination 2 is {(*Q1, Q2*), (*Q1, Q3*), (*Q1, Q4*), (*Q1, Q6*), (*Q2, Q6*), (*Q3, Q4*), (*Q4, Q5*)} the frequently occurred queries with the combination 3 is {(*Q1, Q2, Q6*)}. If the queries *Q1* and *Q2* occur sequentially then the query *Q6* is recommended.

Clustering of Users

The clustering of the users is pursued with respect to the similarity witnessed in their interests. After which the user cluster starts recommending queries to the users with the support of the inference made through the access logs of similar users. For example, the day-wise access of all the users may be considered. Table 3 contains the access information of 5 users with 6 queries. The value 1 indicates that the query *Qi* is accessed by the user *j* where $1 \leq i \leq 6$ and $1 \leq j \leq 5$.

Further, the similarity matrix is generated between the users on day 1 using the symmetric binary similarity measure (see Table 4).

Then, the similar users are clustered using the clustering algorithm (Beeferman, D.*et al.,* 2000)where similarity threshold is 0.5. There are two resultant clusters, Cluster 1 contains {*U1, U2, U3, U4*} and Cluster 2 contains {*U5*}. Similarly we have to find the user-wise cluster for all the days, let us consider the sample clusters in Table 5.

Umagandhi, R. *et al.* (Umagandhi, R. *et al.,* 2013) derived *PrefixSpanBasic* algorithm which generates the frequently clustered users with minimum support of 2 (see Table 6).

While, the users {*U1, U2, U3*} are in a single cluster, fixed through their similar query access the users {*U4, U5*} are observed to be in another cluster. The queries are recommended using the collaborative technique, recommendation for the user *U1* is from the similar queries of the users *U2* and *U3*. Similarly, for the user *U4*, the recommendation is from the intent of the user *U5*.

Table 3. Queries accessed by 5 users

User/ Query	Q1	Q2	Q3	Q4	Q5	Q6
U1	1	0	1	1	0	0
U2	1	0	1	1	0	0
U3	1	0	1	1	1	0
U4	0	0	1	1	0	0
U5	0	1	0	0	1	1

Table 4. Symmetric binary similarity measure

	U1	U2	U3	U4	U5
U1	-	1	0.833	0.833	0
U2	1	-	0.833	0.833	0
U3	0.833	0.833	-	0.667	0.167
U4	0.833	0.833	0.667	-	0.167
U5	0	0	0.167	0.167	-

Table 5. Day-wise clustering of the users

Day	Clusters
Day 1	C1={U1, U2} C2={U3,U4} C3={U5}
Day 2	C1={U1, U2, U3} C2={U4} C3={U5}
Day 3	C1={U1} C2={U2,U3} C3={U4} C4={U5}
Day 4	C1={U1} C2={U2,U3} C3={U4,U5}
Day 5	C1={U1, U2,U3} C3={U4,U5}

Table 6. Frequently clustered users

	U1	U2	U3	U4	U5
U1	-	3	2	0	0
U2	3	-	4	0	0
U3	2	4	-	1	0
U4	0	0	1	-	2
U5	0	0	0	2	-

Concepts Retrieval

The positive and negative concept similarities may also be considered when there is an attribute concept available in the query log file (Umagandhi, R.*et al.*, 2012). The submission of the query to the search engine interface is followed by the pre-processing of the query keywordsapart from the list of web snippets returned to the user. The significant concepts from the clicked documents are retrieved and accumulated in the concept log. The pre-processing of the derived concepts is set through the following ways.

- The concepts are converted into lowercase letters.
- Extra spaces are trimmed.
- All the plurals are converted into singulars. (It is called Lemmatization. Morpha is used for the conversion. It is downloaded from www.informatics.sussex.ac.uk/research)
- Some of the special symbols and words are truncated. (Remove the words like cached, similar etc. and symbols like @, .,; etc.)
- Stop words are removed from the retrieved concepts. (List of Google stop words are downloaded from http://code.google.com/p/andd/downloads/detail?Name=stopwords.csv)

The frequent existence of the concept on the web snippets for a particular query specifies that it is an important concept related to that query. The interestingness of a concept is found by computing the support value. In the concept extraction process, the support value of the unique concepts of length one is initially identified. In case of support value assuring the minimum support threshold, concepts with higher length are generated. Concept gains prominence when it crops up for a minimum of 50% of the clicked documents. The calculation of the support value is restricted to the concepts in the clicked snippets on satisfying the threshold *s*, it is treated as important concepts with positive preferences.Leung, K. W. T.*et al.*, (Leung, K. W. T.,*et al.*, 2010)fixes the maximum length of a concept which is restricted to seven words as it confines the computational time and shuns the extraction of meaningless concepts. The proposed technique in this research also limits the concepts to seven. Maximum number of concept's combinations to be generated for the query *Q* is:

$$Max\_concepts = \sum_{i=1}^{n} 2^{m_i} - 1 \qquad (4)$$

Where m_i is number of concepts in document i and n is number of documents. For example, consider D1, D2 and D3 are clicked documents out of ten snippets which contains:

D1 = {a, b, c, d, e}D2 = {a, b} D3 = {a, c}

For instance, for the three clicked documents, the maximum number of concept's combinations produced is 37. Number of combinations among the concept is nC_r where n is the number of concepts in the document and r is the number of words that is combined. To illustrate, the number of concepts generated with the length of four in the document D1 is $5C_4$ and it is 5. Table 7 through 10 depict that the concept patterns and its support value from the documents D1, D2 and D3.

From Table 7, it is estimated that the concepts a, b and c assure the threshold s and the support value of d and e are 1. The concepts a, b and c are used to create the concepts of length 2. Since the support of "bc" is 1, it is not considered for the next level. Finally, the generated concept patterns and its support value are shown in the Table 10. Maximum number of concepts expected to be generated is 37 with the maximum length of five, but the proposed method generates five concepts with the maximum length of 2.

Next, the relationship between the extracted concepts in the clicked web snippets is identified. Here the similarity measure is produced to obtain the relationship between the concepts. The concepts co-exist in title, abstract, tags or others. The tags are keywords used to retrieve the webpage and it is defined in <meta> tag. The tags are displayed publicly only in few webpage. The format of the <meta> tag is

```
<meta name = "description" content="a description of your site">
<meta name="keywords" content="relevant keywords about your site">
```

Table 7. Concepts with 1 words

Concept Pattern	Support and Confidence
a	3 & 100%
b	2 & 67%
c	2 & 67%
d	1 & 33%
e	1 & 33%

Table 8. Concepts with 2 words

Concept Pattern	Support and Confidence
ab	2 & 67%
ac	2 & 67%
bc	1 & 33%

Table 9. Concepts with 3 words

Concept Pattern	Support and Confidence
abc	1 & 33%

Table 10. Selected concepts

Concept Pattern	Support and Confidence
a	3 & 100%
b	2 & 67%
c	2 & 67%
ab	2 & 67%
ac	2 & 67%

The combined similarity measure is

$$Sim\left(C_i, C_j\right) = \propto * \frac{sf_{title}\left(C_i \cup C_j\right)}{sf_{title}\left(C_i\right) * sf_{title}\left(C_j\right)} + \beta * \frac{sf_{abstract}\left(C_i \cup C_j\right)}{sf_{abstract}\left(C_i\right) * sf_{abstract}\left(C_j\right)} +$$
$$\gamma * \frac{sf_{tags}\left(C_i \cup C_j\right)}{sf_{tags}\left(C_i\right) * sf_{tags}\left(C_j\right)} + \delta * \frac{sf_{others}\left(C_i \cup C_j\right)}{sf_{others}\left(C_i\right) * sf_{others}\left(C_j\right)} \tag{5}$$

where $\propto + \beta + \gamma + \delta = 1$ to warrant that the similarity lies between [0, 1]. is the combined similarity between the concepts C_i and C_j. $sf_{loc}\left(C_i \cup C_j\right)$ is the joint snippet frequencies of the concepts C_i and C_j where $sf_{loc}\left(C\right)$ is the number of snippets containing the concept C and loc = {title, abstract, tags, others}. Here "*others*" indicates the different combinations of concept locations. The proposed work takes into consideration, all the combinations for computing the similarity. Different combination of locations where the concepts C_1 and C_2 may appear is listed in Table 11. For example, in Location number 1, the concept C_1 appears at title whereas the concept C_2 in abstract.

An investigation on the locations {3, 4, 7, 8, 9 and 10} reveals the following observation. If the concepts C_1 and C_2 occur at the location of title, abstract or tags, then the joint snippet frequency $C_1 \cup C_2$ crop up in the maximum of 2 combinations of {(title, abstract), (title, tags), (abstract, tags)}. If any one of the locations is empty then the joint snippet frequency $C_1 \cup C_2$ occurs at the maximum of 1 combination. The support value of the concept C is calculated based on the appearance of C in the title, abstract and tags.

$$Support\left(C_i\right) = \sum_{loc} \propto_j \frac{sf_{loc}\left(C_i\right)}{n} \tag{6}$$

Where loc = {title, abstract, tags}. $\propto_j$ is used to normalize the support value in between [0, 1] where $1 \leq j \leq 3$, C_i is the concept and $1 \leq i \leq m$ where m is number of concepts retrieved from the clicked snippets.

Table 11. Locations of the concepts C_1 and C_2

Location No.	Title	Abstract	Tags	Location No.	Title	Abstract	Tags
1	C_1	C_2	-	7	C_2	C_1	C_1
2	C_1	-	C_2	8	C_2	C_2	C_1
3	C_1	C_2	C_2	9	C_1	C_2	C_1
4	C_1	C_1	C_2	10	C_2	C_1	C_2
5	C_2	C_1	-	11	-	C_1	C_2
6	C_2	-	C_1	12	-	C_2	C_1

Query Recommendations

Top k recommendations for the query Q is generated by the algorithm QRecommender. The overall process of the proposed technique is elaborated in steps listed in the algorithm. The interconnection between the databases is depicted in Figure 4.

Algorithm QRecommender

```
Input: Query Log, Concept Log and Updated User Log
Output: Set of k recommendations
begin
          Step 1: Register and Log in Process of a user and store the
user's information in user    log.
          Step 2: Pre-process the query keywords. Mine and store the web
snippets for the pre-         processed query.
      Step 3: Evaluate the query log about the user's search and navigation-
al behavior.    Identify the favourite query of the user.
          Step 4: Extract the concepts from clicked snippets and stored
in concept log against          the query.
Step 5: Analyze the Concept log and recommend the concepts as queries.
Step 6: Rank the recommendations and it should be self explanatory.
end
```

Experimental Results

The algorithms have been implemented in JDK 1.6.0_24. All the experiments have been performed in Intel Core i3 processor 2.53 GHz with Windows 7 Home Premium (64-bit) and 4 GB RAM. The proposed work has been evaluated by considering the experimental data from AOL search engine query log. The dataset is stored in SQL Server. The log entries from 1-3-2006 to 31-5-2006 are considered (zola.

Figure 4. Data model used in recommendation technique

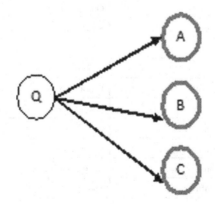

di.unipi.it /smalltext/datasets. html). The data set contains 1975811 log entries and 19131507 words from ~650k users in 174 MB over three months; based on system memory and its speed the pre-processed log entries for the user 1038 are considered. Totally 181 distinct queries are issued by the user 1038 out of 902 log entries. This analysis shows that 80% of the queries are redundant and the users' intents are same at some point. The user 1038 has clicked 318 distinct URLs for 181 distinct queries. Thus in average the user clicked 2.28 pages per query. 69% of the query keywords contain less than 3 terms and the average query length is 2.56. Table 12 shows that the ranking order of 13 queries issued by the user 1038 after considering the individual and combined aspects of the perspectives namely preference and t-measure.

The query recommendations for four different possibilities of users are illustrated below;

Case 1: The query along with the user is a debut to the search process. Here, the recommendation is supplemented either by the top concepts retrieved from the web snippets or by the indexed terms stored against the query in the database.

Case 2: This deals with a query given by a new user. For instance, a query *"herbchambers"* is given by a new user may be considered; it is incredible to generate the favourite query of the user. However, the query cluster is generated. The recommendation contains the following

```
www.herbchambers.com
herb chambers
vespa dealers in boston area
herb chambers bmw
infiniti dealerships in boston
car dealer
volkswagon dealer
car search.com
```

Table 12. Ranking of the queries

Original	Preference	t-measure	Preference + t-measure
didierdrogba	Joe afful	Joe afful	Joe afful
How to take optygen	Low kupono	Liam George	Liam George
Joe afful	Sharlie joseph	How to take optygen	Optygen
Liam George	Optygen	Optygen	How to take optygen
Low kupono	Liam George	Sharlie joseph	Sharlie joseph
Mzbel	didierdrogba	Mzbel	Low kupono
Omar jarun	Omar jarun	didierdrogba	didierdrogba
Optygen	Shane mcfaul	Padraig drew	Mzbel
Optygen soccer	Mzbel	Low kupono	Padraig drew
Padraig drew	Optygen soccer	Optygen soccer	Optygen soccer
Samuel kuffour	How to take optygen	Omar jarun	Omar jarun
Sharlie joseph	Padraig drew	Samuel kuffour	Samuel kuffour
Shane mcfaul	Samuel kuffour	Shane mcfaul	Shane mcfaul

Case 3: This deals with a new query given by the existing user. To illustrate this, the new query "*psychiatric*" given by the user 1038 may be considered. Obviously, the user already exists but the query does not. The favourite query of 1038 is "*Joe afful*". Queries are recommended from the query cluster which contains the similar queries of the input query.. This cluster recommends the subsequent queries

```
Joe afful
psychiatric disorders
cyclothymia
cyclothymia psychiatric disorders
mental health
mental health problems
treatment for psychiatric disorders
```

Case 4: The existence of both the query and the user may be witnessed here. To substantiate this, an existing query "*interview*" given by the already available user 1038 may be considered. Here, the query log is the best evidence for the existence both the user and the query. The recommendations are the favourite query of the user, similar queries and favourite query from the query cluster and the queries from similar users. The recommendations are

```
Joe afful
what to ask on interview
questions to ask employer in interview
interview letters
resume format
```

CONCLUSION AND FUTURE RESEARCH

The query log provided by the search engine is the important repository for this research of query recommendations. In this Chapter, the problem of recommending queries to better capture the search intents of search users has been investigated. The recommendation strategy is based on the favourite query of the user, favourite and similar query from the query cluster and similar queries from the user cluster. The proposed work also generates the frequently occurred query patterns. Through this pattern recommendation is given to the user. The URLs are also recommended to the user by using the URLs clicked by the experts those who have the same intent of the user.

The query analysis and the query recommendation strategies elaborated in this Chapter can be employed irrespective of the category of information retrieval. The primary objective of this proposed work is to formulate a framework in order to offer alternative queries in preference to initial query to retrieve requisite information efficiently with reference to the real search intent of the user. This research work authenticates that recommended queries prove better solutions compared to initial queries. This research results enunciate that the objective is accomplished successfully and proposes significant scope for research in this field. The focus of the experiments conducted by taking advantage of a real large-scale query log is to offer the ranked list of recommended queries. It is firmly trusted that this research with proven results shall offer significant contribution towards web information retrieval and has a substantial impact on the knowledge-based society of today and posterity.

REFERENCES

Agichtein, E., Brill, E., Dumais, S., & Ragno, R. (2006). Learning user interaction models for predicting web search result preferences. In *Proceedings of the 29th annual international ACM SIGIR conference on Research & development in information retrieval*(pp. 3-10). doi:10.1145/1148170.1148175

Antonio, G., & Alessio, S. (2005). The indexable web is more than 11.5 billion pages. *Special interest tracks & posters of the 14th International Conference on World Wide Web.*

Baeza-Yates, R., Carlos, H., & Marcelo, M. (2005). Query recommendation using query logs in search engines. In Current Trends in Database Technology-EDBT 2004 Workshops(pp. 588-596).

Baraglia, R., Carlos, C., Debora, D., Franco Maria, N., Raffaele, P., & Fabrizio, S. (2009). Aging effects on query flow graphs for query suggestion. In *Proceedings of the 18th ACM conference on Information & knowledge management*(pp. 1947-1950). doi:10.1145/1645953.1646272

Beeferman, D., & Berger, A. (2000). Agglomerative clustering of a search engine query log. In *Proceedings of the sixth ACM SIGKDD international conference on Knowledge discovery and data mining*(pp. 407-416). doi:10.1145/347090.347176

Bharat, K., & Andrei, B. (1998). A technique for measuring the relative size & overlap of public web search engines. *Journal on Computer Networks & ISDN Systems*, *30*(1-7), 379-388.

Bodon, F. (2006). *A survey on frequent item set mining. Budapest University of Technology & Economics*. Tech. Rep.

Chen, J. (2010). UpDown Directed Acyclic Graph Approach for Sequential Pattern Mining. *IEEE Transactions on Knowledge and Data Engineering*, *22*(7), 913–928. doi:10.1109/TKDE.2009.135

Cucerzan, S., & Ryen, W. W. (2007). Query suggestion based on user landing pages. In *Proceedings of the 30th annual international ACM SIGIR conference on Research & development in information retrieval*(pp. 875-876). doi:10.1145/1277741.1277953

Dupret, G., & Mendoza, M. (2006). Automatic query recommendation using click-through data. In Professional Practice in Artificial Intelligence (pp. 303-312). doi:10.1007/978-0-387-34749-3_32

Fu, L., Goh, D. H. L., & Foo, S. S. B. (2004). The effect of similarity measures on the quality of query clusters. *Journal of Information Science*, *30*(5), 396–407. doi:10.1177/0165551504046722

Golfarelli, M., Stefano, R., & Paolo, B. (2011). myOLAP: An approach to express & evaluate OLAP preferences. *IEEE Transactions on Knowledge and Data Engineering*, *23*(7), 1050–1064. doi:10.1109/TKDE.2010.196

Khemiri, R., & Fadila, B. (2013). FIMIOQR: Frequent Item sets Mining for Interactive OLAP Query Recommendation. In *DBKDA 2013, the Fifth International Conference on Advances in Databases, Knowledge& Data Applications* (pp. 9-14).

Kleinberg, J. M. (1999). Authoritative sources in a hyperlinked environment. *Journal of the ACM, 46*(5), 604–632. doi:10.1145/324133.324140

Leung, K. W. T., & Lee, D. L. (2010). Deriving concept-based user profiles from search engine logs. *IEEE Transactions on Knowledge and Data Engineering, 22*(7), 969–982. doi:10.1109/TKDE.2009.144

Li, R., Ben, K., Bin, B., Reynold, C., & Eric, L. (2012). DQR: a probabilistic approach to diversified query recommendation. In *Proceedings of the 21st ACM international conference on Information & knowledge management*(pp. 16-25). doi:10.1145/2396761.2396768

Limam, L., David, C., Harald, K., & Lionel, B. (2010). Extracting user interests from search query logs: A clustering approach. *Workshop on Database & Expert Systems Applications* (pp. 5-9). doi:10.1109/DEXA.2010.23

Liu, Y., Junwei, M., Min, Z., Shaoping, M., & Liyun, R. (2011). How do users describe their information need: Query recommendation based on snippet click model. *Expert Systems with Applications, 38*(11), 13847–13856.

Ma, H., Michael, R. L., & Irwin, K. (2010). Diversifying query suggestion results. In *Proc. of AAAI*, 10.

Mark, S. (2008). Ambiguous queries: Test collections need more sense. In *Proceedings of the 31st Annual International ACM SIGIR Conference on Research & Development in Information Retrieval* (pp. 499-506).

Mei, Q., Dengyong, Z., & Kenneth, C. (2008). Query suggestion using hitting time. In *Proceedings of the 17th ACM conference on Information & knowledge management* (pp. 469-478).

Neelam, D., & Sharma, A. K. (2010). Rank Optimization & Query Recommendation in Search Engines using Web Log Mining Techniques. *Journal of Computing, 2*(12).

Neelam, D., & Sharma, A. K. (2011). QUESEM: Towards building a Meta Search Service utilizing Query Semantics. *International Journal of Computer Science, 8*(1).

Paul-Alexandru, Claudiu, S. F., & Wolfgang, N. (2007). Personalized query expansion for the web. In *Proceedings of the 30th annual international ACM SIGIR conference on Research & development in information retrieval* (pp. 7-14).

Pei, J., Jiawei, H., Behzad, M., Jianyong, W., Helen, P., Qiming, C., & Mei-Chun, H. et al. (2004). sequential patterns by pattern-growth: The prefixspan approach. *IEEE Transactions on Knowledge and Data Engineering, 16*(11), 1424–1440. doi:10.1109/TKDE.2004.77

Sanderson, M. (2008). Ambiguous queries: test collections need more sense.*Proceedings of the 31st annual international ACM SIGIR conference on Research & development in information retrieval.* doi:10.1145/1390334.1390420

Silverstein, C., Henzinger, M., Marais, H., & Moricz, M. (1998). *Analysis of a very large AltaVista query log. Technical Report.* Systems Research Center, Compaq Computer Corporation.

Speretta, M., & Gauch, S. (2005). Personalized search based on user search histories. In *Proceedings of the IEEE/WIC/ACM International Conference on Web Intelligence*(pp. 622-628). doi:10.1109/WI.2005.114

Stefanidis, K., Marina, D., & Evaggelia, P. (2009). *You May Also Like results in relational databases.* Lyon, France: Proc. PersDB.

Thada, V., & Sandeep, J. (2011). A Genetic Algorithm Approach for improving the average Relevancy of Retrieved Documents Using Jaccard Similarity Coefficient. *International Journal of Research in IT & Management, 4.*

Umagandhi, R., & Senthilkumar, A. V. (2009). Approaches to find URL click count from Search Engine Query Logs. *International Journal of Computer Information Systems, 4.*

Umagandhi, R., & Senthilkumar, A. V. (2012). Concept based Time Independent Query Recommendations from Search Engine Query Logs. In *Proceedings of the International Conference on computer Applications & Advanced Communications*(pp. 17-18).

Umagandhi, R., &Senthilkumar, A, V. (2013). Time Dependent Approach for Query and URL Recommendations Using Search Engine Query Logs. *IAENG International Journal of Computer Science, 40*(3).

Umagandhi, R., & Senthilkumar, A. V. (2013). Search Query Recommendations using Hybrid User Profile with Query Logs. *International Journal of Computers and Applications, 80*(10), 7–18. doi:10.5120/13895-1227

Umagandhi, R., & Senthilkumar, A. V. (2014). Time Heuristics Ranking Approach for Recommended Queries Using Search Engine Query Logs. *Kuwait Journal of Science, 41*(2), 127–149.

Zahera Hamada, M., & Gamal, F. (2011). Query Recommendation for Improving Search Engine Results. *International Journal of Information Retrieval Research, 1*(1), 45–52. doi:10.4018/ijirr.2011010104

ADDITIONAL READING

Adomavicius, G., & Tuzhilin, A. (2005). Toward the next generation of Recommender systems: A survey of the state-of-the-art & possible extensions. *IEEE Transactions on Knowledge and Data Engineering, 17*(6), 734–749. doi:10.1109/TKDE.2005.99

Baeza-Yates, R., Calderon-Benavides, L., & Gonzalez-Caro, C. (2006). The intention behind web queries. In String processing and information retrieval(pp. 98-109). doi:10.1007/11880561_9

Chatzopoulou, G., Magdalini, E., & Neoklis, P. (2009). Query recommendations for interactive database exploration. InScientific and Statistical Database Management(pp. 3-18). doi:10.1007/978-3-642-02279-1_2

Chen, D., Chen, W., Wang, H., Chen, Z., & Yang, Q. (2012). Beyond ten blue links: enabling user click modeling in federated web search. In *Proceedings of the fifth ACM international conference on Web search and data mining* (pp. 463-472). doi:10.1145/2124295.2124351

Cho, Y. H., Kim, J. K., & Kim, S. H.Yoon HoChoa. (2002). A personalized recommender system based on web usage mining & decision tree induction. *Expert Systems with Applications, 23*(3), 329–342. doi:10.1016/S0957-4174(02)00052-0

Cooley, R., Mobasher, B., & Srivastava, J. (1997). Web mining: Information & pattern discovery on the world wide web. In *Proceedings of the 9th IEEE International Conference on Tools with Artificial Intelligence*. doi:10.1109/TAI.1997.632303

Cui, H., Wen, J. R., Nie, J. Y., & Ma, W. Y. (2003). Query expansion by mining user logs. *IEEE Transactions on Knowledge and Data Engineering, 15*(4), 829–839. doi:10.1109/TKDE.2003.1209002

Jiawei, H., & Micheline, K. (2006). *Data Mining Concepts & Techniques* (2nd ed.). Elsevier.

Joachims, T. (2002). Optimizing search engines using clickthrough data. In*Proceedings of the eighth ACM SIGKDD international conference on Knowledge discovery and data mining*. doi:10.1145/775047.775067

Jones, R., Rey, B., Madani, O., & Greiner, W. (2006). Generating query substitutions. In*ACM Proceedings of the 15th international conference on World Wide Web* (pp. 387-396). doi:10.1145/1135777.1135835

Leung, K. W. T., Ng, W., & Lee, D. L.Dik Lun Lee. (2008). Personalized concept-based clustering of search engine queries. *IEEE Transactions on Knowledge and Data Engineering, 20*(11), 1505–1518. doi:10.1109/TKDE.2008.84

Mobasher, B., Dai, H., Luo, M. N. T., & Nakagawa, M. (2002). Discovery & evaluation of aggregate usage profiles for web personalization. *Data Mining and Knowledge Discovery, 6*(1), 61–82. doi:10.1023/A:1013232803866

Mobasher, B., Dai, H., Luo, T., Sun, Y., & Zhu, J. (2000). Integrating web usage & content mining for more effective personalization. In*Proceedings of the EC-Web* (pp. 165–176). doi:10.1007/3-540-44463-7_15

NPDSearch and Portal Site Survey. (2000). Published by NPD New Media Services.

Sanderson, M. (2008). Ambiguous queries: test collections need more sense. In *Proceedings of the 31st annual international ACM SIGIR conference on Research & development in information retrieval*(pp. 499-506). doi:10.1145/1390334.1390420

Smyth, B. (2007). A community-based approach to personalizing web search. *Computer, 40*(8), 42–50. doi:10.1109/MC.2007.259

Srivastava, T., Prasanna, D., &Vipin, K. (2005). Web mining–concepts, applications & research directions, *Foundations &Advances Data Mining*, Springer Berlin Heidelberg, 275-307.

Umagandhi, R., & Senthilkumar, A. V. (2013). Time Dependent Approach for Query and URL Recommendations Using Search Engine Query Logs. *International Journal of Computer Science, 40*(3).

VanderMeer, D., Dutta, K., & Datta, A. (2000). Enabling scalable online personalization on the web. In *Proceedings of ACM E-Commerce*(pp. 185–196). doi:10.1145/352871.352892

Voorhees, E. M. (1999). The TREC-8 Question Answering Track Report. In TREC, 99, 77-82.

Wang, J., Chen, C., & Peng, B. (2004). Analysis of the user log for a large-scale Chinese search engine, *SouthChinaUniversity of Technology(Natural Science Edition)*, 1-5. Wen J. R., Jian-Yun N. & Hong-Jiang Z., Clustering user queries of a search engine, In *Proceedings of the 10th international conference on World Wide Web* (pp. 162-168).

Xiaobin Fu, Jay Budzik, & Kristian J. Hammond. (2000). Mining navigation history for Recommendation. *Intelligent User Interfaces*, 106–112.

Zhang Zhiyong., &OlfaNasraoui. (2006). Mining search engine query logs for query recommendation. *Proceedings of the 15th International Conference on World Wide Web*, 1039-1040.

APPENDIX: KEY TERMS AND DEFINITIONS

Association Rule: Consider $I = \{i_1, i_2, ..., i_n\}$ is a set of items and $T = \{t_1, t_2, ..., t_n\}$ is a set of transactions where each transaction t_i consists of a subset of items in I. An association rule is of the form,

$$X \Rightarrow Y, X \in I, Y \in I, X \cap Y = \varnothing \tag{7}$$

Association Rules from Query Log File: The generation of associations between the queries in addition to the clicked URLs are stored in the query log file. This is obvious, if the traversal path of the user U_1 for the input query Q_1 is taken for experimenting.

Here the user clicks the documents B and E from the document A. The referring URL for the documents C and D is B. The adjacency matrix representation for the traversal path given in Figure 5 is shown in Box 1.

The association rules generated for the above traversal path is

A =>B, A =>E, B => C, B =>D, AB => C, AB =>D

Figure 5. Traversal path for Q_1 by U_1

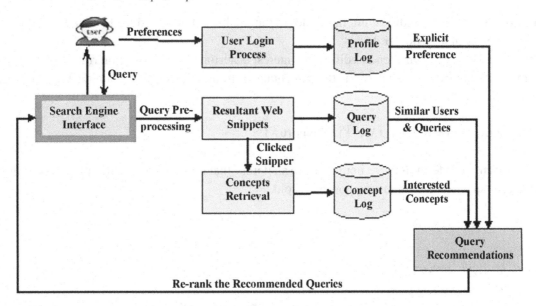

Box 1. Adjacency matrix

	A	B	C	D	E
A	0	1	0	0	1
B	0	0	1	1	0
C	0	0	0	0	0
D	0	0	0	0	0
E	0	0	0	0	0

The association rules generated from the query log may be based on the weights such as in degree, out degree, number of clicks, time spent on the web pages etc. (Fu, L. *et al.*, 2004). The rules are also generated without any pre assigned weights (Neelam, D. *et* al., 2010). The proposed work generates the association rules between the queries and in between the URLs without considering any pre-assigned weights.

Hub: The index pages which bear numerous useful links to relevant content pagesare known as *Hubs*. Generally, a *Hub* identifies the URLs assessed for the query *Q*. A *Hub* can otherwise associate itself with the number of pointers from a page to other pages that is *out-degree*.

Authority: The pages that bear significant, trustworthy and precise information on the topic of search are addressed as *Authorities*. The authority identifies the URL pointed for the query *Q*. In Figure 6, A, B and C are the URLs which have resources for the query Q. For example, number of pointers to a page that is *in-degree* is one simple measure of authority.

From Figure 6,

Hub (*Q*) = Number of out links from *Q* = Authority (A) +Authority (B) +Authority(C) = 3

From Figure 7,

Authority (Q) = Number of in links to Q = Hub (A) +Hub (B) + Hub(C) = 3

Candidate: The usage, candidate implies either to the total set of accessed URLs in a day or the set of triggered queries in a particular day.

Confidence: The term, confidence, edifies the interest criterion of an association rule. The rule *X=>Y* holds in *T* with confidence *c*, where *c* is the percentage of transactions in *T* containing *X* which perhaps comprises *Y* also.

Confidence (*X=>Y*) = Support (*X* U *Y*) / Support(*X*)   (9)

Frequent Item: The term frequent item refers to an item, *I*,that becomes frequent if its support is higher than the user specified minimum support threshold.

Figure 6. Multiple authorities

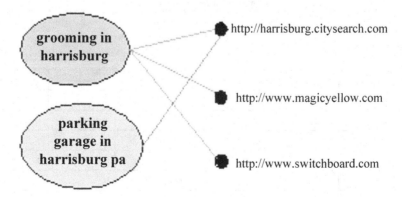

Figure 7. Multiple hubs

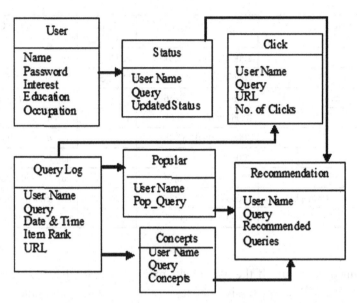

Item/Query: The term, *item* in this context refers to either a query or clicked URL. The queries and the URLs are treated as items when they are recommended individually.

Lift: Lift is a simple correlation measure that compares the rule of confidence with the expected rule of confidence.

Lift(*X=>Y*) = Confidence (*X=>Y*) / Support (*Y*) (10)

Query Log: Search engine leaves the search information to the user for further references in the form of query logs. Query log is an important repository, which records the user's search activities. The search histories are stored in the query log file and it is organized under the attributes <AnonID Query QueryTimeItemRankClickURL>. Table 12 shows the attributes and its description used in the data set and Table 13 shows the sample log entries in the data set.

The first two rows contain the log entry of the user 1038. The user either obtains the information from the web snippets itself or is not satisfied with the result; hence the user does not click any URL. Other rows contain the data for all the attributes. Here the user clicked some of the URL given in the web

Table 12. Aol search engine's attribute and its description

Attribute	Description
AnonID	an anonymous user identifier
Query	the query issued by the user
QueryTime	The date and time on which the query was triggered by the user
ItemRank	If the user clicked on the search result, the rank of the item on which they clicked is listed.
ClickURL	If the user clicked on the search result, the domain portion of the URL in the web snippets is listed.

Table 13. Sample log entries

AnonID	Query	QueryTime	Item Rank	ClickURL
1038	tow truck	2006-03-01 23:17:31	NoClick	NoRank
1038	kris stone	2006-03-1523:19:22	NoClick	NoRank
227	psychiatric disorders	2006-03-02 17:30:36	1	http://www.merck.com
227	cyclothymia	2006-03-02 17:34:08	1	http://www.psycom.net
1038	joeafful	2006-03-05 02:52:48	4	http://www.uslfans.com
1038	joeafful	2006-03-05 02:52:48	6	http://www.northeastconference.org
366	intravenous	2006-03-01 17:16:19	3	http://en.wikipedia.org
647	rabbit hole the broad way play	2006-03-01 22:15:33	2	http://www.entertainment-link.com
309	whectv inrochesterny	2006-05-1114:54:43	1	http://www.10nbc.com

snippets and has attained the result. If the user clicks more than one URL from the returned result for a single query, then there will be successive entries in the access log. The query log entries are pre-processed (Umagandhi, R. *et al.*, 2013) and the unique queries are retrieved. An ID is assigned to each unique query which is shown in Figure 8.

Support of an Item: An item set X has support s in T if $s\%$ of the transactions in T contains X. Support value of an URL is calculated by the access count of the URL by the total number of distinct URLs observed in the data set. Support of a query refers to the count of query submission by the total number of distinct queries.

To exemplify this, the query log of AOL search engine is explored from which the initial 200 log entries, 148 unique URLs and 113 unique queries are retrieved. Noticeably, the recurrence of the URL http://www.google.com for 5 times with a support value of 3% besides, the occurrence of the query "*lotto*" for 12 times with a support value of 10.6% are observed.

Support of a Rule: The rule $X=>Y$ holds in the transaction set T with the support, s, where s is the percentage of transactions in T that contains $X \cup Y$.

$$\text{Support } (X=>Y) = P (X \cup Y) \tag{8}$$

Figure 8. Unique Query with ID

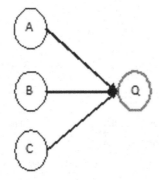

Chapter 9
Web Mining and Analytics for Improving E-Government Services in India

Rajan Gupta
University of Delhi, India

Sunil K. Muttoo
University of Delhi, India

Saibal K. Pal
DRDO, India

ABSTRACT

The ever increasing technology usage and the globalization have given rise to the need of quick, accurate and smarter handling of information by organizations, states, nations and the entire globe. For every nation to be under any form of government, it became mandatory to have shorter turnaround time for their interactions with citizens. This pressure gave rise to the concept of e-Governance. It has been implemented by various nations and even UN reported an increase in E-Governance activities around the world. However, the major problems that need to be addressed by developing nations are digital divide and lack of e-Infrastructure. India started its e-Governance plan through a proposal in 2006 with establishment of National e-Governance Plan popularly known as NeGP headed by Ministry of Communications and Information Technology, Government of India. As per the Electronic Transaction and Aggregation Layer, millions of transactions are taking place on regular basis. Within 2015 itself, over 2 billion transactions have been carried out by the Indian citizens in various categories and sectors like agriculture, health, and the likes. For central government projects alone, around 980 million electronic transactions have taken place, while for state government projects, the combined total of all the states is close to 1.2 billion. With the kind of data getting generated through e-Governance initiative in India, it will open up lot of opportunities for data analysts & mining experts to explore this data and generate insights out of them. The aim of this chapter is to introduce various areas and sectors in India where analytics can be applied for e-Governance related entities like citizens, corporate and government departments. It will be useful for researchers, academicians and students to understand various areas in E-Governance where web mining and data analysis can be applied. The theoretical background has been supported by practical case study for better understanding of the concepts of web analysis and mining in the area of E-Governance.

DOI: 10.4018/978-1-5225-0613-3.ch009

INTRODUCTION

With the rising ubiquity of ICTs, technology becomes an enormously powerful tool to ensure good governance. On one hand, the government is able to incorporate citizens in the process of governance and on the other hand, citizens are able to hold authorities accountable and demand information. The power of any citizen lies in their accessibility to information. E-Governance promotes this notion by promoting access to information in all corners of the nation. This chapter talks about how the idea of E-Governance has taken form over the years and become an indispensable part of how the country is run, focusing on India primarily. It then talks about the related aspects of E-Governance that include the data generation and areas which produce this data. Furthermore, it explores using advanced statistical tools to improve the efficiency of E-Governance and finally discusses some of the case studies that have been conducted on existing E-Governance projects. The aim of this chapter is to get a better understanding of the overall perception of E-Governance in India and how mining and analytics can be incorporated in the related areas.

BACKGROUND

Rise of E-Governance in India

The concept of E-Governance materialized at the turn of the century with the advent of the global wave of a drastic technological change. The arrival of Information and Communications Technology (ICT) paved way for a digitized and networked world facilitating an extensive use of the Internet. This networked globe fostered E-Governance. As stated by Gobind & Rao (2015) UNESCO states that "Governance refers to the exercise of political, economic and administrative authority in the management of a country's affairs, including citizens', the articulation of their interests and exercise of their legal rights and obligations. E-Governance may be understood as the performance of this governance via the electronic medium in order to facilitate an efficient, speedy and transparent process of disseminating information to the public, and other agencies, and for performing government administration activities" (p. 69).

The eighties initiative by National Informatics Centre (NIC) to connect all the district headquarters is considered to be a landmark in the history of E-Governance in India. Consecutively, with the efforts of the government combined with the technology boom, there has been increased emphasis on policy making and using IT for the advancement of E-Governance. Passing the IT Act 2000 by the government was a major forward step towards the further development of E-Governance. With the passing of the act, initiatives and activities under E-Governance got a legal frontier (Weerakkody, 2012). Digital records, signatures, money transfers, notifications, etc. were all now authorized. Since then, there have been programs to compile a comprehensive and dynamic national database that provides information on all the chief E-Governance projects around the country. In 2003, the government approved National E-Governance Action Plan that was to be implemented during the period of 2003-2007 (Babbar & Jain, 2007) and intended to improve infrastructure and establish true governance. Similarly, the Digital India initiative, launched in July 2015 and scheduled for completion by 2019, has given further boost to the E-Governance scenario. The project aims to integrate the various departments in the government and the citizens of our country. The Ministry of Information Technology has over the years worked to ensure implementation and facilitation of E-Governance policies and services. The various ministries and departments like Ministry of Finance, Ministry of Labour, Ministry of Environment and Forests, etc. have also adopted measures that improve E-Governance structure of their ministry. At the state level Andhra Pradesh, Gujarat, Karnataka, Kerala, Madhya Pradesh, Maharashtra, New Delhi and Tamil Nadu, are some of the states that set foremost example for having put E-Governance into operation in their respective areas (Haque, 2002).

As the E-Governance landscape has been on a rise in the country, the government has focused on making technology accessible to rural areas and accommodating citizens from all over the country in it thereby taking important steps at building digital infrastructure and reducing the cost of implementation. It has paid attention to improving the telecommunication system, bettering connectivity and introduced several programs at national and state levels. At present, the government schemes are believed to be reaching millions of people providing them with access to information and increasing their participation in policy making. With information availability becoming a household affair, citizens now demand more accountability, transparency and effectiveness from their governments. The shift in governance not only brings about reduction in costs for the State and for citizens, but also creates an opportunity for interaction and interchange of information (Nandan & Chand, 2007).

The diversity, population and administrative problems that exist in India are the ultimate reason for the development and subsequent success of E-Governance in the country. These factors also play a role in increasing the potential of E-Governance exponentially. Twin Cities Network Services in Andhra Pradesh, Gyandoot in Madhya Pradesh, Bhoomi in Karnataka and WARANA in Maharashtra are some of the projects well known for reducing red-tapism and corruption, all the while improving accessibility to information for citizens and cutting costs (Babbar & Jain, 2007). The 'www.*mygov.in*' website provides an interactive platform to engage citizens in working towards good governance. At present, there are over a million registered members on the website (NIC, 2015; Center, 2015a; Centre, 2015b). Apart from inviting suggestions from the public and introducing competitions, the website also engages people by asking them to design logos and concepts for different projects and departments. More recently, it has launched a crowd-sourcing service where in citizens have been asked to send their views on what should the Prime Minister incorporate in his speech for the upcoming Independence Day. According to the officials, they receive over 500 entries every day (Hebbar, 2015). Overall the governmental digital platforms have seen a tremendous rise in participation by the general public over the past few years.

However, the diversity directs how and what policies are framed so as to serve all the communities in a well-rounded manner. Several problems arise due to the sheer volume of the data that is generated and the variety of languages it is required to be processed in. As there are 22 official languages in India, the services need to be multilingual and should be able to process information obtained in one language into another language. Over time several E-Governance platforms have started provided information in regional languages that takes them one step closer to the goal of providing accessibility to all. With Google leading the way in providing easy online access to multilingual translators, Centre for Development of Advanced Computing (CDAC), India has also employed multilingual computing facilities.

Despite of the advances, there are several milestones that need to be crossed in order to make E-Governance reachable to the high percentage of remote areas in the country. Techniques need to be formulated to process the vast amount of the data that needs to be collected and organized into information every day. Statistical methodologies and analytical tools need to be employed.

Data Generation through E-Governance

E-Governance in India works towards a primary aim - to make information available even in the remotest parts of the country. While the technological advancements help in achieving this goal, there exists the added downside of the massive data that is henceforth generated. The population of India is upwards of 1.25 billion and is set to surpass that of China in the coming years. The foremost form of data is produced in terms of the database of the entire population. Records of all Indian nationals are to be maintained for the effective implementation of E-Governance. Hence this data is produced as a pre-requisite for the larger, yet to be generated information. Besides, as technology and the associated resources become accessible to a larger percentage of the population several factors get incorporated in data generation, with population, diversity and geography playing important roles.

In accordance with the demographics of our country, sources of data generation can be broadly categorized into two – rural and urban. The two sources differ not just in the quantity of technological resource utilized but also in the method of its employment and hence, entail vast differences in the produced data. At the urban level, computing devices are concentrated at individual levels. Majority of the urban population carries individual smart-phones and other computing devices. The work ethics and the urban culture dictate this phenomenon. On the other hand, resources at the rural level, so far, have been shared and community based. This is a result of the cost of obtaining the resource as well as technical proficiency. Apart from the habitat settings, the diverse nature of the population that India comprises also weighs in. With 29 states and 7 union territories the data acquired through E-Governance spreads in more than one way. There are over 85 languages that are spoken across the country. To make E-Governance services truly successful it is important to incorporate people with different spoken languages. A consistent effort has been made over the years to inculcate languages beyond English and Hindi. As a result of this effort, the records that are received through various portals and platforms are an assortment of a multitude of languages. On top of the variety of the languages, there is the added attribute of India being the most populous democracy. Thus data is produced from a massive variety of sources that differ all over the country.

Apart from the sources, the structure or the form in which data is obtained is also an important factor in understanding the magnitude of it all. Mainly, the data can be said to be in two forms - structured and unstructured. The problems in the shift from paper to electronic media are a by-product of the evolution of E-Governance. As the transformation is still underway a lot of the generated data remains in unstructured form. Large amount of paper work and related information from documents are fed into the databases for E-Governance. Therefore the data that could be generated in a structured, program readable form is text heavy and acts as an overhead of E-Governance. Even the structured information that is quantified by the various E-Governance services of different departments are unorganized and therefore add to the volume of our data. For example, several of the government services being offered through E-Governance function as a stand-alone service and are not integrated with each other (Babbar & Jain, 2007). Related data is entered as two completely separate entries and without establishing the required connection. Despite all the attempts, censuses are still inefficient and hence person identity is still not completely established for all the citizens. For this reason the bulk of data lacks efficacy.

After being familiar with the sources and the form of our generated data, we can visualize the real size of this data by recognizing the exponentially increasing web traffic. Data creation and its availability have increased radically in the past decade. Similarly, the ways in which this data can be utilized have also shot up at the same time. At present, the Open Government Data (OGD) Platform India maintains

16,876 resources attributed to 91 different departments which have in all been downloaded 1.54 million times, and have a viewership of three times of that (NIC, 2015). This is only one of the several E-Governance services that are currently available to the public. The global IP traffic is said to be reaching 1.1 zetta-bytes per year in the year 2016 (Peisker & Dalai, 2015). The Internet Service Providers will soon have exhausted the available IPv4 addresses. There is staggering proof of people being more than ever active on the web and India is no different. The E-Governance platforms obtain data from a multitude of sources like Geographical Positioning Services (GPS) devices, department websites, social networking sites, computing devices installed at various stations, and other traditional data sources. The size of data generated is persistently going uphill. In the wake of the size of the data that now needs to be processed into information, the procedure needs to be assisted with powerful analytical tools.

E-Governance Application Areas

The greatest benefit of an efficient E-Governance system is that it puts the citizens in a position of power by providing information and implementing transparency. In order to meet this end it is important to recognize which sectors bring about the most impact into the lives of the common people. Even through the broad areas remain the same across the globe; there can be variations from country to country depending on the geography, demographic and development of the country. The following areas emerge as the most significant ones in terms of E-Governance applications in India – Agriculture, Education, Health, Tourism, Commerce and Trade.

Agriculture

Agriculture is undoubtedly the backbone of India's livelihood even if its share in the economy has declined to less than 15%. According to a story published by the World Bank in 2012, close to three-quarters of the population depends on rural income and nearly 70% of the poor in India live in rural areas (World Bank Group, 2012). Clearly, the consequence of agricultural prosperity cannot be undermined.

The high geographical diversity makes India home to a varied set of intense agriculture practices. The country basically rides on the shoulders of its farmers and their agricultural produce. Not only is the agriculture sector responsible for food security within the country, it is also extremely crucial for exports. Hence it becomes essential that correct information flow be maintained for the farmers in order to keep they updated with the resources at their disposal, to ensure a good yield. Over the past decade the extreme climate changes coupled with inflation and changing political scenarios has left a huge impact on the overall well-being of the farmers. It then becomes necessary to manage the sector with increased efficiency. Through E-Governance the agriculture sector can benefit in the following ways.

- Increasing the agricultural productivity per unit of land is extremely crucial due to the ever increasing population. Through E-Governance, the accurate and much needed information about the climate conditions, forecasts, new technologies, available farm products and market prices of their produce can reach the farmers in an organized and trusted manner. Timely updates will help them adapt to what lies ahead.
- A much needed improvement in the communication between the farmer/users and the government can be brought about. Farmers will be able to voice their concerns and complaints, and put forward their needs in a much more structured manner and track the steps being taken to address their

problems at the same time. The overall administration will progress vastly. The inter-mediatory officers can be supervised better if there is a channel to track their activities through the people they are responsible for.

- Participation of the agrarian community can be brought about in matters that concern them. They can be involved in policy and decision-making through a dedicated platform that not only informs them of the vital changes being brought about, but can also incorporate their views on the matter. The dedicated platform can also be used to bring to the government's notice what products and services are necessary.
- The underrepresented and neglected portions of the community can also be assisted better (Aarti, 2014). By providing them with means to be involved in the bigger picture, their overall conditions can be vastly improved upon.

Education

According to a 2104 UN report, India has the largest population of illiterate adults at 287 million, which equals to 37 per cent of the global total (The Hindu, 2014). There are two main reasons for which E-Governance can be employed in the area of education.

- To track the progress and ensure long term enrollment of the students so that the literacy rate can be improved.
- To better the condition of existing schools and improve the learning process for the students presently enrolled.

The shabby status of most government schools in not unknown to the people. The overall education system needs several necessary changes that E-Governance can help to bring about. Some of them are as follows.

- E-Governance makes it easier to track qualifications of teaching staff across the country at even the remotest levels. A nationwide standard of teaching can be strived for and their performances could be monitored closely to ensure there are no lags in teaching. A hierarchical order of administration can be established to make sure that progress is being made at all levels.
- A dynamic database of schools, resources and staff can be maintained. The database can be used to understand which area becomes priority for improvement. Effective measures can be then taken.
- Interactive mediums of education and administration can be established. New tools of learning and teaching can be applied and made certain that they are performing the required function.
- Most importantly, students, parents and teachers, alike, can voice their complaints and requirements. The government will not only get to know which of its policies are effective, it will also provide a better picture of where improvements can be made and at which level are problems being produced.

Health

Access to basic health care facilities should be enjoyed by all citizens alike. But the Indian scenario is greatly different than the ideal. A major chunk of the population has no proper means to avail health care services or have a doctor available. In such a case, people require a quick and easy way to understand what problems they have. In the health sector E-Governance helps people in a variety of issues. Some of the important applications for E-Governance in health sector are listed below.

- It provides a means to efficiently record the medical facilities available to people in any area. If people have access to this information, they can find out their nearest clinics, hospitals and pharmacies. They can also judge which clinic is well suited for them based on the provided information.
- For remote areas, it creates a way for people to receive medical counseling and a quick diagnosis when a doctor is unavailable. Through an e-healthcare system, areas which are yet to obtain good medical services, people in such areas can benefit massively and receive treatment on a regular basis for common problems.
- E-Governance will create a common platform for all those involved in the process – the healthcare providers, the government and the people (Poonam, Parul, & Kavita, 2013). These groups can come together to ensure best healthcare services are provided to people across the nation. Remote areas can be brought under the radar through an effort from the people as well as the government.

Tourism

The length and breadth of India offers geographical variety that lurks thousands of tourists into the country every year. The World Travel and Tourism Council's report(World Travel and Tourism Council, 2015) says, 'The direct contribution of Travel & Tourism to GDP was INR2,178.1bn (2.0% of total GDP) in 2013, and which rose by 7.5% in 2014, and to rise by 6.4% per annum, from 2014-2024, to INR4,346.4billion (2.1% of total GDP) in 2024'. Both domestic and international tourists are on the rise and therefore, it's important to make their travel as convenient as possible in order to boost the industry further. E-Governance in this sector is not just beneficial from the tourist point of view, but also for the administration of the government. In the area, following schemes can be implemented.

- Comprehensive information can be made available through trusted government portals that provide accurate statistics and relevant data about the numerous travel destinations for the tourists. The tourists can receive information on expenditures, local area, communicate with locals there, get in touch with authorities and overall manage their travel. It will also help the government to promote destinations that are less known and help the local economy.
- Several complaints of frauds and harassments are filed through the year by tourists. Through a dedicated portal it will be easier to identify the criminals and beware fellow tourists. Information can reach the concerned authority as well the public in a timely manner. Hence, the public and government can work together to make the travel hassle free.

Commerce and Trade

The internet revolution has ushered in an era where everything is available on the web. People buy products of daily use over e-commerce websites. Business owners also prefer to advertise and sell their goods online. When there is such an abundance of available platforms, the intervention by E-Governance can help in more than one ways.

- Citizens can receive necessary information of which platforms can be trusted with product quality. The certification and assessment details of the various commerce sites can be made public for the people to judge themselves. It will also make the sellers wary in their activities.
- Government can also use e-commerce to market products from local industries that need more recognition, like handloom industry. Across the country, there are several communities that manufacture unique products but fail to reach the required audience. E-Governance services can aim to improve their conditions.
- As the government has initiated the 'Make in India' project, the use of E-Governance services will help to make the goods accessible around the globe. Qualified government mediums can be used to promote the project and its result to people in all parts of the world and better up the trade.

ROLE OF WEB MINING AND DATA ANALYTICS

Overview

As the size of data grows, it becomes difficult to extract relevant information. The process of quantifying usefulness of a certain information resource also becomes a complex task. With the digitization of most of our everyday activities, online content is increasing rapidly. The role of web mining and data analysis is now more important than ever. Data mining techniques provide a way to recognize patterns automatically and attempt to uncover patterns in data that may not be easily detected otherwise (Kaur &Wasan, 2006). Web mining concentrates on finding trends, patterns and knowledge discovery over the web. It makes use of the information available over the web and is based on web content mining, web structure mining and web usage mining (Purandare, 2008). Data analysis is another related field that also makes use of techniques from data mining and statistics. It is primarily used to make predictions about future trends based on events occurred in the past and uses databases to extract information required to build models that would provide the necessary analysis. The implementation of web mining and data analysis tools provides an effective way to understand and efficiently use the bulk of information that is available.

The most fundamental application of these techniques is in 'knowledge discovery'. By using large and otherwise complex to understand databases, mining and analysis tools can discover important information that helps in decision making. In E-Governance, understanding the trends is essential for the government to be able to make use of the available resources and direct its resources to where they are needed the most. It is also highly essential for the government to understand its citizens, their demands, opinions and problems. Since E-Governance also provides citizens a platform to voice their opinions and concerns, the government can make use of such techniques to understand a general reaction to any new policies or rules passed. Citizen opinion is also spread over a multitude of platforms and simply collecting them from all those sources would be a waste. While the information separately may seem confusing and irrelevant, converging them as the source information to be analyzed will provide a means to understand the general mood of the public (Weng, Fong & Deb, 2011). On the other hand, it also helps citizens to browse through the government portals and find the relevant information. The amount of informative text concerning government policies, decisions and directives that are made available from a number of resources are massive. In addition to the volume of the data being a problem, they are also cross referenced and can be ambiguous as well (Gobind & Rao, 2015). In such a case mining tools can greatly reduce the impediment for citizens to access the information they need.

Developing analytical models also helps define E-Governance services that target specific areas which need attention and improvement. For example, in order to promote the usage of public transport, the government could perform analysis of which routes have enough public transports and which lack in them. They could also identify which areas people prefer to use private transport for, and how will providing more transport options reduce local traffic as well as encourage people to use public transport. In this way, one analysis model can help in several related areas like required construction and infrastructure, heavy traffic routes and so on. The prerequisite source information can also be collected by incorporating real time public opinion and performing web content mining to unearth the vital information from the unstructured data. The study can then be expanded to areas of security and resource management. Similarly, mining and analysis also help in studying crime related data and provides insights into crime rate prediction, hot spot identification, grouping of criminal groups and socio economic analysis of crimes (Chakravorty, 2015). In the education sector, using databases with multidimensional processing pattern that are based on the needs of the departments and citizens provides both the users with control over quality and an overview of the standards of education (Bhanti, Kaushal & Pandey, 2011). Moreover, to provide healthcare over the web, a large amount of data is collected and converted to information that can be dispensed while controlling cost and maintaining quality in patient care (Kaur & Wasan, 2006). Web mining can help address the problem of making relevant information reach the public and analysis can show which techniques are producing the desired results.

Web Mining for E-Governance

Figure 1 describes the three main steps to perform web mining with E-Governance that are Data collection, Pattern discovery and pattern analysis.

Data Collection

Data collection is the primarily step for the web mining in E-Governance. The data can be collected from various E-Government websites. These websites contains data from 3 major sources, server side, registration side and client side. The server side contains information from server ends mainly the data generated from cookies, log files. The client side information consists of records of single client who access multiple websites. The registration information Consist of information gathered from web server through web pages for example log in and log out messages.

Figure 1. Web mining steps for e-governance

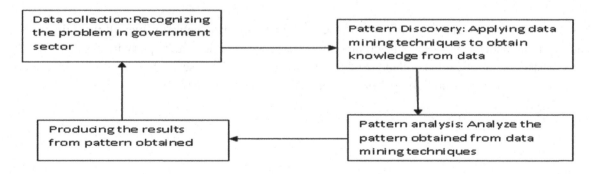

The E-Government data obtained from E-Government websites usually contains redundant data, so it is necessary to convert this data into more useful content for pattern discovery. For this data mining contain various processes like data cleaning which means to remove all the irrelevant information from the data. Data transformation is another method which refers to conversion of data for data analysis on and performing decision making.

Pattern Discovery

After data collection and data preparation another tool is used for implementing web mining in E-Governance that is pattern discovery. Pattern discovery works with the help of various analytical techniques such as statistics, data mining and machine learning.

Statistical Analysis

One of the most common methods for extracting knowledge in data mining is statistical analysis. Statistical model are built on some set of training data. There are many statistical tools available in data mining such as Bayesian network, regression analysis, and correlation analysis. Bayesian network represents relation among various variables. Regression works by mapping a set of attributes to an output variable.

Association Rules

Association or correlation is mainly used to find frequent items sets from a collection of data. This data collected from association rules can help to make various important decisions in E-Governance such as making decisions in health sector or education sector. The association rule for a data is generally large. There are different types of association rules such as Multi association rule, multi- dimensional association rule, quantitative association rule (Bharati and Ramageri, 2010).

Classification and Clustering

Clustering is a technique to group similar class of data. With the help of clustering the dense and spare region of data set can be identified. Clustering in E-Governance can help to form group of states with some specific type of requirement. Data mining provides different types of clustering methods for example: partition clustering, Hierarchical clustering, grid based clustering, soft clustering (Bharati and Ramageri, 2010). Whereas classification can be defined as per Zhou & Le (2007) as "task of mapping the data item with a predefined task" (p. 491).

Pattern Analysis

Pattern analysis is the last step in E-Governance mining. The phase helps to filter all the unimportant data from the pattern discovery. The common methods used for knowledge query mechanism are like SQL. Visualization is another technique of pattern analysis which is used to highlight different pattern and trends in a dataset by assigning different colors to different trends in data.

Implementing Data Analysis

Analysis is an important means for the government to ensure that the administrative ends are functioning properly. In departments like Income Tax, Insurance and Trade and Commerce, analytical tools can be handy to make decisions. For tax collections, predictive models can identify which cases should be given priority, which collectors should be assigned to those cases and how much resource must be allocated to a particular case (Nandan & Chand, 2007). For insurance companies, these can be crucial to recognize defaulters and work on individual cases accordingly. Same technique can be applied by credit bureaus to make judgments about individuals and organizations when debt transactions are concerned. In trade and commerce underwriting is a crucial part of the business. To predict risk exposure analytics models can be extremely helpful and thereafter underwriting can become much easier. Similar models may be applicable for several companies that run on the same structure or target an analogous market.

The government can also track activities and develop these models to ensure that the departments direct their energy productively. The intergovernmental departments' dealings can greatly benefit as much of the work is interlinked and cross-referenced. The departments can interact in a much more industrious manner when they interchange crisp information on the required subject matter. The Government to Business enterprise activities can also progress from analysis. Government can provide companies with information retrieved from the analysis instead of dumping voluminous data on them. The Government to citizen workings will also be at an advantage. Departments can provide citizens with information on frequent mistakes that are made in tax filings and other transactions. People can also receive statistics on frauds and find ways to be more aware. At the same time, the government can find trends in fraud cases such as identity thefts and fraudulent transactions. Maintaining a log of the activities will signal the authorities on any unusual movements. Keeping a track of this data covering departments, enterprises and citizens becomes much better ordered when it is done over the web through government portals where the information will be readily available. Overall it immensely improves the government and citizen interaction.

Implementing Web Mining

Techniques like cluster analysis, association analysis, pattern recognition and correlation analysis are important steps in organizing the unstructured data on the internet. Majority of the content is in the form of text based documents that have no obvious pattern. Hence obtaining information by simply reading the data is very difficult. Employing regular statistics tools is also tricky. In such a case, web mining methods assist in information retrieval. At present the implementation of web mining and data analysis can be seen in various spheres. Social networking sites like Facebook and Twitter use social web mining through hash-tags to generate a list of trending topics. With advanced analysis several lists that are important locally, nationally and globally are produced. The benefit of already existing mining by these platforms this is two-fold. As these two are the most commonly used social platforms, people can actively participate in what is being talked about around the world and be up-to date. Government authorities can directly retrieve information that is of consequence to them in terms of public opinions and reactions. Similar techniques can be executed by government bodies to reach out to a large demographic. It is now common to see Government bodies disseminating significant information through these platforms which immediately reach out to millions of people across the globe.

E-Governance facilities can also be improved through web mining. Officials can obtain data on which services are convenient for users and which are not performing their intended function. They can receive information on how to make services more user-friendly. They can also get data by combining web mining and analytics to discover which portions of the country are actively involved. They can then formulate future actions based on the results. Just like the e-commerce websites that use mining to follow customer behavior, government websites can also use them to produce a personalized experience for their citizens. Incorporating viewer response is an important step in improving website content and design. Being aware of the needs of the citizens is the key to the success of E-Governance services. Web mining not only helps to promote the intended services but also recognize the ones that are required in the near future.

Mining and analysis has been used by the government to promote schemes, and broadcast information. In the capital, data is provided on a regular basis on the condition of metros and buses to endorse their further usage and prove their utility. Metro stations have banners showing statistics of cleanliness and daily commutes. Government officials have also taken to social media and utilized their mining tools to support the growth of projects and campaigns. E-Governance websites have also improved vastly over the years by taking into consideration the overall user experience. But more work can be done in this area to exploit the usefulness of web mining and analysis to its full extent.

CASE STUDY OF MINING AND ANALYTICS IN E-GOVERNANCE

Following the Information Technology (IT) revolution countries across the globe have realized the potential that it bears to change the way public administration is conducted. India has actively been implementing projects that make competent use of technological advancement and has been succeeding too. Several Government divisions have conducted case studies on these projects in order to obtain information and draw results that can help future projects. These case studies help to assess the overall success of the initiative and also highlight the obstacles faced and reasons for failure, if required.

As a part of the Capacity Building initiative under the National E-Governance Plan (NeGP) by the National E-Governance Division (NeGD) a series of case studies were conducted in the period of 2013-2014 that formulated results on various projects implemented in different states and union territories in order to produce appropriate information for policy makers. These case studies were submitted by E-Governance Practitioners from Government and Industry/Research Institutions (Khurana & Dayal, 2014). Each of these case studies bring out the context of the project that has been studied, its objective and outcome, the challenges faced in its implementation and key lessons learnt by the project. Some of the case studies and their results are discussed below. The First case is a real time case study conducted by the authors of this chapter for the inclusion in the current list of cases. Rest other cases are taken from secondary sources.

Case Study 1: E-Transaction Based State-Wise Analysis (Author's Contribution)

E-Transactions are those transactions which are commenced by the consumer electronically from the government entities for the purchase of goods and services. Since the establishment of electronic trading platform consumer style of buying goods and services have changed a lot, and this change is also measured within different states of India. The E-Transaction data collected from government site shows that the state like Andhra Pradesh has largest number of E-Transaction records with more than 600 million E-Transactions. Thus this large size of data can be must be analyzed more comprehensibly to detect further relevant patterns and thereby providing solutions to the government that can help in overall development of the country.

The case that has been studies below is based on different states and union territories of India. The sample contains a total of 36 samples that comprises of twenty nine states and seven union territories. The main purpose of this case study is to distinguish different homogeneous groups of states that are similar in nature. The information gathered from clustering results could be exploited for serving the need of states.

Given that the Indian states are having different infrastructural setup and varied demographic and geographical distribution, there is a need to assess the development of the E-Government in each of these regions. A comparative analysis on similar parameters will give better insights about the status of E-Governance development and will help the policymakers to analyze the situation more critically. Data mining can be used to find clusters of states performing in similar fashion and then based on that, the policy makers can prepare a road map for better development of those states in similar clusters w.r.t. their E-Governance development. There are 4 metrics used from analysis point of view. They are as follows.

1. E-Transaction, which is termed as any E-Governance service availed by the citizen in the country,
2. Population of the respective states,
3. Number of mobile users to access digital platform,
4. Literacy rate in respective states.

The analysis for various clusters is discussed below. Data has been taken from www.etaal.gov.in and the analysis has been conducted using MATLAB 2010a software package. To summarize the data four clusters are suitable for all the above discussed parameters.

E-Transaction vs. Population

Analysis on cluster formation between E-Transaction and population is shown in Figure 2 where number of E-Transactions is shown on Y-axis and population on X-axis. The Table 1 shows four different clusters obtained after clustering. It is concluded from the table that cluster1 contains the states like Tripura, Sikkim, Uttrakhand, Punjab, Puducherry, Odisha, Nagaland, Mizoram, Meghalaya, Manipur, Lakshadweep, Jharkhand, Jammu and Kashmir, Himachal Pradesh, Haryana, Goa, Delhi, Daman and Diu, Dadra and Nagar Haveli, Chhattisgarh, Assam, Arunachal Pradesh, Andaman and Nicobar Islands. All these states have less population as compared to other states of different cluster and therefore accounts low E-Transaction rate. Government must adopt encouraging channels in these states to promote transaction rate. Some measures that government could take to promote E-Transaction are to increase the merchant discount rate, allowing tax benefit to consumers who perform electronic payment for example a tax rebate can be given to consumers who perform electronic transaction for their 50% value. Another method to promote E-Transaction in these states could be mandating some of the government services only by electronic transaction.

The second cluster consists of states like Bihar, Karnataka, Maharashtra, Rajasthan, Tamil Nadu and West Bengal. These states have proportionally very low E-Transaction rates as compared to their

Figure 2. Clustering results of various states based on e-transactions and population

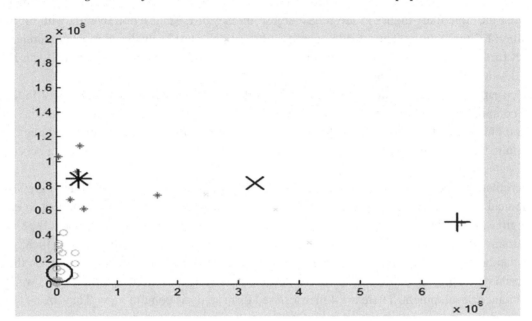

Table 1. Different clusters generated after applying clustering technique on e-transactions and population

CLUSTER 1 Low E-Transaction / Low Population		CLUSTER 2 Medium E-Transaction/ Very High Population	CLUSTER 3 High E-Transaction/ High Population	CLUSTER 4 Very High E-Transaction/ Medium Population
Andaman and Nicobar; Arunachal Pradesh; Assam; Chandigarh; Chhattisgarh; Dadra and Nagar Haveli; Daman and Diu; Delhi; Goa; Haryana; Himachal Pradesh; Manipur; Odisha;	Meghalaya; Mizoram; Nagaland; Puducherry; Punjab; Sikkim; Tripura; Uttarakhand; Jharkhand; Lakshadweep; Jammu and Kashmir	Bihar; Karnataka; Maharashtra; Rajasthan; Tamil Nadu; West Bengal	Gujarat; Kerala; Madhya Pradesh; Uttar Pradesh	Andhra Pradesh

population. Therefore government must adopt special attention in these states to improve E-Transaction rate. Some measures that government must adopt are: To enable E-Transaction approach for government collection for example promoting national E-payment gateway like "PayGov India" for revenue, penalty collection. Another method is to encourage mobile banking and payment channels. A major drawback of electronic transaction is fraudulent activities because of which citizens hesitate while using E-Transaction services. Therefore the government must adopt some awareness mechanism for fraudulent transaction and must ensure consumers that if any fraudulent activity occurred than money will be credited back to the consumer within say a limit of 3 month.

The picture slightly changed for third cluster which consists of states like Gujarat, Kerala, Madhya Pradesh and Uttar Pradesh. It is observed that these states contain large number of E-Transaction rate per population. Government must adopt various measures to improve this number further. The fourth cluster contains only one state that is Andhra Pradesh which tops in E-Transaction rate by registering more than 666.2 million transactions which is much more than the total population of this state. This clustering technique is an example of data mining where no preliminary knowledge exists regarding which states fall into natural group that shows similar behavior for the E-Transaction and population ratio. The data mining tool used here reveals some similar patterns or structures by generating meaningful cluster of states.

Therefore, it can be concluded that government needs to focus on developing infrastructure facilities in certain states more than others. It can be thus seen that dividing the states according to cluster can prove to be useful for policy decision making. This is one of the examples of how data analysis and mining techniques can prove to be helpful.

E-Transaction vs. Mobile Usage

The analysis on cluster formation between E-Transaction and mobile usage is shown in Figure 3 where E-Transaction is shown on Y-axis and mobile usage on X-axis. Table 2 shows division of states on high to low scale. The results of clustering show that states like Andaman and Nicobar, Arunachal Pradesh, Assam, Bihar, Chandigarh, Dadra and Nagar Haveli, Daman and Diu, Goa, Haryana, Jammu and Kashmir, Jharkhand, Lakshadweep, Manipur, Meghalaya, Mizoram, Nagaland, Odisha, Puducherry, Punjab, Sikkim, Tripura and Uttarakhand lie in one cluster.

The next cluster consists of Chhattisgarh, Himachal Pradesh, Karnataka, Maharashtra, Rajasthan, Tamil Nadu and West Bengal. This cluster contain very low E-Transaction rate compared as to mobile users in these states. The third cluster consists of Gujarat, Kerala, Madhya Pradesh and Uttar Pradesh. The E-Transaction rate in these states are small than the mobile users in state. But this ratio is comparatively large than states in cluster 1 and cluster 2. The fourth cluster contains only one state Andhra Pradesh. This state tops in E-Transaction versus mobile usage ratio with E-Transaction rate larger than the total number of mobile users.

Figure 3. Clustering results of various states based on e-transactions and mobile usage

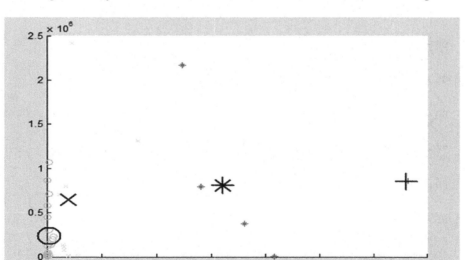

Table 2. Different clusters generated after applying clustering technique on e-transactions and mobile usage

CLUSTER 1 Low E-Transaction/ Low Mobile Users		CLUSTER 2 Medium E-Transaction/ Very High Mobile Users	CLUSTER 3 High E-Transaction/ High Mobile Users	CLUSTER 4 Very High Transaction/ Medium Mobile Users
Andaman and Nicobar; Arunachal Pradesh; Assam; Bihar; Chandigarh; Dadra & Nagar Haveli; Daman and Diu; Delhi; Goa; Haryana; Uttarakhand	Jammu and Kashmir; Jharkhand; Lakshadweep; Manipur; Meghalaya; Mizoram; Nagaland; Odisha; Puducherry; Punjab; Sikkim; Tripura	Chhattisgarh; Himachal Pradesh; Karnataka; Maharashtra; Rajasthan; Tamil Nadu; West Bengal	Gujarat; Kerala; Madhya Pradesh; Uttar Pradesh	Andhra Pradesh

The division of state in clusters based on mobile usage and number of E-Transactions provides insights that states with lower mobile usage and lower number of E-Transactions should be focused upon in terms of provision of better mobile services. This would help increase the mobile usage of people in these states and thereby might affect their E-Transaction frequency. Similar cluster specific measures can be taken which would help in fulfilling the exact needs of the states. This example reproves the importance of data analysis and data mining.

E-Transaction vs. Literacy Rate

This section examines trends in E-Transaction rate per literacy rate in India and gives clusters as shown in Figure 4 where E-Transaction is shown on Y-axis and literacy rate on X-axis. Table 3 shows division

Figure 4. Clustering results of various states based on e-transactions and literacy rate

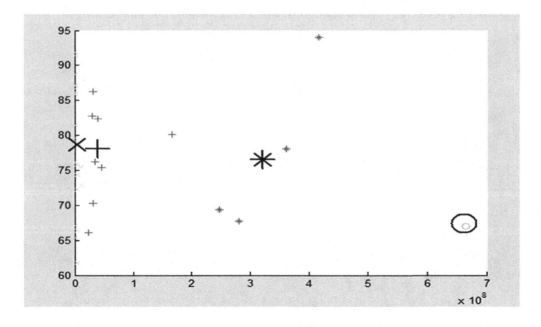

Table 3. Different clusters generated after applying clustering technique on e-transactions and literacy rate

CLUSTER 1 Low E-Transaction / High and Low Literacy Rate		CLUSTER 2 Medium E-Transaction/ High Literacy Rate	CLUSTER 3 High E-Transaction/ Very High and Medium Literacy Rate	Cluster 4 Very High Transaction/ Medium Literacy Rate
Andaman & Nicobar; Arunachal Pradesh; Assam; Bihar; Chandigarh; Dadra & Nagar Haveli; Daman and Diu; Delhi; Goa; Sikkim; Tripura	Haryana; Jammu and Kashmir; Jharkhand; Lakshadweep; Manipur; Meghalaya; Mizoram; Nagaland; Odisha; Puducherry; Punjab; Uttarakhand	Chhattisgarh; Himachal Pradesh; Karnataka; Maharashtra; Tamil Nadu; West Bengal	Gujarat; Kerala; Madhya Pradesh; Uttar Pradesh	Andhra Pradesh

of states on high to low scale. The analysis on cluster formation between E-Transactions and literacy rate shows gives different clusters containing various states. The results are then examined to help government initiatives for improving literacy rate and E-Transaction rate.

The dataset is divided into four clusters where cluster 1 consists of Andaman and Nicobar, Arunachal Pradesh, Assam, Bihar, Chandigarh, Dadra and Nagar Haveli, Daman and Diu, Goa, Haryana, Jammu and Kashmir, Jharkhand, Lakshadweep, Manipur, Meghalaya, Mizoram, Nagaland, Odisha, Puducherry, Punjab, Sikkim, Tripura, Uttarakhand and Delhi. The next cluster consists of Chhattisgarh, Himachal Pradesh, Karnataka, Maharashtra, Tamil Nadu and West Bengal. The third cluster contains Gujarat, Kerala, Madhya Pradesh, Uttar Pradesh and again Andhra Pradesh lies in the fourth cluster.

High literacy rates are likely to correspond with high E-Transaction levels. Focus should thus be laid on maintaining literacy levels in states that have it and promoting the literacy levels in states that are lagging behind on this metric. Focusing on particular states will help in cutting down the cost of administrative procedures in states where it isn't needed. Cluster analysis can thus be seen to be vital in all a lot of cases.

Thus, it can be seen that through simple analytical approach, broad level categorizations can be done which will help the administrative staff to understand the nature and behavior of every state. More in-depth analysis can be carried on the above used data as per specific objectives of the study.

Case Study 2: CHILDLINE 1098 (Khurana & Dayal, 2014)

This project was started by Tata Institute of Social Sciences, Mumbai on an experimental basis in 1996. Starting from 2006 it is conducted under the Integrated Child Protection Scheme (ICPS) of the Ministry of Women and Child Development. At present, CHILDLINE 1098 works as 24 hour helpline number and is operational in 28 states and Union Territories covering 260 cities. The project aims to fulfill the rights of children, and rescue and rehabilitate those in distress. The key findings of the case study are as follows.

- The number of calls made to the helpline has been increasing steadily. Not only does it indicate that the project overall has been a success which means better outreach to children in distress, but it also shows an improved concern for child rights and consciousness on the matter among the general public.

- The entire model of CHILDLINE is based on Public-Private Partnership. The sheer number of stakeholders involved is very large due to the population and geographical area of the country. The project has been progressively linking stakeholders from across to country to report, rescue and rehabilitate children. Despite the loopholes in the partnership, an effective partnership model has emerged from the project.

- Adaptation to the evolving technology is a common obstruction faced by a number of projects. When the helpline was started landline usage was still widespread, but with time the trend has shifted towards mobile phones. The helpline is toll free for landline users but still faces problems with private network providers. After initially being unavailable for mobile calls (at the time of the study), it can now be reached from mobiles for a fee charge.

- The project has not been very efficient in long term rehabilitation. The focus has been maintained on immediate rescue and not closely integrating rescue and rehabilitation and encouraging concentrated efforts for the same from community members, government officials and other stakeholders.

- Child tracking and Analysis through pattern mining made CHILDLINE a very successful 24x7 emergency helpline for rescuing children and link them to long term rehabilitation.

Case Study 3: Andhra Pradesh Transport Department (Rao, 2014)

The E-Governance initiative in Andhra Pradesh at the Transport Department level aimed to computerize all counters and offices in the department. Now the process to obtain a driving license through a reengineered registration process takes less than 24 hours and has introduced transparency. By using IT the department has improved the citizen-government interaction and digitized the entire department. The key findings of the case study are as follows.

- The traditional methods of transactions from the 45 Regional Transport Office(s), RTOs, in Andhra Pradesh was tedious and wasteful of resources. By digitizing the department cost and time of both, the officials and the citizens, can be utilized efficiently. This project has thus shown how implementation of Information Technology can bring about positive changes in administration and change the way citizens are served.

- The project brings out important issues in the implementation of E-Governance services. Lack of awareness of operation of computers among the staff is a common problem across the nation. This can be handled by providing them with appropriate training required for their job, as was done in this project. Another problem arises in the form of job insecurity. With digitization the staff becomes apprehensive about their jobs. The project handled this by motivating their staff and distributing the work load instead of filling new positions.

- Backlogging is a necessary aspect. The manual records need to be converted in digital form so as to maintain backlog data and keep databases up to date.

- Transparency and reducing the role of middle men was achieved by the project. It not only increases the department's productivity but also improves citizens' trust in the officials. The success of the initiative is an indication of the need to adopt this practice in other divisions and departments as well.

- The major analytics used was based on route optimization and analysis of digitized content

Case Study 4: MGNREGA (Sharma & Vincent, 2014)

The ICT Ecosystem project was launched in 2009 for the implementation of MGNREGA and for improving the delivery of services under this act. The village where the project was initially launched has women forming 60% of the workforce. Owing to the gender hierarchy, women in these villages had to be empowered by providing them access to information regarding their entitlements through the Act. Through the project e-Spaces were created for rural women by developing technologies that kept the specific end user in mind. The project provided an important impetus for ensuring that women received the various available services and came to the forefront of the entire scene at a level equivalent with men. The key findings of the case study are:

- The ICT Enabled Ecosystem for MGNREGA was initiated to address the lack of information and awareness among the people that were to benefit from the Act. This lack of awareness prevented the rural population, especially women, from understanding their privileges and using them for the purpose that MGNREGA was established. It also hindered the success of the Act creating discrepancies, administrative lapses and poor accountability on the government's part. Through biometric systems, touch and text-to-speech enabled computers and digital record of all work progress; these problems were largely cut down.
- The technology used in the pilot project was implemented keeping in mind the target user. Along with low literacy rate and unfamiliarity to technology women also are cut off from access to technology due to the socio-economic constructs. The success of the project brings to light important measures that can be replicated in other areas of the country. As a large population of India is still in rural areas, the initiative is essential to make information more accessible to people in these areas.
- An important setback in the success of any project is the lack of participation which arises due to lack of awareness. The ICT Ecosystem project handled the two issues by understanding the situations at the grassroots levels and working with locals to find solutions. While in most cases, women are usually left behind in realizing their rights, the e-Spaces for women boosted their confidence to work with technology, reducing their dependence on men.
- The project also highlighted lack of basic infrastructure as a potent problem in the implementation of projects in rural areas. These include inadequate public transport and roads and inaccessibility to tech centers by local communities. This poses a problem in expansion and up-scaling of projects. But at the same time, it also provided a better understanding of the rural areas, and how projects need to be modified to incorporate their specific needs.

Another case study that focuses on the Gyandoot Project of Dhar district of Madhya Pradesh highlights what steps are overall necessary to ensure that such IT initiatives can succeed (Mansuri, 2013). These are as follows.

- Computerization – as much of the dealings among the government departments are inter-linked, they must be done over a network and digital records should be maintained for them. All the information concerning different departments, divisions and projects must be maintained online.

- Understanding local requirements – the vast geography of the country makes it important to modify regulations and implementation strategies with the change in area. Local languages should be encouraged in discourse. Native problems must be kept in mind.
- Increasing outreach and spreading awareness – unless the general public understands what progress can be made by embracing a certain initiative, they are always resistant to change, especially as they are not comfortable with technology. Awareness about projects, privileges and rights should be spread to encourage participation.
- Working model for E-Governance – learning from existing projects and their case studies, governments and business enterprises can form models that outline a basic working of the steps that need to be undertaken for the E-Governance initiatives. Machine learning approach was used as a part of data analysis.
- Building Information KIOSKS – free public information centers or information kiosks in public spaces can dispense much needed information and improve accessibility. Government departments that inherently need active interaction with the public like grievance cells, social services, payments and billing services, etc. should be identified and made to incorporate such information centers.

In addition to these, several government departments have conducted case studies on their projects in order for future initiatives to benefit from them. These case studies are also available for the assistance of organizations and business enterprises in undertaking such initiatives.

Way Ahead

With the kind of data getting generated through various E-Governance applications, it will be useful to implement various analytical approaches on the data collected through the service transactions. This will be helpful for the various administrative staff and government policymakers to understand the situation better and prepare a more robust roadmap for better E-Governance implementation in India.

- Firstly, the data can be useful in finding the weak and strong areas of E-Governance service transactions across all the states. With the weak areas identification, the service accessibility can be improved and appropriate measures can be taken. For identification of strong and weak areas, data mining and statistical analysis can be used. For financial service oriented transactions, the citizen details can be recorded to study patterns for irregularities and tax evasion. Similarly, the services which are more revenue oriented and which require lesser revenue can be segregated and can be handled accordingly.
- Secondly, various type of service recommendation system can be developed which will encourage the citizen and organizations to use more and more services in related area. This will reduce administration overheads and physical chaos at various centers. Recommendations can be considered as a replacement of marketing activities. As soon as the citizen carries out any E-Transaction, he can be prompted for other similar services. Data Mining is useful in finding associations and frequent patterns which will be helpful in recommending the most frequently used services or the most associated service used by the citizens.

- Thirdly, optimal resource allocation can be planned so that every area can get the resources in appropriate portions of their usage rather than favourism to a particular area in India. Various types of location allocation planning algorithms can be implemented for selecting the location of different service centers. For example allocation of CSCs which are a part of NeGP, can be done using data mining and heuristic approaches. This will help in minimizing the cost of travel for citizens to avail the E-Governance services through the common service centers.
- Fourthly, predictions would be possible for the various industries, areas and service zones in India which would enable the government to be prepared well in advance for introduction of any new service and related infrastructure, if needed. Statistical modeling and Machine learning can help in preparing models that can predict various activities related to E-Governance in India.

FUTURE RESEARCH DIRECTIONS

Further research directions include the practical case studies of data analytics and data mining on the data generated through the electronic transactions of various E-Governance services. Moreover, new service designing is also possible with the help of knowledge discovery through data generated from E-Transactions. It will be helpful for research community, as well as government's key members to study the results based on different types of analytical techniques applied on the transactional data.

Within different ministries, cross comparison can be made for their minister's performance over different E-Government services and necessary measures can be taken to strengthen the weak zones. In a similar manner, different states of India can compete against each other and based on the E-Transactions for various services in different states, rankings could be drawn. These rankings can act as the stepping stone for the central government to assess each state individually and with the help of inclusive growth, India can progress on overall E-Governance development rankings as assessed by United Nations every two years.

CONCLUSION

The overall citizen participation and awareness has greatly improved as a result of government efforts. People now want the officials to be answerable for their actions and hence accountability has also increased. Better access to information plays an important role in this aspect. Owing to the technology revolution major changes have been brought around all over the country in the way administration is carried out. With increased attempts the government has been utilizing the ICTs to improve their services and initiate more E-Governance projects. However the lack of basic infrastructure and low connectivity and literacy rate in most areas prove to be an obstacle in the success of these projects. Nevertheless, the transformation that has been brought about through these projects cannot be undermined even if there is a long way to cover. Data analysis and Web Mining can be really important tools to revolutionize the usage of ICT for Governance. Many campaigns and better coverage of citizen services can be covered if appropriate analytical skills can be imparted along with the digitization of the various services by Government of India.

REFERENCES

Aarti, S. (2014). Data Warehousing & Data Mining Is - A New Paradigm for Good E-Governance. *Asian Journal of Technology & Management Research.*

Babbar, P., & Jain, P. K. (2007). E-Governance in India. *ICOLIS 2007 Kuala Lumpur. LISU FCSIT, 2007,* 363–371.

Bhanti, P., Kaushal, U., &Pandey, A. (2011). E-Governance in Higher Education: Concept and Role of Data Warehousing Techniques. *International Journal of Computer Applications, 18*(1).

Bharati, M., &Ramageri, M. (2010). Data mining techniques and applications. *Data Mining Modules in Emerging Field, 7*(3).

Centre, N. I. (2015a). *MyGov: A Platform for Citizen Engagement towards Good Governance in India.* Retrieved August 5, 2015, from http://www.mygov.in

Centre, N. I. (2015b). *MyGov: Open Government Data (OGD) Platform India.* Retrieved August 5, 2015, from https://data.gov.in/

Chakravorty, S. (2015). Data mining techniques for analyzing murder related structured and unstructured data. *American Journal of Advanced Computing, 2*(2).

Gobind, S., & Rao, L. M. (2015). A Review on Contribution of Data mining in E-Governance Framework. *International Journal of Engineering Research and General Science, 3*(2), 68–75.

Haque, M. S. (2002). E-Governance in India: Its impacts on relations among citizens, politicians and public servants. *International Review of Administrative Sciences, 68*(2), 231–250. doi:10.1177/0020852302682005

Hebbar, N. (2015, August 10). Flood of suggestions after PM seeks input for I-Day address. *The Hindu.* Retrieved August 10, 2015, from http://www.thehindu.com/news/national/flood-of-suggestions-after-pm-seeks-inputs-for-iday-address/article7519493.ece

Kaur, H., & Wasan, S. K. (2006). Empirical study on applications of data mining techniques in healthcare. *Journal of Computer Science, 2*(2), 194–200. doi:10.3844/jcssp.2006.194.200

Khurana, M., & Dayal, A. (2013-14). *CHILDLINE 1098.Case Studies on E-Governance in India.* National Institute for Smart Government.

Mansuri, B. B. (2013). E-GOVERNANCE: A Case Study of Gyandoot Project. *Journal of Contemporary Research in Management, 4*(3).

Nandan, T., & Chand, M. G. (2007, December). Application of Analytics in E-Governance–a next level. In *Foundations of E-Government: 5th International Conference on E-Governance,* (pp. 28-30).

NIC. (2015). *National Informatics Centre (NIC).* Retrieved August 7, 2015, fromhttp://www.nic.in/

Peisker, A., & Dalai, S. (2015). Data Analytics for Rural Development. *Indian Journal of Science and Technology, 8*(S4), 50–60. doi:10.17485/ijst/2015/v8iS4/61494

Purandare, P. (2008). Web Mining: A Key to Improve Business on Web. In *IADIS European Conf. Data Mining*, (pp. 155-159).

Rao, A. K. (2014). *A Case of Process Reengineering of Driving Licence*. Case Studies on E-Governance in India.

Sharma, A., & Vincent, A. (2014). Creating Gender sensitive eSpaces for Mahatma Gandhi National Rural Employment Guarantee Act (MGNREGA). *Case Studies on E-Governance in India*, 6-32.

The Hindu. (2014). India tops in adult illiteracy: U.N. report. *The Hindu*. Retrieved August 8, 2015, from http://www.thehindu.com/features/education/issues/india-tops-in-adult-illiteracy-un-report/article5629981.ece

Weerakkody, V. (2012). *Technology Enabled Transformation of the Public Sector: Advances in E-Government: Advances in E-Government*. IGI Global. doi:10.4018/978-1-4666-1776-6

Weng, C. I., Fong, S., & Deb, S. (2011). *An Analytical Model for Evaluating Public Moods Based on the Internet Comments*. Retrieved from www.excelpublish.com

World Bank Group. (2012). India: Issues and Priorities for Agriculture. *The World Bank*. Retrieved August 7, 2015, from http://www.worldbank.org/en/news/feature/2012/05/17/india-agriculture-issues-priorities

Zhou, P., & Le, Z. (2007). A Framework for Web Usage Mining in Electronic Government. *Integration and Innovation Orient to E-Society*, (2), 487-496.

ADDITIONAL READING

Agarwal, S., Tiwari, M. D., & Tiwari, I. (2013). *E Governance Data Center, Data Warehousing and Data Mining: Vision to Realities*. River Publishers.

Agarwala, K. N., &Tiwari, M. D. (2002).*IT and E-Governance in India*. Macmillan Publishing Company:Incorporated.

Büchner, A. G., & Mulvenna, M. D. (1998). Discovering internet marketing intelligence through online analytical web usage mining. *SIGMOD Record*, 27(4), 54–61. doi:10.1145/306101.306124

Burby, J., & Atchison, S. (2007). *Actionable web analytics: using data to make smart business decisions*. John Wiley & Sons.

Cooley, R., Mobasher, B., & Srivastava, J. (1997, November). Web mining: Information and pattern discovery on the world wide web. In Tools with Artificial Intelligence, 1997.Proceedings.,*Ninth IEEE International Conference on* 558-567, IEEE.

Dykes, B. (2011). *Web analytics action hero: Using analysis to gain insight and optimize your business*. Adobe Press.

Garson, G. D. (2006). *Public information technology and e-governance: Managing the virtual state.* Jones & Bartlett Learning.

Grönlund, Å. (Ed.). (2001). *Electronic Government: Design, Applications and Management: Design, Applications and Management. Idea Group Inc (IGI).* Global.

Gupta, P., & Bagga, R. K. (2008). *Compendium of E-governance Initiatives in India.* Universities Press.

Jansen, B. J. (2009). Understanding user-web interactions via web analytics. Synthesis Lectures on Information Concepts. *Retrieval, and Services, 1*(1), 1–102.

Kosala, R., & Blockeel, H. (2000). Web mining research: A survey. *ACM Sigkdd Explorations Newsletter, 2*(1), 1–15. doi:10.1145/360402.360406

Kumar, T. V. (2015). *E-governance for Smart Cities.*1-43.Springer Singapore.

Kundu, P., Bansal, P., & Choudhary, K. (2013). Record Management Issues under E-Governance. *International Journal of Recent Technology and Engineering, 2*(5), 40–42.

Liu, B. (2007). *Web data mining: exploring hyperlinks, contents, and usage data.* Springer Science & Business Media.

Mukherjee, A., &Biswas, A. (2005).E-Governance in India.*In EuroIMSA,* 429-433.

Mulvenna, M. D., Anand, S. S., & Büchner, A. G. (2000). Personalization on the Net using Web mining: Introduction. *Communications of the ACM, 43*(8), 122–125. doi:10.1145/345124.345165

Panwar, V. (2008). The role of data warehousing & data mining in e-governance.

Phippen, A., Sheppard, L., & Furnell, S. (2004). A practical evaluation of Web analytics. *Internet Research, 14*(4), 284–293. doi:10.1108/10662240410555306

Prabhu, C. S. R. (2013). *E-governance: Concepts and case studies.* PHI Learning Pvt. Ltd.

Rahman, H. (Ed.). (2009). *Social and Political Implications of Data Mining: Knowledge Management in E-Government: Knowledge Management in E-Government. Idea Group Inc (IGI).* Global. doi:10.4018/978-1-60566-230-5

Scime, A. (Ed.). (2005). *Web Mining: applications and techniques.Idea Group Inc (IGI).* Global. doi:10.4018/978-1-59140-414-9

Shah, M. (2007). E-Governance in India: Dream or reality. *International Journal of Education and Development using ICT, 3*(2).

Singh, A. (2014). Data Warehousing & Data Mining Is - A New Paradigm for Good E-Governance. *Asian Journal of Technology & Management Research, 4*(2), 8–18.

Ting, I. H. (2008). Web-mining applications in e-commerce and e-services. *Online Information Review, Springer, 32*(2), 129–132. doi:10.1108/14684520810879773

KEY TERMS AND DEFINITIONS

Clustering: The process of grouping similar items together based on various attributes.

Data Analytics: Data Analytics refers to the science of extracting meaningful information from series of raw data. The data could be primary or secondary which may lead to meaningful insights. It includes the concepts from data mining, statistical analysis, operations research, etc.

Data Mining: Data Mining is a stream of Data Analytics which helps in generating meaningful patterns from large raw data through the process of Knowledge discovery from data. Prominent techniques of data mining are frequent pattern generation, clustering, classification, etc.

Digital India: It refers to the campaign run by Indian government to digitize all the government operations and services in order to make the system more transparent. It's a part of E-Governance.

E-Governance: Electronic Governance or more popularly known as E-Governance refers to the execution of government processes and services through usage of Information and Communication Technologies. The main aim of E-Governance is to provide transparent and accountable governance to the citizens. The government services can be accessed through mobile or web. Popular services of E-Governance in India are IRCTC and MCA21 portals.

Electronic Government: Government which functions and serve the citizens with the help of technology rather than manually.

NeGP: National E-Governance Plan is popularly known as NeGP. It was launched in 2006 by Indian Government when the digitization of government processes started under the scheme of Electronic Governance.

Web Analytics: Web Analytics refers to the science of extracting meaningful information specifically from web data generated through online transactions. The data is generated through users surfing the internet through devices like laptop, desktop, tablets, phone and the likes.

Web Mining: Application of data mining especially on web generated data is referred to as Web Mining. Applying techniques like classification and clustering on web data is categorized under web mining techniques.

Chapter 10
A Dynamic and Scalable Decision Tree Based Mining of Educational Data

Dineshkumar B. Vaghela
Parul University, India

Priyanka Sharma
Raksha Shakti University, India

Kalpdrum Passi
Laurentian University, Canada

ABSTRACT

The explosive growth in the amount of data in the field of biology, education, environmental research, sensor network, stock market, weather forecasting and many more due to vast use of internet in distributed environment has generated an urgent need for new techniques and tools that can intelligently automatically transform the processed data into useful information and knowledge. Hence data mining has become a research are with increasing importance. Since continuation in collection of more data at this scale, formalizing the process of big data analysis will become paramount. Given the vast amount of data are geographically spread across the globe, this means a very large number of models is generated, which raises problems on how to generalize knowledge in order to have a global view of the phenomena across the organization. This is applicable to web-based educational data. In this chapter, the new dynamic and scalable data mining approach has been discussed with educational data.

INTRODUCTION

Web usage mining refers to non-trivial extraction of potentially useful patterns and trends from large web access logs. In the specific context of web-based learning environments, the increasing proliferation of web-based educational systems and the huge amount of information that has been made available has generated a considerable scientific activity in this field. As an increasingly powerful, interactive,

DOI: 10.4018/978-1-5225-0613-3.ch010

and dynamic medium for delivering information, the World Wide Web in combination with information technology has found many applications. One popular application has been for educational use, as in Web-based, distance or distributed learning. The use of the Web as an educational tool has provided learners and educators with a wider range of new and interesting learning experiences and teaching environments that were not possible in traditional education. These platforms contain a considerable amount of e-learning materials and provide some degree of logging to monitor the progress of learning keeping track of learners' activities including content viewed, time spent at a particular subject and activities done. This monitoring trawl provides appropriate data for many different contexts in universities, like providing assistance for a student at the appropriate level, aiding the student's learning process, allocating relevant resources, identifying exceptional students for scholarships and weak students who are likely to fail. This can be possible by processing and analyzing the data using various classification techniques. Decision trees are simple yet effective classification algorithms. One of their main advantages is that they provide human-readable rules of classification. *Decision Tree Induction* algorithm (Quinlan J. R.- 1986) is used for classification by constructing a decision tree. The algorithm constructs decision tree recursively using depth– first divide and conquer approach. At any given node, to further split up the dataset towards identification of a class, the algorithm chooses the most suitable attribute based on the *information gain* value of the attributes. The information gain of an attribute is a measure of the ability of an attribute to minimize the information needed to classify the given entity in the resulting sub-trees.

Decision Tree Construction

Classification is the problem of identifying a category for the given instance whose category is unknown. The classifier tries to classify the given unknown instance based on the data it learns from the training set and features it sees in the instance for which prediction is to be done. This problem arises in various fields ranging from operation research, education, weather forecasting…etc for making decisions. There are wide varieties of classification problems in machine learning domain, all of which cannot be solved using one technique. Therefore, for proving that the results which we are getting from one kind of technique is good enough for us makes it indispensable that we compare the results with other techniques for the given problem. Whilst doing this, we come across the various performance aspects of the algorithm i.e. where it would fail and where it can do remarkably well in classifying the data. One of the most popular techniques for classifying data in Machine Learning domain is Decision Trees. The advantage of using Decision Trees in classifying the data is that they are simple to understand and interpret. Decision tree have been well studied and widely used in the knowledge discovery and decision support system. These trees approximate discrete valued target functions as trees and are widely used practical method for inductive reference. Each line present in the datasets is known as the instance. The instance contains the label and a vector of features present in it. The Decision Trees examines the feature of given instance and comes to a conclusion on what label to assign based on the values present for the various features of that particular instance. Each node in the decision tree is either a decision node or a leaf node. This classifier resembles tree data structure as each decision can have two outcomes, thereby making a binary decision tree that culminates in a label corresponding to each set of given features.

The data classification is a two step process. The first step is training the classifier using training data set. The second step involves predicting the labels for the unknown datasets (or testing datasets). This comes under the training step. Now in order to classify an unknown instance, the attribute values of instance are tested against decision tree and a path is traced from root to leaf node which holds the class prediction for that sample. This comes under the prediction step. The decision trees can easily be converted into classification rules. Decision tree falls under supervised learning techniques as we have known labels in the training data set in order to train the classifier. The various algorithms that are discussed in the subsections given below.

Traditional Method

The traditional algorithm for building decision trees is a greedy algorithm which constructs decision tree in top down recursive manner. A typical algorithm for building decision trees is written below. The algorithm begins with the original set X as the root node. It iterates through each unused attribute of the set X and calculates the information gain (IG). The information gain is calculated by deducting conditional entropy of the given attribute with the total entropy. The formulas needed to calculate information gain along with the formula for calculating information gain is given in the subsection given below. The algorithm then chooses to split on the feature that has the highest information gain. The Set X is then split by the feature obtained in the previous step to produce the subset of data depending on the value of feature. The decision tree is then built recursively until every element in the subset belongs to the same class, in which case, a terminal node is added to the decision tree with a class label same as the class all its elements belong to.

```
function BUILDDECISIONTREE(data, labels)
        if all labels are same then
                return leaf node for that label
        else
                Calculate information gain of all the featured
                choose the feature with highest information gain for splitting
                left=BUILDDECISIONTREE(data with f=0, labels with f=0)
                right=BUILDDECISIONTREE(data with f=1, labels with f=1)
                retrun tree(f, left, right)
        end if
end function
```

Entropy and Information Gain

The information gain from the attribute test on the set of instances X is the expected reduction in entropy. The algorithm computes the information gain of each feature and then chooses the feature with highest information gain for splitting. The formulas needed to calculate information gain along with formula for calculating information gain is given below.

The total entropy is given by the formula:

$$H(X) = -\sum_{i=1}^{n} p\left(xi\right) \log p\left(xi\right) \tag{1}$$

The conditional entropy is given by the formula:

$$H(Y/X) = -\sum_{i=1}^{m}\sum_{j=1}^{n} p\left(yi, xj\right)\log\left(\frac{p\left(yi, xj\right)}{p\left(xj\right)}\right) \qquad (2)$$

and finally, the information gain (IG) is given by the formula:

$$IG(Y/X) = H(X)\text{-}H(Y/X) \qquad (3)$$

The information gain is equal to total entropy for an attribute of a unique class label for each of the given attribute values. Information gain is a good measure for deciding the relevance of attribute in general. However, if we have an attribute that can take large number of distinct values, then splitting feature based on the information gain is not prudent. For example, consider an attribute that contains the instance number of each instance. Now if we use information gain heuristics, this attribute will give the highest information gain value which would depict that we can classify the samples perfectly. This would make the classifier to over fit the training data. Now when we see an unknown instance with value of instance number that is not present in the training set, the classifier would fail to predict the label for it. In order to overcome this problem, a new heuristics is used which uses gain ratio for deciding which feature to split on.

Gain Ratio

The gain ratio biases the decision tree against considering attributes with higher number of distinct values thereby solving the drawback of the information gain. Using gain ratio heuristics for choosing best feature to split upon avoids over fitting of training data. The gain ratio of an attribute is calculated by dividing its information gain with its information value. The formula for calculating information value is given below:

$$IV(Y/X) = -\sum_{j=1}^{n} p\left(y, xj\right)\log\left(p\left(y, xj\right)\right) \qquad (5)$$

The gain ratio (GR) is then given by:

$$GR(Y/X) = IG(Y/X)/IV(Y/X) \ldots\ldots\ldots\ldots (v)$$

Therefore gain ratio is used instead of information gain when searching for best feature to split upon, avoiding the problem posed by using information gain heuristics.

Pruning

In case of traditional algorithms for learning decision trees, when decision trees are built, many of the branches may be reflect noise or outliers in the training data. In order to combat this over fitting, so it is required to identify and remove such branches with the goal of improving classification accuracy on the unseen data. This is called tree pruning.

- **Pre Pruning:** In this the tree construction is halt at early stage. It will not allow splitting a node if this would result in the goodness measure falling below a threshold. The limitation of this is it is difficult to choose an appropriate threshold.
- **Post Pruning:** In this the branches are removed from a "fully grown" tree. This approach gets a sequence of progressively pruned trees. It uses a set of data different from the training data to decide which is the "best pruned tree"

Researchers have developed various decision tree algorithms over a period of time with enhancement in performance and ability to handle various types of data. Some important algorithms are discussed below.

1. **CHID:** CHAID (CHi-squared Automatic Interaction Detector) is a fundamental decision tree learning algorithm. It was developed by Gordon V Kass (Gordan.V.Kass-1980) in 1980. CHAID is easy to interpret, easy to handle and can be used for classification and detection of interaction between variables. CHID is an extension of the AID (Automatic Interaction Detector) and THAID (Theta Automatic Interaction Detector) procedures. It works on principal of adjusted significance testing. After detection of interaction between variables it selects the best attribute for splitting the node which made a child node as a collection of homogeneous values of the selected attribute. The method can handle missing values. It does not imply any pruning method.

2. **CART:** Classification and regression tree (CART) proposed by Breiman *et al.* (Leo Breiman, Jerome H. Friedman, Richard A. Olshen, and Charles J. Stone-1984) constructs binary trees which is also refer as Hierarchical Optimal Discriminate Analysis (HODA). CART is a non-parametric decision tree learning technique that produces either classification or regression trees, depending on whether the dependent variable is categorical or numeric, respectively. The word binary implies that a node in a decision tree can only be split into two groups. CART uses gini index as impurity measure for selecting attribute. The attribute with the largest reduction in impurity is used for splitting the node's records. CART accepts data with numerical or categorical values and also handles missing attribute values. It uses cost-complexity pruning and also generate regression trees.

3. **ID3:** ID3 (Iterative Dichotomiser 3) decision tree algorithm is developed by Quinlan (Quinlan J. R.-1986). In the decision tree method, information gain approach is generally used to determine suitable property for each node of a generated decision tree. Thus, we can select the attribute with the highest information gain (entropy reduction in the level of maximum) as the test attribute of current node. In this way, the information needed to classify the training sample subset obtained from later on partitioning will be the smallest. That is to say, the use of this property to partition the sample set contained in current node will make the mixture degree of different types for all generated sample subsets reduce to a minimum. Therefore, the use of such an information theory approach will effectively reduce the required dividing number of object classification.

4. **C4.5:** C4.5 is an algorithm used to generate a decision tree developed by Ross Quinlan. C4.5 is an extension of Quinlan's earlier ID3 algorithm. The decision trees generated by C4.5 can be used for classification, and for this reason C4.5 is often referred to as a statistical classifier (Zhu Xiaoliang, Wang Jian Yan Hong can and Wu Shangzhuo-2009). C4.5 algorithm uses information gain as splitting criteria. It can accept data with categorical or numerical values. To handle continuous values it generates threshold and then divides attributes with values above the threshold and values equal to or below the threshold. C4.5algorithm can easily handle missing values. As missing attribute values are not utilized in gain calculations by C4.5. Limitations of C4.5 are

a. **Empty Branches:** Constructing tree with meaningful value is one of the crucial steps for rule generation by C4.5 algorithm. In our experiment, we have found many nodes with zero values or close to zero values. These values neither contribute to generate rules nor help to construct any class for classification task. Rather it makes the tree bigger and more complex.

b. **Insignificant Branches:** Numbers of selected discrete attributes create equal number of potential branches to build a decision tree. But all of them are not significant for classification task. These insignificant branches not only reduce the usability of decision

c. **Over Fitting:** Over fitting happens when algorithm model picks up data with uncommon characteristics. This cause many fragmentations is the process distribution. Statistically insignificant nodes with very few samples are known as fragmentations. Generally C4.5 algorithm constructs trees and grows it branches just deep enough to perfectly classify the training examples. This strategy performs well with noise free data. But most of the time this approach over fits the training examples with noisy data.

5. **C5.0/Sec 5:** C5.0 algorithm is an extension of C4.5 algorithm which is also extension of ID3. It is the classification algorithm which applies in big data set. It is better than C4.5 on the speed, memory and the efficiency. C5.0 model works by splitting the sample based on the field that provides the maximum information gain. The C5.0 model can split samples on basis of the biggest information gain field. The sample subset that is get from the former split will be split afterward. The process will continue until the sample subset cannot be split and is usually according to another field. Finally, examine the lowest level split, those sample subsets that don't have remarkable contribution to the model will be rejected. C5.0 is easily handled the multi value attribute and missing attribute from data set (Prof. Nilima Patil and Prof. Rekha Lathi-2012).

6. **Hunt's Algorithm:** Hunt's algorithm generates a Decision tree by top-down or divides and conquers approach. The sample/row data contains more than one class, use an attribute test to split the data into smaller subsets. Hunt's algorithm maintains optimal split for every stage according to some threshold value as greedy fashion (Baik, S. Bala, J.2004). Table 1 shows the comparisons of different algorithms with different parameters.

Distributed Data Mining (DDM)

Data mining technology has emerged as a means for identifying patterns and trends from large quantities of data. The Data Mining technology normally adopts data integration method to generate Data

Table 1. Comparisons between different decision tree algorithms

	ID3	**C4.5**	**C5.0**	**CART**
Type of data	Categorical	Continuous and Categorical	Continuous and Categorical, dates, times, timestamps	continuous and nominal attributes data
Speed	Low	Faster than ID3	Highest	Average
Pruning	No	Pre-pruning	Pre-pruning	Post pruning
Boosting	Not supported	Not supported	Supported	Supported
Missing Values	Can't deal with	Can't deal with	Can deal with	Can deal with
Formula	Use information entropy and information Gain	Use split info and gain ratio	Same as C4.5	Use Gini diversity index

warehouse, on which to gather all data into a central site, and then run an algorithm against that data to extract the useful Module Prediction and knowledge evaluation. However, a single data-mining technique has not been proven appropriate for every domain and data set. Data mining techniques involving in such complex environment must encounter great dynamics due to changes in the system can affect the overall performance of the system. Distributed data mining is originated from the need of mining over decentralized data sources. The field of Distributed Data Mining (DDM) deals with these challenges in analyzing distributed data and offers many algorithmic solutions to perform different data analysis and mining operations in a fundamentally distributed manner that pays careful attention to the resource constraints.

The continuous developments in information and communication technology have recently led to the appearance of distributed computing environments, which comprise several, and different sources of large volumes of data and several computing units. The most prominent example of a distributed environment is the Internet, where increasingly more databases and data streams appear that deal with several areas, such as education, meteorology, oceanography, economy and others. In addition the Internet constitutes the communication medium for geographically distributed information systems.

The application of the classical knowledge discovery process in distributed environments requires the collection of distributed data in a data warehouse for central processing. However, this is usually either ineffective or infeasible for the following reasons:

- **Storage Cost:** It is obvious that the requirements of a central storage system are enormous. A classical example concerns data from the astronomy science, and especially images from earth and space telescopes. The size of such databases is reaching the scales of Exabyte's (1018 bytes) and is increasing at a high pace. The central storage of the data of all telescopes of the planet would require a huge data warehouse of enormous cost.

- **Communication Cost:** The transfer of huge data volumes over network might take extremely much time and also require an unbearable financial cost. Even a small volume of data might create problems in wireless network environments with limited bandwidth. Note also that communication may be a continuous overhead, as distributed databases are not always constant and unchangeable. On the contrary, it is common to have databases that are frequently updated with new data or data streams that constantly record information (e.g. remote sensing sports statistics, etc.).

- **Computational Cost:** The computational cost of mining a central data warehouse is much bigger than the sum of the cost of analyzing smaller parts of the data that could also be done in parallel. In a grid, for example, it is easier to gather the data at a central location. However, a distributed mining approach would make a better exploitation of the available resources.

- **Private and Sensitive Data:** There are many popular data mining applications that deal with sensitive data, such as people's medical and financial records. The central collection of such data is not desirable as it puts their privacy into risk. In certain cases (e.g. banking, telecommunication) the data might belong to different, perhaps competing, organizations that want to exchange knowledge without the exchange of raw private data.

Distributed Data Mining (DDM) (Fu, 2001; Park & Kargupta, 2003) is concerned with the application of the classical Data Mining procedure in a distributed computing environment trying to make the best of the available resources (communication network, computing units and databases). Data Mining takes place both locally at each distributed site and at a global level where the local knowledge is fused in order to discover global knowledge. A typical architecture of a DDM approach is discussed here. The first phase normally involves the analysis of the local database at each distributed site. Then, the discovered knowledge is usually transmitted to a merger site, where the integration of the distributed local models is performed. The results are transmitted back to the distributed databases, so that all sites become updated with the global knowledge. In some approaches, instead of a merger site, the local models are broadcasted to all other sites, so that each site can in parallel compute the global model. Distributed databases may have homogeneous or heterogeneous schema. In the former case, the attributes describing the data are the same in each distributed database. This is often the case when the databases belong to the same organization (e.g. local stores of a chain). In the latter case the attributes differ among the distributed databases. In certain applications a key attribute might be present in the heterogeneous databases, which will allow the association between tuples. In other applications the target attribute for prediction might be common across all distributed databases.

DDM Techniques

The increasing demand to scale up to massive data sets inherently distributed over a network with limited band width and computational resources available motivated the development of the techniques of DDM. A number of approaches and techniques have been proposed in literatures. Some data mining techniques can be used to adapt DDM. Bayesian methods were developed in the framework of statistics for many years. Last ten years, they were applied in the problems of data mining. Decision tree is well-known in data mining. Decision tree technique has been used in DDM. Some statistical techniques such as bagging, boosting and stacking etc., would be extended to combine local models in a distributed environment. The techniques such as Multi-agent Systems, ensemble learning, similarity-based and collective data mining (Chan, P., & Stolfo, S (1998) are presented in DDM literatures. This section mainly present the DDM techniques based on Multi-agent Systems and ensemble learning.

Agent-Based

An agent-based data mining system is a natural choice for mining large sets of inherently distributed data. Many DDM system such as JAM, are based on multi-agent techniques. Multi-Agent Systems (MAS) is a system composed of several agents, capable of reaching goals that are difficult to achieve by an individual system. MAS is the emerging sub field of artificial intelligence that aims to provide both principles for construction of complex systems involving multiple agents and mechanisms for coordination of independent agents' behaviors. Several efforts have been devoted to enable DDM through Mass.

Agent in MAS need to be proactive and autonomous. Agents perceive their environment, dynamically reason out actions based on conditions, and interact with each other. In some applications the knowledge of the agents that guide reasoning and action depend on the existing domain theory. However, in many complex domains this knowledge is a result of the outcome of empirical data analysis in addition to pre-existing domain knowledge. Scalable analysis of data may require advanced data mining for detecting hidden patterns, constructing predictive models, and identifying outliers, among others. In a multi-agent system this knowledge is usually collective. This collective intelligence of a multi-agent system must be developed by distributed domain knowledge and analysis of distributed data observed by different agents.

Such distributed data analysis may be a non-trivial problem when the underlying task is not completely decomposable and computing resources are constrained by several factors such as limited power supply, poor bandwidth connection, and privacy sensitive multi-party data, among others.

Ensemble Learning

Ensemble methods are gaining more and more attention in the machine-learning and data mining communities. By definition, an ensemble is a group of learning models whose predictions are aggregated to give the final prediction. It is widely accepted that an ensemble is usually better than a single classifier given the same amount of training information. A number of effective ensemble generation algorithms have been invented during the past decade, such as bagging (Breiman, 1996), boosting Freund and Schapire, 1996), arcing (Breiman, 1998) and random forest (Breiman, 2001). The effectiveness of the ensemble methods relies on creating a collection of diverse, yet accurate learning

models. Two costs associated with ensemble methods are that they require much more memory to store all the learning models, and it takes much more computation time to get a prediction for an unlabeled data point. Although these extra costs may seem to be negligible with a small research data set, they may become serious when the ensemble method is applied to a large scale real-world data set. In fact, a large scale implementation of ensemble learning can easily generate an ensemble with thousands of learning models (Street and Kim, 2001). A number of effective ensemble generation algorithms have been invented during the past decade, such as bagging (Breiman, 1996), boosting (Freund and Schapire, 1996), arcing (Breiman, 1998) and random forest (Breiman, 2001). The effectiveness of the ensemble methods relies on creating a collection of diverse, yet accurate learning models. Ensemble-based distributed data-mining techniques enable large companies (like Wal Mart) that store data at hundreds of different locations to build learning models locally and then combine all the models for future prediction and knowledge discovery.

Distributed Classifier Learning

Most distributed classifiers have their foundations in ensemble learning (Dietterich, 2000; Opitz & Maclin, 1999; Bauer & Kohavi, 1999; Merz & Pazzani, 1999). The ensemble approach has been applied in various domains to increase the classification accuracy of predictive models. It produces multiple models (base classifiers) – typically from "homogeneous" data subsets – and combines them to enhance accuracy. Typically, voting (weighted or un weighted) schemes are employed to aggregate base classifiers. The ensemble aproach is directly applicable to the distributed scenario. Different models can be generated at different sites and ultimately aggregated using ensemble combining strategies. Fan, et al. (Fan, Stolfo & Zhang, 1999) discussed an Adaboost-based ensemble approach in this perspective. Breiman (Breiman, 1999) considered Arcing as a mean to aggregate multiple blocks of data, especially in on-line setting. An experimental investigation of Stacking (Wolpert, 1992) for combining multiple models was reported elsewhere (Ting & Low, 1997). Homogeneous Distributed Classifiers. One notable ensemble approach to learn distributed classifier is meta-learning framework (Chan & Stolfo, 1993b, 1993a, 1998). It offers a way to mine classifiers from homogeneous, distributed data. In this approach, supervised learning techniques are first used to learn classifiers at local data sites; then meta-level classifiers are learned from a data set generated using the locally learned concepts. The meta-level learning may be applied recursively, producing a hierarchy of meta-classifiers. Java Agent for Meta-learning is reported elsewhere (Stolfo et al., 1997; Lee, Stolfo, & Mok, 1999). Meta-learning follows three main steps:

- Concrete base classifiers at each site using a classifier learning algorithms.
- Collect the base classifiers at a central site. Produce meta-level data from a separate validation set and predictions generated by the base classifier on it.
- Generate the final classifier (meta-classifier) from meta-level data.

The following discourse notes two common techniques for meta-learning from the output of the base classifiers are briefly described in the following.

- **The Arbiter Scheme:** This scheme makes use of a special classifier, called arbiter, for deciding the final class prediction for a given feature vector. The arbiter is learned using a learning algorithm. Classification is performed based on the class predicted by the majority of the base classifiers and the arbiter. It there is a tie, the arbiter's prediction gets the preference.
- **The Combiner Scheme:** The combiner scheme offers an alternate way to perform meta-learning. The combiner classifier is learned in either of the following ways. One way is to learn the combiner from the correct classification and the base classifier outputs. Another possibility is to learn the combiner from the data comprised of the feature vector of the training examples, the correct classifications, and the data comprised of the feature vector of the training examples, the correct classifications, and the base classifier outputs.

Distributed Association Rule Mining

Agrawal and Shafer (1996) discuss three parallel algorithms for mining association rules. One of those, the Count Distribution (CD) algorithm, focuses on minimizing the communication cost, and is therefore suitable for mining association rules in a distributed computing environment. CD uses the Apriori algorithm (Agrawal and Srikant, 1994) locally at each data site. In each pass k of the algorithm, each site generates the same candidate k-itemsets based on the globally frequent itemsets of the previous phase. Then, each site calculates the local support counts of the candidate itemsets and broadcasts them to the rest of the sites, so that global support counts can be computed at each site. Subsequently, each site computes the k-frequent itemsets based on the global counts of the candidate itemsets. The communication complexity of CD in pass k is $O(|Ck|n2)$, where Ck is the set of candidate k-itemsets and n is the number of sites. In addition, CD involves a synchronization step when each site waits to receive the local support counts from every other site.

Another algorithm that is based on Apriori is the Distributed Mining of Association rules (DMA) algorithm (Cheung, Ng, Fu & Fu, 1996), which is also found as Fast Distributed Mining of association rules (FDM) algorithm in (Cheung, Han, Ng, Fu & Fu, 1996). DMA generates a smaller number of candidate itemsets than CD, by pruning at each site the itemsets that are not locally frequent. In addition, it uses polling sites to optimize the exchange of support counts among sites, reducing the communication complexity in pass k to $O(|Ck|n)$, where Ck is the set of candidate k-itemsets and n is the number of sites. However, the performance enhancements of DMA over CD are based on the assumption that the data distributions at the different sites are skewed. When this assumption is violated, DMA actually introduces a larger overhead than CD due to its higher complexity.

The Optimized Distributed Association rule Mining (ODAM) algorithm (Ashrafi, Taniar & Smith, 2004) follows the paradigm of CD and DMA, but attempts to minimize communication and synchronization costs in two ways. At the local mining level, it proposes a technical extension to the Apriori algorithm. It reduces the size of transactions by: i) deleting the items that weren't found frequent in the previous step and ii) deleting duplicate transactions, but keeping track of them through a counter.

It then attempts to fit the remaining transaction into main memory in order to avoid disk access costs.

At the communication level, it minimizes the total message exchange by sending support counts of candidate itemsets to a single site, called receiver. The receiver broadcasts the globally frequent itemsets back to the distributed sites.

Distributed Clustering

Most distributed clustering algorithms have their foundations in parallel computing, and are thus applicable in homogeneous scenarios. They focus on applying center-based clustering algorithms, such as K-Means, K-Harmonic Means and EM, in a parallel fashion (Dhillon & Modha, 1999; Zhang, Hsu & Forman, 2000; Sayal & Scheuermann, 2000). Two approaches exist in this category. The first approach approximates the underlying distance measure by aggregation and the second provides the exact measure by data broadcasting. The approximation approach is sensitive to aggregation ratio and the exact approach involves heavy communication overheads.

Forman and Zhang (Forman & Zhang, 2000) propose a center-based distributed clustering algorithm that only requires the exchange of sufficient statistics, which is essentially an extension of their earlier parallel clustering work (Zhang et al., 2000). The recursive Agglomeration of Clustering Hierarchies by Encircling Tactic (RACHET) (Samatova, Ostrochov, Geist, & Melechko, 2002) is also based on the exchange of sufficient statistics. It particularly collects local dendograms that are merged into a global dendogram. Each local dendogram contains descriptive statistics about the local cluster centroid that is sufficient for the global aggregation. However, both approaches need to iterative until the sufficient statistics converge or the desired quality is achieved.

Decision Trees in Distributed Environment

Training data sets may be distributed across the set of sites for several reasons. For examples, several data sets concerning Credit Card fraud for might be owned by several banks who have security and other competitive reasons for keeping them private. However, they wish to have the model of aggregate data set. Another reason is the large data set not able to fit into a single memory because of their size in terms of terabytes, a parallel approach to process the data at different sites by participating into several subsets.

In Distributed Data mining applications, very large training data sets with several million records are common. Decision trees are very much powerful and excellent technique for both classification and prediction problems. Many decision tree construction algorithms have been proposed to develop and handle large or small training data. Some related algorithms are best for large data sets and some for small data sets. Each algorithm works best for its own criteria. The decision tree algorithms classify categorical and continuous attributes very well but it handles efficiently only a smaller data set. It consumes more time for large datasets. Supervised Learning In Quest (SLIQ) and Scalable Parallelizable Induction of Decision Tree (SPRINT) handles very large datasets. But SLIQ requires that the class labels should be available in main memory beforehand. SPRINT is best suited for large data sets and it removes all these memory restrictions. In distributed environment, the decision tree construction is based on data parallelism. For data parallelism, the entire data set is considered into partitions and each partition is available to its local site. Each local site processor builds a separate tree for its data partition. The ensemble of trees obtained by different processors is combined to obtain the final decision tree.

BACKGROUND

A more common approach is the combination of rules derived from decision trees. The idea is to convert decision trees from two models into decision rules by combining the rules into new rules, reducing their number and finally growing a decision tree of the merged model. The basic fundamentals of the process are first presented in the doctoral thesis of Williams-1990 and over the years, other researchers have contributed by proposing different ways of carrying out intermediate tasks.

Combining Decision Trees

Many of the researchers have work on combining the decision trees in such a way the composite decision tree as a whole should preserve the prediction quality.

Provost-1996 and Hennessy-2001 present an approach to learning and combining rules on disjoint subsets of a full training data. A rule based learning algorithm is used to generate rules on each subset of the training data. The merged model is constructed from satisfactory rules, i.e., rules that are generic enough to be evaluated in the other models. All rules that are considered satisfactory on the full data set are retained as they constitute a superset of the rules generated when learning is done on the full training set. This approach has not been replicated by other researchers. Table 2 summarizes research examples of this approach, specifying the problem (or motivation) and data sets used.

Hall, Chawla and Bowyer-1998 research present as rationale that is not possible do train decision trees in very large data sets because it could overwhelm the computer system's memory by making the learning process very slow. Although a tangible problem in 1998, nowadays, this argument still makes sense as the notion of very large data sets has turned into the big data paradigm. The approach involves breaking down a large data set into n disjoint partitions, then, in parallel, train a decision tree on each. Each model, in this perspective, is considered an independent learner. Globally, models can be viewed as agents learning a little about a domain with the knowledge of each agent to be combined into one

Table 2. Research examples of combination of rules approaches to merge models

Research	Problem/Motivation	Data Sets
Hall, Chawla and Bowyer-1998	Train model in a very large data set	Iris, Pima Indians Diabetes
Bursteinas and Long-2001	Mining data distributed on distant machines	UCI Machine Learning Repository
Andrzejak, Langner and Zabala-2013	Train models for distributed data sets and exceeding RAM sizes	UCI Machine Learning Repository
Strecht, Moreira and Soares-2014	Generalize knowledge in course models at university level	Academic data from University of Porto

knowledge base. Simple experiments to test the feasibility of this approach were done on two datasets: Iris and Pima Indians Diabetes. In both cases, the data sets were split across two processors and then the resulting models merged.

Bursteinas and Long-2001 research aims to develop a technique for mining data which is distributed on distant machines, connected by low transparency connections arguing that there is a lack of algorithms and systems which could perform data mining under such conditions. The merging procedure is divided into two scenarios: one for disjoined partitions and one for overlapped partitions. To evaluate the quality of the method, several experiments have been performed. The results showed the equivalence of combined classifiers with the classifier induced on a monolithic data set. The main advantage of the proposed method is its ability to induce globally applicable classifiers from distributed data without costly data transportation. It can also be applied to parallelize mining of large-scale monolithic data sets. Experiments are performed merging two models in data sets taken from the UCI Machine Learning Repository (C. Blake and C. Merz-1998).

Andrzejak, Langner and Zabala-2013 propose a method for learning in parallel or from distributed data. Factors cited as contributing to this trend include emergence of data sets with exceeding RAM sizes and inherently distributed scenarios such as mobile environments. Also in these cases interpretable models are favored: they facilitate identifying artifacts and understanding the impact of individual variables. The method is compared with ensemble learning, because in a distributed environment, even if the individual learner on each site is interpretable, the overall model usually is not, citing as example the case of voting schemes. To overcome the problem they propose an approach for merging of decision trees (each learned independently) into a single decision tree. The method complements the existing parallel decision trees algorithms by providing interpretable intermediate models and tolerating constraints on bandwidth and RAMS size. The latter properties are achieved by trading RAM and communication constraints for accuracy. The method and the mentioned trade-offs are evaluated in experiments on data sets from the UCI Machine Learning Repository-1998.

Strecht, Moreira and Soares-2014 research on educational data mining starts from the premise that predicting the failure of students in university courses can provide useful information for course and programme managers as well as to explain the drop out phenomenon. The rationale is that while it is important to have models at course level, their number makes it hard to extract knowledge that can be useful at the university level. Therefore, to support decision making at this level, it is important to generalize the knowledge contained in those models. An approach is presented to group and merge interpretable models in order to replace them with more general ones without compromising the quality of predictive performance. The case study is data from the University of Porto, Portugal, which is used for evaluation. The aggregation method consists mainly of intersecting the decision rules of pairs of models of a group recursively, i.e., by adding models along the merging process to previously merged ones. The results obtained are promising, although they suggest alternative approaches to the problem. Decision trees were trained using C5.0 algorithm and F1 was used as evaluation function of the individual and merged models.

THE NEW DYNAMIC AND SCALABLE APPROACH

From the deep literature review the facts have been identified that, most algorithms are memory resident, typically assuming a small data size, not domain-free, static in nature, less efficient in terms of processing and communication overhead. Due to the large volume of data with privacy concern there should be some efficient technique which supports scalable and dynamic classification and prediction capable of handling large distributed data sets and generates the global decision tree without losing the prediction quality.

In this section, the detailed discussions have been provided towards the new dynamic and scalable decision tree merging approach which incorporates of the above problems in distributed environment. In the first sub-section, the architecture for the proposed system has been discussed. In the second sub-section, the algorithm steps at local and coordinator sites have been briefly covered.

Proposed Framework

As shown in Figure 1, the data set D as a whole considered partitioned across different data set sites Si where i=1,2,3,...N. each site Si now process the locally available dataset Di to generate the decision tree using C4.5 algorithm available as J48 in weka tool.

C4.5 is an algorithm used to generate a decision tree developed by Ross Quinlan. C4.5 is an extension of Quinlan's earlier ID3 algorithm. The decision trees generated by C4.5 can be used for classification, and for this reason, C4.5 is often referred to as a statistical classifier. C4.5 builds decision trees from a set of training data in the same way as ID3, using the concept of information entropy. The training data is a set $S = S1, S2...$ of already classified samples. Each sample $Si = X1, X2...$ is a vector where $X1$, $X2...$ represent attributes or features of the sample. The training data is augmented with a vector $C = C1$,

Figure 1. Proposed framework

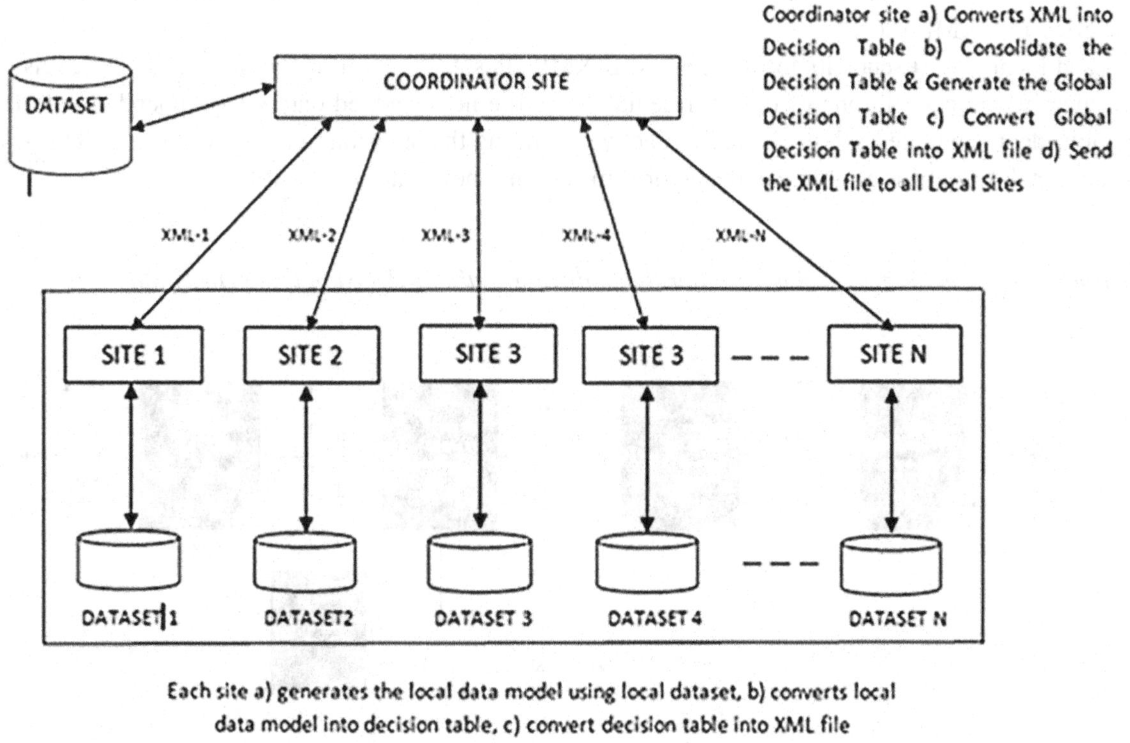

Each site a) generates the local data model using local dataset, b) converts local data model into decision table, c) convert decision table into XML file

C2… Where C1, C2, represent the class to which each sample belongs. At each node of the tree, C4.5 chooses one attribute of the data that most effectively splits its set of samples into subsets enriched in one class or the other. Its criterion is the normalized information gain (difference in entropy) that results from choosing an attribute for splitting the data. The attribute with the highest normalized information gain is chosen to make the decision.

- All the samples in the list belong to the same class. When this happens, it simply creates a leaf node for the decision tree saying to choose that class.
- None of the features provide any information gain. In this case, C4.5 creates a decision node higher up the tree using the expected value of the class.
- Instance of previously-unseen class encountered. Again, C4.5 creates a decision node higher. up the tree using the expected value.

As the decision trees generated at each site occupies larger memory, hence it is converted into decision tables followed by XML files to transmit over the network such that very less network overhead takes place. Each XML file then later available at coordinator site, where actual decision tree merging process takes place.

Proposed System Architecture at Local Site

As shown in the Figure 2, the detailed proposed architecture for dynamic and scalable decision tree generation process has been discussed. The very first step is model Mi creation from the data set Di available at each site. Later the parser converts the decision trees into the decision rule set Ri for each site Si. In the third phase the decision rule set Ri is converted into decision table DTablei which later converted into XML file.

Each local site Si sends its locally generated XML files Xi to coordinator site for further decision tree merging process. In one of the intermediate step, the newly added data set is appended with the previous decision table Dtablei of site Si directly generating the decision tree of new data set. This way the approach becomes scalable, i.e. the algorithm supports new data sets as well.

Figure 2. Proposed system architecture for dynamic and scalable decision tree generation

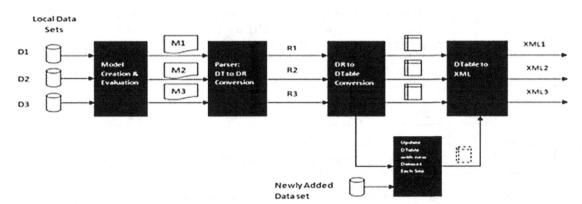

Decision Table Merging Process

As shown in Figure 3, the decision tables Dtablei of all the sites Si where i=1,2,3,…N are merged. At very first the intersection phase is carried out where the common regions i.e. the common rules are found. In the second phase, the less useful disjoint regions are removed from the list. This process is known as filtering. In the third reduction phase, the disjoint regions which can be combined i.e. merged with minor changes are merged to reduce the number of disjoint regions.

Intersection Phase

It is a task to combine the regions of two decision models using a specific method to extract the common components of both, presented in decision table. The set of values (Numerical only) of each region on each model are compared to discover common sets of values across each variable. The class to assign to the merged region is straightforward if the pair of regions have the same class, otherwise class conflict problem arises. Andrzejak, Langer and Zabala-1995 propose three strategies to address this problem. a) Assign the class with the greatest confidence b) Assign the class with the greater probability c) Retrain the model with examples for conflicting class regions, If no conflict arises that class is assigned. Otherwise remove that region from the merged model.

Filter Phase

It is the task to remove the disjoint regions from the intersected model. This is some what pruning operation. In this the regions with the highest relative volume and number of training examples are retained. Strecht, Moreira and Soares-2014 addresses the issue by removing the disjoint regions, and highlighted the case where the models are not merge able if all regions are disjoint.

Reduction Phase

This is applicable when a set of regions have the same class and all variables have equal values except for one. To obtain the simpler merged model, this is the task to find out which can be joined into one.

Figure 3. Decision table merging process to generate the global decision tree

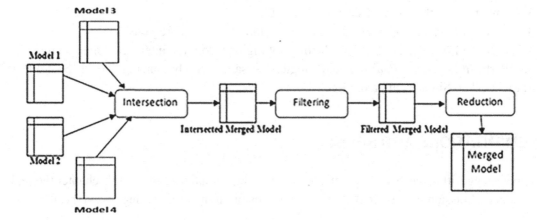

For Nominal Variables: Union of values of variables from all regions. For Numeric Variables: If intervals are contiguous.

Proposed Algorithm

The proposed algorithm supports the scalable and dynamic approach by allowing new data sets to process and update the global decision tree continuously at run time. the algorithm steps at local site and coordinator site have been discussed as below:

```
Input:
        Dataset Di, Dtsi which are the set of training tuples and their as-
sociated class labels (Dtsi is new data set instance at time stamp ts for site
Si) where i=1,2,3,….N
        flag=0 (indicates data set not processed before)
Output:
        Global Decision Tree (GT)
```

Algorithm Steps at Local Site:

Step 1: If flag==0 then perform step-2 to step-5 otherwise perform step-6 to 9.
Step 2: Apply J48 i.e. C4.5 Algorithm on data set Di of each site Si to generate the local decision tree DTi.
Step 3: Convert the Decision Tree DTi into the Decision Table Dtablei at each site Si. flag=1.
Step 4: Sort decision rules in Dtablei in descending order as per class label majority.
Step 5: Perform step 8 and step 9.
Step 6: For each Dtsi perform step 7.
Step 7: Classify Dtsi tuples into Dtablei and update Dtablei accordingly Di= Dtsi U Di.
Step 8: Create the XML file Xi of Dtablei for each site Si.
Step 9: Send Xi file of each Si to coordinator site for further process.

Algorithm Steps at Coordinator Site:

Step 1: Convert the Xi into Dtablei for respective site Si.
Step 2: Merge the Dtablei into Single Table T.
Step 3: Convert T into the Global Decision Tree GT.
Step 3.1: Perform *Intersection Phase:* Finding the common rules i.e. regions.
Step 3.2: Perform *Filter Phase:* Remove the disjoint regions from the intersected merged model.
Step 3.3: Perform *Reduction Phase:* Join the regions of same class but having one attribute differ.
Step 4: Send GT to Si for local prediction.

IMPLEMENTATIONS AND RESULTS

The proposed algorithm has been implemented on the educational data set. In this chapter the real data set of student admission process in different disciplines of engineering colleges have been considered for decision tree merging process. The data sets have been collected from parul university web portal. In the experimental the data set is processed on two different sites to generate the local decision tree models which later merged into a single decision tree as a whole without losing the predication quality. The results are as below:

As shown in Figure 4, each site uses the J48/C4.5 algorithm to generate the local decision tree which in turn later converted into the decision table. In this process the rule set of each discipline as shown in Figure 5 have been separated out for the simplicity.

The decision tree generated will be converted into the decision table using the J48 Parser, which later converted into the XML file as shown in Figure 6 below to transmit it to the remote coordinator site.

Figure 4. Local site decision tree and decision table generation

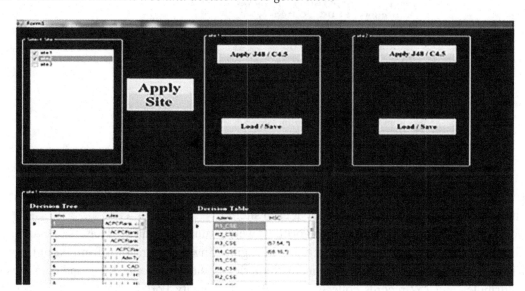

Figure 5. Discipline wise decision rules at one site

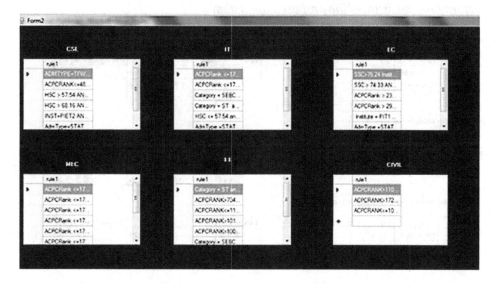

Figure 6. XML file generated from the decision table

```
D:\DINESH SIR PHD\Open Seminar\For Result Dis...

<?xml version="1.0" standalone="yes" ?>
- <NewDataSet>
  - <r1>
      <Hsc>(*,51.3]</Hsc>
      <Ssc>(*,90]</Ssc>
      <AcpRank />
      <Category>ST</Category>
      <admType>STATE</admType>
      <Institute />
      <Branch>CSE</Branch>
    </r1>
  - <r1>
      <Hsc>(*,63.01]</Hsc>
      <Ssc>(*,90]</Ssc>
      <AcpRank>(*,41685]</AcpRank>
      <Category>SEBC</Category>
      <admType>STATE</admType>
      <Institute />
      <Branch>CSE</Branch>
    </r1>
  - <r1>
      <Hsc>(63.01,*)</Hsc>
      <Ssc>(*,71.28]</Ssc>
      <AcpRank />
      <Category />
      <admType>STATE</admType>
      <Institute />
      <Branch>CSE</Branch>
```

The Figure 7 shows various performance measures, and the statistics of the proposed algorithm is better than processing the individual data set at each site.

Performance of Selected classification algorithms were evaluated with two datasets of two different sites. First dataset contains 179 student admission in engineering college records from Parul University Portal (PUP) with 7 attributes (4 Nominal and 3 Numeric) as shown in Table 3. Second dataset is with similar attributes and 152 records collected from Parul University Portal (PUP). For the purpose of

Figure 7. Performance measure of the proposed algorithm

Confusion Matrix for Site-2

	Yes	No		Yes	No	Total	Recognition(%)
Yes	TP=0.648	FN=0	Yes	92	0	92	64.788
No	FP=0.091	TN=0.26	No	13	37	50	35.211
			Total	105	37	142	**90.845**

Confusion Matrix for Site-1

	Yes	No		Yes	No	Total	Recognition(%)
Yes	TP=0.788	FN=0	Yes	141	0	141	78.77
No	FP=0.043	TN=0.168	No	8	30	38	21.052
			Total	149	30	179	**95.53**

Confusion Matrix for Combined Dataset

	Yes	No		Yes	No	Total	Recognition(%)
Yes	TP=0.701	FN=0	Yes	225	0	225	70.09%
No	FP=0.066	TN=0.28	No	6	90	96	67.61%
			Total	231	90	321	**98.13%**

Table 3. Attribute details

Attribute Name	Attribute Type
Institute	Nominal
AdmissionType	Nominal
Category	Nominal
ACPCRank	Numeric
HSC	Numeric
SSC	Numeric
Degree	Nominal

experimentation, Weka© Data Mining open source machine learning software has been used. The J48 algorithm has applied to generate the decision trees at each local site. It is used on i3 processor with 2 GB RAM. With Each algorithm, it has been observed about Accuracy, Precision, Sensitivity and Specificity which can be defined as follows:

- **Accuracy:** The accuracy of a classifier is the percentage of the test set tuples that are correctly classified by the classifier.

Accuracy=(Number of True Positives + Number of True Negatives)/(Number of True Positives + Number of True Negatives + Number of False Positives + Number of False Negatives)

- **Sensitivity:** Sensitivity is also referred as True positive rate i.e. the proportion of positive tuples that are correctly identified.

Sensitivity= (Number of True Positives) / (Number of True Positives + Number of False Negatives)

- **Precision:** precision is defined as the proportion of the true positives against all the positive results (both true positives and false positives)

Precision= (Number of True Positives) / (Number of True Positives + False Positives)

- **Specificity:** Specificity is the True negative rate that is the proportion of negative tuples that are correctly identified.

Specificity= (Number of True Negatives) / (Number of True Negatives + Number of False Positives)

FUTURE RESEARCH DIRECTIONS

In this chapter the web based classification learning with dynamic and scalable data mining approach for distributed environment has been discussed for the educational data i.e. student admission process in different disciplines of engineering institute. The results obtained are very interesting in e-learning system for student admission. The research can be further carried out for dynamic prediction of the missing data based on the decision tree (i.e. of historical data set) and the current real time trends in admission process, so that one can decide his/her admission position. The dynamic approach of generating the decision tables from the previous decision table and newly generated data can be further extended for efficiently to make the prediction more dynamic and accurate without losing the prediction quality.

CONCLUSION

In this chapter, the author has discussed various decision tree based classification algorithms for both central and distributed environment for web-based data. Due to the importance of processing the data set in distributed environment followed by merging the local models, the author has discussed various approaches given by the researchers for decision tree merging process. Later the author has discussed the proposed framework, architecture, and algorithm to merge the decision trees of different sites at one coordinate site. The new approach for merging the decision trees in distributed environment generates the global decision model which predicts the missing classes without losing the quality. The results itself proves the proposed algorithm is more efficient for dynamic and scalable data mining process.

REFERENCES

Amado, N., Gama, J., & Silva, F. (2003). Exploiting Parallelism in Decision Tree Induction. *7th European Conference on Principles and Practice of Knowledge Discovery in Databases*.

Andrzejak, A., Langner, F., & Zabala, S. (2013). Interpretable models from distributed data via merging of decision trees. *2013 IEEE Symposium on Computational Intelligence and Data Mining (CIDM)*. doi:10.1109/CIDM.2013.6597210

Anyanwu, M., & Shiva, S. (2009). Application of Enhanced Decision Tree Algorithm to Churn Analysis. *2009 International Conference on Artificial Intelligence and Pattern Recognition (AIPR-09)*.

Ashrafi, M. Z., Taniar, D., & Smith, K. (2004). ODAM: An Optimal Distributed Association Rule Mining Algorithm. *IEEE Distributed Systems Online*, *5*(3), 1541–4922. doi:10.1109/MDSO.2004.1285877

Baik, S., & Bala, J. (2004). *A Decision Tree Algorithm For Distributed Data Mining*. Academic Press.

Barros, R. C., Cerri, R., Jaskowiak, P. A., & de Carvalho, A. (2011). A Bottom-up Oblique Decision Tree Induction Algorithm. In *Intelligent Systems Design and Applications (ISDA), 2011 11th International Conference on*.

Bauer, E., & Kohavi, R. (1999). An empirical comparison of voting classification algorithms: Bagging, Boosting and variants. *Machine Learning*, *36*(1/2), 105–139. doi:10.1023/A:1007515423169

Bekkerman, R., Bilenko, M., & Langford, J. (Eds.). (2012). *Scaling up Machine Learning: Parallel and Distributed Approaches*. Cambridge University Press.

Ben-Haim, Y., & Tom-Tov, E. (2010). A streaming parallel decision tree algorithm. *Journal of Machine Learning Research, 11*, 849–872.

Blake & Merz. (1998). *UCI Machine Learning Repository*. Academic Press.

Böse, J.-H., Andrzejak, A., & Högqvist, M. (2010). Beyond online aggregation: Parallel and incremental data mining with online mapreduce. ACM. doi:10.1145/1779599.1779602

Breiman, L., Friedman, J. H., Olshen, R. A., & Stone, C. J. (1984). *Classification and Regression Trees*. Belmont, CA: Wadsworth International Group.

Breslow, L.A., & Aha, D.W. (1997). Simplifying decision trees: a survey. *The Knowledge Engineering Review, 12*(1), 1-40.

Bursteinas, B., & Long, J. (2001). Merging distributed classifiers. In *5th World Multi conference on Systemic, Cybernetics and Informatics*.

Caragea, D., Silvescu, A., & Honavar, V. (2004). A framework for learning from distributed data using sufficient statistics and its application to learning decision trees. *Int. J. Hybrid Intell. Syst., 1*(2), 80–89. doi:10.3233/HIS-2004-11-210 PMID:20351798

Carvalho & Freitas. (2004). *A hybrid decision tree/genetic algorithm for coping with the problem of small disjuncts in data mining*. Academic Press.

Chan, P., & Stolfo, S. (1995). Learning arbiter and combiner trees from partitioned data for scaling machine learning.*Proc. Intl. Conf. Knowledge Discovery and Data Mining*.

Chan, P., & Stolfo, S. (1996).Sharing learned models among remote database partitions by local meta-learning. In *Proceedings Second International Conference on Knowledge Discovery and Data Mining*.

Chan & Stolfo. (1996). Sharing Learned Models among Remote Database Partitions by Local Meta-Learning. *KDD-96 Proceedings*.

Chauhan, H., & Chauhan, A. (2013). Implementation of decision tree algorithm c4.5. *International Journal of Scientific and Research Publications, 3*(10).

Dai, W., & Ji, W. (2014). Wei Ji A MapReduce Implementation of C4.5 Decision Tree Algorithm. *International Journal of Database Theory and Application, 7*(1), 49–60. doi:10.14257/ijdta.2014.7.1.05

Ding, Y., & Simonoff, J. S. (2010). An investigation of missing data methods for classification trees applied to binary response data. *Journal of Machine Learning Research, 11*, 131–170.

Freitas. (2000). Understanding the Crucial Differences Between Classification and Discovery of Association Rules. *SIGKDD Explorations, 2*(1), 65.

Gama, J., Rocha, R., & Medas, P. (2003). Accurate decision trees for mining high-speed data streams. In *Proc. of 9th ACM SIGKDD international conference on Knowledge discovery and data mining* (KDD'03). ACM. doi:10.1145/956750.956813

Gorbunov, K. Y., & Lyubetsky, V. (2011, October). The tree nearest on average to a given set of trees. *Problems of Information Transmission, 47*(3), 274–288. doi:10.1134/S0032946011030069

Hall, L., Chawla, N., & Bowyer, K. (1998). Combining decision trees learned in parallel. *Working Notes of the KDD-97 Workshop on Distributed Data Mining.*

Hall, L., Chawla, N., & Bowyer, K. (1998). Decision tree learning on very large data sets. *IEEE International Conference on Systems, Man, and Cybernetics.* doi:10.1109/ICSMC.1998.725047

Kass. (1980). An exploratory Technique for investigation large quantities of categorical data. *Applied Statics, 29*(2), 119-127.

Khoonsari & Motie. (2012). A Comparison of Efficiency and Robustness of ID3 and C4.5 Algorithms Using Dynamic Test and Training Data Sets. *International Journal of Machine Learning and Computing, 2*(5).

Kuhn, Weston, Coulter, & Quinlan. (2014). *C50: C5.0 Decision Trees and Rule-Based Models.* R package version 0.1.0-16.

Li, C., Zhang, Y., & Li, X. (2009, June). OcVFDT: one class very fast decision tree for one-class classification of data streams. In *Proceedings of the Third International Workshop on Knowledge Discovery from Sensor Data* (pp. 79-86). ACM. doi:10.1145/1601966.1601981

Liang, C., Zhang, Y., & Song, Q. (2010). Decision Tree for Dynamic and Uncertain Data Streams. *JMLR: Workshop and Conference Proceedings.*

Liu, B., Hsu, W., & Ma, Y. (1998). Integrating classification and association rule mining. *Proc. 4th Int. Conf. on Knowledge Discovery and Data Mining* (KDD-98), (pp. 80-86). AAAI Press.

Liu, K., & Kargupta, H. (2008). *Distributed data mining bibliography.* Available: http://www.csee.umbc.edu/~hillol/DDMBIB/

Liu, L., Kantarcioglu, M., & Thuraisingham, B. (2009). Privacy Preserving Decision Tree Mining from Perturbed Data. *Proceedings of the 42nd Hawaii International Conference on System Sciences.*

Minguillon & Alfonso. (2002). *On Cascading Small Decision Trees.* (PhD Thesis). University of Barcelona.

Murdopo. (2013). *Distributed Decision Tree Learning for Mining Big Data Streams.* (Master's Thesis). UPC.

Patel & Rana. (2014). A Survey on Decision Tree Algorithm For Classification. *IJEDR, 2*(1).

Patil & Lathi. (2012). *Comparison of C5.0 & CART Classification algorithms using pruning technique.* Academic Press.

Provost, F., & Hennessy, D. (1996). Scaling up: Distributed machine learning with cooperation. In *Proceedings of the 13th National Conference on Artificial Intelligence.*

Provost, F. J., & Hennessy, D. N. (1994). Distributed machine learning: scaling up with coarse-grained parallelism. In *Proceedings of the 2nd International Conference on Intelligent Systems for Molecular Biology.*

Quinlan, J. R. (1986). Induction of decision trees. *Machine Learning, 1*(1), 81-106.

Samatova, N. F., Ostrouchov, G., Geist, A., & Melechko, A. V. (2002). RACHET: An Efficient Cover-Based Merging of Clustering Hierarchies from Distributed Datasets. *Distributed and Parallel Databases, 11*(2), 157–180.

Saravana Kumar, Ananthi, & Devi. (2013). An Approach to Automation Selection of Decision Tree based on Training Data Set. *International Journal of Computer Applications, 64*(21).

Strecht, P. (2015). A Survey of Merging Decision Trees Data Mining Approaches. *Proceedings of the 10th Doctoral Symposium in Informatics Engineering*.

Strecht, P., Mendes-Moreira, J., & Soares, C. (2014). Merging Decision Trees: a case study in predicting student performance. In *Proceedings of 10th International Conference on Advanced Data Mining and Applications*, (pp. 535–548). doi:10.1007/978-3-319-14717-8_42

Totad, Geeta, Prasanna, & Santhosh. (2010). PVGD Prasad Reddy, Scaling Data Mining Algorithms to Large and Distributed Datasets. *International Journal of Database Management Systems, 2*(4).

Williams, G. J. (1990). *Inducing and Combining Multiple Decision Trees*. (PhD thesis). Australian National University.

Yang, H. (2013). *Solving Problems of Imperfect Data Streams by Incremental Decision Trees. Journal of Emerging Technologies in Web Intelligence, 5(3)*.

Yang, H., & Fong, S. (2011). Moderated VFDT in Stream Mining Using Adaptive Tie Threshold and Incremental Pruning. In *Proc. of 13th international conference on Data Warehousing and Knowledge Discovery* (DaWak2011), (LNCS). Springer. doi:10.1007/978-3-642-23544-3_36

Zhu, Wang, & Wu. (2009). *Research and application of the improved algorithm C4.5 on decision tree*. Academic Press.

ADDITIONAL READING

A. Silvescu D. Caragea and V. Honavar. A framework for learning from distributed data using sufficient statistics and its application to learning decision trees. International Journal of Hybrid Intelligent Systems, 2003.

Badr Hssina, Abdelkarim Merbouha, Hanane Ezzikouri, Mohammed Erritali, A comparative study of decision tree ID3 and C4.5, IJACSA-Special Issue.

Chan, P., & Stolfo, S. (1998). Toward scalable learning with non-uniform class and cost distribution: A case study in credit card fraud detection. In Proceeding of the fourth international conference on knowledge discovery and data mining (p.o.). AAAI Press.

Frank, A., & Asuncion, A. "UCI machine learning repository," 2010. [Online]. Available: http://archive.ics.uci.edu/ml

Gama, J., Rocha, R., & Medas, P. Accurate Decision Trees for Mining High-Speed Data Streams," in Proceedings of the ninth ACM SIGKDD international conference on Knowledge discovery and data mining, KDD '03, (New York, NY, USA), pp. 523{528, ACM, 2003. doi:10.1145/956750.956813

Han, J., Kamber, M., & Pei, J. (2011). *Data Mining: Concepts and Techniques*. San Francisco: Morgan Kaufmann.

Jin, C. Luo De-lin and mu Fen-xiang An improve ID3 Decision tree algorithm. IEEE 4th International Conference on computer Science & Education.

Panda, B., Herbach, J., Basu, S., & Bayardo, R. J. (2009). PLANET: Massively parallel learning of tree ensembles with mapreduce. *PVLDB*, *2*(2), 1426–1437.

Prodromidis, A., Chan, P., & Stolfo, S. (2000). Meta-learning in distributed data mining systems: Issues and approaches. In H. Kargupta & P. Chan (Eds.), *Advances of Distributed Data Mining*. AAAI Press.

Thaku, D., Makandaiah, N., & Sharan, R. D. (2010). *Re Optimization of ID3 and C4.5 Decision tree*. IEEE Computer & Communication Technology.

Yael, B.-H., & Elad, T.-T. (2010). A Streaming Parallel Decision Tree Algorithm. *Journal of Machine Learning Research*, *11*, 849–872.

Yael Ben-Haim. (2010). Elad Tom-Tov, A Streaming Parallel Decision Tree Algorithm. *Journal of Machine Learning Research*, *11*, 849–872.

Go¨khan Yavas, Dimitrios Katsaros, O¨ zgu¨ Ulusoy,*, Yannis Manolopoulos, A data mining approach for location prediction in mobile environments, Data & Knowledge Engineering 54 (2005) 121–146, October-2004.

KEY TERMS AND DEFINITIONS

10-Fold-Cross Validation: Break data into 10 sets of size n/10. Train on 9 datasets and test on 1. Repeat 10 times and take a mean accuracy.

Classification: Classification is a data mining function that assigns items in a collection to target categories or classes. The goal of classification is to accurately predict the target class for each case in the data. For example, a classification model could be used to identify loan applicants as low, medium, or high credit risks.

Data Mining: An interdisciplinary subfield of computer science. It is the computational process of discovering patterns in large data sets ("big data") involving methods at the intersection of artificial intelligence, machine learning, statistics, and database systems.

Decision Table: A decision table is an excellent tool to use in both testing and requirements management. Essentially it is a structured exercise to formulate requirements when dealing with complex business rules. Decision tables are used to model complicated logic.

Decision Tree: A decision tree is a decision support tool that uses a tree-like graph or model of decisions and their possible consequences, including chance event outcomes, resource costs, and utility. It is one way to display an algorithm.

Prediction Model: Predictive modeling is a process used in predictive analytics to create a statistical model of future behavior. Predictive analytics is the area of data mining concerned with forecasting probabilities and trends.

Rule Learning: Association rule learning is a method for discovering interesting relations between variables in large databases.

Scalability: Scalability is the capability of a system, network, or process to handle a growing amount of work, or its potential to be enlarged in order to accommodate that growth. Here it refers to support the growth of data set in distributed environment.

Test Data Set: The data set with missing class whose class label is yet to find is known as test data set.

Training Data Set: The data set which is useful to generate the learning model for future prediction is called training data set.

Section 3
Methodologies and Technologies

Chapter 11
Methodologies and Techniques of Web Usage Mining

T. Venkat Narayana Rao
Sreenidhi Institute of Science and Technology, India

D. Hiranmayi
Sreenidhi Institute of Science and Technology, India

ABSTRACT

Web usage mining attempts to discover useful knowledge from the secondary data obtained from the interactions of the users with the Web. It is the type of Web mining activity that involves the automatic discovery of out what users are looking for on the Internet. In this chapter methodology of web usage mining explained in detail which are data collection, data preprocessing, knowledge discovery and pattern analysis. The different Web Usage Mining techniques are described, which are used for knowledge and pattern discovery. These are statistical analysis, sequential patterns, classification, association rule mining, clustering, dependency modeling. Pattern analysis is needed to filter out uninterested rules or patterns from the set found in the pattern discovery phase.

INTRODUCTION

Web mining is the technique of data mining which is used to discover patterns from web. It contains three types of techniques namely web usage mining, web content mining, web structure mining. Web usage mining is the process of extracting information about server logs. This technique is used to extract the information about the users' access. By using web mining we are able to find out for what users are looking about in the internet. This type of mining is used for the collection of web access information about the web pages. This usage data provides the paths leading to access web pages. Web server stores this information automatically in the log files.

Web usage mining is used for companies to produce the information about products and their future business analysis based on the present productive information. This usage data provides the companies to increase their sales. Web usage mining is also useful for e-business of the companies. The use of this type of data mining is used to find the information about customer visiting sites. This helps to know

DOI: 10.4018/978-1-5225-0613-3.ch011

about company's in-depth logging information. This web mining also enables Web based businesses to provide the best access routes to services or other advertisements. When a company advertises for services provided by other companies, the usage mining data allows for the most effective access paths to these portals. In addition, there are typically three main uses for mining in this fashion.

Web usage mining mainly having three main uses:

1. It is used to complete pattern discovery, and used for processing.
2. Content processing which means that converting of web information like text, images to useful forms.
3. Structure processing which means that analyzing the structure of each page in the web site.

Recently, millions of electronic data are included on hundreds of millions data that are previously on-line today. With this significant increase of existing data on the Internet and because of its fast and disordered growth, the World Wide Web has evolved into a network of data with no proper organizational structure. In addition, survival of plentiful data in the network and the varying and heterogeneous nature of the web, web searching has become a tricky procedure for the majority of the users. This makes the users feel confused and at times lost in overloaded data that persist to enlarge. Moreover, e-business and web marketing are quickly developing and significance of anticipate the requirement of their customers is obvious particularly. As a result, guessing the users' interests for improving the usability of web or so called personalization has turn out to be very essential. Web personalization can be depicted as some action that builds the web experience of a user personalized according to the user's interest.

The ease and speed with which business transactions can be carried out over the Web has been a key driving force in the rapid growth of electronic commerce. Specifically, ecommerce activity that involves the end user is undergoing a significant revolution. The ability to track users' browsing behavior down to individual mouse clicks has brought the vendor and end customer closer than ever before. It is now possible for a vendor to personalize his product message for individual customers at a massive scale, a phenomenon that is being referred to as mass customization. The scenario described above is one of many possible applications of Web Usage mining, which is the process of applying data mining techniques to the discovery of usage patterns from Web data, targeted towards various applications.

BACKGROUND

Day by day the data in the web increasing in rapid way. To analyze and process this data is a complex task. The number of pages available on the Web is currently around 1 billion and is increasing at the rate of approximately 1.5 million per day. The Web-based business has been a key driving force for this rapid growth of the Web. Retailers on the Web need the ability to track users" browsing behavior history, which can increase the sale and build a strong customer relationship[8]. This ability also can personalize the retailer's Web pages for different individual customers. Although Web log mining is a relatively new field, it has generated a lot of interest and research in the past ten years. As a sub research field of Web Usage Mining, Web log mining is the process of applying data mining technologies to discover usage patterns from the Web data. One important source to discover such patters is the Web log data that contains users Web browsing history. Most of Web log data is generated automatically by Web servers.

From the last few decades, there has been witnessed an explosive growth in the information available on the World Wide Web (WWW).

Today, web browsers provide easy access to myriad sources of text and multimedia data. More than millions of pages are indexed by search engines, and finding the desired information is not an easy task. The users want to have the effective search tools to find relevant information easily and precisely. The Web service providers want to find the way to predict the users" behaviors and personalize information to reduce the traffic load and design the Web-site suited for the different group of users. This profusion of resources has prompted the need for developing automatic mining techniques on the WWW, thereby giving rise to the term "web mining" (Srivastava, Cooley, Deshpande, & Tan, n.d.). Web mining is the application of data mining techniques to discover patterns from the Web.

WEB DATA

One of the key steps in Knowledge Discovery in Databases (http://www.w3.org/TR/WD-logfile.html). is to create a suitable target data set for the data mining tasks. In Web Mining, data can be collected at the server side, client-side, proxy servers, or obtained from an organization's database (which contains business data or consolidated Web data). Each type of data collection differs not only in terms of the location of the data source (Srivastava, Cooley, Deshpande, & Tan, 2000). But also the kinds of data available, the segment of population from which the data was collected, and its method of implementation. There are many kinds of data that can be used in Web Mining. This paper classifies such data into the following types:

- **Content:** The real data in the Web pages, i.e. the data the Web page was designed to convey to the users. This usually consists of, but is not limited t6;"text and graphics".
- **Structure:** Data which describes the organization of the content. Intra-page structure information includes the arrangement of various HTML or XML tags within a given page. This can be represented as a tree structure, where the (html) tag becomes the root of the tree.
- **Usage:** Data that describes the pattern of usage of Web pages, such as IP addresses, page references, and the date and time of accesses.
- **User Profile:** Data. that provides demographic information about users of the Web site. This includes registration data and customer profile information.

DATA SOURCES

The usage data collected at the different sources will represent the navigation patterns of different segments of the overall Web traffic, ranging from single-user, single-site browsing behavior to multi-user, multi-site access patterns:

Server Level Collection: A Web server log is an important source for performing Web Usage Mining because it explicitly records the browsing behavior of site visitors. The data recorded in server logs reflects the (possibly concurrent) access of a Web site by multiple users. These log files can be stored in various formats such as Common log or Extended log formats. An example of Extended log format is given in Figure 2 (Section 3). However, the site usage data recorded by server logs may not be entirely reliable due to the presence of various levels of caching within the Web environment. Cached page views are not recorded in a server log (Cohen, Krishnamurthy, & Rexford, 1998).

1. In addition, arty important information passed through the POST method will not be available in a server log. Packet sniffing technology is an alternative method to collecting usage data through server logs. Packet sniffers monitor network traffic coming to a Web server and extract usage data directly from TCP/IP packets. The Web server can also store other kinds of usage information such as cookies and query data in separate logs. Cookies are tokens generated by the Web server for individual client browsers in order to automatically track the site visitors. Tracking of individual users is not an easy task due to the stateless connection model of the HTTP protocol. Cookies rely on implicit user cooperation and thus have raised growing concerns regarding user privacy, which will be discussed in Section 6. Query data is also typically generated by online visitors while searching for pages relevant to their information needs. Besides usage data, the server side also provides content data, structure information and Web page meta-information (such as the size of a file and its last modified time.

Client Level Collection: Client-side data collection can be implemented by using a remote agent (such as Java Scripts or Java applets) or by modifying the source code of an existing browser (such as Mosaic or Mozilla) to enhance its data collection capabilities. The implementation of client-side data collection methods requires user cooperation, either in enabling the functionality of the java Scripts and Java applets, or to voluntarily use the modified browser. Client-side collection has an advantage over server-side collection because it ameliorates both the caching and session identification problems. However, Java applets perform no better than server logs in terms of determining the actual view time of a page. In fact, it may incur some additional overhead especially when the Java applet is loaded for the first time. java Scripts, on the other hand, consume little interpretation time but cannot capture all user clicks (such as reload or back buttons). These methods will collect only single-user, single-site browsing behavior. A modified browser is much more versatile and will allow data collection about a single user over multiple Web sites. The most difficult part of using this method is convincing the users to use the browser for their daily browsing activities. This can be done by offering incentives to users who are willing to use the browser, similar to the incentive programs offered by companies such as NetZero (Srivastava, Cooley, Deshpande, & Tan 2000) and All Advantage (Cohen, Krishnamurthy, & Rexford, 1998) that reward users for clicking on banner advertisements while surfing the Web.

Proxy Level Collection: A Web proxy acts as an intermediate level of caching between client browsers and Web servers (Cohen, Krishnamurthy, & Rexford, 1998.). Proxy caching can be used to reduce the loading time of a Web page experienced by users as well as the network traffic load at the server and client sides (Cooley, Mobasher, & Srivastava, 1997). The performance of proxy caches depends on their ability to predict future page requests correctly. Proxy traces may reveal the actual HTTP requests from multiple clients to multiple Web servers. This may serve as a data source for characterizing the browsing behavior of a group of anonymous users, sharing a common proxy server.

DATA ABSTRACTIONS

The information provided by the data sources described above can all be used to construct/identify several data abstractions, notably users, server sessions, episodes, clickstreams, and page views. In order to provide some consistency in the way these terms are defined, the W3C ~reb Characterization Activity (WCA) (Zaïane, 2001) has published a draft of Web term definitions relevant to analyzing Web usage. A user is defined as a single individual that is accessing file from one or more Web servers through a browser. While this definition seems trivial, in practice it is very difficult to uniquely and repeatedly identify users. A user may access the Web through different machines, or use more than one agent on a single machine. A page view consists of every file that contributes to the display on a user's browser at one time. Page views are usually associated with a single user action (such as a mouse-click) and can consist of several files such as frames, graphics, and scripts. When discussing and analyzing user behaviors, it is really the aggregate page view that is of importance. The user does not explicitly ask for "n" frames and "m" graphics to be loaded into his or her browser, the user requests a "Web page." All of the information to determine which files constitute a page view is accessible from the Web server.

A click-stream is a sequential series of page view requests. Again, the data available from the server side does not always provide enough information to reconstruct the full click-stream for a site. Any page view accessed through a client or proxy-level cache will not be "visible" from the server side. A user session is the click-stream of page views for a single user across the entire Web. Typically, only the portion of each user session that is accessing a specific site can be used for analysis, since access information is not publicly available from the vast majority of Web servers. The set of page-views in a user session for a particular Web site is referred to as a server session (also commonly referred to as a visit). A set of server sessions' is the necessary input for any Web Usage analysis or data mining tool. The end of a server session is defined as the point when the user's browsing session at that site has ended. Again, this is a simple concept that is very difficult to track reliably. Any semantically meaningful subset of a user or server session is referred to as an episode by the W3C WCA.

CHALLENGES OF WEB USAGE MINING

There are a number of issues related to web usage mining that affect the utilization of the mined information. Recently, privacy has been defined as one of the problems of data collection in the Web, especially data that are related to query or transaction users or to social networks that have valuable personal information. Web usage mining tools integrate data from different resources: web logs, cookies or explicit user entries, which increase the problem of privacy violation. Many researchers are conscious of this privacy issue and are trying to find some solutions to control the privacy problem in web mining. One of the main proposals to deal with the privacy issue is the Privacy Preferences (P3P) standard, which enables websites to state their privacy practices in a standard format. However, P3P does not solve the problem completely, as it does not answer the issue of which data mining technique should be used over user data (Facca & Lanzi, 2005). In Zaïane (2001) the authors suggest some directives that can applied on the websites to protect user privacy:

- Support of P3P
- Clear disclosure of data and methods to facilitate user understanding of system assumptions about them.
- Provide a number of anonymization methods to help users protect their anonymity.

Moreover, one of the most common problems that face pattern discovery methods is dealing with the huge volumes of data available on the Web, and so the scalability of pattern discovery methods is now a critical issue. Scalability means the rate of memory and time needed for the task, according to the parameters that affect the performance of the algorithms, such as number of users or pages. Another problem is the lack of studies that compare the performance of the different tools, and the reason is the difficulty of finding suitable evaluation criteria. The authors in Korra, Panigrahy, and Jena (2013) propose a multi-level evaluation approach that facilitates the comparison between the performance of the different tools:

- **System Evaluation: This** uses the standard software engineering criteria: memory need, speed, time, scalability and interoperability.
- **Modeling Performance:** This evaluates the web usage mining; machine learning criteria can be used: accuracy, recall and precision.
- **Usability:** These studies the usability features in the tool.

The lack of comparison between existing tools also causes difficulty in finding or choosing the appropriate tool for analyzing data and producing useful knowledge. There are several commercial analysis tools but most of them have limitations in speed, are expensive, inflexible, and difficult to maintain, or give limited results (Pierrakos, Paliouras, Papatheodorou, & Spyropoulos, 2003). Moreover, most of the tools work independently and the results cannot be transferred or used in other tools, which means that most tools do not support interoperability. Most of the tools provide only statistical information without useful knowledge for managers. Also, the visualization of the results should be organized, easy to understand and supported by visual graphs to facilitate knowledge extraction.

WEB USAGE MINING

Requirements of Web Usage Mining

To conduct efficient and effective web usage mining it is necessary to examine what kind of features a Web usage mining system is expected to have. And what kind of challenges may be faced in the process of developing new Web usage mining techniques. A Web usage mining system should be able to:

- Gather useful usage data thoroughly.
- Filter out irrelevant usage data.
- Establish the actual usage data.
- Discover interesting navigation patterns.
- Display the navigation patterns clearly.

- Analyze and interpret the navigation patterns correctly.
- Apply the mining results effectively.

Information Obtained through Web Usage Mining

Web usage mining is used to obtain the following information:

1. **Number of Visitors:** This indicates the count of users who navigates to our website and access one or more pages in the web site.
2. **Visitor Referring Website:** This referring website gives the information about the URL of web site which taken into consideration.
3. **Visitor Referral Website:** This gives the information of URL of website which is referred by particular web site in consideration.
4. **Number of Hits:** This is the number which gives the information about number of times a resource can accessed in a website.
5. **Time and Duration:** This information in the server logs gives the time and duration of a user, how long user can access a particular website.
6. **Path Analysis:** This gives the analysis of the path a particular user can follow while accessing the contents of a website.
7. **Visitor IP Address:** This gives the information of visitor IP address who visited the website.
8. **Browser Type:** This gives the information about the kind of browser used to access the website.
9. **Cookies:** The purpose of cookies is to spot the users and probably prepare a tailor-made websites for them.
10. **Platform:** This provides the information about the OS used in the websites.

HOW TO PERFORM WEB USAGE MINING?

Web usage mining is achieved by reporting the users traffic information based on server log files and other source of server traffic data. Web server logs are initially used by the system administrators and web masters for the purpose of knowing how much traffic is generated and how many requests are failed etc. These files are also used to trace the online behavior of visitors. To collect the web traffic data we are using two techniques: one way is by using web log files and other way is to using "snift" TCP/IP packets as they cross the web site and analyze each web page. After the web traffic data is obtained it combines with relational data bases, to which some data mining techniques are implemented. Through some data mining techniques such as path analysis, sequential analysis, association rules, association and classification rules, visitors behavior patterns are found. Discovery of meaningful patterns from data generated by client-server transactions on one or more Web servers (Dixit & Kiruthika, 2010). Typical Sources of Data:

1. Automatically generated data stored in server access logs, referrer logs, agent logs, and client-side cookies.
2. E-commerce and product-oriented user events (e.g. shopping cart changes, ad or product click-through, etc.
3. User profiles and/or user rating.

METHODOLOGIES OF WEB USAGE MINING

Web server log file contains request of visitors to the web servers as shown in Figure 1. These requests saved in the log file in chronological order. The most common log file formats are common log file or extended common log file.

Web usage mining includes Data collection, data pre-processing, knowledge discovery and pattern analysis are the four major steps that are included in the methodology of web usage mining. Figure 2 depicts complete flow of the events during the process.

Data Collection

Data collected from server side, data collected from proxy server, data collected from client side (Facca & Lanzi, 2003):

1. **Web Servers:** These are the most common log files collected from servers of website. These web servers are the richest among all the other servers through which data is collected. Web servers collect large amount of information into their log files as well as databases they use. Server side data sources contain the information about servers and the websites they use for accessing information. These web servers contain the logging information of all the servers. Sever log usually contain the information about the IP address of the remote host, date and time of the request, the request line as exactly it came from the server side.

Figure 1. Methodology of web usage mining

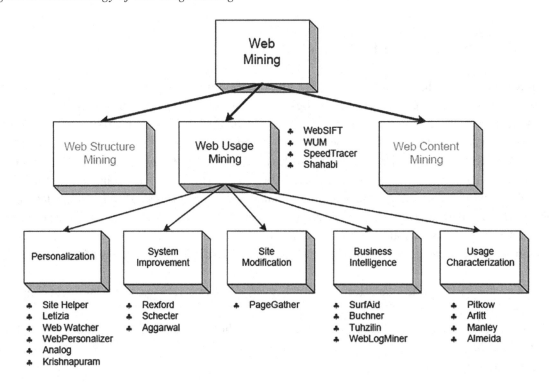

Figure 2. Complete process flow for web usage mining

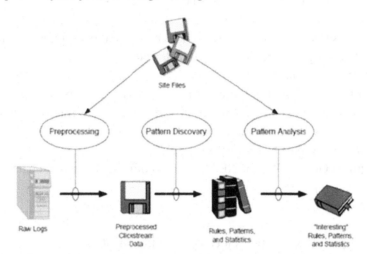

2. **Proxy Servers:** Proxy server's acts as the intermediate level of web servers and client servers. In general collecting data from proxy servers is almost equal to the data collected by the servers. The collected from proxy server includes the data from group of users accessing the web servers. These log files of groups can be maintained by the proxy servers.

3. **Client Servers:** users in general open or access several pages simultaneously and in the mean while they also use the non-browsing pages like Excel, Word etc. for their own personal work, in such cases data recorded in server log only shows the requested time of the web pages and cannot help us to find out which web page and for how long has been really browsed on client machine. Usage data can be tracked on the client side by using java scripts, java applets etc.

Web Log Information

A Web log is a file to which the Web server writes information each time a user requests a resource from that particular site. Examples of the types of information the server preserves include the user's domain, subdomain, and hostname; the resources the user requested (for example, a page or an image map); the time of the request; and any errors returned by the server. Each log provides different and various information about the Web server and its usage data. Most logs use the format of a common log file (Han, Karypis, Kumar, & Mobasher, 2014) or extended log file (Han, Boley, Gini, Gross, Hastings, Karypis, Kumar, & Mobasher, 2003). For example, the following is an example of a file recorded in the extended log format.

#Version: 1.0 #Date: 12-Jan-1996
00:00:00 #Fields: time cs-method
cs-uri 00:34:23 GET /foo/bar.html
12:21:16 GET /foo/bar.html
12:45:52 GET /foo/bar.html
12:57:34 GET /foo/bar.html

The following list shows the information may be stored in a Web log:

- **Authored User:** Username and password if the server requires user authentication.
- **Bytes:** The content-length of the document transferred.
- Entering and exiting date and time.
- **Remote IP Address or Domain Name:** An IP address is a 32-bit host address defined by the Internet Protocol; a domain name is used to determine a unique Internet address for any host on the Internet such as, cs.und.nodak.edu. One IP address is usually defined for one domain name, e.g., cs.und.nodak.edu points to 134.129.216.100.
- **Modus of Request:** GET, POST, or HEAD method of CGI (Common Gateway Interface).
- Number of hits on the page.
- Remote log and agent log.
- Remote URL.
- "request:" The request line exactly as it came from the client.
- Requested URL.
- **Rfc931:** The remote log name of the user.
- **Status:** The HTTP status code returned to the client, e.g., 200 is "ok" and 404 is "not found." The CGI environment variables (Srivastava, Cooley, Deshpande, Tan, n.d.) supply values for many of the above items.

DATA PREPERATION

The information contained in a raw Web server log does not reliably represent a user session file. The Web usage data preparation phase is used to restore users' activities in the Web server log in a reliable and consistent way. This phase should at a minimum achieve the following four major tasks:

1. Removing undesirable entries,
2. Distinguishing among users,
3. Building sessions, and
4. Restoring the contents of a session (Pierrakos, Paliouras, Papatheodorou, & Spyropoulos, 2003).

Removing Undesirable Entries

Web logs contain user activity information, of which some is not closely relevant to usage mining and can be removed without noticeably affecting the mining, for example:

- All log image entries. The HTTP protocol requires a separate connection for every file that is requested from the Web server. Images are automatically downloaded based on the HTML page requested and downloads are recorded in the logs. In the future, images may provide valuable usage information, but the research on image understanding is still in the early stages. Thus, log image entries do not help the usage mining and can be removed.

- Robot assesses. A robot, also known as spider or crawler, is a program that automatically fetches Web pages. Robots are used to feed pages to search engines or other software. Large search engines, like Alta Vista, have many robots working in parallel. As robot-access patterns are usually different from human-access patterns, many of the robot accesses can be detected and removed from the logs.

Distinguishing among Users

User is defined as a single individual that accesses files from one or more Web servers through a browser. A Web log sequentially records users' activities according to the time each occurred. In order to study the actual user behavior, users in the log must be distinguished. Figure 3 is a sample Web site where nodes are pages, edges are hyperlinks, and node A is the entry page of this site. The edges are bi-directional because users can easily use the back button on the browser to return to the previous page. Assume the access data from an IP address recorded on the log are those given in Table 1. Two user paths are identified from the access data: i) A-D-I-H-A-B-F and ii) C-H-B. These two paths are found by heuristics; other possibilities may also exist.

Building Sessions

For logs that span long periods of time, it is very likely that individual users will visit the Web site more than once or their browsing may be interrupted. The goal of session identification is to divide the page accesses of each user into individual sessions. A time threshold is usually used to identify sessions. For example, the previous two paths can be further assigned to three sessions: i) A-D-I-H, ii) A-B-F, and iii) C-H-B if a threshold value of thirty minutes is used.

Figure 3. Applications of web usage mining

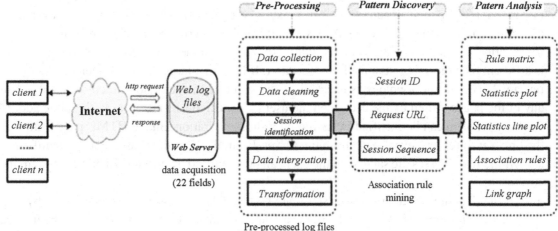

Restoring the Contents of a Session

This task determines if there are important accesses that are not recorded in the access logs. For example, Web caching or using the back button of a browser will cause information discontinuance in logs. The three user sessions previously identified can be restored to obtain the complete sessions: i) A-D-I-D-H, ii) A-B-F, and iii) C-H-A-B.

DATA PREPROCESSING

Some databases are insufficient, inconsistent and include noise in it. To avoid these inconsistency first we have to preprocess the data which is to be stored in the data base that we have to mine. The result is that database became consistent and sufficient to store the data.

The steps involved in the data preprocessing are:

1. **Data Cleaning:** It is the process in which irrelevant data has to be removed from the data which is stored. The irrelevant data have two types in it:
    a. Records having filenames suffixes of JPEG, GIF and CSS.
    b. The records having status code above 299 and below 200 has to be removed.

Improved data quality improves the analysis on it. The Http protocol requires a separate connection for every request from the web server. If a user request to view a particular page along with server log entries graphics and scripts are download in addition to the HTML file. An exception case is Art gallery site where images are more important.

2. **User Identification:** Identification of individual users who access a web site is an important step in web usage mining. Various methods are to be followed for identification of users from the access log. The simplest method is to assign different user id to different IP address. Each user is identified by referring to their IP address. But in Proxy servers many users are sharing the same address and same user uses many browsers. An Extended Log Format overcomes this problem by referrer information, and a user agent. If the IP address of a user is same as previous entry and user agent is different than the user is assumed as a new user. If both IP address and user agent are same then referrer URL and site topology is checked. If the requested page is not directly reachable from any of the pages visited by the user, then the user is identified as a new user in the same address. Caching problem can be rectified by assigning a short expiration time to HTML pages enforcing the browser to retrieve every page from the server. From the IP address user can be identified.
    a. If the IP addresses are same then the user can be identified by different operating system they used.
    b. If the IP address and operating systems are matched then the users can be identified by referring the information. URL of the information is identified first and then by this the user can be identified.
3. **Session Identification:** A user session can be defined as a set of pages visited by the same user within the duration of one particular visit to a web-site. A user may have a single or multiple session's during a period. Once a user was identified, the click stream of each user is portioned into logical clusters.

The method of portioning into sessions is called as Sessionization or Session Reconstruction. A transaction is defined as a subset of user session having homogenous pages. There are three methods in session reconstruction. Two methods depend on time and one on navigation in web topology.

Time Oriented Heuristics: The simplest methods are time oriented in which one method based on total session time and the other based on single page stay time. The set of pages visited by a specific user at a specific time is called page viewing time. It varies from 25.5 minutes to 24 hours while 30 minutes is the default timeout (Cooley, Mobasher, & Srinivastava, 1997). The second method depends on page stay time which is calculated with the difference between two timestamps. If it exceeds 10minutes then the second entry is assumed as a new session. Time based methods are not reliable because users may involve in some other activities after opening the web page and factors such as busy communication line, loading time of components in web page, content size of web pages are not considered.

Navigation-Oriented Heuristics: Uses web topology in graph format. It considers webpage connectivity, however it is not necessary to have hyperlink between two consecutive page requests. If a web page is not connected with previously visited page in a session, then it is considered as a different session. Cooley proposed a referrer based heuristics on the basis of navigation in which referrer URL of a page should exists in the same session. If no referrer is found then it is a first page of anew session. Both the methods are used by many applications. To improve the performance different methods were devised on the basis of Time and Navigation Oriented heuristics by different researchers. Different works were done by researchers for effective reconstruction of sessions.

Web Access Log set is the set of all records in the web access log and stored according to time sequence A User Session Set is obtained from the Web Access Log Set by following rules such as different users are distinguished by different IP address. If the IP addresses are same, the different browsers or operating systems indicate different users and if the IP addresses are same, the different browsers and operation systems are same, the referrer information is taken into account. The Referrer URL field is checked and a new user session is identified if the URL in the Referrer URL field has never been accessed before, or there is a large interval (more than 10 seconds) between the access time of this record and the previous one if the Referrer URL field is empty. If the sessions identified by the previous step contain more than one visit by the same user at different time, the time-oriented heuristics is then used to divide the different visits into different user sessions.

Graphs are also used for session identification. It gives more accurate results for session identification. Web pages are represented as vertices and hyperlinks are represented as edges in a graph. User navigations are modeled as traversals from which frequent patterns can be discovered. i.e., the subtraversals that are contained in a large ratio of traversals.

4. **Path Completion:** Client- or proxy-side caching can often result in missing access references to those pages or objects that have been cached. For Example, if Page A is returned by the user during the same session, the second time when page A will be accessed again, no request is made to the server and it will result in viewing the previously downloaded version of A that was cached on the client side. This results in the second reference to A not being recorded on the server logs (Türkoğlu, 2006). Path Completion should be used acquiring the complete user access path. The incomplete access path of every user session is recognized based on user session identification. If in a start of user session, Referrer as well URL has data value, delete value of Referrer by adding '- Web log pre-processing helps in removal of unwanted click-streams from the log file and also

reduces the size of original file by 40-50%. There are chances of missing pages after constructing transactions due to proxy servers and caching problems (Li, Feng, & Mao, 2008). So missing pages are added as follows: The page request is checked whether it is directly linked to the last page or not. If there is no link with last page check the recent history. If the log record is available in recent history then it is clear that "back" button is used for caching until the page has been reached. If the referrer log is not clear, the site topology can be used for the same effect. If many pages are linked to the requested page, the closest page is the source of new request and so that page is added to the session. There are three approaches in this regard.

a. Reference Length approach: This approach is based on the assumption that the amount of time a user spends on a page correlates to whether the page is a auxiliary page or content page for that user. It is expected that the time spent on auxiliary page is small and content page is more. A reference length can be calculated that estimates the cut off between auxiliary and content references. The length of each reference is estimated by taking the difference between the time of the next reference and the current reference. But the last reference has no next reference. So this approach assumes the last one is always a auxiliary reference.

b. Maximal Forward Reference: A transaction is considered as the set of pages from the visited page until there is a backward reference. Forward reference pages are considered as content pages and the path is taken as index pages. A new transaction is considered when a backward reference is made.

c. Time Window: A time window transaction is framed from triplets of IP address, user identification, and time length of each webpage up to a limit called time window. If time window is large, each transaction will contain all the page references for each user. Time window method is also used as a merge approach in conjunction with one of the previous methods.

Tools Used for Preprocessing

Web based applications are developed by using Active Server Pages which is the most popular scripting language. To access the server logs from windows 2000 *.dll file named logscrpt.dll is used. The MSWCIISLog class contains several methods and properties that can be used either to retrieve log entries or write log entries.

Approaches Used for Data Preprocessing

1. **Pre-Processing Using XML:** Using XML parsers DOM tree structure is created from Logs recorded in the web log. Next step is user identification and session identification is same as given basic algorithm of data preprocessing. Finally, the path completion helps to complete and format the paths in user session, so that these paths can be further used for analysis. After the above steps, transfer the records which are present in XML file into Knowledge base.

2. **Pre-Processing Using Text File:** Data pre-processing is applied on records which are present in the web log file. Steps for pre-processing are: Web log file contains log records in unprocessed form. Before applying cleansing process, attributes in the text file needs to be separated using delimiter as space. These spaces help in identifying exact position of attributes/fields. Steps 3 & 4 are same as in above approach. After the above steps, transfer the records which are present in text file into Knowledge base.

KNOWLEDGE DISCOVERY

It is the key component of web usage mining. Various techniques are used for discovering knowledge which is mentioned below:

Statistical Analysis

Knowledge about visitors to a Web site is extracted with the use of Statistical techniques. Different kinds of descriptive statistical analyses (frequency, mean, median, etc.) on variables such as page views, viewing time and length of a navigational path can be performed by analyzing the session file. The web system report can be potentially useful for improving the system performance, enhancing the security of the System, facilitation the site modification task, and providing support for marketing decisions simply by analyzing the statistical information.

Association Rules

In the context of Web Usage Mining, association rules refer to sets of pages that are accessed together with a support value exceeding some specified threshold. These pages may not be directly connected to one another via hyperlinks. Most common approaches to association discovery are based on the Apriority algorithm.

There are various algorithms for association mining:

- Maximal forward references.
- Markov-Chains.
- Improved AprioriAll.
- Fpgrowth and Prefixspan.
- Custom-built Apriori algorithm.

Clustering

In the case of content-based clustering, the result may be collections of pages or products related to the same topic or category. In usage-based clustering, items that are commonly accessed or purchased together can be automatically organized into groups. Clustering of users tends to establish groups of users exhibiting similar browsing patterns. Such knowledge is especially useful for inferring user demographics in order to perform market segmentation in E-commerce applications or provide personalized Web content to the users.

Clustering can be divided to three types: partitioning, hierarchical and model-based methods:

1. **Partitioning Methods:** This is where the data are divided into k groups (clusters). Various algorithms that can be applied for different purposes (Pani, Panigrahy, Sankar, Ratha, Mandal, & Padhi, 2011):
   a. Algorithms that are used to cluster user sessions:
      i. Leader algorithm.
      ii. Expectation-Maximization (EM).

   iii. Fuzzy clustering.

   iv. Graph partitioning.

   v. Self-Organizing Maps (SOM).

   vi. Ant-based.

   vii. K-means with genetic algorithm.

  b. Algorithms that are used to index page synthesis:

   i. Page Gather.

2. **Hierarchical Methods:** This is where the data is decomposed to create a hierarchical structure of clusters. It uses the Balanced Iterative Reducing and Clustering using Hierarchies (BIRCH) algorithm for clustering user sessions.

3. **Model-Based Methods:** These find the best fit between a given dataset and a mathematical model. There are different algorithms for clustering user sessions (Pani, Panigrahy, Sankar, Ratha, Mandal, & Padhi, 2011):

  a. Auto class.

  b. Self-Organizing.

  c. COBWEB.

  d. ITERATE.

Classification

Classification is the process of mapping of data items into predefined classes. In the web domain everyone is interested in developing user profiles based on the classification. This requires extraction and selection of particular features of a class. Classification can be done by using some supervised algorithms such as Decision trees, naive Bayesian classifiers, k-nearest neighbor's classifiers, and support vector machines.

  There are various algorithms that can be applied for different purposes (Pani, Panigrahy, Sankar, Ratha, Mandal, & Padhi, 2011):

- *Algorithms for extraction rules that represent user interests*:
  - HCV
  - CDL4
- *Algorithms for predicting an interesting page*:
  - RIPPER
  - C4.5
  - Naïve Bayesian
- *Algorithms for classification of sessions according to a concept*:
  - Rough Set Theory

Sequential Patterns

Sequential patterns are used to find out the subsequences from the large amount of sequential data. In web mining sequential patterns are exploited to find the users sequential navigation patterns that appear in user's sequential sessions frequently. For example if A visited a html page, then he must also visit B html page also. Hence A, B are visited in sequential manner by using sequential patterns.

For a deterministic approach, there are several algorithms, such as (Korra, Panigrahy, & Jena, 2013):

- **Spiliopoulou:** Used to extract sequence rules.
- **Paliouras:** Used to cluster navigational patterns.
- **CAPRI:** Used to discover temporally ordered navigational patterns

Also, the stochastic approach has a number of algorithms, such as (Korra, Panigrahy, & Jena, 2013):

- **Borges:** Used to extract navigation patterns from user sessions
- **Markov Models:** Used for next-link prediction.

Pattern Analysis

Pattern analysis is used to filter the uninteresting rules or patterns from the set. Generally pattern analysis consists of knowledge discovery mechanism such as SQL. Content and structure information can be used to find the patterns of content type, certain usage type or page such matches some structure of hyperlink type (Korra, Panigrahy, & Jena, 2013).

APPLICATIONS

The main goal of web usage mining is to study user navigation and their use of web resources. There are various applications for web usage mining in different areas, and such applications are:

- **Personalization of Web Content:** The web usage mining technique can be applied to personalize websites, depending on user profile and behavior. Personalization is important in creating a deeper relationship, to build acceptable marketing strategies, and to automate the promotion of products for potential customers. Also, web usage mining aims to obtain information that supports website design to allow easier and faster access on the part of customers (Zaïane, 2001).
- **System Improvement:** The results produced by web usage mining can be used to improve the performance of web servers and web-based applications. By understanding the behavior of web traffic, polices and strategies can be produced for web caching, network transmission, load balancing and data distribution (Zhang, Zhao, Shang, & Wang, 2009).
- **Security:** Web usage mining can provide patterns that are useful in intrusion, attempted break-ins, fraud, etc. (Nina, Rahman, Bhuiyan, & Ahmed, 2009).
- **Site Design Support:** Usability is one of most important issues in the design and implementation of websites. The results of web usage mining give designers information about user behaviours that help in decisions about any redesign of the content and structure of the website. Moreover, some tools automatically change the structure of the site based on usage patterns discovered (Nina, Rahman, Bhuiyan, & Ahmed, 2009).

- **Enhance E-Learning Environment:** Usage mining tools can be used to track the activities happening within the course's website, and then extract patterns and behaviors that need to be changed, improved or adapted to the course contents. For example, designers can identify the links that are always visited, links never visited, and the cluster of users that visit specific links (Facca & Lanzi, 2005).

- **Business Intelligence:** The primary goal of business intelligence is to help people make good decisions to improve company performance and to maintain competitive advantage in the marketplace, i.e., it helps companies to make the best decisions quickly and easily. Web usage mining is the appropriate technique for extracting information and building a useful and knowledgeable database about customer behaviors. Also, it is very important in determining effective marketing strategies, i.e., those that increase sales and place the company's products on a higher level (Srivastava, Cooley, Deshpande, & Tan, 2000).

Privacy Issues

Privacy is a sensitive topic which has been attracting a lot of attention recently due to rapid growth of e-commerce. It is further complicated by the global and self-regulatory nature of the Web. The issue of privacy revolves around the fact that most users want to maintain strict anonymity on the Web. They are extremely averse to the idea that someone is monitoring the Web sites they visit and the time they spend on those sites. On the other hand, site administrators are interested in finding out the demographics of users as well as the usage statistics of different sections of their Web site. This information would allow them to improve the design of the Web site and would ensure that the content caters to the largest population of users visiting their site. The site administrators also want the ability to identify a user uniquely every time she visits the site, in order to personalize the Web site and improve the browsing experience. The main challenge is to come up with guidelines and rules such that site administrators can perform various analyses on the usage data without compromising the identity of an individual user. Furthermore, there should be strict regulations to prevent the usage data from being exchanged/sold to other sites. The users should be made aware of the privacy policies followed by any given site, so that they can make an informed decision about revealing their personal data. The success of any such guidelines can only be guaranteed if they are backed up by a legal framework. The W3C has an ongoing initiative called Platform for Privacy Preferences (P3P). P3P provides a protocol which allows the site administrators to publish the privacy policies followed by a site in a machine readable format. When the user visits the site for the first time the browser reads the privacy policies followed by the site and then compares that with that security setting configured by the user. If the policies are satisfactory the browser continues requesting pages from the site, otherwise a negotiation protocol is used to arrive at a setting which is acceptable to the user. Another aim of P3P is to provide guidelines for independent organizations which can ensure that sites comply with the policy statement they are publishing (Srivastava, Cooley, Deshpande, & Tan, 2000). The European Union has taken a lead in setting up a regulatory framework for Internet Privacy and has issued a directive which sets guidelines for processing and transfer of personal data (Facca & Lanzi, 2005). Unfortunately in U.S. there is no unifying framework in place, though U.S. Federal Trade Commission (FTC) after a study of commercial Web sites has recommended that Congress develop legislation to regulate the personal information being collected at Web sites (Clarke, 1999).

The Web Personalizer System

The Web Personalizer system uses the architecture shown in Figure 1 to provide a list of recommended hypertext links to a user while browsing through a Web site. Currently, the Web Personalizer system relies solely on anonymous usage data provided by Web server logs and the hypertext structure of a site. The preprocessing steps (http://www.w3.org/Daemon/User/Config/Logging.html) are used to convert the server logs into server sessions. Two different methods, each with its own characteristics, are used to discover aggregate usage profiles represented by a set of URIs. The first method involves the computation of session clusters and the derivation of useful aggregate user profiles from these session clusters. In the second method, we use frequent item sets discovered as part of association rule discovery to directly obtain clusters of URIs based on their usage characteristics (page view clusters). Once the representative usage profiles have been computed, a partial session for the current user (the active session) can be assigned to one or more matching usage profiles. The matching profiles are used as the basis for providing the user with additional recommendations. In order to derive usage profiles from each session cluster, the cluster centroids (the mean vectors) are computed. The mean value for each URI in the mean vector is computed by finding the ratio of the number of occurrences of that URI across all sessions to the total number of sessions in the cluster. Then, the low-support URIs (those with mean value below a certain threshold), are filtered out. For example, if the threshold is set at 0.5, then each usage profile will contain only those URI references that appear in at least 50% of the sessions within its associated session cluster.

For the second method (computing usage profiles directly), the Web Personalizer system uses the Association Rule Hyper graph Partitioning (ARHP) technique. ARHP is well-suited for this task since it can efficiently cluster high-dimensional data sets without requiring dimensionality reduction as a preprocessing step. Furthermore, the ARHP provides automatic filtering capabilities, and does not require distance computations. The ARHP has been used successfully in a variety of domains, including the categorization of Web documents (http://www.w3.org/TR/WD-logfile.html). In this method the set of frequent item sets are used as hyper edges to form a hyper graph. A hyper graph is an extension of a graph in the sense that each hyper edge can connect more than two vertices. The weights associated with each hyper edge are computed based on the confidence of the association rules involving the items in the frequent item set. The hyper graph is then recursively partitioned into a set of clusters. The similarity among items is captured implicitly by the frequent item sets. Each cluster represents a group of items (URIs) that are very frequently accessed together across sessions. The connectivity value of vertex (a URI appearing in the frequent item set) with respect to a cluster measures the percentage of edges with which a vertex is associated. The significance weight of the URI within the resulting profile is obtained as a function of the connectivity value for that URI. In the case of usage profiles derived from session clustering, the weight for a URI is its mean value in the cluster mean session vector. In the case of page view clusters obtained using the ARHP method, the weight is the connectivity value of the item within the cluster. In computing the matching scores, the system normalizes for the size of the clusters and the active session. This corresponds to the intuitive notion that we should see more of the user's active session before obtaining a better match with the larger cluster. Furthermore, a candidate URI is considered to be a better recommendation if it is farther away from the current active session. To capture this notion, the physical link distance between the active session and a URI is measured (this is the smallest path in the site graph between the URI and any of the URIs in the session). The full recommendation set for current active session is computed by collecting all URIs whose recommendation score satisfies a minimum threshold requirement from each matching profile. The URIs in the recommendation set are ranked according to their recommendation score when presented to the user. Details of the specific techniques used in the recommendation process, as well as a set of experiments comparing them can be found at maya.cs.depaul.edu/~mobasher/personalization/.

FUTURE RESEARCH DIRECTIONS

The web usage mining algorithms are more efficient and accurate. But there is a challenge that has to be taken into consideration. Web cleaning is the most important process as researchers say 70% of the time is spent on data pre-processing. But data cleaning becomes difficult when it comes to heterogeneous data. Maintaining accuracy in classifying the data needs to be concentrated. Though many classification techniques exist the quality of clustering is still a question to be answered. The database is huge and it contains large dataset so mining interesting rules adds on to uninterested rules that are huge. These are due to large item set which naturally decrease the efficiency of the mining methodologies. Moreover mining rules from semi structure and unstructured as in the semantic web becomes a great challenge. This leads to time and memory consumption. Research work has to be concentrated on these issues as web data rule the Web. Maintain privacy of the user also peeps in as it is misused in data pre-processing.

CONCLUSION

Web mining is the technique of data mining which is used to discover patterns from web. Section I explains about that introduction of web usage mining and sources of information. Section II describes about the methodology used for web usage mining in detail including the various techniques of knowledge discovery in brief. And concludes with pattern analysis as the last step in the overall of web mining process. Web mining along with semantic web known as semantic web mining is to be concentrated that is evolving which helps us to overcome the cons of web mining. Though various algorithms and techniques have been proposed still work has to be done in discovering new tools to mine the web.

REFERENCES

Clarke, R. (1999). *Internet privacy concerns conf the case for intervention*. Academic Press.

Cohen, E., Krishnamurthy, B., & Rexford, J. (1998). Improving end-to-end performance of the web using server volumes and proxy filters. In *Proceedings of ACM SIGCOMM*. ACM. doi:10.1145/285237.285286

Cooley, R., Mobasher, B., & Srinivastava, J. (1997). Web information and pattern discovery on the world wide web. In *Proceedings of International Conference on Tools with Artificial Intelligence*. IEEE. doi:10.1109/TAI.1997.632303

Cooley, R., Mobasher, B., & Srivastava, J. (1997). Web mining: Information and pattern discovery on the world wide web. In *Proceedings of the Ninth IEEE International Conference on Tools with Artificial Intelligence*. Academic Press. doi:10.1109/TAI.1997.632303

Cooley, R., Mobasher, B., & Srivastava, J. (1999). Data preparation for mining world wide web browsing patterns. *Knowledge and Information Systems, 1*(1), 5–32. doi:10.1007/BF03325089

Dixit, D., & Kiruthika, M. (2010). Preprocessing of web logs. *International Journal on Computer Science and Engineering, 2*(7), 2447–2452.

Facca, F. M., & Lanzi, P. L. (2003). Recent developments in web usage mining research. In *Proceedings of 5th International Conference on Data Warehousing and Knowledge Discovery*. Academic Press. doi:10.1007/978-3-540-45228-7_15

Facca, F. M., & Lanzi, P. L. (2005). Mining interesting knowledge from weblogs: A survey. *Data & Knowledge Engineering, 53*(3), 225–241. doi:10.1016/j.datak.2004.08.001

Han, E., Boley, D., Gini, M., Gross, R., Hastings, K., Karypis, G., Kumar, V., & Mobasher, B. (2003). Document categorization and query generation on the world wide web using web ACE. *Journal of Artificial Intelligence Review*.

Han, E., Karypis, G., Kumar, V., & Mobasher, B. (2014).Clustering based on association rule hyper graphs. In *Proceedings of SIGMOD'97 Workshop on Research Issues in Data Mining and Knowledge Discovery (DMKD'97)*. ACM.

Korra, S. B., Panigraphy, S. K., & Jena, S. K. (2013). Web usage mining: An implementation view. *Journal of Emerging Technologies in Web Intelligence, 5*(3).

Li, Y., Feng, B., & Mao, Q. (2008). Research on path completion technique in web usage mining. In *Proceedings of International Symposium on Computer Science and Computational Technology*. IEEE. doi:10.1109/ISCSCT.2008.151

Nina, S. P., Rahman, M., Bhuiyan, K. I., & Ahmed, K. E. U. (2009). Pattern discovery of web usage mining. In *Proceedings of the International Conference on Computer Technology and Development*. Academic Press.

Pani, S. K., Panigrahy, L., Sankar, V. H., Ratha, B. K., Mandal, A. K., & Padhi, S. K. (2011). Web usage mining: A survey on pattern extraction from web logs. *International Journal of Instrumentation, Control & Automation, 1*.

Pierrakos, D., Paliouras, G., Papatheodorou, C., & Spyropoulos, C. D. (2003). Web usage mining as a tool for personalization: A survey. *User Modeling and User-Adapted Interaction, 13*(4), 311–372. doi:10.1023/A:1026238916441

Srivastava, J., Cooley, R., Deshpande, M., & Tan, P.-N. (2000). Web usage mining: Discovery and applications of usage patterns from web Data. *SIGKDD Explorations, 1*.

Türkoğlu, I. (2006). Extraction of interesting patterns through association rule mining for improvement of website usability. In *Proceedings of the 2006 IEEE/WIC/ACM International Conference of Web Intelligence*. ResulDaş.

Zaïane, O. R. (2001). *Web usage mining for a better web-based learning*. Paper presented at the Conference on Advanced Technology for Education.

Zhang, J., Zhao, P., Shang, L., & Wang, L. (2009). Web usage mining based on fuzzy clustering in identifying target group. *Proceedings of International Colloquium on Computing, Communication, Control, and Management, 4*, 209–212.

KEY TERMS AND DEFINITIONS

Classification: Classify the patterns according to its features.

Knowledge: Required and useful information from huge data.

Methodology: Proper sequence to follow for knows anything.

Pattern-Discovery: Discovering the useful information from the world wide web.

URI: Uniform Resource Identifier.

URL: Unified Resource Locator.

Web: Collection of different web pages.

Web Usage Mining: Mining user behavior and patterns from the web store.

Webs Personalize: It provides list of hyperlinks to user.

Chapter 12
On Visual Information Retrieval Using Multiresolution Techniques for Web Usage Mining Applications

Prashant Srivastava
University of Allahabad, India

Ashish Khare
University of Allahabad, India

ABSTRACT

The proliferation of huge amount of information has made it essential to develop systems that organize and index them for easy access. The advent of World Wide Web has provided immense opportunity to the people across the world to access and share information for different uses ranging from personal to professional. Various web mining techniques are applied to retrieve useful information as well as improvement of existing techniques of mining to search and retrieve useful information from the web. With the growth in the number of devices producing various forms of information, the amount of information is increasing exponentially. Also, these huge amount of information are being shared in the world through various means. Hence, it has become necessary to organize information in such a manner so that access to them is easy and feasible. As the amount of information is increasing rapidly, efficient indexing of information for easy access is becoming quite challenging. Hence, there is a need to search for solutions to solve this problem. The field of information retrieval attempts to solve this problem. Information retrieval is concerned with storage, organization, indexing, and retrieval of information. Information retrieval techniques incorporate several aspects of information to achieve the target of efficient indexing. Since there are several forms of information, their characteristics vary a lot from each other. Image is one such popular form of information which is shared the most among the people around the world. Also, with the presence of numerous image capturing devices, acquisition of image is no longer a difficult task. People enjoy capturing and sharing images through social network. Although image is a complex structure, it is easily understood by people across the world. Also, it has become a popular means of information sharing among people. This chapter discusses information retrieval techniques for image data. Visual

DOI: 10.4018/978-1-5225-0613-3.ch012

Information Retrieval or Content-Based Image Retrieval (CBIR) accepts query in the form of image or image features instead of text. It is concerned with searching and retrieval of images similar to the query given in the form of images. Most of the visual information retrieval techniques are based on processing single resolution of an image. But processing of single resolution of image is not sufficient for efficient retrieval as image is a complex structure and contains varying level of details. Hence, there is a need of multiresolution processing of images. Today, it is very difficult to keep track of number of research papers based on multiresolution analysis as it is widely used for various image-based applications. Also, there are a number of multiresolution techniques available to achieve this. Multiresolution processing has one big advantage that features that are left undetected at one level get detected at another level which is not the case with single resolution analysis. We demonstrate this fact with the help of an experiment using Discrete Wavelet Transform along with the discussion of various multiresolution techniques for visual information retrieval. The experiment helps in explaining the important properties of multiresolution analysis and also provides future scope of research in this field.

INTRODUCTION

We live in the age of information where information is available in various forms such as text, image, audio, and video. Information has been an integral part of our lives. Accurate information is the need of the day for important planning and decision making. Whether manual or machine generated, information plays an important role in our lives and is required for each and every work of our daily lives. There are numerous sources of producing these forms of information. Due to the increase in the number of devices producing these forms of information, it has become practically difficult to manage large volumes of information manually. Hence, there is a need to design such systems which are useful in organization of such forms of information. Such systems are needed so that it is easier for us to get the relevant information whenever and wherever we desire. In other words, we can say that we need some information retrieval systems to search for relevant information in large database. The term information retrieval refers to the arrangement, storage, indexing of useful information in the form of large database (Yates & Neto, 2011). Information retrieval systems facilitate the users to access useful and relevant information from large database. The introduction of World Wide Web (WWW) made the field of information retrieval more interesting. Huge amount of information about every field is available on WWW. After the invention of WWW, large amount of data started getting submitted by all the users of the web around the world. The universal platform has provided users to share data with other users without much constraint. A document submitted by a user gets linked with other documents and is shared among other users. This further increases the amount of information on the web. WWW has given the opportunity to the users to access and share huge amount of information. Add to this, the social networking sites have become one of the largest platforms of data sharing. This has attracted attention of millions of users who are keen on accessing and sharing information. All these platforms have proved to be a big centre of data repository where huge amount of information, of any kind, is available. However, presence of huge amount of information has certain disadvantages. Large number of documents get replicated which further increase the size of web documents. Large amount of unprocessed data creates problems as searching for useful information becomes a difficult task. These problems have caught the attention of computer scientists around the world to develop new and efficient techniques of searching and retrieval of useful information. Searching information from the web is not an easy task. If a user wants to search about anything, he/she has to be very specific about the keywords defining his/her search clearly. Long sentences of simple English fail to retrieve what the user is trying to search. The search criteria have to be clearly defined by the user in order to look for desired information. In other words, the user has to translate his/her information needs into well-defined query understood by the system. The clear definition of query determines the success of information retrieval. An information retrieval system usually finds the information which already exists in the system. The user has to analyze the information according to his/her needs. A user may need to find structured or unstructured information. A user may either get vague or exact information. Depending upon the type of information, a user may proceed with the retrieved information or may further extract useful information from the retrieved one. As mentioned above, information exists in various forms and so there are different types of information retrieval systems for different types of information. One such form of information is image which is one of the most popular forms among all other forms of information. Image finds use in almost all modern applications varying from professional to personal.

The concept information retrieval is not new and was in use in early days. People used to maintain records and retrieved according to their needs. After the invention of papers and printing press, there was a change in the trend of information retrieval. People started storing information in the form of records in files and manually organized them. With the advancement of information technology, card-based storage of information started taking place. In order to retrieve any information cards were used with help of which records were accessed. Later on, with the invention of computers and other electronic devices, the trend shifted to automatic storage, organization and retrieval of information. Attempts were being made to ease the task of storage and retrieval. With the advancement in technology, the task of automated organization and indexing of information became easy and more efficient. Several information retrieval applications were developed to carry out this task.

With the advent of WWW, millions of pages are being posted on the web everyday. It has grown into a large repository of knowledge. Business organizations are interested in getting ideas about how the users are accessing web. It is important for them to understand so as to better push the advertisement of their products. These organizations are keenly interested in keeping track of what the users are accessing on the web and for how long. This has given rise to a new field of web mining known as Web Usage Mining. Web Usage Mining is defined as the application of data mining techniques in order to discover patterns of web access from web data. Web usage Mining techniques are used by business organizations to discover the web usage patterns of users. Web Usage Mining technique consists of three steps: data preprocessing, pattern discovery, and pattern analysis (Srivastava, Cooley, Deshpande, & Tan, 2000). Data preprocessing deals with obtaining suitable data concerned with their needs. This stage involves preprocessing of collected data from multiple sources and converting them into a form suitable for applying data mining operations. This stage is important as it requires useful data for pattern analysis. After preprocessing of data is done, the next step is to understand the pattern of data usage. This is accomplished by applying knowledge extraction algorithms on preprocessed data. This stage involves discovery of usage patterns through the application of various machine learning, pattern recognition, and statistical algorithms. These algorithms are used to extract information such as what kinds of websites are frequently visited by user and for how long. This stage also involves analysis of association and clustering of usage data. The last step is analysis of pattern discovered in the previous step. This stage of web usage mining involves considering useful rules and patterns from the set obtained in pattern discovering stage and discarding useless patterns. This is done in order to understand usage patterns of web users. Web usage mining has proved to be extremely useful for business organizations in order to discover usage pattern of users. This helps them in promoting their products, personalization of user access, improving their sites for easier access etc. Web Usage Mining is an important application of Web mining which deals with applying data mining techniques to web data. As the information is increasing on the web exponentially, more efficient techniques of usage mining are being developed in order to extract useful information from the web.

Web Usage Mining techniques deal with retrieving information about how users access data and what kind of data are frequently accessed. This gives an idea about what users generally search and what are the areas of search. It provides an insight into user preferences, types of web pages users frequently visit and what recommendations and feedback they give about a particular product (Bosnjak, Maric, & Bosnjak, 2009). Based on these information, business organizations especially e-commerce websites personalize contents for the users to make it more user friendly. This helps in improvement of search results.

Web Usage Mining finds application in the field of not only text data but also multimedia data. An interesting application of web usage mining is retrieving information about browsing history and search contents of a user. This helps in improving the rank of search results thereby providing more relevant information to the user. If a user searches about any particular topic using search engine and selects the first result from web page, it can be analyzed that the user is searching in this particular context. This may help search engines to improve search results for the user by discarding irrelevant results that the user prefers not to visit. In this way, web usage mining helps in improving search results and provides more relevant information to the user. Web Usage Mining uses principle of web mining which is used to extract various types of information. In this way, the concept of web usage mining helps in personalization of user data and improves information retrieval. The techniques of web usage mining help in enhancing information retrieval and in turn enhance productivity and throughput.

An important question that arises is that why do we need an information retrieval system. Information exists in various forms and is increasing everyday. It is becoming practically very hard to manage large volumes of information manually. Also, searching information from such a large amount is not an easy task. If the amount of information is small, searching is feasible. But as the amount starts increasing, the traditional method of searching information fails. Hence the need of a system arises that automatically does indexing of information and is able to provide desired information to the user. Information is required not only for personal use but also for other professional use. A medical practitioner may need information from an expert information retrieval system to understand the patient's medical report. An astronomer may require information about the type of image received from spaceships sent to space for gathering information from a planet. All such applications require an efficient information retrieval system. The amount of information has increased from a few bits to billions of bits in recent years. The high speed internet has further added to this amount. Hence, the only way of organizing such a huge amount of information is use of efficient information retrieval systems.

With the availability of various image capturing devices such as smartphones, tablets, webcams etc. image acquisition is quite easy nowadays. Image is one of the most popular forms of data which is shared the most among the people through social network. The result is that we have huge amount of unorganized images. These images have to be stored and organized in such a manner so that access to them is not difficult. Hence, we need some visual information retrieval system to accomplish this task. Content-Based Visual Information Retrieval (CBVIR), Query By Image Content (QBIC), or more popular in scientific fraternity, Content-Based Image Retrieval (CBIR) solves this problem. CBIR is a technique of visual information retrieval where query is given in the form of an image or sketch of the image to the search engine and it processes the query to produce images similar to the query image from the database.

The idea of visual information retrieval is simple. We have an image and we desire to look for images similar to that image. The image is given as a query to image retrieval systems or search engines. The retrieval system extracts the features of the image, thereby constructing a feature vector, compares it with the feature vector of database images and returns the similar image present in the database on the basis of similarity metric. The construction of feature vector is a complex task and research in the field of image retrieval deals with this problem only. Numerous techniques have been developed to construct efficient feature vector varying from gathering local features of an image to global features including combination of both. Today the application of image retrieval varies from natural images to medical and astronomical images.

The origin of visual information retrieval dates back in early 1990s when the term first came into existence (Smeulders, 2000). Information retrieval at that time only meant text-based searching. Searching data using images was totally new and was not much popular. Also, getting an image was not that easy as it is today. Any kind of searching only meant providing query in the form of text. However, with the passage of time, image based information retrieval started getting attention. Nowadays, visual information retrieval has become an active area of research and researchers across the world are exploring new techniques to develop efficient visual information retrieval systems. With the invention of smartphones getting an image is now much easier than it was earlier. But extraction of information from an image is still a challenging problem as different types of images are emerging everyday. Text-based information retrieval is much easier as user is very clear regarding what he/she wants to search. But the same is not the case with images. Being a complex structure, each part of an image conveys different information and finding common feature among all is a challenging problem. Nowadays even text information is conveyed through images. These facts simply prove the importance of images. Hence, there has been a tremendous amount of research in the field of image retrieval to construct an efficient visual information retrieval system. A digital image is a complex structure and based on the features present in the image, a number of basic as well as advanced image retrieval systems exploiting these features have been developed. With the advancements in the field of information technology the trend of more and more automated CBIR systems started arising. There are numerous automated CBIR systems available which accept queries in the form of images rather than text. Some of the popular retrieval systems such as QBIC (http://www.cs.cf.ac.uk/Dave/ISE_Multimedia/node365.html), VisualSEEk (http://www.ee.columbia.edu/ln/dvmm/researchProjects/MultimediaIndexing/VisualSEEk/VisualSEEk.htm), SIMPLIcity (Wang, Li, & Wiederhold) etc. have existed for a long time. Most of these image retrieval systems are specialized for searching natural images. QBIC is one of the earliest CBIR systems. It facilitates use of images as well as video databases. It not only supports image contents as query but also sketches of images drawn by users. SIMPLIcity is another CBIR system which has been in use for a long time. In this, the images are categorized into different categories after performing segmentation. Features of query images are compared with the features of database images and retrieval of similar images is performed through similarity metric. Image retrieval systems based on text have been in use for a long time and are still popular. Text-based retrieval systems take query as text and search for image on the basis of text and keywords. Text-based systems return those results where they find associated keywords taken as query. Early text-based systems were slow and were not much accurate. But due to the introduction of several new text processing techniques, retrieval is now much faster and more accurate. Most of the popular web search engines are text-based. However, such systems have their own limitations. Text-based systems fail to retrieve visually similar images. Text simply conveys what a user wants to search in the form of words instead of visually expressing it. This creates a huge semantic gap between the actual description and its expression. Sometimes a user may want to search something but may not be able to express accurately. This frustrates the very effort of the user and fails to yield useful results. Two images may be conveying same information but their representation may be different. Similarly it may appear that the two images are same but they may be conveying different information. Also, it is practically very tedious to annotate images manually. These limitations engendered CBIR systems. CBIR systems find visually similar images as they accept query in the form of image itself rather than text. Such kind of systems have made web searching more and more popular. With this approach it becomes easier to express the needs of user in an exact fashion. This overcomes the drawback of finding visually similar images by entering text and avoids manual tagging of images which is the case with text-based retrieval. CBIR systems too have certain drawbacks such as image given as query should contain as much less noise as possible as noisy images may not produce desired results. Also, human beings search data more on the basis of semantics rather than features of image. Human beings are more concerned with the type of information they are looking for instead of searching it on the basis of colour, texture, and shape. Modern image retrieval systems combine both text and image features to search for visually similar images. This combination helps in combining advantages of both the features and overcome drawbacks of each other. Search based on image has to overcome a number of challenges based on storage, speed, time, cost, and retrieval quality. All these parameters are difficult to achieve at the same time in a retrieval approach. There are other forms of information retrieval also such as audio-based retrieval systems. In such types of systems, query is provided in the form of speech to the retrieval system and the system coverts speech signal into feature vector which is further used to extract desired images. However, such systems are quite complicated and are in their infancy as well as beyond the scope of this chapter. However, audio-based retrieval systems are still emerging and are coming in the form of smartphone applications.

The growth of large amount of images gives rise to image retrieval systems. As mentioned earlier, image is one of the most popular forms of information which is shared the most among the people around the world. With the invention of various kinds of devices, image capturing has become very easy. Every single second, millions of images get captured and shared through social network. Image is captured not only for personal use but also for scientific, medical and astronomical purposes. Whether it is forensics or biometrics, image is everywhere. Due to these applications huge amount of images are being created. If these images are not managed properly, the users are left with a large number of unorganized images which are of no use. Hence, just like information retrieval systems, we need an image retrieval system to fulfil the task of organizing images for easy access. Some of the advantages of an image retrieval systems are:

- Image retrieval systems help in automatic arrangement of images without requiring any manual intervention. Manual annotation of large number of images is a tedious task. Image retrieval systems make this task easy.
- Image retrieval systems help in automatic tagging of images and also help in automatic categorization of images.
- Image retrieval systems help in getting visually similar images which the text-based retrieval systems fail to achieve. Text-based systems depend only on keywords and phrases describing the system and do not retrieve images on the basis of content of image.
- Image retrieval systems help in achieving the task of organizing images of different types into their respective categories which makes their retrieval easy.
- Image retrieval systems provide proper organization of images due to which the study of different cases dealing with image related applications such as medicine, astronomy etc. become easy.

Although an image is a form of information just like any other form, it conveys much more information than any other form such as text. Also, image is easily understood by the people of the world irrespective of the language they speak as it does not require any specific language to understand.

State-of-the-Art

An image is a complex structure consisting of varying level of details. Retrieval of such complex data requires greater level of processing in order to identify and extract maximum details. Since the inception of the term CBIR, research has been going on to accomplish this task. Image features can be broadly classified into two types- primary features such as colour, texture and shape, and semantic features such as type of image etc. Early image retrieval systems relied more on colour feature. Colour is a visible property of an object and is invariant to some geometrical transformations. A coloured image consists of three components Red, Green and Blue (RGB). Colour based retrieval systems dealt with quantization of these components followed by construction of histogram for feature matching (Smith & Chang, 1996). Most of the colour-based feature use histogram as feature matching tool. Histogram has also been used frequently with texture-based feature. Histogram is still a popular feature for feature vector as it is easy to construct. Histograms give information about occurrence of pixels. However, they fail to give information about mutual occurrence of two pixels. To overcome this drawback (Huang, Kumar, Mitra, & Zhu, 2001) proposed the concept of color correlogram. This method of image indexing introduced the concept of spatial correlation of colours which proved to be very effective for image retrieval. This method of retrieval proved to be better than traditional histogram method of image retrieval. For many years colour remained a popular feature for retrieval. Colour feature was exploited through various techniques and focus of research was on improving the accuracy of retrieval through colour feature only. The trend of image retrieval shifted from colour to texture feature. Texture is still a popular feature which has been used as a single as well as in combination with colour and shape based features. Many texture-based features are being developed and exploited for retrieval. Texture determines the structural arrangement of pixels in an image and gives information about its coarseness, roughness, smoothness etc. Texture features were exploited through Fourier transform (Manjunath & Ma, 1996). Some texture features give information about mutual occurrence of pixels such as Gray-Level Co-occurrence Matrix (GLCM) which the histograms fail to provide. Most texture features use GLCM as feature vector for retrieval. Since texture gives structural arrangement of pixels, it helps in understanding similar images more accurately than colour as colour is only a visible property of any object which does not reveal any information about arrangement of pixels. Modern methods of retrieval exploit texture through local patterns. Local patterns help in determining local features of an image. Other features of image include features such as shape. Shape of an image refers to the shape of the objects present in the image. Shape features have been exploited through moment (Srivastava, Binh, & Khare, 2013) which is the measure of shape of any object, and polygonal shapes (Andreou & Sgouros, 2005)). As compared to colour and texture, shape features generally require segmentation before processing. Lack of good segmentation algorithm makes this task difficult (Khare, Srivastava, & Khare, 2013). Recognizing objects in an image and extracting those objects through segmentation algorithms is also a complex problem. Therefore, shape feature has not been exploited much as compared to colour and texture features. Whereas colour and texture cover local features of an image, shape is generally used to capture global details of an image.

With the growth of more complex type of images, processing of single feature started proving to be insufficient for retrieval. Single feature failed to provide enough details for retrieval hence the trend shifted to combination of features. As compared to single feature, combination of features was able to extract greater details in an image. The combination of primary features such as colour and texture (Wang, Zhang, & Yang, 2012), colour and shape (Gevers & Smeulders, 2000), and colour, texture and shape (Wang, Yu, & Yang, 2011) have been exploited for the purpose of retrieval. Most of the approaches quantized colour components through histogram and utilized texture features through filters and shape through moments. The advantage of combination of features is that it not only extracts greater level of details in an image but also helps in increasing the accuracy of retrieval. The combination also helps in combining the advantages of both the features and in overcoming drawbacks of each other. Feature combination helps in discovering such details of an image which the single feature fails to do.

An image consists of two types of features- local features and global features. Local features cover local details of each section of image and global features consider features from the entire image. Modern retrieval techniques comprise of exploitation of local and global features. Local features include texture features such as Local Binary Pattern (LBP) proposed by Ojala, Pietikainen, and Maenpaa (2002), Local Ternary Pattern (LTP) proposed by Tan and Triggs (2010). LBP encodes surroundings of a pixel into two values 0 and 1 by generating a bitcode and is a simple and efficient texture descriptor. It is sensitive to noise and invariant to gray-level transformations. LTP is an extension of LBP and unlike LBP encodes surrounding of pixels into three values 0, 1, and -1 by using a thresholding constant. It derives greater details from an image as compared to LBP. It is less sensitive to noise as compared to LBP but is not invariant to gray-level transformations. The local features have proved to be very useful for image retrieval. Local features help in encoding local information in order to get fine details of image. These features have been used in combination with other features such as colour and shape. Modern retrieval techniques deal with new features derived from these basic local features. Local patterns such as Local Tetra Pattern (LTrP) (Murala, Maheshwari, & Balasubramanian, 2012), Directional Local Extrema Pattern (DLEP) (Murala, Maheshwari, & Balasubramanian, 2012) both proposed by Murala et al (2012), are some of the examples of this. These features also consider directional information about local features and extract greater details from an image as compared to LBP and LTP. The combination of these features with other features such as shape (Srivastava, Binh, & Khare, 2014) and with SIFT (Yu, Qin, Wan, & Zhang, 2013) through bag-of-feature model has also been practiced. In bag-of-feature model, the images are described by a set of local features. SIFT is used to extract those features which are invariant to transformations.

Image retrieval mainly deals with feature extraction and construction of feature vector. The core area of research in the field of image retrieval is this only. Modern feature extraction techniques involve gathering information from neighbourhood pixels. This concept is being massively used these days through various techniques. Multi-Texton Histogram (MTH) (Liu, Zhang, Hou, & Yang, 2008), Micro-Structure Descriptor (MSD) (Liu, Li, Zhang, & Yu, 2011), Hybrid Information Descriptor (HID) (Zhang et al, 2014) are some of the examples of this. MSD uses the concept of edge orientation similarity. It efficiently combines colour, texture, and shape features for image retrieval. HSD feature tries to imitate physiological structure of human eyes and mechanism of visual perception. It not only incorporates low-level features such as colour, texture and shape but also high-level understanding through combination of features. Such techniques help in construction of powerful feature vectors. Experimental results have proved that these concepts are quite useful and provide good retrieval results. Most of the modern techniques involve combination of these features with other features to construct feature vector. Taking these methods to multiresolution level through various multiresolution techniques is quite useful. The idea has been to use these feature extraction method on more than one resolution of image and then combining them to produce the final result. There are several multiresolution techniques to accomplish this. The focus of this chapter is to study such multiresolution techniques and their applications in the field of image retrieval.

Multiresolution Analysis

As mentioned earlier, an image consists of varying level of details. Every pixel is important and must be considered for feature vector. An image consists of small as well as high resolution objects. In order to construct an efficient feature vector for image retrieval an image has to be processed so as to consider finer level of details. Single resolution of image is not sufficient to extract such a level of detail as processing single resolution of image may not cover varying level of details. This establishes the basis of multiresolution analysis. The basic concept of multiresolution analysis is simple- analysis and processing of images at more than one resolution. The advantage of this concept is that the features that are left at one resolution get considered at another resolution. Objects of small size need high resolution and of large size need coarse view. Studying them at multiple resolutions is advantageous. Some of the important properties useful for the purpose of image retrieval are as follows:

- Multiresolution techniques help in extraction of features at multiple resolutions. Single resolution of image fails to cover those areas of image which require more scaling. This drawback is overcome by multiresolution techniques as they process image at multiple scales. Due to this each area is covered at multiple scales thereby constructing more efficient feature vector which single resolution fails to do so.
- Features that are left undetected at one resolution get detected at another. Multiple scaling of an image tends to cover low as well as high resolution objects and small as well as large size objects. Objects of small size and low resolution are not considered at higher resolution but are covered at low resolution of image. Hence multiple scaling of image is advantageous. This property is not present in single resolution analysis of images. Features are covered in one resolution and it is possible that some of the features may be left out.
- Some multiresolution techniques such as curvelets help in extraction of finer level of details at boundary and edges which are not possible for other features. Single resolution techniques are not able to consider fine details of an image such as those at edges and boundaries. Complex processing is required to achieve this. However, multiresolution techniques such as curvelets achieve this with fewer coefficients.
- Processing of lower level of details at low resolution also reduces time as processing smaller resolution images is faster. As the resolution of image is decreased, the size of matrix becomes small and therefore processing gets faster. This also reduces retrieval time which is an important factor when it comes to information retrieval.

These properties establish the importance of multiresolution analysis and also highlight differences with single resolution analysis. Multiresolution analysis achieves all those things which single resolution analysis fail to do. There are several techniques of achieving multiresolution analysis some of which are wavelets, curvelets, contourlets, shearlet, bandlet, waveatoms etc. All these techniques have a common characteristic of feature extraction at multiple resolutions of image. All these techniques have their own characteristics and their own approach of multiresolution analysis.

Multiresolution Techniques for Visual Information Retrieval

Processing single resolution of an image is insufficient to extract varying level of details. Also, the techniques of retrieval on single resolution of an image when taken to multiresolution level not only gathers greater level of details but also improves the accuracy of existing techniques. Processing of single resolution of image does not construct as efficient feature vector as processing of multiple resolution of image. Multiresolution techniques incorporate multiple resolutions of an image along with features present in the image used for image retrieval. Feature vector constructed for each level are then combined to produce final feature vector which is used for measuring similarity of images with the help of an efficient similarity metric. Feature vector constructed through multiresolution processing have proved to be more efficient as compared to single resolution processing. This observation has made multiresolution techniques more popular among researchers. Modern retrieval techniques incorporate multiresolution analysis of images through various techniques. The idea of multiresolution processing arises from the fact that an image consists of high as well as low resolution objects and observing them at multiple level is advantageous. There are various techniques of multiresolution analysis varying from basic techniques to advanced wavelet based techniques. Some of these techniques are pyramidal structure, subband coding, wavelets, curvelets, contourlets, waveatoms etc. Wavelets are small waves of limited duration and varying frequency. Wavelet transform is analogous to Fourier transform with the difference that wavelets are capable of retaining both frequency and temporal information unlike Fourier transform which retains only frequency information. Several wavelet based techniques have been practiced for image retrieval. Various types of wavelet transform such as Gabor Wavelet Transform, Discrete Wavelet Transform (DWT), Complex Wavelet Transform (CWT), Dual Tree Complex Wavelet Transform (DTCWT) etc. have been used. The most commonly used wavelet transform is Gabor Wavelet Transform. The reason for its popularity is that it acts as a powerful feature descriptor and when combined with feature extraction techniques help in efficient visual classification of objects. Apart from being used as a single feature, Gabor wavelet has been combined with a number of features such as moments (Fu, Li, Harrison, & Belkasim, 2006) where Gabor wavelets of an image are normalized using z-score normalization. The Zernike moments of the image is computed and normalized using z-score normalization. Both these normalized values are then combined to construct feature vector. The method focusses on extraction of texture and shape features and combines them to construct efficient feature vector. The proposed method was tested on face dataset, fingerprint dataset and MPEG-7 shape dataset. Wavelets have been combined with colour as wavelet correlogram (Moghaddam & Tarzjan, 2006) which introduces rotation invariance feature using Gabor wavelets in wavelet correlogram feature. The concept of wavelet correlogram is derived from colour correlogram which analyses spatial correlation of colour pixels. Here, spatial correlation of wavelet coefficients is analyzed to construct feature vector for image retrieval. In wavelet correlogram approach, the first step is computation of coefficients using Gabor wavelet, followed by computation of autocorrelogram. Along with this advanced intelligence based techniques such as genetic algorithm (Tarzjan, Mahdi, & Moghaddam, 2007) have also been used with wavelets for image retrieval where threshold of wavelet correlogram are quantized using genetic algorithms. In this approach, wavelet correlogram approach of CBIR is optimized using new evolutionary algorithm in order to make the task of indexing of images easy and efficient. Gabor wavelet is among the most exploited wavelets since it is a powerful descriptor and extractor. However, there are certain disadvantages associated with it such as it requires large storage space and high computation time for feature extraction. Other wavelet transforms such as Discrete Wavelet Transform (DWT) have also been exploited for feature extraction. DWT represents an

Figure 1. A colored image and its two-level DWT

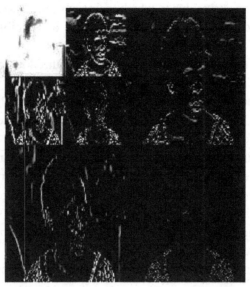

image in the form of discrete sequence of coefficients. Fig 1 shows a coloured image and its two-level DWT. Some of the properties of DWT are very useful for object recognition such as:

- It captures not only frequency content of the signal at different scales but also its temporal content.
- It decomposes the signal into approximation coefficients and detail coefficients.
- It analyses signals at different frequency bands at different resolutions.
- It provides sufficient information for analysis and synthesis.
- It is easier to implement.

DWT has been combined with moments (Srivastava, Prakash, & Khare, 2014) in which geometric moments of normalized DWT coefficients of gray level image are computed to form feature vector for image retrieval (Figure 1). This approach proposes to extract shape feature with the help of moments at multiple resolutions of image. DWT has also been combined with local pattern where Local Extrema Pattern (LEP) of DWT coefficients is computed to construct feature vector (Verma, Balasubramanian, & Murala, 2014). The LEP of DWT coefficients are computed at multiple levels and combined to construct feature vectors to perform indexing and retrieval of images. Along with this, DWT has also been combined with spatial orientation tree (Murala, Maheshwari, Balasubramanian, 2014) where spatial orientation tree of wavelet subbands is computed and combined with colour histogram. Image is divided into subblocks and Spatial Orientation Tree is constructed for each lowpass wavelet coefficient. For each subblock, colour histogram features are constructed followed by indexing of image using vocabulary tree. Inspite of being a powerful feature extractor, there are certain anomalies associated with wavelets such as they fail at edges and do not extract much accurate details when it comes to edges. Some of the limitations of wavelets are:

- Due to nongeometrical nature, wavelets fail to represent objects that are highly anisotropic in nature such as curves due to which their regularity is not exploited.
- At fine scales, large wavelet coefficients are exhibited in two dimensional wavelet transform images.
- Large number of wavelet coefficients is required to properly reconstruct edges in an image.

To overcome this limitation of gathering accurate details at edges, the concept of curvelet transform is introduced. Curvelets are collection of ridgelets which help in extraction of information at the edges. Curvelet transform efficiently represent edges and smooth functions. Through curvelet transform edge information in image is captured more accurately. Curvelet transform is an extension of ridgelet transform at multiple scales. Ridgelet transform provides a sparse definition of smooth functions and straight edges. However, edges are curved structures and ridgelets alone cannot represent them accurately. However, a curved edge is almost a straight line at sufficiently fine scales and hence ridgelets can be applied at sufficiently fine scales to capture curved edges. This implies that ridgelets can be tuned to different orientations and at different scales to create curvelets.

Curvelets have unique properties which distinguish them from wavelets. Some of the properties of curvelets are:

- Curvelets represent edge information in an image more accurately than wavelets.
- Curvelets use fewer coefficients to represent edge information as compared to wavelets.
- Curvelets extract more details from an image in comparison to wavelets.
- Curvelets efficiently represent smooth functions as well as edges with much lower mean squared error which is relatively high in case of wavelets.
- Curvelets completely cover spectrum in frequency domain as compared to Gabor filter which covers only a part of spectrum in frequency domain.
- There is no loss of information in curvelets when it comes to capturing frequency information from images.

These properties of curvelets help in achieving the goal of constructing efficient feature vector for image indexing and retrieval. The retrieval accuracy in case of curvelets has been observed to be more than wavelets and single resolution techniques.

As compared to wavelets, curvelets have not been exploited much. However, curvelets have been used as a single feature (Sumana, Islam, Zhang, & Liu, 2008) in which curvelet coefficients of an image is computed and feature vector is constructed after computing statistical details such as mean. This approach is simple yet efficient. It helps in extraction of texture features at multiple scales of image through curvelet transform. Curvelet has been used in combination with other features such as colour and texture (Youssef, 2012) where curvelet is combined with Region-based vector codebook subband clustering (RBSC) to extract colour and texture information. The integration of colour and texture feature along with curvelet transform coefficient proves to be efficient feature vector for retrieval. Modified form of curvelet is used along with vocabulary tree in (Gonde, Maheshwari, & Balasubramanian, 2013). In this method Gabor wavelet instead of à trous wavelet has been used along with ridgelet transform to compute curvelet coefficients. The original structure of curvelet transform is modified by introducing Gabor wavelet instead if á trous wavelet transform and indexing of image has been done through vocabulary tree. This modified curvelet has been used to construct feature vector to perform retrieval. Apart from these, curvelets have been combined with moments as curvelet moments in (Murtagh & Starck, 2008). The concept of curvelet moments has been introduced on the basis of wavelet moments where curvelet coefficients have been combined with moments at multiple resolutions for image retrieval. Curvelets prove to be better feature vector than wavelets as curvelets are capable of extracting greater edge details with lesser coefficients as compared to wavelets.

Another multiresolution technique that has been used for visual information retrieval is contourlet transform. Contourlet transform helps in obtaining smooth curves with less computational complexity. Contourlet transform includes properties of multiresolution analysis and frequency localization along with precise directionality. It consists of two filter banks namely, Laplacian pyramid and Directional Filter Bank. Laplacian pyramid decomposes image into different scales Direction Filter Bank reveals directional information. Contourlet has been combined with gray level co-occurrence matrix for retrieval in (Nguyen, Do-Hong, Le-Tien, & Bui-Thu, 2010). Contourlet has been combined with Fourier transform for texture and shape extraction from image in (Arun & Menon, 2009). Contourlets are used with normal distribution function where normal distribution functions are used to extract texture feature from the image (Mosleh, Zargari, & Azizi, 2009). Apart from this, contourlet has been combined with colour, texture and spatial features to construct effective feature vector for image retrieval in (Syam & Rao, 2010). Table 1 shows popular image retrieval techniques discussed in this chapter along with their advantages and limitations.

Other multiresolution analysis techniques such as waveatoms have not been exploited much but can act as powerful feature descriptors for image retrieval. Waveatoms have certain properties that overcome the limitations of wavelet transform.

Image Retrieval Using Wavelets

The concept of multiresolution analysis has been exploited for a number of applications. Multiresolution analysis helps in extraction of features at multiple scales in order to construct powerful feature vector. This section discusses CBIR through multiresolution analysis using wavelet. Wavelet being a potential multiresolution technique helps in gathering finer details from an image in the form of coefficients. These coefficients are used in the construction of feature vector. This section uses Discrete Wavelet Transform (DWT) to demonstrate multiresolution CBIR.

Discrete Wavelet Transform

The wavelet series expansion of function $f(x) \in L^2(R)$ relative to the wavelet $\psi(x)$ and scaling function $\varphi(x)$ is defined as

$$f(x) = \sum_k c_{j_0}(k)\varphi_{j_0 k}(x) + \sum_{j=j_0} d_j(k)\psi_{j,k}(x) \qquad (1)$$

where j_0 is an arbitrary starting scale, $c_{j_0}(k)$ are approximation coefficients, $d_j(k)$ are detail coefficients. The expansion of wavelet series defined in eqn (1) maps a continuous variable function into a sequence of coefficients. If the expansion of function results in a sequence of numbers, then the resulting coef-

Table 1. Advantages and limitations of popular image retrieval methods discussed in this chapter

Author	Proposed Method	Advantages	Limitations
Smith and Chang, 1996	Concept of histogram-based feature matching for image retrieval	Efficient use of colour as a feature for image retrieval	Colour used as single feature not sufficient.
Huang et. al, 1997	Concept of color correlogram for image indexing based on statistical concept of correlogram	Novel concept of determining mutual occurrence of colour pixels.	Colour used as single feature not sufficient.
Manjunath and Ma, 1996	Use of Gabor wavelet for analysis of texture for image retrieval	Robustness of Gabor feature and multiresolution texture classification	Texture used as single feature not sufficient to extract enough details from image for efficient image retrieval
Srivastava et. al, 2013	Use of shape feature through geometric moments for image retrieval	Image divided into blocks and matching of shape feature through moments.	Low retrieval speed and accuracy
Andreau and Sgouros, 2005	Use of polygonal shape feature for retrieval	Novel shape feature for visual information retrieval.	Single feature insufficient for efficient retrieval, requires segmentation. Lack of good segmentation makes this task tedious
Wang et. al, 2012	Combination of pseudo-Zernike chromaticity distribution moments and rotation invariant feature vector.	Combination of colour and texture acts as robust feature vector, higher retrieval accuracy	Not suitable for real life applications due to limitations of similarity metric used.
Gevers and Smeulders, 2000	Combination of colour and shape invariant features for retrieval	Multiple features results in efficient feature construction	Processing of features at single resolution.
Wang et. al, 2011	Use of colour, texture and shape feature. Colour feature for colour quantization, texture feature for extracting texture feature and moment feature for shape description.	Combination of multiple features constructs efficient feature vector. High retrieval accuracy	Features exploited at single resolution
Murala et. al, 2012	Proposed new feature Local Tetra Pattern (LTrP) based on Local Binary Pattern	Extraction of more details as compared to LBP and LTP, high retrieval accuracy	Does not exploit diagonal directional information of LTrP
Murala et. al, 2012	Proposed new feature Directional Local Extrema Pattern (DLEP) based on LBP and LTP	Extracts more details as compared to LBP and LTP	Exploitation of feature at single resolution.
Srivastava et. al, 2014	Proposed combination of shape and texture features	Combination of multiple features enhances retrieval accuracy	Exploitation of features at single resolution
Yu et. al, 2013	Combination of SIFT-LBP features to construct Bag-of-Feature (BoF) model	Novel feature BoF	Slow retrieval speed as SIFT computation takes time
Liu et. al, 2008	Combination of histogram and co-occurrence matrix	Combines advantages of histogram and co-occurrence matrix, much efficient than representative image descriptors	Discrimination power limited, fails to represent content of texton images fully.
Liu et. al, 2011	Proposed Microstructure Descriptor (MSD). Based on edge orientation similarity	Effectively combines colour, texture and shape features. Imitates human visual processing	Low retrieval accuracy.
Zhang et. al, 2014	Combines low level features such as colour, texture and shape with high level human visual perception understanding	Combination of primary features along with high level human understanding	Accuracy of method gets affected for some category of images.
Fu et. al, 2006	Combines local and global features through Gabor filter and Zernike moments	Combination of local and global feature extracts greater level of details	Fails to represent multiresolution aspect of the method.

continued on following page

Table 1. Continued

Author	Proposed Method	Advantages	Limitations
Moghaddam and Tarzjan, 2006	Proposed novel feature Wavelet Correlogram based on color correlogram	Introduces rotation invariance feature, spatial correlation of wavelet coefficients	Lack of appropriate optimization scheme produces low accuracy.
Tarzjan et. al, 2007	Combines genetic algorithm and Gabor wavelet for image retrieval	Combination of wavelet with intelligence based algorithm	Retrieval accuracy low.
Srivastava et. al, 2014	Proposed combination of DWT and Geometric moment in multiresolution framework	Combines local and global feature in multiresolution framework	Accuracy low for large image dataset.
Verma et. al, 2014	Proposes multiresolution LEP feature by exploiting LEP in multiresolution framework	Exploitation of local feature at multiple level helps in constructing efficient feature vector.	Low accuracy
Murala et. al, 2012	Combines DWT with vocabulary trees	Performs spatial parent-child relationship for efficient feature extraction.	Exploits only three level of wavelet transform
Sumana et. al, 2008	Used curvelet transform coefficients for image retrieval	Exploits texture feature through curvelet transform	Fails to exploit multiresolution property of curvelets
Youssef, 2012	Used curvelet transform coefficient for retrieval	Combination of multiple features along with multiresolution technique	Fails to exploit multiresolution aspect of curvelet transform efficiently
Gonde et. al, 2012	Modified implementation of curvelet transform for image retrieval by applying Gabor wavelet instead of à trous wavelet	Proposed method when compared with original unmodified curvelet transform produced better results	Retrieval accuracy low, fails to demonstrate multiresolution aspect of modified curvelet transform
Murtagh and Starck, 2008	Proposed the concept of wavelet moments and curvelet moments for image retrieval	Combination of shape feature along with multiresolution technique	Multiresolution property of curvelet missing.
Nguyen-Due et. al, 2010	Proposed a new descriptor contourlet cooccurrence	Combination of contourlet transform and co-occurrence matrix	Exploits only two level of contourlet transform
Arun and Menon, 2009	Exploited rotation invariance property of contourlet transform along with fourier descriptor	Introduces rotation invariance property of contourlet transform along with shape extraction using fourier.	Multiscale property of contourlet transform not exploited properly.
Mosleh et. al, 2009	Proposed texture image retrieval using contourlet transform	Efficiently exploits properties of subband coefficient.	Multiscale property of contourlet transform not exploited properly.
Syam and Rao, 2010	Combined texture colour and spatial features along with contourlet transform	Combination of multiple features along with multiresolution technique	Multiscale property of contourlet transform not exploited properly.

ficients are called discrete wavelet transform of $f(x)$. For this case, the expansion of eqn (1) becomes the DWT transform pair

$$W_\varphi(j_0, k) = \frac{1}{\sqrt{M}} \sum_x f(x) \varphi_{j_0, k}(x) \qquad (2)$$

$$W_{\psi}(j,k) = \frac{1}{\sqrt{M}} \sum_{x} f(x)\psi_{j,k}(x) \tag{3}$$

for $j \geq j_0$ and

$$f(x) = \frac{1}{\sqrt{M}} \sum_{x} f(x)\varphi_{j_0,k}(x) + \frac{1}{\sqrt{M}} \sum_{x} f(x)\psi_{j,k}(x) \tag{4}$$

where j_0 is an arbitrary starting scale, k is an integer index, $f(x)$, $\varphi_{j_0,k}(x)$, and $\psi_{j,k}(x)$ are functions of discrete variable 1, 2, ..., $M-1$.

The one-dimensional transform can be extended to two-dimensional images. In two-dimensions, a two-dimensional scaling function becomes $\varphi(x,y)$ and along with this there are three two-dimensional wavelets $\psi^H(x,y)$, $\psi^V(x,y)$, and $\psi^D(x,y)$. These three wavelets are directionally sensitive and measure gray-level variations for images along different directions- ψ^H measures variations horizontally, ψ^V measures variations vertically and ψ^D measures variations diagonally.

The DWT of function $f(x,y)$ of size $M \times N$ is given as

$$W_{\varphi}(j_0,m,n) = \frac{1}{\sqrt{MN}} \sum_{x=0}^{M-1} \sum_{y=0}^{N-1} f(x,y)\varphi_{j_0,m,n}(x,y) \tag{5}$$

$$W_{\psi}^i(j,m,n) = \frac{1}{\sqrt{MN}} \sum_{x=0}^{M-1} \sum_{y=0}^{N-1} f(x,y)\psi^i_{j,m,n}(x,y) \tag{6}$$

where j_0 is an arbitrary starting scale and the $W_{\psi}^i(j,m,n)$ coefficients define an approximation of $f(x,y)$ at scale j_0. The $W_{\psi}^i(j_0,m,n)$ coefficients add horizontal, vertical, and diagonal details for scales $j \geq j_0$.

Processing of single resolution of an image for image retrieval fails to extract varying level of details. Also, processing of single resolution of image may not detect low resolution of objects in the image. These limitations motivate to exploit multiple resolutions of an image to extract varying level of details and perform content based retrieval of image. This section discusses multiresolution techniques based visual information retrieval through the use of DWT. Here, the concept of wavelets through DWT has been used as a multiresolution technique to demonstrate image retrieval as it is simple to use and understand and is an efficient multiresolution technique for image retrieval. DWT coefficients of image are computed after converting the image into gray-scale. These coefficients are used to form feature vector and are utilized to perform retrieval of visually similar images. The method discussed in this section consists of two parts:

1. Computation of DWT coefficients of gray-scale images.
2. Similarity measurement.

The algorithm for the discussed method is as follows:

```
Input: Query Image f(x, y)
Output: Retrieval results
1.          Convert the image into grayscale.
2.          Resize the grayscale image to size 256 x 256.
3.          Apply 2-D DWT on image to get directional coefficients ψ^H(x,y),
            ψ^V(x,y), and ψ^D(x,y).
4.          Store coefficients in three matrices and construct feature vector.
5.          Compute similarity with database feature vector.
6.          Output.
```

Computation of DWT Coefficients

The two dimensional DWT coefficients of an input grayscale image is computed. The first step is conversion of image into grayscale. This is followed by application of DWT on grayscale images. Application of DWT on an image produces two coefficients- approximation coefficients and detail coefficients. In two dimensions, there is one two dimensional scaling function and three two dimensional wavelets- $\psi^H(x,y)$, $\psi^V(x,y)$, and $\psi^D(x,y)$. These three wavelets are directionally sensitive and measure gray-level variations for images along different directions- $\psi^H(x,y)$ measures variations along rows, $\psi^V(x,y)$ measures variations along columns and $\psi^D(x,y)$ measures variations along diagonals. These detail coefficients are computed for different levels of resolution. For an image of size 256 x 256, the coefficients can be computed upto 7 levels. Following properties of DWT are helpful for image retrieval in their own ways:

1. DWT is easier to implement and provides sufficient information for analysis and synthesis. It decomposes the signal into approximation coefficients and detail coefficients. The detail coefficients are of three types- $\psi^H(x,y)$ which compute coefficients in horizontal direction, $\psi^V(x,y)$ which compute coefficients in vertical direction, $\psi^D(x,y)$ which computes coefficients in diagonal direction. These detail coefficients separately form feature vectors and are used in retrieving visually similar images. These retrieved image sets are further combined to form final set of retrieved images.
2. DWT analyzes the signal at different bands at different resolutions. The coefficients are further analyzed at next resolution which produces three detail coefficients. The coefficients extract features that are left in the previous resolution and further form feature vectors for retrieval.

Similarity Measurement

Similarity measurement is done to retrieve images similar to the query image. Similarity measurement of feature vectors of query image and database image is done to retrieve visually similar images. In similarity measurement, feature vector matching of query image and database image is done for image retrieval. The similarity measurement is done by measuring distance between DWT coefficients of query image and database image. There are several methods of measuring similarity. In the discussed method, the Euclidean distance method has been used to measure similarity between two images. The Euclidean distance method of measuring similarity is as follows. Let the coefficients of the query image be given as $m_Q = (m_{Q1}, m_{Q2}, \ldots, m_{Qn})$ and let the coefficients of the database image be given as $m_{DB} = (m_{DB1}, m_{DB2}, \ldots, m_{DBn})$. Then the Euclidean distance between query image and database image is computed as

$$D(m_Q, m_{DB}) = \sqrt{(m_{Qi} - m_{DBi})^2} \tag{7}$$

There are numerous image datasets to carry out experiments on retrieval such as Corel Image Library, Olivia Image Dataset, Caltech Dataset, GHIM Dataset etc. For experimentation purpose using the discussed method, images from Corel-1K database (http://wang.ist.psu.edu/docs/related/ Accessed April 2014) have been used. Many researchers are of the opinion that Corel dataset has the capability of meeting all the requirements for the evaluation of image retrieval systems because of its large size and diverse contents. The images in this database have been classified into ten different categories namely, Africans, Beaches, Buildings, Buses, Dinosaurs, Elephants, Flowers, Horses, Mountains, Food. Each image is of size either 256 x 384 or 384 x 256 and each category of image consists of 100 images (a total of 1000 images). While performing the experiment the images were rescaled to size 256 x 256. Sample images from each category of database are shown in Figure 2. Each image of this database is taken as query image. If the retrieved images belong to the same category as that of the query image, the retrieval is considered to be successful, otherwise the retrieval fails.

Performance of the discussed method has been measured in terms of precision and recall. Precision has been defined as the ratio of the total number of relevant images retrieved to the total number of images retrieved. Mathematically, precision can be formulated as

$$P = \frac{I_R}{T_R} \tag{8}$$

where I_R denotes total number of relevant images retrieved and T_R denotes total number of images retrieved. Recall is defined as the ratio of total number of relevant images retrieved to the total number of relevant images in the database. Mathematically, recall can be formulated as

Figure 2. Sample images from Corel-1K database

$$R = \frac{I_R}{C_R} \tag{9}$$

where I_R denotes total number of relevant images retrieved and C_R denotes total number of relevant images in the database. In this experiment, $T_R = 10$ and $C_R = 100$.

Retrieval Results

For the purpose of experiment each image has been rescaled to size 256 x 256. DWT coefficients of each image have been computed. Application of DWT on gray-scale images produces three wavelet matrices, namely, horizontal detail, vertical detail, diagonal detail. In this experiment similarity measurement for each of detail coefficients is done separately. This produces three sets of similar images. Union of these three image sets is taken to produce final set of similar images. Recall is computed by counting total number of relevant images in the final set. Similarly, for precision, top n matches for each detail matrix is counted and then union operation is applied on three image sets to produce final set. Precision is evaluated by considering top n matches in the final set. Mathematically, this can be stated as follows. Let f_H be set of similar images obtained from horizontal detail feature vector, f_V be set of similar images obtained from vertical detail feature vector, and f_D be set of similar images obtained from diagonal detail feature vector. Then, the final set of similar images denoted by f_{RS} is given as

$$f_{RS} = f_H \cup f_V \cup f_D \tag{10}$$

Similarly, let f_H^n be set of top n images obtained from horizontal detail feature vector, f_V^n be set of top n images obtained from vertical detail feature vector, and f_D^n be set of top n images obtained from diagonal detail feature vector. Then the final set of top n images denoted by f_{PS}^n is given as

$$f_{PS}^n = f_H^n \cup f_V^n \cup f_D^n \tag{11}$$

The above procedure is repeated for all seven levels of resolution. Feature vector constructed at each level of resolution is used to perform retrieval of similar images. Each level of resolution gathers features which are left undetected at previous levels. This technique is able to cover finer details present in the image which the processing of single resolution fails to do. This property of multi-scale analysis is not present in single resolution processing of image. Hence, it produces results with the help of feature vector constructed at single level only. Hence, single resolution processing of image is not able to gather sufficient details to construct efficient feature vector. In the discussed method, at each level the relevant image set of the previous level is also considered and is combined with current level to produce relevant image set for that level. Retrieval is considered to be good if the values of precision and recall are high. Table 2 and plot in Figure 3 show the average values of precision and recall for all seven levels of resolution of images. From Table 2, Figure 3, and Figure 4 it can be observed that the average values of precision and recall increase with levels of resolution. Due to multiresolution analysis, the features of the image that remain undetected at one level get detected at the next level. It is due to this phenomenon that there is an increase in the values of precision and recall at different levels as shown in Table 2.

Table 2. Average precision and recall for seven levels of resolution

Level	Average Recall (%)	Average Precision (%)
Level 1	13.90	25.29
Level 2	17.93	29.43
Level 3	22.67	31.36
Level 4	28.82	39.05
Level 5	39.18	59.60
Level 6	54.39	76.76
Level 7	67.19	88.78

Figure 3a. Average precision vs. levels of resolution method

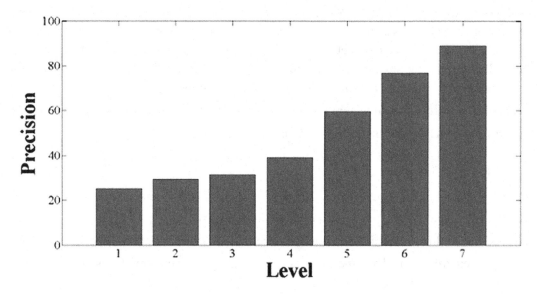

Figure 3b. Average recall vs. levels of resolution for the discussed

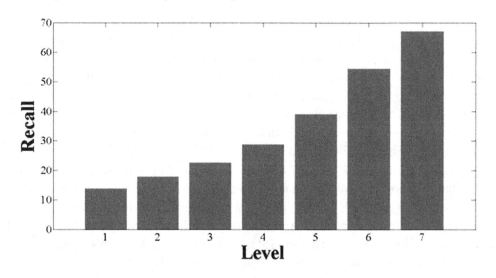

Figure 4. Precision vs. recall curve for the discussed method

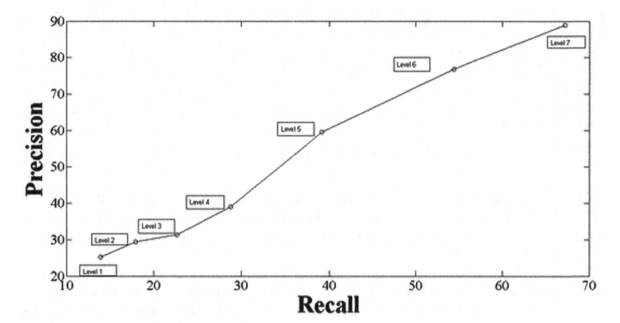

The discussed method is compared with other state-of-the-art methods such as Srivastava et al, 2013, Srivastava et al, 2014, Tarzjan et al, 2007, Srivastava et al, 2014 and Moghaddam and Tarzjan, 2006. Table 3 shows the performance of the proposed method with other methods in terms of precision. From Table 3 it can be observed that the discussed method outperforms the other methods. The experimental results demonstrate that multiresolution techniques not only consider features of image at different levels but also increase the accuracy of image retrieval.

Advantages of Discussed Method

- It is simple but efficient multiresolution technique of retrieving visually similar images which the text-based retrieval methods fail to do.
- Wavelet-based method performs multiresolution analysis and processing of images at more than one resolution. It overcomes the limitations of single resolution processing of images by considering multiple resolutions of image for constructing feature vector, which the single resolution fails to do.
- Experimental results demonstrate the fact that the features left undetected at one level get detected at another.
- Precision and recall values increase with level of resolution thereby demonstrating multiresolution feature extraction property of the discussed method.

Applications of Visual Information Retrieval

With the rapid increase in the number of images through various sources, the importance of image data cannot be denied. People are sharing information through images nowadays more than text. This has

Table 3. Performance comparison of the discussed method with other methods

Methods	Precision (%)
Srivastava et al, 2013	35.94
Srivastava et al, 2014	53.70
Tarzjan et al, 2007	64.30
Srivastava et al, 2014	67.16
Moghaddam and Tarzjan, 2006	64.10
Discussed Method	88.78

led to the development of image retrieval systems very important. Nowadays it is difficult to keep track of the number of applications of image retrieval. From personal use to complex surveillance systems, every application involves the usage of image retrieval. Some of the applications of image retrieval are as follows:

- **Forensics:** The field of image retrieval finds tremendous application in forensics. Large database of forensic data such as fingerprints, face, and other biometric details which help in identifying and nabbing the criminals are stored and retrieved for this purpose. Various new techniques for face recognition and fingerprint recognition are being developed to handle complicated cases.
- **Surveillance:** Large database of human activities is created to identify the activities of suspects. The activity image is captured from the surveillance camera and compared with the activity images stored in a database. This helps in recognizing suspicious activities in order to prevent the country from any deadly attacks. Activity databases are created to record several different activities of human beings so as to identify and retrieve any suspicious activity. Nowadays such kinds of databases have increased due to the increase in terror activities all over the world. Surveillance cameras are being widely used to capture and track activities and then matched with those images stored in activity database. In this way the activities are recognized to avoid any terror activities and to collect proofs against suspects.
- **Astronomy:** Large image database is created in the field of astronomy consisting of images of different celestial bodies, spatial objects, galaxies etc. These images are retrieved to identify any unidentified object or new galaxies for astronomical study. Astronomical images contain noise and are preprocessed before storing in database.
- **Weather Forecast:** Astronomical and spatial images of earth are collected and arranged in the form of database which not only help in predicting weather conditions but also help in predicting any natural disaster in advance. Areal images of earth are collected and stored in a database in order to identify flood affected areas which in turn help in sending relief measures to the affected areas. Also, predicting the arrival of cyclones and areas to be affected due to them also becomes easy due to the image retrieval systems.
- **Medical Imaging:** The field of image retrieval finds massive application in the field of medical imaging. It helps in identification of diseases in various parts of the body such as tumors in brain, stone in gallbladder and kidney etc. medical expert systems automate most of the tasks of medical practitioners and help in analyzing medical reports of patients. Large amount of MRI images are collected and stored in a medical database in order to identify different cases of diseases.

- **Scientific Applications:** Scientific applications such as recognition of animals, leaves etc. require collection and arrangement of large number of images. These images are stored in the form of database which is frequently used for the purpose of identifying class and species of animals and leaves. Also tracking and keeping record of number of animals of certain species are also carried out with the help of image retrieval systems.
- **Personal Use:** People are fond of arranging their holiday images according to their wish. There are several image retrieval systems available for personal use which help in the arrangement of images according to the fields desired by the user. Many modern image retrieval systems in the form of mobile applications for this purpose.
- **Web Usage Mining Applications:** The field of visual information retrieval is also finds application in web usage mining. Business organizations are able to get an idea about the type of websites users frequently visit through web usage mining. This helps in improving search results and also personalizes user contents.

Apart from these applications, there are numerous applications of image retrieval such as disease classification and age detection, vehicle number plate recognition where image retrieval is extensively used.

CONCLUSION AND FUTURE SCOPE

This chapter presented a brief concept of multiresolution techniques based visual information retrieval along with a multiresolution wavelet based method for image retrieval. Instead of processing single resolution of image, multiresolution processing of an image not only captures varying level of details but also increases accuracy of retrieval. This was demonstrated with the help of an experiment using wavelets. Using the concept of multiresolution analysis through wavelets, grayscale images were analyzed at multiple resolutions to construct feature vector for retrieval. The advantages of this method are as follows:

1. Wavelet-based method performs multiresolution analysis and processing of images at more than one level.
2. Features that might go undetected at one resolution are spotted at the next level.

Also, unlike Fourier transform which store frequency information only, wavelet transform stores both frequency and temporal information. The method can be extended by incorporating more features along with wavelets. Also, introducing some normalization technique can make the retrieval system faster. Introducing some intelligence-based technique along with the discussed method can help in reducing semantic gaps to some extent. The method exploited grayscale images for feature vector construction. The method can be extended for colour images as a future scope of chapter.

The application of multiresolution analysis techniques is not limited to image retrieval only. Wide variety of Computer Vision applications such as object recognition, human activity recognition, image fusion, scene analysis etc. is also using multiresolution techniques for better results. The combination of multiresolution techniques with other image features can help in constructing efficient feature vector for these applications. Although, searching of image is based more on semantics rather than specifying features such as colour, texture and shape, image retrieval based on semantic feature is a challenging area of research and requires incorporation of a lot of understanding and other intelligence based techniques.

The field of visual information retrieval is also helpful in web usage mining. Business organizations through web usage mining get an idea about the kind of visual data users frequently visit and access, and are able to improve search results with the help of web usage records. This also helps in optimizing the functionality of web based applications and personalize user content which in turn improves information retrieval. Web usage mining helps in understanding browsing behavior of users and helps in improving search results. Visual information retrieval is a very interesting area of research for scientists across the world. The various methods of retrieval described in this chapter are not only limited to processing of images but can also be exploited for video as well. This chapter focused on the importance of information retrieval through visual data. Presence of huge amount of data has made the task of searching and indexing useful information challenging. Hence, an efficient information retrieval technique has to be proposed in order to improve the indexing and retrieval of information. Also, the presence of different types of data is further making this task challenging. Therefore, efficient information retrieval technique is the need of the day to increase productivity and throughput.

REFERENCES

Andreou, I., & Sgouros, N. M. (2005). Computing, explaining visualizing shape similarity in content-based image retrieval. *Information Processing & Management, 41*(5), 1121–1139. doi:10.1016/j.ipm.2004.08.008

Arun, K. S., & Menon, H. P. (2009). Content based medical image retrieval by combining rotation invariant contourlet features and fourier descriptors. *International Journal of Recent Trends in Engineering, 2*(2).

Bosnjak, S., Maric, M., & Bosnjak, Z. (2009). The role of web usage mining in web applications evaluation. *Management Information System, 5*(1), 31–36.

Fu, X., Li, Y., Harrison, R., & Belkasim, S. (2006). Content-based image retrieval using gabor-zernike features. In *Proceedings of 18th International Conference on Pattern Recognition*, (Vol. 2, pp. 417-420).

Gevers, T., & Smeulders, A. W. (2000). Pictoseek: Combining Color and Shape Invariant Features for Image Retrieval. *IEEE Transactions on Image Processing, 9*(1), 102–119. doi:10.1109/83.817602 PMID:18255376

Gonde, A. B., Maheshwari, R. P., & Balasubramanian, R. (2013). Modified curvelet transform with vocabulary tree for content based image retrieval. *Digital Signal Processing, 23*(1), 142–150. doi:10.1016/j.dsp.2012.04.019

Huang, J., Kumar, S. R., Mitra, M., Zhu, W., & Zabih, R. (2001). *Image Indexing using Color Correlograms*. U.S. Patent 6,246,790.

Khare M., Srivastava R. K., & Khare A. (2013). Moving Object Segmentation in Daubechies Complex Wavelet Domain. *Signal, Image and Video Processing, 8*(3), 635- 650.

Liu, G., Li, Z., Zhang, L., & Xu, Y. (2011). Image retrieval based on microstructure descriptor. *Pattern Recognition, 44*(9), 2123–2133. doi:10.1016/j.patcog.2011.02.003

Liu, G., Zhang, L., Hou, Y., & Yang, J. (2008). Image retrieval based on multi-texton histogram. *Pattern Recognition, 43*(7), 2380–2389. doi:10.1016/j.patcog.2010.02.012

Manjunath, B. S., & Ma, W. X. (1996). Browsing and Retrieval of Image Data. *IEEE Transactions on Pattern Analysis and Machine Intelligence, 18*(8), 837–842. doi:10.1109/34.531803

Moghaddam, H. A., & Tarzjan, M. S. (2006). Gabor Wavelet Correlogram Algorithm for Image Indexing and Retrieval. In *Proceedings of 18th International Conference on Pattern Recognition* (pp. 925–928). doi:10.1109/ICPR.2006.593

Mosleh, A., Zargari, F., & Azizi, R. (2009). Texture image retrieval using contourlet transform. In *Proceedings of IEEE International Symposium on Signals, Circuits and Systems* (pp. 1-4).

Murala, S., Maheshwari, R. P., & Balasubramanian, R. (2012). Directional local extrema patterns: A new descriptor for content-based image retrieval. *International Journal of Multimedia Information Retrieval, 1*(3), 191–203. doi:10.1007/s13735-012-0008-2

Murala, S., Maheshwari, R. P., & Balasubramanian, R. (2012). Expert System Design using Wavelets and Color Vocabulary Trees for Image retrieval. *Expert Systems with Applications*, 39.

Murala, S., Maheshwari, R. P., & Balasubramanian, R. (2012). Local tetra patterns: A new descriptor for content-based image retrieval. *IEEE Transactions on Image Processing, 21*(5), 2874–2886. doi:10.1109/TIP.2012.2188809 PMID:22514130

Murtagh, F., & Starck, J. L. (2008). Wavelet and curvelet moments for image classification: Application to aggregate mixture grading. *Pattern Recognition Letters, 29*(10), 1557–1564. doi:10.1016/j.patrec.2008.03.008

Nguyen-Duc, H., Do-Hong, T., Le-Tien, T., & Bui-Thu, C. (2010). A new descriptor for image retrieval using contourlet co-occurrence. In *Proceedings of Third IEEE International Conference on Communications and Electronics (ICCE)* (pp. 169-174). doi:10.1109/ICCE.2010.5670704

Ojala, T., Pietikainen, M., & Maenpaa, T. (2002). Multiresolution gray-scale and rotation invariant texture classification with local binary patterns. *IEEE Transactions on Pattern Analysis and Machine Intelligence, 24*(7), 971–987. doi:10.1109/TPAMI.2002.1017623

Smeulders, A. W. M., Worring, M., Santini, S., Gupta, A., & Jain, R. (2000). Content-Based Image Retrieval At The End of Early Years. *IEEE Transactions on Pattern Analysis and Machine Intelligence, 22*(12), 1349–1379. doi:10.1109/34.895972

Smith, J. R., & Chang, S. F. (1996). Tools and Techniques for Color Image Retrieval. Electronic Imaging: Science & Technology. *International Society for Optics and Photonics, 2670*, 426–437.

Srivastava, J., Cooley, R., Deshpande, M., & Tan, P. (2000). Web Usage Mining: Discovery and Applications of Usage Patterns for Web Data. *ACM SIGKDD Explorations Newsletter, 1*(2), 12–23. doi:10.1145/846183.846188

Srivastava, P., Binh, N. T., & Khare, A. (2013). Content-Based Image Retrieval using Moments. In *Proceedings of 2nd International Conference on Context Awareness and Application*, (pp. 228-237).

Srivastava, P., Binh, N. T., & Khare, A. (2014). Content-Based Image Retrieval using Moments of Local Ternary Pattern. *Mobile Networks and Applications, 19*(5), 618–625. doi:10.1007/s11036-014-0526-7

Srivastava, P., Prakash, O., & Khare, A. (2014). Content-Based Image Retrieval using Moments of Wavelet Transform. In *Proceedings of International Conference on Control Automation and Information Sciences*, (pp. 159-164). doi:10.1109/ICCAIS.2014.7020550

Sumana, I. J., Islam, M. M., Zhang, D., & Liu, G. (2008). Content-Based Image Retrieval using Curvelet Transform. In *Proceedings of 10th IEEE workshop on Multimedia Signal Processing*, (pp. 11-16).

Syam, B., & Rao, Y. S. (2010). Integrating contourlet features with texture, color and spatial features for effective image retrieval. In *Proceedings of 2nd IEEE International Conference on Information Management and Engineering*, (pp. 289-293). doi:10.1109/ICIME.2010.5477856

Tan, X., & Triggs, B. (2010). Enhanced Local Texture Feature Sets for Face Recognition under Difficult Lighting Conditions. *IEEE Transactions on Image Processing*, *19*(6), 1635–1650. doi:10.1109/TIP.2010.2042645 PMID:20172829

Tarzjan, S. (2007). A Novel Evolutionary Approach for Optimizing Content-based Image Indexing Algorithms. *IEEE Transactions on Systems, Man, and Cybernetics. Part B, Cybernetics*, *37*(1), 139–153. doi:10.1109/TSMCB.2006.880137 PMID:17278567

Verma, M., Balasubramanian, R., & Murala, S. (2014). Multiresolution LEP using Discrete Wavelet Transform. In *Proceedings of 7th IEEE Conference on Contemporary Computing*, (pp. 577-582).

Wang, J. W., Li, J., & Wiederhold, G. (2001). SIMPLIcity: Semantics-Sensitive Integrated Matching for Picture Libraries. *IEEE Transactions on Pattern Analysis and Machine Intelligence*, *23*(9), 947–963. doi:10.1109/34.955109

Wang, X., Yu, Y., & Yang, H. (2011). An Effective Image Retrieval Scheme Using Color, Texture And Shape Features. *Computer Standards & Interfaces*, *33*(1), 59–68. doi:10.1016/j.csi.2010.03.004

Wang, X., Zhang, B., & Yang, H. (2012). Content-based Image Retrieval by Integrating Color and Texture Features. *Multimedia Tools and Applications*, 1–25.

Yates, R. B., & Neto, B. R. (2011). *Modern Information Retrieval*. Pearson.

Youssef, S. M. (2012). ICTEDCT-CBIR: Integrating curvelet transform with enhanced dominant colors extraction and texture analysis for efficient content-based image retrieval. *Computers & Electrical Engineering*, *38*(5), 1358–1376. doi:10.1016/j.compeleceng.2012.05.010

Yu, J., Qin, Z., Wan, T., & Zhang, X. (2013). Feature integration analysis of bag-of- features model for image retrieval. *Neurocomputing*, *120*, 355–364. doi:10.1016/j.neucom.2012.08.061

Zhang, M., Zhang, K., Feng, Q., Wang, J., Kong, J., & Lu, Y. (2014). A novel image retrieval method based on hybrid information descriptors. *Journal of Visual Communication and Image Representation*, *25*(7), 1574–1587.

ADDITIONAL READING

Duda, R. O., Hart, P. E., & Stork, D. G. (2010). *Pattern Classification* (2nd ed.). Wiley.

Dutta R., Joshi D., Li J., & Wang J. Z. (2008). Image Retrieval: Ideas, Influences, and Trends of the New Age. *ACM Computing Surveys, 40*(2), 5:1-5:60.

Eakins, J. P. (2002). Towards Intelligent Image Retrieval. *Pattern Recognition, 35*(1), 3–14. doi:10.1016/S0031-3203(01)00038-3

Gonzalez, R. C., & Woods, R. E. (2002). *Digital Image Processing* (2nd ed.). Prentice Hall of India.

Liu, Y., Zhang, D., Lu, G., & Ma, W. (2007). A Survey of Content-Based Image Retrieval with High-Level Semantics. *Pattern Recognition, 40*(1), 262–282. doi:10.1016/j.patcog.2006.04.045

Manning, C. D., Raghvan, P., & Schütze, H. (2009). *An Introduction to Information Retrieval.* Cambridge University Press.

Starck, J., Candes, E. J., & Donoho, D. L. (2002). The Curvelet Transform for Image Denoising. *IEEE Transactions on Image Processing, 11*(6), 670–684. doi:10.1109/TIP.2002.1014998 PMID:18244665

KEY TERMS AND DEFINITIONS

Content-Based Image Retrieval: Retrieval of similar images on the basis of features present in the image.

Feature Vector: A vector describing about characteristics of an object.

Image Retrieval: Searching of similar images from large database based on query.

Information Retrieval: Arrangement, storage, indexing of useful information in the form of large database.

Multiresolution Analysis: Analysis of a signal at more than one scale/resolution.

Chapter 13

Effectiveness of Web Usage Mining Techniques in Business Application

Ahmed El Azab
Institute of Statistical Studies and Research, Egypt

Mahmood A. Mahmood
Institute of Statistical Studies and Research, Egypt

Abd El-Aziz
Institute of Statistical Studies and Research, Egypt

ABSTRACT

Web usage mining techniques and applications across industries is still exploratory and, despite an increase in academic research, there are challenge of analyze web which quantitatively capture web users' common interests and characterize their underlying tasks. This chapter addresses the problem of how to support web usage mining techniques and applications across industries by combining language of web pages and algorithms that used in web data mining. Existing research in web usage mining techniques tend to focus on finding out how each techniques can apply in different industries fields. However, there is little evidence that researchers have approached the issue of web usage mining across industries. Consequently, the aim of this chapter is to provide an overview of how the web usage mining techniques and applications across industries can be supported.

INTRODUCTION

Nowadays, with the evolution of technology, supported by global and speedy communication network online Web services, has been growth rapidly in the form of created content presents new opportunities and challenges to both producers and consumers of information, the volumes of click stream and client information gathered by Web-based associations in their everyday operations has come to galactic extents.

Web Usage Mining deals with understanding user behavior in interacting with the web site. The aim is to obtain information that may assist web site recognition to better suit the user. The logs include

DOI: 10.4018/978-1-5225-0613-3.ch013

information about the referring pages, user identification, time a user spends at a site and the sequence of pages visited (Rani, 2013).

Data extraction is a field that is concerned with obtaining information from different online databases and services web resources including websites. According of the dynamic nature of the World Wide Web so it become important to find tools for data extraction. end users and application programs have some difficulties when it comes to finding useful data (MOHAPATRA, 2004)

Since 1980 the attempt researches to extract data from the Web are. Two of strategies emerged learning techniques and knowledge engineering techniques also called learning-based and rule-based approaches, respectively. These approaches depends on domain expertise it need programming experience and a good knowledge of the domain in which the data extraction system (Ferrara, E., De Meo, P., Fiumara, G., & Baumgartner, R., 2014)

On the same way, (Tomasz Kaczmarek,et al) in ((Kaczmarek, 2010)) present method part of the extra Spec system called EXT was based on hierarchical execution of XPath commands and regular expressions depending on the structure of processed documents. EXT is capable of processing webpages written in the Polish language in order to extract the information relevant for the needs of expert programmer and team building. But this method not includes development of text processing techniques to cope with fields that are manually filled by humans (Kaczmarek, 2010)

Also web usage mining benefits the capitalist people in some area such as business, industrials and insurance to take a good decision by apply web usage mining recommender system.

Recommender systems have become an important research area since the appearance of the first papers on collaborative filtering in the mid-1990s, The interest in this area still remains high because it constitutes a problem-rich research area and because of the abundance of practical applications that help users to deal with information overload and provide personalized recommendations, content, and services to them. although the roots of recommender systems can be traced back to the extensive work in cognitive science, approximation theory, information retrieval, forecasting theories, and also have links to management science and to consumer choice modeling in marketing, recommender systems emerged as an independent research area in the mid-1990s when researchers started focusing on recommendation problems that explicitly rely on the ratings structure (Mahmood A. Mahmood N. E.-B., 2014).According that recommender system tends to make use of different sources of information (collaborative, social, demographic, content, knowledge-based, geographic, sensors, tags, implicit and explicit data acquisition, etc.), An important research subject in the recommender system field focuses on providing explanations that justify the recommendations the user has received. This is an important aspect of a recommender system because it aids in maintaining a higher degree of user confidence in the results generated by the systems (Mahmood A. Mahmood N. E.-B., 2014) Mahmood and et al in (Mahmood A. Mahmood E. A.-S.-B., 2013)).presented Recommender System for Ground-Level Ozone Predictions. The obtained results demonstrate the effectiveness and the reliability of the proposed recommender system. Resulted experimental values of ground-level Ozone predicted by the proposed recommender system showed similar behavior as the actual tested values of the ground-level Ozone dataset.

Samar and et al in (Samar Mahmoud, 2013) presented An Intelligent Recommender System for Drinking Water Quality to evaluate the performance of the presented recommender system, 5 parameters developed and validated between the year 2000 to 2013, were used. The initial seven years of data was used to develop the forecasting models and the remaining data was used for testing and verifying these models. The obtained results demonstrate the effectiveness and the reliability of the proposed recommender system. Based on the data resulted, the average PH level prediction in a certain time is characterized by a mean absolute error of 0.34. In addition, both experimentally resulted and actual dataset values existed in the healthy region of the PH level for drinking water, which is within the range 6.5 to 8.0 according to the World Health Organization (WHO) drinking water guidelines.

This chapter organized as follows: First sections gives an overview on web mining and web mining taxonomy and its applications. Also Section describes the issues of web usage mining. Also Section 4 introduces Web Usage Mining Languages and Algorithms. On the same way Section explains Effective Web usage mining in Business. Finally, Section presents and discusses the conclusion.

WEB MINING: AN OVERVIEW

There are many definition for web mining the Most popular definition of Web mining is "the application of data mining techniques to extract knowledge from web data, i.e. web content, web structure, and web usage data." As shown in Figure 1. (Rani, 2013) (T. Srivastava, P. Desikan, V. Kumar, 2005) see Figure 1.

Web Content Mining

Most Web content mining and information retrieval applications involve measuring similarity among two or more documents.

Figure 1. Diagram of web mining taxonomy

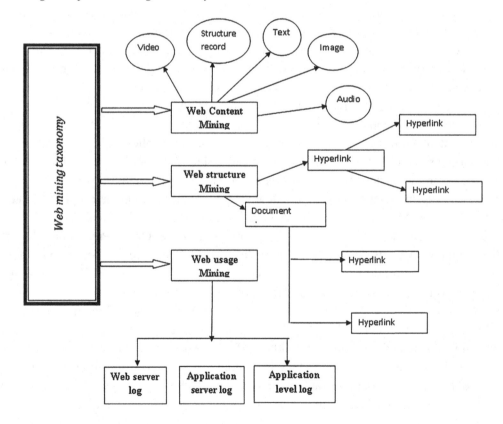

Web Content Mining is the process of retrieving the information from web document into more structure forms. It is related to Data Mining because many Data Mining techniques can be applied in Web Content Mining (Gupta, V., & Lehal, G. S. 2009).

Also Vector representation facilitates similarity computations using vector-space operations (such as Cosine of the angle between two vectors).

For Examples Search engines: measure the similarity between a query (represented as a vector) and the indexed document vectors to return a ranked list of relevant documents.

Document clustering: group documents based on similarity or dissimilarity (distance) among them.

Document categorization: measure the similarity of a new document to be classified with representations of existing categories (such as the mean vector representing a group of document vectors) (Janssens, 2007)

Personalization: recommend documents or items based their similarity to a representation of the user's profile (may be a term vector representing concepts or terms of interest to the user)

Web mining is one of the applications and it's used to discover patterns from the web. The research of the web mining is based on interdisciplinary field and it used techniques from data mining, text mining, databases, statistics, machine learning, multimedia, etc. Web mining has interest based on three categories such as clustering i.e. finding natural groups of users, pages, etc., next one is associations i.e. which URLs tend to request together and finally sequential analysis i.e. the order in which URLs tend to be accessed (Mehtaa, 2012).

Web Structure Mining

Web Structure Mining discovering similarity between sites or discovering web communities Is the target of Web Structure Mining which deals with the discovering and modeling the link structure of the web. This can help in discovering similarity between sites or discovering web communities. Which web structure use of the hyperlink structure of the Web as an (additional) information source the hyperlinks play vital role which pointing to a page has been recognized early on. Texts on hyperlinks in an HTML document which called Anchor which Anchor of predecessor pages were already indexed by the World-Wide Web Worm, one of the first search engines and Web crawlers (McBryan, 1994). Spertus (1997)cited in (Patel, P., Jena, B., & Sahoo, B, 2014) suggested a taxonomy of different types of (hyper-)links that can be found on the Web and discusses how the links can be exploited for various information retrieval tasks on the Web (Patel, P., Jena, B., & Sahoo, B, 2014).

There are challgenes appear with confused structure, people use search engines, trying to focus their search by querying using specific terms/keywords. At the beginning, where large information contained in the Web did not yet have these big parts, search engines used manually-built lists covering common topics. First they maintained an index, containing a list for every word, of all Web pages containing this word. This index was then used in order to answer to the users' queries. However, after a few years, when the Web evolved including millions of pages, the manual maintenance of such indices was very expensive. The automated search engines relying in keyword matching, give results including hundreds (or more) Web pages, most of them of low quality. The need for ranking somehow the importance and relevance of the results was more than evident.

Search engines such as AltaVista, Lycos, Infoseek, HotBot and Excite use some simple heuristics in order to accomplish a page ranking. Such heuristics take into consideration the number of times the term appears in the document, if it appears at the beginning of the text, or at areas considered more important (such as headings, italics, etc) (Fürnkranz, Johannes, 2002).

Web Usage Mining

Web Usage Mining deals with understanding user behavior in interacting with the web site. The aim is to obtain information that may assist web site recognition to better suit the user. The logs include information about the referring pages, user identification, time a user spends at a site and the sequence of pages visited.

There are three main tasks for performing Web Usage Mining or Web Usage Analysis. the tasks for each step and discusses the challenges involved (Rani, 2013).

Preprocessing

The web usage dataset collection, perform preprocessing on the dataset. Because, the data collected from the web is normally diverse, heterogeneous and unstructured. Therefore, it is necessary to do the pre-processing like filtering unnecessary and irrelevant data, predicting and filling the missing values, removing noise, resolving inconsistence before applying the algorithm. Data pre-processing consists of the following processes such as, Data cleaning, User identification, Session identification and Path completion (Choudhary, Durga, and Shreya Sharma., 2015)

Pre-processing consists of converting the usage, content, and structure information contained in the various available data sources into the data abstractions necessary for pattern discovery.

Usage Preprocessing

Difficult task in the Web Usage Mining process is Usage preprocessing, such as the incompleteness of the available data. Unless a client side tracking mechanism is used, only the IP address, agent, and server side click stream are available to identify users server sessions (Srivastava J. C., 2000).

There are some of the typically encountered problems such as:

- **Single IP address/Multiple Server Sessions:** Internet service providers (ISPs) typically have a pool of proxy servers that users access the Web through. A single proxy server may have several users accessing a Web site, potentially over the same time period.
- **Multiple IP Address/Single Server Session:** Some ISPs or privacy tools randomly assign each request from a user to one of several IP addresses. In this case, a single server session can have multiple IP addresses.
- **Multiple IP Address/Single User:** A user that accesses the Web from different machines will have a different IP address from session to session. This makes tracking repeat visits from the same user difficult.
- **Multiple Agent/Singe User:** Again, a user that uses more than one browser, even on the same machine, will appear as multiple users. Assuming each user has now been identified (through cook-

ies, logins, or IP/agent/path analysis), the click-stream for each user must be divided into sessions (Srivastava J. C., 2000). When page request from other servers are not available, it is difficult to know when a user has left a Web site. A thirty minute timeout is often used as the default method of breaking a user's click-stream into sessions. When a session ID is embedded in each URI, the definition of a session is set by the content server. While the exact content served as a result of each user action is often available from the request field in the server logs, it is sometimes necessary to have access to the content server information as well. Since content servers can maintain state variables for each active session, the information necessary to determine exactly what content is served by a user request is not always available in the URI. The final problem encountered when preprocessing usage data is that of inferring cached page references (Mohamed, 2011).

The only verifiable method of tracking cached page views is to monitor usage from the client side. The referrer field for each request can be used to detect some of the instances when cached pages have been viewed.

Content Preprocessing

Content preprocessing consists of converting the text, image, scripts, and other files such as multimedia into forms that are useful for the Web Usage Mining process. Often, this consists of performing content mining such as classification or clustering. While applying data mining to the content of Web sites is an interesting area of research in its own right, in the context of Web Usage Mining the content of a site can be used to filter the input to, or output from the pattern discovery algorithms. For example, results of a classification algorithm could be used to limit the discovered patterns to those containing page views about a certain subject or class of products. (Witten, I. H., Frank, E., 2005). Page views can be intended to convey information (through text, graphics, or other multimedia), gather information from the user, allow navigation (through a list of hypertext links), or some combination uses. The intended use of a page view can also filter the sessions before or after pattern discovery. In order to run content mining algorithms on page views~ the information must first be converted into a quantifiable format. Some version of the vector space model is typically used to accomplish this. Text files can be broken up into vectors of words. Keywords or text descriptions can be substituted for graphics or multimedia. The content of static page views can be easily preprocessed by parsing the HTML and reformatting the information or running additional algorithms as desired. Dynamic page views present more of a challenge. Content servers that employ personalization techniques and/or draw upon databases to construct the page views may be capable of forming more page views than can be practically preprocessed. A given set of server sessions may only access a fraction of the page views possible for a large dynamic site. Also the content may be revised on a regular basis. The content of each page view to be preprocessed must be "assembled", either by an HTTP request from a crawler, or a combination of template, script, and database accesses. If only the portion of page views that are accessed are preprocessed, the output of any classification or clustering algorithms may be skewed (Witten, I. H., Frank, E., 2005).

Structure Preprocessing

The structure of a site is created by the hypertext links between page views. The structure can be obtained and preprocessed in the same manner as the content of a site. Again, dynamic content (and therefore links) pose more problems than static page views. Pattern Discovery Pattern discovery draws upon methods and algorithms developed from several fields such as statistics, data mining, machine learning and pattern recognition. However, it is not the intent of this paper to describe all the available algorithms and techniques derived from these fields.

The kinds of mining activities that have been applied to the Web domain. Methods developed from other fields must take into consideration the different kinds of data abstractions and prior knowledge available for Web Mining. For example, in association rule discovery, the notion of a transaction for market-basket analysis does not take into consideration the order in which items are selected. However, in Web Usage Mining, a server session is an ordered sequence of pages requested by a user. Furthermore, due to the difficulty in identifying unique sessions, additional prior knowledge is required (Okoli et al., 2012).

Statistical Analysis

Statistical techniques are the most common method to extract knowledge about visitors to a Web site. By analyzing the session file, one can perform different kinds of descriptive statistical analyses (frequency, mean, median, etc.) on variables such as page views, viewing time and length of a navigational path. Many Web traffic analysis tools produce a periodic report containing statistical information such as the most frequently accessed pages, average view time of a page or average length of a path through a site (Jaideep Srivastava, 2000) .

Application of Web Data Mining

Web data mining can successfully fix information extraction and the following features incorporated with the web mining program must be fixed if we need to use data mining successfully in creating Web intelligence (Mohamed., 2011).

Web Search-Engine Data Mining

For website optimization web crawls on indexes Websites, and builds and stores large keyword-based indices that help identify sets of Websites that contain specific keywords and phrases. By using a set of tightly restricted keywords and phrases, an experienced user can quickly identify appropriate documents. However, current keyword-based search engines suffer from several deficiencies. First, a subject of any breadth can easily contain tens of thousands of records. This can lead to a look for website returning many document entries (Witten, I. H., Frank, E., 2005), many of which are only partially appropriate to the subject or contain only poor-quality materials. Second, many highly appropriate records may not contain keywords and phrases that explicitly define the subject, a trend known as the polysemy problem. For example, the keyword and key phrase information exploration may turn up many Websites related to other exploration industries, yet fail to identify appropriate papers on knowledge discovery, mathematical analysis, or machine learning because they did not contain the information exploration keyword and key phrase. Depending on these observations, data mining should be integrated with the web search engine service to enhance the excellence of Web searches To do so, For example, a look for the keyword and key phrase information exploration can consist of a few alternatives so that an index-based web search engine can perform a parallel search that will obtain a larger set of records than the search phrases alone would return. The search engine then can look for the set of appropriate Web records obtained so far to select a smaller set of highly appropriate and authoritative records to present to the user. Web-linkage and Web dynamics analysis thus provide the basis for discovering high-quality records.

Web Link Structure Analyzing

Keyword and key phrase or subject, such as investment, an individual would like to find web pages that are not only extremely appropriate, but trustworthy and of high quality. Instantly determining trustworthy Websites for a certain subject will improve a Web search's excellence. The secret of power conceals in Website linkages. These hyperlinks contain quantity of hidden human annotation that can help instantly infer the idea of power. When a Web page's writer makes a web page link directing to another Website, this action can be considered as an approval of that web page. The combined approval of a given web page by different writers on the Web can indicate the value of the site and lead normally to the development of trustworthy Web pages. First, not every web page link symbolizes the approval for a search. Web-page writers make some links for other requirements, such as routing or to provide as compensated ads. Overall, though, if most hyperlinks operate as recommendations, the combined viewpoint will still control. Second, a power that belongs to a professional or aggressive interest will hardly ever have its Web page point to competing authorities' pages. (T. Sunil Kumar; Dr. K. Suvarchala, 2012)

For example, manufacture will likely avoid supporting a product by guaranteeing that no links to that product in their Websites appears. These qualities of web link components have led researchers to consider another essential Website category: locations. A hub is just one Website or web page set that provides selections of links to authorities. Although it may not be popular, or may have only a few links directing to it, a hub provides hyperlinks to a selection of popular websites on a typical subject. These web pages can be list of suggested links on individual home pages, such as suggested referrals websites from a course home-page or a expertly constructed source list on a commercial site A hub unquestioningly confers authority status on websites that focus on a specific subject. Generally, a good hub points to many excellent authorities, and, on the other hand, a page that many good locations point to can be considered a good authority. Such a common encouragement relationship between locations and authorities helps users my own trustworthy. Websites performs development of high quality Web components and sources. Techniques for determining trustworthy Web pages and locations have led to the development of the PageRank1 and HITS3 methods .Some over the counter available Web search engines, such as Google, are built around such methods. By assessing Web links and textual perspective information, these systems can generate better-quality look for results than term-index look for engines.

Automatically Classifying

Web documents Although Yahoo and similar Web listing service systems use human visitors to categorize Web records, inexpensive and improved speed make automated category highly suitable. Common category methods use good and bad illustrations as training sets, then determine each papers a category brand from a set of defined subject groups depending on pre classified papers illustrations. For example, designers can use Yahoo's taxonomy and its associated records as exercising and test places to obtain a Web papers category program. This program groups new Web records by giving groups from the same taxonomy. Developers can obtain great results using typical keyword-based papers category methods, such as Bayesian category, support vector machine, decision-tree introduction, and keyword and key phrase centered organization analysis to categorize Web records. Since hyperlinks contain high quality semantic signs to a page's subject, such semantic information can help achieve even better precision than that possible with genuine keyword-based category. However, since the back-linked web pages around a documents may be loud and thus contain unrelated subjects, innocent use of terms in a document's web page link community can lower precision . For example, many personal home pages may have climate. com connected simply as a save, even though these web pages have no importance to the subject of climate. Tests have shown that combining solid mathematical designs such as Markov unique areas with pleasure brands can considerably improve Web papers category precision. As opposed to many other category techniques, automated category usually does not clearly specify adverse examples: category a pre classified papers connected to, but not which records a certain category definitely limits. Thus, preferably, a Web documents category program should not require clearly marked adverse illustrations. Using positive illustrations alone can be especially useful in Web papers category, forcing some scientists to recommend a category method based on a enhanced support-vector machine program (T. Sunil kumar; Dr. K. Suvarchala, 2012)

Web Page Content and Semantic Structure Mining

Completely automated removal of Website components and semantic material can be difficult given the present restrictions on computerized natural-language parsing. However, semiautomatic techniques can identify a large part of such components. Professionals may still need to specify what types of components and semantic material a particular web page type can have. Then a page-structure-extraction system can evaluate the Website to see whether and how a segment's content suits into one of the components. Designers also can evaluate individual reviews to enhance the training and evaluate procedures and enhance the quality of produced Website components and contents. Specific research of Website exploration systems shows that different types of web pages have different semantic components. For example, a department's home-page, a professor's homepage, and a job marketing web page can all have different components First, to identify the relevant and interesting framework to draw out, either an expert personally identifies this framework for a given Website category, techniques develop to instantly generate such a framework from a set of relabeled Website examples. Second, designers can use Website framework and content removal methods for automatic removal based on Website classes, possible semantic components, and other semantic information. Web page category identification allows to draft out semantic components and material, while getting such components allows validating which category the produced pages are part of. Such a connection mutually increases both procedures. Third, semantic page structure and content recognition will greatly enhance the in depth analysis of Web page contents and the building of a multilayered Web information base. (T. Sunil kumar; Dr. K. Suvarchala, 2012)

Dynamic Web Mining

Web mining can also recognize as dynamics web. How the Web changes in the perspective of its material, components, and accessibility styles. Saving certain pieces of traditional details related to these Web exploration factors helps in discovering changes in material and linkages. In this case, we can evaluate pictures from different time postage stamps to recognize the up-dates. However, as opposed to relational data source systems, the Internet's wide depth and large shop of details create it nearly difficult to consistently shop past pictures or upgrade records (Yu-Hui Tao, 2007).

These restrictions create discovering such changes generally infeasible. Mining Web accessibility activities, on the other hand, is both possible and, in many programs, quite useful. With this strategy, customers can mine Web log information to discover Web page access styles. Assessing and discovering regularities in Web log information can enhance the quality and distribution of Internet information services to the end individual, enhance Web hosting server system performance, and recognize customers for electronic industry. A Web hosting server usually signs up a Web log entry for every Web page accessed. This accessibility includes the asked for URL, the IP address from which the request is started, and a time seal. Web-based e-commerce hosts gather many Web accessibility log details. Popular Web sites can register Web log details that variety hundreds of megabytes each day. Web log directories provide rich details about Web characteristics. Opening these details requires innovative Web log exploration techniques. The success of such programs relies on what and how much legitimate and efficient knowledge we can find out from the raw details. Often, researchers must clean, reduce, and convert these details to recover and evaluate significant and useful details. Second, scientists can use the available URL, time, IP deal with, and Web page content details to create a multidimensional view on the Web log data source and execute a multidimensional OLAP research to find the top customers, top utilized websites, most frequently utilized times, and so on. These results will help find out customers, marketplaces, and other organizations. Third, exploring Web log records can expose organization styles, successive styles, and Web accessibility styles.

Issues of Web Usage Mining

According to Data Mining News, as of 1999, the data mining industry was valued at $1 billion also according to Herb Edelstein, by 1998, the data mining tool market was at $45 million, a 100% increase from 1997. It has been estimated by Internet News that the number of adults using credit cards to purchase goods and services online more than doubled between 1998 and 1999. Furthermore, the report included that by the third quarter of 1999, 19.2 million adults used their credit cards to make online transactions, compared to 9.3 million in 1998 and only 4.9 million in 1997. As such, online transactions are increasing in record numbers.

In the Healthcare E-commerce industry, a recent study showed that by 2004, this industry would surpass the $370 Billion mark in online transactions. Compared with travel, finance, and even the steel industry, healthcare e-commerce is a late bloomer, says the report from Forrester Research (Aldana, 2000), Web mining will be a growing technology as more companies are investing their futures in the Internet. Just in advertising alone, companies are spending most of their revenues trying to publicize their sites and try to attract as many potential customers as they can. With increasing online transactions and the potential of attaining a large set of customers through the Internet, it is no surprise that most Internet companies are devoting most of their sources of revenue to advertising costs.

In the recent years, Internet companies have accumulated over $1 billion in advertising. Advertising by dot.com companies saw growth nearly triple in the third quarter of 1999 compared to the same time period from last year according to a study by Competitive Media Reporting. Including the holiday season, CMR predicted that dotcom's have more than doubled their spending on advertising than the $649.2 million spent offline for all of 1998. According to the CKS Group, they estimated online advertising spending to be $301 million in 1996.

Information Extraction Approaches

Researchers began to use statistical techniques and machine learning algorithms to automatically create information extraction systems for new domains. In the following subsections, overviews of information extraction approaches are presented. In general, approaches of information extraction can be under the category of either supervised, weakly supervised, or unsupervised learning approaches. Supervised learning can be applied for extracting different information including patterns, rules, and sequential information. Moreover, weakly supervised and unsupervised learning methods for information extraction are applied for more global or discourse-oriented approaches to information extraction. The following subsections will demonstrate the work performed by researchers in this field. (Ravi, 2015)

Limitation and Challenges in Web Data Mining

Web information presentation is a noteworthy test in current patterns of data extraction. The conventional plans for getting to the gigantic measures of information that live on the Web on a very basic level expect the content situated, watchword based perspective of Web pages. To accomplish the obliged data we require a high potential web mining procedures to beat the crucial issues. an information situated deliberation will empower another scope of functionalities. Second, at the administration level. Flow web hunt mining backings decisive word, connection address and substance based web look, where information mining will assume an imperative part. Be that as it may, these web crawlers still can't give astounding, astute administrations as a result of a few impediments in web mining which adds to the issue (Marc Bousquet, Katherine Wills, 2003)

Quality of Keyword-Based Searches

The quality of keyword-based searches suffers from several inadequacies such as a search often returns many answers, especially if the keywords posed include words from popular categories such as sports, politics, or entertainment. It overloaded keyword semantics and it can return low-quality results. For instance, contingent upon the connection, a Mac could be a natural product, squeeze, organization or PC and a pursuit can miss numerous exceedingly related pages that don't unequivocally contain the postured essential words and, a quest for the term information mining can miss numerous much respected machine learning or measurable information examination pages (NOOR, 2008)

Effective of Deep-Web Extraction

A research analysts estimated that searchable databases on the Web numbered more than 100,000. These databases provide high-quality, well-maintained information, but are not effectively accessible. Because current Web crawlers cannot query these databases, the data they contain remains invisible to traditional search engines. Conceptually, the deep Web provides an extremely large collection of autonomous and heterogeneous databases, each supporting specific query interfaces with different schema and query constraints. To effectively extract the deep Web, we must integrate these databases and implement efficient web mining approaches (Jiawei Han Kevin, 2002)

- **Self-Organized and Constructed Directories:** A content or type-oriented Web information directory presents an organized picture of a Web sector and supports a semantics-based information search [9], which makes such a directory highly desirable. For example, following organization links like Country > Sports > Football > Players makes searches more efficient. Unfortunately, developers construct such directories manually which limit coverage of these costly directories provide and developers cannot easily scale or adapt them.
- **Semantics-Based Query:** Most keyword- based search engines provide a small set of options for possible keyword combinations, such as Google and Yahoo, provide more advanced search primitives, including ——with exact phrases, without certain words, with restrictions on date and domain site type (Liu, 2003)
- **Human Activities Feedback:** Web page authors provide links to authoritative Web pages and also traverse those Web pages they find most interesting or of highest quality [10][2]. Unfortunately, while human activities and interests change over time, Web links may not be updated to reflect these trends. For example, significant events—such as the 2012 Olympic or the tsunami attack on Japan can change Web site access patterns dramatically, a change that Web linkages often fail to reflect. We have yet to use such human-traversal information for the dynamic, automatic adjustment of Web information services. (Jiawei Han, 2002).
- **Multidimensional Data Analysis and Mining:** Because current Web searches rely on keyword based indices, not the actual data the Web pages contain, search engines provide only limited support for multidimensional Web information analysis and data mining. These challenges and limitation have promoted research into efficiently and effectively discovering and using Internet resources, a quest in which web data mining play an important role (Lancaster, 2003)

Web Mining Tasks

Web mining is the Data Mining technique that automatically discovers or extracts the information from web documents, it consists of following tasks:-

1. **Resource Finding:** It involves the task of retrieving intended web documents. It is the process by which it had been extract the data either online or offline resources available on web.
2. **Information Selection and Pre-Processing:** It involves the automatic selection and pre processing of specific information from retrieved web resources. This process transforms the original retrieved data into information. The data is transformed into useful information by using suitable transformation. The transformation could be renewal of stop words, or it may be aimed for obtaining the desired representation such as finding particular format of data.
3. **Generalization:** It automatically discovers general patterns at individual web sites as well as across multiple sites. Data Mining techniques and machine learning are used in generalization.
4. **Analysis:** It involves the validation and interpretation of the mined patterns. It plays an important role in pattern mining. A human plays an important role in information on knowledge discovery process on web (Thirumala Sree Govada, 2014).

The process of web mining shown in Figure 2.
According to Table 1 there are difference between comparison of WCM, WSM and WUM

Figure 2. Diagram of the Process of web mining

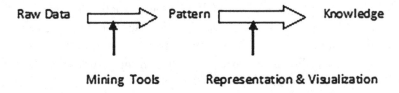

Table 1. Comparison WCM,WSM,WUM

Specifications	Web Content Mining (WCM)	Web Structure Mining	Web Usage Mining
View of data	Structured, Semi Structured and Unstructured	Linking of structure	Interactive data
Type of data used in mining	Primary	Primary	Secondary
Main data	Text document, Hypertext Document	Link Structure	Server Logs, Browser Logs
Representation	Bag of Words, n-grams, Terms, phrases, Concepts or Ontology, Relational, Edge Labeled Graph	Graph	Relational Table, Graph
Method	Machine learning, Statistical Method, Proprietary Algorithm, Association Rules	Proprietary Algorithm,	Machine Learning Statistical Method
Tasks	It describes the discovery of useful information from the web content/ documents.	It tries to discover the model underlying the link structure of the web.	It tries to make sense of data generated by web surfer"s session or behaviour.
Scope	In IR view of data the scope is global while in DB view it is local	Global	Global

Web Usage Mining: Languages and Algorithms

XML languages and a web data mining application which utilizes them to extract complex structural information.

Extensible Graph Markup and Modeling Language (XGMML) is an XML 1.0 application based on Graph Modeling Language (GML) which is used for graph description. XG-MML uses tags to describe nodes and edges of a graph. The purpose of XGMML is to make possible the exchange of graphs between different authoring and browsing tools for graphs. Theconversion of graphs written in GML to XGMML is straight forward. Using Extensible Stylesheet Language (XSL) with XGMML allows the translation of graphs to different formats.

Which Web data mining is one of the current hot topics in computer science. Mining data that has been collected from web server logfiles, is not only useful for studying customer choices, but also helps to better organize web pages. This is accomplished by knowing which web pages are most frequently accessed by the web surfers (Punin, et al.,2002).

Link Analysis Algorithms

There are many algorithms (Aggarwal, 2013) used in web mining .Three Popular algorithms Page Rank, Weighted Page Rank and Weighted Page Content Rank are discussed below.

Page Rank

Page Rank is a numeric value that represents how important a page is on the web. Page Rank is the Google's method of measuring a page's "importance." When all other factors such as Title tag and keywords are taken into account, Google uses Page Rank to adjust

Results so that more "important" pages move up in the results page of a user's search result display. Google Fig.s that when a page links to another page, it is effectively casting a vote for the other page. Google calculates a page's importance from the votes cast for it. How important each vote is taken into account when a page's Page Rank is calculated. It matters because it is one of the factors that determine a page's ranking in the search results. It isn't the only factor that Google uses to rank pages, but it is an important one. The order of ranking in Google works like this:

Find all pages matching the keywords of the search. Adjust the results by Page Rank scores (Aggarwal, 2013)

Weighted Page Rank

Extended Page Rank algorithm- Weighted Page Rank assigns large rank value to more important pages instead of dividing the rankvalue of a page evenly among its outlink pages. The importanceis assigned in terms of weight values to incoming and outgoing links denoted as and respectively. is calculated on the basis of number of incoming links to page n and the number of incoming links to all reference pages of page m.

In is number of incoming links of page n, Ip is number of incoming (Tamanna. 2007).

Weighted Page Content Rank

Weighted Page Content Rank Algorithm (WPCR) is a proposed page ranking algorithm which is used to give a sorted order to the web pages returned by a search engine in response to a user query. WPCR is a numerical value based on which the web pages are given an order. This algorithm employs web structure mining as well as web content mining techniques. Web structure mining is used to calculate the importance of the page and web content mining is used to find how much relevant a page is? Importance here means the popularity of the page i.e. how many pages are pointing to or are referred by this particular page. It can be calculated based on the number of inlinks and outlinks of the page. Relevancy means matching of the page with the fired query. If a page is maximally matched to the query, that becomes more relevant (Aggarwal, 2013)

Comparison of Algorithms

According the rapidly development algorithms were used at web mining we present the difference between coomon three algorithms which Table 2 shows the difference between above three algorithms

Table 2. Comparison of page rank and weighted page rank

Contents	Page Rank	Weighted Page	Weighted Page Content Rank
Mining Technique Used	WSM	WSM	WSM and WCM
Complexity	O(logn)	<O(logn)	<O(logn)
Working Procedure	Computes Scores at index time. Results are sorted on the importance of pages	Assigns large value to more important pages instead of diving the rank value of a page evenly among its outlink pages.	Gives sorted order to the web pages returned by a search engine as a numerical value in response to a user query.
Input/Output parameters	Backlinks	Backlinks and forward links	Backlinks Forward links and content
Advantages	It provides important information about given query by diving rank value equally among its outlink pages	It provides important information about given query and assigning importance in terms of weight values to incoming an outgoing links	It provides important information and relevancy about a given query by using web structure and web content mining
Search Engine	Google	Google	Research Model
Limitations	(1) Page Rank is equally distributed to outgoing links (2) It is purely based on the number of inlinks and outlinks.	(1) While some pages may be irrelevant to a given query, it still receives the highest rank (2) There is a less determination of the relevancy of the pages to a given query	No limitation best as comparison to Page Rank and Weighted Page Rank

The GSP Algorithm

The GSP algorithm, is intended for mining Generalized Sequential Patterns. It extends previous proposal by handling time constraints and taxonomies.

For solving The problem of mining association rules has been refined considering a database storing behavioral facts which occur over time to individuals of the studied population. Thus facts are provided with a time stamp. The concept of sequential pattern is introduced to capture typical behaviors over time, i.e. behaviours sufficiently repeated by individuals to be relevant for the decision maker (Masseglia, 2000).

The PSP Approach

There are problem of a web server log file florent Masseglia, et al., split the problem of mining sequential patterns from a web server log file into the following phases (Masseglia, 2000):-

1. Sort Phase

converts the original access log file into a database d of datasequences is aim of this phase which the access log file is sorted with ip address as a major key and transaction time as the minor key. Furthermore, by group together entries that are sufficiently close according to the user-specified Δt in order to provide temporal transactions. such a transaction is therefore the set of all url names and their access times for the same client where successive log entries are within Δt. a unique time stamp is associated with each such transaction and each url is mapped into integer in order to efficiently manipulate the structure (Ezeife, 2005)

2. Sequence Phase

The general algorithm is utilized to locate the successive arrangements in the database. Methodology continues the key standards of GSP. its inventiveness is to utilize an alternate various leveled structure than in gsp for sorting out hopeful groupings, to enhance productivity of recoveries. the general calculation is like the one in gsp. at every stride, the db is perused for tallying the backing of current competitors (method applicant confirmation). at that point the regular arrangement set can be manufactured. from this set, new competitors are displayed for being managed at the following step (method applicant era). the calculation stops when the longest successive arrangements, installed in the db are found along these lines the hopeful era method yields a vacant arrangement of new applicants. Backing is a capacity giving for every applicant its including quality put away the tree structure (Masseglia, 2000)

Effective Web Mining in Business

Web mining techniques were the major functional areas of businesses. Some examples of deployed systems as well as frameworks for emerging applications yet-to-be-built are discussed. However, the examples are no means to be regarded as solutions to all problems within the framework of business function they are cited in. Their purpose is to illustrate that Web mining techniques have been applied successfully to handle certain kind of problems, providing the evidence of its utility also Neeraj Raheja and V.K.Katiyar cited in (Desikan, P, 2009). proposes an approach for web usage mining based upon web log partition. Neeraj Raheja and V.K.Katiyar have result show how It takes less time and provides popular results in accordance with the existing approach. Some more results may be obtained if the number of cluster formed are changed approach can be changed to 6, 8 or more. However recall and precision may be affected by changing the number of clusters i.e. either may be improved or decayed (Karypis, et al 2000)

Marketing

Marketing is typically defined as: "Marketing is the ongoing process of moving people closer to making a decision to purchase, use, follow or conform to someone else's products, services or values. Simply, if it doesn't facilitate a 'sale', then it's not marketing" Marketing is responsible for keeping the enterprise attentive to market trends, as well as keeping the sales unit aware of where the target segment is. In the following examples, Web mining techniques have been utilized for showcasing items to a client furthermore to recognize conceivable new territories of potential business sector for a venture. Item proposal recommending items to buy is a key issue for all organizations. As the client driven methodology drives the present plans of action, customary block and-mortar stores need to depend on information gathered unequivocally from clients through reviews to offer client driven recommendations.

Product Area and Trend Analysis John Ralston Saul, the Canadian author, essayist and philosopher noted: Businesses would definitely like to see such projections onto the future. Specially, identifying new product areas based on trends is a key for any business to capture markets Adapted from (Al-Azmi, 2013)

Human Resources

In any enterprise, the expansive obligation of Human Resource office is to accurately coordinate the privilege talented work force with the right capacity. HR is additionally dependable to set up approaches, rules and to give devices to representatives and administration to empower a charming work air, solid culture, sound and spare environment, and to guarantee that the association's representatives are reliably getting roused. The accompanying application analyzes how to viably oversee human asset office by keeping up the perfect measure of workforce as far as expense viability. It delineates the utilization of Web mining strategies to decrease pointless human workload.HR Call Centres Human resource departments of large companies often face the task of answering the numerous questions of various employees. As the extent of the organization develops and because of globalization, the assignment turns out to be more troublesome as they not just need to handle the quantity of workers, additionally consider different issues, for example, topographically neighborhood strategies and issues. The majority of these errands are noteworthy to the human asset division as it is their obligation to keep their representatives fulfilled and very much –inform. A possible and popular approach to handle this problem is to have "call-centres" that provide the informative service to the employees. With the advent of Web, most companies have tried to put all their policy information on Web sites for easy perusal by the employees. However, it has been observed that over time, more and more employees seek the advice of the representatives (Regis, 2008).

Sales Management

In an enterprise, sales dealing with the trusts for its diverse divisions and undertakings with the point of amplifying benefit and minimizing the danger. Money related administration itself includes two sorts of issues. The principal kind manages the stores gave to the organization from different sources. These stores could be long haul, (for example, proprietorship value) or short-term, (for example, financing from banks). The second kind manages 'reserve administration'. Here, the objectives include distinguishing issues, for example, methodologies, timetables, and hazard avoidance; for the endeavor to settle on a choice on the amount to contribute and when. In the accompanying case, advancements, for example, web and novel strategies, for example, Web mining can assist focus misrepresentation in exchanges to help an undertaking diminish.

Business opportunity risk evaluation With growing competitive markets, better understanding of customer's requirements and matching those to the enterprise's offerings have gained prominence in an enterprise's decision making processes. Important financial and business forecasts are affected by decisions in such processes and hence these decisions highly influence how an enterprise plans to support its market. For example, a lot of historical data about business sales opportunities are gathered by enterprises for one such analysis. Traditionally, this information of an enterprise's offerings, competitor's offerings and the market's demands are analyzed manually by human experts, using statistical methods, usually using a multi-step process. Correct analysis in such a multi-step process is of prime importance. For example, classifying good (profitable) opportunities as bad (non-profitable) makes the predictions pessimistic and results in lost revenue, whereas classifying bad opportunities (non-profitable) as good opportunities ties up an enterprise's resources, in addition to asking for unrealistic goals (Soley, 2003).

Business Financial Management

Financial Management in a venture manages dealing with the trusts for its diverse divisions and undertakings with the point of amplifying benefit and minimizing the danger. Money related administration itself includes two sorts of issues. The principal kind manages the stores gave to the organization from different sources. These stores could be long haul, (for example, proprietorship value) or short-term, (for example, financing from banks). The second kind manages 'reserve administration'. Here, the objectives include distinguishing issues, for example, methodologies, timetables, and hazard avoidance; for the endeavor to settle on a choice on the amount to contribute and when. In the accompanying case, advancements, for example, web and novel strategies, for example, Web mining can assist focus misrepresentation in exchanges to help an undertaking diminish its risks (Gupta, V., & Lehal, G. S. , 2009).

Role of web mining in e-commerce Financial had AnalysesIt includes reviewing of costs and revenues, calculation and comparative analysis of corporate income statements, analysis of corporate balance sheet and profitability, cash flow statement, analysis of financial markets and sophisticated controlling. Web mining can be an effective tool (Arti, 2015).

Fraud Analysis

Fraud analysis is a large problem faced by many businesses ranging from the telecommunications industry to Web-based stores. Fraud is defined as the use of false representations to gain an unjust advantage or abuse of an organization's resources, such as illegal access to an organization's finances. For example, credit card fraud causes the loss of millions of dollars to credit card management companies like Visa and MasterCard. This motivates organizations to analyze data in order to identify fraud. However, since large amounts of data are necessary for fraud analysis, it becomes difficult for an organization to manually identify fraud from legitimate transactions. This motivates current research in automated analysis of such data, in order to reduce manual screening of individual transactions for fraudulent activity. There are two approaches to reducing fraud - fraud prevention, taking appropriate steps to prevent a fraud from occurring, and fraud detection, identifying fraud as soon as it occurs, thus enabling a quick corrective response. Since it is difficult to predict when a fraud has occurred, fraud detection techniques are usually applied in parallel with fraud prevention techniques (De Decker, 2007).

Fraud Analysis (Case Study)

Ahmed ELAzab (ElAzab. et al, 2015) introduce an approach for detecting fake accounts on Twitter social network, the proposed approach was based on determining the effective features for the detection process. The attributes have been collected from different research, they have been filtered by extensive analysis as a first stage, and then the features have been weighted. Different experiments have been conducted to reach the minimum set of attributes with perceiving the best accuracy results. From more than 22 attributes, the proposed approach has reached only seven effective attributes for fake accounts detection. Although we claim that these attributes can succeed in discovering the fake accounts in other social networks such as Facebook with minor changes according to the unique nature of each social network, however, we need to prepare a dataset to prove our claim. Moreover, providing an analysis to the tweets content of the user can provide more accurate results in the detection process.

Social Media Mining

In general, information extraction is a field that is concerned with obtaining information from different sources. Focusing on online sources such as online databases and web resources services including websites, according of the dynamic nature of the World Wide Web, it became important to find tools for information extraction from the web as end users and application programs have some difficulties when it comes to finding useful information (Alim, Sophia, et al, 2011).

Extracting information from social media had applied different learning approaches as HTML is the common language for implementing Web pages and it is widely supported by The World Wide Web Consortium (W3C). HTML pages can be as a form of semi-structured data in which information follows a nested structure (Ferrara, 2014). This section present different research that have been presented to apply different information extraction approaches on social media.

Culotta, Bekkerman, and McCallumin (Culotta, 2004)had created a system which used the collection of statistical and learning components using real email of two users. In the work of Aron Culotta, et. Al., he depended on the expert-findings, and social network analysis. However,the analysis which is performed by the proposed system lacked a suitable level of reliability and some important information were not considered such as fake email or fake content.

Generally the evolution of technology, supported by global and speedy communication network online Web services, has been growing rapidly which presents new opportunities and challenges to both producers and consumers of information. The volumes of click stream and client information, gathered by web-based associations in their everyday operations, have come to galactic extents. Analysis of such information helps these organizations to focus on the life-time estimation of customers (Mobasher, 2006)

Data mining technique that automatically discovers or extracts the information from web documents in general usually consists of following tasks (Srivastava, Desikan, & Kumar, 2005); (Bhisikar & Sahu, 2013).

- **Resource Finding:** It involves the task of retrieving intended web documents. It is the process by which we extract the data either online or offline resources available on web.
- **Information Selection and Pre-Processing:** It involves the automatic selection and preprocessing of specific information from retrieved web resources. This process transforms the original retrieved data into information. The data is transformed into useful information by using suitable transformation. The transformation could be renewal of stop words, or it may be aimed for obtaining the desired representation such as finding particular format of data.
- **Generalization:** It automatically discovers general patterns at individual web sites as well as across multiple sites. Data Mining techniques and machine learning are used in generalization
- **Analysis:** It involves the validation and interpretation of the mined patterns. It plays an important role in pattern mining. A human plays an important role in information on knowledge discovery process on web

However, in the extraction process, many issues arise for the target of discovering useful information from online pages. One of these issues considering data representation, as website pages can be found in different formats. HTML is designed for present unstructured information, while XML and XHTML are intended for more organized information which elements help the parsers of web crawlers to communicate with the site pages' substance all the more proficiently (Alim, Sophia, et al, 2011)

Production: Shipping and Inventory

Inventory is characterized as the estimation of products available at a certain time case, in an endeavor. Stock can be in distinctive structures like crude material before the company's quality expansion, in procedure amid generation stage, as completed item in its stockroom or in a retail location's conveyance focus holding up to be sold. Stock typically brings about non-esteem added taking care of expenses identified with tied-up capital, protection costs, administration related expense furthermore other outdated stock expenses. Stock administration is characterized as an arrangement of exercises used to do the right stock in ideal spot at perfect time with right amount and right cost. In the accompanying sample application ion, we discuss how Web mining has aided in inventory management (Fernie, 2009)

Predictive Inventory Management in order to help business perform just-in-time inventory, an inventory management system is required to analyze transaction data and accordingly find clusters, each of which is composed of similar items. Since one of significant costs for a business is to maintain an inventory to support sales as well as customers, a successful inventory management helps business decrease cost and increase profit without losing customer satisfaction. An inventory management system should be able to foresee the customers' demand and trends about sale as well; that is, what most customers will buy. (Desikan, P, 2009)

Web Mining in E-Commerce

Ahmad et al, in (Siddiqui, 2013) Tasnim Siddiqui model web mining integrated with the electronic commerce application to improve the performance of e-commerce applications. First Ahmad et al have discussed some important mining techniques which are used in data mining. Then Ahmad et al explained the proposed architecture which contains mainly four components business data, data obtained from consumer's interaction, data warehouse and data analysis. After finishing the task by data analysis

Module it'll produce report which can be utilized by the consumers as well as the e-commerce application owners.

Utilizing Mining to Gain Business Advantages

KFC/Pizza (Al-Azmi, 2013) Hut in Singapore have more than 120 outlets, with a workforce of 5000 Representatives. As a universal fast food establishment, they convey sustenance and refreshments to clients through outlets, drive-through, and by home conveyance. To manage such workload, KFC/Pizza Cabin have utilized a BI instrument; the device was becoming progressively wasteful with every month. Device didn't meet with time necessities to convey business reports. It was additionally had issues with execution benchmarking, in addition to day by day reports over numerous frameworks was dreary. KFC/Pizza Cabin most essential day by day operation was to figure installments required for every day paid laborers, for example, convey staff. The utilized BI instrument, chiefs would take hours and needed to work for additional hours to total up pay accurately. At long last, the old framework reporting was backing off KFC/Pizza Cabin capacity to match and adjust to present and quick changes. Arrangement was to discover another BI apparatus that was present day. KFC/Pizza Hut contracted with Zap, a BI seller, utilizing their item Zap Business Intelligence (Qaqaya, 2008). New arrangement was electronic; it was moreover connected to other outside sources. Corporate information distribution center was rebuilt as to incorporate the point of offers POS, advertising, HR, and the corporate own one of a kind production network. In September 2009, following two month of testing, KFC/Pizza Hut ran live with the new BI apparatus. The workers and administrators were for the most part content with the new instrument. As it was online, and it offered cutting edge BI abilities like dashboards, moment report era, KPI benchmarking, scoreboards, and an extremely easy to understand interface. The advantages of the new device were huge. The change included improved business sector spending, through live upgrades; KFC/Pizza Hut promptly reacted and balanced its promoting effort and offers. Eatery arranging and outlet area administrations were taking into account reports given for the instrument, to adapt to KFC/Pizza Hut procedure of being near its Clients. Client administration was exceptionally enhanced, particularly the home conveyance administration, as the instrument precisely catch the parameters of such conveyances to streamline the conveyance process. In expansion, the POS incorporation into the information distribution center permitted KFC/Pizza Hut to deal with its arrangements what's more, offers per outlet; diverse clients at distinctive areas had exceptionally changed requests.

In brief Web mining extends analysis much further by combining other corporate information with Web traffic data. Practical applications of Web mining technology are abundant, and are by no means the limit to this technology (Arti, 2015). Web mining tools can be extended and programmed to answer almost any question. It can be applied in following areas:

1. Web mining can provide companies managerial insight into visitor profiles, which help top management take strategic actions accordingly.
2. The company can obtain some subjective measurements through Web Mining on the effectiveness of their marketing campaign or marketing research, which will help the business to improve and align their marketing strategies timely.
3. In the business world, structure mining can be quite useful in determining the connection between two or more business Web sites.
4. This allows accounting, customer profile, inventory, and demographic information to be correlated with Web browsing. (Mitta, 2013)
5. Knowledge discovery is obtained from artificial intelligence and machine learning, which uses a datasearch process, to extract information from the data, as well as the relationship between data elements and models from which to discover business rules and business facts. In Knowledge discovery we can use data visualization tools and navigation tools to help developers analyse the data before mining, to further enhance data mining capabilities, visualization systems can be presented with a graphical analysis of multivariate data to help business analysts, knowledge discovery (Arti, 2015).

ADDITIONAL READING

The Deep Web is a part of the internet not accessible to link-crawling search engines like Google. The only way a user can access this portion of the internet is by typing a directed query into a web search form, thereby retrieving content within a database that is not linked. In layman's terms, the only way to access the Deep Web is by conducting a search that is within a particular website.

The Deep Web allows access to my tool box. As Fake ID, Malware, Drugs, Arms, Assassination Services, People trafficking (Kapoor, A., 2011).

The dark Web is the portion of the deep Web that has been intentionally hidden and is inaccessible through standard Web browsers. Dark Web sites serve as a platform for Internet users for whom anonymity is essential, since they not only provide protection from unauthorized users, but also usually include encryption to prevent monitoring. A relatively known source for content that resides on the dark Web is found in the Tor network. The Tor network is an anonymous network that can only be accessed with a special Web browser, called the Tor browser (Tor 2014a). First debuted as The Onion Routing (Tor) project in 2002 by the US Naval Research Laboratory, it was a method for communicating online anonymously.

Another network, I2P, provides many of the same features that Tor does. However, I2P was designed to be a network within the Internet, with traffic staying contained in its borders. Tor provides better anonymous access to the open Internet and I2P provides a more robust and reliable "network within the network" (van Eeten, 2012)The dark web is using for The ability to traverse the Internet with complete anonymity nurtures a platform ripe for what are considered illegal activities in some countries, including controlled substance marketplaces, credit card fraud and identity theft and leaks of sensitive information.

The Dark Web refers to any web page that has been concealed to hide in plain sight or reside within a separate, but public layer of the standard internet. The internet is built around web pages that reference other web pages; if you have a destination web page which has no inbound links you have concealed that page and it cannot be found by users or search engines. One example of this would be a blog posting that has not been published yet. The blog post may exist on the public internet, but unless you know the exact URL, it will never be found. Other examples of Dark Web content and techniques include: Search boxes that will reveal a web page or answer if a special keyword is searched. Try this by searching "distance from Sioux Falls to New York" on Google. Sub-domain names that are never linked to; for example, "internal.brightplanet.com" Relying on special HTTP headers to show a different version of a web page Images that are published but never actually referenced, for example "/image/logo_back. gif" Virtual private networks are another aspect of the Dark Web that exists within the public internet, which often requires additional software to access. TOR (The Onion Router) is a great example. Hidden within the public web is an entire network of different content which can only be accessed by using the TOR network. While personal freedom and privacy are admirable goals of the TOR network, the ability to traverse the internet with complete anonymity nurtures a platform ripe for what is considered illegal activity in some countries, including: Controlled substance marketplaces Armories selling all kinds of weapons Child pornography Unauthorized leaks of sensitive information Money laundering Copyright infringement Credit Card fraud and identity theft Users must use an anonymizer to access TOR Network/ Dark Web websites. The Silk Road, an online marketplace/infamous drug bazaar on the Dark Web, is inaccessible using a normal search engine or web browser (van Eeten, 2012).

FUTURE RESEARCH DIRECTIONS

Web mining techniques were the major functional areas of businesses so Web mining and extract information role important need to be analyze by measure the credibility of information propagated through web.

On the other web mining need to be integrated with the electronic commerce application to improve the performance of e-commerce applications

CONCLUSION

In this chapter, we introduced an overview for web mining, web mining taxonomies, web mining applications, and web mining challenges and limitations. Web usage mining presented in particular, issues of web usage mining, and web usage mining language and algorithms, and finally presented the effectiveness of web usage mining in some area of business such as (Production, Fraud analysis, Business Financial Management, Sales Management, Marketing, Human resource, etc…).

REFERENCES

Aggarwal, Shruti, & Gurpreet. (2013). Improving the Efficiency of Weighted Page Content Rank Algorithm using Clustering Method. *International Journal of Computer Science & Communication Networks, 3*, 231–239.

Aggarwal, S. G. (2013). *Improving the Efficiency of Weighted Page Content Rank Algorithm using Clustering Method.* Academic Press.

Al-Azmi, A. A. (2013). *Data, text and web mining for business intelligence: A survey.* arXiv preprint arXiv:1304.3563

Aldana, W. A. (2000). *Data mining industry: emerging trends and new opportunities.* (Doctoral dissertation). Massachusetts Institute of Technology, Dept. of Electrical Engineering and Computer Science.

Alim, S. (2011). Online social network profile data extraction for vulnerability analysis. *International Journal of Internet Technology and Secured Transactions, 3*(2).

Arti, S. C. (2015). Role of Web Mining in E-Commerce. *International Journal of Advanced Research in Computer and Communication Engineering.*

Bhisikar, P., & Sahu, P. (2013). Overview on Web Mining and Different Technique for Web Personalisation. *International Journal of Engineering Research and Applications, 3*(2).

Bousquet & Wills. (2003). *The Politics of Information The Electronic Mediation of Social Change.* Alt-X Press.

Chaabane, A., Manils, P., & Kaafar, M. A. (2010, September). Digging into anonymous traffic: A deep analysis of the tor anonymizing network. In *Network and System Security (NSS), 2010 4th International Conference on* (pp. 167-174). IEEE. doi:10.1109/NSS.2010.47

Choudhary & Sharma. (2015). Review Paper on Web Content Mining. *International Journal of Research in Engineering and Applied Sciences, 5*(6), 172-176.

Culotta, A. B. (2004). *Extracting social networks and contact information from email and the web.* Academic Press.

De Decker, B. D. (2007). *Advanced Applications for e-ID Cards in Flanders.* Academic Press.

Desikan, P. (2009). *Web Mining for Business Computing.* Academic Press.

El Azab, A., Idrees, A. M., Mahmoud, M. A., & Hefny, H. (2015). Fake Account Detection in Twitter Based on Minimum Weighted Feature set. *World Academy of Science, Engineering and Technology, International Journal of Computer, Electrical, Automation Control and Information Engineering, 10*(1), 13–18.

Ezeife, C. I., & Lu, Y. (2005). Mining web log sequential patterns with position coded pre-order linked wap-tree. *Data Mining and Knowledge Discovery, 10*(1), 5–38. doi:10.1007/s10618-005-0248-3

Fernie, J. (2009). *Logistics and retail management: . emerging issues and new challenges in the retail supply chain.* Kogan Page Publishers.

Ferrara, E. D., De Meo, P., Fiumara, G., & Baumgartner, R. (2014). Web data extraction, applications and techniques. A survey. *Knowledge-Based Systems, 70*, 301–323. doi:10.1016/j.knosys.2014.07.007

Fürnkranz, J. (2002). Web Structure Mining. Exploiting the Graph Structure of the World Wide Web. *Österreichische Gesellschaft für Artificial Intelligence*, 17-26.

Gupta, V., & Lehal, G. S. (2009). A survey of text mining techniques and applications. *Journal of Emerging Technologies in Web Intelligence, 1*(1), 60-76.

Han, J., Cheng, H., Xin, D., & Yan, X. (2007). Frequent pattern mining: Current status and future directions. *Data Mining and Knowledge Discovery, 15*(1), 55–86. doi:10.1007/s10618-006-0059-1

Hassan, H. A. (2014). Query Answering Approach Based on Document Summarization. Query Answering Approach Based on Document Summarization. *International Open Access Journal of Modern Engineering Research, 4*(12).

Hassan, H. D. (2015). Arabic Documents classification method a Step towards Efficient Documents Summarization. *International Journal on Recent and Innovation Trends in Computing and Communication*, 351-359.

Hussein, M. K., & Mousa, M. H. (2010). An Effective Web Mining Algorithm using Link Analysis. *International Journal of Computer Science and Information Technologies, 1*(3), 190-197.

Jaideep Srivastava, R. C.-N. (2000). Web Usage Mining: Discovery and Applications of Usage. *SIGKDD Explorations, 1*(2), 12.

Janssens, F. (2007). *Clustering of scientific fields by integrating text mining and bibliometrics*. Academic Press.

Jiawei Han, K.-C. C. (2002). Data Mining for Web Intelligence. *IEEE International Conference on Data Mining*.

Jiawei Han Kevin, C.-C. C. (2002). *Data Mining for Web Intelligence*. University of Illinois at Urbana-Champaign.

Kaczmarek, T. Z. (2010). Information extraction from web pages for the needs of expert finding. Studies in Logic, Grammar and Rethoric, Logic Philosophy and Computer Science, 141-157.

Kapoor, A., & Solanki, R. (2011). The Susceptible Network. *IITM Journal of Information Technology, 54*.

Kumar & Suvarchala. (2012). A Study: Web Data Mining Challenges and Application for. *IOSR Journal of Computer Engineering, 7*(3), 24-29.

Lancaster, F. W. (2003). *Indexing and abstracting in theory and practice*. London: Facet.

Liu, B. G. (2003). Mining data records in Web pages. In *Proceedings of the ninth ACM SIGKDD international conference on Knowledge discovery and data mining* (pp. 601-606). ACM.. doi:10.1145/956750.956826

Mahmood, A., & Mahmood, E. A.-S.-B. (2013). Recommender system for ground-level Ozone predictions in Kuwait. *IEEE Federated Conference on Computer Science and Information Systems*.

Mahmood, A., & Mahmood, N. E.-B. (2014). An Intel Innovations in Bio-inspired Computing and Applications. Springer.

Masseglia, F. P. (2000). *An efficient algorithm for web usage mining. Networking and Information Systems Journal.*

Mehtaa, P. P. (2012). Web Personalization Concept and Research Issue. *International Journal of Information and Education Technology.*

Mobasher, B. (2006). Web Usage Mining. In *Web Data Mining: Exploring Hyperlinks, Contents and Usage Data.* Academic Press.

Mohamed, F. (2011). Business Intelligence for Emerging e-Business Applications. *Journal of Emerging Technologies in Web Intelligence.*

Mohapatra, R. (2004). *Information extraction from dynamic web sources.* Doctoral dissertation.

Noor, A. B. (2008). Semantic Web: Data Representation. In Partial Fulfillment of the Requirement for the Degree of Master in Information Technology.

Okoli, C., Mehdi, M., & Mesgari, M. (2012). *The people's encyclopedia under the gaze of the sages. A systematic review of scholarly research on Wikipedia.* Academic Press.

Patel, P., Jena, B., & Sahoo, B. (2014). Knowledge Discovery on Web Information Repository. *IJACTA, 1*(2),049-56.

Qaqaya, H. (2008). *The effects of anti-competitive business practices on developing countries and their development prospects.* Academic Press.

Rani, P. (2013). A Review of Web Page Ranking Algorithm. *Revi International Journal of Advanced Research in Computer Engineering & Technology.*

Ravi, K., & Ravi, V. (2015). A survey on opinion mining and sentiment analysis: Tasks, approaches and applications. *Knowledge-Based Systems, 89,* 14–46. doi:10.1016/j.knosys.2015.06.015

Regis, R. (2008). *Strategic human resource management and development.* Excel Books India. Excel Books India.

Samar Mahmoud, N. E.-B. (2013). An Intelligent Recommender System for Drinking Water Quality. *International Conference on Hybrid Intelligent Systems (HIS).*

Shoemaker, P., & Reese, S. D. (2011). *Mediating the message.* Routledge.

Siddiqui, A. T. (2013). *Web Mining Techniques in E-Commerce Applications.* arXiv preprint arXiv:1311.7388

Soley, M. (2003). Culture as an issue in knowledge sharing: A means of competitive advantage. *Electronic Journal of Knowledge Management, 1*(2), 205-212.

Srivastava, J. C., Cooley, R., Deshpande, M., & Tan, P.-N. (2000). Web usage mining: Discovery and applications of usage patterns from web data. *ACM SIGKDD Explorations Newsletter, 1*(2), 12–23. doi:10.1145/846183.846188

Srivastava, T., Desikan, P., & Kumar, V. (2005). Web Mining – Concepts, Applications and Research Directions. Foundations and Advances in Data Mining. *Studies in Fuzziness and Soft Computing*, *180*, 275–307. doi:10.1007/11362197_10

Srivastava, T., Desikan, P., & Kumar, V. (2005). Web Mining – Concepts, Applications and Foundations and Advances in Data Mining. *Studies in Fuzziness and Soft Computing*, *180*, 275–307. doi:10.1007/11362197_10

Stevenson, M., & Greenwood, M. A. (May2006). Learning Information Extraction Patterns Using WordNet.*Proceeding of The Third International WordNet Conference.*

Thirumala Sree Govada, N. L. (2014). Comparative study of various Page Ranking Algorithms in Web Content Mining (WCM). *International Journal of Advanced Research*, *2*(7), 457–464.

van Eeten, M. J., & Mueller, M. (2012). Where is the governance in Internet governance? *New Media & Society*.

Witten, I. H., & Frank, E. (2005). *Data Mining: Practical machine learning tools and techniques*. Morgan Kaufmann.

Yi, L., Liu, B., & Li, X. (2003, August). Eliminating noisy information in web pages for data mining. In *Proceedings of the ninth ACM SIGKDD international conference on Knowledge discovery and data mining* (pp. 296-305). ACM. doi:10.1145/956750.956785

Yu-Hui Tao, T.-P. H.-M. (2007). Web usage mining with intentional browsing data. *International Journal of Expert*.

KEY TERMS AND DEFINITIONS

Data Extraction: Data extraction is a field that is concerned with obtaining information from different online databases and services web resources including websites. According of the dynamic nature of the World Wide Web so it become important to find tools for data extraction. end users and application programs have some difficulties when it comes to finding useful data.

Fraud Analysis: Fraud analysis is a large problem faced by many businesses ranging from the telecommunications industry to Web-based stores. Fraud is defined as the use of false representations to gain an unjust advantage or abuse of an organization's resources, such as illegal access to an organization's finances.

I2P: Was designed to be a network within the Internet, with traffic staying contained in its borders. Tor provides better anonymous access to the open Internet and I2P provides a more robust and reliable "network within the network.

Page Rank: Page Rank is a numeric value that represents how important a page is on the web. Page Rank is the Google's method of measuring a page's "importance." When all other factors such as Title tag and keywords are taken into account, Google uses Page Rank to adjust.

The Deep Web: A part of the internet not accessible to link-crawling search engines like Google. The only way a user can access this portion of the internet is by typing a directed query into a web search form, thereby retrieving content within a database that is not linked. In layman's terms, the only way to access the Deep Web is by conducting a search that is within a particular website.

The GSP Algorithm: GSP algorithm is intended for mining Generalized Sequential Patterns. It extends previous proposal by handling time constraints and taxonomies.

Web Content Mining: Web Content Mining is the process of retrieving the information from web document into more structure forms. It is related to Data Mining because many Data Mining techniques can be applied in Web Content Mining.

Weighted Page Content Rank Algorithm (WPCR): A proposed page ranking algorithm which is used to give a sorted order to the web pages returned by a search engine in response to a user query. WPCR is a numerical value based on which the web pages are given an order.

XGMML: Extensible Graph Markup and Modeling Language) is an XML 1.0 application based on Graph Modeling Language (GML) which is used for graph description. XG-MML uses tags to describe nodes and edges of a graph. The purpose of XGMML is to make possible the exchange of graphs between different authoring and browsing tools for graphs. Theconversion of graphs written in GML to XGMML is straight forward. Using Extensible Stylesheet Language (XSL) with XGMML allows the translation of graphs to different formats.

Chapter 14
Web Harvesting:
Web Data Extraction Techniques for Deep Web Pages

B. Umamageswari
New Prince Shri Bhavani College of Engineering and Technology, India

R. Kalpana
Pondicherry Engineering College, India

ABSTRACT

Web mining is done on huge amounts of data extracted from WWW. Many researchers have developed several state-of-the-art approaches for web data extraction. So far in the literature, the focus is mainly on the techniques used for data region extraction. Applications which are fed with the extracted data, require fetching data spread across multiple web pages which should be crawled automatically. For this to happen, we need to extract not only data regions, but also the navigation links. Data extraction techniques are designed for specific HTML tags; which questions their universal applicability for carrying out information extraction from differently formatted web pages. This chapter focuses on various web data extraction techniques available for different kinds of data rich pages, classification of web data extraction techniques and comparison of those techniques across many useful dimensions.

INTRODUCTION

The information available on the World Wide Web has grown to several zettabytes according to Richard Currier (2013). Estimated size of pages indexed in Google in the last three months is shown in Figure 1. The structured information such as lists and tables containing the target data of interest is embedded in semi-structured web pages which complicates automated extraction.

Many mining applications depend on the data available in this huge repository. The process of automatically retrieving data from websites is known as web data extraction aka Web scraping or Web harvesting. Applications include business intelligence, product intelligence, market intelligence, data analytics, data mashup, meta-search, meta-query etc. Information on WWW is available in different forms. The classification is shown in Figure 2.

DOI: 10.4018/978-1-5225-0613-3.ch014

Figure 1. Size of pages indexed in Google (http://www.worldwidewebsize.com/)

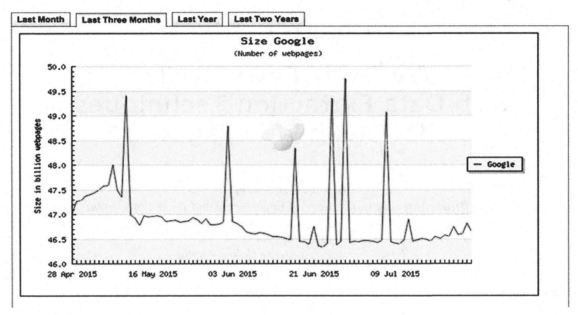

Figure 2. Classification of different forms of information available on WWW

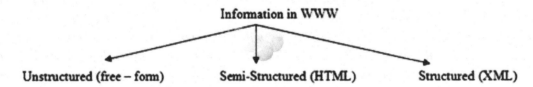

Techniques used for information extraction depends upon the representation of information in WWW. Text mining is a domain which focuses on processing unstructured information. On the other end, extraction of data from structured representation such as XML document can be handled easily using several APIs for ex., JAXP. Our focus is on semi-structured information presented in the form of HTML pages. HTML (Hyper Text Markup Language) is used initially for formatting data and therefore the information is not structured which makes the extraction task cumbersome. Many techniques have been proposed to perform information extraction from HTML pages. Detailed discussion of such techniques is available in the next section.

HTML documents can be represented in various forms. 1. String/Text – Source code of HTML document where a web page is represented using its source code. Certain data extraction tools like OLERA and Trinity etc. use the source code and apply string comparison techniques for information extraction. 2. DOM tree – Many techniques in the literature such as Thresher, DELA, MDR, TPC etc. use DOM tree representation for extraction of information from HTML pages where an HTML page is represented as a tree of HTML elements. 3. Visual (CSS Box) – When the HTML documents are rendered by the browser, each tag is represented as a CSS box. The position and size of box are used by some techniques such as ViDE, ViPER etc for information extraction. 4. Rendered form – it represents the form after being rendered by browsers and tools like Chickenfoot makes use of it for web data extraction which enables user without knowledge in HTML code of the website, to extract data. Figure 3 represents the various representations of HTML documents.

Presentation of Data in HTML Pages

Information is presented in various forms such as tabular form, lists (ordered list, unordered list, definition list, etc.), paragraph, etc. Most of the techniques in the literature are designed for information extraction from a specific presentation format, for ex., Google Set by Tong et al. (2008) is used for extraction from a list, whereas techniques like WWT found by Gupta et al. (2009) are used for information extraction from tabular format and many techniques in the literature such as IEPAD, MDR, OLERA, DELA, DEPTA, ROAD RUNNER etc. are designed for extracting data records. All these formats are in general referred to as web list according to Gatterbauer et al. (2007).

Web List Definition

As defined by Gatterbauer et al. (2007): A list is a series of similar data items or data records. A list is a series of similar data items or data records. A list can be either one-dimensional or two-dimensional; in both variants, no hierarchical or other semantic relationships in between individual list items are implied except for a possible ordering of the items.

Many techniques are designed for information extraction from data rich pages. Therefore, we are going to survey the techniques available for information extraction for different types of data rich pages. There are two types of data rich pages:

Figure 3. Various representations HTML documents

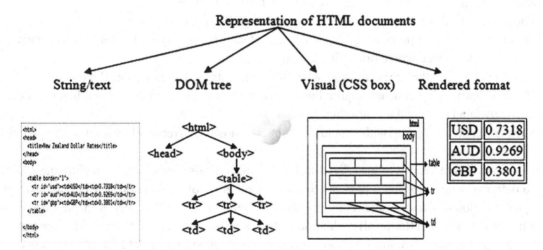

- List pages:
  - Contains a list of one or more data records.
  - Data records may be flat or nested.
  - Similar data records compose a data region.
- Detail pages:
  - Contains details about a single object.
  - Can have relevant as well as other irrelevant information.

Deep vs. Surface Web

Search engines can be used to retrieve pages that are indexed. Crawlers are used to crawl through the links and get the appropriate pages that match the search keywords. All these pages are part of surface web. We get more appropriate information when we do a keyword search in the target web sites directly through form submission. In the back end, the database is queried which results in retrieval of appropriate records which are embedded in HTML template pages and returned to the end user as search results. For ex, book search in Amazon.com using keywords java programming. These template generated web pages are termed as deep web pages and search engines are not capable of retrieving them. Web data extractors play a key role in extracting structured data embedded in template generated web pages which can be fed to many data analytics and data mining applications.

Challenges of Web Data Extraction

Web data extraction systems makes use of techniques derived from Natural Language Processing, Information Retrieval and Machine Learning. Web data extraction system should be applicable to multiple application domains. i.e. it should be domain independent.

Challenges of web data extractors are:

- Requires high degree of human intervention to improve accuracy.
- There exists trade off between level of automation and level of accuracy.
- Should be capable of processing huge volume of data. This is very important for competitive and business intelligence where time critical analysis are done.
- Should not violate the access policies when trying to extract data from social web.
- Machine learning approaches require huge amount of training samples and is a laborious task to manually label them and it is also highly error-prone.
- Should be able to cope up with structural changes that happen frequently with www applications.

This chapter is organized as follows. Section 2 elaborates various state-of-the-art techniques available for web data extraction. Section 3 presents the two broad areas of application of web data extraction techniques. Section 4 discusses the requirements of a web data extractor. Section 5 presents various traditional IR (Information Retrieval) evaluation metrics and custom metrics. Section 6 lists commercial web data extraction tools. Section 7 explores future research directions in the field of web data extraction. Section 8 concludes the chapter.

WEB DATA EXTRACTION TECHNIQUES

General Picture of Web Data Extraction Task

Data in web pages are presented in user-friendly formats and therefore, it is difficult for automated processed to retrieve them, since the structuring of data is done in various ways. The process of extracting data from unstructured or semi-structured web pages and then storing in structured format in RDBMS or other structured file formats such .csv, .xls etc. is known as web data extraction. The general picture of web data extraction is shown in Figure 4.

Data available on world wide web, embedded in HTML pages are referred to as Web data. Web data extraction techniques are broadly classified into two types:

- Data Extraction from free-form text.
- Data Extraction from semi-structured documents.

Data Extraction from Free-Form Text

Tools under this category learn extraction rules and it is used for data extraction from free-form text. All these tools use filtering, POS tagging, semantic tagging in order to determine extraction rules. Most widely used tools in the literature, under this category are:

- **WHISK by Soderland (1999) :** It is a tool which uses training examples for learning a set of extraction rules. It iteratively learns rule starting from the empty set. It requires manual tagging

Figure 4. General picture of web data extraction

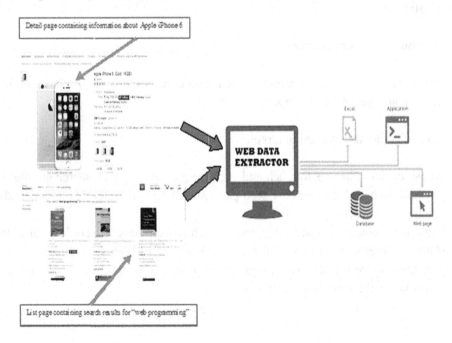

of attributes. Extraction rules are expressed in the form of regular expression and the technique is capable of extracting multiple records from a document.

- **SRV by Freitag et al. (2000) :** This tool can extract only one record from a document. It uses simple or relational token oriented features. Simple feature maps a token to any individual value where as relational feature maps a token to another token. Used for field-level extraction.
- **RAPIER (Robust Automated Production of Information Extraction Rules) by Califf et al. (2003) :** It automatically determines extraction rule when provided the input document and a template indicating the data to be extracted. It extracts only one record of a document. It can be used to perform field-level extraction.

Data Extraction from Semi-Structured Document

Web Pages are written using HTML (HyperText Markup Language). HTML is semi-structured which might introduce error during extraction process.
Possible Errors include:

- Presentation of unstructured data.

Structure or format helps user to easily understand and extract information and it helps data extraction tools greatly to find out target of extraction task. For ex, digital newspaper. Each row has a headline followed by the content or body that contains description of the news. Sophisticated formatting can be done using technologies like CSS which enhances end user view but poses difficulty in automatic extraction.

- Badly constructed HTML documents.

It includes errors such as improper nesting of tags, start tag without end tag etc. HTML pages should follow the W3C standard.

- Missing attributes / optional elements

Some attributes may be missing in certain records and certain elements might be optional. It adds difficulty in arriving at a generalized template.

- Problems in selecting the extraction target.

The page whose content changes for each and every request for ex, web search engine. Ususally we perform a keyword search and the response web page may have some pictures, videos, advertisement etc., depending on the keywords.

This problem can be shown choosing a Web page which content structure could change depending on some factors. One real example of this kind is the resulting page of Web search engines. If we perform a search using an input value we get a result page with some entries. We need to choose the extraction sample such that it keeps the error to a minimum.*f*.

- Problems using scripts or dynamic content.

Dynamic contents can be created using web 2.0 specifications like AJAX, javascript etc. It cannot be treated just like static HTML content because changes happen at any time when the page is loaded. The change can be structural or visual and it may introduce errors during data extraction process which should be taken care of.

Therefore, an ideal web page for data extraction should have the following characteristics:

- It should have structured data representation f.
- HTML code should obey the W3C standard.
- It should not contain nested data elements.
- Used Flash or scripts should not contain data to be extracted f.
- CSS Styles should be used to format elements.

Data Extraction from semi-structured documents can be classified further across four different dimensions:

- Based on the number of input pages it requires.
- Based on the level of human intervention, it requires. (Manual, Wrapper Induction/ semi-supervised, automatic/Unsupervised).
  - **Manually Constructed:** It requires a very high level of human intervention.
  - **Supervised:** Labeled sample is provided based on which wrappers are induced automatically. Therefore, the level of human intervention is high.
  - **Semi Supervised:** Templates are deduced automatically. But human intervention is required for labeling the attributes. Therefore, the level of human intervention is medium.
  - **Unsupervised:** Very little or no human intervention is needed.
- Based on the features or techniques used for data extraction.
- Based on level of extraction.

Level of extraction can be any of these four categories: field-level, record-level, page-level and site-level. The four categories along with the classification of techniques based on level of extraction are shown in Figure 5.

Semi – structured data embedded in web pages are formatted using different HTML tags. We are interested specifically in data regions. Usually, a collection of similar items is formatted as a list using tags such as <OL> (Ordered List), <UL> (Unordered List) and <DL> (Definition List) or as tables (<TABLE>) or as data records using (<DIV>,<SPAN> etc.). In general, they can be referred to as web list according to Gatterbauer et al. (2007).

Representation of Web List and Web List Extraction Techniques

A Web list can be in the form of lists, tables or data records. A web page with different types of web lists is as shown in Figure 6. Navigation list takes us to a similar set of web pages containing data regions of interest. Data region contains one or more data records. Data record contains one or more data items.

Figure 5. Categories of levels of extraction

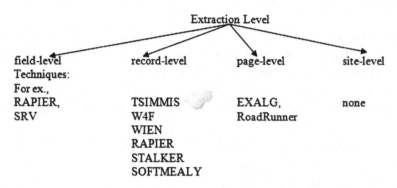

Figure 6. A web page containing different types of web list

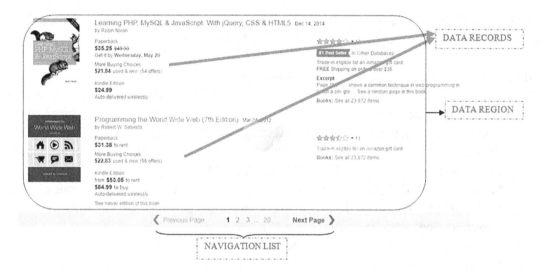

List and Web Tables Extraction Technique

Google Sets by Tong et al. (2002) : This tool is used to generate lists, given a small number of examples of list items. It uses HTML tags to identify lists in a page. It can be used to extract records enclosed within UL, OL, and DL and H1-H6 tags.

Lerman et al. (2001) proposed a technique for automatic data extraction from lists and tables found in web pages. It is based on unsupervised learning algorithm that exploits the regularities found in structure of lists and organization of data for carrying out the extraction task. The limitation of their approach is that the technique requires several pages for identifying list.

Table detection: Wang and Hu (2002) had concluded from their studies genuine tables in most web pages are those enclosed between <table> and </table> tags. They have used a machine learning approach based on layout features, content type feature and word group feature for table detection and extraction.

WWT: This is an unsupervised technique developed by Gupta et al. (2009) for extracting rows from unstructured web lists and to combine multiple lists into a single unified merged table.

Data Region Extractors

Sleiman et al. (2013), have given a detailed survey of several region extractors. The survey is about study of region extractors, along different dimensions such as domain for which it is designed, input to the tool, algorithm used, effectiveness etc. We are going to use that as a foundation for exploring widely used characteristics, when selecting a data extractor for performing IE tasks. Data region consists of a collection of data records. Usually data records are the subject of interest during data extraction. Figure 7 represents an overall classification of data region extractors.

Manually Constructed Extractors/ Web Wrappers

In this category of tools, the user should have profound programming knowledge in order to create wrappers manually using languages such as PERL or specially designed languages.

TSIMMIS by Hammer et al. (1997): In this system, a specification file written using some declarative language which tells where the data of interest is located and how it should be represented as objects, is given as input and it outputs the extracted data in the form of OEM (Object Exchange Model).

W4F by Sahuguet et al. (2001) (World Wide Web Wrapper Factory): It is a JTK used in wrapper generation for which an HTML document from which data need to be extracted is given as input and it outputs NSL (Nested String List) structures. First, the input HTML document is converted into a DOM tree and then extraction rules are applied to the parse tree to obtain NSL structure which is exported to the higher-level application according to the mapping rules.

Supervised Extraction Techniques

It requires comparatively less human intervention compared to previous technique. Here, the user need not manually create a wrapper. Instead, a set of labelled, web pages, is given as input and the system produces wrapper automatically. Some of widely used tools based on this technique are:

WIEN by Kushmerick et al. (1997) (Wrapper Induction for information ExtractioN): In this paper, the authors introduced wrapper induction, which can construct wrappers automatically by generalizing from example query responses. They have used the PAC model which is used in determining bounds on the number of examples needed. They have used oracles for labeling examples. They also used HLRT, a wrapper class designed for retrieving information expressed in tabular form.

SoftMealy by Hsu et al. (1998): Hsu et al. introduced FST (Finite State Transducer) in order to handle variant extraction structures. FST is made of body transducer which is used to extract the data region and tuple transducer for extracting data records within a data region.

Figure 7. Classification of data region extractors

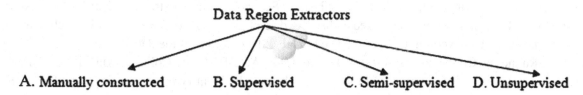

STALKER by Muslea et al. (1999) (Learning Extraction Rules for Semistructured, Web-based Information Sources): This technique is also applicable to differently structured documents and the authors have introduced a concept called Embedded Catalog (EC) formalism. EC of a web page is represented in the form of a tree structure where the leaves represent the attributes to be extracted and the internal nodes represent the list of tuples. It uses a list iteration rule in order to divide the list into individual tuples.

Semi-Supervised Extraction Techniques

Unlike the supervised technique in which labeled examples are needed, these tools require post-effort (i.e. manual labeling after extraction). These techniques are suitable for record-level extraction. User's effort is needed to specify extraction targets using GUI. Therefore, these techniques are classified under semi-supervised extraction techniques.

IEPAD by Chang et al. (2001) (Information Extraction based on PAttern Discovery): This tool is built upon the hypothesis that web pages generated from single server-side template will be having data records structured in a similar way. Thus, this technique uses repetitive patterns to learn template from a set of unlabeled pages. It uses PAT (Pattern Tree) data structure to discover repetitive pattern corresponding to the web page.

OLERA by Chang et al. (2004): It generates extraction rules from roughly labeled examples. It is capable of learning extraction rule, even from a page containing a single data record. This technique uses multiple string alignment technique to find the extraction pattern.

Thresher by Hogue et al. (2005): Users should highlight the data region of interest and label them. It uses tree edit distance, whereas OLERA by Chang et al. (2004) uses string edit distance to find the extraction pattern. Tree edit distance between two trees A and B is the cost associated with the minimum set of operations needed to transform A to B. Here, the set of operations can be node insertion, removal and replacement.

Unsupervised Extraction Techniques

These techniques neither require labeled examples nor user interaction for wrapper induction. Certain un-supervised techniques are used for page-level extraction, such as RoadRunner by Crescenzi et al. (2002), EXALG by Arasu et al. (2003), FivaTech by Kayed et al. (2001) whereas certain others like DeLa Wang et al. (2003) and DEPTA by Zhai et al. (2005) are used for record-level extraction. Since, these techniques do not require user to select data regions of interest, they are extracted automatically by identifying and removing templates. Determining schema is cumbersome and it is up to the user to name the attributes and certain level of post-processing may be needed to obtain the appropriate data.

DeLa (Data Extraction and Label Assignment) by Wang et al. (2003): This tool is capable of extracting nested records and it has two phases: First, it makes use of DSE (Data-rich Section Extraction) by Wang et al. (2002) algorithm which compares DOM trees corresponding two web pages corresponding to same site by removing nodes with similar sub-trees. Secondly, pattern extractor identifies the regular expression. The regular expression is used to discover data objects and then some heuristics such as form element labels and table column names are used to label the columns of the data table.

RoadRunner by Crescenzi et al. (2002): This tool uses ACME (Align, Collapse, Match and Extract) technique in order to induce wrapper from a set of web pages by identifying similarities and differences between them. The outcome of the step is a wrapper which is a pattern used during data extraction.

EXALG (EXtraction ALGorithm): Arasu et al. (2003) presented an approach EXALG for data extraction from template generated web pages which consists of two major steps: i. Differentiating roles and ii. Equivalence classes (EC). According to the authors, if a same token occurs along different paths, then their roles will be different and tokens having the same frequencies of occurrence belong to the same equivalence class. Finally, ECs are used to build the template which is used for data extraction.

DEPTA by Zhai et al. (2005) (Data Extraction Based on Partial Tree Alignment): The authors used visual information for segmenting data records in a web page and used a novel technique called partial tree alignment for extracting data items from identified records. They have used a measure called string edit distance as in OLERA by Chang et al. (2004) for string comparison. The edit distance of two strings, s1 and s2, is defined as the minimum number of mutations required to change one to another where the mutation can be i. change a letter, ii. insert a letter, iii. delete a letter.

MDR by Liu et al. (2004) (Mining Data Records): This technique is used for retrieving data records. It is based on the hypothesis that data records pertaining to similar data objects are formatted using similar HTML tags. It has 3 steps:

- Constructing DOM tree of the page.
- Using a heuristic that each data region should have at least two or more data records with similar structures for data region identification.
- Extracting data records within data regions.

MDR by Liu et al. (2004) is found to be a useful technique in data region extraction and many researchers NET by Liu et al. (2005), ViPER by Simon et al. (2005), PAT by Zhai et al. (2005) used MDR as part of their work.

TPC Miao et al. (2009) (Tag Path Clustering): This technique can be applied only to web pages that satisfy the assumption that a data region should contain data records that are rendered similarly, visually aligned and contain atleast 3 HTML tags. It has the following steps:

- Construct DOM tree and determine DOM paths for every node.
- Determine the triple (p,s,O), where p is a DOM path, s is a visual signal vector which is a binary vector; it contains 1 in position i if the DOM path to the tag at position i is same as p and 0, otherwise and O is a group of individual occurrences of nodes whose DOM path is p.
- Construct a similarity matrix representing visual signals and apply spectral clustering by Ng at al. (2001) to group identical visual signals. Then, find a maximal ancestor for each cluster.
- Identify nested data records using the heuristic that if a visual signal occurs at each point where data records are separated, then the text enclosed by this visual signal represents the relationship between these data records.

STAVIES by Papadakis et al. (2005) (A System for Information Extraction from Unknown Web Data Sources through Automatic Web Wrapper Generation using Clustering Techniques): This technique is used in the automatic data region discovery and data record extraction. It is based on the assumption that the most relevant information is available in leaf nodes and data records have identical structure. HTML code is converted to its strict XHTML version and DOM tree is built. Then, the leaf nodes are extracted and the data region is located by performing hierarchical clustering of leaf nodes and the clusters identified within the data region are returned as data records.

DSE by Wang et al. (2002) (Data-Rich Section Extraction): This technique is based on the assumption that all web pages in a website have similar headers, footers, menus etc. whereas they differ in data regions unless they belong to the same section. After the user provides an input document, then the technique finds a document that can be reached from this document based on a similarity measure computed using URLs. Then, both web pages are transformed into DOM trees. It then, searches for matching node in DOM trees. Removal of those nodes results in two pruned trees constituting data regions. This technique is used in DeLa by Wang et al. (2003).

MSE by Zhao et al. (2006) (Multiple Section Extraction): This technique is based on the assumption that data records in a data region appear consecutively and their content lines are not similar. It is given a set of documents as input. It makes use of two algorithms, namely: Multirecord Extractor (MRE) and Data Section Extractor (DSE) by Wang et al. (2002). MRE is used to discover data regions and DSE by Wang et al. (2002) is used to identify data records composing data regions.

RST by Bing et al. (2011) (Record Segmentation Tree): This technique assumes that similar data records present contiguously form a data region and data records within a data region are formatted using similar tags and they all share a same parent node in the tag tree. The advantage of this technique is that it can handle embedded region and nested region. And also, the authors have introduced a new measure called token-based edit distance. The technique has two major steps, namely record region detection and record segmentation and it determines the similarity between subtrees dynamically and the similarity measure takes into account, the features of the current record region.

FiVaTech by Kayed et al. (2010) (Page-level web data extraction from template pages): It is an unsupervised approach for carrying out page-level extraction task. First, it converts the input web pages to DOM trees. Then, it performs tree merging, which constitutes four steps, namely peer node recognition (i.e. nodes with same names are compared to identify whether they are peer subtrees), multiple string alignment, tandem repeat mining and optional merging. The final step is a schema and template deduction and data extraction.

Trinity by Sleiman et al. (2014) (On Using Trinary Trees for Unsupervised Web Data Extraction): The authors have devised a technique for data extraction based on the hypothesis that templates are shared across web pages and when templates are removed, we get the needed data. The algorithm for construction of trinary tree requires atleast two web pages. It compares the string representation of web pages to find the longest matching substring. The portion of the string before the matching pattern is considered as prefix. The portion of the string in between the matching pattern and its next occurrence is considered as separator and the portion of the string after the matching pattern is considered as suffix. At each step, a node is expanded to the above three nodes. Once the trinary tree is constructed, regular expression is deduced and then, it is used for extracting data.

Table 1 represents the comparison of different data region extraction techniques along different dimensions such as number of input pages required, the level of human intervention needed, features used for data extraction, level of extraction and limitations.

Visual Information Based Extraction Techniques

These techniques utilize several visual clues for data region identification and extraction.

NET by Liu et al. (2005) (Flat and Nested Data Records Extraction): Liu et al. proposed a technique for extraction of both flat and nested records. According to their technique, first a tag tree is built using

Table 1. Comparison of data region extraction techniques across different dimensions

Data Region Extraction Systems	No. of Input Pages Needed	Level of Human Intervention	Features Used for Data Extraction	Limitations	Level of Extraction
TSIMMIS	Single page	Very High, requires sound programming knowledge to write wrappers.	Extraction rules	Requires reconstruction of extraction rule depending upon the structure of the web page	Record-level
W4F	Single Page	Very High, Extraction rules expressed using HEL (HTML Extraction Language) to be written manually.	DOM tree, Extraction rules.	Requires higher level of human intervention.	Record-level
WIEN	Single page	High, Requires manual labeling.	Uses a family of six wrapper classes	Attribute Ordering is required. Therefore, cannot handle missing attributes and permutation of attributes.	Record-level
SOFTMEALY	Single page	High, Requires manual labeling.	Finite State Transducer (FST) for handling missing attributes and attributes permutations.	Cannot handle pages having different structure.	Record-level
STALKER	Single page	High, Requires hand crafting extraction rules.	Uses Node Extraction Rule and List Extraction Rule.	Uses multiple pass scans to handle missing attributes and attributes permutations	Record-level
IEPAD	Single page with multiple records	Medium, Requires manual tagging of extracted template pattern.	PAT trees (binary suffix tree used for identifying repetitive pattern) are used. Center Star Algorithm is used to align strings.	Can be used only for record level extractions. Cannot be used for pages containing single record.	Record-level
OLERA	Single page	Medium, requires labeled examples.	Uses multiple string alignment technique in order to generalize the extraction pattern.	User need to mark the information block of interest.	Record-level
THRESHER	Single page	Medium, requires user highlight the information of interest and label them.	Uses tree edit distance between DOM subtrees for wrapper generation.	Requires substantial manual effort.	Record-level
DELA	Multiple pages with multiple records	Low	DOM trees for Data-rich Section Extraction. Pattern Extractor.	Applicable only for web pages containing more than one data record.	Record-level
ROADRUNNER	Multiple Pages	Low	ACME matching technique is used.	Requires multiple pages for template deduction.	Page-level
EXALG	Multiple Pages	Low	Differentiating roles and equivalence classes (EC) are used.	Requires multiple pages for template deduction.	Page-level
DEPT	Single page with multiple records	Low	HTML TAG tree is used. String Edit Distance is used for substring comparison.	Applicable only for web pages containing more than one data record. Cannot handle nested data records.	Record-level

continued on following page

Table 1. Continued

Data Region Extraction Systems	No. of Input Pages Needed	Level of Human Intervention	Features Used for Data Extraction	Limitations	Level of Extraction
MDR	Single page with multiple records	Low	DOM tree and combinatorial algorithm is used.	Applicable only for web pages containing atleast two or more data records. HTML tag dependent. Does not align data items.	Record-level
TPC	Single page with multiple records	Low	DOM tree and spectral clustering technique are used	Works only for web pages that satisfy the assumption that data records in a data region are rendered similarly and visually aligned and contains atleast 3 HTML tags.	Record-level
STAVIES	Single page with multiple records	Low	DOM tree based. Hierarchical clustering of leaf nodes is done.	Assumes that most information is available in leaf nodes. Suitable only for pages containing identical data record structure.	Record-level
DSE	Single page with multiple records.	Low	DOM tree based.	Requires atleast two web pages with similarly structured data regions.	Page-level
MSE	Multiple pages.	Low	Uses two algorithms: MRE – Multi-Record Extractor and DSE – Dynamic Section Extractor.	Requires atleast two documents.	Record-level
RST	Singe page with two or more records.	Low	DOM tree based. Token-based tree edit distance is used to calculate similarity.	Web page should have more than one data record.	Record-level
FivaTech	Multiple pages containing single or multiple data records.	Low	Tree matching, Tree alignment and mining techniques.	Does not work for malformed HTML pages. Effectiveness highly depends on peer nodes identification.	Page-level
TRINITY	Multiple pages containing single or multiple records.	Low	Trinary tree is obtained by comparing web pages which are used for deducing regular expression.	User has to perform semantic labeling. It does not works well with templates having alternating formatting for the same data.	Record-level

visual clues and then a post-order traversal of tree is performed in order to match sub trees using tree edit distance method and visual clues. Finally, data records are found and data items are aligned.

VIPS by Cai et al. (2003) (VIPS: a Vision-based Page Segmentation Algorithm): This technique uses visual clues such as position, background color, foreground color etc. It involves traversing DOM tree enriched with visual clues and the authors have used 12 heuristics, few to say, if the background color of a node differs from its child nodes then that child is a sub-region; if a table is not having any sub-region, then the adjacent cell also won't be having sub-region and so on. Once sub-regions are identified, they are organized to form tree structure representing the containment relationships and then the tree is returned as output.

VIDE by Liu et al. (2010) (A Vision-Based Approach for Deep Web Data Extraction): It uses Vision based Data Records Extraction technique aka ViDRE by Liu et al. (2006). First, it creates a tree of data regions using VIPS by Cai et al. (2003). Secondly, it finds the largest region present lowest in the tree. Then, the technique groups similar sub-regions using similarity function which is calculated based on features of images, links and text. Then it finds the bounding rectangle for each group. It then creates extraction rule which is given by (x,y,w,h) where x, y represents location of the region and w, h denotes width and height of the bounding box.

ViNTs by Zhao et al. (2005) (Visual Information aNd Tag structure): Learns rules and extract data records from web documents returned by search engine. ViNTs is used for wrapper generation in many search engines for ex., it is used in AllInOneNews by Liu et al. (2007) metasearch engine. Input to the system is set of web pages with atleast four data records and a web page without any data record. First, the input documents are rendered using a browser and css box model of each node is used to extract content lines. A suffix tree is used to find a repetitive pattern that occurs atleast 3 times. Each pattern is used as a separator for dividing the input web page into several regions. It, then learns the extraction rule and finally it selects and merges rules.

Hybrid Information Extraction Techniques

HyLiEn by Fumarola et al. (2011) (Hybrid approach for automatic List discovery and Extraction on the Web): The authors have made a survey of existing list extraction techniques and have shown that existing techniques is not suitable for carrying out general list extraction task by Weninger et al. (2010). They have concluded that DOM based processing alone is insufficient and therefore, they proposed a hybrid approach using visual alignment of list items and non-visual information such as DOM structure of visually aligned items. First, generate the rendered box tree structure for the input web page. Then, generate candidates using visual features and pruning is done using DOM tree structure to eliminate false candidates and finally, list is extracted and returned.

APPLICATIONS

Based on real time applications, Web data extraction techniques can be broadly classified into two types:Organization or Enterprise level techniques and Social web level techniques.

At the organization level, it is useful in performing business engineering, competitive data analysis and helps in making critical business decisions.

At the social web level, it can be used to determine market analysis of human buying behaviors at a large scale. Social media and online social network data can also be analyzed which has significant use in business intelligence, product intelligence and competitive intelligence.

Organization or Enterprise Level Application

Personalized Advertising

End-user will be presented with thematic advertisements along with the content of the web page, ensuring increase in interest towards the advertisement. Ex. Google Adsense.

Customer Help Desk

Usually customer care receives lot of unstructured information in the form of queries, emails, customer phone conversation transcripts, customer review sites etc. Extracting information, classifying and storing them in structured form helps organizations in making important business decisions.

Building Relational Database

It involves collecting information from multiple online sources and integrating them. For ex, Commercial product or services companies want to compare pricing other aspects with their competitors.

Business Intelligence and Competitive Intelligence

Baumgartner et al. (2009) analyzed how to apply Web data extraction techniques and tools to improve market analysis. They discussed about how to acquire the unstructured and semi-structured information using the Lixto Suite and then to perform ETL (Extract, Transform and Load).

Social Applications

Due to the advancements of web 2.0 specifications, many websites evolved which led people to share thoughts, opinions, photos, recipes etc.

Social Networks

Social network consists of millions of people representing relationships between nodes where nodes may represent an entity, groups or organization and edges reprensents relationships between nodes. Ex., Facebook, Twitter, Flikr etc. Social networks are useful to both academic and industrial community. Therefore, Social Networks stay as a field where we can apply web data extraction systems. Applications include obtaining information from relationships between nodes, learning distribution of ties and checking the theory of six degrees of separation, mining patterns from statistical data, finding heuristics. Another interesting application is social bookmarking, a new kind of knowledge sharing, allows user to define hierarchy known as folksonomy and the bookmarks are referred to as tags. Extracting information from social bookmarks is much faster compared to HTML-aware extraction systems

Comparative Shopping

One of the interesting application of Social Web which is used by many commercial organizations is the comparative shopping. It provides a platform to compare prices, features, user experience etc. These services rely on Web data extraction using websites as input.

Mashup Scenarios

A mashup is defined as a website or web application that integrates content of a number of websites of interest. The content is obtained via APIs, embedding RSS or Atom Feeds. To access deep web, complex form queries and web services containing several operations encapsulating application logic can be used.

Opinion Mining

User opinions are expressed in natural language in blogs in the form of reviews, comments, tags, charts etc. Since it is expressed in natural language, they are unstructured and therefore extraction of such information poses serious problem.

Mining of Citation Databases

Web data extraction can be applied to citation databases like Google Scholar, CiteSeer etc. in order to collect scientific digital publications, extract references and citations and build a structured database where users can compare, count number of citations, search etc.

REQUIREMENTS OF A WEB DATA EXTRACTOR

Robust

Web pages structure and content changes frequently and the wrapper should be able to extract data despite those changes. When the wrappers are hand-crafted, we can use the human intelligence to create robust wrappers. In order to create robust wrappers in case of wrapper induction, it should be based on rendered model rathen than source code for ex., class selector, id selector etc.

For ex, consider the following source code,

```
<div id="item" class="content">
 <h3 id="name"> Item Name </h3>
 <div> Dealer <strong id="dealer"> Dealer </strong> </div>
<div> Cost: &rp; <strong id="price"> 100 </strong> </div>
</div>
```

A human developer may decide to use #item (id selector) for selecting the region representing an item rather than class selector .content because ID selector is unique. An induced wrapper won't be able to recognize this and also, different shopping websites may use different names. Thus, induced wrappers should be based on rendered model so that even if the structure and layout changes, the labeling remains the same i.e. price will always be labeled with Price. Technologies like HTML5 contains semantic tags like <time>, <header>, <footer> etc which adds meaning to the document and paves way to design robust wrappers.

Session Management

Web data extractors if integrated onto browser then it handles session management automatically. Session management is needed in websites where multiple requests are made by the client within a session and server wants to keep track of user requests. In case of any disruption, user will be able to proceed from where he has left rather than starting from the scratch. Cookies are small files stored in client machine used for session management. For ex, a client after logging in to a site successfully, the server sends a response which contains cookies that will be stored in the client side. Subsequent requests from the client to the same server includes the stored cookies which are used by the server for identifying the client. In case of disconnection, the server won't ask the client to log on again. When a web data extractor is part of a browser, it need not handle sessions since they will be handled by browser itself whereas if it is itself a HTTP client then it is important that it should support cookies and session management.

Websites with Dynamic Content

Certain websites use scripting languages to present the content dynamically i.e page responds to user initiated events like onmouseover, onmousemove etc. It is easy for designing a wrapper for static web page compared to dynamic web page. In case of dynamic pages, extractor needs to execute scripting code and capture events.

Data Modeling

Extracted data can be structured into different formats such as CSV, XML, RDBMS etc.

Performance

Extractor should not consume too much of resources. Also, it should not be too fast. Otherwise, it results in sending too many requests to the same server resulting in overload which might result in legal action.

User Friendliness

Wrappers should be user friendly. If the end user is not a technical expert, then wrappers should have a rich GUI that helps user in choosing the extraction targets. Certain wrappers require profound programming skills.

$$\text{Prescision (P)} = \frac{tp}{tp + fp} \qquad \text{Recall}\left(R\right) \frac{tp}{tp + fn} \text{ F1 (or) F- measure} = \frac{2PR}{P + R}$$

Table 2. Comparison of visual clue based and hybrid data region extraction techniques across different dimensions

Web Data Extraction Systems	No. of Input Pages Needed	Level of human Intervention	Features Used for Data Extraction	Limitations	Level of Extraction
NET	Single	Low	Post order traversal of visual based tree is used for Flat and Nested record extraction.	Works only for data records.	Record-level
VIPS	Single page with more than one record.	Low	Visual Layout information.	Browser dependent and presence of many small images results in extraction of too many regions.	Record-level
VIDE	Single page with 2 or more records.	Low	Visual rendering of DOM tree boxes, namely AF (Appearance Feature and Layout Feature) are used. Some non-visual information such as same text, frequent symbols and data type are also used.	Cannot handle multi data region deep web pages.	Record-level
ViNTs	Multiple pages with 4 or more records.	Low	Visual rendering of DOM tree boxes.	Cannot be applied to web pages having fewer than 4 data records.	Record-level
HyLiEn	Single page with multiple records.	Low	Visual alignment of items and non-visual information such as DOM structure.	Cannot handle noisy data.	Record-level

Evaluating Accuracy of Web Data Extraction

The data set used for determining efficiency of various web data extraction techniques are not domain specific. Data rich pages from various domains such as real estate, job search, shopping, sports, movies, restaurants etc. are used. Two commonly used metrics in order to evaluate effectiveness of any information retrieval approach are precision and recall. F-Measure is calculated using the precision and recall values. The traditional metrics used for measuring effectiveness of information extractors are shown in Table 4.

Data Sets commonly used include RISE pubic repository, repositories used in EXALG by Arasu et al. (2003) and RoadRunner byCrescenzi et al. (2002) techniques.

For Data Region Extractors

Precision (P) is defined as the ratio of number of regions extracted correctly to the total number of extracted data regions. Recall (R) is defined as the ratio of number of data regions retrieved correctly to the total number of data regions available. F-Measure is defined as weighted harmonic mean of precision and recall. F-Measure aka F1= 2 (P*R)/(P+R).

For List Extractors

Precision (P) is defined as the ratio of number of lists extracted correctly to the total number of lists extracted. Recall (R) is defined as the ratio of number of lists extracted correctly to the total number of lists present in the web page.

Custom Metric

Liu et al. (2010) have proposed a metric called revision in order to measure the performance of an automated extraction algorithm. It represents the percentage of web databases for which the automated extraction solution fails to achieve perfect extraction.

Commercial Web Data Extractors

Table 3 lists the features of various commercial web data extractors:

Table 3. Data extraction tool features

	Input Variables	Script Usage	Output Formats	Complexity	Dynamic Pages	Single / Multiple Pages	Error Treatment	Execution Time	HTML / Other Formats
Dapper	Yes	No	XML, RSS, HTML, Google Gadget, Netvibes Module, PageFlake, Google Maps, Image Loop, Icalendar, Atom Feed, CSV, JSON, XSL, YAML, email	Low	Yes	No	No	Very Good	HTML
XWRAP	No	No	Java	Medium	Yes	No	No	Good	HTML
Lixto	Yes	Yes	XML	Medium	Yes	Yes	No	Very good	HTML
Web Harvest	No	No	XML	Medium	Yes	No	No	Good	HTML
Win Task	By script	Yes	File, Excel, DB	Medium	No	Yes	No	Good	HTML and other formats
Automation Anywhere	No	No	File, Excel, DB, EXE	Low	No	Yes	No	Good	HTML and other formats
Web content extractor	No	No	File, Excel, DB, SQL script File, MySQL script File, HTML, XML, HTTP submit	Low	No	No	No	Poor	HTML

Table 4. Tradional metrics to characterize the effectiveness of information retrieval

Expected		
Extracted	tp – true positive	fp – false positive
	tn – true negative	fn – false negative

Dapper

This tools helps in generating fully server based wrappers and also allows building reusable wrapper repository. It uses ML techniques(Machine Learning) for generation of wrappers and mainly focuses on web pages that can be reached without deep navigation. The tool learns the structure of web page from both positive and negative examples given in the form of labelled web pages and testing is done on similarly structured web pages. Wrappers can be hosted as RESTful web services and can be accessed using web service clients. It also offers commercial APIs.

Denodo6

Denado offers sophisticated GUI for configuring wrappers and allows processing of DOM events while navigating web pages. It supports extraction from deep web pages. It provides a tool called Aracne for document crawling and indexing. It also offers wrapper maintenance functionalities.

Lixto

This tool offers a fully interactive wrapper generation framework. It provides a scalable data transformation environment. It suits well for data extraction from dynamic web applications developed using web 2.0 specifications. It is capable of simulating clicks on DOM elements. Expression Language ELOG is used for data extraction. It can be embedded in Mozilla browser.

Kapowtech

This tool offers a Java-based visual development environment for developing web wrappers. It has a proprietary browser and it has a GUI built on top of a procedural scripting language and stores data in RDBMS.

WebQL

It is a query language used for writing wrappers. WebQL uses HTML DOM tree rather than traditional browser. It also offers IP address anonymization environment.

WinTask

WinTask is a windows tool used for data extraction from websites. It can be used like browser to launch a URL, send userid and password if it is a secure site, perform searches and navigate to web pages which acts as extraction targets. User interaction requires knowing scripts and we need to buy it for unlimited access.

Automation Anywhere

This tool has a sophisticated UI which can record user clicks and movement of mouse. It creates navigation sequence and extract target data. Templates can also be used to realize concrete taks or use the task editor that helps user to create pre-determined action sequences. We need to buy the software to get unlimited access to it.

Web Content Extractor

Allows user to create a project for each extraction site, extracts data and store it in project database. The extracted data can be exported into various formats like txt, HTML, XML, Access and Microsoft Excel (CSV). Only trial version is available as free download. We need to buy the software to get unlimited access just like the previous two softwares.

XWRAP

This tool has a toolkit which has three components: Object and Element Extraction, filter interface extraction and code generation. To use this tool, user need to enter the URL of target website and it also supports customization of extraction process. We need a Java web server like Apache Tomcat to launch XWRAP.

Webharvest

Webharvest is a java based open source web data extraction tool. This tool can be used to collect web pages and extract data from them. It makes use of well established web technologies shuch as XSLT, XQuery and Regular expressions. It is helpful for extraction of data from HTML or XML based websites which constitue the major part of World Wide Web.

FUTURE RESEARCH DIRECTIONS

Generic Web Data Extraction

Manual labeling is tedious and cumbersome task and therefore fully automated web data extraction is of interest to many users. Research challenges in this direction are:

1. How to make accurate extraction of need data (i.e. to how to deal with false positives).
2. How to deal with exponentially increase in size of extraction targets.
3. How to bring in semantic knowledge to the extraction process in order to improve accuracy.

Auto-Adapting Wrappers

Wrappers should get automatically adapted to change in layout and code change of web pages. Auto-adapting wrappers should be capable of healing from such changes by using the knowledge of previous versions of web pages. It should be capable of repairing extraction rules accordingly.

Wrapping from Visual Layouts

Many wrappers were based on HTML code or DOM tree structure and there are few recent approaches which makes use of CSS box model i.e. visual rendering of web pages in browser and it is useful when the extraction targets are layout oriented such as web tables and it also allows creation of domain independent wrappers.

Data Extraction from Non-HTML File Formats

Deducing wrappers for documents in formats like PDF and PostScript is of interest in the recent years. It is guided by visual reasoning process over white space and Gestalt theory which is completely different from designing wrappers for web pages and it can also use algorithms from document understanding community.

Learning to Deal with Web Interactions

The tool can be enhanced with automatic recording of user interactions, making use of efficient wrapping languages which helps in recording, executing and generalizing macros of web interactions so that it models the workflow integration process. Ex. Booking a ticket transaction.

Web Form Understanding and Mapping

To deal with deep web pages, wrappers must be capable of filling out complex web search forms and usage of query interfaces. Such systems should be capable of understanding different form element types, contents and labels and map them to corresponding meta form and vice versa. It should be capable of learning abstract representation of search forms.

CONCLUSION

Customized web documents makes data extraction task cumbersome. This motivated several researchers in designing state-of-the-art techniques for extraction of information from data rich pages. Many data mining and data analytics applications are fed using data, extracted from WWW. Data rich pages are organized in two different ways: i. Detail pages containing information about a single object of interest ii. List pages formatted as tables, data regions containing data records or unordered/ordered lists. Chang et al. (2006) and Laender et. al (2002) have surveyed several state-of-the-art approaches available for information extraction whereas Sleiman et. al (2013) have paid attention to techniques used for data region extraction. This chapter is about techniques available for web data extraction from any sort of data rich pages, need not be specifically data regions. And therefore, it also elaborates on techniques available for list extraction. Finally, comparison of all the above techniques based on dimensions such as the number of input pages needed, level of human intervention, features used for data extraction, level of extraction and limitations had been done. The following are the concluding remarks of this chapter:

- Most of the data rich region extractors rely on DOM tree / Visually rendered tag tree. Therefore, these techniques are applicable only for web pages formatted using HTML.
- There are four classes of information extractors: hand-crafted, supervised, semi-supervised and unsupervised. Much of the research focus is on unsupervised technique because human intervention makes the extraction process time-consuming, specific and error-prone.
- It is very difficult to compare the techniques because evaluation is done on different data sets. Developing data set repository in order to make a fair evaluation of various techniques is required.
- Customizing and personalizing web pages using fast developing web technologies imposes difficulty in carrying out extraction task and therefore, developing an extraction technique that goes well with all, differently formatted web pages is still an active research topic.

REFERENCES

Arasu, A., & Garcia-Molina, H. (2003). Extracting structured data from Web pages.*Proceedings of the ACM SIGMOD International Conference on Management of Data*.

Baumgartner, R., Gatterbauer, W., & Gottlob, G. (2009). Web data extraction system. Encyclopedia of Database Systems, 3465-3471.

Bing, L., Lam, W., & Gu, Y. (2011). Towards a Unified Solution: Data Record Region Detection and Segmentation.*Proc. 20th ACM Int'l Conf. Information and Knowledge Management (CIKM)*. doi:10.1145/2063576.2063761

Bolin, M. (2005). *End-user programming for the web*. (Master's thesis). Massachusetts Institute of Technology.

Cai, D., Yu, S., & Wen, J.-R. Ma & W.-Y. (2003). Extracting Content Structure for Web Pages based on Visual Representation. In *Proc. Fifth Asia Pacific Web Conf.(APWeb)*.

Califf, M., & Mooney, R. (2003). Bottom-up Relational Learning of Pattern Matching Rules for Information Extraction. *Journal of Machine Learning Research*, 177–210.

Chang, C.-H., Kayed, M., Girgis, M. R., & Shaalan, K. F. (2006). A Survey of Web Information Extraction Systems. *IEEE Transactions on Knowledge and Data Engineering*, *18*(10), 1411–1428. doi:10.1109/TKDE.2006.152

Chang, C.-H., & Kuo, S.-C. (2004). OLERA: A Semi-Supervised Approach for Web Data Extraction with Visual Support. *IEEE Intelligent Systems*, *19*(6), 56–64. doi:10.1109/MIS.2004.71

Chang, C.-H., & Lui, S.-C. (2001). IEPAD: Information Extraction based on Pattern Discovery.*Proceedings of the Tenth International Conference on World Wide Web (WWW), Hong-Kong*. doi:10.1145/371920.372182

Crescenzi, V., Mecca, G., & Merialdo, P. (2002). *Roadrunner: Automatic Data Extraction from Data-Intensive Websites*. SIGMOD. doi:10.1145/564691.564778

Currier. (2013). *The amount of data generated worldwide will reach four zettabytes*. Retrieved May 19,2015 from https://vsatglobalseriesblog.wordpress.com/2013/06/21/in-2013-the-amount-of-data-generated-worldwide-will-reach-four-zettabytes/

Estimated size of Google's index. (n.d.). Retrieved August 1, 2015, from http://www.worldwidewebsize.com/

Freitag, D. (2000). Machine Learning for Information Extraction from Informal Domains. *Machine Learning*, *39*(2/3), 169–202. doi:10.1023/A:1007601113994

Fumarola, F., Weninger, T., Barber, R., Malerba, D., & Han, J. (2011). Extracting general lists from web documents: A hybrid approach. *IEA/AIE,* (1), 285–294.

Gatterbauer, W., Bohunsky, P., Herzog, M., Krupl, B., & Pollak, B. (2007). *Towards Domain-Independent Information Extraction from Web Tables*. New York: ACM.

Gupta, R., & Sarawagi, S. (2009). *Answering table augmentation queries from unstructured lists on the web*. PVLDB.

Hammer, J., McHugh, J., & Gracia-Molina, H. (1997). Semistructured data: The TSIMISS experience. *Proceedings of the First East-Europen Symposium on Advances in Databases and Information Systems*.

Hogue, A., & Karger, D. (2005). Thresher: Automating the Unwrapping of Semantic Content from the World Wide.*Proceedings of the 14th International Conference on World Wide Web (WWW)*. doi:10.1145/1060745.1060762

Hsu, C.-N., & Dung, M. (1998). Generating Finite-State Transducers for Semi-Structured Data Extraction from the Web. *Journal of Information Systems*, *23*(8), 521–538. doi:10.1016/S0306-4379(98)00027-1

Kayed, M., & Chang, C.-H. (2010). FiVaTech: Page-level web data extraction from template pages. *IEEE Transactions on Knowledge and Data Engineering*, *22*(2), 249–263. doi:10.1109/TKDE.2009.82

Kushmerick, N., Weld, D., & Doorenbos, R. (1997). Wrapper Induction for Information Extraction. *Proceedings of the Fifteenth International Conference on Artificial Intelligence*.

Laender, F.-H.-A., Ribeiro-Neto, B.-A., da Silva, A.-S., & Teixeria, J.-S. (2002). A Brief Survey of Web Data Extraction Tools. *ACM SIGMOD*, *31*(2), 84–93. doi:10.1145/565117.565137

Lerman, K., Knoblock, C., & Minton, S. (2001). Automatic Data Extraction from Lists and Tables in Web Sources.*Proceedings of the workshop on Advances in Text Extraction and Mining (IJCAI-2001)*.

Liu, B., Grossman, R.-L., & Zhai, Y. (2004). Mining Web Pages for Data Records. *IEEE Intelligent Systems*, *19*(6), 49–55. doi:10.1109/MIS.2004.68

Liu, B., & Zhai, Y. (2005). NET – A System for Extracting Web Data from Flat and Nested Data Records. *WISE, 2005*, 487–495.

Liu, K.-L., Meng, W., Qiu, J., Yu, C.-T., Raghavan, V., Wu, Z., & Zhao, H. et al. (2007). AllInOneNews: Development and Evaluation of a Large-Scale News Metasearch Engine.*Proceedings ACM SIGMOD International Conference Management of Data.* doi:10.1145/1247480.1247601

Liu, W., Meng, X., & Meng, W. (2006). Vision-Based Web Data Records Extraction. *ProceedingsInternational Workshop Web and Databases (WebDB).*

Liu, W., Meng, X., & Meng, W. (2010). ViDE: A Vision based approach for Deep Web Data Extraction. *IEEE Transactions on Knowledge and Data Engineering, 22*(3), 447–460. doi:10.1109/TKDE.2009.109

Miao, G., Tatemura, J., Hsiung, W.-P., Sawires, A., & Moser, L. E. (2009). Extracting Data Records from the Web using Tag Path Clustering.*Proceedings International Conference World Wide Web (WWW).* doi:10.1145/1526709.1526841

Muslea, I., Minton, S., & Knoblock, C. (1999). A Hierarchical Approach to Wrapper Induction.*Proceedings of the Third International Conference on Autonomous Agents* (AA-99). doi:10.1145/301136.301191

Ng, A.-Y., Jordan, M.-I., & Weiss, Y. (2001). *On Spectral Clustering:Analysis and an Algorithm. In Proceedings Neural Information Processing Systems* (pp. 849–856). NIPS.

Papadakis, N., Skoutas, D., Topoulos, K.-R., & Varvarigou, T.-A. (2005). STAVIES: A System for Information Extraction from Unknown Web Data Sources through Automatic Web Wrapper Generation using Clustering Techniques. *IEEE Transactions on Knowledge and Data Engineering, 17*(12), 1638–1652. doi:10.1109/TKDE.2005.203

RISE: Repository of Online Information Sources Used in Information Extraction Tasks. (n.d.). Retrieved May 19,2015 from http://www.isi.edu/integration/RISE/

Sahuguet, A., & Azavant, F. (2001). Building Intelligent Web Applications using Lightweight Wrappers. *IEEE Transactions on Data and Knowledge Engineering, 36*(3), 283–316. doi:10.1016/S0169-023X(00)00051-3

Simon, K., & Lausen, G. (2005). ViPER: Augmenting Automatic Information Extraction with Visual perceptions.*Proceedings 14th ACM International Conference on Information and Knowledge Management (CIKM).* doi:10.1145/1099554.1099672

Sleiman, H.-A., & Corchuelo, R. (2013). A survey of region extractors from web documents. *IEEE Transactions on Knowledge and Data Engineering, 25*(9), 1960–1981. doi:10.1109/TKDE.2012.135

Sleiman, H.-A., & Corchuelo, R. (2014). Trinity: On Using Trinary Trees for Unsupervised Web Data Extraction. *IEEE Transactions on Knowledge and Data Engineering, 26*(6), 1544–1556. doi:10.1109/TKDE.2013.161

Soderland, S. (1999). Learning information extraction rules for semi-structured and free text. *Machine Learning, 34*(1-3), 233–272. doi:10.1023/A:1007562322031

Tong, S., & Dean, J. (2008). *System and methods for automatically creating lists.* US Patent: 7350187.

Wang, J., & Lochovsky, F.-H. (2002). Data-Rich Section Extraction from HTML Pages. *Proceedings of the Third International Conference on Web Information Systems Engineering (WISE).*

Wang, J., & Lochovsky, F.-H. (2003). Data extraction and Label Assignment for Web databases. *Proceedings of the Twelfth International Conference on World Wide Web (WWW).* doi:10.1145/775152.775179

Wang, Y., & Hu, J. (2002), A.machine learning based approach for table detection on the web. *Eleventh International World Wide Web Conference.* doi:10.1145/511446.511478

Weninger, T., Fumarola, F., Barber, R., Han, J., & Malerba, D. (2010). Unexpected Results in Automatic List Extraction on the web. *SIGKDD Explorations, 12*(2).

Zhai, Y., & Liu, B. (2005). Web Data Extraction Based on Partial Tree Alignment. *Proceedings of the 14th International Conference on World Wide Web (WWW).* doi:10.1145/1060745.1060761

Zhao, H., Meng, W., Wu, Z., Raghavan, V., & Yu, C.-T. (2005). Fully Automatic Wrapper Generation for Search Engines. *Proceedings of the International Conference on World Wide Web (WWW).* doi:10.1145/1060745.1060760

Zhao, H., Meng, W., & Yu, C.-T. (2006). Automatic Extraction of Dynamic Record Sections from Search Engine Result Pages. *Proceedings of the 32nd International Conference on Very Large Data Bases (VLDB).*

ADDITIONAL READING

Cohen, W. W. (2003). Learning and discovering structure in web pages. *IEEE Data Eng. Bul.,* (26), pp. 3–10.

Embley, D.-W., Campbell, D.-M., Jiang, Y.-S., Liddle, S.-W., Ng, Y.-K., Quass, D., & Smith, R.-D. (1999). Conceptual model-based data extraction. *Journal Data & Knowledge Engineering, 31*(3), 227–251. doi:10.1016/S0169-023X(99)00027-0

Gupta, S., Kaiser, G., Neistadt, D., & Grimm, P. (2003). DOM based Content Extraction of HTML Documents. *WWW '03 Proceedings of the 12th international conference on World Wide Web,* pp. 207 – 214.

Hu, Y., Xin, G., Song, R., Hu, G., Shi, S., Cao, Y., & Li, H. (2005). Title Extraction from bodies of HTML documents and its application to web page retrieval. *SIGIR '05 Proceedings of the 28th annual international ACM SIGIR conference on Research and development in information retrieval,* pp. 250–257.

Mantratzis, C., Orgun, M., & Classidy, S. (2005). Separating XHTML content from navigation clutter using DOM-structure block analysis. *HYPERTEXT '05 Proceedings of the sixteenth ACM conference on Hypertext and hypermedia,* pp. 145 – 147.

Weninger, T., Hsu, H.-W., & Han, J. (2010). CETR: Content Extraction via Tag Ratios. *Proceedings of the 19th International Conference on World Wide Web,* pp. 971-980. doi:10.1145/1772690.1772789

Zhang, Y., Mukherjee, R., & Soetarman, B. (2012). Concept Extraction for Online Shopping. *ICEC'12 Proceedings of the 14th Annual International Conference on Electronic Commerce,* pp. 48 – 53.

Ziegler, C.-N., Vogele, C., & Viermetz, M. (2009). Distilling Informative Content from HTML News Pages. *WI-IAT '09 Proceedings of the 2009 IEEE/WIC/ACM International Joint Conference on Web Intelligence and Intelligent Agent Technology,* (01), pp. 707 – 712.

KEY TERMS AND DEFINITIONS

DOM Tree: Nodes of documents like HTML, XML etc. are organized in the form of tree structure called DOM tree and the tree structure can be accessed by using Document Object Model API.

Hyper Text Markup Language: A semistructured format for defining content of webpages in WWW.

Information Retrieval: A process of obtaining information resources relevant to an information need from the collection of resources.

Precision: Precision indicates what proportion of the retrieved documents is relevant.

Recall: Recall indicates what proportion of all the relevant documents have been retrieved from the collection.

Resilience: It is defined as the ability to withstand change.

Server-Side Template: HTML template used in server-side for generating web pages, by embedding data records retrieved from database.

Supervised: It is a method which requires manually labeled training samples for web data extraction.

Unsupervised: This method automatically deduces the template for data extraction and makes use of it for data extraction.

Web Harvesting: The process of automatically retrieving data from websites is known as web harvesting or web scraping.

Web Wrapper: A procedure, that might implement one or many different classes of algorithms, which seeks and finds data required by a human user, extracting them from unstructured (or semistructured) Web sources, and transforming them into structured data, merging and unifying this information for further processing, in a semi-automatic or fully automatic way.

Compilation of References

Aarti, S. (2014). Data Warehousing & Data Mining Is - A New Paradigm for Good E-Governance. *Asian Journal of Technology & Management Research.*

Abe, K., Taketa, T., Nunokawa, H., & Shiratori, N. (2001). An effective search method for distributed information systems using a self-organizing information retrieval network. *Electronics and Communications in Japan (Part I Communications), 84*(3), 29–37.

Abhishek, T., & Chauhan, R.K. (2011). Knowledge Discovery in Databases-An Introduction to Data Mining. New Delhi: Galgotia Publications.

Ackland, R., Gibson, R., Lusoli, W., & Ward, S. (2010). Engaging with the public? Assessing the online presence and communication practices of the nanotechnology industry. *Social Science Computer Review, 28*(4), 443–465.

Adachi, F., Washio, T., Fujimoto, A., Motoda, H., & Hanafusa, H. (2005). Multi-structure information retrieval method based on transformation invariance. *New Generation Computing, 23*(4), 291–313.

Adnan, M., Nagi, M., Kianmehr, K., Tahboub, R., Ridley, M., & Rokne, J. (2011). Promoting where, when and what? An analysis of web logs by integrating data mining and social network techniques to guide ecommerce business promotions. *Social Network Analysis and Mining, 1*(3), 173–185.

Adomavicius, G., & Tuzhilin, A. (2005). Toward the next generation of Recommender systems: A survey of the state-of-the-art & possible extensions. *IEEE Transactions on Knowledge and Data Engineering, 17*(6), 734–749. doi:10.1109/TKDE.2005.99

Aggarwal, S. G. (2013). *Improving the Efficiency of Weighted Page Content Rank Algorithm using Clustering Method.* Academic Press.

Aggarwal, Shruti, & Gurpreet. (2013). Improving the Efficiency of Weighted Page Content Rank Algorithm using Clustering Method. *International Journal of Computer Science & Communication Networks, 3,* 231–239.

Agichtein, E., Brill, E., Dumais, S., & Ragno, R. (2006). Learning user interaction models for predicting web search result preferences. In *Proceedings of the 29th annual international ACM SIGIR conference on Research & development in information retrieval*(pp. 3-10). doi:10.1145/1148170.1148175

Agosti, M., Crivellari, F., & Di Nunzio, G. M. (2012). Web log analysis: A review of a decade of studies about information acquisition, inspection and interpretation of user interaction. *Data Mining and Knowledge Discovery, 24*(3), 663–696.

Agrawal, R., & Mehta, M. (1996). *SPRINT: A scalable parallel classifier for data mining.* Paper presented at the 22nd International Conference on Very Large Databases (VLDB 1996), Mumbai, India.

Agrawal, R., & Srikant, R. (1995). *Mining sequential patterns*. Paper presented at the 11th International Conference on Data Engineering (ICDE 1995), Taipei, Taiwan.

Akbar, T., & Ha, S. (2011). Landslide hazard zoning along Himalaya Kaghan Valley of Pakistan-by integration of GPS, GIS, and remote sensing technology. *Landslides*, *8*(4), 527–540. doi:10.1007/s10346-011-0260-1

Al-Azmi, A. A. (2013). *Data, text and web mining for business intelligence: A survey*. arXiv preprint arXiv:1304.3563

Aldana, W. A. (2000). *Data mining industry: emerging trends and new opportunities*. (Doctoral dissertation). Massachusetts Institute of Technology, Dept. of Electrical Engineering and Computer Science.

AleEbrahim, N., & Fathian, M. (2013). Summarising customer online reviews using a new text mining approach. *International Journal of Business Information Systems*, *13*(3), 343–358.

Aleotti, P., & Chowdhury, R. (1999). Landslide hazard assessment: Summary review and new perspectives. *Bulletin of Engineering Geology and the Environment*, *58*(1), 21–44. doi:10.1007/s100640050066

Al-Hassan, A. A., Alshameri, F., & Sibley, E. H. (2013). A research case study: Difficulties and recommendations when using a textual data mining tool. *Information & Management*, *50*(7), 540–552.

Alim, S. (2011). Online social network profile data extraction for vulnerability analysis. *International Journal of Internet Technology and Secured Transactions*, *3*(2).

Al-Kassab, M. (2009). A Monte Carlo Comparison between Ridge and Principal Components Regression Methods. *Applied Mathematical Sciences*, *3*(42), 2085–2098.

Al-Maskari, A., & Sanderson, M. (2010). A review of factors influencing user satisfaction in information retrieval. *Journal of the American Society for Information Science and Technology*, *61*(5), 859–868.

Al-Sabhan, W., Mulligan, M., & Blackburn, G. A. (2003). A real-time hydrological model for flood prediction using GIS and the WWW. *Computers, Environment and Urban Systems*, *27*(1), 9–32. doi:10.1016/S0198-9715(01)00010-2

Alvin, R. C. (2002). *Methods of Multivariate Analysis* (2nd ed.). Wiley Interscience.

Amado, N., Gama, J., & Silva, F. (2003). Exploiting Parallelism in Decision Tree Induction. *7th European Conference on Principles and Practice of Knowledge Discovery in Databases*.

Amemiya, T. (1985). *Advanced Econometrics*. Cambridge, MA: Harvard University Press.

Anderson, Lew, & Peterson. (2003). Evaluating Predictive Models of Species' Distributions: Criteria for Selecting Optimal Models. *Ecological Modeling, 162,* 211-232.

Andreou, I., & Sgouros, N. M. (2005). Computing, explaining visualizing shape similarity in content-based image retrieval. *Information Processing & Management*, *41*(5), 1121–1139. doi:10.1016/j.ipm.2004.08.008

Andrzejak, A., Langner, F., & Zabala, S. (2013). Interpretable models from distributed data via merging of decision trees. *2013 IEEE Symposium on Computational Intelligence and Data Mining (CIDM)*. doi:10.1109/CIDM.2013.6597210

Antonio, G., & Alessio, S. (2005). The indexable web is more than 11.5 billion pages. *Special interest tracks & posters of the 14th International Conference on World Wide Web*.

Anyanwu, M., & Shiva, S. (2009). Application of Enhanced Decision Tree Algorithm to Churn Analysis. *2009 International Conference on Artificial Intelligence and Pattern Recognition (AIPR-09)*.

Arasu, A., & Garcia-Molina, H. (2003). Extracting structured data from Web pages. *Proceedings of the ACM SIGMOD International Conference on Management of Data*.

Arbee, L. P., Wu, & Chen. (2001). Enabling personalized recommendation on the web based on user interests & behaviors. In *11th International Workshop on research Issues Data Engineering*.

Arbelaitz, O., Gurrutxaga, I., Lojo, A., Muguerza, J., Perez, J. M., & Perona, I. (2013). Web usage and content mining to extract knowledge for modelling the users of the Bidasoa Turismo website and to adapt it. *Expert Systems with Applications*, *40*(18), 7478–7491.

Arora, M. K., Das Gupta, A. S., & Gupta, R. P. (2004). An artificial neural network approach for landslide hazard zonation in the Bhagirathi (Ganga) Valley, Himalayas. *International Journal of Remote Sensing*, *25*(3), 559–572. doi:10.1080/0143116031000156819

Arora, S. K., Youtie, J., Shapira, P., Gao, L., & Ma, T. T. (2013). Entry strategies in an emerging technology: A pilot web-based study of graphene firms. *Scientometrics*, *95*(3), 1189–1207.

Arti, S. C. (2015). Role of Web Mining in E-Commerce. *International Journal of Advanced Research in Computer and Communication Engineering*.

Arun, K. S., & Menon, H. P. (2009). Content based medical image retrieval by combining rotation invariant contourlet features and fourier descriptors. *International Journal of Recent Trends in Engineering*, *2*(2).

Ashrafi, M. Z., Taniar, D., & Smith, K. (2004). ODAM: An Optimal Distributed Association Rule Mining Algorithm. *IEEE Distributed Systems Online*, *5*(3), 1541–4922. doi:10.1109/MDSO.2004.1285877

Asllani, A., & Lari, A. (2007). Using genetic algorithm and multiple criteria web-site optimizations. *European Journal of Operational Research*, *176*(3), 1767–1777.

Auf der Heide, E. (1989). Disaster Response: Principles of Preparation and Coordination, Mosby. Online Book. Retrieved from http://coe-dmha.org/dr

Ayalew, L., & Yamagishi, H. (2005). The application of GIS-based logistic regression for landslide susceptibility mapping in the Kakuda-Yahiko Mountains, Central Japan. *Geophysical Journal of the Royal Astronomical Society*, *65*, 15–31.

Babbar, P., & Jain, P. K. (2007). E-Governance in India. *ICOLIS 2007 Kuala Lumpur. LISU FCSIT*, *2007*, 363–371.

Baeza-Yates, R. (2004). Web usage mining search engines. In *Web mining: Applications & techniques* (pp. 307-321). Academic Press.

Baeza-Yates, R., Carlos, H., & Marcelo, M. (2005). Query recommendation using query logs in search engines. In Current Trends in Database Technology-EDBT 2004 Workshops(pp. 588-596).

Baik, S., & Bala, J. (2004). *A Decision Tree Algorithm For Distributed Data Mining*. Academic Press.

Balsubramani, K., & Kumaraswamy, K. (2013). Application of geospatial technology and information value technique in landslide hazard zonation mapping: A case study of Giri Valley, Himachal Pradesh. *Disaster Advances*, *6*, 38–47.

Baraglia, R., Carlos, C., Debora, D., Franco Maria, N., Raffaele, P., & Fabrizio, S. (2009). Aging effects on query flow graphs for query suggestion. In *Proceedings of the 18th ACM conference on Information & knowledge management*(pp. 1947-1950). doi:10.1145/1645953.1646272

Baroň, I., & Supper, R. (2013). Application and reliability of techniques for landslide site investigation, monitoring and early warning—outcomes from a questionnaire study. *Natural Hazards and Earth System Sciences*, *13*(12), 3157–3168. doi:10.5194/nhess-13-3157-2013

Barredo, J. I., Benavides, A., Hervas, J., & Van Westen, C. J. (2000). Comparing heuristic landslide hazard assessment techniques using GIS in the Tirajana basin, Gran Canaria Island, Spain. *International Journal of Applied Earth Observation and Geoinformation*, *2*(1), 9–23. doi:10.1016/S0303-2434(00)85022-9

Barros, R. C., Cerri, R., Jaskowiak, P. A., & de Carvalho, A. (2011). A Bottom-up Oblique Decision Tree Induction Algorithm. In *Intelligent Systems Design and Applications (ISDA),201111th International Conference on.*

Bashir, S., & Rauber, A. (2011). On the relationship between query characteristics and IR functions retrieval bias. *Journal of the American Society for Information Science and Technology*, *62*(8), 1515–1532.

Battistini, A., Segoni, S., Manzo, G., Catani, F., & Casagli, N. (2013). Web data mining for automatic inventory of geohazards at national scale. *Applied Geography (Sevenoaks, England)*, *43*, 147–158.

Bauer, E., & Kohavi, R. (1999). An empirical comparison of voting classification algorithms: Bagging, Boosting and variants. *Machine Learning*, *36*(1/2), 105–139. doi:10.1023/A:1007515423169

Baumgartner, R., Gatterbauer, W., & Gottlob, G. (2009). Web data extraction system. Encyclopedia of Database Systems, 3465-3471.

Baum, R. L., Savage, W. Z., & Godt, J. W. (2002). U.S. geological survey open-file report:Vol. 02. *TRIGRS—a Fortran program for transient rainfall infiltration and grid-based regional slope stability analysis* (p. 424).

Bayir. (n.d.). *A New Reactive Method for Processing Web Usage Data*. Retrieved from http://etd.lib.metu.edu.tr/upload/12607323/index.pdf

Bayir, M. A., Toroslu, I. H., Demirbas, M., & Cosar, A. (2012). Discovering better navigation sequences for the session construction problem. *Data & Knowledge Engineering*, *73*, 58–72.

Beeferman, D., & Berger, A. (2000). Agglomerative clustering of a search engine query log. In *Proceedings of the sixth ACM SIGKDD international conference on Knowledge discovery and data mining*(pp. 407-416). doi:10.1145/347090.347176

Bekkerman, R., Bilenko, M., & Langford, J. (Eds.). (2012). *Scaling up Machine Learning: Parallel and Distributed Approaches*. Cambridge University Press.

Belsley, D. A., Kuh, E., & Welsch, R. F. (1980). *Regression Diagnostics: Identifying influential data sources of collinearity*. New York: John Wiley & Sons. doi:10.1002/0471725153

Ben-Haim, Y., & Tom-Tov, E. (2010). A streaming parallel decision tree algorithm. *Journal of Machine Learning Research*, *11*, 849–872.

Benoît, G., & Agarwal, N. (2012). All-visual retrieval: How people search and respond to an affect-driven visual information retrieval system. *Proceedings of the American Society for Information Science and Technology*, *49*(1), 1–4.

Berendt, B. (2012). More than modelling and hiding: Towards a comprehensive view of web mining and privacy. *Data Mining and Knowledge Discovery*, *24*(3), 697–737.

Berendt, B., & Spiliopoulou, M. (2000). Analysis of navigation behaviour in web sites integrating multiple information systems. *The VLDB Journal*, *9*(1), 56–75.

Berry, M. J. A., & Linoff, G. S. (2000). *Mastering Data Mining*. New York: Wiley.

Berson, A., Thearling, K., & Stephen, J. (1999). *Building Data Mining Applications for CRM*. McGraw-Hill.

Besbes, G., & Baazaoui-Zghal, H. (2015). Modular ontologies and CBR-based hybrid system for web information retrieval. *Multimedia Tools and Applications*, *74*(18), 8053–8077.

Bhanti, P., Kaushal, U., &Pandey, A. (2011). E-Governance in Higher Education: Concept and Role of Data Warehousing Techniques. *International Journal of Computer Applications, 18*(1).

Bharat, K., & Andrei, B. (1998). A technique for measuring the relative size & overlap of public web search engines. *Journal on Computer Networks & ISDN Systems, 30*(1-7), 379-388.

Bharati, M., &Ramageri, M. (2010). Data mining techniques and applications. *Data Mining Modules in Emerging Field, 7*(3).

Bhisikar, P., & Sahu, P. (2013). Overview on Web Mining and Different Technique for Web Personalisation. *International Journal of Engineering Research and Applications, 3*(2).

Bing, L., Lam, W., & Gu, Y. (2011). Towards a Unified Solution: Data Record Region Detection and Segmentation.*Proc. 20th ACM Int'l Conf. Information and Knowledge Management (CIKM)*. doi:10.1145/2063576.2063761

Blake & Merz. (1998). *UCI Machine Learning Repository*. Academic Press.

Blanke, T., Lalmas, M., & Huibers, T. (2012). A framework for the theoretical evaluation of XML retrieval. *Journal of the American Society for Information Science and Technology, 63*(12), 2463–2473.

Bodon, F. (2006). *A survey on frequent item set mining. Budapest University of Technology & Economics*. Tech. Rep.

Bolin, M. (2005). *End-user programming for the web*. (Master's thesis). Massachusetts Institute of Technology.

Borges, J., & Levene, M. (1999). Data Mining of user navigation patterns, In *Proceedings of the WEBKDD'99 Workshop on Web Usage Analysis & User Profiling* (pp. 31–36). Academic Press.

Borges, J., & Levene, M. (2000). Data mining of user navigation patterns. In Proceedings of WEBKDD 99 Workshop on Web Usage Analysis and User Profiling (pp. 31-36). doi:10.1007/3-540-44934-5_6

Borges, J., & Levene, M. (2006). Ranking pages by topology and popularity within web sites.World Wide Web Journal, 9, 301-316.

Borges, J., & Levene, M. (2007). Testing the predictive power of variable history web usage. *Soft Computing, 11*(8), 717–727.

Böse, J.-H., Andrzejak, A., & Högqvist, M. (2010). Beyond online aggregation: Parallel and incremental data mining with online mapreduce. ACM. doi:10.1145/1779599.1779602

Bosnjak, S., Maric, M., & Bosnjak, Z. (2009). The role of web usage mining in web applications evaluation. *Management Information System, 5*(1), 31–36.

Bousquet & Wills. (2003). *The Politics of Information The Electronic Mediation of Social Change*. Alt-X Press.

Breiman, L., Friedman, J. H., Olshen, R. A., & Stone, C. J. (1984). *Classification and Regression Trees*. Belmont, CA: Wadsworth International Group.

Breslow,L.A., & Aha,D.W. (1997). Simplifying decision trees: a survey. *The Knowledge Engineering Review, 12*(1), 1-40.

Buchner, A. G., & Mulvenna, M. D. (1998). Discovering Internet Marketing Intelligence through Online Analytical Web Usage Mining. *ACM SIGMOD, 27*(4), 54–61. doi:10.1145/306101.306124

Bui, D., Pradhan, B., Lofman, O., & Dick, O. (2012). Landslide susceptibility assessment in the Hoa Binh Province of Vietnam: A comparison of the Levenberg-Marquardt and Bayesian regularized neural networks. *Geophysical Journal of the Royal Astronomical Society, 172*, 12–29.

Burke, R. (2007). Hybrid web recommender systems. In *The adaptive web*. Springer Berlin Heidelberg.

Bursteinas, B., & Long, J. (2001). Merging distributed classifiers. In *5th World Multi conference on Systemic, Cybernetics and Informatics*.

Butenuth, M., Frey, D., Nielsen, A. A., & Skriver, H. (2011). Infrastructure assessment for disaster management using multi-sensor and multi-temporal remote sensing imagery. *International Journal of Remote Sensing*, *32*(23), 8575–8594. doi:10.1080/01431161.2010.542204

Cai, D., Yu, S., & Wen, J.-R. Ma & W.-Y. (2003). Extracting Content Structure for Web Pages based on Visual Representation. In *Proc. Fifth Asia Pacific Web Conf.(APWeb)*.

Califf, M., & Mooney, R. (2003). Bottom-up Relational Learning of Pattern Matching Rules for Information Extraction. *Journal of Machine Learning Research*, 177–210.

Calvello, M., Cascini, L., & Mastroianni, S. (2013). Landslide zoning over large areas from a sample inventory by means of scale-dependant terrain units. *Geophysical Journal of the Royal Astronomical Society*, *182*, 33–48.

Camdevyren, H., Demyr, N., Kanik, A., & Keskyn, S. (2005). Use of principal component scores in multiple linear regression models for prediction of Chlorophyll-a in reservoirs. *Ecological Modelling*, *181*(4), 581–589. doi:10.1016/j.ecolmodel.2004.06.043

Cao, H., Jiang, D., Pei, J., He, Q., Liao, Z., Chen, E., & Li, H. (2008). Context-aware query suggestion by mining click-through & session data, In *Proceedings of the 14th ACM SIGKDD international conference on Knowledge discovery & data mining* (pp. 875-883). doi:10.1145/1401890.1401995

Caragea, D., Silvescu, A., & Honavar, V. (2004). A framework for learning from distributed data using sufficient statistics and its application to learning decision trees. *Int. J. Hybrid Intell. Syst.*, *1*(2), 80–89. doi:10.3233/HIS-2004-11-210 PMID:20351798

Cardinali, M., Reichenbach, P., Guzzetti, F., Ardizzone, F., Antonini, G., Galli, M., & Salvati, P. et al. (2002). A geomorphological approach to estimation of landslide hazards and risks in Umbria, Central Italy. *Natural Hazards and Earth System Sciences*, *2*(1/2), 57–72. doi:10.5194/nhess-2-57-2002

Carmona, C. J., Ramirez-Gallego, S., Torres, F., Bernal, E., del Jesus, M. J., & Garcia, S. (2012). Web usage mining to improve the design of an e-commerce website: OrOliveSur.com. *Expert Systems with Applications*, *39*(12), 11243–11249.

Carrara, A., Cardinali, M., Detti, R., Guzzetti, F., Pasqui, V., & Reichenbach, P. (1991). GIS techniques and statistical models in evaluating landslide hazard. *Earth Surface Processes and Landforms*, *16*(5), 427–445. doi:10.1002/esp.3290160505

Carrara, A., Guzzetti, F., Cardinali, M., & Reichenbach, P. (1999). Use of GIS technology in the prediction and monitoring of landslide hazard. *Natural Hazards*, *20*(2–3), 117–135. doi:10.1023/A:1008097111310

Carvalho & Freitas. (2004). *A hybrid decision tree/genetic algorithm for coping with the problem of small disjuncts in data mining*. Academic Press.

Castells, P., Vargas, S., & Wang, J. (2011). *Novelty and diversity metrics for recommender systems: Choice, discovery and relevance*. Paper presented at the 33rd European Conference on IR Research (ECIR 2011), Dublin, Ireland.

Centre, N. I. (2015a). *MyGov: A Platform for Citizen Engagement towards Good Governance in India*. Retrieved August 5, 2015, from http://www.mygov.in

Centre, N. I. (2015b). *MyGov: Open Government Data (OGD) Platform India*. Retrieved August 5, 2015, from https://data.gov.in/

Chaabane, A., Manils, P., & Kaafar, M. A. (2010, September). Digging into anonymous traffic: A deep analysis of the tor anonymizing network. In *Network and System Security (NSS), 2010 4th International Conference on* (pp. 167-174). IEEE. doi:10.1109/NSS.2010.47

Chakrabarti, S., Dom, B., Gibson, D., Kleinberg, J., Kumar, S., Raghavan, P., & Tomkins, A. et al. (1999). Mining the link structure of the world wide web. *IEEE Computer*, *32*(8), 60–67. doi:10.1109/2.781636

Chakravorty, S. (2015). Data mining techniques for analyzing murder related structured and unstructured data. *American Journal of Advanced Computing*, *2*(2).

Champatiray, P., Dimri, S., Lakhera, R., & Sati, S. (2007). Fuzzy based methods for landslide hazard assessment in active seismic zone of Himalaya. *Landslides*, *4*(2), 101–110. doi:10.1007/s10346-006-0068-6

Chan & Stolfo. (1996). Sharing Learned Models among Remote Database Partitions by Local Meta-Learning. *KDD-96 Proceedings*.

Chang, G., Healy, M. J., McHugh, J. A. M., &Wang, J. T. L. (2001). *Mining the World Wide Web: An Information Search Approach*. Kluwer Academic Publishers.

Chang, C.-H., Kayed, M., Girgis, M. R., & Shaalan, K. F. (2006). A Survey of Web Information Extraction Systems. *IEEE Transactions on Knowledge and Data Engineering*, *18*(10), 1411–1428. doi:10.1109/TKDE.2006.152

Chang, C.-H., & Kuo, S.-C. (2004). OLERA: A Semi-Supervised Approach for Web Data Extraction with Visual Support. *IEEE Intelligent Systems*, *19*(6), 56–64. doi:10.1109/MIS.2004.71

Chang, C.-H., & Lui, S.-C. (2001). IEPAD: Information Extraction based on Pattern Discovery.*Proceedings of the Tenth International Conference on World Wide Web (WWW), Hong-Kong*. doi:10.1145/371920.372182

Chang, K., & Chiang, S. (2009). An integrated model for predicting rainfall induced Landslides. *Geophysical Journal of the Royal Astronomical Society*, *105*, 366–373.

Chan, P., & Stolfo, S. (1995). Learning arbiter and combiner trees from partitioned data for scaling machine learning. *Proc. Intl. Conf. Knowledge Discovery and Data Mining*.

Chan, P., & Stolfo, S. (1996).Sharing learned models among remote database partitions by local meta-learning. In *Proceedings Second International Conference on Knowledge Discovery and Data Mining*.

Chauhan, H., & Chauhan, A. (2013). Implementation of decision tree algorithm c4.5. *International Journal of Scientific and Research Publications, 3*(10).

Chelboard, F., Baum, R., & Godt, J. (2006). U S Geological Survey Open file report:Vol. 2006-1064. *Rainfall Thresholds for Forecasting Landslides in the Seattle, Washington, Area- Exceedance and Probability* (pp. 1–17). Reston: Verginia.

Chen, H., Zou, B., & Bian, N. (2009). Optimization of web search engine and its application to web mining. *Wuhan University Journal of Natural Sciences*, *14*(2), 115–118.

Chen, J. (2010). UpDown Directed Acyclic Graph Approach for Sequential Pattern Mining. *IEEE Transactions on Knowledge and Data Engineering*, *22*(7), 913–928. doi:10.1109/TKDE.2009.135

Chen, L., Wu, J., Zheng, Z., Lyu, M. R., & Wu, Z. (2014). Modeling and exploiting tag relevance for web service mining. *Knowledge and Information Systems*, *39*(1), 153–173.

Chen, M. S., Park, J. S., & Yu, P. S. (1996). Data mining for path traversal patterns in a web environment. In *Proceedings of the 16th International Conference on Distributed Computing Systems* (pp. 385-392). doi:10.1109/ICDCS.1996.507986

Chen, Z., Fu, A. W. C., & Tong, F. C. H. (2003). Optimal algorithms for finding user access sessions from very large web logs. *World Wide Web (Bussum), 6*(3), 259–279.

Cheung, K. S. K., & Vogel, D. (2005). Complexity reduction in lattice-based information retrieval. *Information Retrieval, 8*(2), 285–299.

Chevalier, M. (2008). Zdravko Markov and Daniel T. Larose, Data mining the web: Uncovering patterns in web content, structure, and usage. *Information Retrieval, 11*(2), 169–174.

Chipman, J. S. (1979). Efficiency of least squares estimation of linear trend when residuals are autocorrelated. *Econometrica, 47*(1), 115–128. doi:10.2307/1912350

Choudhary & Sharma. (2015). Review Paper on Web Content Mining. *International Journal of Research in Engineering and Applied Sciences, 5*(6), 172-176.

Cho, Y. H., Kim, J. K., & Kim, S. H. (2002). A personalized recommender system based on web usage mining & decision tree induction. *Expert Systems with Applications, 23*(3), 329–342. doi:10.1016/S0957-4174(02)00052-0

Chung, C. F., Fabbri, A. G., & van Westen, C. J. (1995). Multivariate Regression Analysis for Landslide Hazard Zonation. In A. Carrara & F. Guzzetti (Eds.), *Geographical Information Systems in Assessing Natural Hazards* (pp. 107–142). Dordrecht, The Netherlands: Kluwer Academic Publishers. doi:10.1007/978-94-015-8404-3_7

Ciszak, L. (2008). Application of Clustering and Association Methods in Data Cleaning. In *Proc. of Int. Multiconference on Computer Science and Information Technology.*

Clarke, R. (1999). *Internet privacy concerns conf the case for intervention.* Academic Press.

Cleverdon, C. (1967). The Cranfield tests on index language devices. *Aslib Proceedings, 19*(6), 173–194.

Cochrane, D., & Orcutt, G. H. (1949). Application of Least Squares Relationships Containing Autocorrelated Error Terms. *Journal of the American Statistical Association, 44*, 32–61.

Codocedo, V., Lykourentzou, I., & Napoli, A. (2014). A semantic approach to concept lattice-based information retrieval. *Annals of Mathematics and Artificial Intelligence, 72*(1), 169–195.

Cohen, E., Krishnamurthy, B., & Rexford, J. (1998). Improving end-to-end performance of the web using server volumes and proxy filters. In *Proceedings of ACM SIGCOMM*. ACM. doi:10.1145/285237.285286

Cole, C. (2011). A theory of information need for information retrieval that connects information to knowledge. *Journal of the American Society for Information Science and Technology, 62*(7), 1216–1231.

Cooley, R., Mobasher, B., & Srivastava, J. (1997). Web mining: Information and pattern discovery on the World Wide Web. In *International Conference on Tools with Artificial Intelligence* (pp. 558-567).

Cooley, R., Mobasher, B., & Srivastava, J. (1997). *Grouping web page references into transactions for mining World Wide Web browsing patterns. Technical Report Tr. 97-021*. Minneapolis, MN: University of Minnesota, Dept. of Computer Science.

Cooley, R., Mobasher, B., & Srivastava, J. (1997). Web mining: Information & pattern discovery on the world wide web. In *Proceedings of the 9th IEEE International Conference on Tools with Artificial Intelligence*. doi:10.1109/TAI.1997.632303

Cooley, R., Mobasher, B., & Srivastava, J. (1999). Data preparation for mining World Wide Web browsing patterns. *Journal of Knowledge and Information Systems, 1*(1), 5–32.

Cooley, R., Mobasher, B., & Srivastava, J. (1999). Data preparation for mining world wide web browsing patterns. *Knowledge and Information Systems, 1*(1), 5–32. doi:10.1007/BF03325089

Cordon, O., Moya, F., & Zarco, C. (2004). *Fuzzy logic and multi-objective evolutionary algorithms as soft computing tools for persistent query learning in text retrieval environments.* Paper presented at the 14th IEEE International Conference on Fuzzy Systems (FUZZ–IEEE 2004), Budapest, Hungary.

Cordon, O., Viedma, E., Pujalte, C., Luque, M., & Zarco, C. (2003). A review on the application of evolutionary computation of information retrieval. *International Journal of Approximate Reasoning, 34*(3), 241–263.

Crescenzi, V., Mecca, G., & Merialdo, P. (2002). *Roadrunner: Automatic Data Extraction from Data-Intensive Websites.* SIGMOD. doi:10.1145/564691.564778

Cucerzan, S., & Ryen, W. W. (2007). Query suggestion based on user landing pages. In *Proceedings of the 30th annual international ACM SIGIR conference on Research & development in information retrieval*(pp. 875-876). doi:10.1145/1277741.1277953

Culotta, A. B. (2004). *Extracting social networks and contact information from email and the web.* Academic Press.

Cummins, R., & O'Riordan, C. (2006). Evolving local and global weighting schemes in information retrieval. *Information Retrieval, 9*(3), 311–330.

Currier. (2013). *The amount of data generated worldwide will reach four zettabytes.* Retrieved May 19,2015 from https://vsatglobalseriesblog.wordpress.com/2013/06/21/in-2013-the-amount-of-data-generated-worldwide-will-reach-four-zettabytes/

Dahl, M., Mortensen, L., Veihe, A., & Jensen, N. (2010). A simple qualitative approach for mapping regional landslide susceptibility in the Faroe Islands. *Natural Hazards and Earth System Sciences, 10*(2), 159–170. doi:10.5194/nhess-10-159-2010

Dai, E. C., Lee, C. F., & Nagi, Y. Y. (2002). Landslide risk assessment and management: An overview. *Engineering Geology, 64*(1), 65–87. doi:10.1016/S0013-7952(01)00093-X

Dai, W., & Ji, W. (2014). Wei Ji A MapReduce Implementation of C4.5 Decision Tree Algorithm. *International Journal of Database Theory and Application, 7*(1), 49–60. doi:10.14257/ijdta.2014.7.1.05

Daniel, L. T. (2005). *Discovering Knowledge in Data.* Wiley Interscience.

De Decker, B. D. (2007). *Advanced Applications for e-ID Cards in Flanders.* Academic Press.

Deng, H. (1999). Multicriteria analysis with fuzzy pairwise comparisons. *International Journal of Approximate Reasoning, 21*(3), 215–231. doi:10.1016/S0888-613X(99)00025-0

Deshpande, M., & Karypis, G. (2004). Selective Markov models for predicting web page accesses. *ACM Transactions on Internet Technology, 4*(4), 163–184. doi:10.1145/990301.990304

Desikan, P. (2009). *Web Mining for Business Computing.* Academic Press.

Devi, B. N., Devi, Y. R., Rani, B. P., & Rao, R. R. (2012). Design and implementation of web usage mining intelligent system in the field of e-commerce. *Procedia Engineering, 30,* 20–27.

Di, B., Zeng, H., Zhang, M., Ustin, S. L., Tang, Y., Wang, Z., & Zhang, B. et al. (2010). Quantifying the spatial distribution of soil mass wasting processes after the 2008 earthquake in Wenchuan, China: A case study of the Longmenshan area. *Remote Sensing of Environment, 114*(4), 761–771. doi:10.1016/j.rse.2009.11.011

Dijkstra, T. (1985). *Latent variables in linear stochastic models: Reflections on maximum likelihood and partial least squares methods* (2nd ed.). Amsterdam, The Netherlands: Sociometric Research Foundation.

Dimopoulos, C., Makris, C., Panagis, Y., Theodoridis, E., & Tsakalidis, A. (2010). A web page usage prediction scheme using sequence indexing and clustering techniques. *Data & Knowledge Engineering, 69*(4), 371–382.

Ding, Y., & Simonoff, J. S. (2010). An investigation of missing data methods for classification trees applied to binary response data. *Journal of Machine Learning Research, 11*, 131–170.

Dixit, D., & Kiruthika, M. (2010). Preprocessing of web logs. *International Journal on Computer Science and Engineering, 2*(7), 2447–2452.

Doğan, E., Sert, M., & Yazıcı, A. (2011). A flexible and scalable audio information retrieval system for mixed-type audio signals. *International Journal of Intelligent Systems, 26*(10), 952–970.

Domingues, M. A., Soares, C., & Jorge, A. M. (2013). Using statistics, visualization and data mining for monitoring the quality of meta-data in web portals. *Information Systems and e-Business Management, 11*(4), 569–595.

Dong, Y., Zhuang, Y., & Tai, X. (2007). A novel incremental mining algorithm of frequent patterns for web usage mining. *Wuhan University Journal of Natural Sciences, 12*(5), 777–782.

Dumais, S. (2003). Data-driven approaches to information access. *Cognitive Science, 27*(3), 491–524.

Dunham, M. H. (2003). *Data Mining Introductory & Advanced Topics*. Prentice Hall.

Dupret, G., & Mendoza, M. (2006). Automatic query recommendation using click-through data. In Professional Practice in Artificial Intelligence (pp. 303-312). doi:10.1007/978-0-387-34749-3_32

Efremenkova, V. M., & Krukovskaya, N. V. (2009). Information monitoring in the area of science-intensive technologies: Optimisation of information retrieval. *Scientific and Technical Information Processing, 36*(1), 26–38.

Efron, M. (2011). Information search and retrieval in microblogs. *Journal of the American Society for Information Science and Technology, 62*(6), 996–1008.

Efron, M., & Winget, M. (2010). Query polyrepresentation for ranking retrieval systems without relevance judgments. *Journal of the American Society for Information Science and Technology, 61*(6), 1081–1091.

Eirinaki, M., & Vazirgiannis, M. (2003). Web mining for web personalization. *ACM Transactions on Internet Technology, 3*(1), 1–27. doi:10.1145/643477.643478

El Azab, A., Idrees, A. M., Mahmoud, M. A., & Hefny, H. (2015). Fake Account Detection in Twitter Based on Minimum Weighted Feature set. *World Academy of Science, Engineering and Technology, International Journal of Computer, Electrical, Automation Control and Information Engineering, 10*(1), 13–18.

El-Khair, I. A. (2007). Arabic information retrieval. *Annual Review of Information Science & Technology, 41*(1), 505–533.

EM-DAT. (2007). Emergency Disasters Data Base, Brussels, Belgium. Centre for Research on the Epidemiology of Disasters. Ecole de Santé, Publique, Université Catholique de Louvain.

EMDAT. (2010). Emergency Disasters Data Base, Brussels, Belgium. Centre for Research on the Epidemiology of Disasters. Ecole de Santé, PubliqueUniversité Catholique de Louvain.

Ercanglu, M. (2005). Landslide susceptibility assessment of SE Bartin (West Black Sea region, Turkey) by artificial neural networks. *Natural Hazards and Earth System Sciences, 5*(6), 979–992. doi:10.5194/nhess-5-979-2005

Estimated size of Google's index. (n.d.). Retrieved August 1, 2015, from http://www.worldwidewebsize.com/

Etnoteam S. P. A. Marzo . (2000). Retrieved from http://ww.etnoteam.it/webquality

Etzioni, O. (1996). The World Wide Web: Quagmire or Gold Mine. Communications of the ACM, 39(11), 65-68.

Etzioni, O. (1996). The World Wide Web: Quagmine or gold mine. *Communications of the ACM, 39*(11), 65–68.

Etzioni, O. (1996). The World Wide Web: Quagmire or gold mine. *Communications of the ACM, 39*(11), 65–68. doi:10.1145/240455.240473

Ezeife, C. I., & Lu, Y. (2005). Mining web log sequential patterns with position coded pre-order linked WAP-Tree. *Data Mining and Knowledge Discovery, 10*(1), 5–38.

Ezeife, C. I., & Lu, Y. (2005). Mining web log sequential patterns with position coded pre-order linked wap-tree. *Data Mining and Knowledge Discovery, 10*(1), 5–38. doi:10.1007/s10618-005-0248-3

Facca, F. M., & Lanzi, P. L. (2003). Recent developments in web usage mining research. In *Proceedings of 5th International Conference on Data Warehousing and Knowledge Discovery.* Academic Press. doi:10.1007/978-3-540-45228-7_15

Facca, F. M., & Lanzi, P. L. (2005). Mining interesting knowledge from weblogs: A survey. *Data & Knowledge Engineering, 53*(3), 225–241. doi:10.1016/j.datak.2004.08.001

Farah, M., & Vanderpooten, D. (2008). An outranking approach for information retrieval. *Information Retrieval, 11*(4), 315–334.

Fengrong, J. (2004). *Study of web usage mining and discovery of browse interest.* (Thesis). Beijing Science and Technology University, Beijing, China.

Feng, Z., & Chin, K. W. (2015). A novel data centric information retrieval protocol for queries in delay tolerant networks. *Journal of Network and Systems Management, 23*(4), 870–901.

Fernández-Luna, J. M., Huete, J. F., & MacFarlane, A. (2009). Introduction to the special issue on teaching and learning in information retrieval. *Information Retrieval, 12*(2), 99–101.

Fernie, J. (2009). *Logistics and retail management: . emerging issues and new challenges in the retail supply chain.* Kogan Page Publishers.

Ferrara, E. D., De Meo, P., Fiumara, G., & Baumgartner, R. (2014). Web data extraction, applications and techniques. A survey. *Knowledge-Based Systems, 70*, 301–323. doi:10.1016/j.knosys.2014.07.007

Fidel, R. (1993). Qualitative methods in information retrieval research. *Library & Information Science Research, 15*(3), 219–247.

Fisher, J., Craig, A., & Bentley, J. (2007). Moving from a web presence to e-commerce: The importance of a business-web strategy for small-business owners. *Electronic Markets, 17*(4), 253–262.

Foley, C., & Smeaton, A. F. (2010). Division of labour and sharing of knowledge for synchronous collaborative information retrieval. *Information Processing & Management, 46*(6), 762–772.

Fragos, K., & Maistros, Y. (2006). A goodness of fit test approach in information retrieval. *Information Retrieval, 9*(3), 331–342.

Freitag, D. (2000). Machine Learning for Information Extraction from Informal Domains. *Machine Learning, 39*(2/3), 169–202. doi:10.1023/A:1007601113994

Freitas. (2000). Understanding the Crucial Differences Between Classification and Discovery of Association Rules. *SIGKDD Explorations, 2*(1), 65.

Friedman, J. H. (1997). *Data mining and statistics: what is the connection?*. Keynote Speech of the 29th Symposium on the Interface: Computing Science and Statistics, Houston, TX.

Fu, Budzik, & Hammond. (2000). Mining navigation history for Recommendation. *Intelligent User Interfaces*, 106–112.

Fujimoto, H., Etoh, M., Kinno, A., & Akinaga, Y. (2011). Web user profiling on proxy logs and its evaluation in personalization. In X. Du, W. Fan, J. Wang, Z. Peng, & M. Sharaf (Eds.), *Web technologies and applications.* Lecture notes in computer science (pp. 107–118). Berlin, Germany: Springer–Verlag.

Fu, L., Goh, D. H. L., & Foo, S. S. B. (2004). The effect of similarity measures on the quality of query clusters. *Journal of Information Science*, *30*(5), 396–407. doi:10.1177/0165551504046722

Fumarola, F., Weninger, T., Barber, R., Malerba, D., & Han, J. (2011). Extracting general lists from web documents: A hybrid approach. *IEA/AIE,* (1), 285–294.

Fürnkranz, J. (2002). Web Structure Mining. Exploiting the Graph Structure of the World Wide Web. *Österreichische Gesellschaft für Artificial Intelligence*, 17-26.

Fu, X., Li, Y., Harrison, R., & Belkasim, S. (2006). Content-based image retrieval using gabor-zernike features. In *Proceedings of 18th International Conference on Pattern Recognition*, (Vol. 2, pp. 417-420).

Gabet, E., Burbank, D., Putkonen, J., Pratt-Situala, B., & Ojha, T. (2004). Rainfall thresholds for landsliding in the Himalaya of Nepal. *Geophysical Journal of the Royal Astronomical Society*, *63*, 131–143.

Gama, J., Rocha, R., & Medas, P. (2003). Accurate decision trees for mining high-speed data streams. In *Proc. of 9th ACM SIGKDD international conference on Knowledge discovery and data mining* (KDD'03). ACM. doi:10.1145/956750.956813

Gandhi, M., Jeyebalan, K., Kallukalam, J., Rapkin, A., Reilly, P., & Widodo, N. (2004). *Web Research Infrastructure Project Final Report*. Cornell University.

Garcia, P., Amandi, A., Schiaffino, S., & Campo, M. (2007). Evaluating Bayesian networks precision for detecting students learning styles. *Computers & Education*, *49*(3), 794–808.

Gatterbauer, W., Bohunsky, P., Herzog, M., Krupl, B., & Pollak, B. (2007). *Towards Domain-Independent Information Extraction from Web Tables*. New York: ACM.

Gevers, T., & Smeulders, A. W. (2000). Pictoseek: Combining Color and Shape Invariant Features for Image Retrieval. *IEEE Transactions on Image Processing*, *9*(1), 102–119. doi:10.1109/83.817602 PMID:18255376

Ghorab, M. R., Zhou, D., O'Connor, A., & Wade, V. (2013). Personalised information retrieval: Survey and classification. *User Modeling and User-Adapted Interaction*, *23*(4), 381–443.

Ghosh, S., Van Westen, C., Carranza, E., Ghoshal, T., Sarkar, N., & Surendranath, M. (2009). A quantitative approach for improving BIS (Indian) method of medium-scale landslide susceptibility. *Journal of the Geological Society of India*, *74*(5), 625–638. doi:10.1007/s12594-009-0167-9

Gianoutsos, S., & Grundy, J. (1996). *Collaborative work with the World Wide Web: Adding CSCW support to a web browser*. Paper presented at the 1996 ACM Conference on Computer Supported Cooperative Work (CSCW 1996), Boston, MA.

Giudici, P. (2003). *Applied Data-Mining: Statistical Methods for Business and Industry*. West Sussex, UK: John Wiley and Sons.

Glenn, M. J. (2007). *Making Sense of Data-A practical guide to exploratory data analysis and data mining. New Jersy*. Wiley-Interscience.

Gobind, S., & Rao, L. M. (2015). A Review on Contribution of Data mining in E-Governance Framework. *International Journal of Engineering Research and General Science, 3*(2), 68–75.

Godd, A., & Wold, H. (1964). *Econometic Model Suideliy.* North Holland.

Godoy, D., Schiaffino, S., & Amandi, A. (2004). Interface agents personalizing web-based tasks. *Cognitive Systems Research Journal, 5*(3), 207–222.

Gök, A., Waterworth, A., & Shapira, P. (2015). Use of web mining in studying innovation. *Scientometrics, 102*(1), 653–671. PMID:26696691

Golfarelli, M., Stefano, R., & Paolo, B. (2011). myOLAP: An approach to express & evaluate OLAP preferences. *IEEE Transactions on Knowledge and Data Engineering, 23*(7), 1050–1064. doi:10.1109/TKDE.2010.196

Golovchinsky, G., Qvarfordt, O., & Pickens, J. (2009). Collaborative information seeking. *Computer, 42*(3), 47–51.

Gonde, A. B., Maheshwari, R. P., & Balasubramanian, R. (2013). Modified curvelet transform with vocabulary tree for content based image retrieval. *Digital Signal Processing, 23*(1), 142–150. doi:10.1016/j.dsp.2012.04.019

Gorbunov, K. Y., & Lyubetsky, V. (2011, October). The tree nearest on average to a given set of trees. *Problems of Information Transmission, 47*(3), 274–288. doi:10.1134/S0032946011030069

Gorsevski, P. V., & Jankowski, P. (2008). Discerning landslide susceptibility using rough sets. *Computers, Environment and Urban Systems, 32*(1), 53–65. doi:10.1016/j.compenvurbsys.2007.04.001

GSI. (2006). *Geological Survey of India.* Landslide Hazard Studies.

Gupta, V., & Lehal, G. S. (2009). A survey of text mining techniques and applications. *Journal of Emerging Technologies in Web Intelligence, 1*(1), 60-76.

Gupta, R. P., & Joshi, B. C. (1990). Landslide hazard zoning using the GIS approach—a case-study from the Ramganga Catchment, Himalayas. *Engineering Geology, 28*(1–2), 119–131. doi:10.1016/0013-7952(90)90037-2

Gupta, R., & Sarawagi, S. (2009). *Answering table augmentation queries from unstructured lists on the web.* PVLDB.

Gupta, Y., Saini, A., & Saxena, A. K. (2015). A new fuzzy logic based ranking function for efficient Information Retrieval system. *Expert Systems with Applications, 42*(3), 1223–1234.

Guzzetti, F., Carrara, A., Cardinali, M., & Reichenbach, P. (1999). Landslide hazard evaluation: A review of current techniques and their application in a multi study, Central Italy. *Geophysical Journal of the Royal Astronomical Society, 31,* 181–216.

Guzzetti, F., Reichenbach, P., Cardinali, M., Galli, M., & Ardizzone, F. (2005). Probablistic landslide hazard assessment at the basin scale. *Geophysical Journal of the Royal Astronomical Society, 72,* 272–299.

Hall, L., Chawla, N., & Bowyer, K. (1998). Combining decision trees learned in parallel. *Working Notes of the KDD-97 Workshop on Distributed Data Mining.*

Hall, L., Chawla, N., & Bowyer, K. (1998). Decision tree learning on very large data sets. *IEEE International Conference on Systems, Man, and Cybernetics.* doi:10.1109/ICSMC.1998.725047

Hammer, J., McHugh, J., & Gracia-Molina, H. (1997). Semistructured data: The TSIMISS experience.*Proceedings of the First East-Europen Symposium on Advances in Databases and Information Systems.*

Han, E., Boley, D., Gini, M., Gross, R., Hastings, K., Karypis, G., Kumar, V., & Mobasher, B. (2003). Document categorization and query generation on the world wide web using web ACE. *Journal of Artificial Intelligence Review.*

Hanani, U., Shapira, B., & Shoval, P. (2001). Information filtering: Overview of issues, research & systems. *User Modeling and User-Adapted Interaction, 11*(3), 203–259. doi:10.1023/A:1011196000674

Hand, D., Mannila, H., & Smyth, P. (2001). *Principles of Data Mining*. Cambridge, MA: MIT Press.

Han, E., Karypis, G., Kumar, V., & Mobasher, B. (2014).Clustering based on association rule hyper graphs. In *Proceedings of SIGMOD'97 Workshop on Research Issues in Data Mining and Knowledge Discovery (DMKD'97)*. ACM.

Han, J., Cheng, H., Xin, D., & Yan, X. (2007). Frequent pattern mining: Current status and future directions. *Data Mining and Knowledge Discovery, 15*(1), 55–86. doi:10.1007/s10618-006-0059-1

Han, J., & Kamber, M. (2001). *Data mining: Concepts and techniques*. San Francisco, CA: Academic Press.

Han, J., & Kamber, M. (2006). *Data Mining: Concepts and Techniques*. San Francisco, CA: Morgan Kaufmann Publishers.

Hanjalic, A. (2012). New grand challenge for multimedia information retrieval: Bridging the utility gap. *International Journal of Multimedia Information Retrieval, 1*(3), 139–152.

Hansen, P., & Jarvelin, K. (2005). Collaborative information retrieval in an information-intensive domain. *Information Processing & Management, 41*(5), 1101–1119.

Haque, M. S. (2002). E-Governance in India: Its impacts on relations among citizens, politicians and public servants. *International Review of Administrative Sciences, 68*(2), 231–250. doi:10.1177/0020852302682005

Hassan, H. A. (2014). Query Answering Approach Based on Document Summarization. Query Answering Approach Based on Document Summarization. *International Open Access Journal of Modern Engineering Research, 4*(12).

Hassan, H. D. (2015). Arabic Documents classification method a Step towards Efficient Documents Summarization. *International Journal on Recent and Innovation Trends in Computing and Communication*, 351-359.

Hastaoglu, K. O., & Sanli, D. U. (2011). Monitoring Koyulhisar landslide using rapid static GPS: A strategy to remove biases from vertical velocities. *Natural Hazards, 58*(3), 1275–1294. doi:10.1007/s11069-011-9728-5

Hastie, T., Tibshirani, R., & Friedman, J. (2009). *The Elements of Statistical Learning-Data Mining, Inference, and Prediction*. Retrieved from http://statweb.stanford.edu/~tibs/ElemStatLearn

Haveliwala, T. H. (2003). Topic-sensitive PageRank: A context-sensitive ranking algorithm for web search. *IEEE Transactions on Knowledge and Data Engineering, 15*(4), 784–796.

Hearst, M. A., & Rosner, D. (2008). Tag clouds: Data analysis tool or social signaller? In *Hawaii International Conference on System Sciences,Proceedings of the 41st Annual*.

Hearst, M. A., & Rosner, D. (2008). Tag clouds: Data analysis tool or social signaller? In *Proceedings of 41st Hawaii International Conference on System Sciences (HICSS 2008), Social Spaces minitrack*.

Hebbar, N. (2015, August 10). Flood of suggestions after PM seeks input for I-Day address. *The Hindu*. Retrieved August 10, 2015, from http://www.thehindu.com/news/national/flood-of-suggestions-after-pm-seeks-inputs-for-iday-address/article7519493.ece

Hjørland, B. (2015). Classical databases and knowledge organization: A case for Boolean retrieval and human decision-making during searches. *Journal of the Association for Information Science and Technology, 66*(8), 1559–1575.

Hoekstra, R., ten Bosch, O., & Harteveld, F. (2012). Automated data collection from web sources for official statistics: First experiences. *Statistical Journal of the IAOS: Journal of the International Association for Official Statistics, 28*(3/4), 99–111.

Hoenkamp, E., & Bruza, P. (2015). How everyday language can and will boost effective information retrieval. *Journal of the Association for Information Science and Technology, 66*(8), 1546–1558.

Hogue, A., & Karger, D. (2005). Thresher: Automating the Unwrapping of Semantic Content from the World Wide. *Proceedings of the 14th International Conference on World Wide Web (WWW)*. doi:10.1145/1060745.1060762

Hong, T. P., Lin, K. Y., & Wang, S. L. (2002). Mining linguistic browsing patterns in the World Wide Web. *Soft Computing, 6*(5), 329–336.

Hong, Y., Adler, R., & Huffman, G. (2006). Evaluation of the NASA multi-satellite precipitation analysis potential in global landslide hazard assessment. *Geophysical Research Letters*.

Hsu, C.-N., & Dung, M. (1998). Generating Finite-State Transducers for Semi-Structured Data Extraction from the Web. *Journal of Information Systems, 23*(8), 521–538. doi:10.1016/S0306-4379(98)00027-1

Hsu, D. F., & Taksa, I. (2005). Comparing rank and score combination methods for data fusion in information retrieval. *Information Retrieval, 8*(3), 449–480.

Huang, J., Kumar, S. R., Mitra, M., Zhu, W., & Zabih, R. (2001). *Image Indexing using Color Correlograms*. U.S. Patent 6,246,790.

Huang, C. K., Chien, L. F., & Oyang, Y. J. (2003, May). Relevant term suggestion interactive web search based on contextual information query session logs. *Journal of the American Society for Information Science and Technology, 54*(7), 638–649. doi:10.1002/asi.10256

Hung, Y. S., Chen, K. L. B., Yang, C. T., & Deng, G. F. (2013). Web usage mining for analysing elder self-care behavior patterns. *Expert Systems with Applications, 40*(2), 775–783.

Hussein, M. K., & Mousa, M. H. (2010). An Effective Web Mining Algorithm using Link Analysis. *International Journal of Computer Science and Information Technologies, 1*(3), 190-197.

IFRC. (2011). *World Disaster Report*. International Federation of Red Cross and Red Crescent Societies. Available online: http://www.ifrc.org/

Ivory, M. Y. (2001). *An Empirical foundation for Automated Web Interface Evaluation, Doctoral dissertations, University of California*. Berkeley, CA: Computer Science Department.

Jade, S., & Sarkar, S. (1993). Statistical models for slope stability classification. *Engineering Geology, 36*(1-2), 91–98. doi:10.1016/0013-7952(93)90021-4

Jaideep Srivastava, R. C.-N. (2000). Web Usage Mining: Discovery and Applications of Usage. *SIGKDD Explorations, 1*(2), 12.

Jain, R. K., Jain, S., Thakur, S. S., & Kasana, R. S. (2009). Web user categorization and behaviour study based on refreshing. *IJANA, 1*(2), 69–75.

Jaiswal, P., van Westen, C., & Jetten, V. (2010). Quantitative assessment of direct and indirect landslide risk along transportation lines in southern India. *Natural Hazards and Earth System Sciences, 10*(6), 1253–1267. doi:10.5194/nhess-10-1253-2010

Janssens, F. (2007). *Clustering of scientific fields by integrating text mining and bibliometrics*. Academic Press.

Jiang, S., Song, X., & Huang, Q. (2014). Relative image similarity learning with contextual information for Internet cross-media retrieval. *Multimedia Systems, 20*(6), 645–657.

Jiawei Han Kevin, C.-C. C. (2002). *Data Mining for Web Intelligence.* University of Illinois at Urbana-Champaign.

Jiawei Han, K.-C. C. (2002). Data Mining for Web Intelligence. *IEEE International Conference on Data Mining.*

Joho, H., Hannah, D., & Jose, J. M. (2009). *Revisiting IR techniques for collaborative search strategies.* Paper presented at the 31st European Conference on IR Research (ECIR 2009), Toulouse, France.

Jung, J. J. (2007). Ontological framework based on contextual mediation for collaborative information retrieval. *Information Retrieval, 10*(1), 85–109.

Jung, J. J. (2009). Consensus-based evaluation framework for distributed information retrieval systems. *Knowledge and Information Systems, 18*(2), 199–211.

Kaczmarek, T. Z. (2010). Information extraction from web pages for the needs of expert finding. Studies in Logic, Grammar and Rethoric, Logic Philosophy and Computer Science, 141-157.

Kamdar, T., & Joshi, A. (2005). Using incremental web log mining to create adaptive web servers. *International Journal on Digital Libraries, 5*(2), 133–150.

Kao, S. J., & Hsu, I. C. (2007). Semantic Web approach to smart link generation for web navigations. *Software, Practice & Experience, 37*(8), 857–879.

Kapoor, A., & Solanki, R. (2011). The Susceptible Network. *IITM Journal of Information Technology, 54.*

Kasemsap, K. (2014a). The role of social networking in global business environments. In P. Smith & T. Cockburn (Eds.), *Impact of emerging digital technologies on leadership in global business* (pp. 183–201). Hershey, PA: IGI Global.

Kasemsap, K. (2014b). The role of social media in the knowledge-based organizations. In I. Lee (Ed.), *Integrating social media into business practice, applications, management, and models* (pp. 254–275). Hershey, PA: IGI Global.

Kasemsap, K. (2015a). Theory of cognitive constructivism. In M. Al-Suqri & A. Al-Aufi (Eds.), *Information seeking behavior and technology adoption: Theories and trends* (pp. 1–25). Hershey, PA: IGI Global.

Kasemsap, K. (2015b). The role of data mining for business intelligence in knowledge management. In A. Azevedo & M. Santos (Eds.), *Integration of data mining in business intelligence systems* (pp. 12–33). Hershey, PA: IGI Global.

Kasemsap, K. (2015c). The role of social media in international advertising. In N. Taşkıran & R. Yılmaz (Eds.), *Handbook of research on effective advertising strategies in the social media age* (pp. 171–196). Hershey, PA: IGI Global.

Kasemsap, K. (2015d). The role of customer relationship management in the global business environments. In T. Tsiakis (Ed.), *Trends and innovations in marketing information systems* (pp. 130–156). Hershey, PA: IGI Global.

Kasemsap, K. (2016a). The roles of knowledge management and organizational innovation in global business. In G. Jamil, J. Poças-Rascão, F. Ribeiro, & A. Malheiro da Silva (Eds.), *Handbook of research on information architecture and management in modern organizations* (pp. 130–153). Hershey, PA: IGI Global.

Kasemsap, K. (2016b). The roles of e-learning, organizational learning, and knowledge management in the learning organizations. In E. Railean, G. Walker, A. Elçi, & L. Jackson (Eds.), *Handbook of research on applied learning theory and design in modern education* (pp. 786–816). Hershey, PA: IGI Global.

Kasemsap, K. (2016c). Examining the roles of virtual team and information technology in global business. In C. Graham (Ed.), *Strategic management and leadership for systems development in virtual spaces* (pp. 1–21). Hershey, PA: IGI Global.

Kashyap, A., Hristidis, V., & Petropoulos, M. (2010). *FACeTOR: Cost-driven exploration of faceted query results.* Paper presented at the 19th ACM Conference on Information and Knowledge Management (CIKM 2010), Toronto, Canada.

Kass. (1980). An exploratory Technique for investigation large quantities of categorical data. *Applied Statics, 29*(2), 119-127.

Katz, J. S., & Cothey, V. (2006). Web indicators for complex innovation systems. *Research Evaluation, 15*(2), 85–95.

Kaur, H., & Wasan, S. K. (2006). Empirical study on applications of data mining techniques in healthcare. *Journal of Computer Science, 2*(2), 194–200. doi:10.3844/jcssp.2006.194.200

Kayed, M., & Chang, C.-H. (2010). FiVaTech: Page-level web data extraction from template pages. *IEEE Transactions on Knowledge and Data Engineering, 22*(2), 249–263. doi:10.1109/TKDE.2009.82

Keikha, M., Crestani, F., & Carman, M. J. (2012). Employing document dependency in blog search. *Journal of the American Society for Information Science and Technology, 63*(2), 354–365.

Kelly, D., & Sugimoto, C. R. (2013). A systematic review of interactive information retrieval evaluation studies, 1967–2006. *Journal of the American Society for Information Science and Technology, 64*(4), 745–770.

Keßler, C. (2012). What is the difference? A cognitive dissimilarity measure for information retrieval result sets. *Knowledge and Information Systems, 30*(2), 319–340.

Khare M., Srivastava R. K., & Khare A. (2013). Moving Object Segmentation in Daubechies Complex Wavelet Domain. *Signal, Image and Video Processing, 8*(3), 635- 650.

Khemiri, R., & Fadila, B. (2013). FIMIOQR: Frequent Item sets Mining for Interactive OLAP Query Recommendation. In *DBKDA 2013, the Fifth International Conference on Advances in Databases, Knowledge& Data Applications* (pp. 9-14).

Khoonsari & Motie. (2012). A Comparison of Efficiency and Robustness of ID3 and C4.5 Algorithms Using Dynamic Test and Training Data Sets. *International Journal of Machine Learning and Computing, 2*(5).

Khribi, M. K., Jemni, M., & Nasraoui, O. (2009). Automatic Recommendations for E-Learning Personalization Based on Web Usage Mining Techniques & Information Retrieval. *Journal of Educational Technology & Society, 12*(4), 30–42.

Khurana, M., & Dayal, A. (2013-14). *CHILDLINE 1098.Case Studies on E-Governance in India.* National Institute for Smart Government.

Kim, & Mueller. (1978). *Factor analysis: Statistical methods and practical issues.* Beverly Hills, CA: Sage Publications.

Kim, & Mueller. (1978). *Introduction to Factor Analysis-What it is and how to do it.* Sage Publications, Inc.

Kim, Breslin, Yang, & Kim. (2008). Social semantic cloud of tag: Semantic model for social tagging. In *Agent and Multi-Agent Systems: Technologies and Applications.* Springer Berlin Heidelberg.

Kim, E., Kim, W., & Lee, Y. (2000). Purchase propensity prediction of EC customer by combining multiple classifiers based on GA. In *International Conference on Electronic Commerce* (pp. 274–280).

Kim, J. K., Cho, Y. H., Kim, W. J., Kim, J. R., & Suh, J. H. (2002). A personalized recommendation procedure for Internet shopping support. *Electronic Commerce Research and Applications, 1*(3/4), 301–313.

Kleinbaum, D. G., Kupper, L. L., & Muller, K. E. (1998). *Applied Regression Analysis and Other Multivariate Methods.* Belmont, CA: Duxbury Press.

Kleinberg, J. M. (1999). Authoritative sources in a hyperlinked environment. *Journal of the ACM, 46*(5), 604–632. doi:10.1145/324133.324140

Knautz, K., Soubusta, S., & Stock, W. G. (2008). Tag clusters as information retrieval interfaces. In *Proceedings of System Sciences (HICSS), 2010 43rd Hawaii International Conference.* doi:10.1109/HICSS.2010.360

Kobiyama, M., Mendonça, M., Moreno, D. A., Marcelino, I. P. V. O., Marcelino, E. V., Gonçalves, E. F., & Rudorff, F. M. et al. (2006). *Prevenção de Desastres Naturais* (pp. 20–25). Florianópolis, Brazil: Organic Trading.

Kohavi, R., Masand, B., Spiliopoulou, M., & Srivastava, J. (2002). Web mining. *Data Mining and Knowledge Discovery*, *6*(1), 5–8.

Kohavi, R., Mason, L., Parekh, R., & Zheng, Z. (2004). Lessons and challenges from mining retail e-commerce data. *Machine Learning*, *57*(1-2), 83–113. doi:10.1023/B:MACH.0000035473.11134.83

Komac, M. (2006). A landslide susceptibility model and multivariate statistics in perialpine Slovenia. *Geomorphology*, *74*, 17–28. doi:10.1016/j.geomorph.2005.07.005

Korra, S. B., Panigraphy, S. K., & Jena, S. K. (2013). Web usage mining: An implementation view. *Journal of Emerging Technologies in Web Intelligence*, *5*(3).

Kosala, R., & Blockeel, H. (2000). Web mining research: A survey. *ACM SIGKDD Explorations Newsletter*, *2*(1), 1–15. doi:10.1145/360402.360406

Kovar, K., & Natchtnebel, H. P. (1995). *Application of Geographic Information Systems in Hydrology and Water Resources Management. Hydro GIS 93*. Oxford, UK: IAHS Press.

Kreines, M. G. (2009). Models and technologies for the extraction of aggregated knowledge to control processes of the retrieval of non-structured information. *Journal of Computer and Systems Sciences International*, *48*(2), 272–281.

Krishna, A. P., & Kumar, S. (2013). Landslide hazard assessment along a mountain highway in the Indian Himalayan Region (IHR) using remote sensing and computational models. Article In *Proceedings of Spie- The International Society. Optical Engineering (Redondo Beach, Calif.)*. doi:10.1117/12.2029080

Krishna, V., Jose, J., & Suri, N. N. R. R. (2014). Design and development of a web-enabled data mining system employing JEE technologies. *Sadhana*, *39*(6), 1259–1270.

Kuhn, Weston, Coulter, & Quinlan. (2014). *C50: C5.0 Decision Trees and Rule-Based Models*. R package version 0.1.0-16.

Kumar & Suvarchala. (2012). A Study: Web Data Mining Challenges and Application for. *IOSR Journal of Computer Engineering, 7*(3), 24-29.

Kumar, R., & Pande, I. C. (1972). Deformation of rocks of Simla Hills. *Geologische Rundschau*, *61*(2), 430–441. doi:10.1007/BF01896326

Kuo, Hentrich, Good, & Wilkinson. (2007). Tag clouds for summarizing web search results. In *Proceedings of the 16th international conference on World Wide Web*.

Kushmerick, N., McKee, J., & Toolan, F. (2000, January). Towards zero-input personalization: Referrer-based page prediction. In *Adaptive Hypermedia and Adaptive Web-Based Systems* (pp. 133–143). Springer Berlin Heidelberg. doi:10.1007/3-540-44595-1_13

Kushmerick, N., Weld, D., & Doorenbos, R. (1997). Wrapper Induction for Information Extraction.*Proceedings of the Fifteenth International Conference on Artificial Intelligence*.

Ladwig, P., Anderson, A. A., Brossard, D., Scheufele, D. A., & Shaw, B. (2010). Narrowing the nano discourse? *Materials Today*, *13*(5), 52–54.

Laender, F.-H.-A., Ribeiro-Neto, B.-A., da Silva, A.-S., & Teixeria, J.-S. (2002). A Brief Survey of Web Data Extraction Tools. *ACM SIGMOD*, *31*(2), 84–93. doi:10.1145/565117.565137

Lancaster, F. W. (2003). *Indexing and abstracting in theory and practice.* London: Facet.

Lancaster, F. W., & Warner, A. I. (1993). *Information retrieval today.* Arlington, VA: Information Resources Press.

Lang, H., Wang, B., Jones, G., Li, J. T., Ding, F., & Liu, Y. X. (2008). Query performance prediction for information retrieval based on covering topic score. *Journal of Computer Science and Technology, 23*(4), 590–601.

Langley, P. (1999). User modeling adaptive interfaces, In *Proceedings of the Seventh International Conference on User Modeling* (pp. 357–370). Academic Press.

Larsen, B., Ingwersen, P., & Lund, B. (2009). Data fusion according to the principle of polyrepresentation. *Journal of the American Society for Information Science and Technology, 60*(4), 646–654.

Lazcorreta, E., Botella, F., & Fernandez-Caballero, A. (2008). Towards personalized recommendation by two-step modified Apriori data mining algorithm. *Expert Systems with Applications, 35*(3), 1422–1429.

Lee, C. H., & Fu, Y. H. (2008). *Web usage mining based on clustering of browsing features.* Paper presented at the Eighth International Conference on Intelligent Systems Design and Applications (ISDA 2008), Kaohsiung, Taiwan.

Lee, C. H., Lo, Y. L., & Fu, Y. H. (2011). *A novel production model based on hierarchical characteristic of website.* Elsevier.

Lee, C., Huang, C., Lee, J., Pan, K., Lin, M., & Dong, J. (2008). Statistical approach to storm event-induced landslides susceptibility. *Natural Hazards and Earth System Sciences, 8*(4), 941–960. doi:10.5194/nhess-8-941-2008

Lee, J. T., Seo, J., Jeon, J., & Rim, H. C. (2011). Sentence-based relevance flow analysis for high accuracy retrieval. *Journal of the American Society for Information Science and Technology, 62*(9), 1666–1675.

Lee, S., & Choi, J. (2004). Landslide susceptibility mapping using GIS and the weight-of-evidence model. *International Journal of Geographical Information Science, 18*(8), 789–814. doi:10.1080/13658810410001702003

Lee, S., & Dan, N. T. (2005). Probabilistic landslide susceptibility mapping in the Lai Chau province of Vietnam: Focus on the relationship between tectonic fractures and landslides. *Environmental Geology, 48*(6), 778–787. doi:10.1007/s00254-005-0019-x

Lee, S., & Pradhan, B. (2006). Probabilistic landslide hazards and risk mapping on Penang Island, Malaysia. *Journal of Earth System Science, 115*(6), 661–672. doi:10.1007/s12040-006-0004-0

Lee, S., & Talib, J. A. (2005). Probabilistic landslide susceptibility and factor effect analysis. *Environmental Geology, 47*(7), 982–990. doi:10.1007/s00254-005-1228-z

Lerman, K., Knoblock, C., & Minton, S. (2001). Automatic Data Extraction from Lists and Tables in Web Sources. *Proceedings of the workshop on Advances in Text Extraction and Mining (IJCAI-2001).*

Leung, K. W. T., & Lee, D. L. (2010). Deriving concept-based user profiles from search engine logs. *IEEE Transactions on Knowledge and Data Engineering, 22*(7), 969–982. doi:10.1109/TKDE.2009.144

Liang, C., Zhang, Y., & Song, Q. (2010). Decision Tree for Dynamic and Uncertain Data Streams. *JMLR: Workshop and Conference Proceedings.*

Liao, S. H., Chen, Y. J., & Lin, Y. T. (2011). Mining customer knowledge to implement online shopping and home delivery for hypermarkets. *Expert Systems with Applications, 38*(4), 3982–3991.

Li, C., Zhang, Y., & Li, X. (2009, June). OcVFDT: one class very fast decision tree for one-class classification of data streams. In *Proceedings of the Third International Workshop on Knowledge Discovery from Sensor Data* (pp. 79-86). ACM. doi:10.1145/1601966.1601981

Lieherman, R., & Letizia. (1995). An agent that assists web browsing. In *Proceedings of the 1995 International Joint Conference on Artificial Intelligence.* Montreal, Canada: IEEE.

Li, J., & Zaïane, O. R. (2004). Combining usage, content, and structure data to improve web site recommendation. In *E-Commerce and Web Technologies* (pp. 305–315). Springer Berlin Heidelberg. doi:10.1007/978-3-540-30077-9_31

Li, J., Zhang, G. Y., Gu, G. C., & Li, J. L. (2003). The design and implementation of web mining in web sites security. *Journal of Marine Science and Application, 2*(1), 81–86.

Lillis, D., Toolan, F., Mur, A., Peng, L., Collier, R., & Dunnion, J. (2006). Probability-based fusion of information retrieval result sets. *Artificial Intelligence, 25*(1), 179–191.

Limam, L., David, C., Harald, K., & Lionel, B. (2010). Extracting user interests from search query logs: A clustering approach. *Workshop on Database & Expert Systems Applications* (pp. 5-9). doi:10.1109/DEXA.2010.23

Lin, C., Alvarez, S., & Ruiz, C. (2000). *Collaborative recommendation via adaptive association rule mining.* Academic Press.

Lin, C. W., & Hong, T. P. (2013). A survey of fuzzy web mining. *Wiley Interdisciplinary Reviews: Data Mining and Knowledge Discovery, 3*(3), 190–199.

Lin, J. G., & Huang, H. H. (2003). Web mining for electronics business application. In *Proceedings of the Fourth International Conference on Parallel and Distribution Computing, Application and Techniques* (pp. 872-876). Academic Press.

Link, A. N., Rowe, B. R., & Wood, D. W. (2011). Information about information: Public investments in information retrieval research. *Journal of the Knowledge Economy, 2*(2), 192–200.

Lin, S., & Xie, I. (2013). Behavioral changes in transmuting multisession successive searches over the web. *Journal of the American Society for Information Science and Technology, 64*(6), 1259–1283.

Li, R., Ben, K., Bin, B., Reynold, C., & Eric, L. (2012). DQR: a probabilistic approach to diversified query recommendation. In *Proceedings of the 21st ACM international conference on Information & knowledge management*(pp. 16-25). doi:10.1145/2396761.2396768

Little, M. A., McSharry, P. E., Roberts, S. J., Costello, D. A. E., & Moroz, I. M. (2009). Exploiting Nonlinear Recurrence and Fractal Scaling Properties for Voice Disorder Detection. *Biomedical Engineering Online.* PMID:17594480

Liu, B., Hsu, W., & Ma, Y. (1998). Integrating classification and association rule mining. *Proc. 4th Int. Conf. on Knowledge Discovery and Data Mining* (KDD-98), (pp. 80-86). AAAI Press.

Liu, K., & Kargupta, H. (2008). *Distributed data mining bibliography.* Available: http://www.csee.umbc.edu/~hillol/DDMBIB/

Liu, W., Meng, X., & Meng, W. (2006). Vision-Based Web Data Records Extraction. *ProceedingsInternational Workshop Web and Databases (WebDB).*

Liu, B. G. (2003). Mining data records in Web pages. In *Proceedings of the ninth ACM SIGKDD international conference on Knowledge discovery and data mining* (pp. 601-606). ACM.. doi:10.1145/956750.956826

Liu, B., Grossman, R.-L., & Zhai, Y. (2004). Mining Web Pages for Data Records. *IEEE Intelligent Systems, 19*(6), 49–55. doi:10.1109/MIS.2004.68

Liu, B., & Zhai, Y. (2005). NET – A System for Extracting Web Data from Flat and Nested Data Records. *WISE, 2005*, 487–495.

Liu, G., Li, Z., Zhang, L., & Xu, Y. (2011). Image retrieval based on microstructure descriptor. *Pattern Recognition, 44*(9), 2123–2133. doi:10.1016/j.patcog.2011.02.003

Liu, G., Zhang, L., Hou, Y., & Yang, J. (2008). Image retrieval based on multi-texton histogram. *Pattern Recognition, 43*(7), 2380–2389. doi:10.1016/j.patcog.2010.02.012

Liu, J., & Belkin, N. J. (2015). Personalizing information retrieval for multi-session tasks: Examining the roles of task stage, task type, and topic knowledge on the interpretation of dwell time as an indicator of document usefulness. *Journal of the Association for Information Science and Technology, 66*(1), 58–81.

Liu, K.-L., Meng, W., Qiu, J., Yu, C.-T., Raghavan, V., Wu, Z., & Zhao, H. et al. (2007). AllInOneNews: Development and Evaluation of a Large-Scale News Metasearch Engine.*Proceedings ACM SIGMOD International Conference Management of Data*. doi:10.1145/1247480.1247601

Liu, L., Kantarcioglu, M., & Thuraisingham, B. (2009). Privacy Preserving Decision Tree Mining from Perturbed Data. *Proceedings of the 42nd Hawaii International Conference on System Sciences*.

Liu, W., Meng, X., & Meng, W. (2010). ViDE: A Vision based approach for Deep Web Data Extraction. *IEEE Transactions on Knowledge and Data Engineering, 22*(3), 447–460. doi:10.1109/TKDE.2009.109

Liu, X. (2013). Generating metadata for cyberlearning resources through information retrieval and meta-search. *Journal of the American Society for Information Science and Technology, 64*(4), 771–786.

Liu, Y., Junwei, M., Min, Z., Shaoping, M., & Liyun, R. (2011). How do users describe their information need: Query recommendation based on snippet click model. *Expert Systems with Applications, 38*(11), 13847–13856.

Liu, Y., Zhang, M., Cen, R., Ru, L., & Ma, S. (2007). Data cleansing for web information retrieval using query independent features. *Journal of the American Society for Information Science and Technology, 58*(12), 1884–1898.

Li, Y., Feng, B., & Mao, Q. (2008). Research on path completion technique in web usage mining. In *Proceedings of International Symposium on Computer Science and Computational Technology*. IEEE. doi:10.1109/ISCSCT.2008.151

Li, Y., Xu, S., & Wang, B. (2010). Chinese Query Recommendation by Weighted SimRank. *Journal of Chinese Information Processing, 24*(3), 3–10.

Lorentzen, D. G. (2014). Webometrics benefitting from web mining? An investigation of methods and applications of two research fields. *Scientometrics, 99*(2), 409–445.

Lorenzi, F., Ricci, F., Tostes, R. M., & Brasil, R. (2005). Case-based recommender systems: A unifying view. In Intelligent Techniques Web Personalisation. Springer.

Luk, R. W. P., Leong, H. V., Dillon, T. S., Chan, A. T. S., Croft, W. B., & Allan, J. (2002). A survey in indexing and searching XML documents. *Journal of the American Society for Information Science and Technology, 53*(6), 415–437.

Macpherson, K. (2004). An information processing model of undergraduate electronic database information retrieval. *Journal of the American Society for Information Science and Technology, 55*(4), 333–347.

Ma, H., Michael, R. L., & Irwin, K. (2010). Diversifying query suggestion results. In *Proc. of AAAI*, 10.

Mahmood, A., & Mahmood, E. A.-S.-B. (2013). Recommender system for ground-level Ozone predictions in Kuwait. *IEEE Federated Conference on Computer Science and Information Systems*.

Mahmood, A., & Mahmood, N. E.-B. (2014). An Intel Innovations in Bio-inspired Computing and Applications. Springer.

Maleki-Dizaji, S., Siddiqi, J., Soltan-Zadeh, Y., & Rahman, F. (2014). Adaptive information retrieval system via modelling user behaviour. *Journal of Ambient Intelligence and Humanized Computing*, *5*(1), 105–110.

Mandl, T. (2008). Recent developments in the evaluation of information retrieval systems: Moving towards diversity and practical relevance. *Informatica*, *32*(1), 27–38.

Manfre´, L. A., Hirata, E., Silva, J. B., Shinohara, E. J., Giannotti, M. A., Larocca, A. P. C., & Quintanilha, J. A. (2012). An analysis of geospatial technologies for risk and natural disaster management. *ISPRS International Journal of Geo-Information*, *1*(2), 166–185. doi:10.3390/ijgi1020166

Manjunath, B. S., & Ma, W. X. (1996). Browsing and Retrieval of Image Data. *IEEE Transactions on Pattern Analysis and Machine Intelligence*, *18*(8), 837–842. doi:10.1109/34.531803

Mannila, H., & Ronkainen, P. (1997). *Similarity of event sequences*. Paper presented at the Fourth International Workshop on Temporal Representation and Reasoning (TIME 1997), Daytona Beach, FL.

Mansourian, A., Rajabifard, A., & Valadan Zoej, M. J. (2005). SDI Conceptual Modelling for Disaster Management. In *Proceedings of the ISPRS Workshop on Service and Application of Spatial Data Infrastructure*.

Mansuri, B. B. (2013). E-GOVERNANCE: A Case Study of Gyandoot Project. *Journal of Contemporary Research in Management*, *4*(3).

Markov, Z., & Larose, D. T. (2007). *Data mining the web: Uncovering patterns in web content, structure, and usage*. Hoboken, NJ: Wiley–Interscience.

Mark, S. (2008). Ambiguous queries: Test collections need more sense. In *Proceedings of the 31st Annual International ACM SIGIR Conference on Research & Development in Information Retrieval* (pp. 499-506).

Marta, B., & Michele, M. (2010). *Maximum Likelihood Estimation of Factor Models on Data Sets With Arbitrary Pattern of Missing Data*. European Central Bank, Working Paper Series, No. 1189.

Masand, B., & Spiliopoulou, M. (1999). *Workshop on web usage analysis & user profiling*. ACM.

Mascaro, C. M., & Goggins, S. (2010). *Collaborative information seeking in an online political group environment*. Paper presented at the Second International Workshop on Collaborative Information Seeking at CSCW 2010, Savannah, GA.

Masseglia, F. P. (2000). *An efficient algorithm for web usage mining*. *Networking and Information Systems Journal*.

Masseglia, F., Poncelet, P., Teisseire, M., & Marascu, A. (2008). Web usage mining: Extracting unexpected periods from web logs. *Data Mining and Knowledge Discovery*, *16*(1), 39–65.

Masseglia, F., Teisseire, M., & Poncelet, P. (2003). HDM: A client/server/engine architecture for real-time web usage mining. *Knowledge and Information Systems*, *5*(4), 439–465.

McCabe, T. J. (1976). A Complexity Measure. *IEEE Transactions on Software Engineering*, *SE-2*(4), 308–320. doi:10.1109/TSE.1976.233837

Mehrotra, G. S., Sarkar, S., Kanungo, D. P., & Mahadevaiah, K. (1996). Terrain analysis and spatial assessment of landslide hazards in parts of Sikkim Himalaya. *Geological Society of India*, *47*, 491–498.

Mehtaa, P. P. (2012). Web Personalization Concept and Research Issue. *International Journal of Information and Education Technology*.

Mei, Q., Dengyong, Z., & Kenneth, C. (2008). Query suggestion using hitting time. In *Proceedings of the 17th ACM conference on Information & knowledge management* (pp. 469-478).

Mei, Q., Zhou, D., & Church, K. (2008). Query suggestion using hitting time. In *Proceedings of the 17th ACM conference on Information & knowledge management* (pp.469-478). ACM.

Mel'nikov, V. O., Melikyan, G. S., & Maksimov, O. A. (2009). Characteristics of information retrieval systems on the Internet: Theoretical and practical aspects. *Automatic Documentation and Mathematical Linguistics, 43*(1), 42–50.

Menasce, D. A., Almeida, V. A., Fonseca, R., & Mendes, M. A. (1999). A methodology for workload characterization of e-commerce sites. In *Proceedings of ACM E-Commerce* (pp. 119–128). doi:10.1145/336992.337024

Miao, G., Tatemura, J., Hsiung, W.-P., Sawires, A., & Moser, L. E. (2009). Extracting Data Records from the Web using Tag Path Clustering.*Proceedings International Conference World Wide Web (WWW)*. doi:10.1145/1526709.1526841

Mikhailov, L., & Tsvetinov, P. (2004). Evaluation of services using a fuzzy analytic hierarchy process. *Applied Soft Computing, 5*(1), 23–33. doi:10.1016/j.asoc.2004.04.001

Min, D. H., & Han, I. (2005). Detection of the customer time-variant pattern for improving recommender systems. *Expert Systems with Applications, 28*(2), 189–199.

Minguillon & Alfonso. (2002). *On Cascading Small Decision Trees*. (PhD Thesis). University of Barcelona.

Mitchell, T., Caruana, R., Freitag, D., McDermott, J., & Zabowski, D. (1994). Experience with a learning personal assistant. *Communications of the ACM, 37*(7), 81–91. doi:10.1145/176789.176798

Mobasher, B. (2006). Web Usage Mining. In *Web Data Mining: Exploring Hyperlinks, Contents and Usage Data*. Academic Press.

Mobasher, B., Cooley, R., & Srivastava, J. (1999). *Creating adaptive web sites through usage-based clustering of URLs*. Paper presented at the 1999 IEEE Knowledge and Data Engineering Exchange Workshop (KDEX 1999), Chicago, IL.

Mobasher, B., Cooley, R., & Srivastava, J. (2000a). Automatic personalization based on web usage mining. *Communications of the ACM, 43*(8), 142–151. doi:10.1145/345124.345169

Mobasher, B., Dai, H., Luo, M. N. T., & Nakagawa, M. (2002). Discovery & evaluation of aggregate usage profiles for web personalization. *Data Mining and Knowledge Discovery, 6*(1), 61–82. doi:10.1023/A:1013232803866

Mobasher, B., Dai, H., Luo, T., & Nakagawa, M. (2002). Discovery and evaluation of aggregate usage profiles for web personalization. *Data Mining and Knowledge Discovery, 6*(1), 61–82.

Mobasher, B., Dai, H., Luo, T., Sun, Y., & Zhu, J. (2000b). Integrating web usage & content mining for more effective personalization. In *Proceedings of the EC-Web* (pp. 165–176). doi:10.1007/3-540-44463-7_15

Moghadasi, S. I., Ravana, S. D., & Raman, S. N. (2013). Low-cost evaluation techniques for information retrieval systems: A review. *Journal of Informetrics, 7*(2), 301–312.

Moghaddam, H. A., & Tarzjan, M. S. (2006). Gabor Wavelet Correlogram Algorithm for Image Indexing and Retrieval. In *Proceedings of 18th International Conference on Pattern Recognition* (pp. 925–928). doi:10.1109/ICPR.2006.593

Mohamed, F. (2011). Business Intelligence for Emerging e-Business Applications. *Journal of Emerging Technologies in Web Intelligence*.

Mohapatra, R. (2004). *Information extraction from dynamic web sources*. Doctoral dissertation.

Moraveji, N., Morris, M., Morris, D., Czerwinski, M., & Riche, N. H. (2011). *ClassSearch: Facilitating the development of web search skills through social learning.* Paper presented at the the 29th Annual ACM Conference on Human Factors in Computing Systems (CHI 2011), Vancouver, Canada.

Morris, M. R., & Morris, D. (2011). *Understanding the potential for collaborative search technologies in clinical settings.* Paper presented at the Third Workshop on Collaborative Information Retrieval (CIR 2011), Glasgow, United Kingdom.

Morris, M. R., Paepcke, A., & Winograd, T. (2006). *TeamSearch: Comparing techniques for co-present collaborative search of digital media.* Paper presented at the First IEEE International Workshop on Horizontal Interactive Human-Computer Systems (TableTop 2006), Adelaide, Australia.

Mosleh, A., Zargari, F., & Azizi, R. (2009). Texture image retrieval using contourlet transform. In *Proceedings of IEEE International Symposium on Signals, Circuits and Systems* (pp. 1-4).

Murala, S., Maheshwari, R. P., & Balasubramanian, R. (2012). Directional local extrema patterns: A new descriptor for content-based image retrieval. *International Journal of Multimedia Information Retrieval, 1*(3), 191–203. doi:10.1007/s13735-012-0008-2

Murala, S., Maheshwari, R. P., & Balasubramanian, R. (2012). Expert System Design using Wavelets and Color Vocabulary Trees for Image retrieval. *Expert Systems with Applications, 39.*

Murala, S., Maheshwari, R. P., & Balasubramanian, R. (2012). Local tetra patterns: A new descriptor for content-based image retrieval. *IEEE Transactions on Image Processing, 21*(5), 2874–2886. doi:10.1109/TIP.2012.2188809 PMID:22514130

Murata, T. (2007). Discovery of user communities based on terms of web log data. *New Generation Computing, 25*(3), 293–303.

Murdopo. (2013). *Distributed Decision Tree Learning for Mining Big Data Streams.* (Master's Thesis). UPC.

Murtagh, F., & Starck, J. L. (2008). Wavelet and curvelet moments for image classification: Application to aggregate mixture grading. *Pattern Recognition Letters, 29*(10), 1557–1564. doi:10.1016/j.patrec.2008.03.008

Muslea, I., Minton, S., & Knoblock, C. (1999). A Hierarchical Approach to Wrapper Induction. *Proceedings of the Third International Conference on Autonomous Agents* (AA-99). doi:10.1145/301136.301191

Nagarajan, R., Mukherjee, A., Roy, A., & Khire, M. V. (1998). Temporal remote sensing data and GIS application in landslide hazard zonation of part of Western Ghat, India. *International Journal of Remote Sensing, 19*(4), 573–585. doi:10.1080/014311698215865

Nagarajan, R., Roy, A., Vinodkumar, R., & Khire, M. (2000). Landslide hazard susceptibility mapping based on terrain and climatic factors for tropical monsoon region. *Engineering Geology, 58,* 275–287.

Naithani, A. (2007). Macro landslide hazard zonation mapping using uni-variate statistical analysis in parts of Garhwal Himalaya. *Journal of the Geological Society of India, 70,* 353–368.

Naithani, A. K. (1999). The Himalayan Landslides. *Employment News, 23*(47), 20–26.

Nandan, T., & Chand, M. G. (2007, December). Application of Analytics in E-Governance–a next level. In *Foundations of E-Government: 5th International Conference on E-Governance,* (pp. 28-30).

Natarajan, R., & Shekar, B. (2005). Interestingness of association rules in data mining: Issues relevant to e-commerce. *Sadhana, 30*(2/3), 291–309.

Neelam, D., & Sharma, A. K. (2010). Rank Optimization & Query Recommendation in Search Engines using Web Log Mining Techniques. *Journal of Computing, 2*(12).

Neelam, D., & Sharma, A. K. (2011). QUESEM: Towards building a Meta Search Service utilizing Query Semantics. *International Journal of Computer Science, 8*(1).

Nestorov, S., Abiteboul, S., & Motwani, R. (1998). Extracting schema from semistructured data. In ACM SIGMOD. doi:10.1145/276305.276331

Ng, A.-Y., Jordan, M.-I., & Weiss, Y. (2001). *On Spectral Clustering:Analysis and an Algorithm. In Proceedings Neural Information Processing Systems* (pp. 849–856). NIPS.

Nguyen-Duc, H., Do-Hong, T., Le-Tien, T., & Bui-Thu, C. (2010). A new descriptor for image retrieval using contourlet co-occurrence. In *Proceedings of Third IEEE International Conference on Communications and Electronics (ICCE)* (pp. 169-174). doi:10.1109/ICCE.2010.5670704

NIC. (2015). *National Informatics Centre (NIC)*. Retrieved August 7, 2015, fromhttp://www.nic.in/

Nielsen, J. (1996). *Top ten mistakes in Web design*. Jakob Nielsen's Alertbox. Retrieved from www.useit.com/alertbox/9605.html

Nielsen, J. (2000). *Designing Web Usability: the practice for simplicity*. Indianapolis, IN: New Riders.

Nina, S. P., Rahman, M., Bhuiyan, K. I., & Ahmed, K. E. U. (2009). Pattern discovery of web usage mining. In *Proceedings of the International Conference on Computer Technology and Development*. Academic Press.

Niwa, S., Doi, T., & Honiden, S. (2006). Web Page Recommender System based on Folksonomy Mining. In *Proc. of the Third International Conference on Inforrmation Technology: New Generation (ITNG'06)*.

Noor, A. B. (2008). Semantic Web: Data Representation. In Partial Fulfillment of the Requirement for the Degree of Master in Information Technology.

Ojala, T., Pietikainen, M., & Maenpaa, T. (2002). Multiresolution gray-scale and rotation invariant texture classification with local binary patterns. *IEEE Transactions on Pattern Analysis and Machine Intelligence, 24*(7), 971–987. doi:10.1109/TPAMI.2002.1017623

Okoli, C., Mehdi, M., & Mesgari, M. (2012). *The people's encyclopedia under the gaze of the sages. A systematic review of scholarly research on Wikipedia*. Academic Press.

Oren, E. (1996). The World Wide Web: Quagmire or gold mine. *Communications of the ACM, 39*(11), 65–68.

Ou, J. C., Lee, C. H., & Chen, M. S. (2008). Efficient algorithms for incremental web log mining with dynamic thresholds. *The VLDB Journal, 7*(4), 827–845.

Oyama, K., Kageura, K., Kando, N., Kimura, M., Maruyama, K., Yoshioka, M., & Takahashi, K. (2003). Development of an information retrieval system suitable for large-scale scholarly databases. *Systems and Computers in Japan, 34*(6), 44–58.

Pabarskaite, Z., & Raudys, A. (2007). A process of knowledge discovery from web log data: Systematization and critical review. *Journal of Intelligent Information Systems, 28*(1), 79–104.

Pachauri, A. K., & Pant, M. (1992). Landslide hazard mapping based on geological attributes. *Engineering Geology, 32*(1-2), 81–100. doi:10.1016/0013-7952(92)90020-Y

Palcic, I., & Lalic, B. (2009). Analytical Hierarchy Process as a tool for selecting and evaluating projects. *International Journal of Simulation Modelling, 8*(1), 16–26. doi:10.2507/IJSIMM08(1)2.112

Pandia, , Pani, , & Padhi, , Panigrahy, & Ramakrishna. (2011). A Review of Trends in Research on Web Mining.International Journal of Instrumentation. *Control and Automation, 1*(1), 37–41.

Pani, S. K., Panigrahy, L., Sankar, V. H., Ratha, B. K., Mandal, A. K., & Padhi, S. K. (2011). Web usage mining: A survey on pattern extraction from web logs. *International Journal of Instrumentation, Control & Automation, 1*.

Panikkar, S., & Subramaniyan, V. (1997). Landslide hazard analysis of the area around Dehra Dun and Mussoorie, Uttar Pradesh. *Current Science, 73*, 1117–1123.

Papadakis, N., Skoutas, D., Topoulos, K.-R., & Varvarigou, T.-A. (2005). STAVIES: A System for Information Extraction from Unknown Web Data Sources through Automatic Web Wrapper Generation using Clustering Techniques. *IEEE Transactions on Knowledge and Data Engineering, 17*(12), 1638–1652. doi:10.1109/TKDE.2005.203

Pardeshi, S. D., Autade, S. E., & Pardeshi, S. S. (2013). *Landslide hazard assessment: recent trends and techniques.* Springer Plus. doi:.10.1186/2193-1801-2-523

Park, D. C., El-Sharkawi, M. A., Marks, R. J. II, Atlas, L. E., & Damborg, M. J. (1991). Electric load forecasting using an artificial neural network. *IEEE Transactions on Power Engineering, 6*(2), 442–449. doi:10.1109/59.76685

Park, D. H., Kim, H. K., Choi, I. Y., & Kim, J. K. (2012). A literature review and classification of recommender systems research. *Expert Systems with Applications, 39*(11), 10059–10072.

Park, J. S., Chen, M. S., & Yu, P. S. (1997). Using a hash-based method with transaction trimming for mining association rules. *IEEE Transactions on Knowledge and Data Engineering, 9*(5), 813–825.

Patel & Rana. (2014). A Survey on Decision Tree Algorithm For Classification. *IJEDR, 2*(1).

Patel, P., Jena, B., & Sahoo, B. (2014). Knowledge Discovery on Web Information Repository. *IJACTA, 1*(2),049-56.

Patil & Lathi. (2012). *Comparison of C5.0 & CART Classification algorithms using pruning technique.* Academic Press.

Paul-Alexandru, Claudiu, S. F., & Wolfgang, N. (2007). Personalized query expansion for the web. In *Proceedings of the 30th annual international ACM SIGIR conference on Research & development in information retrieval* (pp. 7-14).

Pei, J., Han, J., Mortazavi-asl, B., & Zhu, H. (2000). Mining access patterns efficiently from web logs. In *Proceedings of the 4th Pacific-Asia Conf. on Knowledge Discovery and Data Mining* (pp. 396-407). doi:10.1007/3-540-45571-X_47

Pei, J., Jiawei, H., Behzad, M., Jianyong, W., Helen, P., Qiming, C., & Mei-Chun, H. et al. (2004). sequential patterns by pattern-growth: The prefixspan approach. *IEEE Transactions on Knowledge and Data Engineering, 16*(11), 1424–1440. doi:10.1109/TKDE.2004.77

Peisker, A., & Dalai, S. (2015). Data Analytics for Rural Development. *Indian Journal of Science and Technology, 8*(S4), 50–60. doi:10.17485/ijst/2015/v8iS4/61494

Perkowitz, M., & Etzioni, O. (1997). *Adaptive web sites: An AI challenge.* Paper presented at the 15th International Joint Conference on Artificial Intelligence (IJCAI 1997), Nagoya, Japan.

Perkowitz, M., & Etzioni, O. (1998). Adaptive web sites: Automatically synthesizing web pages. In *Proceedings of the 15th National Conference on Artificial Intelligence.*

Perkowitz, M., & Etzioni, O. (1998). Adaptive web sites: automatically synthesizing web pages. In *Proceedings of the Fifteenth National Conf. on Artificial Intelligence (AAAI)* (pp. 727-732).

Perkowitz, M., & Etzioni, O. (2000). Towards adaptive web sites: Conceptual framework and case study. *Artificial Intelligence, 118*(1/2), 245–275.

Pierrakos, Paliouras, Papatheodorou, & Spyropoulos. (2003). Web Usage Mining as a Tool for Personalization: A Survey, User Modeling& User-Adapted Interaction. Kluwer Academic Publishers.

Pierrakos, D., Paliouras, G., Papatheodorou, C., & Spyropoulos, C. (2003). Web usage mining as a tool for personalization: A survey. *User Modeling and User-Adapted Interaction, 13*(4), 311–372. doi:10.1023/A:1026238916441

Pighin, M., & Brajnik, G. (2000). A formative evaluation of information retrieval techniques applied to software catalogues. *Journal of Systems and Software, 52*(2), 131–138.

Pirolli, P., Pitkow, J., & Rao, R. (1996). Silk from a sow's ear: extracting usable structures from the web. In *Proceedings of Conference on Human Factors in Computing Systems (SIGCHI)* (pp. 118-125).

Pitkow, J. (1997). In search of reliable usage data on the www. In *Sixth International World Wide Web Conference* (pp. 451-463).

Pitkow, J., & Pirolli, P. (1999). Mining longest repeating sub sequences to predict www surfing. In *Proceedings of the 2nd USENIX Symposium on Internet Technologies & Systems.*

Pitkow, J., & Pirolli, P. (1999). Mining longest repeating subsequences to predict WWW surfing. *Proceedings of 2nd USENIX Symp. Internet Technologies and Systems* (pp. 139-150).

Piwowarski, B., & Gallinari, P. (2005). A Bayesian framework for XML information retrieval: Searching and learning with the INEX collection. *Information Retrieval, 8*(4), 655–681.

Pradha, B. (2010). Remote sensing and GIS-based landslide hazard analysis and cross-validation using multivariate logistic regression model on three test areas in Malaysia. *Advances in Space Research, 45*(10), 1244–1256. doi:10.1016/j.asr.2010.01.006

Pradhan, B., & Lee, S. (2009). Landslide risk analysis using artificial neural network model focussing on different training sites. *International Journal of Physical Sciences, 4*, 1–15.

Pregibon, D. (1997). *Data Mining.* Statistical Computing and Graphics.

Preuth, T., Glade, T., & Demoulin, A. (2010). Stability analysis of a human-influenced landslides in eastern Belgium. *Geophysical Journal of the Royal Astronomical Society, 120*, 4–98.

Provost, F. J., & Hennessy, D. N. (1994). Distributed machine learning: scaling up with coarse-grained parallelism. In *Proceedings of the 2nd International Conference on Intelligent Systems for Molecular Biology.*

Provost, F., & Hennessy, D. (1996). Scaling up: Distributed machine learning with cooperation. In *Proceedings of the 13th National Conference on Artificial Intelligence.*

Purandare, P. (2008). Web Mining: A Key to Improve Business on Web. In *IADIS European Conf. Data Mining,* (pp. 155-159).

Qaqaya, H. (2008). *The effects of anti-competitive business practices on developing countries and their development prospects.* Academic Press.

Qin, J., Zhou, Y., Chau, M., & Chen, H. (2006). Multilingual web retrieval: An experiment in English–Chinese business intelligence. *Journal of the American Society for Information Science and Technology, 57*(5), 671–683.

Quinlan, J. R. (1986). Induction of decision trees. *Machine Learning, 1*(1), 81-106.

Quinlan, J. R. (1996). Bagging, boosting, and C4.5. In *Proc. 13th National Conference on Artificial Intelligence (AAAI'96).*

Rahimi, R., Shakery, A., & King, I. (2015). Multilingual information retrieval in the language modeling framework. *Information Retrieval Journal, 18*(3), 246–281.

Rajaraman, A., & Ullman, J. D. (2014). *Mining of Massive Datasets.* New York: Cambridge University Press.

Rani, P. (2013). A Review of Web Page Ranking Algorithm. *Revi International Journal of Advanced Research in Computer Engineering & Technology.*

Rao, A. K. (2014). *A Case of Process Reengineering of Driving Licence.* Case Studies on E-Governance in India.

Ravi, K., & Ravi, V. (2015). A survey on opinion mining and sentiment analysis: Tasks, approaches and applications. *Knowledge-Based Systems, 89,* 14–46. doi:10.1016/j.knosys.2015.06.015

Razavi. (2005). *Canonical Correlation Analysis for Data Reduction in Data Mining Applied to Predictive Models for Breast Cancer Recurrence. In Connecting Medical Informatics and Bio-Informatics* (pp. 175–180). ENMI.

Regis, R. (2008). *Strategic human resource management and development.* Excel Books India. Excel Books India.

Resnick, P., & Varian, H. R. (1997). Recommender systems. *Communications of the ACM, 40*(3), 56–58. doi:10.1145/245108.245121

Ricci, F., Rokach, L., Shapira, B., & Kantor, P. B. (2011). Recommender Systems. Springer.

RISE: Repository of Online Information Sources Used in Information Extraction Tasks. (n.d.). Retrieved May 19,2015 from http://www.isi.edu/integration/RISE/

Rivadeneira, A. W., Gruen, D. M., Muller, M. J., & Millen, D. R. (2007). Getting our head in the clouds: Toward evaluation studies of tagclouds. In *Proceedings of the SIGCHI Conference on Human Factors in Computing Systems.* doi:10.1145/1240624.1240775

Robertson, S. E., Walker, S., & Hancock-Beaulieu, M. (2000). Experimentation as a way of life: Okapi at TREC. *Information Processing & Management, 36*(1), 95–108.

Ross, T. J. (1997). *Fuzzy logic with engineering applications.* Singapore: McGraw–Hill.

Rubens, N. O. (2006). The application of fuzzy logic to the construction of the ranking function of information retrieval system. *Computer Modeling and New Technologies, 10*(1), 20–27.

Rusiñol, M., de las Heras, L. P., & Terrades, O. R. (2014). Flowchart recognition for non-textual information retrieval in patent search. *Information Retrieval, 17*(5/6), 545–562.

Rusmussen, C. (1996). *Website.* Retrieved from http://www.cs.toronto.edu/~delve/data/bank/desc.html

Russell, T. (2006). Cloudalicious: Folksonomy over time. In *Proceedings of the 6th ACM/IEEEC-CS Joint Conference on Digital Libraries.* doi:10.1145/1141753.1141859

Ruthven, I. (2008). Interactive information retrieval. *Annual Review of Information Science & Technology, 42*(1), 43–91.

Saaty, T. L. (1980). *The Analytical Hierarchy Process.* New York: McGraw – Hill.

Saaty, T. L. (1994). How to make a decision: The analytic hierarchy process. *Interfaces, 24*(6), 19–43. doi:10.1287/inte.24.6.19

Saha, A. (2003). *Introduction to artificial Neural Network Models.* Retrieved from http://www.geocities.com/adotsaha/-NNinExcel.html

Saha, A. K., Gupta, R. P., & Arora, M. K. (2002). GIS-based landslide hazard zonation in the Bhagirathi (Ganga) Valley, Himalayas. *International Journal of Remote Sensing, 23*(2), 357–369. doi:10.1080/01431160010014260

Sahuguet, A., & Azavant, F. (2001). Building Intelligent Web Applications using Lightweight Wrappers. *IEEE Transactions on Data and Knowledge Engineering, 36*(3), 283–316. doi:10.1016/S0169-023X(00)00051-3

Samar Mahmoud, N. E.-B. (2013). An Intelligent Recommender System for Drinking Water Quality.*International Conference on Hybrid Intelligent Systems (HIS)*.

Samatova, N. F., Ostrouchov, G., Geist, A., & Melechko, A. V. (2002). RACHET: An Efficient Cover- Based Merging of Clustering Hierarchies from Distributed Datasets. *Distributed and Parallel Databases, 11*(2), 157–180.

Sanderson, M. (2008). Ambiguous queries: test collections need more sense.*Proceedings of the 31st annual international ACM SIGIR conference on Research & development in information retrieval*. doi:10.1145/1390334.1390420

Saravana Kumar, Ananthi, & Devi. (2013). An Approach to Automation Selection of Decision Tree based on Training Data Set. *International Journal of Computer Applications, 64*(21).

Sarkar, S., & Kanungo, D. P. (2004). An integrated approach for landslide susceptibility mapping using remote sensing and GIS. *Photogrammetric Engineering and Remote Sensing, 70*(5), 617–625. doi:10.14358/PERS.70.5.617

Sarkar, S., Kanungo, D., & Mehrotra, G. (1995). Landslide hazard zonation: A case study of garhwal Himalaya, India. *Mountain Research and Development, 15*(4), 301–309. doi:10.2307/3673806

Sarukkai, R. (2000). Link prediction and path analysis using markov chains. In *Proceedings of the 9ᵗʰ International WWW Conference* (pp. 377-386). doi:10.1016/S1389-1286(00)00044-X

Sarwar, B., Karypis, G., Konstan, J., & Riedl, J. (2001). Item-based collaborative filtering recommendation algorithms. In*ACM Proceedings of the 10th international conference on World Wide Web* (pp. 285-295). doi:10.1145/371920.372071

Schafer, J. B., Konstan, J. A., & Reidl, R. (2001). E-commerce recommendation applications. *Data Mining and Knowledge Discovery, 5*(5), 115–153. doi:10.1023/A:1009804230409

Schenker, A., Last, M., & Kandel, A. (2005). Design and implementation of a web mining system for organizing search engine results. *International Journal of Intelligent Systems, 20*(6), 607–625.

Schiaffino, S., & Amandi, A. (2006). Polite personal agent. *IEEE Intelligent Systems, 21*(1), 12–19.

Scime, A. (2004). Guest editor's introduction: Special issue on web content mining. *Journal of Intelligent Information Systems, 22*(3), 211–213.

Seifert, C., Kump, B., Kienreich, W., Granitzer, G., & Granitzer, M. (2008). On the beauty and usability of tag clouds. In *Information Visualisation, 2008. IV'08.12th International Conference*. doi:10.1109/IV.2008.89

Senkul, P., & Salin, S. (2012). Improving pattern quality in web usage mining by using semantic information. *Knowledge and Information Systems, 30*(3), 527–541.

Sha, H., Liu, T., Qin, P., Sun, Y., & Liu, Q. (2013). EPLogCleaner: Improving data quality of enterprise proxy logs for efficient web usage mining. *Procedia Computer Science, 17*, 812–818.

Shah, C. (2012). *Collaborative information seeking: The art and science of making the whole greater than the sum of all*. New York, NY: Springer–Verlag.

Shah, C., Pickens, J., & Golovchinsky, G. (2010). Role-based results redistribution for collaborative information retrieval. *Information Processing & Management, 46*(6), 773–781.

Sharma, A., & Vincent, A. (2014). Creating Gender sensitive eSpaces for Mahatma Gandhi National Rural Employment Guarantee Act (MGNREGA). *Case Studies on E-Governance in India*, 6-32.

Shchekotykhin, K., Jannach, D., & Friedrich, G. (2010). xCrawl: A high-recall crawling method for web mining. *Knowledge and Information Systems, 25*(2), 303–326.

Shoemaker, P., & Reese, S. D. (2011). *Mediating the message*. Routledge.

Shukla, D., & Singhai, R. (2011). Analysis of user's web browsing behavior using Markov chain model. *International Journal of Advanced Networking & Applications, 2*(5).

Shyu, M. L., Haruechaiyasak, C., & Chen, S. C. (2006). Mining user access patterns with traversal constraint for predicting web page requests. *Knowledge and Information Systems, 10*(4), 515–528.

Siddiqui, A. T. (2013). *Web Mining Techniques in E-Commerce Applications*. arXiv preprint arXiv:1311.7388

Si, L., Callan, J., Cetintas, S., & Yuan, H. (2008). An effective and efficient results merging strategy for multilingual information retrieval in federated search environments. *Information Retrieval, 11*(1), 1–24.

Silverstein, C., Henzinger, M., Marais, H., & Moricz, M. (1998). *Analysis of a very large AltaVista query log. Technical Report*. Systems Research Center, Compaq Computer Corporation.

Simon, K., & Lausen, G. (2005). ViPER: Augmenting Automatic Information Extraction with Visual perceptions. *Proceedings 14th ACM International Conference on Information and Knowledge Management (CIKM)*. doi:10.1145/1099554.1099672

Sinclair, J., & Cardew-Hall, M. (2007). The folksonomy tag cloud: When is it useful? *Journal of Information Science, 34*(1), 15–29. doi:10.1177/0165551506078083

Sleiman, H.-A., & Corchuelo, R. (2013). A survey of region extractors from web documents. *IEEE Transactions on Knowledge and Data Engineering, 25*(9), 1960–1981. doi:10.1109/TKDE.2012.135

Sleiman, H.-A., & Corchuelo, R. (2014). Trinity: On Using Trinary Trees for Unsupervised Web Data Extraction. *IEEE Transactions on Knowledge and Data Engineering, 26*(6), 1544–1556. doi:10.1109/TKDE.2013.161

Smeulders, A. W. M., Worring, M., Santini, S., Gupta, A., & Jain, R. (2000). Content-Based Image Retrieval At The End of Early Years. *IEEE Transactions on Pattern Analysis and Machine Intelligence, 22*(12), 1349–1379. doi:10.1109/34.895972

Smith, J. R., & Chang, S. F. (1996). Tools and Techniques for Color Image Retrieval. Electronic Imaging: Science & Technology. *International Society for Optics and Photonics, 2670*, 426–437.

Sobkowicz, P., Kaschesky, M., & Bouchard, G. (2012). Opinion mining in social media: Modeling, simulating, and forecasting political opinions in the web. *Government Information Quarterly, 29*(4), 470–479.

Soderland, S. (1999). Learning information extraction rules for semi-structured and free text. *Machine Learning, 34*(1-3), 233–272. doi:10.1023/A:1007562322031

Soley, M. (2003). Culture as an issue in knowledge sharing: A means of competitive advantage. *Electronic Journal of Knowledge Management, 1*(2), 205-212.

Soulier, L., Tamine, L., & Bahsoun, W. (2013). *A collaborative document ranking model for a multi-faceted search*. Paper presented at the Ninth Asia Information Retrieval Society Conference (AIRS 2013), Singapore.

Soulier, L., Tamine, L., & Bahsoun, W. (2014). On domain expertise-based roles in collaborative information retrieval. *Information Processing & Management, 50*(5), 752–774.

Speretta, M., & Gauch, S. (2005). Personalized search based on user search histories. In *Proceedings of the IEEE/WIC/ACM International Conference on Web Intelligence* (pp. 622-628). doi:10.1109/WI.2005.114

Spiliopoulou, M. (1999). Data mining for the web. In *Principles of Data Mining & Knowledge Discovery* (pp. 588–589). Academic Press.

Spiliopoulou, M. (2000). Web usage mining for web site evaluation. *Communications of the ACM, 43*(8), 127–134. doi:10.1145/345124.345167

Spiliopoulou, M., & Pohle, C. (2001). Data mining for measuring and improving the success of web sites. *Data Mining and Knowledge Discovery, 5*(1/2), 85–114.

Srikant, R., & Yang, Y. (2001). Mining web logs to improve website organization. In *Proceedings of the 10th International Conference on World Wide Web* (pp. 430 – 437). doi:10.1145/371920.372097

Srivastava, T., Prasanna, D., &Vipin, K. (2005). Web mining–concepts, applications & research directions. In *Foundations & Advances Data Mining*. Springer Berlin Heidelberg.

Srivastava.Desikan, J. P., & Kumar, V. (2002). Web Mining:*Accomplishments and Future Directions. National Science Foundation Workshop on Next Generation Data Mining*.

Srivastava, J., Cooley, R., Deshpanda, M., & Tan, P. N. (2000). Web Usage Mining: Discovery and applications of usage patterns from web data. *ACM SIGKDD., 1*(2), 12. doi:10.1145/846183.846188

Srivastava, J., Cooley, R., Deshpande, M., & Tan, P.-N. (2000). Web usage mining: Discovery and applications of usage patterns from web Data. *SIGKDD Explorations*, 1.

Srivastava, P., Binh, N. T., & Khare, A. (2013). Content-Based Image Retrieval using Moments. In *Proceedings of 2nd International Conference on Context Awareness and Application*, (pp. 228-237).

Srivastava, P., Binh, N. T., & Khare, A. (2014). Content-Based Image Retrieval using Moments of Local Ternary Pattern. *Mobile Networks and Applications, 19*(5), 618–625. doi:10.1007/s11036-014-0526-7

Srivastava, P., Prakash, O., & Khare, A. (2014). Content-Based Image Retrieval using Moments of Wavelet Transform. In *Proceedings of International Conference on Control Automation and Information Sciences*, (pp. 159-164). doi:10.1109/ICCAIS.2014.7020550

Srivastava, T., Desikan, P., & Kumar, V. (2005). Web Mining – Concepts, Applications and Research Directions. Foundations and Advances in Data Mining. *Studies in Fuzziness and Soft Computing, 180*, 275–307. doi:10.1007/11362197_10

Stefanidis, K., Marina, D., & Evaggelia, P. (2009). *You May Also Like results in relational databases*. Lyon, France: Proc. PersDB.

Steichen, B., Ashman, H., & Wade, V. (2012). A comparative survey of personalised information retrieval and adaptive hypermedia techniques. *Information Processing & Management, 48*(4), 698–724.

Stevenson, M., & Greenwood, M. A. (May2006). Learning Information Extraction Patterns Using WordNet.*Proceeding of The Third International WordNet Conference*.

Strecht, P. (2015). A Survey of Merging Decision Trees Data Mining Approaches. *Proceedings of the 10th Doctoral Symposium in Informatics Engineering*.

Strecht, P., Mendes-Moreira, J., & Soares, C. (2014). Merging Decision Trees: a case study in predicting student performance. In *Proceedings of 10th International Conference on Advanced Data Mining and Applications*, (pp. 535–548). doi:10.1007/978-3-319-14717-8_42

Subtil, P., Mouaddib, N., & Faucout, O. (1996). *A fuzzy information retrieval and management system and its applications*. Paper presented at the 1996 ACM Symposium on Applied Computing (SAC 1996), Philadelphia, PA.

Sumana, I. J., Islam, M. M., Zhang, D., & Liu, G. (2008). Content-Based Image Retrieval using Curvelet Transform. In *Proceedings of 10th IEEE workshop on Multimedia Signal Processing*, (pp. 11-16).

Syam, B., & Rao, Y. S. (2010). Integrating contourlet features with texture, color and spatial features for effective image retrieval. In *Proceedings of 2nd IEEE International Conference on Information Management and Engineering*, (pp. 289-293). doi:10.1109/ICIME.2010.5477856

Tamine-Lechani, L., Boughanem, M., & Daoud, M. (2010). Evaluation of contextual information retrieval effectiveness: Overview of issues and research. *Knowledge and Information Systems*, *24*(1), 1–34.

Taneja, A., & Chauhan, R. K. (2011). A Theoretical Framework for Comparison of Data Mining Technique. *International Journal of Advanced Research in Computer Science*, *2*(3), 28–33.

Tan, X., & Triggs, B. (2010). Enhanced Local Texture Feature Sets for Face Recognition under Difficult Lighting Conditions. *IEEE Transactions on Image Processing*, *19*(6), 1635–1650. doi:10.1109/TIP.2010.2042645 PMID:20172829

Tao, Y. H., Hong, T. P., Lin, W. Y., & Chiu, W. Y. (2009). A practical extension of web usage mining with intentional browsing data toward usage. *Expert Systems with Applications*, *36*(2), 3937–3945.

Tao, Y. H., Hong, T. P., & Su, Y. M. (2006). Improving browsing time estimation with intentional behaviour data. *International Journal of Computer Science and Network Security*, *6*(12), 35–39.

Tao, Y. H., Su, Y. M., & Hong, T. P. (2008). Web usage mining algorithm with intentional browsing data. *Expert Systems with Applications*, *35*(4), 1893–1904.

Tarzjan, S. (2007). A Novel Evolutionary Approach for Optimizing Content-based Image Indexing Algorithms. *IEEE Transactions on Systems, Man, and Cybernetics. Part B, Cybernetics*, *37*(1), 139–153. doi:10.1109/TSMCB.2006.880137 PMID:17278567

Thada, V., & Sandeep, J. (2011). A Genetic Algorithm Approach for improving the average Relevancy of Retrieved Documents Using Jaccard Similarity Coefficient. *International Journal of Research in IT & Management*, *4*.

The Hindu. (2014). India tops in adult illiteracy: U.N. report. *The Hindu*. Retrieved August 8, 2015, from http://www.thehindu.com/features/education/issues/india-tops-in-adult-illiteracy-un-report/article5629981.ece

Theil, H. (1966). *Applied Economic Forecasting*. North Holland.

Thelwall, M. (2012). A history of webometrics. *Bulletin of the American Society for Information Science and Technology*, *38*(6), 18–23.

Thirumala Sree Govada, N. L. (2014). Comparative study of various Page Ranking Algorithms in Web Content Mining (WCM). *International Journal of Advanced Research*, *2*(7), 457–464.

Thomas, D. S. K., Eturĝay, K., & Kemeç, S. (2007). The role of Geographic Information System/Remote Sensing in Disaster Management. In H. Rodríguez, E. L. Quarantelli, & R. Dynes (Eds.), *Handbook of Disaster Research* (pp. 83–96). Newark, NJ: Springer. doi:10.1007/978-0-387-32353-4_5

Tong, S., & Dean, J. (2008). *System and methods for automatically creating lists*. US Patent: 7350187.

Tonon, A., Demartini, G., & Cudré-Mauroux, P. (2015). Pooling-based continuous evaluation of information retrieval systems. *Information Retrieval Journal*, *18*(5), 445–472.

Totad, Geeta, Prasanna, & Santhosh. (2010). PVGD Prasad Reddy, Scaling Data Mining Algorithms to Large and Distributed Datasets. *International Journal of Database Management Systems, 2*(4).

Trant, J. (2009). Studying social tagging and folksonomy: A review and framework. *Journal of Digital Information*, *10*(1).

Tseng, V. S., Lin, K. W., & Chang, J. C. (2008). Prediction of user navigation patterns by mining the temporal web usage evolution. *Soft Computing*, *12*(2), 157–163.

Türkoğlu, I. (2006). Extraction of interesting patterns through association rule mining for improvement of website usability. In *Proceedings of the 2006 IEEE/WIC/ACM International Conference of Web Intelligence*. ResulDaş.

Tuzhilin, A. (2012). Customer relationship management and web mining: The next frontier. *Data Mining and Knowledge Discovery*, *24*(3), 584–612.

UCI-Machine Learning Repository: Center for Machine Learning and Intelligent Systems. (2014). Retrieved from http://archive.ics.uci.edu/ml/datasets.html

Umagandhi, R., & Senthilkumar, A. V. (2009). Approaches to find URL click count from Search Engine Query Logs. *International Journal of Computer Information Systems*, *4*.

Umagandhi, R., &Senthilkumar, A, V. (2013). Time Dependent Approach for Query and URL Recommendations Using Search Engine Query Logs. *IAENG International Journal of Computer Science*, *40*(3).

Umagandhi, R., & Senthilkumar, A. V. (2012). Concept based Time Independent Query Recommendations from Search Engine Query Logs. In *Proceedings of the International Conference on computer Applications & Advanced Communications*(pp. 17-18).

Umagandhi, R., & Senthilkumar, A. V. (2013). Search Query Recommendations using Hybrid User Profile with Query Logs. *International Journal of Computers and Applications*, *80*(10), 7–18. doi:10.5120/13895-1227

Umagandhi, R., & Senthilkumar, A. V. (2014). Time Heuristics Ranking Approach for Recommended Queries Using Search Engine Query Logs. *Kuwait Journal of Science*, *41*(2), 127–149.

Valet. (n.d.). Retrieved from http://valet.webthing.com/access/url.html

van de Lei, T. E., & Cunningham, S. W. (2006). *Use of the Internet for future-oriented technology analysis*. Paper presented at the Second International Seville Seminar on Future-Oriented Technology Analysis: Impact of FTA Approaches on Policy and Decision-Making, Seville, Spain.

van Eeten, M. J., & Mueller, M. (2012). Where is the governance in Internet governance? *New Media & Society*.

van Wel, L., & Royakkers, L. (2004). Ethical issues in web data mining. *Ethics and Information Technology*, *6*(2), 129–140.

Van Westen, C. J. (1994). GIS in landslide hazard zonation: a review, with examples from the Andes of Colombia. In M. Price & I. Heywood (Eds.), *Mountain environments and geographic information system* (pp. 135–165). London: Taylor and Francis.

VanderMeer, D., Dutta, K., & Datta, A. (2000). Enabling scalable online personalization on the web. In *Proceedings of ACM E-Commerce* (pp. 185–196). doi:10.1145/352871.352892

Varnes, D. J. (1984). Landslide Hazard Zonation: a review of principles and practice. UNESCO.

Vasina, E. N., Golitsyna, O. L., & Maksimov, N. V. (2007). The architecture of a computerized information retrieval system: Technologies and aids of retrieving in documentary information resources. *Scientific and Technical Information Processing*, *34*(3), 117–130.

Verma, A., Tiwari, M. K., & Mishra, N. (2011). Minimizing time risk in on-line bidding: An adaptive information retrieval based approach. *Expert Systems with Applications*, *38*(4), 3679–3689.

Verma, M., Balasubramanian, R., & Murala, S. (2014). Multiresolution LEP using Discrete Wavelet Transform. In *Proceedings of 7th IEEE Conference on Contemporary Computing*, (pp. 577-582).

Villaverde, J., Godoy, D., & Amandi, A. (2006). Learning styles' recognition in e-learning environments with feed-forward neural networks. *Journal of Computer Assisted Learning*, 22(3), 197–206.

Voorhees, E. M. (1998). *Variations in relevance judgments and the measurement of retrieval effectiveness*. Paper presented at the 21st Annual International ACM Conference on Research and Development in Information Retrieval (SIGIR 1998), Melbourne, Australia.

Wang, J., & Lochovsky, F.-H. (2002). Data-Rich Section Extraction from HTML Pages. *Proceedings of the Third International Conference on Web Information Systems Engineering (WISE)*.

Wang, H., & Sassa, K. (2005). Comparative evaluation of landslide susceptibility in Minamata area, Japan. *Environmental Geology*, 47(7), 956–966. doi:10.1007/s00254-005-1225-2

Wang, J. W., Li, J., & Wiederhold, G. (2001). SIMPLIcity: Semantics-Sensitive Integrated Matching for Picture Libraries. *IEEE Transactions on Pattern Analysis and Machine Intelligence*, 23(9), 947–963. doi:10.1109/34.955109

Wang, J., Chen, C., & Peng, B. (2004). *Analysis of the user log for a large-scale Chinese search engine*. South China University of Technology.

Wang, J., & Lochovsky, F.-H. (2003). Data extraction and Label Assignment for Web databases.*Proceedings of the Twelfth International Conference on World Wide Web (WWW)*. doi:10.1145/775152.775179

Wang, X., Yu, Y., & Yang, H. (2011). An Effective Image Retrieval Scheme Using Color, Texture And Shape Features. *Computer Standards & Interfaces*, 33(1), 59–68. doi:10.1016/j.csi.2010.03.004

Wang, X., Zhang, B., & Yang, H. (2012). Content-based Image Retrieval by Integrating Color and Texture Features. *Multimedia Tools and Applications*, 1–25.

Wang, Y. T., & Lee, A. J. T. (2011). Mining web navigation patterns with a path traversal graph. *Expert Systems with Applications*, 38(6), 7112–7122.

Wang, Y., & Hu, J. (2002), A.machine learning based approach for table detection on the web.*Eleventh International World Wide Web Conference*. doi:10.1145/511446.511478

Weerakkody, V. (2012). *Technology Enabled Transformation of the Public Sector: Advances in E-Government: Advances in E-Government*. IGI Global. doi:10.4018/978-1-4666-1776-6

Weiss, G. M., & Davison, B. D. (2010). *To appear in the Handbook of Technology Management* (H. Bidgoli, Ed.). John Wiley and Sons.

Weng, C. I., Fong, S., & Deb, S. (2011). *An Analytical Model for Evaluating Public Moods Based on the Internet Comments*. Retrieved from www.excelpublish.com

Weninger, T., Fumarola, F., Barber, R., Han, J., & Malerba, D. (2010). Unexpected Results in Automatic List Extraction on the web. *SIGKDD Explorations*, 12(2).

Wen, J. R., Jian-Yun, N., & Hong-Jiang, Z. (n.d.). Clustering user queries of a search engine. In *Proceedings of the 10th international conference on World Wide Web* (pp. 162-168).

White, R. W., Bilenko, M., & Cucerzan, S. (2007). Studying the use of popular destinations to enhance web search interaction. In *Proceedings of the 30th Annual International ACM SIGIR Conference on Research & Development Information Retrieval* (pp. 159–166). doi:10.1145/1277741.1277771

Wikantika, K., Sinaga, A., Hadi, F., & Darmawan, S. (2007). Quick assessment on identification of damaged building and land-use changes in the post-tsunami disaster with a quick-look image of IKONOS and Quickbird (A case study in Meulaboh City, Aceh). *International Journal of Remote Sensing, 28*(13-14), 3037–3044. doi:10.1080/01431160601091845

Williams, G. J. (1990). *Inducing and Combining Multiple Decision Trees.* (PhD thesis). Australian National University.

Willmott, C. J., & Matsuura, K. (2005). Advantages of the mean absolute error (MAE) over the root mean square (RMSE) in assessing average model performance. *Climate Research, 30,* 79–82. doi:10.3354/cr030079

Witten, I. H., & Frank, E. (2005). *Data Mining: Practical machine learning tools and techniques.* Morgan Kaufmann.

World Bank Group. (2012). India: Issues and Priorities for Agriculture. *The World Bank.* Retrieved August 7, 2015, from http://www.worldbank.org/en/news/feature/2012/05/17/india-agriculture-issues-priorities

Wu, S., Li, J., Zeng, X., & Bi, Y. (2014). Adaptive data fusion methods in information retrieval. *Journal of the Association for Information Science and Technology, 65*(10), 2048–2061.

Xu, Y., & Benaroch, M. (2005). Information retrieval with a hybrid automatic query expansion and data fusion procedure. *Information Retrieval, 8*(1), 41–65.

Yadav, S. B. (2010). A conceptual model for user-centered quality information retrieval on the World Wide Web. *Journal of Intelligent Information Systems, 35*(1), 91–121.

Yadla, S., Hayes, J. H., & Dekhtyar, A. (2005). Tracing requirements to defect reports: An application of information retrieval techniques. *Innovations in Systems and Software Engineering, 1*(2), 116–124.

Yalcin, A. (2008). GIS – based landslide susceptibility mapping using analytical hierarchy process and bivariate statistics in Ardesen (Turkey): Comparison of results and confirmations. *Catena, 72*(1), 1–12. doi:10.1016/j.catena.2007.01.003

Yang, C. C., Yang, H., Jiang, L., & Zhang, M. (2012). *Social media mining for drug safety signal detection.* Paper presented at the 2012 International Workshop on Smart Health and Wellbeing (SHB 2012). New York, NY.

Yang, H., & Fong, S. (2011). Moderated VFDT in Stream Mining Using Adaptive Tie Threshold and Incremental Pruning. In *Proc. of 13th international conference on Data Warehousing and Knowledge Discovery* (DaWak2011), (LNCS). Springer. doi:10.1007/978-3-642-23544-3_36

Yang, H. (2013). *Solving Problems of Imperfect Data Streams by Incremental Decision Trees. Journal of Emerging Technologies in Web Intelligence, 5(3).*

Yang, M. D., Su, T. C., Hsu, C. H., Chang, K. C., & Wu, A. M. (2007). Mapping of the 26 December 2004 tsunami disaster by using FORMOSAT-2 images. *International Journal of Remote Sensing, 28*(13-14), 3071–3091. doi:10.1080/01431160601094500

Yannibelli, V., Godoy, D., & Amandi, A. (2006). A genetic algorithm approach to recognize students learning styles. *Interactive Learning Environments, 14*(1), 55–78.

Yates, R. B., & Berthier, R. (1999). *Modern information retrieval.* Boston, MA: Addison–Wesley.

Yates, R. B., & Neto, B. R. (2011). *Modern Information Retrieval.* Pearson.

Yen, B., Hu, P., & Wang, M. (2005). *Towards effective web site designs: A framework for modeling, design evaluation and enhancement.* Paper presented at the 2005 IEEE International Conference on e-Technology, e-Commerce and e-Service (EEE 2005), Hong Kong.

Ye, Z., He, B., Wang, L., & Luo, T. (2013). Utilizing term proximity for blog post retrieval. *Journal of the American Society for Information Science and Technology, 64*(11), 2278–2298.

Ye, Z., Huang, J. X., He, B., & Lin, H. (2012). Mining a multilingual association dictionary from Wikipedia for cross-language information retrieval. *Journal of the American Society for Information Science and Technology, 63*(12), 2474–2487.

Yi, L., Liu, B., & Li, X. (2003, August). Eliminating noisy information in web pages for data mining. In *Proceedings of the ninth ACM SIGKDD international conference on Knowledge discovery and data mining* (pp. 296-305). ACM. doi:10.1145/956750.956785

Yilmaz, I. (2009). Landslide susceptibility mapping using frequency ratio, logistic regression, artificial neural networks and their comparison: A case study from Kat landslides (Tokat-Turkey). *Computers & Geosciences, 35*(6), 1125–1138. doi:10.1016/j.cageo.2008.08.007

Yin, P. Y., & Guo, Y. M. (2013). Optimization of multi-criteria website structure based on enhanced tabu search and web usage mining. *Applied Mathematics and Computation, 219*(24), 11082–11095.

Youssef, S. M. (2012). ICTEDCT-CBIR: Integrating curvelet transform with enhanced dominant colors extraction and texture analysis for efficient content-based image retrieval. *Computers & Electrical Engineering, 38*(5), 1358–1376. doi:10.1016/j.compeleceng.2012.05.010

Youtie, J., Hicks, D., Shapira, P., & Horsley, T. (2012). Pathways from discovery to commercialisation: Using web sources to track small and medium-sized enterprise strategies in emerging nanotechnologies. *Technology Analysis and Strategic Management, 24*(10), 981–995.

Yu, P. (1999). *Data mining and personalization technologies.* Paper presented at the Sixth IEEE International Conference on Database Systems for Advanced Applications (DASFAA 1999), Hsinchu, Taiwan.

Yuhaniz, S. S., & Vladimirova, T. (2009). An onboard automatic change detection system for disaster monitoring. *International Journal of Remote Sensing, 30*(23), 6121–6139. doi:10.1080/01431160902810638

Yu-Hui Tao, T.-P. H.-M. (2007). Web usage mining with intentional browsing data. *International Journal of Expert.*

Yu, J., Qin, Z., Wan, T., & Zhang, X. (2013). Feature integration analysis of bag-of- features model for image retrieval. *Neurocomputing, 120,* 355–364. doi:10.1016/j.neucom.2012.08.061

Yun, C. H., & Chen, M. S. (2000). *Using pattern-join and purchase-combination for mining transaction patterns in an electronic commerce environment.* Paper presented at the 24th Annual International Computer Software and Applications Conference (COMP–SAC 2000), Taipei, Taiwan.

Yun, B. H., & Seo, C. H. (2003). Semantic-based information retrieval for content management and security. *Computational Intelligence, 19*(2), 87–110.

Zadeh, L. A. (1965). Fuzzy sets. *Information and Control, 8*(3), 338–353.

Zadeh, L. A. (1997). Toward a theory of fuzzy information granulation and its centrality in human reasoning and fuzzy logic. *Fuzzy Sets and Systems, 90*(2), 111–127.

Zahera Hamada, M., & Gamal, F. (2011). Query Recommendation for Improving Search Engine Results. *International Journal of Information Retrieval Research, 1*(1), 45–52. doi:10.4018/ijirr.2011010104

Zaïane, O. R. (2001). *Web usage mining for a better web-based learning.* Paper presented at the Conference on Advanced Technology for Education.

Zaki, M. J., & Meira, W. Jr. (2014). *Data mining and analysis: fundamental concepts and algorithms*. New York: Cambridge University Press.

Zhai, Y., & Liu, B. (2005). Web Data Extraction Based on Partial Tree Alignment.*Proceedings of the 14th International Conference on World Wide Web (WWW)*. doi:10.1145/1060745.1060761

Zhang, H., Song, H., & Xu, X. (2007). Semantic session analysis for web usage mining. *Wuhan University Journal of Natural Sciences, 12*(5), 773–776.

Zhang, J., Zhao, P., Shang, L., & Wang, L. (2009). Web usage mining based on fuzzy clustering in identifying target group. *Proceedings of International Colloquium on Computing, Communication, Control, and Management, 4*, 209–212.

Zhang, M., Zhang, K., Feng, Q., Wang, J., Kong, J., & Lu, Y. (2014). A novel image retrieval method based on hybrid information descriptors. *Journal of Visual Communication and Image Representation, 25*(7), 1574–1587.

Zhang, Y., & Jiao, J. (2007). An associative classification-based recommendation system for personalization in B2C e-commerce applications. *Expert Systems with Applications, 33*(2), 357–367.

Zhao, H., Meng, W., Wu, Z., Raghavan, V., & Yu, C.-T. (2005). Fully Automatic Wrapper Generation for Search Engines. *Proceedings of the International Conference on World Wide Web (WWW)*. doi:10.1145/1060745.1060760

Zhao, H., Meng, W., & Yu, C.-T. (2006). Automatic Extraction of Dynamic Record Sections from Search Engine Result Pages.*Proceedings of the 32nd International Conference on Very Large Data Bases (VLDB)*.

Zhou, P., & Le, Z. (2007). A Framework for Web Usage Mining in Electronic Government. *Integration and Innovation Orient to E-Society,* (2), 487-496.

Zhu, J., Hong, J., & Hughes, J. (2002). Using Markov chains for link prediction in adaptive web sites.*Proceedings of Software Computing in an Imperfect World (LNCS)*, (vol. 2311, pp. 60-73). Springer-Verlag. doi:10.1007/3-540-46019-5_5

Zhu, Wang, & Wu. (2009). *Research and application of the improved algorithm C4.5 on decision tree*. Academic Press.

Zhu, H., & Hall, P. (1993). Test data adequacy measurement. *Journal of Software Engineering, 8*(1), 21–30. doi:10.1049/sej.1993.0004

About the Contributors

A. V. Senthil Kumar obtained his BSc Degree (Physics) in 1987, P.G.Diploma in Computer Applications in 1988, MCA in 1991 from Bharathiar University. He obtained his Master of Philosophy in Computer Science from Bharathidasan University, Trichy during 2005 and his Ph.D in Computer Science from Vinayaka Missions University during 2009. To his credit he has industrial experience for five years as System Analyst in a Garment Export Company. Later he took up teaching and attached to CMS College of Science and Commerce, Coimbatore and now he is working as a Director & Professor in the Department of Research and PG in Computer Applications, Hindusthan College of Arts and Science, Coimbatore, India since 05/03/2010. He has to his credit 5 Book Chapters, 74 papers in International Journals, 2 papers in National Journals, 22 papers in International Conferences, 5 papers in National Conferences, and edited three books in Data Mining, Mobile Computing, and in Fuzzy Expert Systems (IGI Global, USA). He is an Editor-in-Chief for 5 International Journals. Key Member for India, Machine Intelligence Research Lab (MIR Labs). He is an Editorial Board Member and Reviewer for various International Journals. He is also a Committee member for various International Conferences. He is a Life member of International Association of Engineers (IAENG), Systems Society of India (SSI), member of The Indian Science Congress Association, member of Internet Society (ISOC), International Association of Computer Science and Information Technology (IACSIT), Indian Association for Research in Computing Science (IARCS), and committee member for various International Conferences. He has got many awards from National and International Societies.

* * *

Hiranmayi Dhappuri is pursuing m tech 2nd year and published paper on agile methodology in international journal of computer science and information technology. Interested in data mining and big data concepts.

Abd El-Aziz has completed his PhD degree in June 2014 in information science and technology from Anna University, Chennai-25, India. He has received his BSc, and Master of computer science in 1995 and 2006 respectively from Faculty of Science, Cairo University. Now, He is a lecturer in the Institute of Statistical Studies and Research, Cairo University, Egypt. He has 11 years' experience in Teaching at Cairo University, Egypt. He has published 25 papers in International Journals and Conferences. His research interests include database system, database security, Data Mining, Big data, Cloud computing, and XML security.

Rajan Gupta is currently Research Scholar with University of Delhi. His area of interest includes E-Governance, Public Information Systems, Multimedia Data processing and Data Analysis. He has over 25 publications at national and international forums.

Kijpokin Kasemsap received his BEng degree in Mechanical Engineering from King Mongkut's University of Technology Thonburi, his MBA degree from Ramkhamhaeng University, and his DBA degree in Human Resource Management from Suan Sunandha Rajabhat University. He is a Special Lecturer at Faculty of Management Sciences, Suan Sunandha Rajabhat University based in Bangkok, Thailand. He is a Member of International Association of Engineers (IAENG), International Association of Engineers and Scientists (IAEST), International Economics Development and Research Center (IEDRC), International Association of Computer Science and Information Technology (IACSIT), International Foundation for Research and Development (IFRD), and International Innovative Scientific and Research Organization (IISRO). He also serves on the International Advisory Committee (IAC) for International Association of Academicians and Researchers (INAAR). He has numerous original research articles in top international journals, conference proceedings, and book chapters on business management, human resource management, and knowledge management published internationally.

Ashish Khare received Doctor of Philosophy degree in Computer Science in 2007 from University of Allahabad, India. He was a Post-Doctoral fellow at Gwangju Institute of Science and Technology, Gwangju, South Korea in 2007-2008. Currently, he is an Associate Professor in Computer Science at University of Allahabad, India. He was a Visiting Professor in Gwangju Institute of Science and Technology, Gwangju, South Korea in 2015. He has published more than 100 papers in international journals as well as conference proceedings. He wrote two book chapters and edited a book. He has supervised a number of Ph.D. theses. His research interest includes Image Processing and Computer Vision, Application of Wavelet Transform, Human Action Recognition and Behaviour Understanding, and Soft Computing Techniques.

Akhouri Pramod Krishna is Professor and Head of the Department of Remote Sensing, Birla Institute of Technology (BIT), Mesra, Ranchi. His specialisation is in Earth Resources Technology comprising Remote Sensing and Environmental Geosciences with extensive research experience and interests in Natural Hazards and Disaster Management, Natural Resources Management, Glacier and Climate Change studies, etc.

Akshay Kumar received the B.Sc. degree in Geology (with honours) and M.Sc degree in Applied Geology from Ranchi University, Ranchi, India. He also received M.Tech Degree in Remote Sensing from the Birla Institute of Technology, Mesra, India, in 2011. He is currently pursuing Ph.D degree in Remote Sensing from the Birla Institute of Technology, Mesra, Ranchi. His research interest lies in coal mining hazard, water resource management, ground water, land degradation, risk mapping, glacier studies in Himalaya and soft computing techniques in natural hazard and environmental problems.

Ratnesh Kumar received his PhD in November 2010 from Dr. Hari Singh Gour University (formerly, Sagar University) Sagar, MP, India. He completed his Master's in Computer Applications (MCA) in 2001 and BSc with Electronics as special subject in 1998 from the same university. His field of study is operating system, data structures, compiler designing, web mining, and information retrieval. He has published more than 15 research papers and has authored a book. Presently he is working as PGT at Kendriya Vidyalaya, Ara, Bihar.

Umamageswari Kumaresan is an assistant professor at the Dept. of IT, in New Prince Shri Bhavani College of Engineering and Technology. She received her B.Tech in Computer Science and Engineering from Pondicherry Engineering College in 2005, her M.Tech in Computer Science and Engineering from Bharath University in 2010, and currently pursuing Ph.D. degree in Computer Science and Engineering in Pondicherrry Engineering College respectively. Her research interests include web mining, web data extraction, information security and sentiment analysis.

Mahmood A. Mahmood is an Assistant Professor (Staff Member) in the institute of statistical studies and Research Computer science and Information.

Alok Bhushan Mukherjee is currently pursuing PhD in Remote Sensing and is performing investigation on the complexities of urban system. Earlier he had M-tech in Remote Sensing, while M.Sc in Information Science and B.Sc in Mathematics respectively. His research interests lies in the analysis of urban system, decision sciences, uncertainty analysis and sensitivity analysis using statistical modelling.

Saibal Kumar Pal is a senior research scientist at DRDO, Delhi, INDIA. He has a PhD in Computer Science. His areas of Interest are Information Security, Computational Intelligence, Multimedia Technologies & Electronic Governance.

Kalpana Ramanujam is currently working as Professor in the Department of Computer Science and Engineering at Pondicherry Engineering College, Puducherry, India. She received her B.Tech. degree in Computer Science and Engineering from Pondicherry University, Puducherry, India in the year 1996 and M. Tech. degree in Computer Science and Engineering from Pondicherry University, Puducherry in1998. She completed her Ph.D in Computer Science & Engineering in the year 2013 in the field of Parallel Computing Systems. She joined as Lecturer in Department of Computer Science & Engineering, Pondicherry Engineering College, Puducherry in the year 2000. Subsequently she was promoted as Assistant Professor in the Department of Computer Science & Engineering, Pondicherry Engineering College, Puducherry in the year 2007 and elevated as Associate Professor in the year 2010. She is presently holding the post of Professor. Her areas of interest include Parallel Computing Systems, High Performance Computing, Web services and Distributed Computing. She has published more than 30 research papers in International Journals / Conferences. She is also a member of ISTE.

Priyanka Sharma is currently working as Professor in MCA department of Raksha Shakti University. Her research area is Data Mining, Cloud Computing and Artificial Intelligence. She is currently guiding many PhD scholars from Gujarat Technological University, Chandkheda. She has an excellent research and teaching experience. She has published papers in many international and national journals. She also has presented many papers in national and international conferences.

Rahul Singhai received his PhD in July 2011 from Dr. Hari Singh Gour University (formerly, Sagar University) Sagar, MP, India. He completed his M.Phil in Computer Science from Madurai Kamraj University, Tamilnadu and Master's in Computer Applications (MCA) from the Dr. Hari Singh Gour

University. His field of study is Data Mining, operating system, Computer Network and information retrieval. He has published and presented more than 20 research papers and has authored a book. He is an active members of several academic & Professional bodies. Presentlly he is working as senior assistant professor at Devi Ahilya University, Indore.

G. Sreedhar is working as a Associate Professor in the Department of Computer Science, Rashtiya Sanskrit Vidyapeetha (Deemed University), Tirupati, India since 2001. G. Sreedhar received his Ph.D in Computer Science and Technology from Sri Krishnadevaraya University, Anantapur, India in the year 2011. He has over 15 years of Experience in Teaching and Research in the field of Computer Science. He published more than 15 research papers related to web engineering in reputed international journals. He published 4 books from reputed international publications and he presented more than 15 research papers in various national and international conferences. He handled research projects in computer science funded by University Grants Commission, Government of India. He is a member in various professional bodies like academic council, board of studies and editorial board member in various international journals in the field of computer science, Information Technology and other related fields. He has proven knowledge in the field of Computer Science and allied research areas.

Prashant Srivastava received B.Sc. degree in Computer Science and Mathematics in 2008 and M.Sc. degree in Computer Science in 2010 from University of Allahabad, India. Currently, he is pursuing Doctor of Philosophy in Computer Science from Department of Electronics and Communication, University of Allahabad, India. His area of research is Content-Based Image Retrieval. His research interest includes Image Processing and Computer Vision, Content-Based Image Retrieval, and Pattern Recognition.

Abhishek Taneja is an Assistant Professor of Computer Science at S A Jain College, Ambala City (India). His teaching experience includes Data Mining, System Analysis and Design, Computer Graphics & Multimedia, and Software Engineering. Abhishek is an active researcher in the field of Predictive Data Mining and is currently working on a University Grant Commission, New Delhi sponsored project. Abhishek Taneja received his doctorate and MCA degree in Computer Science and Applications from Kurukshetra University, Kurukshetra. He did his Master's in Business Economics from G J University of Science & Technology, Hisar (India). Abhishek has authored books on Data Mining, Computer Graphics and Multimedia. He has published several papers in reputed journals and conference proceedings.

R. Umagandhi obtained her UG Degree B.Sc Mathematics in 1995, PG Degree Master of Computer Applications in 1998 from Kongunadu Arts and Science College, Bharathiar University, Coimbatore. She has obtained her Master of Philosophy in computer Science from Manonmaniam Sundaranar University, Tirunelvelli during the year 2003 and Ph.D in Computer Science from Bharathiar University during 2014. She is working as an Associate Professor and Head, Department of Computer Technology Kongunadu Arts and Science College, Coimbatore for the past 16 Years. She is an active member of Indian Science Congress (ISCA). She is a Life member in International Association of Engineers (IAENG) and Reviewer in various National and International Journals. She has published 15 papers in International Journals and Conferences. Her research interests include database system, database security, Data Mining and Web Mining.

Dineshkumar B. Vaghela is currently pursuing his PhD in Distributed Data Mining from Gujarat Technological University, Chandkheda. He has total 11 years of teaching experience. He has published papers in many international and national journals. He also has presented many papers in national and international conferences. He has guided more than 15 students to complete their dissertation thesis of Master of CSE.

Paresh V. Virparia joined the Department of Computer Science of Sardar Patel University, Vallabh Vidyanagar in 1989 and currently working as a Director and Professor. He completed his MCA in 1989 from Sardar Patel University and Ph. D. in 2002 from Sardar Patel University. SEVEN research scholars have completed their Ph.D. (Computer Science) under his guidance. Currently, SEVEN students are doing their Ph. D. under the guidance of him. Also, three students have completed their M.Phil. (Comp. Sc.) under his supervision. His publications include 40 papers in International Journal, 16 papers in National Journals and 47 papers in national conferences/seminars. His research interests include the areas of Computer Simulation & Modeling, Data Mining, Networking and IT enabled services. He is an editor and editorial review board member in several journals/magazines.

Index

I

I2P 345, 349

image retrieval 298, 300-307, 309, 312-314, 317-319, 323

information retrieval 1-4, 8-11, 28, 80-81, 84, 87, 95, 118, 176, 190, 199-200, 213-214, 233, 297-302, 306, 309, 312, 317, 319-320, 323, 325-327, 354, 369, 378

Internet 1-2, 4, 10, 13, 28-29, 106, 169, 187-190, 197, 199, 224, 227, 229, 233, 247-248, 254, 275-276, 292, 300, 332-333, 344-345, 349

K

knowledge 2-9, 12, 30-31, 78, 83, 92-93, 95, 97, 99, 103, 107, 109, 115-116, 118-119, 122, 138-141, 143-144, 146, 152, 159, 168-170, 197-198, 201, 230, 232, 237, 243, 247-249, 254-256, 259-260, 275, 277, 280, 282, 289, 291, 294, 296, 299, 325-326, 330, 333, 353, 359, 366, 373

L

landslides 6, 141-153, 155-156, 158-159, 166

land use 141, 143, 145, 150, 152, 155-157, 166

lineament density 145, 156, 166

lineaments 155-156, 166

lithology 143, 145, 147, 150, 155-156, 166

M

machine learning 97, 99, 107, 115, 118-119, 140, 232, 249, 260, 267, 272, 299, 327, 330, 334, 354, 358, 371

Markov chain model 29, 31-37, 75-76, 78

Mean Adjusted Error (MAE) 135

Mean Square Error (MSE) 129-130, 135

methodology 81, 84, 106, 108, 123, 125, 153, 155-156, 172, 176, 193, 195, 199-200, 275, 282, 294, 296, 339

modified coefficient of efficiency 125, 129-132, 135

multiresolution analysis 298, 305-306, 309, 315, 319, 323

N

natural hazards 141-142, 152, 154, 158-159

NeGP 223, 234, 247

Number of Predictors 135

P

Page Rank 337, 349

pattern analysis 97, 100, 107-108, 110, 115, 140, 231-232, 275, 282, 291, 294, 299

Pattern Discovery 30, 97, 107-108, 110, 115, 231-232, 275, 280, 296, 299, 328-330, 360

precision 8, 35, 267, 314-317, 332, 339, 369-370, 378

prediction model 125, 129, 273

privacy 6, 184, 187, 193, 197-198, 256, 261, 279, 292, 294, 345

R

recall 8, 314-317, 339, 369-370, 378

Recommendation Systems 93, 95, 115

Relative Relief 166

remote sensing 147, 152-153, 155, 166

Resilience 378

RMSE 125, 129-131, 135-136

R-Square 116, 125, 129, 135-136

rule learning 273

S

scalability 5, 106-107, 273, 280

search 1-4, 6, 8-13, 29, 35, 81-83, 87, 93-96, 98, 103, 109, 115, 145, 168, 173, 176-177, 183-184, 188, 193, 198-204, 206, 208, 211, 213, 220-222, 277, 297-302, 320, 327-328, 330-331, 334, 337, 344-345, 349-350, 354, 356, 365, 367, 369, 373

Server-Side Template 360, 378

similarity metric 81-82, 84-85, 88, 301, 306

slope 141, 143-145, 147, 150-151, 153, 155-156, 166

social bookmarking 81-82, 84, 88, 366

standards 3, 152, 169, 183-184, 189-190, 193, 197-198, 231, 339

supervised 149, 250, 256, 258, 290, 334, 359-360, 378

T

tag cloud 80-86, 88-89

tagging 80, 83, 85, 87-88, 302, 355

technology 2-4, 6, 8, 11, 28, 81, 98, 139-140, 147, 152-153, 155, 223-226, 234, 243, 247, 249, 253-254, 299, 301, 324, 333, 342, 344

test data set 273

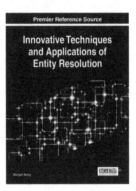